# Charles Wesley

# Charles Wesley

*Life, Literature and Legacy*

*Edited by*
Kenneth G. C. Newport and
Ted A. Campbell

 EPWORTH

British Library Cataloguing in Publication data

A catalogue record for this book is available
from the British Library

978 0 7162 0607 1

First published in 2007
by Epworth
4 John Wesley Road
Werrington
Peterborough PE4 6ZP

Typeset by Regent Typesetting, London
Printed and bound in Great Britain by
William Clowes Ltd, Beccles, Suffolk

# Contents

In Memoriam

Frank Baker (1910–99)

# Preface

Few Anglican clergymen are as well known as John and Charles Wesley. Despite the recognition of the names, however, there is much misunderstanding as to the relative roles of the two brothers in the progress and development of what was to become the Methodist tradition. In popular perspective at least, and probably in an academic one too, it is John and not Charles who was largely responsible for the birth and growth of the movement; and it was John and not Charles who gave that section of the wider Christian body its theological profile, ecclesial distinctiveness and evangelical appeal. To be sure, Charles was there as a support. He gave his brother's thoughts and theology wings by translating them into poetic form, and particularly by writing some of the most inspiring of all English hymns. But in the last analysis it is to John and not Charles that we may trace the origins of Methodism. Similarly it is to John and not Charles that any credit due for the calling into existence of a movement that has had such a powerful and positive influence on human society must be attributed. At least, that is the received popular wisdom.

It is not the purpose of this volume to argue for a complete reversal in this perception. Any attempt to mount such an argument would be pointless, for there can be no doubt at all that John Wesley was a man of almost unparalleled energy whose tireless work in establishing the Methodist movement was the single most important contribution to the development of that tradition. (Though it ought not to be forgotten that it was Charles and not John who first established the Oxford 'holy club'.) John's commitment and zeal for the gospel was staggering; his influence profound. It is proper, then, that it is 24 May, the day of *John* Wesley's 'strange warming of the heart', that is the day when Anglicans and Methodists alike remember the brothers and their contribution to the broader Christian spiritual heritage. Charles' own 'Day of Pentecost' as he called it, when his heart was 'strangely palpitated', had come three days earlier but in the end it was John's experience that was to have the greater and wider consequence. And from that point on, Charles has been in his brother's shadow. John was the real 'head' if Charles was the 'heart'. John was the leader, Charles followed. John was the preacher, Charles the poet. This popular conception is probably reflected even in the Anglican Collect for 24 May: 'God of mercy, who inspired John and Charles Wesley with zeal for your gospel: grant to all your people boldness to proclaim your word and ever to rejoice in singing your praises . . .' John proclaimed, Charles composed. If such a division of labour is not in fact intended in the Collect, it is nevertheless at least lodged in the minds of many a Christian – Methodist, Anglican or otherwise. This book seeks to balance this perception rather than to reverse it, and to present a picture of Charles that is in keeping with the surviving evidence. In short, the 28 essays here contained show, so the editors believe, that Charles Wesley was much more than the 'Sweet Singer of Methodism'.

The fact that this book appears in 2007 is not without significance, for this year marks the tercentenary of Charles' birth. Hence this is a fitting point at which to reflect upon the 'life, literature and legacy' of a man who has not only had a spiritual role to play in the life of many believers, but is also a significant historical figure and an able theologian.

The essays in this volume hence reflect something of the renaissance of scholarship on Charles Wesley which is witnessed to also in the growing number of scholarly publications related to Charles Wesley research that have already appeared. The Bibliography supplies details. In particular, a number of new critical editions of Charles Wesley primary texts have been published in the last 25 years. These include the work on Methodist hymnals conducted in the 1980s, which involved critical scholarly background work both in the UK (*Hymns & Psalms*, 1983) and in the USA (*The United Methodist Hymnal*, 1989), and the heavily annotated edition of the 1780 hymn book that was completed as part of the bicennnial edition of John Wesley's works.[1] Perhaps the most pressing need of all, a fully accurate edition of Charles' journal (previous editions by Jackson and Telford fall short of this ideal), has now been completed and will also appear in 2007.[2] Similarly, we now have Charles' sermons[3] and his hymns and other poetical compositions.[4] As a result of this scholarly work, scholars working in this area now have available a much wider range of Charles Wesley sources in critical editions than have been available in the past. And the situation is set to improve further. Work is now well under way on the task of bringing to publication a two-volume edition of Charles' letters.[5]

At the same time, Charles Wesley research was offered in the Wesleyan Studies working group of the Oxford Institutes of Methodist Theological Studies from 1982 and in the Wesleyan Studies Group of the American Academy of Religion from 1983. A further major development was the founding of the Charles Wesley Society in 1990 (http://www.wesleysociety.org) by S T Kimbrough Jr. This brought together Charles Wesley scholars from around the world and has accelerated Charles Wesley scholarship through its annual meetings, its newsletter, its *Proceedings*, and its publication of a series of reprints (with critical introductions) of many of Charles Wesley's original collections of poetry and hymns. A hitherto largely unsung but crucial development has been the work of Gareth Lloyd, whose meticulous scholarship and dedication have resulted not only in the identification and logging of many hundreds of Charles Wesley items now housed in the John Rylands University Library of Manchester, but also extensively annotated printed catalogues of them.[6] It is doubtless the case that Lloyd's work will provide the basic data pool for generations of Charles Wesley scholars to come. His contribution has been immense.

One of the themes that emerges in the following essays is that of Charles Wesley's more conservative ecclesiastical leanings in comparison to those of his brother John. Although this has been generally known (for example, Charles' stated opposition to John's ordinations in 1784), it becomes very clear

in these essays that from the middle of the 1750s, when Charles ceased itinerating as a Methodist preacher, the relationship between the two brothers
became increasingly strained at this point (see essays by John Lenton and
Richard Heitzenrater, and Gareth Lloyd's essay on Charles' letters). Moreover,
as Lloyd points out in the very first chapter of this book, the extent of this
rift was concealed, or at the very least down-played, by Methodist historians
anxious to portray the essential unity of the two brothers in their evangelical
mission. This difference in ecclesiastical sensitivities may well reflect the difference between the characters of the brothers noted in John Newton's essay:
John Wesley's independent character gives rise to his consistent focus on the
distinct mission of the Methodist movement; Charles Wesley's sense of loyalty to family and church offers a more 'catholic' perspective expressed in his
hymns on a very broad range of Christian liturgical and doctrinal topics. The
point is taken up by Ted Campbell, whose essay suggests that John Wesley's
concern with distinctive Methodist identity accounts for his preference for
Charles' hymns on the 'way of salvation' in the 1780 *Collection of Hymns for
the Use of the People Called Methodists*, whereas Charles' hymns themselves
have a much broader focus on Christian liturgical and doctrinal topics. This
is not to rob Methodists of one whom they are used to counting as their own,
but rather to present Charles to a wider audience. Seen in the round, Charles
emerges not just as the 'Sweet Singer of Methodism', but as a powerful voice
for the Christian faith as a whole.

The relevance of Charles Wesley's characterological, ecclesiastical, and
theological distinction from his brother can be seen in two ways. On the one
hand, Charles' legacy in hymns is far better known in the Christian community beyond Methodist churches than any of his brother's publications.
So a recent hymnal supplement from the Episcopal Church in the USA takes
its title, *Wonder, Love, and Praise*, from a line in Charles Wesley's hymn 'Love
divine, all loves excelling'. On the other hand, as Methodist churches grow
towards the goal of communion with other Christian communities (including Anglicans), Charles Wesley's broader relevance to Methodists beyond his
hymns on the 'way of salvation' and Christian experience becomes more and
more important. For example, Charles Wesley scholarship has figured prominently in international dialogues on Wesleyan and Eastern Orthodox spirituality, and this scholarship has come from Orthodox as well as from Methodist
and Nazarene scholars (much of this research is summarized in the chapter
by S T Kimbrough Jr). Charles' relationship to the Roman Catholic tradition is
masterfully explored here by Peter Nockles, while his unremitting criticisms
of Calvinism, yet his acceptance of Calvinists such as Whitefield and the Lady
Huntingdon, is put in context by Geoffrey Wainwright.

The contributions of a number of other authors found in this book seek further to outline Charles' theological views and his contribution to the development of theology in the eighteenth century. Vickers argues that Charles was
a not unimportant figure in the context of debates concerning the doctrine of
the Trinity and the revival thereof. Tyson presents us with a thorough examination of Charles' view of the cross and the way of salvation. Cruickshank
and Webster explore Charles' approach to suffering and his understanding of
the 'supernatural' respectively. No one who has read much of Charles could

be in any doubt that here was a man soaked in biblical language and whose religious language was articulate to a sometimes astonishing degree. Some of this is explored by Chilcote whose close study of Charles' language of faith is illuminating. The final chapter in this book, by Susan White, is timely: this may be the tercentenary of Charles' birth, but his is perhaps still a voice that is well worth hearing.

Charles, though, was not simply a man of theology, but of history, and to understand him properly he must be put in a proper historical context. In this book such is suggested by the work of the eminent scholar of the 'long' eighteenth century, Jeremy Gregory, who shows how Charles fits into his own context and is illustrative of that period. Henry Rack puts Charles in the context of the development of early Methodism and shows just how central Charles was to the movement and how he helped shape and fashion it. The story of Charles Wesley cannot be told without a thorough study of his prose works, and this presents a problem, for some of what Charles wrote he put into a (sometimes infuriating) form of shorthand. But the code is not indecipherable and the effort needed to unlock the script is often well spent. Here Wesley scholars are indebted to the late Dr Oliver Beckerlegge, since it was he who pioneered the work on Charles' shorthand script. In the chapter on Charles' use of shorthand (updated by Kenneth Newport) Beckerlegge gives an account of why and in what circumstances Charles turned to shorthand, how important the shorthand sections of Charles' writings are, and gives a very brief overview of how that script is to be read. If we are fully to appreciate Charles' role in early Methodism, this shorthand script needs to be accessed. It gives a picture of Charles that is at a considerable distance from that of a quiet hymn writer working away in his Bristol attic. He had very determined views that were not always in accord with those of his brother.

Another major contribution of the authors presented here is the exploration of Charles' family and personal life. Olleson looks at Charles' relationship with his children (and in the process explores a little of his relationship with his wife Sally), while Lawrence explores the whole area of Charles and marriage. Forsaith reconstructs Charles' relationship with John Fletcher, with whom Charles had an extensive correspondence – much of which was of a highly personal nature. Wallace's major study of Charles and Susanna, based on years of painstaking research into Susanna's writings as well as Charles', is a major contribution to our knowledge of Charles and again helps others to see Charles in a broader perspective. Indeed, all these chapters on Charles' relationships and personal life help further to paint a picture of Charles that is more fully rounded as we begin to see Charles as a real flesh-and-blood eighteenth-century son, father, husband, confidant, pastor and friend.

None of this is of course to deny Charles Wesley's place as an almost unparalleled poet (at least when he had spiritual matters in view). Such is explored here in historical and linguistic context by Dick Watson, while the 'afterlife' of what Charles had to say is the subject of Andrew Pratt's study of the significance (or otherwise) of Charles to contemporary hymnody. Frank Baker's typically meticulous study of the reception history of Charles' *Christmas Hymns* shows by example how such texts developed as they meandered their way through the eighteenth century and beyond. The tradition was not static. In a ground-breaking study Carlton Young explains something of the musical context of Charles' poetical compositions, showing that Charles was by no means unaware of the musical trends of his age and that while he might have been more interested in the musical careers of his sons he was not without an understanding (informed by his wife), or view, of how his own work might fare once available outside of a context that he could control.

The essays presented here are scholarly. They represent the cutting edge of Charles Wesley scholarship and in some cases touch upon historical, textual and theological issues that go far beyond the confines of early Methodism. However, a dry academic volume is far from what the editors had in mind when this project began, and it is hoped that the balance between academic rigour and accessibility has been struck. It is hoped too that the total of this book is greater than the sum of its constituent parts. The detail of the chapters provide the building materials for the mosaic; but standing back, it is hoped, one begins to catch sight of the overall picture. It is still somewhat hazy. Some of the lines are blurred. Some of the detail is obscured. More work needs to be done. The conversation needs to continue, and if this book has contributed to keeping the discussion live, one major objective will have been achieved.

Charles Wesley, the editors believe, is a figure from the past who continues to have much to say for today. We hope that the book will not only be informative, but perhaps even 'inspiring' as Charles' voice is heard from within its pages. As we pass the milestone of the tercentenary of Charles' birth, it is a pleasure to present these essays to the reader.

## Notes

1 *BE*, 7.

2 S T Kimbrough and Kenneth G. C. Newport, eds. *The Journal of Charles Wesley* (Nashville: Abingdon, 2007).

3 *Sermons*.

4 *Unpublished Poetry* and *PW*.

5 Kenneth G. C. Newport and Gareth Lloyd, *The Letters of Charles Wesley* (Oxford: Oxford University Press, forthcoming).

6 See especially Gareth Lloyd, *Catalogue of the Charles Wesley Papers*, 2 vols (Manchester: John Rylands University Library of Manchester, 1994).

# Acknowledgements

The writing of any book is in practice a team effort, especially in the case of a volume of collected essays. It goes without saying that the 28 contributors to this volume (the count includes the Revd Dr Donald A. Bullen who compiled the Bibliography) have all played a major part. The journey has been a long one, and the editors have been fortunate in having colleagues who have responded quickly to requests for clarifications, additions and amendments, and have done so with good grace. It is a particular pleasure that we have been able to include work by two colleagues who are sadly no longer with us: the late Frank Baker and the late Oliver Beckerlegge. The editors are grateful for the permission of the Charles Wesley Society for permission to reprint (with some editorial changes) previously published work of these scholars.

The team that has been involved in the production of this book is, however, much larger than simply the sum of those whose names appear in it. Family and friends, librarians and academic colleagues have doubtless made invaluable contributions to each and every chapter. We cannot list them all, but without their support chapters would not have been written, sources would not have been supplied and creative discussions would not have been had. The editors express their thanks to all such persons and in particular to Rose-Marie, Matthew, Stephen and Sarah (Newport), to Dr Suzanne Schwarz and Dr J'annine Jobling; and to Dale Marie (Campbell).

Thanks are also due to Professor Gerald Pillay and Dr Terry Phillips of Liverpool Hope University, who, as Vice-Chancellor and Dean of Humanities respectively, offered constant encouragement and practical support to enable this book to become a reality. In the same manner, we offer thanks to Garrett-Evangelical Theological Seminary, the Claremont School of Theology, and Perkins School of Theology of Southern Methodist University for their support for Dr Campbell during the period of his work on this book. A particular word of thanks is in order for Page Thomas, Jim McMillin and the staff of Bridwell Library (SMU), who assisted Dr Campbell in final editing for this work.

Tony Williams worked on this book and his careful eye for detail has left its mark on almost every page. The editors are deeply appreciative of his efforts and of those of the staff at Epworth Press whose professionalism and skill have made this volume what it is.

The book is dedicated to the memory of Dr Frank Baker (1910–99), one of whose essays appears (reprinted) in this volume. A native of Yorkshire, Baker spent much of the period of the Second World War collecting Wesleyana throughout Britain – he recalled one evening when the sirens were wailing in the city of Manchester and a book dealer allowed him to spend the night (with bombs falling in the city) working through his collection. When asked how he could afford to collect valuable materials on a Methodist preacher's stipend, Baker replied, 'These are my cigarettes.' His collection became the centrepiece of the Baker Collection of Wesleyana at Duke University, where he served as Professor of English Church History from 1960 to 1980. Baker's work in Wesleyan studies lay in the background of the renaissance of studies of John and Charles Wesley in the late twentieth century, and he was one of the founding members of the Charles Wesley Society in 1990. It is our distinct honour to dedicate this Charles Wesley tercentenary volume to his memory.

Kenneth G. C. Newport

Ted A. Campbell

*The Feast of St Michael and All Angels, 2006*

# Abbreviations

MARC        Methodist Archives and Research Centre, The John Rylands University Library of Manchester.

*CWJ*        Thomas Jackson, ed., *The Journal of the Rev. Charles Wesley, M.A., sometime student of Christ Church, Oxford: to which are appended selections from his correspondence and poetry with an introduction and occasional notes by Thomas Jackson,* Wesleyan Methodist Book Room, 1849, Grand Rapids: Baker Book House, 1980, 2 vols.

*BE*        The Bicentennial Edition of the Works of John Wesley, Nashville: Abingdon Press, 1976– .

*Life*        Thomas Jackson, *The life of . . . Charles Wesley . . . comprising a review of his poetry: sketches of the rise and progress of Methodism: with notices of contemporary events and characters,* John Mason, 1841.

*Sermons*        Kenneth G. C. Newport, ed., *The Sermons of Charles Wesley: A critical edition with introduction and notes,* Oxford: Oxford University Press, 2001.

*Works*        Thomas Jackson, ed., *The Works of John Wesley,* London: John Mason, 1831.

*Unpublished Poetry*        S T Kimbrough Jr and Oliver A. Beckerlegge, eds, *The Unpublished Poetry of Charles Wesley,* 3 vols, Abingdon/Kingswood, 1988, 1990, 1992.

*PW*        G. Osborn, *The Poetical Works of John and Charles Wesley . . . together with the poems of Charles Wesley not before published,* 13 vols, Wesleyan-Methodist Conference Office, 1869–72.

JRUL        John Rylands University Library.

# 1. Charles Wesley and his Biographers[1]

## GARETH LLOYD

Charles Wesley was one of the most important leaders of the Evangelical Revival, an event that saw the birth of Methodism and related movements that still occupy a prominent place in the twenty-first-century Church. Regarded by his contemporaries as a man of exceptional gifts, Charles played an invaluable part in promoting and consolidating the Wesleyan wing of the Revival during its difficult formative years. There was also of course his literary genius: Charles' poetry is regarded as one of the greatest gifts of Methodism to the global Church, and more than 200 years after his death his hymns continue to be sung around the world by Christians of every denomination. At a time when few people read the sermons of John Wesley or George Whitefield, even non-churchgoers are familiar with such timeless works as 'Love divine all loves excelling' and 'Hark the herald angels sing'. When President George W. Bush used a line from a Charles Wesley hymn as the title of his autobiography he had reason to expect that most people would be at least familiar with the name of its author.[2]

Charles Wesley is a significant figure whose ministry has a continuing popular resonance greater than that of any of his evangelical contemporaries. One would expect his story to have been well told already by popular biographers and historians alike; but this is not the case. With the exception of his poetry,[3] his life and work have in fact been largely neglected. Until recently there has been no complete edition of his letters or adequate text of his journal, though one will be forthcoming in 2007,[4] and the most detailed biography was published as long ago as 1841.[5] This neglect of one of the co-founders of the Methodist movement indicates an ambivalence towards Charles Wesley that continues to cast a shadow over his reputation.

Any attempt to re-evaluate the place of Charles Wesley in church history has to deal with the problem posed by existing scholarship (or indeed the lack of it), and in particular has to ask why he appears to have been such a problem figure. This chapter will therefore outline the major weaknesses of existing Charles Wesley biographical scholarship and seek to uncover why, as we approach the 300th anniversary of his birth, Charles Wesley, the prince of hymn writers, remains something of an embarrassment to the Church that he helped to found.

## Early biographical works

Charles Wesley's earliest biographer was the London physician John Whitehead in 1793.[6] In addition to spending a short time as a Methodist preacher, Whitehead had nursed both Wesley brothers during their final illnesses: moreover, as John's literary executor, he had unrivalled access to personal papers as well as to a wide circle of family and friends. He was therefore ideally placed to provide an accurate and detailed picture of the great hymn writer and co-founder of the Methodist movement. Whitehead's book is based principally on Charles' manuscript journal covering the years 1736 to 1756, and within those defined limits it is an excellent source of information containing extensive extracts from a previously unpublished work.

Nineteenth-century scholars were to rely to a greater extent on the journal than on other sources. This was in part a result of its accessibility through Whitehead and Thomas Jackson's edition of 1849.[7] Also, the journal's lengthy descriptions of episodes from the early years of the Revival lent themselves to portraying Charles and Methodism in a heroic light. However, there are obvious problems with using just one primary source. Charles was aged 27 when the journal commences and there is very little of the document surviving for the period after 1751; even before that date there are considerable gaps[8] and the manuscript terminates completely in 1756.[9] The end of the journal coincides with Charles' withdrawal from the travelling ministry and that represents the effective end of Whitehead's narrative, more than thirty years before his subject died. This is all the more striking when one considers developments during the last three decades of Charles' life, as Methodism evolved from a network of Anglican societies into a *de facto* denomination. It has also been argued that these years witnessed the dissolution of the working and personal relationship between the Wesley brothers,[10] a notion that historians have been reluctant to entertain.[11] It is significant that out of a book containing 275 pages, Whitehead covers this important period in just five, dismissing the whole of his subject's later life and ministry in a few sentences.

As a man who knew him well, Whitehead does, however, offer a unique insight into Charles' character, and in so doing indicates the reasons for his failure to venture outside the 'journal years'. For Whitehead, as for many scholars, one of the most controversial aspects of Charles Wesley was his sudden retirement as a travelling preacher. This is rooted in the fact that the itinerancy has always been regarded as one of the most important characteristics of Methodism; early publications are full of accounts of tireless journeys after the model of John Wesley, regardless of persecution and family circumstances. Whitehead freely acknowledged that Charles Wesley's sudden abandonment of his vocation created hostility and resentment:

> Not a few have attributed his conduct . . . to lack of zeal and true vital religion; and I confess that I was once of that opinion; but I have since been more perfectly informed . . . [12]

According to Whitehead, Charles abandoned the itinerancy because of the opposition of some preachers for his support of the Church of England.

Tension was aggravated by Charles' outspoken criticism of the ability of a number of the lay itinerants, and this unhappy combination led to his decision to withdraw from the forefront of the movement in favour of a settled ministry in London and Bristol.[13]

There can be little doubt that Whitehead avoided detailed discussion of the later years of Charles' life because of his subject's controversial reputation and the extreme dislike felt for him in certain quarters. In the years leading up to 1756, Charles had undergone a change of heart. From being one of the most radical clergymen in England, whose irregular activities led to a threat of excommunication, he had turned into an outspoken Anglican loyalist. By arguing in favour of Methodism remaining within the Church of England, he ran counter to the views of some of his contemporaries. In his refusal to discuss this subject in detail, Whitehead was politic as well as discreet; the controversies in which Charles had been involved remained current for several decades after he died.

In his final summing up, Whitehead provided another explanation why Charles has been a problem figure for Methodist scholarship. He is described as possessed:

> of a warm and lively disposition, of great frankness and integrity . . . His love of simplicity, and utter abhorrence of hypocrisy . . . made him sometimes appear severe on those who assumed a consequence . . . or were pert and forward in talking of themselves and others. These persons were sure of meeting with a reproof from him, which some might perhaps call precipitate and imprudent . . . [14]

We begin to see why Charles could be unpopular. His biographers have faced the dilemma of portraying as a Methodist hero a man who was the movement's co-founder and one of the greatest of hymn writers but who ultimately fell short of expectations and was regarded in some quarters as an enemy of Methodism.

Other early historians were equally reluctant to examine Charles' later career. In his early history of the Methodist movement,[15] the minister William Myles omitted him altogether except for a fleeting reference to his membership of the Oxford Holy Club. Even allowing for the fact that Myles' work is just 24 pages in length, this is still a surprising omission.

In his influential *Methodist Memorial*,[16] Charles Atmore refused any explanation of Charles' abrupt withdrawal from the itinerancy, but instead made the following observation:

> It is not easy to ascertain, with any precision, the reasons which induced him to desist from travelling; and from taking the same active part in the government of the societies . . . Some have imputed his conduct to this cause, and others to that: perhaps the safest and best way, is to let it rest till the secrets of all hearts shall be disclosed.[17]

Atmore's work is a brief narration of the bare facts of Charles' life. His evaluation of his subject's character is extracted almost word for word from

Whitehead, despite the fact that Atmore, like Myles, was a younger contemporary of Charles and would also have been able to draw on the recollections of colleagues in the ministry.[18] Atmore was in fact one of the preachers who were hostile to Charles' support of the Church of England,[19] and it is likely that only a desire not to cause controversy prevented him from a more critical evaluation.

The next published assessment of Charles Wesley's character appeared in the preface to an edition of his sermons, published in 1816.[20] It has been generally assumed that Charles' widow Sarah wrote this introduction;[21] a more likely candidate, considering that Sarah was aged 90 in the year of publication, is the couple's daughter Sarah junior,[22] who took a keen interest in the preservation of her father's memory and was described by her uncle John Wesley as having the 'pen of a ready writer'.[23]

As one might expect, there is little of a controversial nature in this short pen-picture, although it is interesting to note the detailed comparison in the temperaments of the two Wesley brothers. John is described as:

> born with a temper which scarcely any injuries could provoke, ingratitude ruffle, or contradiction weary. This disposition peculiarly qualified him to govern . . . his gentleness and forbearance rendered him so much the object of love among the people . . . that they considered their 'sovereign pastor as a sovereign good'.[24]

By contrast, Charles was:

> full of sensibility and fire . . . The peculiar virtue of John was forgiveness . . . Equally generous and kind was his brother . . . but he could not replace his confidence where he had experienced treachery. This formed some variation in their conduct, as also the higher church principles of Charles.[25]

This assessment of the character of the Wesleys is plausible, although the effect of Charles' fiery temperament on events and relationships is not examined.

## The work of Thomas Jackson

For many years the definitive and indeed the only major biography of Charles Wesley was the two-volume life by the minister Thomas Jackson, published in 1841. This remains the most complete treatment, and the conclusions that Jackson reached had an impact which still influences scholarship. This is regrettable as Jackson's portrayal was highly distorted, based on a selective reading of source material which had itself been tampered with.

Jackson's approach is made clear in his introduction where he states that his purpose is the advancement of Christian piety and the propagation of Protestant doctrine.[26] He also declares his intention of correcting criticism of John Wesley[27] and offering a Methodist opinion on the development of the relationship with the Church of England.[28] Jackson and Charles Wesley stood on different sides of this particular thorny fence, as is made clear in the body of the work. An unbiased critical assessment appears to have been low on the list of Jackson's priorities.

The first 50 years of Charles' life are covered by Jackson in exhaustive detail, with extensive extracts from the journal, supported for the first time by other printed and manuscript sources. Examination of Jackson's use of this material is fundamental to an appreciation of the traditionally weak state of Charles Wesley scholarship. His use of extracts is highly selective, and close perusal of the manuscript journal[29] and letters[30] reveals that phrases, sentences and even entire pages are omitted from Jackson's printed work. This is particularly the case where there is criticism of John Wesley and the preachers. One example of many occurs on page 124 of Volume 2, where the transcription of the journal entry for 26 October 1756 changes one preacher's description of the Church of England as 'Old Peg' to the more innocuous 'church'. One can see in the original document where Jackson has marked passages that are to be omitted.[31] Jackson's heavy hand of censorship was applied in the same way to his edition of a number of Charles' letters which Jackson included as an appendix to the journal.[32]

There are other glaring weaknesses in Jackson's work. Charles frequently used shorthand in his personal papers and such passages often reflect his most intimate and controversial opinions, yet Jackson missed these entirely.[33] The recent (2007) publication of a new edition of Charles' journal will, it is true, enable scholarship to be corrected on some of the main points to which the shorthand sections of the MS relate. However, it remains the case that until very recently indeed scholars working on Charles Wesley had only a highly defective edition of the journal with which to work, and hence Jackson's legacy has been a lasting one.

It is evident from Jackson's use of his sources that he was prepared to go only so far in his discussion of his subject, for fear of presenting the early Methodists in an unfavourable light. He was not alone in this attitude, nor was Charles Wesley the only Methodist whose contribution was sanitized by nineteenth-century historians. In his introduction to a printed edition of John Wesley's account of his abortive engagement to Grace Murray, the editor J. A. Leger has this to say concerning an earlier published transcript of this important document:

> Verbal alterations are pretty numerous wherever the editor has thought fit to improve upon Wesley's eighteenth-century style and grammatical forms. Nor is it easy to understand why so many clauses, sentences, and paragraphs have been suppressed, some of them quite essential to the perspicuity of the narrative . . . The most striking features of Grace's strange experiences have been also carefully left out.[34]

Leger's comments could equally be applied to Jackson's handling of Charles Wesley's journal and correspondence, key documents for the study of evangelical history.

Jackson would have experienced particular difficulty in the second volume of his biography consisting of a detailed study of Wesley's life after his retirement from the itinerancy in 1756. This was a challenge that previous scholars had avoided, but because the controversies of the 1790s were now over,[35] Jackson felt able to address some sensitive areas. He was therefore to acknowledge some, but by no means all, of the difficult aspects of Charles' character and conduct, while understating their impact on events and relationships. One of his major themes was the dispute concerning the growing call for Methodist separation from the Anglican Church – this was to be expected, given the importance of the issue and Charles' prominent role in the controversy. Possible division had been discussed by the annual Conference between the Wesley brothers and their preachers as early as 1744, only to be firmly rejected.[36] In 1755 matters came to a head with the revelation that some lay preachers were administering Communion, which if unchallenged would have signified a break with the Anglican Church.[37] This crisis was the main point of debate at the Conferences of 1755 and 1756. Jackson's sympathies are clearly with the preachers and against his subject, whose impetuous and inflexible manner is remarked upon.[38] In this and other nineteenth-century Methodist works, Charles is invariably portrayed as a man driven by prejudice and blind loyalty to the Anglican Establishment.[39]

One would assume from reading Jackson that, with the occasional exception of Charles himself, conflicts of opinion within early Methodism were generally worked out on a high moral ground without personal rancour. This is particularly the case with the preachers, for whom Jackson displays considerable sympathy.[40] The truth is different, for it is clear from the primary sources that several of the preachers disliked Charles intensely,[41] resenting what they viewed as his obsessive loyalty to a persecuting Church.[42] Jackson makes a point of denying that such was the case; following a description of John Wesley's controversial American ordinations in 1784, he states the following:

> Some persons have thought that the part which Mr Wesley took in opposition to his brother's ordinations, and against the administration of the sacraments . . . must have rendered him an object of dislike and jealousy among the Methodist preachers generally. But this is a mistake. Those who knew him best were convinced of his integrity and conscientiousness; and though they might dissent from his views of ecclesiastical order, they admired the man whom they saw to be as generous as he was upright.[43]

While it is true that Charles enjoyed the respect and possibly even the affection of some of the preachers like Samuel Bradburn and Joseph Benson,[44] others felt very differently – including men who went on to occupy the highest offices in the Methodist Church.

Jackson, as a minister of many years standing, served alongside veteran preachers like Adam Clarke, Thomas Vasey and Henry Moore, all of whom had personal knowledge of the Wesleys, and he must have been aware of the animosity felt towards Charles and his supporters. In any case, he knew that Charles was outspoken and possessed of a fiery temper – he describes him as a man 'generally happy in the application of epithets. Whether he intends to praise or blame, the names, which he gives to the parties whom he designs to characterize are usually appropriate and striking.'[45] It is unrealistic to expect from human nature – even that of Methodist preachers – that such feelings were never reciprocated. Jackson's description of the relationship between John and Charles Wesley is similarly unconvincing. The primary sources confirm that the two were close until middle age, both on a personal level and as co-evangelists. The beginnings of a divergence can be seen from the time of Charles' marriage in 1749; later that year John's engagement to Grace Murray was ended, principally by his brother's interference, and relations between them were never the same again.[46] Charles' retirement from the itinerancy, very much against John's wishes,[47] and the increasing bitterness concerning the Church of England, completed their partial estrangement. While Jackson acknowledges the differences, he does not examine in any detail the effect on their relationship, which by the late 1750s was one of mutual hurt and mistrust.

It is clear that Jackson had extreme difficulty in making Charles' later life fit into the accepted Victorian picture of early Methodism, torn between the demands of iconography and the reality of a man who in Mabel Brailsford's words was 'brilliant, unhappy and strangely inhibited'.[48] As a result, important aspects of his portrayal are unconvincing, tainted by denominational loyalty and a reluctance to draw uncomfortable conclusions. More than a hundred years after his death, Jackson is still the principal authority on the life and work of Charles Wesley. His edition of the journal has never been superseded and his biography remains the most detailed secondary source. How influential Jackson has been will be seen in the rest of this chapter.

## Twentieth-century scholarship

The next major biography of Charles Wesley was written by John Telford and published in 1900,[49] enlarged and revised from an earlier version issued in 1886 by the Religious Tract Society.[50] In his introduction, Telford claims that all available sources had been used, with the emphasis on the journal, the letters and 'Thomas Jackson's painstaking and judicious biography, which has been called the best history of Methodism'.[51] It should come as no surprise that Telford's book duplicates some of the weaknesses apparent in earlier works. The last 30 years of his subject's life are covered in just 51 pages out of a total of 309,[52] and a considerable portion of that is devoted to a description of Charles' happy marriage and family life.

Telford does not comment in detail on important episodes like the Grace Murray affair or the American ordinations of 1784, to both of which he allocates just two pages apiece. The defensive attitude, so often adopted by scholars when commenting on Charles' less attractive characteristics, is evident in the following observation:

> He was not always wise in the action which he took . . . No-one who understands his character would expect that he should be. Charles Wesley was not a calm judicious statesman like his brother, but a poet, with all a poet's emotion and impulsiveness. He was never made to stand alone, but to work with others who might be roused and cheered by his devotion and his love.[53]

Telford does, however, include some quotations from original documents, which inevitably provoke questions concerning aspects of Charles' personality. One such instance is John Wesley's writing to his brother in the following words: 'Your gross bigotry lies here, in putting a man on a level with an adulterer, because he differs from you as to church government. What miserable confounding the degrees of good and evil is this!'[54] The quotation is included without comment as to the significance of such strong language applied to a man described elsewhere by Telford as 'humble, free from all self-seeking and affectionate'.[55] This apparent contradiction demands an explanation deeper than Telford is prepared to give. Such a treatment of Charles, partly laudatory and partly negative, helped to elevate and isolate his brother as the supreme hero of Methodism.

In 1919, Dora Jones published *Charles Wesley: a Study*.[56] In her preface, Jones declared her reliance on Telford, who in her judgement had replaced Jackson as the standard biography.[57] Despite this assertion, she also stated that Jackson's edition of the journal was her main source of biographical information,[58] although she acknowledged that it was incomplete.[59] Jones includes only printed works in her 'list of the principal authorities'[60] and it appears unlikely that she made extensive use of manuscript material. By her own admission, Jones' work represented only a 'short sketch' and 'introduction'.[61]

In 1948 Frank Baker published a volume containing lengthy extracts from Charles' correspondence, much of which was previously unpublished.[62] Baker was the first scholar to concentrate exclusively on this material as a preliminary to a full edition of the letters, a project that was never completed. Baker's work is among the most revealing on the subject. His use of original sources, albeit largely confined to letters that Charles wrote, as opposed to those that he received, opened up a range of material. The book is, however, limited in length, and his commentary does not contain much in the way of new insight.

Like many other Charles Wesley scholars, Baker was a Methodist minister and this is reflected in his delicate handling of controversial issues. With regard to Charles' forcible prevention of John's marriage to Grace Murray in 1749, Baker has this to say:

> That Charles planned to outwit his brother seems certain; that he did so from the worthiest of motives even more certain. The thought of his brother's marrying at all was bad enough. But from the evidence which he possessed at the time it seemed that John Wesley was not only in danger of 'marrying beneath himself' but – a much more serious matter – of bringing scandal on his own good name and that of the Church . . . he acted hastily, passionately, but as the loyal servant of God.[63]

In this passage, Baker reveals a sympathy with his subject which seems to stand in the way of objective analysis. The Grace Murray affair illustrated a negative side of Charles' personality as well as the changing dynamics of the relationship between the brothers. As will be made clear later, Charles' motives for destroying his brother's engagement were both complex and discreditable.

Baker's treatment of Charles' relations with the preachers also lacks conviction. This is exemplified by the following passage:

> Although even the preachers who differed from Charles Wesley realised his sterling sincerity, his self-effacing humility, a measure of estrangement came between them. The cause was not any deficiency in the abilities or morals of a few preachers, but the tendency of a growing number to favour a breach with the Church of England.[64]

As with Telford, there is the emphasis on the positive aspects of Charles' personality and little direct reference to the negative traits; one of the contributing factors to Charles Wesley's unpopularity was precisely his sharp criticism of the abilities of several of the itinerants.

One of the most radical ventures into Charles Wesley scholarship was Mabel Brailsford's *A Tale of Two Brothers: John & Charles Wesley*, which appeared in 1954. She was the first biographer to have the fraternal relationship as her main theme and the only biographer so far to attempt a detailed and dispassionate examination of the Wesleys' bitter disagreements. Brailsford declares her intention in the foreword:

> For all practical purposes, John Wesley and his brother . . . parted company as co-evangelists half-way through their working life, and the disharmony between them, both public and private, was fostered by Charles up to the time of his death, and, by his own direction beyond it. The events and motives which occasioned this breach form the chief subject of this book . . . It is a tale of treachery . . . and of the loneliness of a man, robbed of what he held most dear, and deserted as he said, 'in his utmost need,' by his brother and fellow-worker.[65]

Brailsford acknowledged that her work was based largely on the published journals of the two men,[66] and she cites as a problem the fact that very few of Charles' letters had been published and edited.[67] Her observations on Jackson are insightful and could also be applied to other works on Charles Wesley:

> The discreet two-volume biography, written by Dr Thomas Jackson . . . suffers from the reticencies [sic] of its period and fails to paint a convincing picture . . . The author is biased by his sympathy as a fellow minister and tongue-tied, when he should be outspoken.[68]

However, Jackson's work remained very influential. Brailsford describes his depiction of early Methodism as 'clear and faithful, and I have followed it without question'.[69] In addition to Jackson, her main authorities were other printed sources such as *The Annals of Westminster School* and *John Wesley's Last Love*, although she did consult the original manuscript of which the latter is an edited transcript. It is unlikely that Brailsford made extensive use of the large collection of surviving primary material such as Charles' letters; that she was still able to reach different conclusions from those of other scholars is testimony to the complaisance of earlier work on the subject.

The central role of Charles in destroying his brother's engagement to Grace Murray is described in detail[70] and is seen as the turning point in their relationship.[71] Her treatment of this complex affair appears well argued. It is Brailsford's contention that concern over the future of Methodism was not Charles' only reason for opposing the match, but that he was reluctant to accept any relationship with John that threatened the fraternal bond.[72] In his efforts to thwart John's plans, Charles rode from Bristol to the north of England to ensure Murray's marriage to the Methodist preacher John Bennet. Using John Wesley's own account of the affair,[73] Brailsford reveals a side of Charles which earlier biographers had ignored or merely implied. In order to justify his behaviour, Charles placed the blame on John's shoulders: he attacked him before meetings of the Methodist society in Newcastle, describing him as a seducer of another man's wife (on the grounds that Murray was already promised to Bennet) and damning him as a 'child of the devil'.[74] Charles' attitude is all the more striking when one considers that his own entry into matrimony earlier that same year would not have been possible without John's active co-operation. Despite withdrawing his accusations, Charles never expressed remorse. On the contrary, towards the end of that year of 1749, he wrote an account of the episode vindicating his conduct and circulated it among the preachers.[75] It is hardly surprising that John withheld from his brother news of his marriage in February 1751 to Mary Vazeille until after the wedding. The unhappiness of John's married life should not be used as justification of Charles' behaviour, or to disguise the insight this episode provides into a rather volatile personality.

While concentrating on relations between Charles and John, Brailsford also reveals something of the tension that existed between Charles and the itinerants.[76] Regardless of the particular issues, the younger Wesley's mode of expression could not but give offence. The mistrust with which he was regarded by at least some of his brother's helpers is indicated in the following passage:

> Such intemperate language, combined with his somewhat slighting estimate of their abilities . . . did nothing to endear him to the rank and file of the preachers. This, together with his intimate friendship with the Countess of Huntingdon, and her aristocratic circle, made his own doctrine suspect, and the double charge of Calvinism and snobbery began with some truth to be made against him.[77]

Whether or not one agrees with Brailsford's conclusions, her at times radical reassessment of important aspects of Charles' life demands an acknowledgement of her work. It is surprising therefore that her book is rarely mentioned, and her arguments have yet to be examined in detail by other scholars.[78]

In recent years several popular biographies of Charles Wesley have been written, beginning with Frederick Gill's work in 1964[79] and this remains one of the best, offering a sound introduction to Charles' life. Some of Gill's statements are, however, inaccurate, such as his assertion that 'we have no voluminous records as of John [Wesley]'.[80] This is simply not the case, for while it is true that there is more material surviving for his brother, there are several thousand Charles Wesley manuscripts accessible to the public in archive repositories, particularly the Methodist Archives in Manchester.[81] Gill's statement is particularly surprising as he acknowledges the staff of the Methodist Archives Centre for their assistance.[82] Whatever form his access to the Archives took, Gill did not make extensive use of the Centre's Charles Wesley collection, which includes the manuscript journal and over six hundred letters, relying instead, by his own admission, on the Jackson edition of the journal and secondary sources.[83]

Gill is extremely generous in his treatment of his subject. His chapter describing the Grace Murray affair is titled 'Charles to the Rescue' and he describes John's attachment to Murray as a 'strange interlude . . . the kindest explanation is that he was a sick man at the time'.[84] His brother's interference in John's personal life is defended as follows:

> Charles acted impetuously, but with good reason . . . Charles' attitude has been criticised as interfering and inconsiderate, but he could hardly have stood aside. His deep concern for the welfare of the Church, and never more than when he rode the length of England to save his brother from such a venture.[85]

In his discussion of the American ordinations of 1784, Gill is more supportive of Charles' stand than earlier scholars but perhaps goes too far in his advocacy; his subject was not driven by prejudice but rather by commendable consistency and 'complete loyalty to his Methodist principles'.[86] His viewpoint is summed up by his description of the argument between Charles and the preacher John Hampson;[87] Charles is described as speaking with 'characteristic bluntness' while Hampson's response is 'rude'. Gill's conclusion is, however, valuable, displaying perception of the problem that Charles represents:

> Charles' attempts to preserve its [Methodism's] original aim had failed. As a result, his memory has suffered; with some there remains a lingering coolness, while to others his logical emphasis has been unwelcome, and in general no popular or clear-cut image has survived.[88]

Biographical treatments since Gill have been largely unimpressive. The chapter on Charles in the official history of the Methodist Church should be considered as little more than a general introduction.[89] Of 29 pages, 17 are devoted to a discussion of the hymns.[90] Arnold Dallimore's life of Charles Wesley[91] skates over the surface of the controversies of the later years, but he does provide additional evidence of Charles' rather unstable nature by quoting the Calvinistic preacher John Cennick: 'He [Charles Wesley] fell into a violent passion and affrighted all at the table . . . He called Calvin the first-born son of the Devil and set all his people into a bitter hatred of me.'[92] Dallimore does not, however, address in any detail the causes of the friction between the Wesley brothers, or the dispute with the preachers – a significant episode like the Norwich Sacramental dispute of 1760[93] is dismissed in three paragraphs with no comment as to its outcome.[94] One of the most impressive works on Charles should have been *Charles Wesley: A reader*,[95] an extensive edited collection of extracts from letters, sermons and the journal, presented in a visually attractive form by a major academic publishing house. In reality, the value of this work is diminished by glaring textual inaccuracies.[96] This unfortunate fact considerably lessens the impact made by the extensive use of unknown or previously unpublished manuscript material.

The most recent biography is by T. Crichton Mitchell, published in 1994.[97] Even allowing for the fact that the book was obviously intended for a general audience, it is still noteworthy for its lack of depth and insight. The foreword describes Charles as a 'vastly complex person, embodying the tension between the free spirit of the Evangelical Revival and the liturgical traditions of the English Church'.[98] What the reader is then presented with is a simplistic spiritual biography, written from a sympathetic evangelical perspective. In the introduction, Mitchell promises to bring Charles out from the shadow of his brother 'insofar as the records allow'[99] and attributes the previous scholarly neglect of his subject to Wesley's own carelessness in preserving personal papers. It is difficult to see how that conclusion could be reached, when one considers that during the course of his research, Baker transcribed 600 of Charles' letters.[100] Mitchell himself refers in the introduction to the existence of thousands of manuscripts[101] but cites only printed works; and the letters and journal extracts that he uses are all from published sources, most notably Jackson's edition and Baker. The promise in the foreword that the portrayal of Charles would not be characterized by 'uncritical adulation'[102] is not fulfilled in the main body of the work.[103]

## The case for a reassessment

The preceding survey of the biographical treatment of Charles Wesley explains why a new study is long overdue. Ever since his own lifetime he has posed problems for denominational scholarship, and the aggressively pro-Anglican viewpoint that Charles represented has been seen as rather an embarrassment. Coupled with his difficult personality, his refusal to compromise his principles made it hard for denominational historians to portray him sympathetically; intertwined with this reluctance to address certain issues was a reliance on corrupted texts, which in the case of the journal is itself fragmentary.

The main authorities on Charles have traditionally been Methodists, or connected with other evangelical churches. This has resulted in varying degrees of bias. Charles Wesley scholars have seemed reluctant to comment on or reveal material critical of the Wesleys or their followers, but most have been prevented by the importance of the issues from ignoring this aspect entirely. This has resulted in somewhat conflicting interpretations, portraying Charles as both a great Methodist and as an obstacle to the movement's seemingly natural progression to denominational status. This is not to say that such an interpretation is incorrect, for Charles was a complicated man living in volatile times; but there are still many gaps in our understanding.

It is valuable to consider briefly the differences in the scholarly treatment of the two Wesleys. John has been discussed and analysed in many academic and popular works; Charles on the other hand remains an obscure figure, seemingly fixed in his role as Methodist bard. His ministry and place within the evangelical movement is seen as secondary, a side-show to the John Wesley main event. By consistently downplaying the significance of the controversies of early Methodism, scholars have minimized and distorted not only Charles' role, but also that of a substantial body of opinion. Personal papers of the period reveal that Charles was not alone in fighting against separatist trends;[104] it was in fact a bitter struggle that continued for many years after his death, and the end result was a Methodist Church which, in Britain at least, possessed a unique character with deep roots in the movement's Anglican past. Yet his biographers have dismissed Charles' sympathizers as 'croakers and busy-bodies'.[105] The treatment of Charles and his circle can in fact be seen as an example of the victors writing history; Jackson and Telford wrote with the advantage of the hindsight provided by a flourishing Methodist Church.

The possibility that advocates of separation were not entirely representative of the views of the movement as a whole is significant.[106] The dominant school of opinion has given the impression that the bond between Methodism and the Anglican Church was progressively weakened by a number of factors, one of which was the wish of the people as championed by the itinerants.[107] If this argument can be shown to be flawed then it casts doubt on the traditional view of Charles Wesley as a man who was marginalized and out of touch. This would open the way for a new evaluation of his contribution and allow a new understanding of the evolution of early Methodism.

## Notes

1 This chapter was originally published in the *Bulletin of the John Rylands University Library of Manchester*, vol. 82, 1, pp. 81–99 under the title 'Charles Wesley and his Biographers: An Exercise in Methodist Hagiography'. It is reproduced here by courtesy of the University Librarian and Director, The John Rylands University Library, The University of Manchester.

2 George W. Bush, *A Charge to Keep* (New York: William Morrow & Company, 1999).

3 Discussed by several leading authorities including John Ernest Rattenbury, *The Evangelical Doctrines of Charles Wesley's Hymns* (London: Epworth Press, 1941), and Teresa Berger, *Theology in Hymns? A study of the relationship of doxology and theology* (Nashville: Kingswood Books, 1989).

4 *The Journal of Charles Wesley*, eds S T Kimbrough and Kenneth G. C. Newport (Nashville: Abingdon, 2007).

5 Thomas Jackson, *The Life of the Rev. Charles Wesley, sometime Student of Christ-Church Oxford*, 2 vols (London: Wesleyan Methodist Conference Office, 1841).

6 John Whitehead, *Some Account of the Life of the Rev. Charles Wesley, M.A., Late Student of Christ-Church Oxford, collected from his private journal* (London: Stephen Couchman, 1793).

7 *The Journal of the Rev. Charles Wesley, M.A., sometime Student of Christ-Church, Oxford . . .*, ed. Thomas Jackson, 2 vols. (London: Wesleyan Methodist Book Room, 1849) (hereafter referred to as *CWJ*).

8 For example, 1 January to 4 January 1738; 27 December 1738 to 1 January 1739; 22 September 1741 to 3 January 1743; 29 December 1747 to 13 January 1748 and 16 September to 21 October 1749.

9 Charles Wesley, MSJ 9 March 1736 – 6 November 1756; reference MARC, DDCW, 10/2.

10 Mabel Richmond Brailsford, *A Tale of Two Brothers: John & Charles Wesley* (London: Rupert Hart-Davis, 1954), 11.

11 For example, *Charles Wesley: A reader*, ed. John R. Tyson (Oxford and New York: Oxford University Press, 1989), 9.

12 Whitehead, *Charles Wesley*, 270.

13 Whitehead, *Charles Wesley*, 270.

14 Whitehead, *Charles Wesley*, 274.

15 William Myles, *A Short Chronological History of the Methodists* (Rochdale: J. Hartley, 1798).

16 Charles Atmore, *The Methodist Memorial; being an impartial sketch of the lives and characters of the preachers, who have departed this life since the commencement of the work of God, among the people called Methodists* (Bristol: Richard Edwards, 1801).

17 Atmore, *The Methodist Memorial*, 482.

18 Atmore's colleagues in London in 1797 and 1798 included James Creighton, Adam Clarke and John Pawson, all of whom had personal knowledge of Wesley.

19 John Pawson, *The Letters of John Pawson (Methodist Itinerant, 1762–1806)*, ed. John C. Bowmer and John A. Vickers (Peterborough: World Methodist Historical Society, 1994), 1.59.

20 Charles Wesley, *Sermons by the late . . . Charles Wesley . . . with a memoir of the author by the editor* (London: Baldwin, Cradock and Joy, 1816).

21 For example, Tyson, *Charles Wesley*, 9 and Frank Baker, *A Union Catalogue of the Publications of John and Charles Wesley* (Durham, NC: Duke University, 1966), 205.

22 John Tyson does suggest Sarah junior as an alternative candidate. John R. Tyson, *Charles Wesley on Sanctification: A biographical and theological study* (Grand Rapids: Francis Asbury Press of Zondervan Publishing House, 1986), 316. See further Chapter 12 below.

23 Quoted by Frederick C. Gill, *Charles Wesley the First Methodist* (London: Lutterworth Press, 1964), 228.

24 Charles Wesley, *Sermons*, xxxi.

25 Charles Wesley, *Sermons*, xxxii–xxxiii.

26 Jackson, *Life*, 1:viii–ix.

27 Jackson, *Life*, vi.

28 Jackson, *Life*, vii–viii.

29 Principally the bound manuscript journal catalogued as MARC DDCW, 10/2. Also, part of the manuscript collection catalogued as MARC, DDCW consists of either loose sheets from the journal or so-called 'Journal Letters', which are essentially journal extracts sent as letters – see for example MARC, DDCW, 6/1–29. It is possible that these formed the original draft of the bound journal catalogued as MARC, DDCW, 10/2.

30 Most of these are to be found in the Wesley papers at the MARC and are catalogued as collections DDCW and DDWes.

31 For example, out of 15 lines comprising the manuscript journal entry for 13 May 1750, only four were reproduced by Jackson in his edition of the journal. The missing 11 lines are erased in pencil in the original document. See MARC, DDCW, 10/2 *in loc* and CWJ, 2:71.

32 For example, in his manuscript journal for 12 June 1751 Charles describes some of the preachers as 'worthless, senseless, graceless men'. MARC, DDCW, 10/2. This is omitted from Jackson's printed version. *CWJ*, 2:82.

33 For example, manuscript journal entries for 26 June 1748, 17 November 1749 and 9 February 1750. MARC, DDCW, 10/2.

34 John Wesley, *John Wesley's Last Love*, ed. J. A. Leger (London: J. M. Dent & Sons Ltd, 1910), vi.

35 These included such questions as Methodist preachers being allowed to administer Communion and the holding of Methodist services during the hours of Anglican worship.

36 *Minutes of the Methodist Conferences from the first held in London by the late Rev. John Wesley, A.M. in the Year 1744* (London: Methodist Conference Office, 1812), 1.9.

37 Frank Baker, *John Wesley and the Church of England* (London: Epworth Press, 1970), 162–7.

38 Jackson, *Life*, 2.74.

39 For example, 'Charles Wesley, whose mind, less noble than his heart, was perpetually fettered by his High-Church sentiments . . . he seemed incapable of progress.' Stevens, *History of Methodism*, 1.311.

40 For example, Jackson, *Life*, 2.130–1.

41 For example, in one letter of 8 August 1787 to [Charles Atmore], John Pawson referred to Charles' bigotry and the fire of hell that was burning in his breast. *Letters of John Pawson,* ed. Bowmer and Vickers, 1.46.

42 See, for example, the letter of 28 April 1788 from John Pawson to [Charles Atmore]. *Letters of John Pawson,* ed. Bowmer and Vickers, 1.62.

43 Jackson, *Life*, 2.446.

44 For example, the letter from Samuel Bradburn to Samuel Bardsley [April 1788]. Quoted by Jackson, *Charles Wesley*, 2.446.

45 Jackson, *Life*, 2.75.

46 Frank Baker, *Charles Wesley as Revealed by his Letters* (London: Epworth Press, 1948), 74.

47 *BE*, 26.573.

48 Brailsford, *A Tale of Two Brothers*, 12.

49 John Telford, *The Life of the Rev. Charles Wesley, M.A.* (London: Wesleyan Methodist Book Room, 1900).

50 All citations in this work to Telford's *Life of the Rev. Charles Wesley* are based on the 1900 edition.

51 Telford, *Charles Wesley*, xiv.

52 Telford, *Charles Wesley*, 201–15 and 255–92.

53 Telford, *Charles Wesley*, xiii.

54 Telford, *Charles Wesley*, 204.

55 Telford, *Charles Wesley*, xiii.

56 [Dora] M. Jones, *Charles Wesley: A study* (London: Skeffington, 1919).

57 Jones, *Charles Wesley*, viii.

58 Jones, *Charles Wesley*, vii–viii.

59 Jones, *Charles Wesley*, viii.

60 Jones, *Charles Wesley*, viii and xi–xii.

61 Jones, *Charles Wesley*, vii.

62 Frank Baker, *Charles Wesley.*

63 Baker, *Charles Wesley as Revealed*, 72.

64 Baker, *Charles Wesley as Revealed*, 90.

65  Brailsford, *A Tale of Two Brothers*, 11.

66  While it is not stated explicitly, it is clear from the context of the foreword that Brailsford was referring to the published journals rather than the manuscripts. Brailsford, *A Tale of Two Brothers*, 12.

67  Brailsford, *A Tale of Two Brothers*, 12.

68  Brailsford, *A Tale of Two Brothers*, 12.

69  Brailsford, *A Tale of Two Brothers*, 12.

70  Brailsford, *A Tale of Two Brothers*, 175–215.

71  Brailsford, *A Tale of Two Brothers*, 12–13.

72  Brailsford, *A Tale of Two Brothers*, 196.

73  *John Wesley's Last Love*, ed. Leger.

74  Quoted by Brailsford, *A Tale of Two Brothers*, 198.

75  Brailsford, *A Tale of Two Brothers*, 212.

76  Brailsford, *A Tale of Two Brothers*, 251–2.

77  Brailsford, *A Tale of Two Brothers*, 252.

78  Tyson cites Brailsford in his footnotes to *Charles Wesley on Sanctification*, 18. Likewise, in the text of the *Reader*, 4, 8 and 21. Gill describes her book as 'interesting and well-written, but covering familiar ground'. Gill, *Charles Wesley*, 11. Arnold Dallimore in his *A Heart Set Free: The life of Charles Wesley* (Welwyn: Evangelical Press, 1988), does not mention Brailsford in his select bibliography.

79  Gill, *Charles Wesley*.

80  Gill, *Charles Wesley*, 11.

81  There are other substantial deposits at other institutions including Wesley College in Bristol and Drew, Emory and Duke Universities in the United States.

82  Gill, *Charles Wesley*, 9.

83  Gill, *Charles Wesley*, 11.

84  Gill, *Charles Wesley*, 146.

85  Gill, *Charles Wesley*, 148.

86  Gill, *Charles Wesley*, 197.

87  Gill, *Charles Wesley*, 219.

88  Gill, *Charles Wesley*, 234.

89  W. F. Lofthouse, 'Charles Wesley', in *A History of the Methodist Church in Great Britain*, ed. Gordon Rupp and Rupert Davies, 4 vols (London: Epworth Press, 1965–88), 1.115–44.

90  Lofthouse, 'Charles Wesley', 127–44.

91  Dallimore, *Charles Wesley*.

92  Dallimore, *Charles Wesley*, 97.

93  In 1760, the three resident itinerant preachers in Norwich began to administer Communion. This led to a major dispute involving both Wesley brothers. The preachers eventually agreed to desist.

94  Dallimore, *Charles Wesley*, 203.

95  *Charles Wesley*, ed. Tyson.

96  Examples of these are given by S T Kimbrough Jr in his review of the *Reader*. *Methodist History*, 29.1 (1990), 54–8.

97  T. Crichton Mitchell, *Charles Wesley: Man with the dancing heart* (Kansas City: Beacon Hill Press, 1994).

98  Mitchell, *Charles Wesley*, 9.

99  Mitchell, *Charles Wesley*, 11.

100  Baker, *Charles Wesley*, 4.

101  Mitchell, *Charles Wesley*, 12.

102 Mitchell, *Charles Wesley*, 9–10.

103 It is difficult to find any reference in Mitchell's work that is critical of Charles. His approach is illustrated by the affectionate descriptive terms which he frequently applies to his subject, such as the 'Methodist Music man' or the 'man with the dancing heart'.

104 See, for example, the series of letters written between 1773 and 1774 from the important London Methodist John Horton to Charles Wesley. Reference MARC, DDPr, 1/41–8.

105 Jackson, *Charles Wesley*, 2:137.

106 For a recent discussion of this important issue see Gordon Rupp, *Religion in England 1688–1791*, ed. Henry and Owen Chadwick, *Oxford History of the Christian Church* (Oxford: Clarendon Press, 1986), 444–8.

107 For example, 'although respect for the personal authority of [John] Wesley restrained the Methodist societies from formal separation until after his death, that action was ultimately inevitable. Nor was it surprising that the majority of the Methodist converts, drawn from the ranks of dissenters or the classes neglected by the ministrations of the Church, should sit loose to the relics of Anglican religious practice retained by their leaders. Their interest lay in the new church organization evolved by John Wesley, not in the old system in which he had been reared.' Norman Sykes, *Church and State in England in the XVIII Century* (Cambridge: Cambridge University Press, 1934), 394. Note also Simon's comment that 'A small minority of the people might desire to keep the Methodist Societies within the fold of the Established Church, but the great majority wished to receive the Sacraments from their own preachers. There seemed every likelihood of a great division . . . at [John] Wesley's death', John S. Simon, *John Wesley: The last phase*, 2nd edn (London: Epworth Press, 1962), 330–1.

## 2. Charles Wesley and the Eighteenth Century[1]

### JEREMY GREGORY

Scholars of the eighteenth century have seldom known how to place, or indeed known what to do with, Charles Wesley, and have thus tended virtually to ignore him altogether. Tellingly, two powerfully argued and hugely influential social and political interpretations of the period which did give some weight to Methodism – those by E. P. Thompson[2] and J. C. D Clark,[3] who, however else they may have disagreed about the trajectory of eighteenth-century society, were agreed that Methodism was essentially a reactionary and pro-establishment social and political force – hardly mention Charles as an individual in their analyses of the movement (he does not, for instance, feature in their indexes whereas John Wesley does). This may be surprising since both historians have sustained treatments of the Methodist revival which, on the face of it, could profitably have acknowledged the younger Wesley's input more fully. For example, in the course of his notorious discussion of Methodism, Thompson analysed Methodist hymns for their psychosexual nature (without properly mentioning their author),[4] and Clark's vision of John Wesley as a staunch pro-government (even Tory) supporter would probably have made more sense if he had been talking about Charles.[5] This is so since Charles' political verse (which was not published in his lifetime),[6] ardent royalism (he, with John, was accused of being a Jacobite in the 1740s, despite his near-veneration of the Hanoverian monarchs),[7] hostile views about the American War of Independence,[8] and friendship with members of the London social elite (who were fascinated by his talented musical sons, a fascination not always shared by other Methodists),[9] may well fit him more readily into Clark's model of an *ancien regime* figure than his brother, who was arguably more on the fringes of the eighteenth-century Establishment.[10] There is also no mention of Charles Wesley in John Brewer's wide-ranging account of eighteenth-century culture, despite the fact that he includes a discussion of church music and hymns (and does in fact mention John Wesley).[11] As sometimes happens to younger brothers, Charles has clearly been overshadowed by his elder sibling in the general historical record.

Whatever the lack of treatment of Charles Wesley by social, political and cultural historians, even historians of religion (including Methodist historians, despite the protestations of Frederick Gill and Gordon Rupp)[12] have too readily assumed that he was just an imitation, or version, of his brother (hence the myriad blanket catch-all references to 'the Wesleys'). Such scholars have really only been interested in Charles Wesley for the ways in which he concurred with or differed from John, and have been reluctant to consider him in his own right. But whereas the other contributions to this book will highlight and emphasize Charles Wesley's individual contribution and achievements, his impact on his age, and, in some cases, his uniqueness, this essay will explore the ways in which Charles Wesley reflected and refracted the period in which he lived. In so doing, I want to examine Charles Wesley as an eighteenth-century figure, his long life spanning most of the century – although in this, as in other areas, he was beaten by the even longer life of his more famous sibling.

Trying to see Charles Wesley in his eighteenth-century context immediately poses the question of how we should relate him to a period conventionally characterized by and associated with labels, terms and concepts such as 'the Enlightenment', 'the Age of Reason', and 'secularization'. In discussions of both John and Charles Wesley, with their stress on the 'religion of the heart', most historians have viewed them as being in some ways counter-cultural. Indeed, they have often portrayed the Wesley brothers as reacting against the dominant trends of the time; depending on the stance of the historian, that reaction has been seen as either 'backward looking' or 'forward looking'.[13] In this, Charles, with his often blunt, passionate and forthright personality, and especially as the author of intensely spiritual hymns, has sometimes been categorized as a proto-Romantic counter to the Age of Reason.[14] But it can be argued that both John and Charles Wesley should better be seen as children of their age, and as products of their time, rather than as reactions against it.[15] In Charles' case, someone educated at Westminster and Christ Church could never have been totally counter-cultural, and, throughout his life, the associations he made at both school and university played a significant part in linking him to the wider eighteenth-century world. As is well known, he was the school and university friend of William Murray (later Earl Mansfield, Lord Chief Justice of England), but there were plenty of other schoolfriends and college connections who helped win over a broader acceptance of early Methodism. In 1748, for instance, while preaching 'to many serious souls' at Fishponds, near Bristol, Charles noticed 'a coach with Mrs Knight, Miss Cheyne, Mr Edwin, and Sir William Bunbury. The latter challenged me for his old school fellow, in the face of the sun, and was not ashamed to join heartily in our hymns', and Bunbury later sent a servant who had behaved rudely to Wesley to a constable for punishment.[16] This is not, of course, to claim that all Charles' former school and college friends supported the Methodist project – in fact one accused him in 1743 of 'running mad'[17] – but it reminds us that it is hard to detach him from his age.

Understanding the relationship between an individual and his or her context is a highly complex matter which broaches questions about determinism and human agency, as well as the extent to which individuals are necessarily conditioned by the period in which they live. The undertaking also raises the issue of whether there was just one eighteenth century into which Charles Wesley can be placed, or whether, as some modern scholars would emphasize, were there a number of possibly contradictory but overlapping eighteenth centuries into which he could be located (and indeed everyone else who lived in the period).[18] Moreover, from a postmodern perspective, some psychoanalysts and literary critics might ask how far there was a coherent being called 'Charles Wesley' who can be put into an eighteenth-century context (however we define that context).[19] Furthermore, how far can we in the twenty-first century objectively understand either Charles Wesley the personality, or the period we label 'the eighteenth century', without bringing our own prejudices and standpoints to both? These questions are more readily raised than answered. Nevertheless, they may be worth airing, since they go to the heart of some of the issues associated with biographical or single-figure projects such as this book. For most of the twentieth century, the dominant historiographical trend, inspired in part by Marxist scholarship, was to downplay the part played by individuals in shaping history and to stress instead the importance of collectivities and groups, and the role of impersonal economic and social structural forces.[20] This led some historians in the mid-twentieth century to argue that the biography was not a proper historical method,[21] although during the last twenty years or so there has been a rehabilitation of the significance of the lives of individuals such as Charles Wesley, and the recognition of human agency, with the proviso that the individual concerned can only be understood as illustrative of wider trends.[22]

It would not be unfair to say that, to a large degree, Wesley and Methodist studies have been relatively untouched by these developments, and the 'great man/great men' approach to history has lasted much longer here than for most other topics. Approaches to Methodism are still dominated by discussions of its (assumed) principal founder, although in recent years there has been, at least among social historians of religion, a move away from a fixation with the leading personalities to a greater concentration on the Methodists and Wesleyans, and in particular to the 'ordinary' men and women who encountered, took on board, and shaped the Methodist message.[23] It could be argued that part of Charles Wesley's significance was that without him these 'ordinary' people would not have left an historical record since it was often in letters to him that they wrote about their religious experiences,[24] and in this he probably had a larger part to play than his brother in giving a voice to those who would otherwise have been hidden from history.

One of the central problems in placing Charles Wesley within an eighteenth-century context is that scholars of Methodism often work within accounts of the period which are outmoded and ignore many of the ways in which our knowledge about eighteenth-century Britain has changed. During the past twenty years or so, there has been a vast explosion of scholarship on what is fashionably called 'the long eighteenth century' which has opened up a much more multifaceted set of interpretations of the time, and which means that some of our traditional understandings of the period (on which much Methodist scholarship is still premised) have been challenged or modified on a number of levels. Scholarly work on all aspects of history (whether religious, political, social, economic, cultural or intellectual) has unearthed a much more complex and dynamic society than the traditional characterization of this as the 'dull' century in British history implied. New topics, such as women's and gender history, and the rise of consumer society (which have an important bearing on the history of early Methodism), have opened up additional areas for debate, while familiar subjects such as the agricultural and industrial revolutions, and the unreformed political system (topics which have been used as reference points by some historians of Methodism) have received fresh consideration which has, in some cases, significantly modified older interpretations.[25] A challenge for historians of Methodism is to place Charles Wesley within these newer interpretations of the period. The challenge is also to make their findings accessible to a wider audience, since accounts of Methodism are often internally driven (sometimes, it seems, trying to fight battles about the nature of Methodism, and finding – perhaps forcing – connections between the eighteenth century and the present), and they seldom seem to have much to say to the more general historian, who is bemused by such navel gazing. But in acting as a broker between historians of Methodism and historians of the eighteenth century, Charles may be a more useful figure than his brother.

Perhaps the most obvious way in which our understanding of the eighteenth century has changed in the last quarter of a century (and which has a clear bearing on how we locate Charles Wesley within his age) has been the transformation in our understanding of the eighteenth-century Church of England, and the place of religion more broadly in the period.[26] Older histories viewed this both as an age of secularization and as a nadir in the history of the Anglican Church.[27] In this scenario, Methodism was seen as a backlash against the pastoral torpor of the established Church, as well as a counter-cultural throwback to an age of religious fervour and excitement. In this context, it is worth stressing that many of the ways in which the pessimistic history of the eighteenth-century Church of England was written, both in the nineteenth and in much of the twentieth centuries, was from what has been called a 'Methodist perspective',[28] with John's (and to some extent Charles') criticisms of the Anglican Church being cited as proof of the shortcomings of that institution – although their negative comments were often taken out of context, and generally were not balanced by the enormous amount of affection which both brothers, and especially Charles, could feel towards it. A telling instance of this is the way in which the influential nineteenth-century Methodist scholar Thomas Jackson edited and published Charles' journal. In the index there are only four references to the Church of England – and they are bracketed under the heading 'low state of'[29] – despite the fact that there are a large number of times when the Church is mentioned in the journal which could be interpreted in a very different light.[30] Indeed, from 1737 to 1739, precisely when some scholars have seen Methodism emerging as a reaction to the perceived shortcomings of the Anglican Church, Wesley found 'comfort'[31] from the church services he attended, and during this period Charles, as throughout the rest of his life, was an advocate for frequent Communion (in late February 1738, for example, he was communicating nearly every day).[32]

If John's relationship to the Church of England can be regarded as complex,[33] Charles' was certainly so. He could (like John) be sharply critical of contemporary Church practice, leading him to lament on a number of occasions the situation of 'our desolate Mother the Church of England', or, at other times, 'the ship, the shattered, sinking Church of England'.[34] But these phrases are pithily symbolic of Charles' attitude towards the established Church: he saw it as a mother who needed to be saved, and as a ship which needed to be rescued. His criticisms of the established Church can thus be viewed as an attempt to salvage and revive it, and to eradicate 'modern' vices which, in his opinion, had betrayed the true ideals of the institution. He was particularly critical of those whom he considered to be 'our modern Pharisees . . . these men [who] cry out "The Church, the Church", when they will not hear the Church themselves, but despise her authority, teach contrary to her Articles and Homilies, and break her canons',[35] and here he envisaged his role as reminding the Church what its true teachings were, believing himself to be more Anglican than the Anglicans. What is also striking is how far he understood his own 'rediscovery' of Reformation principles to be really an unearthing of true Anglican doctrine. Just before his conversion he had been reading Luther on salvation by faith alone and he noted: 'I am astonished I should ever think this is a new doctrine: especially when our Articles and Homilies stand unrepealed and the key of knowledge is not yet taken away.'[36]

Throughout Charles' life as a priest he repeatedly made claims which echoed his 1748 statement that 'all our desire is the salvation of souls and the establishment of the Church of England'.[37] In this he saw his mission as increasing people's affection for the Church, taking special pride in bringing them back to the Anglican fold. He frequently congratulated himself on encouraging his followers to take Communion in church, observing, for instance, when at York Minster in 1756 that '[t]hey were forced to consecrate twice, the congregation being doubled and trebled through my exhortation and example'.[38] In the same year he spoke approvingly of the Methodist society in Leeds who 'were unanimous to stay in the Church, because the Lord stays in it, and multiplies his witness therein, more than in any other Church in Christendom',[39] and when in Ireland in 1748 he 'took occasion to vindicate the Methodists from the slander that they rail against the clergy. I enlarged on the respect due to them, prayed particularly for the Bishops, and laid it on their conscience to make mention of them all in their prayers.'[40] And although Wesley was eventually happy to preach anywhere, it is striking how often his outdoor preaching was conducted in churchyards, as if to demonstrate his umbilical attachment to the institution.[41] By the 1750s he maintained that 'experience convinces me more and more that the Methodists can never prosper, or even stand their ground unless they continue steadfast in the ordinances [of the Church]',[42] and that 'Scripture comes with double weight to me in a Church'.[43] He was, rather against John's wish, buried in Marylebone churchyard, writing to the incumbent from his death-bed, 'Sir, whatever the world may have thought of me, I have lived, and I die, in the communion of the Church of England, and I will be buried in the yard of my parish church.'[44] It may be that one reason why Charles Wesley has not been much studied by Methodist historians is because he does not fit easily into the received picture of Methodism gradually distancing itself from the Church. If anything, his trajectory was to become increasingly Anglican,[45] and in this he could be placed into a model of eighteenth-century character types who went from youthful rebellion to a more conservative stance in their old age (and as such he has clear affinities with other eighteenth-century figures such as William Wordsworth and Samuel Taylor Coleridge).[46]

But in discussing Charles' relationship to the Church of England, I do not want to rehearse the magnificent research of Gareth Lloyd on some of these issues, in particular the ways in which Lloyd has shown that Charles advocated the Church–Methodist position in Conference and elsewhere, acting almost as an 'Anglican conscience' against what he felt were John's tendencies towards nonconformity.[47] Rather, I want to note some recent scholarship which has emphasized the ways in which, long before the Wesley brothers' 'conversion' in May 1738, Anglicanism had itself been undergoing a movement of renewal and reform. This was witnessed most obviously by the creation of the religious societies, the societies for the reformation of manners, the Society for Promoting Christian Knowledge, and the Society for the Propagation of the Gospel in Foreign Parts; but the impulse for reform can also be seen in the attempts of the Church's hierarchy to improve the quality of the standards of pastoral care more generally.[48] For some historians at least, this reforming temper remained a constant current throughout the century, which has led them to argue that the Church in the eighteenth century should be seen as continuing the work of the Reformation.[49] This is not to say that some of this scholarship is not in itself controversial. W. R. Ward (himself a Methodist), for instance, warned some time ago that in his opinion the fashionable rehabilitation of the eighteenth-century Church was going much faster than the evidence warranted.[50] But the activity outlined above (the existence of which cannot be doubted, even if its general significance can be) does suggest that we should view Charles' relationship to the Church in which he was born, ordained (deacon by John Potter, Bishop of Oxford, and priest by Edmund Gibson, Bishop of London, two of the luminaries of the Hanoverian Church), and, so he claimed, lived and died, in a more nuanced way than most accounts of the rise of Methodism would have it. Methodist scholarship is usually premised on the given fact of a moribund and ineffective established Church, but it may be that the Wesleys themselves are evidence of a lively Anglican culture, and much of what has been considered to be Methodist innovation should perhaps be seen as emerging from within an Anglican Church which was itself experimenting with developments in pastoral care.[51]

We can also point to the ways in which Charles' undoubted lasting contribution to Christian piety – his hymns – articulated an Anglican rather than a distinctively Methodist religiosity. To put it another way, Charles' Methodist hymns articulated an Anglican spirituality, and drew deeply on his eighteenth-century context. As is well known, his *Hymns on the Lord's Supper* (1745), for instance, were almost wholly indebted in terms of subject matter and imagery to the devotional treatise by Daniel Brevint (c. 1616–95, and dean of Lincoln Cathedral), *The Christian Sacrament and Sacrifice* (1673);[52] and his *Hymns on the Trinity* (1767) were based on the high-churchman William Jones' *The Catholic Doctrine of a Trinity Proved by Arguments . . . Expressed in the Terms of the Holy Scripture* (1756).[53] A full assessment of Wesley's hymnody will be found elsewhere in this volume, but it is worth stressing here that placed alongside the full range of eighteenth-century verse and poetry they are perhaps more in tune with their time than some scholars have claimed. Since the 1980s, our understanding of eighteenth-century poetry has been transformed by Roger Lonsdale's influential collections which have alerted us to the sheer range of verse in the period, and which have shown how far religious sentiment, emotion and imagination were embedded within the so-called Age of Reason. While this is not the place to rehearse the debates among literary scholars about the merits of using terms such as 'pre-' or 'proto-' Romantic to discuss some of this material, it is clear that eighteenth-century writing was much more varied than some accounts (usually from a 'Romantic' perspective) have claimed. Given this, Wesley's ('pre-Romantic') verse can be seen to fit not only into the Anglican tradition, but also into a context of religious and imaginative writing which was part of, not apart from, the general literature of the age, and from which in some cases (such as the poems of Elizabeth Singer Rowe) he drew heavily.[54] He was – in common with many other eighteenth-century men and women – a great admirer of Edward Young's *Night Thoughts* (1742), claiming in 1754 that 'no writings but the inspired are more useful to me'.[55] Charles also wrote in a number of characteristically eighteenth-century poetic genres such as the elegy, and poems on the death of friends and relations, which again place him firmly within the mainstream of the religious literary culture of the period. And similarly, as a great admirer of Handel (he wrote poems about him), Wesley was participating in the broader Anglican artistic culture of the time.[56]

But although those studies of Charles Wesley which do exist highlight his attachment to the Church, they find it hard to square with some aspects of his behaviour which, especially, from 1739 to the early 1750s, seemed to undermine Anglican practice (and there is some suggestion that in the years immediately after 1739 he was more radical in his innovations than John).[57] What perhaps needs to be emphasized is that eighteenth-century Anglicanism could be more flexible and more pragmatic than either Methodist or later Anglican writers have acknowledged. To take one instance which has received very little serious attention from his biographers: Charles' time in Georgia in 1736. This is usually regarded as a complete failure, and as such is seen to have little to do with the rest of his life. T. Crichton Mitchell's biography of Charles blames his lack of pastoral success during his time in Georgia on the fact that he was not yet an 'Evangelical'.[58] This begs all kinds of questions about how we should define 'Evangelical', and it may be that 'Methodist' handling of Charles' biography has tended to exaggerate the nature of the divide of May 1738 (as seen in Jackson's editorial insertion for Part 2 of Wesley's journal: 'From December 3 1736 when he landed in England to May 21 1738, when he received the Christian salvation'). Even a cursory reading of Wesley's journal and correspondence indicates that for him 'heartfelt' religion was possible before 1738, and there was much talk of 'new birth' before that date.[59] There are certainly moments – such as his observation in Georgia that 'it were endless to mention all the Scriptures which have been for so many . . . adapted to my circumstances'[60] – which are at least suggestive of a biblicism and a personal relationship with God, as was his behaviour during the storm on his way back from Georgia which certainly displayed a sense of the religion of the heart.[61]

There are several points worth noting about his experience in Georgia as James Oglethorpe's secretary, where he spent much of his time in Anglican pastoral work, and which may have had a greater bearing on his later life than biographers have tended to assume. First, the ways in which the Church of England operated in North America as a missionary institution, lacking the structures, fabrics and personnel of the Church at home, may have made it easier for Charles to have a flexible attitude to the practices of the Church in England after 1738. In Georgia there were, for example, no properly consecrated places of worship. Charles preached in the storehouse ('our tabernacle at present'), and in the guardroom, and even outside;[62] and, given the pressing situation, it was customary to rely on lay readers – perhaps even lay preachers. Benjamin Ingham's situation is instructive – he was only a deacon, and was appointed as a lay reader to the Georgia mission, but there is evidence (including that from Charles' journal) that he preached.[63] Given the rudimentary nature of church furnishings, Wesley baptized by immersion,[64] a practice which, while not unknown in the contemporary Anglican Church at home, was certainly unusual. Quite what effect witnessing the functioning of the Anglican Church in Georgia had on Charles' understanding of how the Church might operate in necessity has not been fully thought through, but it may well have been that Charles' experience of working for the Church in a missionary context shaped what he felt the Church could do in what he considered the home mission field. For example, was his early encouragement of lay preachers after 1739 in any way influenced by what he saw of the role of lay readers in the colonial Church? Likewise, the pastoral initiatives developed in Georgia within the framework of the Anglican Church – such as the 'Charlestown' ('Charleston') hymnal of 1737 – need more consideration for their effect on Charles' later hymnody. And Charles' few weeks in Boston (experiencing the Church of England as a 'nonconformist Church' to the New England Congregationalist establishment) needs further exploration. To what extent did his experience of the Church as a nonconformist Church encourage him later to support some of the tactics developed by nonconformists in England?

Second (and in a way which would help connect religious history with the wider history of the century), the Wesley brothers' sojourn in North America could benefit from being integrated into the recent spate of scholarship on the transatlantic world and Britain's imperial mission.[65] In this, Charles could usefully be viewed as a broker of information about Georgia to the London scene, appearing on his return before the Board of Trade to answer questions about jurisdictional disputes between the colonies of Georgia and Carolina,[66] and representing the case of a Boston high-churchman whom Wesley felt had 'true primitive piety' and who wanted to be ordained by the bishop of London to work as missionary for the Society of the Propagation of the Gospel in New England.[67] He was also perturbed by the 'shocking instances' of cruelty he witnessed to negro slaves at the hands of the planters.[68]

Third, Charles' correspondence reveals that he kept in contact with those who were in North America for much of the rest of his life, which is suggestive of the ways that his North American trip had a more lasting impact than the bare record of a nine-month visit would suggest. His autobiographical letter of 1785 to Thomas Bradbury Chandler was to a future American Episcopalian bishop, and in a postscript to the letter Wesley called Samuel Seabury – the first American Episcopalian bishop – 'a REAL "primitive bishop"',[69] reporting with relief that Seabury considered the American Methodists to be true members of the Episcopal Church, which mirrored his own views of the relationship between Methodism and Anglicanism.

If Charles' Anglicanism would repay greater attention than it has hitherto received, and which would, I argue, locate him more firmly within his century than the counter-cultural interpretation would have it, there are other ways in which Wesley can be placed more centrally into recent eighteenth-century scholarship with profit. One of the most important historiographical developments during the past 20 years has been to widen and complicate what might be meant by 'the Enlightenment'. Traditional scholarship, heavily based on a French model of the Enlightenment, viewed it as an anti-religious force,[70] and in this the Wesleys, and Methodism more generally, could be portrayed as a counter-Enlightenment backlash.[71] More recently, scholars working on British history have argued that the Enlightenment was not necessarily anti-religious, and the late Roy Porter, in a seminal essay, argued that in the English Enlightenment piety and reason could go hand in hand.[72] Moreover, Charles Wesley himself can be put into an 'Enlightenment' framework, complicating the view of the Wesleys as 'anti' or 'counter' Enlightenment.[73] The lynchpin of Charles' theology – Arminianism and universal redemption – endlessly reiterated in his correspondence, his journal, and his hymns, was not only the dominant theology of the Church of England (again indicative of the fact that we need to understand Wesley as an Anglican), but its central premises can be understood as chiming in with the Enlightenment emphasis on optimism, human potential and the essential equality of humankind.[74] Likewise, Wesley's emphasis on evidence and experience can be seen as echoing Enlightenment traits. This is not to say that Wesley was directly influenced by Enlightenment thought, or that we need to speak of a *Zeitgeist*, but it is to argue that there was at least an elective affinity between his central concerns and those usually viewed as belonging to the Enlightenment. And on another level, the language of 'enlightenment' itself surely has a close correlation with the transformation and illumination Wesley associated with religious experience and understanding, and he frequently spoke of religious experience using light metaphors. For instance, on seeing the changes Methodism had brought to the people of Tyril Pass in Ireland in 1748, he observed they 'were wicked to a proverb . . . but how the scene is entirely changed . . . They are turned from darkness to light!'[75]

It can also be argued that the whole thrust of Charles Wesley's religious message was – in Enlightenment fashion – the centrality of experience and feeling. His fundamental criticism of William Law, for example, whom he much admired, was that Law's understanding of 'new birth' was just a theory; converts would not really know that they had experienced a new birth, whereas Wesley was convinced of the need actually to feel the experience.[76] Indeed it is the accounts of the religious experiences of Methodists in their letters to Charles Wesley which constitute an important untapped source for how Methodism affected the lives and consciousness of ordinary men and women. But if Wesley put great emphasis on sensation and empiricism, he was – again in Enlightenment fashion – keen to ensure that the experience was a genuine one, and that the convert was neither deluded nor fabricating their feelings (and in any case this needed to be tempered by reason, in a characteristically eighteenth-century balance). His concern with experience and feeling should in any case be understood as part of an eighteenth-century emphasis on empiricism and sentiment (seen in such a typically eighteenth-century virtue as benevolence) rather than as what might be thought to be a full-blooded Romanticism.[77]

Wesley can be linked to the Enlightenment in other ways. In the last decade or so, it has been fashionable to argue that one of the key hallmarks of the Enlightenment in England was the concern with 'politeness' and sociability. A number of historians, such as Paul Langford and Lawrence Klein,[78] have explored the secular aspects of what might be deemed polite behaviour, but Charles Wesley valued this attribute as well for religious reasons. Recently, David Hempton has rightly urged us to examine the noisy and impolite side of early Methodism, and the ways in which Methodism could challenge cultural and social conventions.[79] Wesley's journal, for instance, noted the stones, dirt and eggs thrown at the early Methodists.[80] And, as befitting someone so passionately interested in sound and music, his journal also records the din associated with early Methodism, as in the screaming women in Bristol he noted in the early 1740s,[81] in the 'roaring stamping, blaspheming . . . and ringing the bells' in anti-Methodist riots,[82] and in the shouting and singing matches between himself and his opponents (which Charles won by 'lifting up [his] voice like a Trumpet').[83] But Charles Wesley was more concerned about the ways in which politeness, proper behaviour and Methodism could go hand in hand, and he seems to have wanted to distance both himself and the Methodist movement from those whom he deemed to be unruly. It is true that he was disdainful of what he considered to be the affected and the superficial politeness of Bath (which he named 'the Sodom of our Land'),[84] but after a return visit to Cork he was pleased to report in 1748 that 'much good has been done already in this place. Outward wickedness has disappeared, outward religion succeeded. Swearing is seldom heard in the streets; churches and altars are crowded to the astonishment of our adversaries.'[85] A remarkable instance of the transforming power of Methodism admired by Charles can be found in the following account:

one poor wretch told me, before his wife, that he had lived in drunkenness, adultery, and all the works of the devil, for twenty-one years had beat her every day of the time; and never had any remorse till he heard us; but now he goes constantly to Church, behaves lovingly to his wife, abhors the thing that is evil, especially his old sins.[86]

These quotations are interesting not only for Wesley's recognition of the value of 'polite' behaviour, but also for his emphasis on the significance of 'outward' religious conduct and the reformation of manners[87] (and thus bringing him closer to the dominant characteristics of the age), when scholars have usually emphasized the centrality of 'inward' manifestations of religion to the Methodist movement. In 1745 'before preaching I read them the late Act against swearing, of which 100 had been sent to my brother'.[88] He also noted that it was 'the exemplary behaviour' of some of the societies which 'convinced the ministers that this new sect, everywhere spoken against is no other than the sect of the Nazarenes, or real Christians'.[89] Wesley also recognized that the eighteenth-century social elite found the 'fits and trances' associated with early Methodism to be one of the stumbling blocks for joining the movement.[90]

Related to eighteenth-century concepts of politeness was the period's interest in sociability. When leaving Georgia, General Oglethorpe recommended Charles to abandon the celibate life and marry: 'you are of a social temper, and would find in a married state the difficulties of working out your salvation exceedingly lessened, and your helps as much increased'.[91] Charles' domestic life can indeed link him to the vigorous scholarship on eighteenth-century marriage and sexuality. Ever since Lawrence Stone's pioneering study of *The Family, Sex, and Marriage, 1500–1800* (1977), which placed great stress on the eighteenth century as a crucial period for what he termed the rise of 'affective individualism' (and how far does this in itself connect to Methodism?), the companionate marriage, and the development of a new world for children, which supposedly replaced older patterns of a patriarchal family where there were distances between husbands and wives, and between parents and children, social historians have debated how far these were indeed new experiences in the eighteenth century.[92] But whatever the limits of Stone's analysis, the relationship between Charles Wesley and Sarah Gwynne was certainly companionate and compassionate (calling her 'my dearest Sally', 'my dearest partner', 'my best of friends');[93] and, given the number of their progeny, their relationship hardly fits Thompson's picture of a repressed and repressive Methodist sexuality. To a large extent they also shared a spiritual journey, although for the first years of his marriage Charles was happy to leave 'my partner for my master'.[94] And while Wesley's children can hardly have been typical, what we know of his relations with them, at least as revealed through his correspondence, hardly fits into Stone's characterization of the supposedly harsh world of Wesleyan child-rearing (based on reading Susanna Wesley's much-quoted description of how she brought up her children).[95] As Charles Wesley's own family indicates, the Epworth household was not the only model of the Methodist family on offer in the eighteenth century. He himself appears to have doted on his children, and it was partly because of the musical needs of his talented sons that Charles and his family left Bristol for London in 1771. Moreover, did Charles stop writing his introspective journal on 5 November 1756[96] (interestingly at around the same time that he ceased itinerating) because by then there was less need for such introspection: did he now have happiness in his family life?

Within the broad concept of sociability, one of the developments of the eighteenth century which has received a fair amount of scholarly consideration is its penchant for clubs and associational life.[97] Methodism itself has sometimes been viewed as a joint-stock association typical of the age,[98] and in many ways its societies should be seen as religious variants of the 'secular' clubs which have attracted the attention of historians. The original Oxford gathering which Charles convened in 1729 was called the 'holy *club*', and the Wesleys' interest in societies (with Charles often taking the initiative in establishing them) is a salutary warning against an over-concentration on the individualism sometimes associated with the Methodist movement. It is not perhaps too far fetched to argue that Charles Wesley was himself to a certain extent 'clubbable' (he had an extensive wine cellar).[99] His links to the world of eighteenth-century sociability and clubbability may be worth pursuing, and he may even have viewed 'clubbability' as a way of furthering the Methodist cause. From the 1740s, he was a friend of Priscilla Wilford (stage name Stevens) who became the third wife of the London theatre-manager John Rich. She joined the Methodists, and with Charles's advice converted the Rich family to Methodism.[100] The concert series Charles promoted (both in his London home in Chesterfield Street, Marylebone, and elsewhere) can also be placed within a growing body of literature which has seen music-making as one of the key ways in which eighteenth-century men and women participated in the world of sociability.[101] And in the 1770s he was part of – though admittedly on the fringes of – Dr Johnson's club, and knew David Garrick, Charles Burney, as well as Hannah More and William Wilberforce (who first met Wesley at one of More's gatherings in 1786).[102] Moreover, the similarities between Wesley and Samuel Johnson deserve more exploration.[103] Not only did Johnson (whom Boswell claimed was 'in a dignified manner, a Methodist')[104] speak more approvingly of the Wesley brothers as individuals than some of his statements about the Methodists as a group might have suggested, but certain of his character traits, such as a mixture of optimistic sociability, and the tendency to depression, seem to have echoes in Charles Wesley's temperament.[105]

As well as research into the Enlightenment, politeness, the family, and sociability, a topic which has became fashionable for historians of the eighteenth century following the publication of Linda Colley's *Britons: Forging the nation, 1707–1837* is that of national identity.[106] Colley argued that it was during this period that men and women began to think of themselves as 'British' rather than as 'English' or 'Scots', or having a more regional affiliation. Charles Wesley can certainly be placed within a fiercely nationalistic camp. In 1746, during the panic of the Jacobite uprising, the love feast he led in Newcastle resulted in 'a mighty prayer for the Church and nation'.[107] There is also something almost John Bullish about his hatred of the French (which is clearly related to his anti-Catholicism),[108] as in his boast to Sarah in 1759 (during the threat of a French invasion of Britain): 'wherever I am I press all into service of our nation against the French'.[109] Moreover, in line with Colley's suggestion that behind the concept of 'Britishness' were ideas about the British being God's elect nation, was his belief that 'our nation' had God on its side (as witnessed in his hope in the same year: 'But if God be for us, who can be against us?').[110] But Wesley does complicate her argument somewhat: he rarely, if ever, talked about his 'Britishness', but there are a number of times when he talked about his 'Englishness'.[111]

The topics of the Enlightenment, politeness, sociability, the family, and national identity can be seen as aspects of a broader debate about the nature of eighteenth-century society and social relations, and the part played by the

Wesleys and Methodism in either maintaining or changing these. Ever since Elie Halévy and Robert Wearmouth's classic studies of the social consequences of Methodism – which the former linked to the avoidance of a British-style French Revolution, and the latter to the birth of a working-class consciousness – historians have debated the social purchase of Methodism, wondering how far it was a religion for or of the people.[112] What is clear is that, whatever the social outcomes of the movement, Charles Wesley – however much he associated with the poor (he once called them 'my best friends')[113] – saw himself (he once claimed rank as a gentleman in an argument with a JP),[114] and they saw him, as a gentleman. On a number of occasions he preached in assembly rooms (the seat of eighteenth-century politeness),[115] and he was pleased when the elite took the lead in promoting 'true vital Christianity'.[116] As the son of a clergyman, and being an Oxford-educated clergyman himself, it could hardly have been otherwise.

Charles' understanding of society and social relations drew deeply on traditional paternalist ideals. He seems to have believed in a hierarchical yet organic community, and he was certainly inclusive, incorporating all in his vision, such as tinners, miners, colliers and keelmen. At Birstall in 1743, in a phrase from Luke 14 and redolent of imagery often used by his brother, Charles remembered that 'I called the poor and maimed and halt and blind to the great supper'.[117] In one episode, in an almost textbook illustration of E. P. Thompson's concept of the eighteenth-century 'moral economy',[118] Charles was met by about a thousand colliers who complained about the price of corn, in a way in which Thompson envisaged eighteenth-century crowds treating with members of the local elite prior to a food riot. Charles was able to calm them down, and, so he claimed, 'singing stopped a riot'.[119] In this, as elsewhere, Wesley seems more readily to have operated under Thompson's vision of a paternalistic moral economy rather than under the harsher world envisaged by Thompson's description of Methodism in *The Making of the English Working Class*.

In trying to place Wesley within the eighteenth century, the historian is fortunate to have an abundance of primary material (much of which is as yet under-utilized). One of the sources (but of course not the only one) for understanding Charles Wesley is his journal. Although a later essay will be devoted to the journal, it is worth noting here that the keeping of journals and autobiographies (whether or nor intended for publication) was one of the characteristic genres of the age, and has been linked to the period's preoccupation with Enlightenment individualism.[120] The keeping of a journal to record the details of this life has also been connected with the supposed secular priorities of the age. But, as we have seen, our understanding of the Enlightenment can now embrace religious concerns, and Charles' journal should really be understood within the tradition of spiritual autobiographies going back to St Augustine. Charles' journal more readily fits into this genre than his brother's, which is far more of a publicly orientated record of the achievements of the Methodist movement rather than an account of his religious beliefs.[121] What is also striking is the heightened language of Charles' journal when discussing religious matters, which in places is echoed in later hymns.[122]

But if Charles Wesley's journal is much more of a spiritual autobiography

than his brother's (containing as it does far more evidence of religious introspection and soul-searching), it can also be viewed as a medical diary, and
in this the journal is a useful record of Charles' many illnesses. There is, of
course, a close correlation between Wesley's religious and his medical life. He
seems frequently to have thought during his many periods of illness that he
was about to die, noting in 1738 that 'at eleven I waked in extreme pain, which
I thought would quickly separate soul and body'.[123] Helped by the lavish
funding of the Wellcome Institute, issues of medicine, health and 'the body'
have been hot topics for eighteenth-century historians. But while historians
of medicine such as Roy Porter have paid some attention to John Wesley's
medical writings, and in particular to his *Primitive Physick*,[124] Charles' journal would also merit some discussion since it reveals much about eighteenth-
century maladies: pleurisy, flux, distemper, headache, toothache, dysentery,
fevers, bowel complaints, lumbago, rheumatism and depression are frequently mentioned, as well as the prescriptions for them such as bleedings, vomit-
ings, purgings, taking laudanum and 'the bark', and smoking tobacco. Wesley
also records his interest in experimenting with contemporary fads such as
vegetarianism and milk diets, as well as his desire to have indulged in such
fashionable cures as sea-bathing in Margate, had he had the time (which in
typically Methodist fashion he did not).[125] *Inter alia*, then, Charles Wesley's
journal, and to some extent his letters, shed light on eighteenth-century medical practice as opposed to merely prescriptive literature.

If the journal is in part a spiritual autobiography and a medical diary, it is a
multi-genred text in that (together with his letters) it can also be seen in part
as travel writing, another characteristically eighteenth-century genre.[126] His
illnesses often seem to have been brought about by travel: 'riding with the
wind and rain in my face', he noted, 'has brought back my old companion,
the toothache'.[127] If his journal has more descriptive accounts of his spiritual
life, it also has more sustained descriptions of geography, topography, the
state of the roads and the weather (interestingly his time in America became a
reference for assessing the magnitude of a storm)[128] than his brother's, and the
writing is often vivid and immediate, as when in Ireland in 1748 he wrote: 'the
continuous rain and sharp wind here full in my teeth'.[129] The nexus between
spiritual and travel writing itself needs further exploration: both, of course,
involved journeys, and Charles used coach trips as opportunities for evangelism. David Hempton has noted how mobile the Methodists were, and Charles
clearly fits into this pattern: with perhaps pardonable exaggeration Thomas
Jackson claimed that his itinerary has 'seldom been equalled, and perhaps in
no instance surpassed, at least since the apostolic times'.[130] Charles also seems
to have travelled at speed (he was, after all, a man with a mission), telling his
companion in 1753: 'I never slack my pace for way or weather.'[131]

If the main thrust of this essay has been to show how Charles Wesley can be
linked to some of the recent developments within eighteenth-century studies,
in what ways can research into Charles Wesley benefit the historian interested
in the eighteenth century more generally? Over a decade ago, W. A. Speck,
reviewing some of the new scholarship on the period, asked, 'Will the real
eighteenth century stand up?'[132] How far, he wondered, was it a period of
secularization and change, anticipating modernity, or how far was it a more

traditional society, with its links to the early modern period? But it may be, as Speck himself suggested, that we should not view those perennial concerns of the historian, 'continuity' and 'change', as being necessarily in antagonism. 'Traditional' religious priorities could be agents of change and innovation, and new genres and ways of behaving could be vehicles for older priorities and concerns. Some of the topics discussed above, such as medicine and health, life-writing, family relations, politeness, sociability and clubbability, have usually been seen by eighteenth-century historians within the framework of a modernizing secular analysis. For instance, Roy Porter's many works on illness and medicine have attempted to chart the ways in which scientific and Enlightenment understandings replaced religious views and interpretations, eighteenth-century autobiographies and travel writings have been understood to explore the delights of the here and now, and the family is discussed within a secular, this-worldly context. The importance of Charles Wesley to the eighteenth-century historian is to show that, at least for him, these supposedly secular concerns all had profoundly religious connotations.

## Notes

1 Many years ago Maldwyn Edwards wrote a book-length study of John Wesley with a similar title to this essay: *John Wesley and the Eighteenth Century: A study of his social and political influence* (London: Epworth Press, 1st edn, 1933, rev. edn, 1955). Edwards summarized the aim of the book (p. 167): 'We are concerned to show the influence of John Wesley's work on England', but admitted '[i]t would be equally possible to show the effect of England on John Wesley's work'. (ibid). In this essay, as perhaps reflects the changing methods of historians and historical biographers during the last century, the priorities will be reversed, and I will be more concerned with the effects of historical context on Charles Wesley than with Charles' effect on his context. I am grateful to Gareth Lloyd for commenting on a draft of this essay, and for pointing me to references from the Archive in his care; and to David Bebbington, Phyllis Mack, Henry Rack and John Walsh for reading an earlier version.

2 E. P. Thompson, *The Making of the English Working Class* (1963, rev. edn 1968, with new preface, 1980). On Thompson's complex attitude towards Methodism, see David Hempton and John Walsh, 'E. P. Thompson and Methodism', in *God and Mammon: Protestants, money and the market, 1790–1860*, ed. Mark A. Noll (New York: Oxford University Press, 2001), pp. 99–120.

3 J. C. D. Clark, *English Society, 1688–1832: Ideology, social structure and political practice during the ancient regime* (Cambridge, 1985, rev. edn, 2000).

4 Thompson, *Working Class*, p. 408, refers to the hymns of 'John and Charles Wesley', echoing the way in which even in the eighteenth century John subsumed Charles' unique contributions under the fiction of joint publication, and on p. 410 there is a single (surely negative) reference to Charles writing hymns on the cult of death. Although there is a discussion of (Charles') Methodist hymns in Thompson's text, they are listed in the index under the heading 'Methodism and Sexuality'.

5 Clark, *English Society*, 235–44.

6 For Charles' political verse, see S T Kimbrough Jr and Oliver A. Beckerlegge,

eds, *The Unpublished Poetry of Charles Wesley*, 3 vols (Nashville: Abingdon/ Kingswood, 1988–92), 1.41–167.

7 Charles certainly portrayed himself as a staunch supporter of the Hanoverian monarchy, going so far as to take extra oaths during the Jacobite scares in 1744 to 'show my loyalty unquestionable': *CWJ*, 1.361. In 1737 he waited on George II at Hampton Court with the Oxford Address (1.73). In 1739 he noted, 'afterwards I enforced obedience to the powers that be from Rom. XIII, and showed the scandalous inconsistency of your high-churchmen, who disclaim resistance, and yet practice it, continually speaking evil of dignities, nay of the ruler of the people, as well as of those who are put in authority under him' (1.183). Statements such as this might complicate the idea that the Wesleys had aligned themselves with the 'reversionary interest': Hempton, *Methodism*, 80–1. Wesley also wrote poems for George II's birthday: MARC, CW Box 5.

8 *Unpublished Poetry*, 1.41–40.

9 MARC, Wesley family letters, 1/86–1/96 are letters from William Legge, Earl of Dartmouth, Lady Bathurst, the Duchess of Ancaster, Daines Barrington, and John Egerton, the Bishop of Durham about his musical sons. Members of the elite also subscribed to the musical concerts held in the Wesley family home during the 1770s and 1780s. For example, the concert held on 3 January 1780 was attended by the Earl of Dartmouth, the Earl of Mornington, Sir Edward Walpole and a host of gentry: MARC, DDCW, 8/21

10 On John Wesley's more ambivalent attitude to the establishment, see David Hempton, 'John Wesley and England's *Ancien Regime*', in his *The Religion of the People: Methodism and popular religion* (London, 1996), 77–90.

11 John Brewer, *The Pleasures of the Imagination: English culture in the eighteenth century* (London, 1997).

12 Frederick C. Gill, *Charles Wesley: The first Methodist* (London: Lutterworth Press, 1961); E. Gordon Rupp, *Religion in England, 1688–1791* (Oxford, 1986), 407–16.

13 For a discussion of the Wesleys and Methodism as counter-cultural and reactionary, see David Hempton, *Empire of the Spirit*, 11, 32, 201, and, in a different way, Thompson, *Working Class*. For the forward-looking and 'progressive' effects of the Wesleys' message, see R. F. Wearmouth's trilogy: *Methodism and the Working Class Movements of England, 1800–1850* (London, 1937), *Methodism and the Common People of the Eighteenth Century* (London, 1945), and *Some Working Class Movements of the Nineteenth Century* (London, 1948).

14 For the 'proto-Romantic' nature of Charles Wesley's hymns, see Gill, *Charles Wesley*, 209 and F. C. Gill, *The Romantic Movement and Methodism* (London, 1937), 63–71.

15 For some suggestive thoughts about how the Wesleys and Methodism fit into the age, see B. Semmel, *The Methodist Revolution* (1973), although his view of the enlightenment context needs modification.

16 *CWJ*, 2.15–16.

17 *CWJ*, 1.93.

18 On different models see, W. A. Speck, 'Will the real eighteenth century stand up?', *Historical Journal*, 34 (1991), 203–6.

19 Terry Eagleton, 'Knock-me-down Romantic', *London Review of Books*, 25 (12) (19 June 2003), 7; see the remarks in Keith Thomas, *Changing Conceptions of National Biography: The Oxford DNB in historical perspective* (Cambridge University Press, 2005), 50–3.

20 Paul M. Kendall, *The Art of Biography* (New York, 1965).

21 Stanley Fish, 'Just published: minutiae without meaning', *New York Times*, 7 September 1999, Section A, 19.

22 See Barbara Tuchman, 'Biography as a Prism of History', in *Telling Lives: The biographer's art*, ed. Marc Pachter (Washington, DC, 1979); T. C. W. Blanning and David Cannadine, eds, *History and Biography: Essays in honour of Derek Beales* (Cambridge University Press, 1996) and Lloyd E. Ambrosius, ed, *Writing Biography: Historians and their craft* (Lincoln, Neb.; London: University of Nebraska Press, 2004).

23 For a scintillating example of this, see Hempton, *Empire of the Spirit*.

24 MARC, Early Methodist Volume contains ms accounts of the religious experiences of early Methodists in letters to Charles Wesley from 1740 until his death. Some of these have now been published: K. Morgan, 'Methodist Testimonials . . .', in J. Barry and K. Morgan, eds, *Reformation and Revival in Eighteenth-Century England* (Bristol Record Society, 1994), 75–104. The Early Methodist volume is discussed in Bruce Hindmarsh, *The Evangelical Conversion Narrative: Spiritual autobiography in Early Modern England* (Oxford University Press, 2005), chapter 4.

25 For some of the recent burgeoning bibliography on these themes, see J. Gregory and John Stevenson, *The Longman Companion to Eighteenth-Century Britain, 1688–1830* (1999). A new edition is currently in preparation.

26 Contributions to this reassessment are: *The Church of England, c. 1689–c. 1833: From Toleration to Tractarianism*, ed. J. Walsh, C. Haydon and S. Taylor (Cambridge, 1993); Mark Smith, *Religion in Industrial Society: Oldham and Saddleworth, 1740–1865* (Oxford, 1994); Jeremy Gregory, *Restoration, Reformation, and Reform, 1660–1828: Archbishops of Canterbury and their diocese* (Oxford, 2000); J. Gregory and J. S. Chamberlain, eds, *The National Church in Local Perspective: The Church of England and the regions, 1660–1800* (Boydell, 2003).

27 See, in particular, C. J Abbey and J. H. Overton, *The English Church in the Eighteenth Century*, 2 vols (London, 1878); J. Stoughton, *Religion in England under Queen Anne and the Georges, 1702–1800*, 2 vols (London, 1878); and J. H. Overton and F. C. Relton, *The English Church from the Accession of George I to the End of the Eighteenth Century, 1714–1800* (London, 1906).

28 The phrase is J. H. Plumb's, *In the Light of History* (London: Allen Lane, 1972), 37.

29 *CWJ*, 2: index.

30 For some more positive views of the Church of England in Charles' journal, see *CWJ*, 1.56, 67, 82, 165; 2.126, 128, 129, 132, 133, 138.

31 *CWJ*, 1.56 (found 'comfort with the sacrament at St Paul's'), *CWJ*, 1.84 ('received comfort from the lessons and anthems' at Christ Church, Oxford).

32 *CWJ*, 1.82–4.

33 See, for example, Jeremy Gregory, '"In the Church I will live and die": John Wesley, the Church of England, and Methodism', in William Gibson and Robert G. Ingram, eds, *Religious Identities in Britain, 1660–1832* (Ashgate, 2005), 147–78.

34 *CWJ*, 1.262–3, 370.

35 *CWJ*, 1.191.

36 *CWJ*, 1.88.

37 *CWJ*, 2.23. See also John Lawson, 'Charles Wesley: A Man of the Prayer Book', *Proceedings of the Charles Wesley Society*, 1 (1994), 85–119.

38 *CWJ*, 2.119.

39 *CWJ*, 2.117.

40  *CWJ*, 2.22.

41  For example, *CWJ*, 1.165 2; *CWJ*, 2.127.

42  *CWJ*, 2.132.

43  *CWJ*, 2.133.

44  Quoted in Gill, *Charles Wesley*, 225.

45  Although he did continue to allow and even encourage 'non-Anglican' practices such as lay preaching, and his personal preference was to work in a Methodist circuit rather than in an Anglican parish.

46  For Wordsworth, see Stephen Gill, *William Wordsworth: A life* (Oxford: Clarendon Press, 1989), 347–423; for Coleridge, see Richard Holmes, *Coleridge: Darker reflections* (London, 1998), 530–60.

47  Gareth Lloyd, *Charles Wesley and the Struggle for Methodist Identity* (Oxford, forthcoming).

48  J. Spurr, 'The Church , the societies, and the moral revolution of 1688', in Walsh, Haydon and Taylor, *Church of England*, 127–42; Craig Rose, 'The origins and ideals of the SPCK, 1699–1766', idem, 172–90; Tina Isaacs, 'The Anglican hierarchy and the Reformation of Manners, 1688–1738', *Journal of Ecclesiastical History*, 33 (1982), 391–411; Gillian Wagner, 'Spreading the Word: the Church and SPG in North America: Thomas Coram and Anglicanism in New England', *Journal of the Canadian Church Historical Society*, XLV (2003), 65–76; S. Taylor, 'Bishop Edmund Gibson's proposals for Church Reform', in S. Taylor ed., *From Cranmer to Davidson: A Church of England Miscellany*, Church of England Record Society, 172–86; R. A. Burns, 'A Hanoverian legacy? Diocesan reform in the Church of England, c. 1688–c. 1883', in Walsh, Haydon and Taylor, *Church of England*, 265–82.

49  See Jeremy Gregory, 'The Eighteenth-Century Reformation: The pastoral task of Anglican clergy after 1689', in Walsh, Haydon and Taylor, *Church of England*, 67–85; 'The making of a Protestant nation: "Success" and "Failure" in England's Long Reformation', in Nicholas Tyacke, ed., *England's Long Reformation, 1500–1800* (1998), 307–33; Jonathan Barry, 'Bristol as a Reformation City, c. 1640–c. 1780', in Tyacke, *Long Reformation*, 261–84; Jeremy Gregory, *Restoration, Reformation, and Reform, 1660–1828: Archbishops of Canterbury and their diocese* (Oxford: Oxford University Press, 2000).

50  W. R. Ward, review of J. Gascoigne, *Cambridge in the Age of the Enlightenment: Science, religion and politics from the Restoration to the French Revolution* (Cambridge, 1989), in *History*, 73 (1990), 497.

51  Gregory, 'I live and die in the Church of England', 162–4.

52  The preface to the hymns included a shortened edition of Brevint's original treatise, which is indicative of its influence on their thinking. See Geoffrey Wainwright, '"Our Elder Brethren Join": The Wesleys' *Hymns on the Lord's Supper* and Patristic Revival in England', *Proceedings of the Charles Wesley Society*, 1 (1994), especially 12–17.

53  For Jones, see *Oxford Dictionary of National Biography*.

54  See Roger Lonsdale, ed., *The New Oxford Book of Eighteenth-Century Verse* (Oxford, 1984); *Eighteenth-century Women Poets: An Oxford anthology* (Oxford, 1990). For Wesley's indebtedness to the poems of Elizabeth Rowe, see James Dale, 'Holy Larceny? Elizabeth Rowe's poetry in Charles Wesley's Hymns', *Proceedings of the Charles Wesley Society*, 3 (1996), 5–20. See also James Dale, *The Theological and Literary Qualities of the Poetry of Charles Wesley in Relation to the Standards of his Age*, Cambridge University PhD thesis, 1961.

55  *CWJ*, 2.106.

56 For Wesley's poems on Handel, see *Unpublished Poetry*, 3.381–2. For Anglican artistic activity, see Jeremy Gregory, 'Anglicanism and the Arts: Religion, Culture and Politics in the Eighteenth Century', in Jeremy Black and Jeremy Gregory, eds, *Culture, Politics and Society in Britain, 1660–1800* (Manchester, 1991), 82–109; and Jonathan Barry, 'Cultural Patronage and the Anglican crisis: Bristol, c. 1689–1775', in Walsh, Haydon and Taylor, *Church of England*, 191–208, which is particularly useful given that Wesley lived in Bristol for over two decades.

57 He clearly caused disquiet for the church authorities who in 1738 and 1739 had a series of interviews with him: *CWJ*, 1.129, 132–3, 135–6, 143, 156. It is worth noting, too, Wesley's early scathing verses about the Church:

Leaders who turn the lame out of the way,
Shepherds who watch to make the sheep their prey,
Preachers who dare their own report deny,
Patrons of Arius' or Socinius' lie,
Who scoff the Gospel truths as idle tales,
Heathenish Priests, and mitred infidels!

(From 'An Elegy on the Death of Robert Jones, Esqr': quoted in *CWJ*, 2.298–99). In 1785 Wesley said that he no longer agreed with these lines, but his brother claimed: 'Your verse is a sad truth. I see fifty times more of England than you do, and I find few exceptions to it': *The Letters of the Revd. John Wesley, M.A.*, ed. John Telford, 8 vols (London, 1931), 7.288; John Wesley to Charles Wesley, 13 September 1785.

58 T. Crichton Mitchell, *Charles Wesley: Man with the dancing heart* (Kansas, 1994), 52–3.

59 For example, *CWJ*, 1.73.

60 *CWJ*, 1.17.

61 *CWJ*, 1.49–52.

62 *CWJ*, 1.13, 27.

63 *CWJ*, 1.13.

64 *CWJ*, 1.4.

65 See *The Oxford History of the British Empire*, vol. 2, *The Eighteenth Century*, ed. P. J. Marshall (Oxford, 1998); David Armitage and Michael Braddick eds, *The British Atlantic World, 1500–1800* (Basingstoke, 2002); David Armitage, *Greater Britain: Essays in Atlantic history, 1516–1776* (Ashgate Variorum, 2004).

66 *CWJ*, 1.71–2.

67 *CWJ*, 1.60.

68 *CWJ*, 1.36.

69 MARC DDWes, 1/38, Charles Wesley to Dr Chandler, 28 April 1785.

70 Classic studies of the Enlightenment include Paul Hazard, *European Thought in the Eighteenth Century* (Harmondsworth, 1965); Peter Gay, *The Enlightenment: An interpretation* (London, 1967).

71 See Thompson, *Working Class*.

72 Roy Porter, 'The Enlightenment in England', in R. Porter and M. Teich, eds, *The Enlightenment in National Context* (Cambridge, 1981), 1–18. However, in some of Porter's later and more extended considerations of the themes, he tended to see the Enlightenment as a secularizing force: R. Porter, *The Enlightenment* (Basingstoke, 1990), *Enlightenment: Britain and the creation of the modern world* (London: Penguin, 2001). See also Sheridan Gilley's pioneering article: 'Christianity and the

Enlightenment: An Historical Survey', *History of European Ideas*, 1 (1981), 103–21.

73 For thoughtful discussions of the relationship between the Evangelical Revival more broadly and the Enlightenment, see David Bebbington, 'Revival and Enlightenment in Eighteenth-Century England', in Andrew Walker and Kristin Aune, eds, *On Revival: A Critical Examination* (Paternoster Press, 2003), 71–86; and David Hempton, *Methodism: Empire of the Spirit* (Yale, 2005), 32–54. My take on this is that rather than seeing 'Enlightenment' and 'Evangelicalism'/'Enthusiasm' as polarities, we should acknowledge that what we might term 'Enlightenment' might include certain 'evangelical' qualities and vice versa.

74 For suggestions of the links between Arminianism, Methodist theology and Enlightenment thought, see Semmel, *Methodist Revolution*, 87–109. Semmel, however, argued that Wesleyanism should be seen as a liberalizing force. I think we can agree that there are affinities between Methodism and the Enlightenment without forcing either into a liberalizing framework.

75 *CWJ*, 2.2

76 *CWJ*, 2.191.

77 And even 'Romantic' writers may have placed more stress on 'reason' than is sometimes suggested: see Jon Mee, *Romanticism, Enthusiasm and Regulation: Poetics and the policing of culture in the Romantic period* (Oxford, 2003).

78 Paul Langford, *A Polite and Commercial People: England, 1727–1783* (Oxford: Oxford University Press, 1989); Lawrence Klein, 'The Third Earl of Shaftesbury and the Progress of Politeness', *Eighteenth-Century Studies*, 18 (1984–5), 186–214; *Shaftesbury and the Culture of Politeness: Moral discourse and cultural politics in eighteenth century England* (Cambridge: Cambridge University Press, 1994); 'Politeness and the Interpretation of the British Eighteenth Century', *The Historical Journal*, 4 (2002), 869–98.

79 Hempton, *Methodism: Empire of the Spirit*, 56.

80 *CWJ*, 1.268, 302.

81 *CWJ*, 1.172.

82 *CWJ*, 1.428. But he did indulge in some of the pastimes of 'polite' society such as visiting 'Mr Pope's gardens' at Twickenham.

83 *CWJ*, 1.430, 174.

84 *CWJ*, 1.286.

85 *CWJ*, 2.19.

86 *CWJ*, 2.24.

87 R. B. Shoemaker, 'Reforming the city: the reformation of manners campaign in London, 1690–1738', in *Stilling the Grumbling Hive: The response to social and economic problems in England, 1689–1750*, eds L. Davidson *et al.*, (Stroud, 1993), 391–411; and S. Burtt, 'The societies for the reformation of manners: between John Locke and the devil in Augustan England', in *The Margins of Orthodoxy: Heterodox writing and cultural response, 1650–1750*, ed. R. Lund (Cambridge, 1995), 149–69. Some of this literature has tended to separate out 'the reformation of manners' from the concern with religious revival, but for Charles they went hand in hand.

88 *CWJ*, 1.425.

89 *CWJ*, 1.433.

90 *CWJ*, 1.136. See Ann Taves, *Fits, Trances and Visions: Experiencing religion and explaining experience from Wesley to James* (Princeton, 1999).

91 *CWJ*, 1.35.

92 For some of this literature, see John Gillis, *For Better, For Worse: British marriages 1600 to the present* (Oxford, 1985); Alan MacFarlane, *Marriage and Love in*

*England, 1300–1840* (Oxford, 1986); R. T. Vann, 'Review Essay', *Journal of Family History* (1979), 308–15; Joanne Bailey, *Unquiet Lives: Marriage and marriage breakdown in England, 1660–1800* (Cambridge, 2003).

93  See the correspondence between them in the MARC.

94  *CWJ*, 2.53.

95  Stone, *Family*, 467–8. For a useful discussion of the letter, see Elizabeth Kurtz Lynch, 'John Wesley's editorial hand in Susanna Annesley Wesley's 1732 "Education" letter', in *John Wesley: Tercentenary Essays*, ed. Jeremy Gregory, Special Edition of the *Bulletin of the John Rylands University Library of Manchester*, 85 (2005), 195–208.

96  Scholars are unclear whether he did in fact continue writing a journal which has now been lost. See S T Kimbrough and Kenneth G. C. Newport, eds, *The Journal of Charles Wesley* (Nashville, forthcoming), introduction.

97  Peter Clark, *British Clubs and Societies, 1500–1800: The origins of an associational world* (Oxford, 2000). It is worth noting that Clark's view of his subject is entirely secular and he does not refer to any of the religious societies that might have been considered part of his purview.

98  John Walsh, 'Religious societies: Methodist and Evangelical, 1738–1800', in W. J. Sheils and Diana Wood, eds, *Voluntary Religion*, 23 (1986), 279–302.

99  MARC: DDW, 8/15, Charles Wesley, MS housekeeping expenses, 1778–82.

100  *Oxford Dictionary of National Biography*.

101  Clive T. Probyn, *The Sociable Humanist: The life and works of James Harris 1709–1780: provincial culture in eighteenth-century England* (Oxford, 1991). See also the discussion in Brewer, *Pleasures of the Imagination*, 531–72.

102  Gill, *Charles Wesley*, 185. Anne Stott, *Hannah More: The first Victorian* (Oxford, 2003), 109, also notes this.

103  Scholars have also differed over whether Johnson was more of an Enlightenment or anti-Enlightenment figure: see the contrasting treatments in John Cannon, *Samuel Johnson and the Politics of Hanoverian England* (Oxford, 1994) and J. C. D. Clark, *Samuel Johnson: Literature, religion, and English cultural politics from the Restoration to Romanticism* (Cambridge, 1994).

104  James Boswell, *Life of Johnson*, ed. R. W. Chapman (Oxford, 1980), 324.

105  See E. G. Rupp, 'The religion of Samuel Johnson', in his *Religion in England, 1688–1791* (Clarendon Press: Oxford, 1986), 539–52; M. J. Quinlan, *Samuel Johnson: A layman's religion* (Madison, 1964). See also C. Chaplin, *The Religious Thought of Samuel Johnson* (Ann Arbor, 1968) and C. Pierce, *The Religious Life of Samuel Johnson* (1983). Henry Rack considers that Charles Wesley had 'almost a manic depressive personality': *Reasonable Enthusiast*, 252.

106  Linda Colley, *Britons: Forging the nation, 1707–1837* (Yale, 1992). For some of the scholarship which has modified or taken issue with her interpretation, see T. Claydon and Ian McBride, eds, *Protestantism and National Identity: Britain and Ireland, 1650–1850* (Cambridge, 1998); M. Pittock, *Inventing and Resisting Britain: Cultural identities in Britain and Ireland, 1685–1789* (Basingstoke: Macmillan, 1997); and L. Brockliss and D. Eastwood, eds, *A Union of Multiple Identities: The British Isles, 1750–1850* (1997).

107  *CWJ*, 1.436.

108  Seen for example in the three anti-Popish hymns, almost certainly composed by Charles and added to the eighth edition of John Wesley's, *A Word To a Protestant* (8th edn, London, 1745), 7–12 (cited in Hempton, *Methodism and Politics*, 33). For further discussion of this, see the chapter by Peter Nockles below.

109  MARC, 7/18, Charles Wesley to Sarah Wesley, 9 July 1759.

110  *CWJ*, 2.256.

111  *CWJ*, 2.256

112  E. Halévy, *A History of the English People in the Nineteenth Century*, vols 1–4 (London, 1949–51); *The Birth of Methodism in England* (Chicago, 1971); and the works by Wearmouth cited in footnote 13. For comments, see J. D. Walsh, 'Elie Halévy and the Birth of Methodism', *Transactions of the Royal Historical Society*, 5th series, 25 (1975), 1–20.

113  *CWJ*, 1.402.

114  *CWJ*, 1.384.

115  *CWJ*, 2.16.

116  *CWJ*, 2.22.

117  *CWJ*, 1.313. For the importance of all being invited to the 'great supper' to John Wesley, see John Walsh, *John Wesley, 1703–1791: A bicentennial tribute* (London: Friends of Dr Williams's Library, 1993), 17.

118  E. P. Thompson, 'The moral economy of the English Crowd in the Eighteenth Century', *Past and Present*, 50 (1971), 76–136.

119  *CWJ*, 1.249.

120  See Donald A. Stauffer, *The Art of Biography in Eighteenth-Century England* (Princeton, 1941).

121  See the comments by W. R. Ward , 'Introduction', *The Works of John Wesley*, vol. 18, *Journal and Diaries*, ed. R. P. Heitzenrater and W. R. Ward (Nashville, 1988), 1, 29.

122  A recurring phrase to describe a religious experience was 'we were all in a flame' (*CWJ*, 1.175), 'the flame was kindled (1, 263, and 1, 270), which was reworked in the hymn: 'O thou who camest from above' as 'kindle a flame of sacred love'.

123  *CWJ*, 1.82.

124  See Deborah Madden, 'Experience and the common interest of mankind: the enlightened empiricism of John Wesley's *Primitive Physick*', *British Journal for Eighteenth-Century Studies*, 26 (2003), 41–54.

125  DDCW, 7/83, CW to Sarah Wesley, 13 September 1755.

126  Malcolm Andrews, *The Search for the Picturesque: Landscape aesthetic and tourism in Britain, 1760–1800* (Aldershot, 1989).

127  *CWJ*, 2.33.

128  *CWJ*, 2.74.

129  *CWJ*, 2.11.

130  *CWJ*, 1: Introduction.

131  *CWJ*, 2.46.

132  Speck, 'Real Eighteenth Century'.

# 3. Charles Wesley and Early Methodism

## HENRY D. RACK

## Introduction

In his brief obituary of his brother in 1788 John Wesley claimed that 'his least praise was his talent for poetry'.[1] This judgement may seem curious, but it can serve as a motto for this essay. Poetry and hymns will be dealt with elsewhere in this book. 'Early Methodism', for the purposes of this essay, will be taken to involve the whole of Charles Wesley's lifetime, though his activities were most extensive and intensive during the 1740s. Although consideration of his relationship with his brother is unavoidable, this will be discussed in detail elsewhere in this book.[2] The main purpose of this essay is to explain Charles' relationship with the Methodist movement more generally as evangelist, pastor, overseer and policy-maker. In 1756 he made his last extended evangelistic journey, and (perhaps not coincidentally) his surviving journal terminates at this point. Yet we shall see that his influence on the development of Methodism still continued in other ways.

## Charles Wesley as 'the first Methodist'

In his various accounts of the origins and nature of 'Methodism', John Wesley often traced it back to his days in Oxford. In *A Short Account of the People Called Methodists* (1781) he observed that 'the first rise of Methodism (so-called) was in November 1729 when four of us met together in Oxford'.[3] Other 'rises' (he said) followed. The first (undated) application of the name he attributed to a 'young gentleman of Christ Church', identified elsewhere as John Higham.[4] In the *Large Minutes* of 1770 the origin of Methodism is ascribed to 'two young men' (evidently the Wesleys) 'reading the Bible in 1729'.[5] Modern research suggests that the so-called 'Holy Club' was a looser and less Wesley-centred organization than has traditionally been supposed.[6] But what concerns us here is Charles Wesley's role in the origin of Oxford Methodism. John's 'four of us' or 'two young men' should, some have claimed, be replaced by Charles Wesley alone as 'the first Methodist'.[7]

Strictly speaking, the only *specific* evidence for this claim is found in a letter by Charles to Dr Thomas Bradbury Chandler in 1785. In this he describes how he turned from frivolity to seriousness during his second year in college:

I went to the weekly sacrament, and persuaded two or three young scholars to accompany me, and to observe the method of study prescribed by
the statutes of the university. This gained me the harmless nickname of
Methodist. In half a year, my brother left his curacy at Epworth, and came
to our assistance. We then proceeded regularly in our studies and in doing
what good we could to the bodies and souls of men.[8]

Several points need to be made about this account. Surviving letters from
the spring of 1729 certainly describe Charles' efforts at self-reformation and
attempts to influence two friends.[9] But these letters do not describe an organized group, nor is there any mention of the nickname 'Methodist'. Charles
also omits the fact that John Wesley was already present in Oxford in the
summer of 1729 and sometimes met with Charles and his friends.[10] While it is
perfectly possible that 'Methodist' was applied to Charles and his friends in
1729, the first contemporary evidence for this use is in 1732.[11]

Later accounts of the origins of Methodism by either Wesley need to be
read with caution, but Charles' especially so. John, too, was concerned to
emphasize continuity with the Oxford activities and ideals, and to refute hostile pictures of the later movement which stressed its irregularities and un-
Anglican nature. But Charles was not only writing over fifty years after the
events described, but also had a particular purpose in mind in his account
to Chandler. This was to claim that 'our only desire was, to do all the good
we could, as ministers of the Church of England, to which we were firmly
attached, both by education and principle. (My brother still thinks her the
best constituted national church in the world).' Throughout the letter he
emphasized that their only purpose was to 'serve God and the Church of
England'; that 'the lost sheep of the [Anglican] fold' were their principal care.
He admitted that they preached in houses and fields, but only when forced
out of parish churches and 'never in church hours'. He claimed that they regularly preached against separation from the Church and that he and John 'beat
down' the lay preachers wishing to do so. But now, he claimed, his brother
had betrayed the original Methodist principles by his ordinations in 1784 and
would not recognize that ordination meant separation. Charles' picture of
himself as the originator of 'Methodism' looks like an implicit claim to be the
correct interpreter of its character.

This account, like some of his brother's, omits a great deal. The claim that
Methodism was bound to the Church of England and constantly conformed
to it until John Wesley betrayed it through his ordinations is particularly misleading. The 1738 conversion, and the doctrinal implications it had,
are not mentioned. The post-conversion irregularities (shared equally by
Charles with his brother) are played down, though some critics almost from
the first claimed that they implied separation from the Church, especially
the use of lay preachers. The claim to a united front with John against the
preachers on the separation question glossed over the fact that by 1755 the
brothers were already in serious disagreement. Finally, Charles' settlement
in Bristol and then London after 1756 was hardly that of a model Anglican
priest, for he was preaching and administering Communion in unconse-
crated buildings.

## Charles Wesley's early evangelism: from conversion to marriage (1738–49)[1]

What is obscured in both Wesleys' retrospective accounts of the origins and development of Methodism is the extent to which it became a more irregular and less 'Anglican' movement after 1738. Their protestations of loyalty to the Church of England were sincerely meant, but almost from the first co-existed uneasily with John Wesley's other claim that Methodism was open to people of all denominations.

Judging by entries in Charles' journal, his occasional expressions of loyalty to the Church in the 1740s were provoked by specific challenges. In 1743, before 'poor Moravianised Mr Hall', he strongly avowed 'my inviolable attachment to the Church of England'.[12] In 1744, provoked by charges of Jacobitism, he claimed that 'I am as true a Church of England man and as loyal a subject as any man in the Kingdom.'[13] Yet he had earlier affirmed that 'by the grace of God, I shall preach the word in season, out of season, though they [the bishops] and all men forbid me'.[14]

In the 1740s Charles was, after initial hesitations, certainly as irregular as his brother. What decided both of them in the end were the needs of the gospel and the 'fruits' of the work. They proved that the irregularities were approved by God. Thus, influenced by Whitefield's example, John 'consented to be more vile' by preaching in the open air in April 1739.[15] Charles first preached in a field on 29 May, but scrupled preaching 'in another's parish till I had been refused the church'. By 19 June he was justifying Whitefield's irregularities to the Archbishop of Canterbury, because his success was a 'spiritual sign and sufficient proof of his call'. On 24 June he preached in Moorfields, encouraged by the day's lessons and psalms at St Paul's which 'put fresh life into me . . . My load was gone and all my doubts and scruples.'[16]

Lay preaching was more of a problem for both brothers, but in the end this, too, was justified by results. In May 1739 Whitefield and Charles 'declared against' lay preaching.[17] Observing Howell Harris' abilities may have helped to make lay preaching acceptable, for in November 1740 Charles resisted attempts to persuade him to speak against Harris' preaching.[18] He showed no qualms over allowing the lay preachers to join the clergy at the first Methodist Conference in 1744.[19] By April 1746, encountering people who had 'tasted the love of Christ, mostly under the preaching of our lay helpers', he commented, 'How can anyone dare deny that they are sent by God?' He wished that all who had the 'outward call' [i.e. the clergy] 'were as inwardly moved by the Holy Ghost to preach!'[20] In August 1748 Charles defended their preaching by declaring 'the matter of fact, that when God sent any one forth, and owned him by repeated conversions, we dare not reject him'.[21] Although more cautious about the Cornish 'exhorters' who had 'sprung up' in 1746, he 'found no reason to doubt their having been used by God thus far'. He only 'advised and charged them not to stretch themselves beyond their line, by speaking out of the Society, or fancying themselves public teachers'.[22]

In the period before his marriage, Charles appears to have been as actively and extensively engaged as John in preaching, pastoral care and the exercise of discipline. His journeys were, at least in some measure, co-ordinated with his brother's, though this was to be a matter for dispute between them later. They appear to have commuted alternately between London and Bristol in 1738; both travelled into Wales in 1739–40; then to the Midlands and the north in 1741–2; to Cornwall in 1743; Ireland was added in 1747. Up to this point Charles' journeys repeated John's, though we shall see that after his marriage they became more restricted. Though John usually preceded Charles in breaking new ground, Charles made prolonged follow-up visits, notably in Ireland, which significantly consolidated the work.

## Charles Wesley's early evangelism: after marriage (1749–56)

Up to the point of his marriage, then, it seems plain that Charles was no less of an itinerant than was John and that the two worked in concert. In two letters written in October 1753, however, John Wesley claimed that Charles had ceased to co-ordinate his journeys with his brother long before his (John's) marriage in 1751. He therefore demanded:

> Either act really in connexion with me, or never pretend to it . . . By acting in connexion with me I mean, take counsel with me once or twice a year as to the places where you will labour . . . At present you are so far from this that I do not even know when and where you intend to go.[23]

Charles apparently blamed any lack of consultation on John's marriage. John then claimed that Charles followed supposed divine inspirations rather than reason. He continued: 'You do not, will not act in concert with me. Not since I married only . . . but for ten years past and upward, you have no more acted in connexion with me than Mr Whitefield has done.'[24] John is claiming here, then, that from as far back as 1743, or even earlier, his brother was out of step with his own work. Was this fair or correct? It is hard to be sure. John Wesley certainly liked to control other people's lives and the movements of his preachers. We have seen that the brothers certainly followed each other – and closely – into new areas, in the early to middle 1740s and very possibly up to Charles' marriage in 1749. Though not explicit, it also looks as though the intention was for one of them to be in London or Bristol while the other was travelling elsewhere. Unless Charles was making excuses, this seems to be confirmed by letters to John Bennet in 1750 in which he says that he could not yet travel north but must 'hover between Bristol and London' until John returned from Ireland. Once he had arrived back and visited Bristol and Cornwall, one of the brothers would visit the north.[25] It may be that John exaggerated Charles' vagaries and lack of consultation or at least their effects, though Charles does seem to have spent an increasing amount of time in Wales in 1748–9 because of his courtship of Sarah Gwynne.

Charles evidently intended to continue to travel after his marriage. On 19 February 1749 his future wife agreed that he could keep up his 'vegetable diet' and travelling. She even, against her mother's wishes, agreed that he could go to Ireland and that she 'should be glad herself to visit the many gracious souls' there.[26] Charles' journal shows that he did continue to travel and that Sarah sometimes accompanied him, even as late as August 1753.[27] But there were now some restrictions and diversions. Trips to Ludlow and elsewhere were devoted mainly to meeting the Gwynnes and other families and friends. Ireland was never visited again; nor Cornwall after 1753. Scotland was apparently never visited at all, though it appears that he had intended to follow up his brother's first visit there in 1751. His journey was, however, hindered by illness and at Newcastle he met a preacher who reported adversely on the Scottish response to his preaching. Charles then sent another preacher into Scotland, apparently as a substitute for himself.[28]

John's outburst in 1753 is likely to have been provoked by more recent events than he claimed. Family visits distracted Charles; health was a recurring problem. But there was also Charles' intervention in the Grace Murray affair, when he married her to John Bennet to prevent his brother from wedding her. It has been argued that, perhaps not surprisingly, this did lasting damage to the relationship between the brothers and their trust in each other.[29] John's marriage to Mrs Vazeille in February 1751 made matters worse, for Charles and Mrs John Wesley were mutually distrustful.

Charles' journeys after his marriage were also influenced by his increasing distrust of the travelling preachers' abilities, characters and loyalty to the Church of England. This was in sharp contrast with his earlier defences of them. In September 1750 John had hoped that Charles would travel north and recruit more travelling preachers, but illness prevented the journey. Then came the scandal of James Wheatley's sexual misconduct which provoked the Wesleys into agreeing that the preachers' characters must be investigated and that Charles should be the one to do this in 1751.[30]

Charles' letters show a deep distrust of the preachers' abilities, though John urged restraint since they needed the men, and ultimately he preferred 'grace before gifts'.[31] Charles disagreed and, in a letter to Lady Huntingdon in August 1751, claimed that 'unless a sudden remedy be found, the preachers will destroy the work of God'. Leaving their trades had made them aspire to be 'gentlemen'. The only remedy is to return all but a few to their trades. Then they can preach locally, with occasional forays farther afield. New recruits must be closely examined by the Wesleys. Charles, however, had another motive for these drastic proposals which may reflect the recent loss of trust between the brothers: he confided to Lady Huntingdon that he wished to 'break his [John Wesley's] power' by preventing the preachers from 'depending on him for bread'. This would 'reduce his authority within due bounds, as well as guard against that rashness and credulity of his which has kept me in continual awe and bondage for many years'. He will insist on the preachers 'working . . . as the single condition of my acting in concert with him'.[32] Unfortunately for Charles, this letter fell into his brother's hands. In response, after claiming that he had no wish to cling to power, John tartly remarked that he could not understand how Charles, given his regular income, could draw on the connexional class money.[33]

So recent disputes and ill feeling probably help to explain John's outburst about the lack of 'connexion' in October 1753. Further reasons for division appear in 1754–5. The story is well known of how Charles panicked in face of the preachers' pressure for ordination which seemed to imply separation from the Church. Fearing that his brother was on the verge of giving way, Charles busily rallied those like-minded with himself to press John to resist. The upshot was that at the Conference of 1755 John produced a statement arguing that, whether or not separation was 'lawful', it was not 'expedient'. Yet one wonders how far Charles agreed with some of John's quite radical views on the defects of church courts, canon law and even the Book of Common Prayer, as well as his narrow definition of the Church of England and conformity to it.[34] John was here reflecting not only his own doubts, but also the impact made on him by criticisms from the preachers, which he confessed he could not easily answer.[35]

Charles continued to worry that John might eventually conclude that ordination and separation had become 'expedient'. In correspondence with the Wesley brothers, Samuel Walker, the evangelical curate of Truro, attacked lay preaching. Suitable preachers should seek ordination and the rest be restricted to being 'inspectors or readers' in certain societies. John Wesley did not agree, but Charles effectively did: 'the regulations you propose are the same in substance which I have long been contending for in vain', he informed Walker. He claimed that he would have left Methodism in 1752 if his brother and some of the preachers had not signed a letter affirming their union and loyalty to the Church.[36] Charles was already implying the position he would summarize in 1760: 'My chief concern upon earth, I said, was the prosperity of the Church of England; my next, that of the Methodists; my third, that of the preachers.'[37]

Charles repeatedly made it clear in the 1750s, and later, that he stayed with the Methodists mainly to save them from being led into separation. His journeys north, for example, in 1751, 1755 and finally in 1756 show signs of being substantially with this purpose in view. John continued to see him as unpredictable and unco-operative. In June and July 1755 he wished Charles to go to Cornwall, unless he substituted for John in London. Charles appeared to have the excuse that his wife was about to give birth. At all events his failure to meet his brother's wishes led John to write: 'I shall wonder if Wales or Margate [for family visits] or something did not hinder your taking any step that I desire or which might save my time or strength.'[38]

Charles took his last extended journey – to the north – late in 1756. The reasons for his subsequent withdrawal from the itinerancy have been variously explained. Sally Wesley, his daughter, always defensive of her father's and uncle's reputations, thought it was not due to health or family considerations (which might have reflected on his sense of duty). She believed it was to avoid conflicts with his brother and the preachers.[39] Thomas Jackson and Luke Tyerman tended to agree.[40] Frank Baker suggested health and family commitments, while noting Charles' growing awareness of the preachers' hostility and the congenial 'Church Methodist' tone of the societies in Bristol and London to which he now mainly ministered.[41] Gareth Lloyd opts for family commitments rather than health problems and points out that ceasing to itinerate did not stop Charles from stirring up opposition to his brother and the preachers over threats to separate, and eventually John's ordinations.[42]

Whatever his reasons for the withdrawal, it looks as though Charles was feeling the itinerancy to be a burden. In a letter in July 1755 he speaks rather mysteriously of Lady Huntingdon saying that his 'redemption draws nigh'.

He is heartily tired of his role and wishes to 'call no man master'. Referring to his support from the book fund he says that £100 a year will not 'buy my liberty' and he would be glad if it was no longer paid to him.[43] In the event, however, he retained it to the end of his life.

## Charles Wesley and Methodism after 1756

So far as we know, Charles did not, for the rest of his life, venture beyond the south of England. Residing first in Bristol and then in London (from 1771), his travels became restricted mainly to the environs of these cities and visits to family and friends. Attempts were made from time to time to persuade him to travel further, but in vain. He does seem to have expressed a particular fondness for Newcastle upon Tyne. It was probably in 1760 that he wrote to his wife that 'if the Lord gives strength, I am willing to go to Yorkshire, or to Newcastle, or to anywhere to spread the glad tidings'.[44] This claim may reflect uneasiness after receiving a severe letter in April 1760 from Joseph Cownley, a preacher from Newcastle, which concluded:

> Give me leave now to press you to do what I think is your bounden duty. I mean, to visit the north this summer. We have excused you to the poor people, till we can do it no longer. If you refuse to come now, we can say neither more nor less about it, than, that you cannot, because you will not. If you could not preach at all, it would do them good only to see your face.[45]

On other occasions Charles sent greetings to Newcastle friends and as late as 1773 claimed that 'I do not want a heart to visit my very dear friends at Newcastle, but a body.'[46]

John also tried to stir him up to travel. In 1760 there was a crisis in Norwich when some of the preachers administered Communion without authorization. Charles resisted John's wish that he visit Norwich on the grounds that he believed his brother would not act before the Conference when (Charles believed) the preachers would vote for separation. He then led an outcry in the London society against preachers who had taken licences as Dissenting preachers.[47] On various occasions John regretted Charles' delays in coming to London. In 1766 he urged him to come to Leeds for the Conference. He could travel by coach, stay for two days and it would be good for his health.[48] In the early 1770s he was complaining that Charles did not support him at the Conferences.[49] Charles resisted, claiming that he could do little good there, though he did attend one at Bristol as late as 1786.[50]

Although there has been speculation about Charles' reasons for ceasing to itinerate, it is arguable that what is more remarkable is that he had persisted in doing so for nearly twenty years. This must be attributed to his sense of duty, if only the duty (as he saw it) of staying with Methodism to resist threats of separation. It will be recalled that in 1785 he claimed to Dr Chandler that in 1735 he had expected to spend his days in Oxford but for pressure from his brother.

In Georgia he had questioned 'whether I could have a small village remote from any town, where I may hide myself from all business and all company'.[51]

In January 1739 even his brother and others 'set upon me, but I could not agree to settle at Oxford without further direction from God'.[52] He rejoiced when a possible Anglican living went to someone else.[53] He was certainly tempted at times to give up preaching and retire to Oxford and 'attend to my own improvement'.[54] Soon after his marriage, which cut off the possibility of returning to college, he spoke of 'making the most of a short life' by studying all morning and visiting in the afternoons and was alarmed at the thought of mixing in 'the great world'.[55] Yet even after he ceased to itinerate, he seems to have resisted offers of Anglican livings and opted to stay with the Methodists.[56]

Settling in Bristol as resident minister, with only limited forays elsewhere except for fairly frequent visits to London, Charles remained in the western city until moving to the metropolis in 1771. His pattern of life was not quite the 'retirement' which he had professed to desire earlier. In 1758 he claimed that 'I cannot away with more than three or at most four in company. A crowd ever [sic probably 'even'] of religious people dissipates me, unless we spend the whole time in worship.' He professed a desire not to stir from home except to visit the sick and preach. In 1759 he wished to care for his health by refusing to preach every night as his brother expected.[57] This was in London, but in 1758 he had claimed that he did not care for the city and would not mind if he never saw it again. However, by 1760 he told his wife that 'as I shall probably take much more public care upon me than I have ever done heretofore, my office will require me to spend more time in town, *perhaps to settle here'.*[58] In reality he enjoyed what appears to have been an active social life in addition to his Methodist duties, and without obvious signs of distaste. In part this was because in London he was attempting to further the careers of his musical sons by seeking patrons and hosting concerts in his home to avoid more worldly venues. This still earned censures from some Methodists and did not improve Charles' reputation among them.[59] What further alienated some of the preachers was his virtual monopoly of the City Road pulpit which some claimed also caused the London membership figures to stagnate for many years.[60]

Both before and after his cessation from itinerating, as we have seen, Charles saw it as his duty to counteract anti-Anglican sentiments and threats of separation. Though unwilling and indeed incapable, by his own confession, to contemplate taking on the leadership of Methodism if he outlived his brother, Charles was determined that it should be led in what he saw as the right direction. Though in the end John Wesley opted, from necessity, for the Conference to succeed him as a collective leader, both he and Charles for a time had hopes of a clerical leader and one (in Charles' mind at least) not subject to the preachers. In the 1770s it was hoped that the Revd Mark Davis might fill the bill, but he was found to be unsuitable.[61]

It is not clear what Charles thought of the 1784 Deed of Declaration which vested the succession in 100 self-perpetuating preachers. But he and those who thought like him made their hostility only too clear in response to John Wesley's ordinations for America and Scotland.[62]

What needs to be emphasized, in the light of Lloyd's recent work, is that Charles was not, as has often been assumed or implied, a solitary or at least unrepresentative voice opposing the inevitability of Methodism moving towards outright separation from the Church of England. This threat was seen by at least a section of Methodism as an unwelcome threat and one to be resisted as by no means as inevitable as it may seem in retrospect. Certainly a significant, though unknown, proportion of Methodists did not wish for separation but instead desired to retain ties with the Church of England and in a more conservative and less flexible manner than John Wesley. They were certainly opposed to the ordinations and Methodist sacraments. Some chapels opposed them into the early years of the nineteenth century. Some of the preachers and rank and file shared these sentiments, but what was even more important was the fact that influential leading laymen, notably trustees in London, Bristol and other major centres, agreed.[63] The importance and influence of such people and the curbs they could impose on John Wesley can already be glimpsed in the behaviour of a powerful committee set up in 1767 to settle connexional debts.[64] To John's annoyance they made proposals for handling financial and trust affairs. Several of them became trustees of City Road chapel later.

The trustees of City Road and the Bristol New Room had final control of those pulpits, which caused much trouble in the 1790s.[65] At Bristol, Henry Durbin and William Pine, allies of Charles Wesley, rejected attempts to give control to John and the preachers.[66] After John Wesley's death, trustees with 'Church Methodist' sympathies figured in a series of conflicts with the preachers in the Conference over control of the Book Room and helped to fill the committee supporting Dr John Whitehead in his struggle with the preachers over his biography of John Wesley and payment for it. That biography blamed the preachers and not John Wesley for the controversial ordinations and saw the events of 1784 as destroying what Whitehead saw as the distinctive position of Methodism as a bridge between Anglicanism and Dissent.[67] Rightly or wrongly, however, John Pawson (a leading preacher) thought that Whitehead's erroneous views (as he saw them) of the preachers' 'ambitions' were due to his use of Charles Wesley's papers. Pawson himself claimed that the preachers had had no thought of ordination until John Wesley sprang his plan on his 'select committee' including Pawson. They unanimously opposed it, Pawson claimed, but he saw that Wesley would have his way.[68] Pawson was very hostile to Charles Wesley and he was evidently ignorant of the events of 1755 or ignored them. Neither his nor Whitehead's views of the forces behind the ordinations are entirely reliable. But what is evident is that the 'Church Methodists' of the 1790s and their role in the divisions which followed John Wesley's death are part of Charles Wesley's legacy.

## Charles Wesley as pastor

The notorious clashes between Charles and his brother on ordination and separation, along with their apparently growing lack of co-ordination, at least after the 1740s, tend to overshadow the significance of Charles' pastoral work. It is understandable that this was most extensive and in some ways most intensive in the early years of the Revival. Not only was he still a bachelor, but he was also learning to care for new, raw converts drawn in by his fiery preaching. As a preacher, Charles was evidently more passionate and emotional than his brother. John neatly hit off the contrast as: 'In connexion [reasoned argument] I beat you; but in strong, pointed *sentences* you beat me.'[69] Charles was liable at times to depend on sudden inspirations for preaching, and in later years some thought he offered poor fare.[70] But preaching did not stand alone. As Whitefield recognized in summoning John Wesley to Bristol in 1739, those he had awakened were 'ripe for bands'.[71] Charles was equally in demand for such work.[72]

In 1739 and the early 1740s Charles' journal frequently included examples of individuals being interrogated about their religious experience and claims to conversion. In September and October 1739 he wrote that 'this afternoon I conferred with Thomas Tucker and Eliz. Shirdock, both clearly justified', along with a number of others. 'I appointed any who had been converted through my ministry to call upon me after expounding.' There follow brief accounts of a number of conversion experiences. Or again, 'Today I talked with several who have lately found rest to their souls.' Several are named.[73] He also writes of 'hours of conference', letters relating conversion experiences and 'thanksgiving-notes'.[74] There was also the special category of condemned criminals, whose souls (after initial doubts about death-bed repentances) Charles delighted to save.[75]

Pastoral care of this kind, though most frequent in extended visits to London and Bristol, also occurred elsewhere. At Wednesbury in May 1743, 'I spent the morning in conference with several who have received the atonement under my brother etc.'[76]

Types of experience briefly recorded in the journal can be seen narrated in detail in a revealing series of letters to Charles from recent converts. Nearly thirty of these are artless, first-hand accounts, recorded within a few months of conversion and untouched by editorial intervention. They also, incidentally, reveal interestingly varied degrees of literacy.[77] It is likely that these letters were from people who felt particularly indebted for their conversions to Charles or at least to Charles and John. It is common to find them first attracted to, or awakened by, George Whitefield; but then more deeply affected and finally converted by one of the Wesleys. Elizabeth Halfpenny was convicted of sin by Whitefield, affected by John Wesley and found forgiveness under Charles.[78] Sarah Barber was awakened by Whitefield, shown she had no faith by John Wesley and apparently experienced justification through Charles' prayers.[79] Common though this type of pattern was, Whitefield certainly brought some all the way to salvation, as Charles found in Sheffield in 1751.[80]

From these accounts it is difficult to see much difference between the impact of John and Charles as pastors.[81] Yet one sometimes has the impression that Charles may have been found a more obviously affectionate and warmly sympathetic pastor than John. John Gambold, an early observer of Oxford Methodism, thought Charles 'a man made for friendship'.[82] This may be contrasted with the harsh judgement of John Hampson, John Wesley's first biographer, that John apparently lacked 'attachments' that 'partook of the genius of friendship'.[83] But Hampson had little knowledge of the younger, less self-contained Wesley.

Charles does seem to have worked harder than John to maintain friendships or colleagueships with those who had fallen out with the brothers. This was certainly the case with John Bennet, though here Charles may have felt that he had a special obligation to maintain old ties, given his role in engineering Bennet's marriage, to frustrate his brother. A series of letters in 1752 by which Charles sought in vain to retain Bennet's allegiance to Methodism concluded, 'Your afflicted, but affectionate friend.'[84]

There are other noticeable differences between the brothers in response to bereavements. Both show the traditional belief that death is within God's will and leads to a happier state for believers. Children could be seen as fortunate, when dying early, to escape later occasions for sin. Charles, arguably, had an excessive love of death and periodic longing for it. This is reflected in such hymns as 'Rejoice for a brother deceased' and 'O lovely appearance of death'. Entries in his journal include looking 'with envy on the corpse in the coffin' and claiming that 'a funeral is one of our greatest festivals'.[85] He could also be severe on what he saw as inordinate grieving. To Elizabeth Briggs he wrote that, 'it is time for you to think of your translated father rather than your desolate self; or I shall begin to suspect you love yourself rather than him'.[86]

John Wesley, however, seems exceptionally insensitive to mourners. To his sister Martha he wrote that 'the death of your child is a great instance of the goodness of God towards you'. She had often grumbled at the time used up by children, but now she had 'nothing to do but serve our Lord'.[87] Charles was more sympathetic and more subtle. To Joseph Cownley on the loss of his wife, though he began conventionally 'It is the Lord, let him do as seemeth him good . . .', he added, 'He does not forbid you to feel your loss like Ezekiel.' It is a 'great thing' that you can submit and 'patiently bear your irreparable loss'. 'By and by you will *feel* the comfort of *calm* and perfect resignation.'[88] To William Marriott on the death of a son he wrote, 'Jesus wept – to see his creature weeping; therefore he does not disapprove you feeling your loss.' He adds a poem which helps to explain his sensitivity, since it was written for the loss of his own son years before.[89]

Charles' affectionate feelings for friends and indeed for his own family were tempered, it should be added, by a dread of the threat of worldliness. William Perronet was urged to avoid temptation: 'You did not go to London to keep company but to mind your business . . . Improve your leisure hours, that is all the time you are not at the hospital.'[90] Ebenezer Blackwell, a London banker and confidant of the Wesleys, was warned about the dangers of engaging too much 'with the gentlemen of your club'. This might insensibly lead him into the 'ways and spirit of the world' and to remaining silent in the presence of 'idle words and oaths'.[91]

Rather more like his brother in another respect, Charles also learnt from observation and experience to be more open to the varieties of religious experience. But from the same sources, and perhaps more often, he was led to greater scepticism about accepting exaggerated claims at first sight. The real test became 'fruits'. Against the Moravian advocates of 'stillness' – waiting on God for salvation and avoiding use of any means of grace – Charles, like John, was gratified to find examples of people converted while receiving Holy Communion. Several examples of this are recorded in the conversion letters received in 1740–2 and they may well have been requested for this reason.[92] Speaking to a young woman, Charles 'found she was in Christ before me, but her not using my expressions hindered my perceiving it'. This compares with John Wesley's recognition of the reality of justification regardless of the jargon used in describing it.[93]

On the other hand, Charles became increasingly sceptical – more so than John – about naïve conversion claims. In February 1743 a woman had told him that 'she had a constant sense of forgiveness'. But under Charles' probing she proved 'full of the gall of bitterness' towards a fellow-member. In June he concluded that 'we have certainly been too rash and easy in allowing persons for believers on their own testimony'. He now doubted whether one could infallibly identify cases of justification 'at the time'. Only fruits could prove it.[94]

Charles' attitude to the supernatural was also more cautious than John's. It is true that, like most evangelicals, he believed in divine intervention as displayed in 'particular providences' and 'judgements' – cases where God saved the godly from danger and opponents suffered death or injury.[95] But as early as January 1739 he remarked, 'We had some discussions about agitations' (convulsions under evangelical preaching)· 'no sign of grace in my humble opinion'. To Count Zinzendorf he expressed his dislike of 'motions, visions, dreams'.[96] A girl confessed to him that her 'fits and cryings out' were 'all feigned, that Mr Wesley might take notice of her'. He was aware of the possibility of sincere but unconsciously imitative and contagious hysteria.[97] Yet he also believed that Satan could use 'natural' phenomena 'to hinder the work of God'; in Newcastle, specifically to deter the gentry from attending Methodist preaching. The remedy was to put the offenders aside, when they soon quietened down.[98]

Two underlying reasons may be suggested for Charles' greater caution, even scepticism, than John, at least about claims to conversion and perfection. Probably each reinforced the other. One reason was theological, for on at least two issues Charles differed from his brother. On what he called 'the wilderness state', John published two sermons in 1760.[99] He made a sharp distinction between 'darkness' (an uncommon and unnecessary loss of faith) and 'heaviness' (a more or less normal anxiety which is not a ground for despair). Charles, however, believed that the former condition is one into which believers are 'generally' led. Indeed, he seems to have thought that God might deliberately withhold his presence as a spiritual discipline. John regarded this as a false teaching of the 'mystics', and unscriptural. According to John, God never leaves us, though we may leave him.[100]

The brothers also differed on 'perfection'. In the 1740s Charles seems to speak optimistically of the prospect of complete dominion over sin.[101] But whatever his early views, he later became more pessimistic, especially after the Bell and Maxfield excesses in the early 1760s.[102] Progress was to come by discipline and affliction rather than through a sudden act of faith. Perfection was likely to be reached only near the time of death. But John in later life increasingly insisted that perfection could be received at any time, by simple faith. He thought Charles set the standard too high to be attained at all in this life, whereas his own more restricted view of it as a condition of love without conscious sin, is attainable now.[103]

The other underlying reason for the contrast between the brothers on all these issues was temperamental. Charles was constitutionally more melancholy and subject to depression than John. Like some other people, he thought John excessively optimistic and credulous and a bad judge of character. In particular he seemed particularly credulous about claims to justification and perfection. John himself once remarked to Charles that 'many times you see further into men than I do'.[104] Yet John Pawson, who was hostile to Charles, thought John as good a judge of character as his brother and quotes him as saying, 'My brother suspects everybody and is continually imposed upon; but I trust everybody and I am never imposed upon.'[105] This was surely an exaggeration. John was certainly very ready to accept people at face value, especially if they appeared to show signs of his favourite types of piety. Whitehead, his biographer, thought he was a man 'remarkably free from jealousy and suspicion and therefore very open to imposition'.[106] Charles had good reason to be suspicious about some Methodist claims to holiness, even if he was excessively critical and suspicious of some of the preachers.

Charles' pastoral practice was, then, influenced by temperament, theological presuppositions and the lessons of experience. His most intense probing of converts seems to have been from 1739 into the early 1740s. Letters to him about religious experience continued to be sent after this period up to and including the 1780s, though these generally deal with life after conversion. Along with these are accounts of edifying death-beds. It is not clear whether these letters came unsolicited from old acquaintances or admirers, or were requested by Charles. His contact with, and knowledge of, rank and file Methodists outside the Bristol and London areas naturally diminished after 1756 and in those centres tended to be coloured by the presence of Church-loving associates. His letters to his wife now reveal more about patrons and friends than strictly pastoral interests, but this may be due to a proper reticence which had not applied to his private and unpublished journal. It is touching to find an echo of earlier times when, during a visit to Bristol in 1778 he accompanied his brother to Kingswood where they 'enjoyed a feast indeed with our beloved colliers'.[107]

## Conclusions

What were Charles Wesley's contributions to early Methodism beyond his hymn-writing? In the first few years of the Revival he was as active as his brother in travelling, preaching, pastoral work and oversight. Even if his travels lacked correlation with John's after 1743 (as his brother later claimed), and they certainly seemed to have done so after his marriage, Charles had nevertheless helped to further and deepen the work in new areas as well as old ones. He also catered for Bristol and London in his brother's absence, even if not as predictably as John desired. Though his journeys after his marriage became less extended, they only became restricted effectively to the Bristol area and south-east after 1756. Until he finally settled in London from 1771 it appears that Charles, though resident in Bristol, paid fairly frequent visits to the capital and so continued to fill, in some measure, the gap left by his brother's absences. It appears that once removed to London he rarely visited Bristol. Yet it is important to recognize the effects of his long-term ministry in both places, which consolidated two leading societies and fortified their pro-Anglican sentiments.

If Charles' purging of the preachers had gone as far as wished in 1751, it is probable that the itinerant system would have been undermined. Yet it may be that his actions did remove some weak links. For whatever reasons, it is worth noting that about two dozen preachers did disappear between 1751 and 1754.[108] Charles' opposition to ordination and separation in the 1750s, despite involving unpleasant intrigues against his brother, helped to stave off the very real threat of a secession from the Church of England. Had this happened at such an early stage, it would almost certainly have narrowed, weakened and perhaps permanently damaged Methodism's appeal as an alternative to conventional Anglicanism without the stigma and limitations of Dissent. The movement was in a much stronger position to face a gradual separation later in the century.

Charles' opposition to Methodist ordinations and his efforts to maintain the Anglican connection may appear to have been a fight against the inevitable. But whether or not this is so, it needs to be recognized that he reflected and represented a significant body of Methodist opinion, not least among influential trustees and other leading laymen in major centres as well as a section of the travelling preachers. Their influence, it is argued, can be seen as early as the 1760s and in the conflicts which followed John Wesley's death. The continuing resistance to Methodist sacraments in some places after the Plan of Pacification of 1795 is evidence of the strength of 'Church Methodists'. Their role and that of their lay leaders in John Wesley's later years deserve further investigation. The point of view they represented is arguably another of Charles Wesley's significant legacies. Those who wished for ordination and a more self-sufficient Methodism were retained partly by John Wesley's capacity for compromise, through his concessions where such pressures were greatest. Yet Charles and those he represented were a standing reminder of an older, more conservative Methodism, even if one less restrictive than Charles liked to remember .

Perhaps John Wesley's claim that Charles' 'least praise was his talent for poetry' meant that he had the fuller range of his brother's activities in mind. The memorial tablet in City Road chapel certainly reflected this. It praised his achievement as an 'unrivalled' Christian poet and his power as a preacher to be both a 'son of consolation' and a 'son of thunder'. Uniting with his brother in 'the plan of itinerant preaching', it claims, led him to 'contributing largely . . . by his labours . . . to the first formation of the Methodist Society in these Kingdoms'. He was also – and Charles would certainly have welcomed this tribute – 'a sincere friend of the Church of England'.[109]

## Notes

1 John Wesley, *Works,* ed. Thomas Jackson, 14 vols (London: Wesleyan Conference Office, 1872), XIII, 514.

2 See Chapter 4 below.

3 *BE*, 9.430 from his *Concise Ecclesiastical History*. Compare *A Short History of Methodism* (1765) in *BE*, 9.368.

4 *Short History*, in *BE*, 9, 368; *Character of a Methodist* (1742), in *BE*, 9.32.

5 *Works* (1872) VIII, 299.

6 See R. P. Heitzenrater, *Wesley and the People Called Methodists* (Nashville: Abingdon Press, 1995), 38–52.

7 Hence the sub-title of F. C. Gill, *Charles Wesley: The first Methodist* (London: Epworth Press, 1964).

8 MARC, DDWes, 1/38, 29 April 1785; also printed in J. B. Tyson, *Charles Wesley: A reader* (New York: Oxford University Press, 1989), 58–61.

9 For these see MARC, DDCW, 1/1–3 and extracts in Frank Baker, *Charles Wesley as Revealed by his Letters* (London: Epworth Press, 1948), 10–16.

10 V. H. H. Green, *Young Mr Wesley* (London: Arnold, 1961), 122, 153; Heitzenrater, *Wesley and the People Called Methodists*, 38.

11 R. P. Heitzenrater, *The Elusive Mr Wesley*, 2nd edn (Nashville: Abingdon Press, 2003), 64.

12 *CWJ*, 1.320.

13 *CWJ*, 1.358.

14 *CWJ*, 1.320.

15 *BE*, 19.46.

16 *CWJ*, 1.150, 154–5.

17 *CWJ*, 1.149.

18 *CWJ*, 1.259.

19 *BE*, 20.34; *CWJ*, 1.67–8.

20 *CWJ*, 1.413; compare John Wesley to Samuel Walker in 1756, defending lay preachers and claiming he would rather have the inward (divine) call than the outward (human) call: John Wesley, *Letters*, ed. J. Telford, 8 vols (London: Epworth Press, 1931), VIII, 195.

21 *CWJ*, 2.16.

22 *CWJ*, 1.419.

23 *BE*, 26.527.

24 *BE*, 26.528.

25 MARC, DDCW, 1/34, 36, 37.

26 *CWJ*, 2.52–3.

27 *CWJ*, 2.95.

28 For Cornish visits, see Thomas Jackson, *Life of Charles Wesley*, 2 vols (London: John Mason, 1841), II, 21–3, quoting two letters and dating both to 1753. Gareth Lloyd, in his calendar of *The Charles Wesley Papers* (Manchester: JRUL, 1994), dates the first (MARC, DDCW, 7/99) 1753, but the second in *The Wesley Family Papers* (Manchester: JRUL, 1993) (MARC, DD, Wes 4/42) as 1752. For Scotland, see John Wesley, *BE*, 26.449 and *CWJ*, 2.290, 291–2. A letter from an unidentified 'St Mungo's' on 25 April 1754 might perhaps be in Scotland or Cornwall (MARC, DDCW, 1/51).

29 Gareth Lloyd, 'Charles Wesley: A New Evaluation of his Life and Ministry', unpublished PhD dissertation (University of Liverpool, 2002), chapter 4.

30 For the Wheatley affair, see John Wesley to Wheatley in *BE*, 26.64–5; E. J. Bellamy, *James Wheatley and Norwich Methodism in the 1750s* (Peterborough: Methodist Publishing House for World Methodist Historical Society, 1996).

31 *BE*, 26.472–3.

32  Charles Wesley to Lady Huntingdon by an amanuensis: MARC, PLP, 113.2.5. Wrongly dated 4 August 1752 but really 1751. Most of the letter is printed in Baker, *Charles Wesley*, 183–5.

33  *BE*, 26.479 (in December 1751).

34  The statement is printed from a copy made for Charles Wesley in Frank Baker, *John Wesley and the Church of England* (London: Epworth Press, 1970), 326–40. Original in a notebook in MARC, DDCW, 8/1. For the context see Baker, same work, 164–6.

35  See letter to Samuel Walker of Truro, 24 September 1755, in *BE*, 26.592–6.

36  For the Walker and Wesley correspondence, see G. C. B. Davies, *Early Cornish Evangelicals* (London: SPCK, 1951), chapters 5 and 6; *BE*, 26.582–86, 592–6, 606–8, 611–13 (John Wesley and Walker); Charles Wesley and Walker in Davies, 106–7, 114–15).

37  L. Tyerman, *Life and Times of John Wesley*, 3 vols (London: Hodder and Stoughton, 1871), II, 387–8; Baker, *Charles Wesley*, 102–3.

38  *BE*, 26.562, 565, 573.

39  Sally Wesley to Adam Clarke in Wesley College, Bristol MSS D6/1/ 276–300; MARC, DDWes, 6/15 offering material for his projected life of John Wesley.

40  Tyerman, *John Wesley*, II, 271–2; Jackson, *Life*, 2.135–7.

41  Baker, *Charles Wesley*, 104–5, 117–18.

42  G. Lloyd, 'Charles Wesley', 205–9.

43  MARC, DDCW, 1/53: to Samuel Lloyd, 5 July 1755.

44  MARC, DDCW, 5/97 and *CWJ*, 2.210–11. A reference to the 'new chapel' would normally mean City Road and therefore a date after November 1778. This is possible, but references to medical advice resemble those in MARC, DDCW, 7/5, 7/7 dated May 1760, the same month as this letter.

45  MARC, DDPr. 2/16; Jackson, *Charles Wesley*, II, 196; Tyerman, *John Wesley*, II, 387.

46  To Joseph Cownley, February 1763 and 1765 or 1766: MARC, DDCW, 1/57, 5/110. For 1773 see Baker, *Charles Wesley*, 104.

47  Baker, *Charles Wesley*, 98–103.

48  John Wesley, *Letters*, V, 16–17.

49  For example, 30 May 1773: John Wesley, *Letters*, VI, 29.

50  MARC, DDWes, 4/37, 50.

51  Baker, *Charles Wesley*, 118.

52  *CWJ*, 1.139.

53  *CWJ*, 1.142, 143.

54  For example, 10 August 1739: *CWJ*, 1.158.

55  MARC, DDCW, 5/67; Baker, *Charles Wesley*, 118–19; MARC, DDCW, 1/23.

56  Offer from Mrs Gumley in 1759: MARC, DDCW, 5/99 and *CWJ*, 2.212.

57  Baker, *Charles Wesley*, 118.

58  MARC, DDCW, 7/2; Baker, *Charles Wesley*, 107.

59  For his defence in 1779 see Baker, *Charles Wesley*, 113–14.

60  Tyerman, *John Wesley*, III, 299–300; but criticized by G. Lloyd, 'Charles Wesley', 249–53.

61  See MARC, DDCW, 1/61–4, 7/60; D Pr. 1/41–8; Baker, *Charles Wesley*, 129–30; G. Lloyd, 'Charles Wesley', 240–6.

62  Baker, *Charles Wesley*, 129–40; Baker, *Charles Wesley and the Church of England*, 256–82; H. D. Rack, *Reasonable Enthusiast: John Wesley and the rise of Methodism*, 3rd edn (London. Epworth Press, 2002), 518–21.

63  G. Lloyd, 'Charles Wesley', chapter 8 , especially 247–85.

64  For this little-known episode see MARC (uncatalogued) Joseph Sutcliffe, MS 'History of Methodism' folios 678–81 to be discussed in the Introduction to my edition of the Methodist Conferences in the forthcoming as *BE*, vol. 10.

65  E. B. Perkins, *Methodist Preaching Houses and the Law* (London: Epworth Press, 1952), 54–6.

66  MARC, 'Letters Chiefly to the Wesleys', 2.72, 2.117 and G. Lloyd, 'Charles Wesley', 267–72.

67  For these interlocking disputes see H. D. Rack, 'Wesley Portrayed: Character and Criticism in some Early Biographies of John Wesley', *Methodist History*, XLIII:2 (2005), 91–2, 98–101.

68  Pawson on Whitehead: *Letters of John Pawson*, ed. J.C. Bowmer and John Vickers, 3 vols (Peterborough: Methodist Publishing House for World Methodist Historical Society, 1994–95), II, 43–72. On Whitehead, Wesley and the preachers see notes on Pawson's lost biography of Whitehead, in MARC, Tyerman MSS (uncatalogued) III, folios 43–72, especially 53–4 on the ordinations.

69  John Wesley, *Letters*, V, 16.

70  For Charles as preacher, see Newport, *Sermons*, 28–47.

71  *BE*, 25.605, 612.

72  For some discussion of Charles as pastor, see Baker, *Charles Wesley*, 117–28.

73  *CWJ*, 1.174, 176–7, 193.

74  *CWJ*, 1.207, 226, 217–18, 270.

75  *CWJ*, 1.117, 120–3.

76  *CWJ*, 1.307; similarly in Cornwall, 323.

77  These early letters are included in a collection addressed to Charles in MARC EMV, 1–153 along with later correspondence. Most of the early accounts are from London in 1740–1, but six from Bristol in 1742. The latter are published by Kenneth Morgan in *Reformation and Revival in Eighteenth Century Bristol*, ed. J. Barry and K. Morgan (Bristol Record Society Publications, XLV, Bristol Record Society, 1994), 75–104. These and other early accounts are analysed in H. D. Rack, *Early Methodist Experience: Some prototypical accounts* (Oxford: Religious Experience Research Unit, Westminster College, Occasional Papers Second Series No. 4, 1997).

78  MARC, EMV, 87 and Morgan in Barry and Morgan, 91–4.

79  MARC EMV, 7; similar case in *CWJ*, 1.178.

80  *CWJ*, 2.87.

81  For an excellent analysis of John as pastor, see M. Schmidt, *John Wesley: A Theological Biography*, English translation, 3 vols (London: Epworth Press), II(2), 118–74.

82  Originally in the *Arminian Magazine*, 1798, partly reprinted in L. Tyerman, *The Oxford Methodists* (London: Hodder and Stoughton, 1873). See 157 for remark on Charles Wesley.

83  John Hampson, *Memoirs of John Wesley*, 3 vols (Sunderland: for the author, 1791), III, 199.

84  MARC, DDCW, 1/43, 44, 47.

85  *CWJ*, 1.263, 304.

86  MARC, DDCW, 7/119.

87  *BE*, 26.90–1. For other examples *BE*, 26.587–8 and John Wesley, *Letters*, VIII, 283.

88  Baker, *Charles Wesley*, 123.

89  MARC, DDCW, 7/116.

90 MARC, DDCW, 1/15a.

91 MARC, DDCW, 1/46; Baker, *Charles Wesley*, 126 prints with some minor errors.

92 See, for example, MARC EMV, 16, Thomas Cooper.

93 *CWJ*, 2.25; John Wesley, *BE*, 22, 114.

94 *CWJ*, 1.303, 315.

95 See, for example, rain ceasing during preaching; members saved from danger and sinners damaged; healing by prayer; demons cast out: *CWJ* 1.415, 241, 352, 120, 180.

96 *CWJ*, 1.140, 148.

97 *CWJ*, 1.247, 314.

98 *CWJ*, 1.243, 316, 314.

99 'The Wilderness State' and 'Heaviness through Manifold Temptations': sermons 46 and 47 in *BE*, 2.205–37 and A. C. Outler's introduction, *BE*, 2.202–4.

100 *CWJ*, 1.165, 174; *BE*, 2.203, 208, 219.

101 *CWJ*, 1.280 (in 1740).

102 See further, Kenneth G. C. Newport and Gareth Lloyd, 'George Bell and Early Methodist Enthusiasm: A New Source from the Manchester Archives', *Bulletin of the John Rylands University Library of Manchester*, 80 (1998), 89–101.

103 See H. D. Rack, *Reasonable Enthusiast*, 395–401. For John's arguments with Charles, see John Wesley, *Letters*, IV, 187–8; V, 20, 38–9, 41, 88, 93, 316; and to Miss March VI, 88.

104 John Wesley, *Letters*, VII, 272.

105 MARC, Tyerman MSS, III, folio 50 from notes on Pawson's lost life of Dr Whitehead.

106 John Whitehead, *Life of John Wesley and Charles Wesley*, 2 vols (London: S. Couchman, 1793–6).

107 MARC, DDCW, 7/36.

108 Tyerman, *John Wesley*, II, 126–7.

109 Quoted by G. J. Stevenson, *City Road Chapel, London* (London: G. J. Stevenson, 1872), 348.

# 4. Brothers in Arms: The Partnership of John and Charles Wesley[1]

## JOHN A. NEWTON

In his life of Dr Johnson, James Boswell records a conversation he had with the great man in 1778. Johnson, quite incidentally, provides an interesting comparison of the two Wesley brothers, in respect of their different temperaments. Boswell's account runs as follows:

> Of John Wesley he [Johnson] said, 'He can talk well on any subject.'
> BOSWELL: [who, as usual, is keen to draw Johnson out by putting him to the question] 'Pray, Sir, what has he made of his story of a ghost?'
> JOHNSON: 'Why, Sir, he believes it; but not on sufficient authority. He did not take time enough to examine the girl. It was at Newcastle, where the ghost was said to have appeared to a young woman several times, mentioning something about the right to an old house, advising application to be made to an attorney, which was done; and, at the same time, saying the attorney would do nothing, which proved to be the fact. "This (says John) is a proof that a ghost knows our thoughts." Now (laughing) it is not necessary to know our thoughts, to tell that an attorney will sometimes do nothing. Charles Wesley, who is a more stationary man, does not believe the story. I am sorry that John did not take more pains to inquire into the evidence for it.'[2]

Johnson's description of Charles Wesley as 'a more stationary man' than John appears to mean that he is more fixed in his views, less volatile and subject to change in his convictions than his older brother. Vivian Green, in his *Young Mr Wesley*, speaks of the Epworth ghost or poltergeist ('Old Jeffrey'), and similar events, as buttressing the adolescent John Wesley's 'natural credulity'.[3] John certainly held a lifelong belief in apparitions and witches – beliefs which were more common among educated people of the seventeenth century than those of the eighteenth.

Charles, on the other hand, though fervent, even passionate, in temperament, was much more hard-headed and sceptical than John in his attitude to allegedly supernatural or abnormal phenomena. His considered judgement (1743) about the convulsive paroxysms which accompanied the earliest Methodist preaching, from 1739, was that, 'some were counterfeit, others could be controlled, the remainder he could not accept as divine signs'.[4]

We can perhaps gain a clearer impression of the temperamental differences between the brothers if we compare them with their parents. John's character bears an unmistakable likeness to that of his mother; he is, in the deepest sense, 'son to Susanna'. Charles, for his part, shared many of his father's traits of character, both his strengths and his weaknesses. Despite his tendency to credit accounts of supernatural interventions more readily than Charles, John is generally as calm and reasonable as Charles is passionate and poetic. Susanna's prayers and meditations have a strongly rational and intellectual strain in them, as well as expressing a personal religious fervour and a lively faith. In the same way, John, as a mature theologian, insists that 'all irrational religion is false religion',[5] and continually addresses his earnest appeals to 'Men of Reason and Religion'.[6] Even as a small child, he showed a strong inclination to reasonableness. When offered fruit or anything else between meals, Jacky, as he was known as a child in his family, would be quite likely to respond with the measured reply, 'I thank you, I will think of it.'[7] Samuel, the rector and father of the family, seems to have found the child's eminent reasonableness irritating at times, and he once remarked to Susanna that he did not believe Jack would attend to the most pressing needs of nature, unless he could give a reason for it. The child is father of the man; and John retained this characteristic all through his adult life.

Charles, by contrast, tended to be volatile, quick-tempered, impatient, like his father. It may well have been in part the reflex of his poetic nature. Certainly, the man who would leap from his horse after a journey, rush into the house, and demand at once pen and paper to scribe down the words of a hymn he had just composed while riding, was, on his own admission, not greatly endowed with the gift of patience. In an early letter to John, written from Christ Church, Oxford, (20 January 1727/28), Charles could admit,

> Tis an ill wind that blows nobody good! That same favourable blast, at which my father may say, 'Ego in portu navigo' [I have reached port] has quite overset my patience, which as you know is but a slight vessel at best, and at present is sadly at a loss for ballast. 'Settled for life – at least for years!['] You can't imagine what a violent effect those few words had upon this gentle reader.[8]

Charles's father had evidently being telling him that he was now comfortably off, with his scholarship at Oxford, and his future assured. Charles, in his letter to John, takes quite a different view, and proceeds to bemoan, in no uncertain terms, his acute lack of clothes and money – a student complaint by no means limited to the eighteenth century!

A year later, in another Oxford letter to John, dated 5 January 1729 (NS), Charles contrasts his own poor aptitude for study with John's avid gift for learning:

> In my pursuit of knowledge I own I have this advantage of you in some things. My brothers were born before me; I start at twenty. But then I'm sure I'm less indebted to nature than you. I'm very desirous of knowledge, but can't bear the drudgery of coming at it near as well as you could. In reading anything difficult I'm bewildered in a much shorter time than I believe you

used to be at your first setting out. My head will by no means keep pace
with my heart, and I'm afraid I shan't reconcile it in haste to the extraordinary business of thinking.[9]

Charles' confession, 'My head will by no means keep pace with my heart',
might well stand as the key to his life story, for good as well as ill. It is not a
phrase that could easily be applied to brother John. Charles' impulsiveness
and impatience challenge comparison with the same traits of character that
we see in his father. Susanna Wesley, in her detailed letter to John (24 July
1732), giving an account of her child-rearing and educational methods, lists
the 'bye-laws' or rules which she drew up for her large brood of children.
Rule Number One, which stands out, both by pride of place and length of
exposition, reads as follows:

> It had been observed that cowardice and fear of punishment often lead
> children into lying; till they get custom of it which they cannot leave. To
> prevent this, a law was made that whoever was charged with a fault, if they
> would ingenuously confess it, and promise to amend, should not be beaten.
> This rule prevented a great deal of lying; and would have done more, if
> one in the family would have observed it. But he could not be prevailed on,
> and therefore was often imposed upon by false colours and equivocations,
> which none would have used but one had they been kindly dealt with; and
> some in spite of all would always speak truth plainly.[10]

There is no prize for guessing who the 'one in the family' was, who would not
keep to the rule, and who punished the child, even when it had confessed.
Such an enlightened, reasonable principle as Susanna's evidently could not
withstand the sudden anger of Samuel. Even when he had broken the rule, 'he
could not be prevailed on', Susanna recalls – no doubt by her own reasoned
entreaty – but insisted on going his own headstrong way. Charles had something of the same hasty temper, just as John embodied the calm, reasoned
attitude of his mother.

Another way of exploring the temperamental difference between the two
brothers is to look at their personalities in terms of the masculine and feminine elements in their personal make-up. John's feminine side was highly developed. He related well to women as friends and colleagues, and was noted for
his sensitivity and tact. Charles, by contrast, was much more the rough, blunt
male, sometimes unbridled in his anger and vehement in speech in a way
that John rarely was. The same contrast emerges from a study of their preaching styles. There has survived, from the pen of a sympathetic Dissenter, a
vivid account of Charles' preaching in the open air at Bristol in 1740. Joseph
Williams of Kidderminster writes of Charles:

> He preached about an hour, from 2 Corin. V.17–21, in such a manner as I
> have seldom, if ever, heard any Minister preach; that is, though I have heard
> many a finer sermon, according to the common taste, yet I have scarcely
> ever heard an Minister discover [i.e. reveal] such evident signs of a most
> vehement desire, or labour so earnestly to convince his hearers that they

were all by nature in a state of enmity against God, consequently in a damnable state, and needed reconciliation to God.

Williams goes on to describe how Charles then, having wounded the conscience of his hearers, proceeds to pour in the oil and wine of the gospel, 'and used a great variety of the most moving arguments and expostulations, in order to persuade, allure, instigate, and, if possible, compel all to come to Christ and believe in him for pardon and salvation'.[11]

We note here the ardour and vehemence of Charles' preaching, and his passionate longing to bring people to Christ. Nor does this account stand alone. It is corroborated by Thomas Jackson in his major life of Charles, where he assures the reader:

> There was nothing artificial in his sermons. To a strictly logical arrangement, and the arts of secular oratory, he was indifferent. His discourses were effusions of the heart, rather than the offspring of the intellect, or of the imagination . . . [in his preaching] . . . the tears ran down his cheeks; his tongue was loosed; and he poured forth the truth of God, in the very phraseology of inspiration, with an effort that was overwhelming.[12]

If we turn to John's preaching, we are immediately conscious of a markedly different style. Bishop Edward King, the Anglican Bishop of Lincoln (1829–1910), was a great admirer of John Wesley. King deplored what he called 'tail-lashing' in the pulpit, that is, self-display, affectation, or exhibitionism in preaching. John Wesley was clearly of the same mind, as his instructions to his preachers reveal. Writing to a Lincolnshire Methodist in 1753, Wesley says, 'I . . . advise all our preachers not to preach above an hour at a time, prayer and all; and not to speak louder either in preaching or prayer than the number of hearers requires.'[13] He deprecated the touch of 'enthusiasm' which showed itself in William Brammah's 'screaming' in the pulpit.[14] He urged his preachers to speak 'in the plainest manner'[15] possible – no exaggeration, no flowery language, no pseudo-learning. To Sally Mallet, one of his few women preachers, he urges: 'You are not to judge by your own feeling, but by the word of God. Never scream. Never speak above the natural pitch of your voice; it is disgustful to the hearers. It gives them pain, not pleasure. And it is destroying yourself. It is offering God murder for sacrifice . . .'[16]

Contemporary accounts of John's own preaching make clear the force of his appeal to the heart as well as the head, and yet suggest a predominant tone of calm, reasoned appeal. Horace Walpole's celebrated and unsympathetic description of his hearing Wesley preach at Bath in 1766 would seem to bear this out. Walpole records that Wesley 'spoke his sermon so fast, and with so little accent, that I am sure he has often uttered it, for it was like a lesson. There were parts and eloquence in it; but towards the end he exalted his voice, and acted very ugly enthusiasm.'[17]

We turn now to the hymns of Methodism, in which Charles made his supreme contribution to the Revival and to the devotion of the whole Christian Church. In Henry Rack's words, Charles Wesley, like Isaac Watts, 'Contrived to express profound religious ideas coupled with intense yet controlled religious

feeling.'[18] Charles used his classical education and his profound knowledge of
the scriptures to the full; but he was also not afraid to use sensuous, personal,
even erotic imagery to express his Christian experience. His evening hymn,
'How do thy mercies close me round', for example, contains the verses:

> Jesus protect, my fears be gone!
> Naught can the Rock of Ages move;
> Safe in thy arms lay me down,
> Thy arms of everlasting love.

> While Thou art intimately nigh,
> Who, who shall violate my rest?
> Sin, earth and hell I now defy;
> I lean upon my Saviour's breast.[19]

Of course, scriptural echoes are present here – the Old Testament assurance
that 'Underneath are the everlasting arms'; and the portrait in John's Gospel
of the Beloved Disciple leaning back, during the Last Supper, on the breast
of Jesus (John 13.23). Yet Charles has unmistakably heightened the emotional
force of the language.

John Wesley, as the critical editor of his brother's hymns, and as one who
kept his own feelings on a much tighter rein than did Charles, could not
approve this kind of emotional language. He was always on the look out,
like a rigorous censor, for what he called 'fondling' terms of endearment, as
applied to the believer's relationship with the Lord Jesus. It is well known
that he omitted the hymn 'Jesu, Lover of my soul' from the 1780 hymn book,
though he did include it in some of the shorter, less official collections. It was
the opening couplet to which he took exception, with its, to him, over-intimate
and personal plea,

> Jesu, Lover of my soul,
> Let me to Thy bosom fly . . .

Charles, with the inspiration of a major religious poet, and with the experience of the ecstasy of happy love, could give powerful expression to his deepest feelings. John, who had not the same poetic gift, who never knew happy
married love, and who was so eminently reasonable in character, never found
it easy to come to terms with his deepest feelings. (At Aldersgate Street, at the
turning point of 24 May 1738, his familiar journal entry deserves close scrutiny in this respect. What did he mean by the phrase, 'I felt my heart strangely
warmed'? Was he merely saying that this experience simply heightened feelings he had known before – that is, they were strange in a matter of degree,
rather than of kind? Or does 'strangely' imply that here was a radically new
experience of powerful religious feeling, which shook him to the depths, precisely because he had never experienced the like before?)

Certainly, John does not seem to have found it easy to come to terms with
his emotional depths, either in his personal relationships or in his personal
religion. To take a specific example: though he consistently encouraged his

people to press on to entire sanctification, or Christian Perfection, he never claimed to have reached that state himself. He was once present at a Methodist Lovefeast in Yorkshire, at which several members freely testified to having been made perfect in love. Wesley said nothing; so that one layman, with typical Yorkshire bluntness, was bold enough to draw attention to their leader's silence on the matter. John Wesley, drawing himself up to his full height of five feet three inches or so, permitted himself only an oracular statement from St Paul, 'By the grace of God, I am what I am!' – and sat down again without another word. That incident was typical, not only of his notorious unwillingness to claim personal experience of entire sanctification, but also of his diffidence in expressing publicly – either in speech or writing – his own most profound and personal religious feelings.

Again, in churchmanship, we can readily detect a notable difference between John and Charles. Both had been brought up in the high church atmosphere of the Epworth parsonage, by parents who were not cradle Anglicans but had joined the Church of England from personal choice and conviction. Both brothers were deeply attached to their mother Church, in which they had been baptized, brought up and ordained. John's ringing declaration, 'I live and die a member of the Church of England',[20] has become as much part of Methodist tradition as his missionary avowal, 'I look upon the whole world as my parish.'[21] And yet, when it came to specific policy decisions involving the Methodist Societies and their relation to the Church of England, John and Charles often disagreed. Charles once sharply and epigrammatically pointed up the basic difference between them when he made the explicit claim that 'all the difference between my brother and me was that my brother's first object was the Methodists and then the Church; mine was first the Church and then the Methodists. Our different judgement of persons was owing to our different tempers, his all hopes and mine all fears.'[22] Of course, ideally, neither brother would have wanted to make a choice between the interests of the Mother Church and those of the Methodist connexion. Yet sometimes events constrained John, as leader of the Methodist people, to make some very hard choices indeed. It might just conceivably have been different had the Church of England not been, from 1717 to 1852, without its 'vocal organs'; that is to say, lacking the active leadership and guidance of its Convocation. For political reasons, that body was in abeyance for the whole of the adult lives of the Wesleys – and far beyond. In other words, during the entire period of the rise and progress of the eighteenth-century Methodist movement in England, the Anglican Church had no means of coming to terms with it in a corporate, considered, formal way. That may well be accounted as one of the tragedies of eighteenth-century church history; but such was the fact.

In consequence, John Wesley, in guiding and directing the Methodist movement, found himself time and again in an ambiguous set of circumstances, in which he deemed compromise, however distasteful, to be inevitable. To take one or two of the most obvious examples: John was as adamant as Charles that the Methodists were not Dissenters. Their leaders had no desire to break away from the Established Church. They encouraged their followers to attend its services, and, where possible, to receive its sacraments. Yet as the Methodist movement spread, meeting-houses were built for purposes of shared prayer, fellowship, exposition of the scriptures and, as for example at the New Room, Bristol, from 1739, for providing a school for poor children and a dispensary with free medicines for the poor.

These buildings were used for Methodist worship, but they were neither Anglican nor Dissenting meeting-places. They were not licensed by law as Dissenting chapels, and therefore had no legal protection against the depredations of the mob, who might break in and cause damage with impunity. John Wesley was therefore driven, with extreme reluctance, but nevertheless conscientiously, to license them as Dissenting meeting-houses under the Toleration Act. Charles was incensed and wrote on the back of the licence for the New Room, Bristol, his angry protest against a legal document which he held to be absurd and unnecessary.[23] He did not make clear, however, what alternative course of action he would have taken, had he been in John Wesley's shoes and seeking to protect the humble preaching houses where the Methodist Societies gathered.

Charles' opposition to John's Bristol ordinations in 1784 was entirely predictable and equally emphatic. He not only lampooned John's action in verse dashed off for the occasion – 'Wesley his hands on Coke has laid, But who laid hands on him?'[24] – but also coined the pithy, memorable judgement that 'ordination is separation'. In this instance, Charles was in all probability being more realistic and far-sighted than his brother. That John, in Anglican priest's orders, should have taken to himself the Episcopal prerogative of ordination, was a clear breach of the discipline and order of the Church. Yet he did so only in what he perceived to be a situation of acute pastoral and missionary need, in terms of the severe lack of clergy in America, and having unsuccessfully appealed to the Bishop of London, in whose diocese North America lay, to take such remedial action himself.

Charles, then, was much more the stiff high churchman than John. In this regard, as in others, he resembled his father, Samuel, the Rector of Epworth. John, though a loyal churchman, proved in practice much more flexible with regard to Anglican order. Here, I think, he was the son of his mother, and may be seen as reverting – perhaps unconsciously – to his Puritan, nonconformist ancestry. Susanna was prepared to withstand her husband when, during his absence from the parish at Convocation, she began to hold simple services of worship in her kitchen, to which a considerable number of local people came. To Samuel, informed of what was happening by his curate, she was usurping a clergyman's prerogative, and he pressed her in his letters to stop holding the meetings. She defended her action, courteously but vigorously; claimed she was meeting a spiritual need; and argued that genuine benefit was resulting from these meetings for prayer; denied that she was preaching; and finally refused to desist unless Samuel explicitly ordered her to do so. When it came to the crunch, the rector gave way, and Susanna continued her lay ministry, no doubt to the chagrin of the curate.[25]

Again, when Thomas Maxfield, one of John Wesley's young lay helpers, began to preach without Mr Wesley's authorization, it was Susanna who intervened on his behalf. John had ridden post-haste from Bristol to London on hearing of this new development of lay preaching, and greeted his mother on his arrival with the curt words, 'Thomas Maxfield has turned preacher, I find.' Susanna's reply is well known, and represents again her willingness to sanction a modification of strict Anglican church order, for the sake of the furtherance of the gospel. She calmly admonished her son: 'John, you know what my sentiments have been. You cannot suspect me of favouring readily anything of this kind. But take care what you do with respect to that young man, for he is as surely called of God to preach as you are. Examine what have been the fruits of his preaching, and hear him also yourself.'[26] John listened to this wise counsel, heard the young man preach, and acknowledged, 'It is the Lord!' (And so began the order of Methodist lay preachers. One can well imagine what Samuel Wesley's advice would have been in the same circumstances! He would surely have cracked the whip of discipline and insisted on the requirements of Anglican church order.)

Charles Wesley did not, of course, deny the right of lay men and women to preach; but he was exceedingly jealous of their pretensions, and continually concerned lest they should exceed the limits which John Wesley, as their leader, had prescribed for them. He was furious when some of the preachers in Yorkshire began to celebrate the sacrament of Holy Communion. He resented it deeply when a number of them advocated separation from the Church of England, when this issue surfaced in the Conference, as it did more than once. He was of the opinion that his brother John deferred far too much to the views of the preachers, and wanted them kept under much tighter control. In all this, we may say that Charles is the son of his father, and a stiff Church of England man who lacked the flexibility and pragmatism we see both in John and in their mother, Susanna. It is fittingly symbolic that both Samuel and Charles lie buried in Anglican consecrated ground; Susanna and John do not. Samuel was buried in Epworth churchyard, and Charles was interred in the graveyard of St Marylebone parish church in London. Charles' body was carried to its grave by eight Anglican clergy who acted as his pall-bearers. Susanna's body, on the other hand, was laid to rest in the great Puritan burial-ground of Bunhill Fields, across the road from Wesley's chapel, London, where John's own earthly remains were buried.

The differences in temperament between the two brothers, and the friction that arose when so often they did not see eye to eye, are both illustrated by a letter from John to Charles, written on 31 October 1753. John upbraids Charles for not acting 'in connexion' with him over the course of the previous ten years, because, says John, Charles has repeatedly failed to keep him informed as to his plans and his preaching journeys. John asks: 'In journeying, which of us lays his plans according to reason? Either you move (quite contrary to me) by those impressions which you account divine, or (which is worse) *pro ratione voluntas* [taking your own will for reason].'[27] The implications of John's complaint seem plain. He, John, plans his preaching journeys carefully, on a rational scheme. Charles, in John's view, simply takes off on impulse, or because of what he accounts – without any consultation with John, the director of the whole Methodist mission – as a divinely given leading or inspiration. We do not have Charles' view of the matter, but John's strictures are in keeping with what we know of Charles' nature from other sources.

As early as their Oxford days, they recognized that, though brothers and close friends, they were unlike in temperament and in outlook. Charles, writing to John from Oxford on 20 January 1727/28, comments: 'I wish the person who says I'm like you had [mo]re reasons for so saying.'[28] They certainly were two very different men; and yet, for all their differences, they needed each other, for in many ways their gifts were complementary. John had outstanding gifts of organization and pastoral care; but he also had a very strong will, liked his own way, and had a marked tendency to authoritarianism. He was not nicknamed 'Pope John' for nothing. He himself needed what he insisted every Christian should have, namely, a 'candid friend'; that is to say, someone who would, as and when necessary, speak plainly to him, challenge his actions and perhaps constrain him to think again about what he was planning to do. This is precisely what Charles was able to do for John. Again, John's calm rationality was complemented by Charles' emotional fire and poetic temperament. On the other hand, Charles, who suffered from poor health – Henry Rack describes him as 'almost a manic-depressive personality'[29] – needed John's steadying support in his darker moments. Both the calm rationality and the emotional passion were essential to the work of the Revival, and each brother would have been profoundly the poorer without the other.

I have dwelt at some length on the differences between John and Charles, because these are part of the fascination of their joint story. Yet for all their differences, at the deepest level they were united, as brothers in arms. Both were committed to the preaching of the gospel, to reaching the unchurched, to making known to all the unsearchable riches of Christ. Both had a keen compassion for the poor, and were ardent in their desire to relieve both spiritual poverty and physical destitution. John Wesley in 1747 advised the London Methodist Stewards, 'Put yourself in the place of every poor man, and deal with him as you would God should deal with you';[30] and as an old man, he could be seen in one bitter winter season, tramping the streets of London through snow and slush, collecting from friends and colleagues money to relieve the sufferings of the poor members of the London societies. He once preached, in one of the parish churches of the city, to a well-to-do congregation on the text: 'You brood of vipers, who warned you to flee from the wrath to come?' One angry member of the congregation confronted him after the service and demanded to know how Mr Wesley had dared to preach such a sermon to so eminently respectable a congregation. If Wesley had been going to preach on that text, urged his critic, he should have preached it to the riffraff of Spitalfields, one of the poorest and roughest parts of the capital. Not at all, Wesley responded; 'If I had been preaching to the poor of Spitalfields, my text should have been "Behold the Lamb of God, who takes away the sin of the world"!'

Likewise, Charles' hymns express the same evangelical concern for the poorest of the poor. Indeed, he makes such compassion one of the supreme tests of whether a professing Christian really does have the Spirit of Jesus at work in his or her heart and life. Take, for instance, one of his hymns which is a prayer for the gift of the Spirit of Christ to be poured out upon the believer:

Jesus, the gift divine I know,
The gift divine I ask of thee;

That living water now bestow –
Thy Spirit and thyself, on me;
Thou, Lord, of life the fountain art;
Now let me find thee in my heart.

He goes on to pray that the fruit of the Spirit may be manifest in his whole life, but especially in a caring, sacrificial ministry to those in greatest need:

Thy mind throughout my life be shown,
While, listening to the sufferer's cry,
The widow's and the orphan's groan,
On mercy's wings I swiftly fly,
The poor and helpless to relieve,
My life, my all, for them to give.

Thus may I show thy Spir't within,
Which purges me from every stain;
Unspotted from the world and sin,
My faith's integrity maintain;
The truth of my religion prove
By perfect purity and love.[31]

Despite differences of interpretation and emphasis, John and Charles also shared a longing to attain to Christian perfection, to have the mind that was in Christ, to walk as Christ walked, to grow into perfect love. When it came to the deepest things of God, to justice and mercy and the love of the Lord, they were at one. They shared so much in their lives and in their faith. They had known a common upbringing in a loving home at Epworth; they were together at Oxford in the Holy Club; they had ventured to America in the service of Christ; they had experienced an evangelical conversion of heart and mind; they were both evangelists to the people of England and beyond; they both sang of the Good News of Jesus Christ in an abundant outpouring of hymns.

It is, fittingly enough, in the setting of one of Charles' greatest hymns that we gain a final glimpse of how close to each other the brothers were. The year is 1788. Charles, though the younger brother, has recently died. John, now an old man of 85, is conducting a service at Bolton in Lancashire. There is a children's choir, whose sweet voices touch the heart of the old apostle, and he confesses that he has not heard better singing anywhere in the kingdom. Then he gives out the first lines of Charles' hymn, 'Wrestling Jacob'. With the loss of his brother still fresh in his experience, he recites the opening lines:

Come, O thou Traveller unknown,
Whom still I hold, but cannot see!
My company before is gone,
And I am left alone with thee . . .

And then the old man – all his lifelong calm self-control forgotten – breaks down in tears in the sight of the whole congregation.[32] Those tears set the seal on a partnership of a lifetime, of two brothers in arms, a partnership which was central to the Methodist Revival, and one which, by the mercy of God, still bears fruit.

## Notes

1 This chapter was first published as an article in the *Proceedings of the Charles Wesley Society* 5 (1998), 11–21 and is reprinted here, with a few minor changes, by permission.

2 James Boswell, *The Life of Samuel Johnson* (London: Folio Society, 1968), 2 vols, 2.245.

3 V. H. H. Green, *The Young Mr. Wesley: A study of John Wesley and Oxford* (London: Edward Arnold, 1961), 59.

4 *Dictionary of National Biography*, s.n. Charles Wesley.

5 John Wesley, *An Earnest Appeal to Men of Reason and Religion (with Farther Appeal to Men of Religion and Reason)*, 8th edn (London, 1796).

6 Wesley, *An Earnest Appeal*.

7 Telford, *Life of John Wesley* (London: Hodder and Stoughton, 1886), 21.

8 *BE*, 25.230.

9 *BE*, 25.236.

10 Adam Clarke, *Memoirs of the Wesley Family* (London, 1823), 266.

11 Cited in Gill, *Charles Wesley, First Methodist*, 97. The full text of Williams' remarks can be found in Newport, *Sermons*, 30–1.

12 Jackson, *Life*, 2.468–9 and see further Newport, *Sermons*, 28–47.

13 John Telford, ed., *The Letters of the Rev. John Wesley M.A.* (Epworth Press, 1931), 8 vols, 3.97 [hereinafter cited as Wesley, *Letters*].

14 Wesley, *Letters*, 5.347. Letter of 28 November 1772.

15 Wesley, *Letters*, 6.186.

16 Wesley, *Letters*, 8.190.

17 Cited in Rack, *Reasonable Enthusiast*, 346.

18 Rack, *Reasonable Enthusiast*, 256.

19 *BE*, 7.353.

20 'I am a Church of England Man and as I said fifty years ago, so I say still, in the Church of England I will live and die, unless I am thrust out.' Letter to Henry Moore, 6 May 1788.

21 'I look on all the world as my parish; thus far I mean, that, in whatever part of it I am, I judge it meet, right, and my bounden duty, to declare unto all that are willing to hear, the glad tidings of salvation.' On 16 August 1739 Wesley met the Bishop of Bristol and had a long conversation which he recorded. He was challenged as to his right to preach in the parishes of other clergy. Wesley argued that as a Fellow of Lincoln College he was ordained with a right to preach anywhere and that his duty was to preach to all the gospel message. The words 'I look on all the world as my parish' first appeared shortly before this incident in a letter from John Wesley to John Clayton (see *BE*, 25.616).

22 Wesley, *Letters*, 8.267.

23 The document has survived; see MARC, DDCW, 6.48.

24 Quoted by Rack, *Reasonable Enthusiast*, 518.

25 See John A. Newton, *Susanna Wesley and the Puritan Tradition in Methodism* (Peterborough: Epworth Press, 2002), 85–6.

26 H. Moore, *The Life of the Rev. John Wesley A.M.*, 2 vols (1824–5), 1.506.

27 *BE*, 26.528.

28 *BE*, 25.230.

29 Rack, *Reasonable Enthusiast*, 252.

30 N. Curnock, ed., *The Journal of the Rev. John Wesley A.M.* 8 vols (Robert Culley, 1909–16), 3.301.

31 *Hymns and Psalms*, 318.

32 See further, Rack, *Reasonable Enthusiast*, 530 and Tyerman, 3.526, 527.

# 5. Charles Wesley and Susanna

## CHARLES WALLACE

No less than the rest of his siblings, Charles Wesley grew up under his mother's strong influence. Susanna Wesley was his more present parent and his first teacher, both roles continuing well into his adulthood and ending only with her death in 1742. The decisive role she played in his formation eventually led to the theological tensions that developed between them after his evangelical conversion in 1738, though in her last years she finally acknowledged and proudly supported his and his brother's work. Her influence on him continued after her death, and Charles returned the favour by helping shape her reputation. This essay explores a fascinating and important two-way relationship.

Born Susanna Annesley in London in 1669, Charles' mother was the precocious twenty-fifth and final child of the well-known moderate Puritan divine Samuel Annesley and his second wife Mary White. Well educated at home in her father's library, she showed an early 'dissenting' streak of her own by deciding at age 12 to leave her family's faith tradition and join the Church of England. Intriguingly, such a move did not unduly strain Susanna's relationship with her parents, but it did set the stage for her marriage in 1688 to another converted Nonconformist, Samuel Wesley. After a brief time in the metropolis where their first son Samuel was born, the couple moved to the young priest's first parish, South Ormsby, in Lincolnshire, in 1691 and then in 1697 to Epworth in another section of the same county. Six children were born in the former place, though only three of them, all girls, survived. In the family's latter and better-known home they were joined by ten or twelve more (such are the difficulties in determining exact numbers in days of high birth rates and high infant mortality), of which only six survived, four girls and two boys. Following her husband's death in 1735, Susanna lived in turn with four of her children: daughter Emily in nearby Gainsborough; son Samuel in Tiverton, Devon; daughter Martha in three quick moves from Wooton in Wiltshire, to Salisbury and then to London; and finally John, settling into his newly acquired London headquarters, the Foundery, in late 1739.

For her seven daughters who could not expect additional formal education, Susanna Wesley also served as their secondary teacher, home-schooling them beyond childhood with the aid of the rectory library, the set of catechetical writings she created in her 'spare' time, and spirited daily conversation for as long as they all lived under the same roof. Her three sons received the same early upbringing, but experienced her in a new way when they left Epworth to attend public schools in London, and afterwards when they went up to

Oxford. She doted on her eldest, Samuel junior, writing voluminous letters of advice and encouragement when he began at Westminster School, and years later deferred to him and depended upon him (even living with him for a time) after the death of Samuel senior. Given her middle son's prominence, it is not surprising that Methodist historiography (having more primary material with which to work) and Methodist hagiography (seeking early signs of his chosenness) has discovered and debated the impact she wielded on John, particularly as an early adviser in the realm of 'practical divinity'. Fewer letters and stories remain to illustrate the remarkable mother's impact on her youngest son Charles, and there has been little inclination to focus on their relationship, but the investigation contributes to a better rounded picture of this less studied figure whom this book celebrates.

Charles Wesley's relationship with his mother divides easily into several subsections: his experience growing up in the Epworth rectory (with hints of how that affected his later life); the subtle and not always easy shift to a more adult-to-adult connection, culminating in a debate between him and Susanna, who proved to be the loving theological critic of his early impulsive Methodism; and a final phase, in which Susanna acknowledged not only dependence on, but pride in, her Methodist sons, and in which Charles helped fashion his mother's legacy, notably with the enigmatic epitaph he composed for her tombstone.

## Saturday's child: an Epworth upbringing

Among the variety of complications that Susanna Wesley faced in her 17 to 19 pregnancies and childbirths, Charles' premature arrival as the last son and next to last child on 18 December 1707 (about a month shy of her own 39th birthday) was not particularly dramatic, though it was notable enough for friend, physician and early biographer John Whitehead to pass on a bit of family lore. Charles was, he writes,

> several weeks ahead of his time . . . [and] appeared dead rather than alive when he was born. He did not cry, nor open his eyes, and was kept wrapt up in soft wool until the time when he should have been born according to the usual course of nature, and then he opened his eyes and cried.[1]

Neither this nor other details of Charles' infancy have received the same pious treatment as one incident in young John Wesley's life – even though he went through the same experience. A little over a year later, as a babe in arms Charles escaped the devastating rectory fire that rendered the family temporarily homeless and provided a piece of Wesleyan legend, the last-minute rescue of his older brother from a blazing upper-storey room. While John thereafter saw himself as a 'brand plucked from the burning', so was Charles, and indeed, so was every member of the family.

It is not completely clear from where Charles' given name came, but it may reflect the family's religious and political positioning. All but one of his siblings' names resonate either with the Bible (e.g. Kezia and Jedidiah), with family precedent (e.g. Annesley), or with both (e.g. Samuel and John).[2] Only his oldest surviving sister Emilia shared a non-biblical, non-family name with Charles, and while hers seems a rather neutral choice, his might represent a conscious ecclesiastical and political statement, especially for Susanna. In the normal course of things the grandson of two Dissenting ministers who had been ejected from their livings at the Restoration would decidedly *not* have received the name of the very monarch whom parliamentary forces had driven out and eventually captured and executed a generation before. Even less likely would they celebrate his son, who helped restore the monarchy and episcopal authority, and lived a private life charitably described as 'irregular'. But Samuel and Susanna were both converts from Nonconformity to high-church or 'Caroline' Anglicanism, and by baptizing their son Charles in 1707 they may have been indicating not only their high churchmanship, but also their approval of the Stuart monarchy.[3] At the time of Charles' birth, Queen Anne reigned, last of the Stuarts, with no surviving children and a set of ministers who seemed to be restraining her Tory affinities. Moreover, her accession several years earlier had helped heal a marital quarrel between the Wesley parents, who could not agree on the rightfulness of King William's reign following the death of Queen Mary. When Anne succeeded, they could finally concur: both the conscientious nonjuror Susanna and her somewhat more pragmatically political husband Samuel, who had been ready to accept Parliament's choice of William in the first place.[4] In short, the Wesley family of Epworth found themselves most comfortable in the emerging Tory party, and the naming of their youngest son reflects that.[5]

Legend and politics aside, the Epworth rectory functioned as a (necessarily) methodical centre for child-rearing and education, and here Charles, like his siblings, 'received the first rudiments of learning . . . under the pious care of his mother'.[6] Her method is well known from the long letter her son John solicited from her in 1732,[7] but there she is recalling practices already observable in earlier letters and journal entries. Several years before the fire struck in early 1709 she had been collecting materials from her reading, sifting her own spiritual experience, and putting together for her children a 'little manual' of her own theological and ecclesiastical perspectives. It included her reflections on natural and revealed religion, her reasons for joining the Established Church, and directions for receiving the sacrament. However, as she wrote to her son Samuel, then at Westminster School in London, 'before I could finish my design the flames consumed this with all the rest of my writings'.[8] She did not abandon the project, however, and seems to have reconceived it as a set of commentaries on the key documents that the Church catechism focused on in the Book of Common Prayer. These included a commentary on the Apostles' Creed, dated 13 January 1710, and an exposition of the Ten Commandments, begun some time in early to mid-1711, but apparently never completed. Finally, though there is no evidence of an attempt to exposit the Lord's Prayer, she did reclaim something of the project that was lost in the fire by composing an extended dialogue on 'natural and revealed religion' between 'Mother' and 'Emilia' dated early 1712.[9]

At about that same time, three years after the fire, she seized the opportunity to continue her educational work not only on paper, but in face-to-face tutorials with her children. In the winter of 1711–12 while her husband Samuel was attending the Church's Convocation in London, she had discovered a recent publication detailing the work of Danish missionaries in India. The book inspired her, as she wrote to him, 'to do somewhat more than I do', beginning with her children and employing the 'following method':

> I take such a proportion of time as I can best spare every night to discourse with each child by itself on something that relates to its principal concerns. On Monday I talk with Molly, on Tuesday with Hetty, Wednesday with Nancy, Thursday with Jacky, Friday with Patty, Saturday with Charles, and with Emily and Sukey together on Sunday.[10]

Charles thus was 'Saturday's child', with a special weekly share of his mother's attention already at about age four. As the letter 'on educating my family' reveals, there came further maternal focus at age five, that birthday typically having been set aside in the family for a first reading lesson. By the end of that day the 'average' Wesley child, Charles included, knew his or her letters and was then put to spelling and then reading the first verse of Genesis, and before long whole chapters of holy writ and other works.[11]

The educational process may have centred on the six hours a day the children spent in their home school, but that was only part of the 'regular method of living' that Susanna Wesley sought to inculcate. Along with the schooling, that basic routine consisted of a 'regular course of sleeping' into which the infants were coaxed, a fairly intense mealtime regimen (with a clear prohibition of 'drinking or eating between meals'), and a set of behavioural expectations that effectively eliminated 'taking God's name in vain, cursing and swearing, profaneness, obscenity, rude, ill-bred names'. Not surprisingly, the good order she initially achieved did not survive the farming out of the children to other families while the rectory was being rebuilt following the 1709 fire. At a distance Susanna was not able to restrain the questionable company they might keep (servants, for instance, and 'bad' children) and the objectionable habits they might adopt. They fell into lax observance of the Sabbath, the 'knowledge of several songs and bad things', and 'a clownish accent and many rude ways'.[12] One can sense here not just a parental nervousness about impiety or immorality, but perhaps also a London-bred antipathy toward country ways, especially given her husband Samuel's interest in the various societies currently existing in the metropolis and elsewhere that aimed at the 'reformation of manners'.[13]

At any rate, by the time the four-year-old Charles was coming into consciousness as a member of the family – with his own special Saturday evening mother–son tutorial – Susanna was already engaged in a programme of 'strict reform' in the new rectory. Previous usage had already included the Lord's Prayer and other short prayers and collects, a short catechism, and the memorizing of brief portions of scripture – all accounting for the ease with which biblical quotation and allusion would later flow in Charles' verse. The new regime involved in addition the teaming up of pairs of older and younger siblings who read one another a chapter from each Testament, and 'the Psalms for the day', probably as appointed in the Book of Common Prayer.[14] Further, in direct competition with any rowdy songs that might have infected her children out in the town, she adopted the custom of *singing* psalms at the beginning and end of the school day. Likely they used one of the metrical versions available at the time, either the old standby from the sixteenth century, *The Whole Book of Psalmes Collected into English Meeter*, better known with reference to its authors as 'Sternhold and Hopkins', or the more recent *New Version of the Psalms of David*, usually identified as 'Tate and Brady'. In either case, one can well imagine the growing force of both biblical paraphrase and common metre in the mind and heart of the future hymn writer.[15]

Susanna listed a number of 'by-laws observed among us' designed to prevent and correct any lying, disobedience, quarrelling, Sabbath breaking and the like, but the general principle behind her child-rearing method was the oft-recreated phrase 'break their wills' or 'conquer their stubbornness', together with the corollary that they 'be taught to fear the rod and cry softly'. Though these grate on the twenty-first-century ear, they represented a progressive voice in the early eighteenth century – not at all a mindless and sadistic example of child abuse, but an attempt at appropriate and 'timely correction', a distillation of her own Puritan upbringing and the latest Enlightenment thought of no less a luminary than John Locke, whose *Some Thoughts Concerning Education* she seems to have read.[16] Though there is no direct evidence that Charles ever merited corporal punishment during his Epworth childhood, he no doubt often enough incurred some form of parental correction.

Charles certainly bought into his mother's theory, if not always her practice, in the raising of his own children. Writing to his wife Sally years later, not long after the birth of their first child, he urged her to adopt the 'most important of all Locke's rules . . . in which the whole *secret* of education consists – make it your invariable rule to *cross his will*, in some one instance at least, every day of your life'. However, by the time their second son, Charles junior, came along, he was already backing off ('Persuade him, and you need never compel him', he wrote to her). And a decade or so later, it is clear the boy's talents were trumping family child-rearing tradition. Originally intending him for the priesthood, but finding a gifted young musician on his hands, he admitted defeat. 'My friends advised me not to cross his inclination', he wrote to a woman who objected to the boy playing concerts. 'Indeed I could not if I would. There is no way of hindering his being a musician but cutting off his fingers.'[17]

Charles paid closer attention to one other of Susanna's 'by-laws', 'that no girl be taught to work [i.e., do needlework] till she can read very well'.[18] Though the three Wesley brothers would ultimately have more educational and vocational opportunities than their sisters, as far as schooling in the Epworth rectory went, girls were valued as much as boys. Charles, who grew up in the company of seven sisters and only one brother (brother Samuel no longer being at home), surely sensed the importance of female education. And, as Frank Baker indicates, he later encouraged his own daughter Sally in numerous letters to read history, 'practical divinity' (Thomas à Kempis, William Law's *Serious Call*), and poetry (Edward Young's *Night Thoughts*) and to try her own hand at writing poetry.[19]

Clearly the Epworth upbringing and Susanna's leading part in it decisively affected Charles' future, the more so because much of it was unconsciously appropriated at an early age. Without denigrating the important role of father, sisters, brothers, or later extra-familial influences, we might usefully look for her hovering in the background as we follow Charles' life and work in other chapters of this book. For instance, in addition to the way he raised his own children, note how his own marriage to the much younger but well-educated Sarah Gwynne in April 1749 recalls a maternal influence. In the first place it was 'marrying up' into a 'genteel' Welsh family which offered not only social status, but also evangelical Anglican credentials of which Susanna would have been proud.[20] Second, it was a happy match, an exception that proves the rule: *one* of the Wesley children, at least, could establish a successful 'companionate marriage' in the early modern ideal described by Lawrence Stone and exemplified (more or less!) by Samuel and Susanna Wesley. Or, put another way, we ought to be more wary of adopting the traditional interpretation that blames John Wesley's 'troubled relationships with women' on 'the influence of his mother and the predominantly feminine atmosphere of the Epworth rectory'.[21] If Charles (not to mention eldest brother Samuel, who also married happily) could be raised in the same mother- and sister-dominated home and yet find a measure of marital bliss, John's oft-remarked problems with women might owe more to his own personality and less to an overweening Susanna or her child-rearing regimen.[22]

Epworth rectory life also provided a template for Charles' home life. Though he did his share of early itinerating for the Methodists even after his marriage, his gravitation toward a more settled family existence in Bristol and finally in his mother's native London reflects an approach to being a 'Church' Methodist that Susanna, with her high church principles *and* her Puritan ways, could well appreciate. Suburban life in Marylebone brought the best of both worlds: the culture that the Wesley family had pined for in distant Epworth, together with a home in which his wife could carry out home schooling in the Susanna tradition, and in which the boys could play house concerts, free from the negative influence of 'bad music and bad musicians'. It also put Charles in touch with a set of Methodists who more than most supported his churchmanship in opposition to John's increasing move toward 'separation' from the Church. As he wrote to his brother in 1785 urging no further ordination of preachers, 'This letter is a debt to our parents, and to our brother, as well as to you, and to your faithful friend.'[23]

Supported by the £100 per annum that John promised him from the profit of book sales, whatever Sarah Wesley might contribute from her funds, and whatever he could glean from the boys' subscription concerts, Charles Wesley the West End householder was able to enjoy a middle-class existence. However, he could not forget the times of financial difficulty that his mother fretted over while trying to make ends meet as mistress of the Epworth rectory. Thus, following his mother in this way as well, he had more than a *spiritual* 'charge to keep', and his 'strict account' of household expenses shows he attended to it faithfully. For instance, in 1782 the family received a little over £382, but spent over £430, which he broke down by the four traditional quarters of the year and meticulously by key expense categories.[24] If the family in this instance seems not to have lived within its means, there is no sense that it ever fell into the near poverty that Susanna described in a letter to her brother the East India merchant, a time in the summer of 1705 that found Samuel in debtors' prison and Susanna begging from the Archbishop of York in order to feed her family. That dramatic occasion occurred before Charles' birth, but it was likely emblematic of the rocky financial situation in which the Epworth Wesleys often found themselves, a situation well remembered by the family.[25] Such experience in childhood no doubt contributed to the Wesleyan sensitivity to the poor, and indeed Charles wrote numerous hymns reflecting on the importance of 'gospel poverty' and 'perfect poverty', as S T Kimbrough has clearly demonstrated.[26]

However, such experience growing up might also (and at the same time) motivate one away from such idealism and toward the sort of comfortable existence concerning which brother John often warned Methodists.[27] Living fairly well as a settled family man and remembering his own childhood and adolescence, it is not surprising that Charles would turn his poetic talents to the concerns of families. His *Hymns for the Use of Families and on Various Occasions* (1767)[28] reveals his sensitivity to the issues of the home, as he wrote under such rubrics as 'For a woman near the time of her travail', 'At sending a child to the boarding-school', 'A mother's act of resignation on the death of a child', and even 'To be sung at the tea-table'. By turns affecting and complacent, aimed it seems more at the middling sort and the well-off, and not always his best poetry, such work nevertheless reminds us again of the imaginative influence that family life – his own in Bristol and London as well as his childhood at Epworth – held over him.[29]

## Mother as mentor and loving critic

Maternal nurture and instruction did not end when Charles left for Westminster in 1716 and afterwards to Christ Church in 1726. Vacations meant that he returned home from time to time, and Susanna kept up with him the custom of long-distance mentoring by post that she had begun years before with her oldest son Samuel and later followed also with John. Though few letters have survived, especially early on, correspondence continued between the two until her death, and in it we may see her playing a number of roles: Charles' protective mother and spiritual adviser, later his loving theological critic, and finally, a clear supporter as well as something of a suppliant, a frail and dependent elderly mother.

The nurturing mother naturally worried about her son getting enough to eat! In a letter to John (8 June 1725), she commented tartly on how Charles had been misused by his brother Samuel's wife Ursula, who had apparently curtailed his kitchen privileges while the three of them were visiting her father. 'The case was somewhat mended here', Susanna remarked in summarizing the different authority that greeted the travellers when they arrived at her home, 'for I would so far overrule in my own house as to let him fill his belly'.[30] Before long, Charles would be leaving Westminster for Oxford, and would thus no longer need to put up with such 'ungenteel' behaviour from his sister-in-law, but a passing comment in another letter to John in November 1726 shows that Susanna was still worried about 'poor starving Charles', by then just a month into his university career.[31] The following spring she persisted in her concern, inquiring, 'Jacky, do you really think Charles has [victuals] enough?'[32] A letter from Charles to John in 1729 indicates not only the former's occasional lack of appetite, but also his continuing dependence on the Epworth family for such basic items as 'my Cloaths'.[33] And as late as 1732 the ever-vigilant mother, clear that university attainments provided no cover for unhealthy behaviour, berated him and his brother, both, for not taking proper care of themselves while on the road from Epworth to Oxford:

> I must tell ye, Mr. John Wesley, Fellow of Lincoln, and Mr. Charles Wesley, Student of Christ Church, that ye are two scrubby travelers and sink your characters strangely by eating nothing on the road to save charges. I wonder ye are not ashamed of yourselves. Surely if ye will but give yourselves leave to think a little, ye will return to a better mind.[34]

Susanna wanted to ensure that her children were fed in other ways, as well. Years before, she had written to her daughter Sukey in the preface to her commentary on the Creed, 'I love your body and do earnestly beseech Almighty God to bless it with health and all things necessary for its comfort and support in this world. But my tenderest regard is for your immortal soul and for its eternal happiness.'[35] Though her daughters seem to have been the primary intended audience of this and her other catechetical writings, her sons received the same attention in the long letters she addressed to them. All her children understood her continuing devotion to their spiritual well-being, a natural outgrowth of the way in which they had been raised in the Epworth rectory.

In Charles' case, his mother's continuing influence is discernible in what might be called his 'Oxford conversion'. Prior to 1729, his student career showed no special inclination toward piety, studies and social life both claiming his attention and energy. Near the end of his life he recalled his first year at Christ Church having 'been lost in diversions', though in his second year 'diligence' led him both to 'serious thinking' and attendance at the weekly sacrament.[36] John later commented that any mention of religion prior to this time inevitably elicited the reply, 'What! would you have me be a saint all at once?' Nevertheless, he began to awake from his spiritual slumber and in discussing it with John in a letter of 22 January 1729 he was ready to attribute 'what God has begun in me' to Susanna. ''Tis owing in great measure to somebody's [prayers] (my mother's most likely) that I am come to think as I do.'[37] Several months later he confirmed his sense of dependence on her guidance in another letter to John, who was then acting as his father's curate and thus in daily contact with their parents. Worried about his inattention in 'public prayers' and the 'heartlessness of which he himself is the cause', Charles resolved to continue struggling. 'I *must*, I *will*, in spite of Nature and the Devil, take pains: while my strength lasts, I *will* put it to the utmost stretch . . .' He concluded, 'You may show this if you think proper to my mother, for I would gladly have a letter from her upon this subject.'[38]

Why would Charles look to his mother? Bonds of affection, no doubt, but also an awareness that she had good spiritual sense, based on pious habits and clear thinking. Bible and Prayer Book were plainly part of her daily, as well as weekly, practice, and they became similarly familiar to Charles at his mother's knee. In addition, though, we might pause briefly here to consider what additional authors she read, wrestled with in her diaries, drew on in her own 'catechetical writings', and recommended in her letters. Many of them, of course, would have found place on any divine's bookshelves or list of approved theological writings in the early eighteenth century. In fact Charles' grandfather and father both possessed well-stocked libraries. The former, a wide-ranging collection, provided grist for Susanna's precocious decision as a 12-year-old to join the Church of England. The latter became a main source of intellectual and spiritual nurture during her married years. In addition, his father Samuel had helped devise several bibliographies, including the one found in *Advice to a Young Clergyman*, that Jackson reprinted in his *Life . . . of Charles Wesley.*[39] Susanna's access to theological learning may have come through the men in her life (and not from any formal education), but it registered with Charles and his Oxford-educated brothers no less than with the Wesley girls that she participated in contemporary theological discussion with energy and understanding.

We have already noticed her interest in John Locke on child rearing and on the Society for the Propagation of the Gospel volume detailing the Danish mission to India. However, Susanna's writing reveals other favourites who may be seen similarly to have influenced Charles, at least indirectly. Among them were men like John Pearson, royalist Bishop of Chester in the late seventeenth century, from whose *Exposition of the Creed* Susanna generously cribbed (without attribution) in her own 1710 explication of the Creed. Also present is the blind Welsh priest Richard Lucas, whose extensive writings on Christian perfection engaged Susanna significantly and who stands as an important backdrop to the thinking of Charles and John on what became a major Wesleyan emphasis.[40] William Beveridge, Bishop of St Asaph and St David from 1704 to 1708, was another such influence. He also preached and wrote extensively on holiness, as well as on conscience, and Susanna meditated extensively on his work. One element from Beveridge that she copied into her journal suggestively foreshadows elements of the evangelical revival (and one of John's most memorable phrases). Beveridge refers to 'an experimental knowledge whereby a man hath the sense or experience of those perfections upon his own heart, which he knows and believes to be in God, whereby his thoughts and conceptions are so strangely enlarged, that he seems to apprehend him that is altogether incomprehensible'. A 'strangely enlarged' heart is not exactly a 'strangely warmed' one, but that Susanna was pondering it in her meditation some thirty years prior to the revival her sons experienced and led, is significant.[41]

The same might be said about her reading and/or recommendation of a host of writers: among others, the philosopher John Norris, spiritual writers like Thomas à Kempis, Henry Scougal, Lorenzo Scupoli, Jeremy Taylor, William Law and Blaise Pascal, the borderline Anglican heretic Samuel Clarke, her father's friend Richard Baxter, and the poet-priest George Herbert.[42] In addition to reading John Locke's work on educating children, Susanna also read his major epistemological work, *Essay Concerning Human Understanding*, which she discussed in a letter to a neighbouring clergyman.[43] None of this demonstrates a direct influence on Charles' theological development – all of the writers cited were obviously 'in the air' and did not require a mother's *imprimatur* for him to discover and savour them. Nevertheless, the fact that names like Baxter, Law, Pascal and Thomas à Kempis pop up in his journals and correspondence, and Scougal and Norris are referenced in his sermons, is not beside the point.[44]

Beyond the authors that Charles might have been introduced to by his mother – or whose impact on him had been reinforced by her – are a number of key themes, such as the ones she listed under the 'ways and means of religion' whose 'serious use' she recommended in a 1718 journal entry:

> prayer, reading, meditation, frequenting public worship, the sacrament, fasting, or at least abstinence, self-denial in other instances, etc., which will revive the spirit of piety, the sense of God, of good and evil, strengthen faith, encourage hope and perfect obedience.[45]

Close to John's frequent later celebrations of the 'means of grace', it was also echoed in Charles' clever polemic against the Moravians, a poem of 23 stanzas first published in their *Hymns and Sacred Poems* in 1740.[46]

Within that important set of practices, Charles especially followed his mother in emphasizing the Eucharist. As John Newton has noted, 'Her stress on the operation of the Spirit in the sacrament' is 'often echoed in Charles Wesley's *Hymns on the Lord's Supper*'.[47] It also seems clear that her theology of the real presence had some bearing on Charles. In a 1732 letter to John (sent together with one to Charles) she affirmed Christ's real presence, but refrained from claiming to know how it came about: 'however this divine institution may seem to others, to me 'tis full of mystery. Who can account for the operation of God's Holy Spirit? Or define the manner of his working upon the spirit in man . . . ?' Here we may detect an anticipation of Charles's equally balanced poetic explication of sacramental theology:

> O the depth of love divine,
> Th' Unfathomable Grace!
> Who shall say how Bread and Wine
> God into Man conveys?[48]

Again, such approaches were part of the common currency of Christian discourse and practice in late seventeenth- and early eighteenth-century England. Nevertheless, Susanna's shaping influence should not be underestimated.

Thankfully, parenting rarely represents moral, theological or spiritual cloning. Instead, a young adult often achieves independence and a sense of his or her own vocation by pushing against parental norms. This truism (as well as its antagonistic opposite, 'Mother knows best') is amply illustrated in the relationship of Susanna and Charles roughly from the time of his evangelical conversion in mid-1738 until a year or so before her death in 1742. Having

trained up her child in a rich theological and practical mix of dissenting and
Establishment Christianity, Susanna had to confront a son who felt his own
experience leading him to deeper gospel truth. Having made his own emotionally satisfying evangelical discovery, Charles chafed under his mother's
resistance to it. For a brief while, mother and son became theological opponents – though from an early twenty-first-century perspective, their disagreement sounds less like a major rift and more like another psychological
commonplace, Freud's 'narcissism of small differences'.

In any case, the controversy also fed on the Wesley family's particular situation. Samuel senior had died in 1735, and Susanna had to leave Epworth
rectory and would spend the rest of her life under the care of her children.
Dependent on all her children at the time that Charles and John returned
from Georgia and experienced evangelical conversions in the spring of 1738,
she relied especially on her son Samuel, who died prematurely in the autumn
of 1739, but not before he had mounted his own theological critique of his
young brothers' activities. Nevertheless, at about the time of his death she had
moved in with John at the Foundery in London, where she would live out her
life, and her opinions gradually re-merged with those of her sons.

Only a few days after Charles and John experienced their 1738 conversions,
another alarmed mother, Elizabeth Hutton, wrote to Samuel junior about their
new opinions, which she characterized as 'wild speech', particularly John telling a gathering in the Hutton house that he 'was not a Christian' prior to his
evangelical experience five days before. Nervous – for good reason – about
her son and daughter following the Wesleys, she urged Samuel to 'put a stop
to such madness'.[49] While putting the best face on Mrs Hutton's account of
his brothers, Samuel nevertheless replied that he would try to intervene with
them and closed by assuring her that he would 'heartily pray God to stop
the progress of this lunacy'.[50] Thus an intrafamily division was set up, with
Susanna and Samuel (her trusted oldest son) facing off against the 'enthusiastic' innovations of John and Charles.

A series of letters reveals the story. The first extant letter from Susanna
to Charles following the Elizabeth Hutton–Samuel Wesley exchange demonstrates that the two were communicating well as of 19 October 1738. Mother is
expressing 'much pleasure' that his 'mind is somewhat easier than formerly',
though she is gently probing his new belief system as well, writing, 'I would
gladly know what your notion is of justifying faith, because you speak of it as
a thing you have but lately obtained.'[51] The exchange quickly developed into a
disputation, which Charles characterized in his endorsement on his mother's
next letter (6 December 1738) as 'My mother (not clear) of faith'. From her perspective there was perfect clarity, just not the sort he might readily appreciate.
She wrote provocatively, 'I do not judge it necessary for us to know the precise
time of our conversion', and

> I think you are fallen into an odd way of thinking. You say that till within
> a few months you had no spiritual life nor any justifying faith. Now this
> is as if a man should affirm he was not alive in his infancy, because, when
> an infant he did not know he was alive. A strange way of arguing, this! Do
> you not consider that there's some analogy in spiritual to natural life? A

man must first be born and then pass through the several stages of infancy, childhood, and youth, before he attain to maturity. So Christians are first born of water and the spirit and then go through many degrees of grace, be first infants, or babes in Christ, as St. Paul calls them, before they become strong Christians. For spiritual strength is the work of time, as well as of God's Holy Spirit.

Despite the spiritual combat, she could still conclude the letter with her 'tender love and blessing' and wishes for a 'cheerful Christmas and happy New Year'.[52]

Late that same winter (8 March 1738/39) she wrote to Samuel expressing some of her disagreements with Charles. She had begun another letter to him, she wrote, but decided that her prospective move to London the following month with her daughter Martha would provide a better, face-to-face opportunity for her to 'fully speak my sentiments of their new notions, more than I can do by writing'. She also recounted a brief visit from the rising star of the Revival, George Whitefield, whom she questioned about whether her 'sons were not for making some innovations in the church'. Whitefield allayed her fears, saying the Wesley brothers were actually working 'to reconcile dissenters to our communion'.[53] A couple of weeks later, those fears were relayed back to John in more pointed form. 'My mother tells me she fears a formal schism is already begun among you', Samuel wrote, 'though you and Charles are ignorant of it. For God's sake take care of that, and banish extemporary expositions, and extemporary prayers.'[54] However, Susanna was vulnerable enough and amenable enough to Charles and John that she could not sustain total opposition, especially in close proximity to them in London. In fact, Samuel complained in a letter to her only a few days before his death, 'It was with exceeding concern and grief, I heard you had countenanced a spreading delusion, so far as to be one of Jack's congregation. Is it not enough that I am bereft of both my brothers, but must my mother follow too?'[55] Clearly, she was nervous about what seemed to be unhealthy innovation in the work of her two younger sons, but also at her stage of life she was ready to look for support in the movement that John and Charles were organizing.

## A final reconciliation?

Whether and to what extent Susanna quizzed them in person about their innovations, the tone of her writing changed. Her next letter to Charles contains no hint of theological difference. Samuel had died, and John and Charles had journeyed to his home in Devon to comfort their sister-in-law and niece. Her letter reflected on Samuel's death, thanked Charles for his 'care of my temporal affairs', and expressed nothing more contentious than 'the comfortable hope of my dear son's salvation'.[56] She signalled a more formal change of loyalty in her next letter to Charles just before the New Year, in which, acknowledging her eldest's death, she expressed gratitude for John, 'whom henceforward I shall call Son Wesley'. Ever an independent woman, she nevertheless now blessed God for the success of her sons' ministry, admitted her need of their company ('in the most literal sense I am become a little child and want continual succour') and, in general, of 'religious conference when I can obtain it', and confessed to a 'want of faith in the blessed Jesus'.[57]

But the practical theologian had not completely lost her edge. By the time of her next letter to Charles in early October 1740, she was trying to scold her youngest son out of a spiritual slump of his own.

> I cannot conceive why you affirm yourself to be not Christian; which is, in effect, to tell Christ to his face that you have nothing to thank him for, since you are not the better for anything he hath yet done or suffered for you. Oh, what great dishonour, what wondrous ingratitude, is this to the ever-blessed Jesus! I think myself far from being so good a Christian as you are, or as I ought to be; but God forbid that I should renounce the little Christianity I have: nay, rather let me grow in grace and in the knowledge of our Lord and Saviour Jesus Christ. Amen.[58]

Recovery from grief and a more settled sense of herself as a member of John's Methodist community at the Foundery helped bring her back to form. So, too, did a final burst of controversial work on behalf of her sons, as they began to define themselves against Calvinist predestinarianism on the one side and Moravian quietism on the other. The magisterial Susanna is once again visible in the final letter we have from Susanna to Charles and in the anonymous pamphlet she wrote (and John published) against George Whitefield.[59] Reconciled to her sons, indeed collaborating with them in the months immediately preceding her death, she could boast about them to the Countess of Huntingdon in July 1741:

> I've known few (if any) that have laboured more diligently and unweariedly in the service of our dear Lord. And, blessed be his great name, he hath set his seal to their ministry and hath made them instrumental in bringing many souls to God. And though in the eye of the world they appear despicable, men of no estate or figure, and daily suffer contempt, reproach and shame among men, yet to me they appear more honourable than they would do if the one were Archbishop of Canterbury and the other of York; for I esteem the reproach of Christ greater riches than all the treasures in England.[60]

All the ingredients for a satisfying hagiographical narrative were in place, the only necessary addition being a holy death, surrounded by faithful family and friends. On 30 July 1742, she obliged, and John Wesley provided the account in his published journal, bolstered with excerpts from two of his mother's letters: one, her account of the semi-public prayer services she conducted in the Epworth rectory during her husband's absence in February 1711/12, and the other, her famous 1732 memoir of how she educated her family.[61]

John's description contained one sour note: the epitaph authored by Charles. This 'last word', which he later published in his *Hymns and Sacred Poems* (1749), takes the story of mother and son in a slightly more problematical direction. It reads:

Here lies the body of Mrs. Susannah [sic] Wesley, the youngest and last
surviving daughter of Dr. Samuel Annesley.

In sure and steadfast hope to rise
And claim her mansion in the skies,
A Christian here her flesh laid down,
The cross exchanging for a crown.

True daughter of affliction she,
Inured to pain and misery,
Mourned a long night of griefs and fears,
A legal night of seventy years.

The Father then revealed his Son,
Him in the broken bread made known.
She knew and felt her sins forgiven,
And found the earnest of her heaven.

Meet for the fellowship above,
She heard the call, 'Arise, my love'.
I come, her dying looks replied,
And lamb-like, as her Lord, she died.

The first and last stanzas are conventional enough, the sort of evangelical
poetry that might grace any eighteenth-century grave in Bunhill Fields or any
Anglican churchyard. The middle quatrains, however, contain pointed reference to Susanna. Although the 'legal night of seventy years' might have some
reference to the more-or-less official limit of a human lifetime, the 'threescore
years and ten' of Psalm 90, it is hard not to read it also as a judgement on her
piety prior to being touched by her sons' Revival. One can almost hear the
subtext: 'Mother did her best all her life, but was "not clear" of faith until she
finally saw things our way'. The following stanza calls up an incident from
1739, when – at age 70 – Susanna reported her own conversion experience (or,
more correctly, her assurance of divine pardon) during Holy Communion.
She told John, 'While my son Hall was pronouncing those words, in delivering the cup to me, "The blood of our Lord Jesus Christ, which was given for
thee", the words struck through my heart, and I knew God for Christ's sake
had forgiven me all my sins.'[62] In this instance she had indeed adapted her
own eucharistic piety in the direction of her sons' doctrine of assurance, but
framing her life only from the perspective of the early years of the Revival
might lead the unwary to erroneously assume that she lacked a rich devotional life and a sense of divine love for most of her threescore years and ten. In
fact, that devotional life can be regarded as a wellspring (if not *the* wellspring)
from which her sons' revival flowed.

Charles' need to set his mother's record straight after her death depends
in part on a desire to reinforce the conversionist narrative that was becoming normative for the nascent Methodist movement. Even good religious folk
needed to know and feel their sins forgiven – clergy and other 'preachers

of righteousness' (such as Susanna) not excepted. But there is an additional focus, an evangelical sub-narrative that seems intent on demonstrating the spiritual travail and triumph of women, especially mothers. Charles had experienced the opposition of several strong women by the time of Susanna's death. We have already noticed the difficulty that another mother (and clergy wife) Elizabeth Hutton presented when she criticized Charles and John to their elder brother Samuel. Like Susanna, she had evangelically inclined young adult children, and her objections were not that far from Susanna's initial reactions to the events of May 1738. The following month Charles faced off against a similarly minded parent, the mother of his friends Charles and William Delamotte, in Bexley. After preaching, he 'accosted Mrs. Delamotte in her pew', and the next day visited her at home, where she berated him for his 'false doctrine', complained 'It is hard people must have their children seduced in their absence', and, when he owned up to believing in 'instantaneous faith', she 'ran out of the house'. He worked with her patiently, though, and within a month she had realized the error of her ways, apologized for her earlier behaviour and finally invited him 'to rejoice with her, in the experience of the divine goodness'.[63] Not completely parallel, but surely in his mind at the time of Susanna's death, was the case of Mrs Hannah Richardson, whose up-and-down spiritual life he chronicled in a popular prose tract. Recounting Richardson's final triumph in words that he later echoed on his mother's tombstone, God 'took away the veil from her heart and revealed himself in her in a manner the world knoweth not of'.[64] It was important that women, and particularly mothers, be included (and be seen to be included) within the economy of the Methodist movement.

Charles was present neither at his mother's death nor her funeral, so it was particularly fitting that he should have the honour of writing her epitaph. It could not be so straightforward, simple or classical as the maternal tribute he had admired on a visit to Pope's house in Twickenham after returning from Georgia.[65] In his verse, the young poet, priest and evangelist would have to show his love *and* demonstrate his independence, both of which he owed to his mother, in a more complex way. So employing the rhetoric of the Revival, he expressed his love in the biblical diction she had helped him learn, celebrating the 'crown' and the 'mansion in the skies' she had now attained. It was a rhetoric that resonated with the sacred space and sacred occasion to which it bore witness. Her heritage and his were represented in her interment in a Dissenters' burying ground using a church burial service just across from the Methodist headquarters that had served as her last home. His dependence on that triple tradition of British Protestantism allowed for a celebration of its latest emphasis: 'She knew and felt her sins forgiven.' Yet, however full of his new evangelical discovery Charles may have been (certainly no more so than the young Susanna when she declared her own spiritual independence from her father), he was, know it or not, also acknowledging a profound theological debt to his mother.[66] The tercentenary of Charles Wesley's birth provides *us* with an appropriate opportunity to affirm that debt with new awareness: the one who bore him was indeed one of his most prominent theological mentors.

# Notes

1 John Whitehead, *The Life of the Rev. John Wesley . . . with the Life of the Rev. Charles Wesley . . .* (Auburn and Buffalo: John E. Beardsley, 1844), 65.

2 Frank Baker, 'Investigating Wesley Family Traditions', *Methodist History*, 26.3 (April 1988), 162.

3 As David Cressy observes, 'Names like Elizabeth, Anne, James, and Charles may also have marked respect for the monarchy, akin to the way that catholics chose names for their association with patron saints', *Birth, Marriage, and Death: Ritual, religion, and the life-cycle in Tudor and Stuart England* (Oxford: Oxford University Press, 1997), 161.

4 Charles Wallace, ed., *Susanna Wesley: The complete writings* (New York: Oxford University Press, 1997), 34–9; Vivian H. H. Green, *The Young Mr. Wesley: A study of John Wesley and Oxford* (New York: St Martin's Press, 1961), 43.

5 Scott Smith-Bannister's study of representative parishes in the early modern period indicates that 'Charles' was not an uncommon boy's name. First appearing in the top-50 list in the decade 1560–9, the name rose to a ranking of 19th in 1640–9, and thence in subsequent decades to 15th, 12th, 12th, 14th, and, finally to 13th in 1690 9, the decade preceding Charles' birth and the last one included in the study. (In that same last decade John, as always, was the most popular boy's name, and 'Samuel' ranked 10th.) *Names and Naming Patterns in England, 1538–1700* (Oxford: Clarendon Press, 1997), 191–6.

6 Whitehead, *Life of John Wesley*, 66.

7 Wallace, *Susanna*, 367–73. For a recent analysis of the document's provenance, see Elizabeth Kurtz Lynch, 'John Wesley's Editorial Hand in Susanna Annesley Wesley's 1732 "Education" Letter', *Bulletin of the John Rylands University Library of Manchester*, 85.2–3 (Summer and Autumn, 2003), 195–208.

8 Wallace, *Susanna*, 71.

9 Wallace, *Susanna*, 236, 377–454.

10 Wallace, *Susanna*, 80.

11 Wallace, *Susanna*, 371.

12 Wallace, *Susanna*, 369, 371–2.

13 Richard P. Heitzenrater, *Mirror and Memory: Reflections on early Methodism* (Nashville: Abingdon, 1989), 42–5; Henry Rack, *Reasonable Enthusiast: John Wesley and the rise of Methodism*, 3rd edn (London: Epworth, 2002), 53.

14 Wallace, *Susanna*, 372.

15 Kenneth D. Shields, 'Charles Wesley as Poet', *Charles Wesley: Poet and theologian*, S T Kimbrough Jr, ed. (Nashville: Abingdon, 1992), 49.

16 Wallace, *Susanna*, 368.

17 Baker, *Charles Wesley as Revealed by His Letters*, 109–10.

18 Wallace, *Susanna*, 373.

19 Baker, *Charles Wesley as Revealed by His Letters*, 115–16.

20 Baker, *Charles Wesley as Revealed by His Letters*, 54–67; Henry D. Rack, 'Wesley, Charles (1707–1788)', *Oxford Dictionary of National Biography* (Oxford: Oxford University Press, 2004).

21 Rack, *Reasonable Enthusiast*, 56.

22 G. Elsie Harrison, *Son to Susanna: The private life of John Wesley* (London: Ivor Nicholson and Watson, 1937), 323–4.

23 Baker, *Charles Wesley as Revealed by His Letters*, 104, 107, 113, 138.

24 MARC, DDCW, 8/15. This fascinating unpaginated notebook and its

companions reveal what the Wesleys spent their money on after moving to London in 1771. Included are items of food and drink, furniture, servants, clothes, washing, concert expenses, etc.

25  Wallace, *Susanna*, 97–8.

26  S T Kimbrough Jr, 'Perfection Revisited: Charles Wesley's Theology of "Gospel Poverty" and "Perfect Poverty"', *The Poor and the People Called Methodists*, Richard P. Heitzenrater (Nashville: Abingdon, 2002), 101–19.

27  John Wesley, 'The Works of John Wesley', *The Works of John Wesley*, Thomas Jackson, vol. 13 (London: John Mason, 1831), 225–7.

28  Reprinted in *PW*, 7.1–200.

29  Charles Wesley, *Hymns for the Use of Families, and on Various Occasions* (Bristol: William Pine, 1767), 44–48, 67–8, 71–2, 81–2, 165–9.

30  Wallace, *Susanna*, 107. The family was at the time residing in Wroot, the small nearby parish that Samuel Wesley held along with Epworth from about the summer of 1724.

31  Wallace, *Susanna*, 126. Samuel junior had been a major benefactor of his younger brother. Employed as an usher (assistant schoolmaster) at Westminster from 1713 until his move to Blundell's School in Tiverton in 1733, he urged the family to send Charles, and looked out for him there, both academically and financially. Samuel married Ursula Berry in 1724, who might have assumed something of a maternal role toward Charles for his final two years at Westminster. See Tabraham, *Brother Charles*, 10.

32  Wallace, *Susanna*, 135.

33  *PWHS*, 2 (1900), 222–3.

34  Wallace, *Susanna*, 153.

35  Wallace, *Susanna*, 379. She completed this work in January 1710, not quite a year after the rectory fire. See also the title page of her 'Religious Conference', which she wrote out in a generous fair hand 'for the use of my children, 1711/12'. The superscription from Galatians 4 has an even more poignant meaning in this context than when Paul first wrote it: 'I write unto you little Children, of whom I travail in Birth again, until Christ be Formed in you.'

36  Charles Wesley to Thomas Chandler, 28 April 1785. John R. Tyson, *Charles Wesley: A reader* (New York and Oxford: Oxford University Press, 1989), 59.

37  Baker, *Charles Wesley as Revealed by His Letters*, 10–11.

38  Charles Wesley to John Wesley, 5 May 1729; Baker, *Charles Wesley as Revealed by His Letters*, 13.

39  Wallace, '"Some Stated Employment of Your Mind": Reading, Writing, and Religion in the Life of Susanna Wesley', *Church History*, 58.3 (September 1989), 356; Jackson, *Life*, 2.500–34.

40  On Beveridge, see Wallace, *Susanna*, 378–97; on Lucas, see Wallace, *Susanna*, 325–32, 340–2, 344–51.

41  Wallace, *Susanna*, 262; see also 118, 260–5, 275, 313–15, 351–2.

42  On Norris, see Wallace, 122–3, 443; on à Kempis, see 107–9; on Clarke, Scupoli, Scougal, and Baxter, 151–3; on Taylor, 110–11; on Law, 161, 473; on Pascal, *inter alia*, 256, 285–8, 328; on Herbert, *inter alia*, 70–1, 228, 332–3.

43  Wallace, *Susanna*, 85–6.

44  *CWJ*, 1.47, 75, 277; 2.128, 278. Newport, *Sermons*, 17–18, 67–8, 138, 149–50, 357. In the last instance, Charles' version of one of John's sermons contains a sentence from Norris that Susanna had also used, but not acknowledged, in her letter of 1 January 1733/34. See Wallace, *Susanna*, 162.

45 Wallace, *Susanna*, 294.

46 Tyson, *Charles Wesley*, 267–9.

47 John Newton, *Susanna Wesley and the Puritan Tradition in Methodism* (London: Epworth Press, 2002), 148.

48 Wallace, *Susanna*, 149; John Wesley and Charles Wesley, *Hymns on the Last Supper* (Bristol: Felix Farley, 1745), 41.

49 Joseph Priestly, ed., *Original Letters by the Rev. John Wesley . . . with Other Curious Papers . . .* (Birmingham: Thomas Pearson, 1791), 67–71.

50 Priestly, *Original Letters*, 74–5.

51 Wallace, *Susanna*, 174.

52 Wallace, *Susanna*, 176–7.

53 Wallace, *Susanna*, 178–9.

54 Priestly, *Original Letters*, 96.

54 Priestly, *Original Letters*, 109–10.

55 Wallace, *Susanna*, 179.

57 Wallace, *Susanna*, 180.

58 Wallace, *Susanna*, 186.

59 Wallace, *Susanna*, 188–90, 466–79. The letter to Charles is dated 28 April 1741, and the pamphlet was published that same year: *Some Remarks on a Letter from the Reverend Mr. Whitefield to the Reverend Mr. Wesley, in a Letter from a Gentlewoman to her Friend*.

60 Wallace, *Susanna*, 190.

61 *BE*, 19.284–91

62 *BE*, 19.93 (3 September 1739)

63 *CWJ*, 1.109–10, 116–17, 125. Interestingly this dramatic interaction all took place immediately after Charles received letters (now lost) from Susanna , 'heavily complaining of my brother's forsaking her, and requiring me to accept of the first preferment that offered, on pain of disobedience. This a little disquieted me' (1.108).

64 Thomas R. Albin, 'Charles Wesley's Other Prose Writings', *Charles Wesley: Poet and theologian*, ed. S T Kimbrough Jr. (Nashville: Abingdon, 1992), 91. Cf. Charles Wesley, *CWJ*, 1.268.

65 He had been 'sensibly affected with the plain Latin sentence on the Obelisk, in memory of [Pope's] mother – *Ah Editha, Matrum optima, Mulierum amantissima, vale!* [Ah Editha, the best of mothers, the most loving of women, farewell!]' Whitehead, *Life of John Wesley*, 93.

66 For a psychological perspective that might have applicability to Charles and Susanna, see Donald Capps, *Men, Religion, and Melancholia: James, Otto, Jung, and Erikson* (New Haven and London: Yale University Press, 1997).

# 6. Charles Wesley and the Preachers

## JOHN LENTON

## Introduction

On 15 March 1760 the itinerant preacher Francis Gilbert wrote to Charles Wesley about the travelling preachers, describing them as those 'who are in Connection with your Brother & You'. For Gilbert, as for most Methodists of the period, the two brothers were of equal importance and the preachers were best defined as being in connexion with *both* the brothers. Later, and certainly from the perspective of the nineteenth century, Charles may have been seen as less important than his elder brother, but not in 1760.[1] This chapter will examine the role of Charles as a leader of the preachers and his relationship with them. In particular it will use his correspondence with them as a focus. In the past he has been seen as an opponent of the preachers, seeking to purge them of unworthy members, and also acting against their claims to administer Communion. This chapter will attempt to paint a wider picture, showing that the old one was only part of a complex relationship which developed over the period.

## The importance of Charles in relation to the preachers

Charles' older brother John later declared he had invited the preachers to be his 'sons in the Gospel'.[2] However, the first reference to 'sons' in John's published journal shows Charles acting the more important role. On 8 March 1741 John wrote to the preacher John Cennick: 'You came to Kingswood upon my brother's sending for you. You served under *him* as a son.' It appears that Charles had begun the whole process of encouraging lay itinerant preachers, or at least that is the implication of this early example.[3] But this was to change, for it is certain that in later years it was John who decided the stations of the preachers, moved them and invited them to Conference. For 50 years John travelled throughout the Connexion, carrying on a correspondence with individuals in every circuit, checking up on the preachers. John was very much the leader of Methodism, and this is shown not least by his work with the preachers, but though Charles' place in the movement may have been second to that of John in the later years, this was not the case at the beginning.

It was, for example, Charles rather than his brother who in all probability founded the 'Holy Club' in Oxford, and he was certainly the first of the two men to experience conversion in 1738 – to be followed three days later by his brother. It was Charles too who, in April 1740, took the first steps in breaking with the Moravians while John wavered.[4] And, at least until the 1750s, Charles travelled the country as an equal partner with John, leading and encouraging the preachers. Indeed, in some respects it was Charles who led the way. It was Charles who first preached at Gwennap Pit and converted most of the early Methodist leaders in the Wednesbury area. As early as 1740 he took Thomas Maxfield with him on a preaching tour, thereby helping to train one of the first of the lay itinerants.[5] Even when Charles settled down, first in Bristol and later in London, he continued to play in both cities the leading part in his brother's absence and, as Newport has shown, preached actively in both places until shortly before his death.[6] When the preachers Richard Boardman and Joseph Pilmore were about to go to the chief North American colonies in 1769, they consulted with Charles about the great step they were taking. In Pilmore's words: 'He spoke freely and kindly to us about the voyage and the important business in which we had engaged: he sent us forth with his blessing in the name of the Lord.'[7] Charles remained interested and much involved in all the Methodist societies, both those he had founded and ones that he had never visited.

It is also clear that Charles corresponded with many of the preachers and continued to do so until his death in 1788. Many of these letters, both the 'in' and the 'out' letters, that is those written to Charles and those by him, have survived and provide a useful correction to the idea that it was only John who directed and led the preachers. Certainly the itinerants themselves did not think this, although they accepted that John was the brother who was always at their Conference so that his will was paramount on the most important aspect of stationing. When they wrote to Charles they usually ended the letter by describing themselves as 'your affectionate son in the Gospel' which was exactly as they wrote to John Wesley. It is that collection of letters between Charles Wesley and the preachers that provides the focus of the work presented in this chapter. As we shall see, they certainly merit detailed analysis.

There are 89 known letters from Charles to 29 different individuals, and 82 by preachers to Charles from at least 36 different individuals. Both lists will doubtless be further extended as work on the letters continues.[8] An analysis by date is shown in Table 6.1.

**Table 6.1: Letters written to and from Charles Wesley**

|       | *Undated* | *1740s* | *1750s* | *1760s* | *1770s* | *1780s* |
|-------|-----------|---------|---------|---------|---------|---------|
| Out   | 2         | 12      | 28      | 13      | 26      | 8       |
| In    | 1         | 3 (all three are from 1741 and 1742) | 11 (mainly from 1755 and after) | 36 (most are before 1764) | 15 | 16 |

This distribution suggests that Charles rarely kept letters from the preachers until about 1755, presumably because he had by then settled down and had a base where they could be kept.

Individuals with whom Charles corresponded over a long period include Joseph Cownley (from at least 1748 to 1778), John Nelson (letters dated 1746–72), Vincent Perronet (letters dated 1749–79)[9] and Howell Harris (letters dated 1740–57). Other preachers whose correspondence is numerically significant if not of broad date coverage include John Bennet (15 letters dated between 1750 and 1752), Mark Davis (6 letters dated between 1765 and 1774), Walter Sellon (letters dated between 1754 and 1755) and John Valton (letters dated between 1779 and 1787). In the early period Charles also corresponded with Thomas Maxfield, William Holland, Thomas Hardwick, John Cennick and Thomas Mitchell. In the middle period correspondents included William Grimshaw, Thomas Lee, Thomas Walsh, Christopher Hopper, John Downes, John Johnson, Alexander Coats, Francis Gilbert and Nicholas Gilbert. In the late period he wrote to the aged John Haime about his memoirs and to the bigamist Richard Moss whom he rebuked. Charles wrote also to younger men such as John Atlay, Francis Woolf, Joseph Benson, James Creighton, Joseph Pilmore, Richard Dillon, Thomas Rankin, Joseph Bradford and Samuel Bradburn. He received at least one letter from John Pawson, John Atlay and Thomas Carlill. These names include the well known and those of whom almost nothing otherwise is heard.[10]

There appears to be no correspondence with some leading preachers of the middle and later periods such as Alexander Mather, William Thompson, Thomas Hanby or with Thomas Coke. No letters written to preachers survive after 1781 except those to Samuel Bradburn. Charles considered most of these to be men who advised his brother to follow a course that was in their own interest, rather than that of the Church. Certainly, Mather and Thomas Olivers are named in a letter of 1773 to Mark Davis as poisoning the minds of many Methodists against Wesley's plan to employ Davis in London as an Anglican minister, working in conjunction with the Methodist societies.[11]

There are other frustrating gaps. For example, there is no surviving correspondence between Charles and the early preacher Thomas Richards, despite the fact that the two men are known to have been very close. There are no letters to John Jones, even though the two men enjoyed friendly relations over many years – six letters from Jones to Charles have, however, survived. Letters of the late period to younger preachers with whom he was clearly friendly, such as Henry Moore, have similarly not survived. For only 13 of the correspondents do we have at least one letter in each direction; in other words, for 38 correspondents we only have a letter (or letters) in one direction. For example, there are no letters extant from Samuel Bradburn to Charles, even though the number and the warmth of Charles' letters to Bradburn speak volumes for their friendship. It would have been good to get Bradburn's side of the story. Several preachers referred to Charles' failure to reply to their letters. They usually put this down to his health, but also sometimes wondered if they had offended him. Perhaps this is the less organized poet at work.

Seven of these correspondents were Church of England clergymen, who had been or still were Wesley's travelling preachers. These included John Fletcher (considered at length elsewhere in this book),[12] Walter Sellon of Bredon (Leicestershire), William Grimshaw of Haworth (Yorkshire), Vincent

Perronet of Shoreham (Kent), the Irishmen James Creighton and Richard Dillon, both of whom were without livings, and Joseph Pilmore, who had been a Methodist itinerant but was ordained Anglican priest in Philadelphia in 1785. Several others, including Nicholas and Francis Gilbert, were would-be clergymen but had not in fact been ordained. Many correspondents possessed social standing; this was true not just of the clergymen, but also of John Valton, the placeman son of a courtier, and of Francis Gilbert, who came from wealthy planter stock in the Caribbean. Similarly Joseph Benson, Joseph Cownley and the Welsh religious leader Howell Harris were all men of social standing.[13]

The accident of preservation by one individual or another is rather frustrating, since at best what these potentially illuminating documents can give is merely a glimpse of a much more rounded and complicated picture. However, even from the little that has survived there is much to be learned regarding the importance that Charles and the itinerants both seem to have attached to their mutual relationship, not only in the early period but throughout his life.

## Leading the preachers in the 1740s

In the 1740s Charles was the evangelistic preacher, pioneering new areas, venturing like his brother to places neither had been before. He preached in the open air, encouraged converts and engaged in arduous travel in sometimes hazardous circumstances. Like his brother he did not at first welcome lay preaching and was rather unhappy with some of the lay leaders.[14] However, when such developments did take place, Charles was quick to realize the potential advantages and worked closely with lay preachers like Thomas Maxfield, John Bennet and John Nelson. Another early leader, the itinerant Thomas Richards (1717–98), acted for some time as Charles' travelling secretary, making copies of his journals for use by others at the letter-reading days which were held at that period, sometimes at Conference.[15] Newport also cites the letter to Thomas Hardwick of 1747 as evidence of Charles' personal encouragement of lay preaching.[16] At this same time, both Wesleys were attacked for preaching in the open air and encroaching into other ministers' parishes. The preachers were also threatened and physically abused (for preaching at all) and on such occasions Charles stood with them, preaching at their side and travelling in their company just as his brother did. A good example of Charles working with two ordinary lay preachers in this early period is taken from the following entry from Charles' journal in early 1744:

Took John Healey's account of their treatment at Nottingham. The Mayor sent for Thomas Westal. John went with him. Thomas desired time to read the oath, which they offered him; upon which Mr Mayor threatened to send him to prison. While he was making his mittimus, J[ohn] Healey asked, 'Does not the law allow a man three hours to consider of it?' This checked their haste; and they permitted him to hear first what he should swear to. He said it was all very good, and what he had often heard Mr Wesleys [sic] say, that King George was our rightful King, and no other; and he would take this oath with all his heart.

They had first asked J[ohn] Healey if he would take the oaths. He answered, 'I will take them now; but I would not before I heard Mr Wesleys [*sic*]; for I was a Jacobite till they convinced me of the truth; and of His Majesty's right.' 'See the old Jesuit', cries one of the venerable Aldermen: 'he has all his paces, I warrant you!' Another on T[homas] Westal's holding his hand to his eyes, cried, 'See, see! he is confessing his sins!' They treated them like Faithful and Christian at Vanity-fair, only they did not burn them yet, or even put them in the cage. They demanded their horses for the King's service, and would not believe them that they had none till they sent and searched.[17]

Charles was clearly identifying himself with the preachers at this point, and the way he wrote about them was sympathetic and supportive. There is more in this vein in the primary sources though it is unnecessary to cite it at length here. It is difficult in this first period to distinguish between the two brothers' attitude to and relationship with the preachers.

## The 1750s: purging the preachers

With Charles' marriage in 1749 and settlement in Bristol later that year, his relationship with the preachers started to change. This was inevitable as Charles' marriage and home life had an effect on his travels and so on Charles' previously close engagement with the preachers in the work of the Revival. The early period of Charles' ministry, and of his relationship with the preachers, had come to a close.

From 1751 onwards Charles took it on himself (with John's sometimes reluctant agreement) to purge the preachers, examining most and turning quite a few out of the itinerancy. Charles' predilection for the Church of England meant that this was the main focus of his concern in relation to the preachers for much of the next 40 years.

The first example of such purging was at a Conference Charles Wesley held at Leeds in September 1751. Assembled with Charles and two other clergymen (Grimshaw and Milner) were 11 preachers, including Nelson, Shent and Bennet, so the group included most of the leading preachers in the area. According to Charles' account, the meeting began with a hymn:

Arise thou Jealous GOD arise
Thy sifting power exert,
Look through us with thy flaming eyes
And search out every heart.

Our inmost souls thy Spirit knows,
And let him now display
Whom thou hast for thy glory chose
And purge the rest away . . .[18]

Charles then continued:

> After prayer I began, without design, to speak of the qualifications, work
> and trials of a preacher; and what I thought requisite in men who act in
> concert. As to preliminaries and principles we all agreed . . . At Three we
> met again. But first I talked to Mortimer, whom I admitted; and to William
> Darney, whom I rejected.[19]

Darney was to be the first of many preachers who were suspended from the
itinerancy. Charles said that at the same time Webb and Trathen 'came afterwards but were not admitted'. Darney soon returned to the itinerancy, though
his career was to be chequered and he probably eventually left the itinerancy, but not Methodism, in 1768. Thomas Webb, who had preached alongside Charles Wesley in Wednesbury and elsewhere in 1744, was permanently
excluded, apparently for preaching Calvinism. David Trathen, a Cornishman,
accused of preaching predestinarianism, was also excluded at this time by
John Wesley, but for his actions rather than his beliefs – at least that was John
Bennet's account of the matter.[20]

There were others who, in addition to Webb, Trathen and Darney, were similarly purged at this time. These included Thomas Westell, James Wheatley,
Eleazer Webster, Robert Gillespie, 'James Watson',[21] Michael Fenwick and
John Maddern. It must be questioned, however, just how well Charles knew
the details of the lives, beliefs and conduct of the preachers that he was purging. For example, there was no 'James' Watson at this time, though that is how
Charles named him. There was a Matthew Watson who was a local preacher
in Leeds, and would have scarcely been known to Charles, which is perhaps
why he had difficulty in even getting his name correct. Charles' argument
was that 'the tinner, barber, thatcher, forgot himself with his business and
immediately set up for a gentleman', and therefore needed to be purged. He
was not always right.[22]

Another example of such purging of a preacher is Michael Fenwick, in his
case for the second time. In 1752 Charles wrote about Michael Fenwick:

> I went to the room that I might hear with my own ears one of whom many
> strange things had been told me. But such a preacher have I never heard,
> and hope I never shall again. It was beyond description. I cannot say he
> preached false doctrine or true, or any doctrine at all, but pure unmixed
> nonsense. Not one sentence did he utter that could do the least good to
> any one soul. Now and then a text of Scripture, or a verse quotation was
> dragged in by the head or shoulders. I could scarce refrain from stopping
> him. He set my blood a galloping and threw me into such a sweat that I
> expected the fever to follow.[23]

What is not always remembered is that a preacher such as Michael Fenwick,
though doubtless annoying to John as well to Charles Wesley (he slept through
at least one of John's sermons),[24] remained in the itinerancy until his old age.
Charles expelled him at least twice (1751 and 1752) but Fenwick was allowed
to return by John. The same happened to others.

A week after the journal entry concerning Michael Fenwick, Charles was again purging preachers, this time Robert Gillespie who had been an itinerant since 1748. Gillespie was expelled by Charles in 1751 but was allowed back in 1752. Little is known about him apart from this story from a letter Charles wrote to John Bennet:

> Your last helped on the work of God for which he has sent me into his vineyard at this time: and it supplied me with more abundant proof of R.G.'s utter unworthiness to preach the Gospel. I have accordingly stopped him, and shall tomorrow send him back to his proper business. A friend of ours (without God's counsel) made a preacher of a tailor. I with God's help shall make a tailor of him again.
>
> You will not (I am persuaded) rejoice in evil, but in evil prevented and good secured by this thing. And pray earnestly for me, that the Lord may guide and direct me in my most important concern – to purge the Church, beginning with the labourers.
>
> For this end, I say again in God's name, come and help me. On [the] 6th of September I trust to see Leeds: on Wednesday, September 11th to meet in conference as many of the preachers as can be got together. Bring all you can; and give notice everywhere I have silenced another scandalous preacher, and sent a third back to his trade.[25]

Again, as with Fenwick, it is clear that Gillespie did not stay purged. John must have let him back yet again! Robert Gillespie is found preaching in the Isle of Wight in the Wiltshire circuit in 1753. Though Charles purged some of the preachers, it would appear that John allowed many of those purged by him to return.

Purging the preachers should of course be seen as part of Charles' high view of the calling of the preachers. This is supported in this last letter by his clear belief that the recipient Bennet, a lay preacher himself, will only want to help Charles in this. It is also true that in this period relationships between the brothers can only be described as uneasy. On the one hand John wanted Charles to travel more. On the other Charles, when he did travel, was using his power to purge below-standard preachers whom John later allowed to return. No wonder each regarded the other with some concern.

## The 1750s and later: Charles the reconciler

However, where standards were not in question, with the preachers and with others, Charles was usually concerned with reconciliation rather than conflict. It is noticeable that where John broke with individuals, such as John Bennet himself for example, it was Charles who wrote letters which show attempts to reconcile, even though he might have realized the difficulty of his task. The quarrel with Bennet has been the object of much significant research. The latest biography of Bennet shows the rift between Bennet and John Wesley developing after Bennet's marriage to Grace Murray in October 1749. Charles was trying to hold the two together. As late as 25 September 1751

Charles wrote to Bennet: 'we shall never be separated, in time or in Eternity'; 'My heart is more committed to you than ever, & our dear Sister' (Grace). As has been noted already. in September 1751 Charles Wesley (not John) convened a meeting of the Northern preachers at Leeds. The next day they went to Birstall and 'concluded the happy day with John Bennet in prayer'. On 13 September Charles let Bennet 'preach in the evening, to the satisfaction of all'. Nevertheless in October Bennet wrote to Charles accusing both brothers of adopting underhand practices: 'you, as well as your brother, . . . assume arbitrary power'.[26] On 26 October Charles replied:

Had you received my last before you wrote yours of the 12th Instant, it might have saved us both a little Trouble. By this time you know my whole mind, both concerning yours & R[obert] Swindells: . . . yet permit me to add a few sincere, although soft words. You think you have reason not only to suspect my sincerity but positively to affirm that I use improper unscriptural things and assume arbitrary power. Therefore you cannot in conscience give me the right hand of fellowship . . .

I appeal to your own calmer judgment . . . I design never to quarrel with John Bennet, though John Bennet does all he can to force me. But I will not be forced. The second blow makes the quarrel and that with God's help I will never give. Try again, ( if you are not weary of ceaseless provocations) and I will still; answer you with words of Peace and Love . . . Love is not easily provoked. If you loved me as I do you, you could not so hastily think evil of me . . .

The Manchester brethren's behaviour toward T[homas] Web[b] I know not. My advice to them I know, which was not to receive him or D[avid] T[rathen] because they both had declared to me they would preach doctrines which I was sure would stir up strife.

Farewell.

With this letter went a shorter one to Grace Bennet:

Dear Grace,
You ask me 'What have you done? W[illiam] Shent has made a separation.' If it be so, (it is not yet plain to me) then W[illiam] Shent has done it, not I. Neither is it in his, or any man's power to separate J[ohn] B[ennet] & me. For my heart shall not be broken off from you, use me as ye will.
Your faithful & affectionate CW.[27]

Charles wrote as one who was against the breach, trying to reconcile both Bennets even at this late stage and determined not to return the blow which would solidify the quarrel. His efforts ended in failure as Bennet refused to 'try again'. Later letters show how Charles continued to try, even into 1752, to reconcile Bennet. On the other hand, in view of Charles' purging of the other preachers, it could be said that Bennett was right to be as suspicious of Charles as he clearly was of John.

Charles' attempts to reconcile preachers was a feature of his later relationships with them. The Perronet brothers ceased to itinerate for the Wesleys after 1756, but Charles remained on good terms with them, even though he disagreed strongly with their virulent anti-church views. Joseph Pilmore is another example of a preacher out of favour with John with whom Charles continued to correspond warmly. Another example is provided by the case of John Jones, who had been John Wesley's right-hand man in Bristol and London in the 1750s and early 1760s. In 1770 Jones became ordained and eventually settled as Vicar of Harwich. John was never reconciled to Jones' withdrawal from Methodism, despite the fact that it had been a decision Jones took on grounds of poor health. Charles, on the other hand, remained in friendly correspondence with Jones and tried to moderate his brother's views. Jones wrote to Charles in 1780 that he had 'told John over and over again that the only reason he left was because of ill health. He loves and esteems the Wesleys as much as ever and has never denied his links to them. But if John will not believe him. What can he do?'[28]

## Charles, the preachers and separation

In 1756 Charles wrote a letter to Samuel Walker which has been much discussed and needs quoting at length:

> Lay-preaching it must be allowed is a Partial separation; & may, but need not, end in a Total one. The probability of it has made me tremble for years past; and kept me from leaving the Methodists. I stay not so much to do good, as to prevent evil. I stand in the way of my Brother's violent Counsellors, the object of both their Fear and Hate . . .
> All I can desire of him is: 1. to cut off all their Hopes of ever leaving the Church of England. 2. to put a stop to any new preachers till he has entirely regulated, disciplined and secured the old ones.[29]

Of these two hopes, the first could not be maintained after Charles' death, and the second was never even a remote possibility. The reference to John's 'violent counsellors' in 1756 is interesting, though its precise reference is not clear. One of those to whom he was probably referring was Thomas Walsh, the saintly Irish Catholic convert, who had celebrated the sacrament in 1754 and argued for it at the 1755 Conference. He was in London in 1756, and having been previously John's right-hand man in Ireland was acting in a similar capacity in 1756–8. 'Violent' does not seem the right description for Walsh. Also dangerous in Charles' view were the Perronet brothers, sons of John's influential friend Vincent Perronet, Vicar of Shoreham in Kent. Shoreham was a place close to London to which John Wesley frequently retired in the winter period for quiet, rest and Vincent's sage advice. The two sons, Edward and Charles, were less peaceful than their father. Having joined the Wesleyan itinerancy from 1747, they retained a certain amount of independence because of their social standing and their parentage. Edward was the more important of the two brothers. Following his marriage in 1748, he eventually settled in Canterbury where he started his own independent church, right under the Archbishop's nose. This was typical of the man who in 1756 published an attack in verse on the Church in 279 pages called 'The Mitre'. It was so vitu-perative that John Wesley attempted to buy up every copy.[30] Charles' 'violent' exactly matches its tone.

In 1755 Charles wrote to John a letter which summed up his problems with some of the preachers:

> one . . . thing occurs to me now, which might in great measure prevent the mischiefs which will probably ensue after our death; and that is *greater, much greater deliberation and care in admitting Preachers*. Consider seriously, if we have not been too easy and too hasty in this matter. Let us pray God to show us, if this has been the principal cause, why so many of our preachers have lamentably miscarried. Ought any new preacher to be received before we know that he is grounded, not only in the doctrines we teach, but in the discipline also, and particularly in the communion of the Church of England? Ought we not to try what he can answer a Baptist, a Quaker, a Papist as well as a Predestinarian and a Moravian. If we do not insist on that natural affection for our desolate mother as a prerequisite, yet should we not be well assured that the candidate is no enemy to the Church?[31]

Charles remained convinced that John had too generous and trusting an attitude towards the peccadilloes of his preachers. He remained suspicious of some of John's advisers and where they were leading him. Certainly a study of Charles' letters after 1750 shows that they contained a constant refrain, at least to his closer friends, concerning the dangers of 'separation' from the Church of England.

## Charles, money and the preachers

From 1749 Charles had a financial link to the preachers. The money, agreed for his family's support in the marriage settlement with the Gwynne family that year, came from the sale of publications, sales which were mostly carried out by the preachers. In this context there are three important surviving manu-script volumes of Charles, all dated to 1749. In these volumes there is a listing, in Charles' own hand, of the subscribers to his 1749 publication *Hymns and Sacred Poems*. Interestingly, these subscribers are arranged not by place alone, but also by the name of the preacher who is responsible for the collection of the subscriptions, so that Charles could directly approach those who were not selling as well as he thought they should.[32] There is also a letter dated March 1750 in which Charles asked John Bennet for lists of the subscribers. It is clearly the case that this requirement and expectation that the preachers would collect the money from Charles' subscribers and be questioned about an apparent lack of sales, would be likely to make the relationship between Charles and the preachers even more tense. Just as Pawson grumbled later about John's insistence on preachers acting as booksellers, so earlier preachers would grumble about money going to Charles, who after 1756 was so much less visible in the connexion as a whole.[33]

## Later criticisms

Despite (or perhaps because of) the fact that he depended financially upon them, Charles remained often critical of the preachers, often centring on their preaching abilities. In October 1756 he wrote to John about Alexander Coats, a Scotsman stationed in Yorkshire: 'Alex. Coats is come. He may have both sense and grace: but I wish he had a little more utterance. I am of George Whitefield's mind, that he will never do for Leeds. He is a barbarian to me, I am sure, for I can't understand one word in three which he speaks.'[34] This was probably an unfair criticism of Coats, who had been preaching in England, probably from 1741, and hence should be regarded as one of the earliest preachers. Coats was proficient in Greek, Hebrew and Latin, and later learned Gaelic. His preaching enjoyed considerable success; John Crosse, the future clergyman, was converted by Coats and there were other accounts of this kind of success, which, one might have thought, would have been pleasing to Charles. Coats died in 1765, still in the work and by then the oldest living lay preacher. The kind of criticism of the preachers made by Charles would, at least in Coats' case, appear to have been unjustified.[35]

Relations did not get easier with the passage of years. In 1760 Charles was writing concerning his suspicions of John Murlin's sincerity. He was also concerned to see Paul Greenwood and had summoned the preacher for what would no doubt have been an uncomfortable interview.[36]

Thomas Jackson, Charles Wesley's biographer, in writing to Adam Clarke in 1829 and reporting his purchase for the Wesleyan Conference of Charles Wesley's manuscript papers, says: 'they might in the hands of our enemies, some of them at least, have been used to a very mischievous purpose; considering the high church principles of Mr C. Wesley, and the sarcastic language in which he often applied them to the lay preachers'.[37] This gives a typical nineteenth-century picture of the relationship of Charles to the preachers and hints at what Jackson had discovered in the papers, some of which are explored here. But the ill-feeling could be felt and expressed on both sides. Hence, much came to be written after Charles' death, usually by one of the preachers themselves, of Charles's attitude towards them. For example, Pawson wrote

> It is well known that Mr Charles Wesley was much prejudiced in favour of the clergy through the whole course of his life, and that it was hard necessity that obliged him in any degree to continue the lay preachers . . . he was glad of their assistance when he did not preach himself, and accordingly on a Sunday evening, he would always have a lay preacher appointed as well as himself, lest a shower of rain or an agreeable visit should prevent his attending.[38]

This obviously refers to Charles' declining years in London, though it should be said in Charles' defence that he was often not well during this period. John Pawson is the best known and perhaps the most pungent of those preachers who commented adversely on Charles. His hostility and doubts about Charles' edifying end have been described by Henry Rack as 'shocking,' but are not untypical of Pawson's general jaundiced views on others, not least his fellow preachers.[39] The Irish clergyman James Creighton was an interested and relatively unprejudiced observer of all this in the late 1780s. He described Charles' relationship with the preachers in a private letter to his sister in Ireland:

> He [Charles Wesley] does not approve of many things which his brother does, and he sees how many of the [preachers] flatter him to get favour with him [John Wesley] to make him think well of them. He speaks much of humility, and some don't like him because he sees through them, for he is very discerning.[40]

It is not irrelevant to point out that while at least eleven of the preachers christened their son 'John Wesley', none are known to have chosen the names 'Charles Wesley', and there are relatively few 'Charles' who could have been named after Charles Wesley.[41]

## Charles and Conference

In the early years Charles was always at the Conference of the preachers, and indeed it is difficult to imagine that John would have held a Conference without Charles being present, at least in the 1740s, though the 1751 Conference, to which reference has been made above, was convened in Leeds by Charles without John being present. However, as Charles' travelling declined so his attendance at the Conference became less frequent, a development that becomes noticeable in the mid-1750s. In 1755 there is a letter from Charles to his wife which was written from Rotherham on his journey south afterwards. In it Charles informs his wife that he had 'Done with Conference forever.' In the event, however, Charles did attend several more Conferences, though the 1755 letter perhaps indicated his true views and state of mind. In 1759 Charles attended Conference in London and wrote he felt like 'scampering away to Margate' immediately after Conference had ended. Charles attended in 1776 (London) and again in 1783 (Bristol), though he there referred to it as 'his brother's Conference', a significant reference. His declared purpose for his presence in 1783 was 'not to edify himself or others but purely to please his brother'.[42]

## Charles, the preachers and the societies

Despite an apparent deterioration in the relationship Charles had with some of the preachers, it is nevertheless clear that, even after the early 1750s, some of the leaders of the societies were quick to appeal to Charles at key points in the development of the movement. William Ellis, about to become a preacher, wrote to Charles in December 1762 to ask for his help in dealing with those who claimed perfection.[43] Ellis and other leaders of the London Society hoped Charles would deal firmly with Thomas Maxfield and George Bell in the problems of 'enthusiasm' of late 1762 and early 1763. The leaders were looking for firmness and decision, failed to find it in John and so turned instead to his younger brother.[44]

During the late 1760s there was a pattern of Charles coming to London to supply for John in the summer – for example, in 1762 he spent August to December in London and in 1763 and 1764 he arrived in London in May. By 1768 he was looking for a house in the capital, although he did not move there until 1771. After that he maintained a pattern of returning to Bristol in the summer when travel was easier and maintained a house in Bristol until 1782.

One of the best known visits made by Charles to Bristol in later life occurred in 1776, portrayed in the beautiful cartoons executed by his daughter Sarah who accompanied her father on that occasion. The junior preacher Thomas Tennant is shown by Sarah as about to 'introduce him [Charles] to a host of Colliers'. It is worth noting in this context that it was the *preacher* doing the introductions, which is perhaps not what might have been expected in this late period of Charles' career when the relationship with the preachers was not all that it had once been.

Charles' last tour of the northern societies was in 1756, although he remained interested in what was happening there for the rest of his life. He might have concentrated his ministry almost exclusively in London and Bristol, but he did remain in touch with developments elsewhere in the Connexion. Preachers often wrote to him with news asking for advice and help; for example in 1759 James Jones, who was based in Staffordshire for over ten years and was treated by the Wesleys for most of the time as a travelling preacher, wrote to Charles about the business of the Wednesbury House. He knew Charles was concerned about the practicalities of where the local Methodists could worship. In 1760, John Johnson, a preacher based in Ireland, wrote a long letter to Charles about the state of the society in Cork. It had been 12 years since Charles had last been in that place, but Johnson knew that Charles was still concerned with the progress of the work there, even though it was unlikely that Charles would ever see Cork again.[45] In the same year Thomas Briscoe wrote to Charles from Athlone, telling him the exciting story of Briscoe's own voyage to Ireland when storms made them think all was lost. Briscoe also told Charles about the state of the Circuit and asked for his prayers, which was a regular request in these letters. The preacher knew that Charles cared about them and the societies, even in remote Irish circuits like Athlone, and believed his prayers were still effective. Twenty years later it was a different preacher, Thomas Carlill, who wrote to Charles. He too had gone to Ireland, but was unhappy about his situation there and the prevalence of Dissenting 'Arians', not least in Methodist congregations. Again he was sure that Charles would be interested in the state of Methodism in Ireland.[46]

## Charles, the preachers and ordination

Charles' polemical poems about the preachers' claims to administer the sacrament encapsulate many of the differences between the Wesley brothers. Such is the short hymn on Numbers 16.10: 'And seek ye the priesthood also?', published in 1762.

Raised from the people's lowest lees,
Guard, Lord, thy preaching witnesses,
And let their pride the honour claim
Of sealing covenants in thy name:
Rather than suffer them to dare
Usurp the priestly character,
Save from the arrogant offense,
And snatch them uncorrupted thence.[47]

Later in 1779 he wrote bitterly:

With tears we own: They *did* run well!
But where is now their fervent zeal,
Their meek humility.
Their upright heart, their single eye,
Their vows the Lord to magnify
And live, and die for Thee?

The love of ease, and earthly things,
The pride from which contention springs,
The fond desire of praise,
Have imperceptibly stole in,
Brought back the old besetting sin
And poison'd all their grace.[48]

And yet, while attacking the preachers for trying to 'usurp the priestly character', Charles was quite prepared to write to them and even help them in
their ambition to become properly ordained clergymen of the Church. This
was true of Francis Gilbert who wrote to him about this in 1761, also of Mark
Davis, who was a close associate of Charles among the preachers in the 1760s
and early 1770s. Davis and Charles wrote to each other frequently before
Conference, planning how Davis should best act as Charles' spokesman at
Conference. In the process Charles sympathized with Davis over his wish to
be ordained. When Davis had been ordained, Charles seems to have quarrelled with him in 1772 over a horse.[49]

Later, in the 1780s, Charles wrote to the Methodist preacher Joseph Pilmore,
encouraging him to go back to America. Pilmore had been one of the first two
Methodist missionaries to go to the American colonies and had made a great
impression in both Philadelphia and New York and in undertaking a pioneering journey down into the Southern Colonies. However, Pilmore had become
unpopular with Wesley and been withdrawn from America. On his return to
England the preacher had at first not been received back into the itinerancy,
though in the end he was readmitted. Even after his return as an itinerant he
had remained interested in going back to the colonies and, after the peace was
made in 1783, looked for the opportunity to return. Charles wrote Pilmore a
letter of introduction to the newly appointed American bishop to get Pilmore
ordained by the Anglican Church there. Pilmore's letter of thanks has survived and testifies to Charles' continuing interest in his protégé.

## Good relations

With many of the preachers Charles Wesley had a reasonably good relationship. John Nelson was one of the most important of Wesley's preachers from
the early 1740s up to his death in 1774. He corresponded regularly with Charles
Wesley over an extended period. The following extract from a typical letter of
Nelson's in 1756 shows something of these good relations. Nelson wrote:

> Sir, I will assure you my heart is as your heart as concerning the Church,
> for by the help of God I hope to continue in the way wherein I was called. I
> heard some words dropped at Newcastle that made me uneasy: that some
> of our preachers had taken upon them to administer the sacrament in the
> south. That was day men[50] and they seemed to justify it. But I replied that if
> you and your Brother allowed it I would turn my back on you and all that
> join in that covenant. Then I heard no more about it as long as I stayed in the
> north. Brother Shent[51] told me about them as I come through Leeds, but he
> is entirely in my mind that if we separate from the Church God will leave
> us, as he hath done all that hath separated before us. The work seems to be
> at a stand at Leeds, I hear, at present. Brother Jones is very strong in grace
> though weak in body. He joins in love to you, so doth my wife. This with
> my best love to you and your dear wife. I beg an interest in your prayers as
> you have in mine daily.

> From your unworthy Brother in Christ and son to serve in the gospel,

> John Nelson[52]

Even towards the end of Charles' life, when there were more quarrels
between the brothers and Charles might be thought of as being more distant from the preachers, this was not necessarily the case. Henry Moore, who
entered the ministry in 1778, was a young Irish favourite of John's, and had
been brought to work in London in 1784–86. Moore later wrote about Charles
in that period as follows:

> Mr Charles Wesley also treated me with a most fatherly spirit, which sur-
> prised me the more, as there were almost continual disputes between the
> brothers about these things [Deed of Declaration, America, ordinations]
> in which, at Mr [John] Wesley's particular desire, I was generally present;
> and yet Mr Charles Wesley never showed any difference in his behaviour
> towards me.[53]

In 1777 William Linnell,[54] who had been a travelling preacher for three years
between 1770 and 1773, died in Cumbria. Charles Wesley wrote his epitaph,
which may seem no strange thing, but by 1777 Linnell had been in Cumbria
for six years and hence a long way away from Charles in the south. Linnell's
wife (née Eleanor Blenkinsop from Brampton in Cumbria) was presumably
completely unknown to Charles. Nevertheless Charles wrote epitaphs for
both Linnell and his wife, which surely suggests something of the regard in

which Charles held them. This is perhaps a little surprising in view of the supposed hostility towards the preachers on the part of Charles by this time.

There is a very late letter written by Charles in August 1787 to a preacher whose wife had recovered from what had seemed to be a terminal illness. The following is a typical passage from it. (Charles, it seems, was so much better than John at sympathizing with the preachers and retained his empathy with others to the end.)

> I never could give her up, but still hoped against hope that she be restored to you lest you should have sorrow upon sorrow. The Society prayed one night and, I believe, stopped the spirit in her flight . . . My eyes fail for writing more Give my most fatherly blessing to Her whom you have Received as from the dead.[55]

Perhaps the best letter which shows Charles' concern for all the preachers is one of the last of all his letters to survive. It is dated 13 January 1788 and was written to Samuel Bradburn.[56]

> Dear Sam,
> Send, if you cannot bring me word, how your Sophia[57] fares? Whether Mrs. Brettell[58] is brought to bed, and of what? How he does? How the Governor, and John Atlay, and Samuel Tooth.[59] I am known as a dead man out of mind, and am content. Send me the history of your Covenant Night. I would gladly join you, in renewing the Covenant at West Street . . .[60] When saw you Lady Mary? Call on me in your way to her the next time, and I will send a message by you. What day does my Brother depart for Bristol or when? When the Doctor?[61]
> Adieu.

In this one short letter the now aged Charles, who was soon to pass away, asked about two preachers and two preachers' wives in a way that suggests that, despite the water that had by this time passed under the bridge, he continued to hold these preachers at least in some regard and had a genuine concern to know of their well-being. (Admittedly Charles is also trying to find out what his brother is doing and what Thomas Coke, John's chief adviser, whom he disliked and mistrusted, is about.) The recipient, Samuel Bradburn, was the preacher who sat up all night with Charles Wesley on the night before Wesley's death. It was not one of the London stewards or one of Charles' many wealthy London friends, but one of the London preachers who, when the need arose, sat in for the absent older brother.[62]

## Charles and women preachers

Charles' attitude to women preachers seems at first sight to have been like that of the majority of men, one of opposition; in 1743, for example, he opposed a woman public speaker at Evesham.[63] However, Sarah Perrin's letters to Charles justify a brief discussion of this point.

Active in the movement from its birth at the beginning of the 1740s, Sarah Perrin made a fleeting appearance in the published Wesley papers, and from those references it is clear that she was a friend of both the brothers, but particularly of Charles. Perrin served for a time as the housekeeper at the New Room in Bristol before marrying Dr John Jones, one of the Wesleys' most respected preachers and one who corresponded with Charles for a long period. With the exception of such scraps of information and her letters to Charles, very little is known about her life or contribution to Methodism's formative years and she has never been regarded as a figure worthy of study in her own right. Hence Perrin is not mentioned in the standard works on early Methodist women by Paul Chilcote, Earl Kent Brown or Dorothy Valenze, and even in a recent biographical work on her husband she is referred to only in passing.[64]

However, Perrin clearly was exhorting and 'labouring publicly' in Leominster and other places in the 1740s and wrote to Charles about it. Unfortunately we do not have his replies, but what we do have are his annotations on the letters that Perrin has sent to him. These annotations include the brief and to the point remark, 'S. Perrin prophesying!'[65] The comments that Charles wrote do not seem adverse and it is possible that at this stage he was not against Sarah Perrin's public speaking or 'prophesying'. Similarly in 1758 Charles met the Quaker woman minister, Mercy Bell of York, and evidently thought highly of her. However, we also have a letter from Mark Davis at Conference in 1765 written to Charles, from which it is clear that both Davis and he were by this time against women preaching and (in Davis' view) that John Wesley had therefore not allowed the question to be discussed because he knew Davis was prepared to oppose it.[66]

## After Charles' death

When Charles died in 1788, the relationships between his family and the preachers continued and were not particularly difficult. By this time Charles' two sons, Samuel and Charles Jr, had already drifted away from Methodism and relations between them and their father's former acquaintances were always complex. Charles' widow, who survived to 1822, and their daughter Sally who lived with her and died in 1828, however, maintained close relations with many of the preachers, particularly those who came to City Road in London. To some extent this was because both Charles' widow and his daughter were in possession of Wesley relics and stories about the past. Those who saw themselves as historians of the Connexion, men like Henry Moore, Adam Clarke or, in a later generation, Thomas Jackson and James Everett, naturally cultivated their links with survivors of the family. Just as Mary Fletcher and Mary Tooth at Madeley saw themselves as the protectors of John Fletcher's reputation, so Sarah and Sally Wesley saw themselves as the protectors of Charles' fame and reputation. With John leaving no family surviving, Charles' family became the obvious focus for 'Wesley' events, so that even Charles' son Samuel might be encouraged to come to great Wesleyan celebrations. Problems did occasionally arise over access to Charles' papers, which belonged to Charles junior as his father's heir. After Sally's death, Charles, who was less interested in them and needed the money, sold most of them to the Conference. These problems were, however, relatively mild in comparison with those which arose over John's papers among the executors who were preachers (or former preachers) themselves.[67]


## Conclusion

In conclusion, it needs to be admitted that the traditional view of Charles' relationship to the preachers, as expressed most famously in his verse of suspicion and 'purging', is not entirely wrong. Charles was indeed suspicious of many of the preachers and he doubtless purged many and almost certainly wanted to have done more in this regard. John, however, was, from Charles' perspective, too lenient towards the preachers and allowed many of those whom Charles had expelled to return to the work. Charles, as the brother concerned about retaining Methodism within the Church, was always suspicious of the preachers' ambitions to seek independence outside the mother Church of the country and take most Methodists with them. His dislike was returned by Coke, Pawson and others. It has to be said too that Charles was often right in the judgements he made. However, relations were made worse by his acerbic verse, his failure to travel and the financial relationship which was forced upon the preachers as a result of the expected sale of Charles' books. Charles' failure to work closely with his brother led to his increasing suspicions of what he and they were trying to do.

However, there was another Charles not so well known or celebrated who emerges, at least partially, from the very fragmented record that has survived. This Charles was not only the fiery preacher who began the summoning of lay preachers to become 'sons in the Gospel' and itinerant preachers. This was not only the Charles who was a leader of the preachers of the 1740s. This was a Charles who could genuinely feel the empathy with the bereaved preacher which his older brother John found so difficult to understand, a Charles who attempted reconciliation with John and Grace Bennet and remained on good terms with the Perronets and John Jones long after they had become estranged from the more angular John Wesley. This was the Charles who appeared as kindness itself to the young Henry Moore and to whom the stout Yorkshire mason-preacher John Nelson wrote so regularly, not least when he was embarrassingly short of money. It was for this Charles that the preacher Samuel Bradburn, later to sit as President in John Wesley's chair, sat up on Charles' last night on earth, as the representative of all the itinerant preachers for someone who had shared their leadership for so long.


## Notes

1 MS letter of Francis Gilbert at Bristol to CW (MARC, PLP MAM, 2/54). Francis Gilbert (1725–79) was the younger brother of Nathaniel Gilbert, planter of Antigua. He fled to England where he became a Methodist and began to travel as

a preacher in 1758. He had money and may well have acted as a local preacher in the period after 1764 when he was living first in Kendal and later in Chester.

2 John Lenton, *My Sons in the Gospel* (Loughborough: Wesley Historical Society, 2000), 3.

3 *BE*, 19 186 (journal for 8 March 1741). The emphasis is mine.

4 Colin J. Podmore, *The History of the Moravian Church in England 1728–60* (Oxford: Clarendon Press, 1998), 67.

5 *Charles Wesley Papers*, ed. G. Lloyd (Manchester, 1994 [hereinafter *CWP*]), vol. 1.114–5, quoting MARC, DDPr CW, 6/31. Baker, *Charles Wesley as Revealed by his Letters*, 82. The argument as to who was the first itinerant preacher was probably settled by Frank Baker in 'Thomas Maxfield's first sermon', in *Proceedings of the Wesley Historical Society*, 27 (1949), 7–15.

6 Newport, *Sermons*, 38–9.

7 J. P. Lockwood, *The Western Pioneers . . . Boardman and . . . Pilmoor* (London: Wesleyan Conference Office, 1881), 69–70.

8 See Chapter 19 below.

9 Vincent Perronet, William Grimshaw, Richard Dillon and James Creighton were all clergymen who preached to many Methodist societies.

10 See the list at <http://www.gcah.org/WesleyPreachers/WesPreachersIntro.htm>

11 MS copy letter in Lloyd, *CWP*, 1.27–8 and MARC, DDCW, 1/62.

12 See Chapter 7 below.

13 All would agree that Thomas Coke was a Methodist preacher. He was also an ordained Anglican clergyman. Benson was appointed by Lady Huntingdon to Trevecca. Cownley had been a solicitor's clerk.

14 See R. P. Heitzenrater, *Wesley and the People Called Methodists* (Nashville: Abingdon, 1995), 115–16 for examples.

15 I am indebted to Richard Heitzenrater for this information. Richards became a master at Kingswood in 1748, married the housekeeper there in 1749 and was ordained in 1750, becoming curate at St Sepulchre's, Holborn, for 30 years.

16 Newport, *Sermons*, 20.

17 John R. Tyson, *A Charles Wesley Reader* (New York: Oxford University Press, 1989), 405.

18 Jackson, *Life*, 1.84–5.

19 Jackson, ibid; for Darney see also *BE*, 20.171 n. 12 and *BE*, 26.537 n. 20.

20 For Webb, see *Arminian Magazine*, 1779, 315; *BE*, 20.111 n. 15 and *BE*, 26.487 n.15, *CWJ*, 345, 348–9; S. R. Valentine, *Mirror of the Soul: The Diary of an Early Methodist Preacher John Bennet 1714–54* (Peterborough: Epworth Press, 2002), 215. For Trathen, see Jackson, *Life*, 1.583; S. R. Valentine, *John Bennet and the Origins of Methodism and the Evangelical Revival in England* (Lanham: Scarecrow Press, 1997), 147 n. 174–5, 259, 265; *Mirror of the Soul: The diary of an early Methodist preacher, John Bennet, 1714–1754* ed. S. R. Valentine (Peterborough: Methodist Publishing House, c2002), 154, 159, 188–94, 215.

21 On which see immediately below; Charles seems to have Matthew Watson in mind.

22 In the 1747 and 1751 Minutes, Matthew Watson is listed as assisting in one place after Shent and before Appleyard, so he was local to Leeds. He was invited by Charles Wesley to the September Conference at Leeds. He was still preaching in the area in 1753, 1756 and 1758/9. Nelson said he was buried 10 November 1763, having preached 17 years (Laycock *Great Haworth Round*, 80, 256). Charles

Wesley's notebook (mostly 1751) MARC DDCW, 8/5 in *CWP*, 2.87–8. This shows no fewer than ten preachers purged by Charles in 1751, which was a significant loss given the maximum of 69 preachers then available to the Wesleys. No wonder John let many back!

23 *CWJ*, 2.77–8, cf. Baker, *Charles Wesley as Revealed by his Letters*, 85. The letter has not survived.

24 *WJW*, 21; 117 n. 57.

25 Baker, *Charles Wesley as Revealed by his Letters*, 86. See also, Heitzenrater, *Wesley and the People Called Methodists*, 185, which makes it clear that 'RG' was Robert Gillespie. *BE*, 26.530 n. 15 provides the Isle of Wight reference.

26 Valentine, *John Bennet and the Origins of Methodism and the Evangelical Revival in England*, chapter 19. Valentine does not appear to have used the important letter of 26 October quoted immediately below.

27 The original MS letter is at Drew University (ref. 2135-6-4):03 26 Oct 1751 CW London to Bennet.

28 MARC, DDPr, 1/94 John Jones 17/6/1780 to CW.

29 *PWHS* 15, 70–1.

30 For Walsh, see T. Jackson (ed.), *Early Methodist Preachers* 3, 14–292. John Wesley described him as 'that man of God'. For the Perronets, see for example, the *Dictionary of Evangelical Biography*; and Tyerman, *Life and Times*, 2.198–258 (esp. 241–4) for 'The Mitre'.

31 Quoted in Tyson, *Reader*, 419–20.

32 Lloyd, *CWP*, 2.104 (MARC, DDCW, 8/18–20).

33 The letter extract to Bennet is in MARC, DDCW, 9/17b. For one grumble see Pawson, *Letters* 3.105–6.

34 Baker, *Charles Wesley as Revealed by his Letters*, 88.

35 For Coats, see *Methodist Magazine* (1821) 50, *Wesleyan Methodist Magazine* (1841) 3–4, Elliott Binns (1953) 316, *WJW* 22, 23 n. 96.

36 *CWP*, 1.108, letter of 17 March 1760.

37 Perkins Library, Duke University NC, Frank Baker Collection, Loose Presidential book 119. P6 of the Mss. The letter is dated 22 July 1829.

38 Everett and Tyerman, Mss 657B at MARC. I owe this reference to Gareth Lloyd.

39 *Methodist History*, 43 (2005), 93–4.

40 MS copy letters of James Creighton to his sister at the Clark Collection, Lake Junaluska Museum NC, in Creighton Letter Book P47 7/2/1788.

41 Fourteen of the preachers named a son 'Charles.' However, three fathers were called Charles themselves, one son was born in 1723 and another named after his father's friend Charles Atmore. One named his son after he left the itinerancy, five before they entered, while they were only local preachers. One, Thomas Wride, named him after a relative Charles Harrison. That leaves only five preachers who, while travelling, may have called their son after Charles Wesley. One of those was John Nelson who corresponded frequently with Charles Wesley. Nelson's descendant thinks it quite likely the son was named after Charles Wesley, since no earlier Charleses are known in the family.

42 *CWP*, 1.91, II 26–7, 19 July 1759, II 65 DDCW, 7/86).

43 MS Letter to CW ELLW (23 December 1762) EMV:56 in MARC.

44 Newport, *Sermons*, 25–6.

45 James Jones Handsworth to CW (London: 24 December 1759) re: Wednesbury House MARC EMV 95, John Johnson to CW (7 February 1760) MARC, EMV, 91.

46  Briscoe at Athlone to CW (Bristol 17/11/1760) MARC, DDPr, 2/8. Carlill to CW (Bishops Court, Ireland 8/11/1780) MARC, DDPr, 2/9.

47  *Short Hymns on Select Passages* (1762) as quoted in Tyson, *Reader*, 425. JW added a note to the first line 'Query?'

48  Kimbrough and Beckerlegge, *Unpublished Poetry*, 3.37–9, headed 'For some of the preachers Written 10 October 1779'.

49  MARC, DDCW, 7/11 about 'the Christian behaviour of CW when shamefully treated by a hypocritical clergyman'. See *CWP*, 2.82.

50  Paid by the day, so only temporary 'journeymen'.

51  William Shent (1715–87), barber and preacher of Leeds (entered 1747) was a convert of Nelson's.

52  At least nine letters survive from Nelson to Charles Wesley 1755–72. Two letters from Charles Wesley to Nelson survive (1746 and 1760). In these surviving letters Nelson always signed himself to Charles in this way referring to himself as a 'son to serve in the gospel'.

53  Mrs Richard Smith, *The Life of the Rev Mr Henry Moore . . .* (London: Simpkin Marshall, etc., 1844).

54  Linnell had been brought up in Buckinghamshire at a time when Charles was in Bristol, see the article on him in *Cumbria WHS Journal*, 40 (1997) 15–17 by J. Williamson. For the epitaphs and more information on the Linnells, see Kimbrough and Beckerlegge, *Unpublished Poetry*, 3.325.

55  Drew University, UMC Archives (ref. 2135–6–4:11) original letter CW to 'My dear Bro.' (Bristol, 31 August 1787).

56  Samuel Bradburn, entered 1774, was then in his third year stationed in London. The letter is in the World Methodist Museum, Lake Junaluska, NC. Methodist Manuscript Book, p. 8, original letter CW to Samuel Bradburn (London: 13 January 1788).

57  Sophia was Samuel Bradburn's second wife, married 1786. She was the former Sophia Cooke, with money of her own, prominent in Gloucester where she had played a leading part with Raikes in starting a Sunday School.

58  Wife of the itinerant preacher Jeremiah Brettell, who had a daughter, Maria, in 1788. She was the former Rebecca King (married 1786) whom Charles Wesley may have known well as she was the daughter of John King, a Bristol class leader and trustee.

59  John Atlay was the long-term Book Steward, who in August 1788 deserted John Wesley and joined the rebellious Dewsbury Trustees. Samuel Tooth was a former Preacher who had built Wesley's Chapel in City Road, London in 1778.

60  West Street Chapel.

61  Dr Coke.

62  G. J. Stevenson, *The Methodist Hymn Book* (London, 1876), 523.

63  *CWJ*, 1:307.

64  Paul Chilcote, *John Wesley and the Women Preachers of Early Methodism* (Lanham: Scarecrow Press, 1991); Earl Kent Brown, *Women in Mr Wesley's Methodism* (Lampeter: Edwin Mellen, 1983); Deborah Valenze, *Prophetic Sons and Daughters: Female preaching and popular religion in industrial England* (Princeton: Princeton University Press, 1985); A. B. Sackett, *John Jones: First After the Wesleys*, WHS Publication, 7 (1972).

65  Gareth Lloyd's article, 'Sarah Perrin (1721–1787) – Early Methodist Exhorter', *Methodist History*, 41 (2003), 79–88.

66  Whitehead, *Life of the Rev John Wesley*, 1.338.

67  Jackson, *Life*, 1.iii–iv.

# 7. Charles Wesley and John Fletcher

## PETER FORSAITH

In his friend John Gambold's telling phrase, Charles Wesley was 'a man born for friendship'.[1] This chapter explores that gregarious propensity by way of his friendship with another evangelical clergyman, John Fletcher (1729–85), who became Vicar of Madeley in Shropshire. The singular focus should not detract from the perspective of Charles' wide circle of friends, but rather should be seen as an example of it. From school and university these included William Murray who, as Lord Mansfield, became Lord Chief Justice. There were friends in the musical and literary spheres too, most notably G. F. Handel; in addition there were Charles' own neighbours and relations such as Lord Mornington and, of course, members of his own and his wife's families. Inevitably perhaps, many of his friends were evangelical clergy who shared his interests and to a greater or lesser extent identified with the Methodist movement. These included William Grimshaw, the reputedly irascible incumbent of Haworth, Yorkshire, and the irenic Vincent Perronet, Vicar of Shoreham in Kent, to name only two: a thorough survey of Charles' circle of friendship would hence be a considerable undertaking.

This chapter could, then, equally have been written about one of a range of such evangelical clergy friendly to Charles. However, it is hoped that this snapshot of his relationship with Fletcher will give at least some indication of how that broader story, were it told in full, might appear. Again, this chapter might have explored broader eighteenth-century notions of male friendship, exemplified between Charles Wesley the Englishman and Fletcher, who was born a Swiss. Langford notes that if the English were judged slow to make friends (Charles Wesley may have been an exception here), a friendship once made was a lifelong commitment.[2] If this contrasted with norms of continental friendship, it may have been one of the features of English life which attracted Fletcher and made the country his adopted home: 'O for quietness and English friends' he wrote to Perronet in 1779 during a visit back to his continental homeland,[3] reflecting perhaps the polite taciturnity which was reputedly characteristic of the English social male.[4] Yet the correspondence indicates an animated warmth which both Wesley and Fletcher found came naturally.

This chapter does not, however, treat in any detail such broader themes, but rather focuses very precisely on the Charles Wesley–John Fletcher relationship. This is appropriate here for at least three reasons. First, both Wesley and Fletcher were men of central prominence in Wesley's Methodism. Such is seen in rather clear form by the fact that in a synthesized engraving of Wesley's first Conference held in the City Road chapel, Wesley and Fletcher occupy the pulpit with John Wesley. This was a focal hegemony of late eighteenth-century Methodism, and the story of this friendship is the story from its very heart. Second, it is appropriate since there is a substantial surviving archive of Fletcher's correspondence which readily enables the friendship to be mapped and analysed with some clarity. Third, the focus of this chapter is appropriate since in some ways it was an attraction of opposite poles. Thus, for example, Fletcher was a generation younger than Charles; he was not English by birth and (as far as is known) neither was he particularly literary or musical. What is more, unlike Charles who, even after his marriage, engaged in some periods of extensive travel (at least in the very early years) and thereafter had a ministry shared at least between London and Bristol, Fletcher by contrast buried himself almost entirely in the work and life of his Shropshire parish and for many years saw little of his friend.

Inevitably, a considerable proportion of the narrative will be occupied by Fletcher. Relative to Charles, Fletcher is something of an unknown and there is comparatively little work on the life and work of this man or detailed assessment of his place within early Methodism.[5] Yet both have suffered historically and biographically from being labelled 'Methodist'. As John Wesley's brother and colleague, Charles' Methodist allegiance has excluded him from consideration within mainstream studies of the established Church while Methodist historians have been faintly alienated by his staunch Church of England loyalty. Much the same might be said of John Fletcher who, like Charles, can justifiably be said to have put the Church before the Methodists.[6]

Charles Wesley was a man of warmth. As a poet and as a family man he knew the warmth of emotion; and on occasion he could display warmth of temper. John Fletcher was (according to John Wesley) 'all on fire – but it was the fire of love'.[7] Fletcher was, almost uniquely and certainly pre-eminently, an ordained evangelical who sided solidly with the Wesleys' Methodist connexion beyond the doctrinal debacle of the 1770s and into the incipient sectarianism of the 1780s.

Charles first came to know Fletcher around the time of Fletcher's ordination,[8] in March 1757. What we know of their friendship survives through extant manuscript letters.[9] An obstacle in mapping both the course and qualities of their relationship is that while some 90 holograph letters from Fletcher to Charles survive, and these range from 1757 to 1785, only six from Charles' side are known, and those are from later years. However, the fullness and fluency of Fletcher's letters enables the construction of the geography of their friendship to be undertaken with reasonable confidence.

The first letter from Fletcher to Charles is autobiographically framed within a familiar template of evangelical personal testimony.[10] Fletcher's childhood waywardness and burden of sin are expressively, subjectively and lengthily contrasted with the ineluctable dawning of divine grace. What the letter only fleetingly hints at is Fletcher's Swiss origins, though we know that he was born of a well-to-do and well-placed family, that he attended Geneva University briefly and came to England around 1749 after a frustrated military career. Patrick Streiff has considered in some depth the implications of the social, national, religious and family influences of his early life.[11]

In England, Fletcher became tutor to the sons of Thomas Hill, MP for Shrewsbury, whose wife had been a girlhood friend of Sarah Gwynne[12], and during much of the 1750s his life was divided between London and Shropshire. In 1753: 'as I was going into the country . . . I met a poor woman who . . . was a Christian: the pleasure and profit I found in her conversation made me forget I was upon a journey.'[13] Making excuses for his delay, Mrs Hill suggested he risked being considered Methodist. 'I ask'd what she meant by a Methodist and when she had told me I say'd that I would be one of them if there was realy such a people in England.'[14]

So in London he sought out Methodists and went to 'west street and Hog Lane every Sunday'.[15] It was here that he first heard Charles Wesley preach – apparently at the fashionable Huguenot church of Les Grecs, Hog Lane. West Street was a former Huguenot chapel that John Wesley had taken over. Fletcher's evangelical conversion followed in January 1754. Yet it was not until some years later that he really came into the Wesleys' orbit.

This initial letter (docketed by Charles as 'Mr Fletcher's experience'), probably responded to a request for a narrative of his religious experience, and if so may have been requested as a means by which Fletcher's Methodist credentials could be established. Surviving letters indicate that the relationship between Charles and Fletcher moved rapidly from this point from formal and formulaic to a level of intimacy. By late 1759 Fletcher was able to declare eloquently how Charles' fellowship was vital to his religious equilibrium:

> I am so certain of your salvation, that I demand no other place in Heaven than that which I may find at your feet: I even doubt that Paradise will be Paradise without you sharing it with me: & the mere idea raised in my mind by your question whether we might one day be separated cuts me to the heart and bathes my eyes in tears.[16]

To what extent such affection was reciprocated is unclear. But at the least, Fletcher had found a mentor and Charles Wesley a protégé.

For 12 years, from 1758 to 1770, Fletcher wrote to Charles in French. Why Fletcher should choose to write to his friend in this language is a bit of a puzzle, although it was the *lingua franca* of polite society.[17] Possibly Charles Wesley did not reply in the same language: Fletcher testily remarked in one letter 'I await *a reply in French*', apparently inferring sloth on his correspondent's part.[18] Fletcher's chosen language of correspondence may equally have arisen from a shared French-speaking ministry in London from about 1758. Indeed, Fletcher's introduction to English society had initially been through the francophone expatriate Huguenot community in London and he retained links with them.[19] Moreover, at that time French prisoners (from the Seven Years War) were incarcerated near London and, at Lady Huntingdon's behest, Fletcher established a ministry (which Charles Wesley shared) among them. Letters of 1758 to 1760 also mention a similar circle of friends with demonstrably French roots such as Colonel Gallatin and Mme Carteret.

In 1759 Fletcher was seeking a French Bible for Charles, possibly a New Testament which survives.[20] In 1762 Charles wrote to his wife that he had ventured to preach in French (whether this was extempore or not we cannot tell). But how far this explains the correspondence in French with Fletcher is an open question. Years later, in a letter dated 19 December 1782, Fletcher forwarded Charles Wesley some writings in French for his perusal, adding, perhaps pointedly, 'if you have not forgot your French'. While this letter is largely in English, Fletcher interjected some French into it. Charles found it necessary to interline his own translation of what Fletcher had written, perhaps suggesting a lesser fluency in French at this point on the part of the now fairly elderly Charles.[21]

By 1760 Fletcher was a rising star in the evangelical firmament. His tutorial work for the Hills was at an end, the sons having been sent to Cambridge to escape Methodist infection. Yet he retained the Hills' support (behind whom lay the backing of an influential Shropshire Whig–evangelical hegemony)[22] as well as being favoured by the Wesleys, Lady Huntingdon and their set. A probable future either as curate of a London parish or chaplain to a sympathetic aristocrat, while establishing himself as an itinerant preacher, might have lain ahead. However, Fletcher's sights were actually set on the obscure and challenging parish of Madeley in the heart of proto-industrial Shropshire, to which he had been appointed titular curate on his ordination. When at length he was offered the parish, again through the good offices of Thomas Hill, his friends were divided. John Wesley was aghast, dismissing it as 'the devil's snare' and consistently schemed for a quarter-century to wheedle Fletcher away from the parish.[23] What he never could grasp was, as Bishop Nuelsen pithily put it, 'for Wesley the world was his parish, for Fletcher his parish was his world'.[24]

Charles Wesley, on the other hand, and Lady Huntingdon too, gave cautious approval. He had already advised Fletcher not to resist providence, and this seemed a clear instance to Fletcher of 'a chain of providences I could not break'.[25] In Fletcher's early years at Madeley, Charles diligently watched over his young protégé as the new and sometimes naïve vicar sought to make his mark upon the 'sheep . . . without a shepherd'[26] to whom he believed he was divinely called (while ever ready to hear the heavenly voice calling him elsewhere).

It may be that Charles had mixed feelings as he read at a distance of progress and setbacks in the parish. Almost inevitably his mind would have gone back to his father's difficulties in Epworth where a faithful Christian ministry had been spurned by many of the population. So in 1776, when Fletcher was ill, he cautioned Fletcher not to return to duties before he was better: 'My Father lost his life by wilfully officiating before his strength returned.'[27] Possibly he reflected on his own career, which could easily have taken him to a parish – and still might. In 1761 Fletcher counselled him about accepting a church and it would be tempting to believe that Fletcher's appointment had ignited a hankering for parish ministry. Nor was that the last time Charles considered such a possibility: in 1764 he was apparently offered Drayton in Oxfordshire.[28]

If he was envious of Fletcher on this point, such might explain why he never visited his friend in Shropshire. It became a bone of contention. Fletcher could recognize that in Charles' busy and productive life, letter writing was not always a priority and he might wait weeks or months for a reply. While that irked him, he could make allowances. What became increasingly frustrating was Charles' (apparently) reiterated but unfulfilled promised to come to Madeley. Mild affront was succeeded by annoyance, which in turn became amused resignation. Yet Fletcher was clearly needled.[29]

Perhaps this apparent tension over the issue of the long-awaited but never-seen visit highlights differing models of friendship between the two men. Fletcher could not have been an easy person to have as a friend. He was an individual of considerable intensity who demanded a high level of commitment from himself and allegiance from his friends. James Ireland would at one point say of Fletcher, 'I would have divided the last shilling with him.'[30] It must be stressed that these were relationships of reciprocity. Fletcher's own devotion, late in life, to his wife was deep and mutual and exemplifies the intensity, intimacy and commitment which seems characteristic of his significant relationships, including that with Charles.

Charles Wesley was hardly able to return such intimacy. He had many friends with calls on his loyalty, time and interests. He was married, with the cares of a family which increased with the years. Further, as John Wesley's brother he needed to consider the political and ecclesiastical positioning of the Methodists. His relationship with his brother comes out in several chapters in this book, and it is evident that Charles could and did sometimes subsume his personal feelings within the greater interests of the 'connexion'. So despite a long and mutual friendship with Lady Huntingdon, her last letter of appeal to Charles in the heat of the 1771 dogmatic row was ostentatiously docketed by him, perhaps intentionally ambiguously, 'Unanswered by J. W.'s Brother'.[31]

This brings us to consider the *ménage à trois* between Charles, his brother John and his friend John Fletcher. The Wesley brothers' contradictory chemistry was compounded of fraternal loyalty, sibling rivalry, past family reference points, divine graciousness, human stubbornness and a naked fear of the wrath to come. To factor into that equation someone like Fletcher who seemed both independent and subservient was to provoke a reaction. It was, however, a delayed reaction. During Fletcher's lifetime his considerable personal spirituality more than allayed jealousy or resentment.

Fletcher's reputation as eminent exemplar of Christian holiness, in John Wesley's scheme, has remained undisputed even by opponents of Wesley's theological system.[32] In his own lifetime, no matter his self-perception as a worthless worm, he was widely respected as a saint. After his early death his reputation soared: superlatives about him were freely traded and Madeley became a place of pilgrimage, the 'Mecca of Methodism'.[33] On this John Wesley quickly capitalized. His life of Fletcher burnished the subject's reputation and attached it firmly to Wesley and his cause.[34] From being a free spirit, Fletcher was depicted as Wesley's theological mastiff, his preferred successor and bosom acquaintance. Yet from Wesley's account certain voices are strangely absent. Few of Fletcher's friends contributed, and Charles Wesley was virtually unmentioned: his promised elegy never materialized.[35]

The reality is that tensions went back many years. If the correspondence is an accurate reflection, as Fletcher's friendship with Charles Wesley strengthened, that with brother John never progressed beyond the formal. While Fletcher wrote to Charles as *Mon très cher ami*, to John Wesley it was mostly 'Revd and Dear Sir'. In a nutshell, he loved Charles as his brother in Christ, but John Wesley as his father in God. His letters to John look as though they have been carefully drafted; to Charles he poured his heart onto the page unreservedly. With John he may have anticipated that the letter might become public. To Charles he wrote entirely confidentially.

So to Charles, Fletcher was at times openly critical of John. He could hardly have been ignorant of the tensions between them, while recognizing too that beneath the unease lay a fierce mutual loyalty and respect. When in early 1760 Fletcher finally left the Hills and took rooms in fashionable St James, he reported that John Wesley was annoyed.[36] Charles Wesley's letters of the time indicate that he too was engaged in ministry among 'the quality' and empathized with Fletcher's move.

Tensions surfaced again some two years later over the emergence in Wesley's London 'society' of a group claiming Christian perfection for themselves. Fletcher had been part of this 'society' and evidently knew (and probably empathized with) some of the group, as well as sharing perfectionist aspirations and sympathizing with their millennial views. One of the leaders was Thomas Maxfield, reputedly Methodism's first lay preacher who subsequently took Anglican orders. In 1763 John Wesley complained of his 'speaking evil' about him to Fletcher 'for six weeks together'.[37] Wesley, fairly peremptorily, dismissed Maxfield and others from membership.

The divisiveness and extremity of the group was probably exaggerated:[38] certainly Wesley's reaction appeared intolerant and Maxfield was more moderate than others. Fletcher, in distant Shropshire, could only go by report. He was unwilling to take sides since he only knew the facts partially, but did know people involved and was not prepared to condemn them as schismatic, whatever John Wesley had done. Moreover, there was apparently some suspicion that Fletcher himself was clandestinely supporting or advising 'the perfects', which he unsurprisingly resented and felt the need to defend himself. But foremost, he insisted he was non-partisan, a position which was to become a hallmark of his career, though seldom appreciated.[39]

Charles Wesley, who was generally suspicious of both lay power and religious extremes, might have been a prickly correspondent. Yet Fletcher confidently (and presumably confidentially) assured him that 'I am not a party man',[40] corresponded with hardly anyone else, and was sceptical about claims to perfection. Nevertheless Fletcher refused to distance himself from the 'perfects', writing occasionally to Maxfield and possibly to others as well. Fletcher recorded an attempted *rapprochement* in early 1765, when Maxfield assisted John Wesley at Spitalfields (an event generally omitted from accounts of the crisis) and welcomed Maxfield to Madeley for six weeks late that summer and again the following year. Maxfield preached among the colliers; Fletcher found little to criticize and much to commend. Sadly, he concluded to Charles Wesley, he had 'lost hope of seeing a public reunion between your brother and M[axfiel]d. They are not made for each other'; adding obliquely, 'Whoever would be the first among us, let him be the Servant of all.'[41]

The episode with Maxfield demonstrates, over several years, several qualities of Charles Wesley's friendship. First, he allowed Fletcher his independence, then he supported his non-partisan neutrality, and third, his (implied) affability is in contrast to his brother's. Yet if Fletcher felt able to confide to

Charles Wesley his frustration with John's indomitability, that did not extend to direct criticism. So in 1765, just when Fletcher was identifying solidly with local evangelical clergy and welcoming the outcast Maxfield to officiate in the parish, a Methodist itinerant, Alexander Mather, was stationed nearby. If Fletcher did resent the appointment his criticisms were tangential; he had forbidden Mather the year before to preach in the parish and told Charles Wesley that his brother had avoided the issue when visiting Madeley.[42]

It is unfortunate that a five-year lacuna in surviving correspondence (1765–70) denies precise plotting of the continuing friendship through years of growing confidence and expansion in Fletcher's ministry and life, years which saw the establishment of Lady Huntingdon's College at Trevecca and Fletcher's appointment as its 'President', about which John Wesley commented sourly to Charles.[43] During this period Fletcher did spend time with Charles Wesley, but his friendship with the Bristol sugar and wine merchant, James Ireland, also developed. On returning in August 1770 from a visit with Ireland to mainland Europe, Fletcher re-stated his continuing affection for Charles Wesley:

My very dear Friend
The waters of the Ocean and the Mediterranean have not quenched my spark of brotherly love for you, I have a great desire to see you to converse about the mysteries of the Kingdom of Heaven . . .[44]

However, such relaxed benignities were to be short lived, for their world was soon to change radically. On Charles Wesley's side, the life he had long lived of superintending the Methodist societies in Bristol and London was altered by removal to London, increasing immersion in family life and disengagement from a Methodist ecclesia which he sensed (correctly) was moving away from the established Church. Fletcher himself cautioned Charles about his changing lifestyle: 'You have your enemies as well as your brother, they complain of your love for musick, company, fine people, great folks and the wane of your former zeal & frugality. I need not put you in mind to cut off sinful appearances . . .'[45]

The vitriolic and damaging 'Calvinistic controversy' which absorbed Fletcher's mind, energy and health was to come to define his historic reputation and be the acid test of his relations with the Wesleys. Its outbreak and course has been described and dissected elsewhere.[46] Whitefield's death in 1770, Wesley's injudicious phrasing of his 1770 'Minutes' and Lady Huntingdon's intractable fury led inexorably to the fraction of a movement whose doctrinal mantra had hitherto been to agree to disagree.[47]

Polemically, Fletcher has generally been perceived as 'Wesley's bulldog', the heroic champion of Wesleyan Arminianism who remained faithful although all others had fled.[48] However, he was drawn into the dispute unwillingly, intending merely to defend Wesley against what he considered unfair defamation. He tried to withdraw his *Vindication* from publication when he recognized its potential for damage, but the printer would only take instructions from Mr Wesley, not from the author. Fletcher was correct: the publication of his *Vindication* launched a protracted bout of vindictive pamphleteering which destroyed most semblance of remaining harmony between the disparate evangelical factions.

Fletcher's *Checks to Antinomianism*, acclaimed for their dogmatic and polemical qualities by opponents as well as supporters, essentially defended the Arminian position rather than demolishing Calvinism – although at times that seems a fine distinction. Fletcher abhorred sectarianism or schism, so perhaps the most significant of his publications in the 1770s were the *Scripture Scales* and *Plan of Reconciliation*. After the long and arduous arguments of successive *Checks*, these set out human freewill and divine sovereignty as being two sides of the same coin, truth in paradox, urging the warring sides to make peace with each other.

It was too little, too late. The damage had been done, and henceforth Fletcher was revered or reviled for his doctrinal stance and his part in splitting the evangelical revival. The image was reinforced a decade later, when Wesley's 1786 life majored on Fletcher's polemical achievements and his loyalty to Wesley and his connexion.

In reality Fletcher strove for peace and harmony and as far as possible kept his friendships with evangelicals on the other side of the divide in good repair. He continued an amicable correspondence with Lady Huntingdon, and as late as 1781 Richard Hill preached at Madeley. James Ireland, to whom Fletcher was drawn ever closer, refused to take sides, as did many other lay evangelicals, for whom a non-aligned position was easier than for the clergy.

In all this Charles Wesley was in something of an invidious position. He too believed profoundly that unity was the essence of the Church and yet his hymns declared the free, open and unconditional love of God, the very position which was the cause of the conflict. While he was friendly with evangelical clergy and others, including Lady Huntingdon, yet he was John Wesley's brother. Fletcher's letters to Charles form a kind of backstage subscript to the drama which was being publicly enacted.

At the outset of the controversy Fletcher preferred to entrust Charles with correcting or editing his writings, evidently fearing that John Wesley was too hurried and would go straight to press rather than consulting the author. So Charles became an intermediary figure:

> Your brother has corrected my other book and will print it . . . but I should be glad to see his corrections . . . I should be glad you were at Bristol to correct the press according to your old promise . . . [49]

and:

> thank you for all you[r] care and diligence in correcting both my manuscripts and the press.[50]

Yet Fletcher voiced frustration to Charles about him and his brother:

> My very dear Brother
> Where are you? . . . Your brother is in Scotland and you are in the land of forgetfulness.[51]

Or

> In your 2 last You say 'you have seen Mr. T[oplady]'s book and his argumts. for repr.[obation]' Indeed I have not. I know nothing of what passes or what is published in London or Bristol . . .[52]

When he published his *Equal Check* in 1774–5, he retained editorial control, and used his Shrewsbury printer.

By the mid-1770s Fletcher's friendship with Charles Wesley seems to have cooled significantly. Reasons for this are not immediately obvious. On Fletcher's side his experience during the Controversy had been that under duress, the Wesleys' brotherly relationship became dominant. No more could Fletcher be confident that Charles was independent of John. Moreover, Fletcher had found elsewhere, in James Ireland, another close friend who mirrored his own basic hunger for harmony and was determinedly neutral. On Charles Wesley's side his preoccupation with family life and growing dislike of the laicization and sectarianism of Methodism distanced him from the scenes and themes of action. He also sensed his age. Approaching his three-score years and ten he wrote to Fletcher: 'I have hardly recovered my late journeys. Do not expect to weather another winter.'[53] And there was yet another factor: in 1775 John Wesley, at 72 still generally vigorous and active, fell seriously ill in Ireland. His life was despaired of and Fletcher wrote to Charles Wesley:

> The same post which brought me yours, brought me a letter from Ireland informing me of the danger of your dear brother my dear Father. What can you and I do? What, but stand still and see the salvation of God?[54]

However, the danger passed, so on 8 August a relieved Fletcher wrote to Charles Wesley: 'Your brother is preserved, and I trust you are spared for good also.'[55]

If, or when, John Wesley died, the question of a 'successor' to lead the Methodists would be a live issue. In July Fletcher had mooted this to Charles Wesley:

> The Methodists will not expect from you your brother's labours, but they have (I think) a right to expect that you will preside over them . . . Should your brother be called to his reward, I would not be free to go to London.[56]

Already by 1773 John Wesley had asked Fletcher to be nominated his heir-apparent. Fletcher wittily responded that such a proposal 'would make me take to my horse and gallop away'.[57] The prospect of Fletcher succeeding John Wesley has consistently puzzled commentators such as Southey who have found it impossible to match Wesley's leadership qualities with Fletcher's preferred subsidiarity and obscurity.[58] Why was John Fletcher considered Wesley's 'designated successor',[59] even by John Wesley himself? John Wesley was critical of Fletcher's inability to discipline his own parish, so how might he exercise the iron control which Wesley asserted over his societies? Among the factors usually cited (Fletcher's doctrinal position, his acknowledged

saintliness and Anglican ordination), the question of Charles Wesley's influence has not entered the discussion. However, the extent to which Charles
may have had a hand in this is a question worth careful consideration and one
that may shed some light on an otherwise rather dimly lit corner of Methodist
history. What we do know is that Charles Wesley wrote to Walter Sellon on
26 June 1774 stating that he hoped Fletcher would succeed his brother.[60] As
has already become clear, this was a time of real crisis about the future of
the movement. Not surprisingly, then, Charles' priority was clear: Methodism
should absolutely remain within the established Church and whoever was to
lead the Methodist people must of necessity be an ordained clergyman. But
by 1774 such men were hard to find. Most had sided with the Calvinists and
were hence alienated from Wesley. To whom, then, might Charles turn?

Among eligible evangelical clergy, Fletcher was undoubtedly pre-eminent.
Sympathetic older candidates like Sellon or Perronet were tied to parishes;
the minute trickle of younger clergy still under Wesley's influence – such as
Thomas Coke – were too inexperienced. Fletcher had demonstrated his experience, energy and intellectual powers as well as his support for Wesley. And,
although Fletcher was in a parish, John Wesley had consistently attempted since
1760 to seduce him away from it, perhaps reflecting a longer-term strategy.

If Charles Wesley had not made the suggestion, he was strongly supportive of it. Wesley's 1773 letter was probably written from Shoreham following a consultation with Vincent Perronet, the 'Archbishop of the Methodists'.
Charles was probably present and possibly argued for his erstwhile protégé,
although this remains (not unreasonable) speculation in the absence of any
hard evidence. If he did argue thus, it might well explain John Wesley's unlikely choice and, given Fletcher's reluctance, the discernible distancing between
him and Charles thereafter. As is noted below, in 1785 Charles stated very
directly that he wanted John Fletcher and his wife to 'gather up the wreck'
after his and his brother's deaths.[61]

Both the succession question and the Calvinistic controversy of the early
1770s were domestic diversions which masked a more far-reaching international crisis: unrest in the American colonies. By the time the crisis broke
in 1775 Fletcher's relationship with the Wesleys had altered loyalties. In 1774
Fletcher apparently considered seriously a suggestion by Lord Dartmouth,
Secretary for the Colonies, of preferment, possibly in North America, of which
the Wesleys knew nothing. This may be further indication of Fletcher's cooled
friendship with Charles Wesley, a relationship under the terms of which
Fletcher had once promised to take no serious step without consulting him.[62]

As the American situation became increasingly volatile, Fletcher, who was
(as he declared) a republican by birth and upbringing but a constitutional
monarchist by adoption,[63] declared his unequivocal loyalist position on the
issue. His unashamedly pro-government 1776 publication, the *Vindication of
Mr Wesley's Calm Address*, submitted to Lord Dartmouth for approbation, was
followed by *American Patriotism Farther Confronted* and *The Bible and the Sword*.
It seems anomalous that in a later generation the author of such vehement
anti-republicanism would become so revered in American Methodism since
American independence provided a springboard for vigorous and substantial
transatlantic expansion of the Methodist community.

CHARLES WESLEY AND JOHN FLETCHER

Charles Wesley's position on America was equivocal. Forty years before, he had witnessed anti-government murmurings in Boston. While he empathized with the rebels' case, his instincts, reason and beliefs supported responsible and representative rule through king in parliament. On this issue there was little to divide Charles from his brother: in fact John underwent a *volte-face* on America, drawing him closer to Charles' position. However, Fletcher's stance seems more firmly pro-government, viewing both royal and parliamentary authority as unquestionably divine and to be unquestioningly obeyed.

Whatever his public sentiments, in the face of political realism John Wesley moved to a pragmatic accommodation of the outcome of the American revolution, addressing both the pastoral needs of the new nation and the missionary opportunities it offered. This course led inexorably to the most serious split between him and his brother, over the spurious 1784 ordinations for America in the face of Anglican obduracy about ecclesiastical provision for the former colonies. John Fletcher's attitude is unclear; but he did not voice opposition and at Wesley's 1784 Conference he characteristically played the part of peacemaker.[64]

Charles Wesley probably became suspicious of American intentions, advising Fletcher 'With the poetry of yr. Poem on the Peace I can find no fault. Concerning the Peace itself, yr. information was very imperfect.'[65] Evidently Fletcher offered some defence, to which Charles riposted: 'You think I know nothing about the Peace; I think you know nothing about it yet I wish your Poem good sale.'[66] He warned Fletcher, 'Be not too sanguine for the American Methodists',[67] and cautioned him against their 'prelatical spirit', which he feared would spread to British Methodism, adding further 'I fear the Fanatical Spirit also. I cannot explain this, in writing.'[68]

This letter was to be the last Charles wrote to his friend, for Fletcher died suddenly in August 1785 having contracted typhoid while sick visiting in the parish. Since Fletcher's marriage in November 1781, Charles had habitually written to both John and Mary Fletcher. Mrs Fletcher, as Mary Bosanquet, had been something of a Methodist personage in her own right, forming and leading her Christian communities first in Leytonstone in Essex and then at Cross Hall in Yorkshire. Certainly she is now considered to have been the most significant woman preacher to have John Wesley's imprimatur. As Fletcher's widow she maintained his ministry in Madeley parish for 30 years, until her own death in 1815.[69]

In this last letter, too, having written to each individually, Charles Wesley penned a section to them both. Anticipating that they would long outlive him and his brother, he made the extraordinary proposal that John and Mary Fletcher form a husband and wife consortium to lead the Methodists:

I trust you are reserved (after mine and my B[rother]'s departure) to gather up the Wreck. Be sure, the Sheep will be scatter'd . . . Methodism will be broken into 1000 pieces.
. . . You must stand still & see – the Design & the Salvation of God.[70]

This at least strengthens the suggestion that Charles was behind his brother's proposal 12 years previously that he be named as his heir

As Charles Wesley's friendship embraced Mary Fletcher, so John Fletcher was drawn into Charles' family circle. As Charles was open with his friendships, so he was open with his family. Virtually every letter of Fletcher's concludes with greetings to Sarah Wesley, 'your very dear wife',[71] who was virtually Fletcher's contemporary. Charles Wesley made him godfather to his two daughters Sarah and Susanna, ('Sally' and 'Suky'). While Suky died in 1762 at 11 months, Sarah lived long, although in 1785 her father pessimistically wrote to Fletcher, 'Happy w[oul]d Sally be to die like her God sister. I am not without hope she will live to be a Xtian.'[72] In fact young Sally turned out to be a gifted and vivacious young lady: both her Uncle John and Samuel Johnson delighted in her company. Unmarried, she lived with her bachelor brother Charles until their deaths in the 1820s. How she appreciated her evangelical godfather is unknown. If she did not share his faith she probably respected his care and attention in her early years.

Just as Charles Wesley enjoyed the warmth of his family circle, so too did he enjoy the warmth of a wider circle of friendship. John Fletcher was just one among many, mostly evangelical, clergy, whom Charles Wesley numbered as friends, and many of whom made their mark on the social and religious life of their time. Among friends from university, John Gambold became a Moravian bishop, and George Whitefield developed an extraordinary transatlantic evangelistic influence. Others were parish clergy who to a greater or lesser extent allied themselves to the Methodist movement. Pre-eminent was Vincent Perronet: not merely a friend but trusted and wise adviser who died only a few months before Fletcher in 1785. Howel Harris, the leading evangelical in Wales, and Martin Madan, the Bishop of Peterborough's brother and chaplain to the Lock Hospital, were among others. Indeed, Charles Wesley's letters to his wife read as a catalogue not only of evangelical activity but of life among people he knew and trusted and loved. These are clergy and laity; family and associates; those from musical and literary circles. Among evangelical aristocracy were Lord Dartmouth and Lady Huntingdon. Unlike his brother, Charles did not spurn 'the quality'; Lord Mornington was a relative, and members of the Gwynne family were well established in society. With his old school friend Lord Mansfield, now Lord Chief Justice of England, he was able to use his influence 50 years on in the case of two escaped slaves.

In August 1785 Sarah Wesley was in London and wrote to Charles, who was in Bristol, with the news that John Fletcher was dead.[73] A generation younger, it must have come as a sad blow to Charles Wesley who pinned great hope for the future of the Methodist people on men like Fletcher. Yet Sarah included it among several items of news, as if it was of lesser interest. This suggests, again, that the friendship between these two men had faded and also that it may anyway have been a more significant relationship for Fletcher than it was for Charles. It would also have been another reminder of mortality for Charles Wesley, who was himself approaching 80 and feeling the infirmities of age and the concurrent demise of friends. In the event Charles lived nearly three more years, being carried to his grave by eight fellow clergymen of the Church of England.

## Notes

1 Tyson, *Charles Wesley*, 8.

2 P. Langford, *Englishness Identified* (Oxford: Oxford University Press, 2000), 249.

3 John Fletcher to William Perronet, 2 December 1779 (MARC, Fletcher fol., 55).

4 See M. Cohen, 'Manliness, Effeminacy and the French: Gender and the Construction of National Character in Eighteenth-Century England', in T. Hitchcock and M. Cohen, eds, *English Masculinities* (London: Longman, 1999), 46ff.

5 For recent treatments, see particularly P. Streiff, *Reluctant Saint* (Peterborough: Epworth Press, 2001 [an English translation of his *Jean Guillaume de la Fléchère/ John William Fletcher; Ein Beitrag zur Geschichte des Methodismus* (Frankfurt: Lang, 1984]) and P. Forsaith, 'The Correspondence of Rev John Fletcher with Rev Charles Wesley' (unpublished PhD thesis, Oxford Brookes University, 2003). Older biographies, such as by J. Wesley, *A Short Account of the Life and Death of the Rev John Fletcher* (London, 1786) and L. Tyerman, *Wesley's Designated Successor* (London: Hodder, 1882) are to be treated with caution, although J. Benson, *The Life of the Rev John de la Flechere* (London, 1806) is generally sound.

6 CW–JW, quoted in Newport, *Sermons*, 25.

7 John Wesley to Lady Maxwell, 8 February 1772, (in Telford, J. ed., *Letters of John Wesley* (8 vols, London: Epworth, 1931) (hereafter *JWL*), v: 304.

8 For Fletcher's ordinations see W. R. Davies, 'John Fletcher's Georgian Ordinations and Madeley Curacy', in *PWHS*, xxxvi/3 (1968), 139–42. Even given any laxity in the eighteenth-century national Church it is difficult to understand how Fletcher obtained orders, for he was neither a university graduate nor naturalized English. Further, his Methodistical enthusiasm must have shouted to anyone with a passing acquaintance and would have been little recommendation to any bishop; James Beauclerk, Bishop of Hereford, in whose diocese was Madeley parish, was noted as being particularly diligent. Thomas Hill MP, Fletcher's employer and sponsor/patron through whom ordination was procured, must have carried a great deal of influence.

9 A comprehensive calendar of Fletcher's correspondence is in Streiff, *Reluctant Saint*, but see also Forsaith, 'Correspondence'. The majority of the letters are at MARC.

10 John Fletcher to Charles Wesley, 10 May 1757 (MARC, Fletcher, Fol. 65); see also *PWHS*, 33 (1961/2), 25.

11 Streiff, *Reluctant Saint*, 3 ff.

12 B. Coulton in 'Tutor to the Hills: The Early Career of John Fletcher', in *PWHS*, 47 (3), (1989), 97.

13 John Fletcher to Charles Wesley, 10 May 1757 (MARC, Fletcher, Fol. 65); see also *PWHS*, 33 (1961/2), 25.

14 John Fletcher to Charles Wesley, 10 May 1757 (MARC, Fletcher, Fol. 65); see also *PWHS*, 33 (1961/2), 25.

15 John Fletcher to Charles Wesley, 10 May 1757 (MARC, Fletcher, Fol. 65); see also *PWHS*, 33 (1961/2), 25.

16 John Fletcher to Charles Wesley, 15 November 1759 (MARC, Fletcher, Fol. 6): 'Je suis si assuré de votre salut, que je ne demande point d'autre place dans le Ciel que celle que je pourai y avoir à vos pieds: Je doute meme si le Paradis seroit un Paradis sans vous pour le partager avec moi: & la seule idée que votre question

m'a fait naitre qu'un jour nous pourions etre separés me serre le cœur & baigne mes yeux de larmes.' Hereafter, where original texts are in French, the original will be given in footnotes.

17  Cohen, *English Masculinities*, 55–7.

18  John Fletcher to Charles Wesley, 4 September 1759 (MARC, Fletcher, Fol. 4), 'j'attens une Reponse en François'.

19  See Forsaith, 'Correspondence', 297ff.

20  John Fletcher to Charles Wesley, April 1759 (MARC, Fletcher, Fol. 58). Charles Wesley's French New Testament survives (MARC, MAW/CW 274).

21  John Fletcher to Charles Wesley, 19 December 1782 (Drew University, NJ: Fletcher papers, 1306–5–3.01).

22  Lewis Namier, *The Structure of Politics at the Accession of George III* (London: Macmillan, 1957), 235ff.

23  Forsaith, 'Correspondence', 241–2.

24  J. Nuelsen, *Jean Guillaume de la Flechere; der erste Schweizerische Methodist* (Zürich: 1929), 11.

25  John Fletcher to Lady Huntingdon, 28 October 1760, quoted in Tyerman, *Wesley's Designated Successor*, 58.

26  John Fletcher to Charles Wesley, 26 December 1759 (MARC, Fletcher, Fol. 2).

27  Charles Wesley to John Fletcher, 12 September 1776 (MARC, DDCW, 1/66).

28  John Fletcher to Charles Wesley, 12 October 1761; 1759 (MARC, Fletcher, Fol. 84); Charles Wesley to Sarah Wesley, 27 July 1766 (MARC, DDCW, 5/99).

29  See Forsaith, 'Correspondence', 233–4.

30  J. Ireland to Mary Fletcher, 6 November 1785 (MARC, MAM, Fl.4/1/14).

31  Lady Huntingdon to Charles Wesley, 8 June 1771 (MARC, DDWES, 1: Wesley Family Letters & Papers, fol. 4.24).

32  J. C. Ryle, *Christian Leaders of the 18th Century* (London, 1885), 386 states 'Mistaken, as I think he was, on some points . . . He was a man of rare grace . . .'.

33  B. Trinder, *The Industrial Revolution in Shropshire* (Chichester: Phillimore, 1973), 267.

34  Wesley, *Life and Death of the Rev. John Fletcher*.

35  Wesley, *Life and Death of the Rev. John Fletcher*; JW–CW, 6 April 1786 (in *JWL*, vii, 323–4).

36  John Fletcher to Charles Wesley, 15/22 January 1760 (MARC, Fletcher, Fol. 63) (Votre frere parut fache . . . il dit qu'il aimeroit mieux en paier la rente pour rien plutot que me vour perdu *parmi les riches*: 'Your brother seemed vexed . . . he said he would rather pay the rent for nothing than see me lost among the rich'.).

37  JW – 'A Friend', May 1763 (in *JWL*, iv: 211).

38  See G. Lloyd, '"A Cloud of Perfect Witnesses": John Wesley and the London Disturbances 1760–1763', *The Asbury Theological Journal*, 56/2, 57/1 (2001–2), 116–36.

39  Fletcher's letters to Charles Wesley of 1762 especially support this.

40  'Je ne suis pas un home a parti', JF–CW, 20 Sepember 1762 (MARC, Fletcher, Fol. 1).

41  'J'ai perdu l'Esperance de voir une reunion publique entre votre frere & M-d. Ils ne sont pas faits l'un pour l'autre.' John Fletcher to Charles Wesley, 8 August 1765 (MARC, Fletcher, Fol. 29).

42  John Fletcher to Charles Wesley, 22 August 1764 (MARC, Fletcher, Fol. 86).

43  John Fletcher to Charles Wesley, 14 May 1768 (in *JWL*, v, 88).

44  'Les eaux de l'Ocean et de la Méditerranéen'ont pas éteient mon éteincelle

d'amour fraternal pour vous, J'ai grande envie de vous voir pour mentretenir avec vous sur les mysteres du Roiaume des Cieux.' JF–CW, 10 August 1770 (MARC, Fletcher, Fol. 33).

45 John Fletcher to Charles Wesley, 13 October 1771 (Woodruff Library, Emory University: John Wesley papers, Box 2).

46 See Streiff, *Reluctant Saint*; and Rack, *Reasonable Enthusiast*.

47 See Rack, *Reasonable Enthusiast*, 200–2.

48 Rack, *Reasonable Enthusiast*, 457.

49 John Fletcher to Charles Wesley 21 September 1771 (MARC, Fletcher, Fol. 37).

50 John Fletcher to Charles Wesley, 16 January 1773 (MARC, Fletcher, Fol. 46).

51 John Fletcher to Charles Wesley, 31 May 1772 (MARC, Fletcher, Fol. 44).

52 John Fletcher to Charles Wesley, 20 April 1773 (MARC, Fletcher, Fol. 87).

53 John Fletcher to Charles Wesley, 12 September 1776 (MARC, DDCW, 1/66).

54 John Fletcher to Charles Wesley, 2 July 1775 (John Wesley's Chapel, 'The New Room', Bristol).

55 John Fletcher to Charles Wesley, 8 August 1775 (MARC, Fletcher Fol. 52).

56 John Fletcher to Charles Wesley, 2 July 1775 (MARC, Fletcher Fol. 52).

57 John Fletcher to John Wesley, 9 January 1776 (MARC, Fletcher Fol. 103).

58 R. Southey, *The Life of John Wesley: And the Rise and Progress of Methodism* (London: Longman, 1820), chapter xxx.

59 Hence the title of of Tyerman's work, *Wesley's Designated Successor*.

60 Charles Wesley to W Sellon, 26 June 1774 (MARC, Everett–Tyerman volumes, 2:15).

61 John Fletcher to Charles Wesley, 21 June 1785 (MARC, DDCW, 1/75).

62 John Fletcher to Charles Wesley, 26 December 1763 (MARC, Fletcher 36.1).

63 Streiff, *Reluctant Saint*, 190.

64 John S. Stamp, 'Memoir of the Rev. Charles Atmore', in *Wesleyan Methodist Magazine*, 1845, 14–15.

65 John Fletcher to Charles Wesley, 21 May 1785 (Wesley's Chapel, London, LDWMM 1992/403); J. Fletcher, *Essai sur le paix de 1783* (London, 1784).

66 John Fletcher to Charles Wesley, 21 June 1785 (MARC, DDCW, 1/75).

67 John Fletcher to Charles Wesley, 21 June 1785 (MARC, DDCW, 1/75)

68 Charles Wesley to John Fletcher, 21 June 1785 (MARC, DDCW, 1/75).

69 See H. Moore, *The Life of Mrs Mary Fletcher* (Birmingham: J. Peart, 1817).

70 Charles Wesley to John Fletcher, 21 June 1785 (MARC, DDCW, 1/75).

71 'Votre très chere epouse.'

72 Charles Wesley to John Fletcher, 21 June 1785 (MARC, DDCW, 1/75).

73 Sarah Wesley to Charles Wesley, 18 August 1785 (MARC, DDCW, 6/42).

# 8. Charles Wesley and his Children[1]

## PHILIP OLLESON

The family life of Charles Wesley has not always received its due share of attention from his biographers, who have understandably concentrated their attentions on the more public aspects of his ministry.[2] Yet the domestic sphere assumed for Charles an importance that it never had for his brother John, and any biographical study needs to take account of this important area of his life, and his relationships with the members of his family circle: his wife Sarah (1726–1822), his daughter Sally (1759–1828),[3] and his sons Charles (1757–1834) and Samuel (1766–1837).[4] In this chapter I focus on Charles Wesley's attitudes to family life and his relationships with his children, drawing on the evidence of his journals, letters and poetry, on unpublished family papers, and on contemporary testimony.[5]

When confronted with information from such sources, one of the biographer's first concerns is with context: the extent to which the picture of family life and parental attitudes that emerges is typical of its time and the position in society of those involved. Accordingly, I begin by considering prevalent attitudes to the education and upbringing of children in eighteenth-century England, and in particular those attitudes prevalent within Methodism. I go on to examine the childhood and early upbringing of the Wesley children. From the point of view both of parents and of children the evidence here is uneven, favouring Charles and his sons at the expense of his wife Sarah and his daughter Sally, and written in terms of the activities of the children rather than the attitudes of the parents. There is remarkably little on the contribution of Sarah Wesley, but in the light of what we know about the general harmony of their marriage, we can only assume that she shared Charles' views and attitudes. As far as the children are concerned, most of the main sources of information relate to Charles and Samuel, on account of their celebrity as musical child prodigies. Regrettably, there is less on Sally, who, lacking the outstanding musical abilities of her brothers, was less in the public eye and attracted correspondingly less attention.

During his last decade, the most significant events in Charles' family life were his dealings with Samuel, at the time going through a troubled adolescence and early adulthood. Of the three Wesley children, Samuel was the most musically gifted; he also comprehensively rejected the values of his family and of Methodism, to the sorrow of the family and the scandal of the entire Methodist community. Most of Samuel's later life was after Charles' death, and is thus not of direct relevance here. But his involvement with and conversion to Roman Catholicism and his long-standing love affair with Charlotte Louisa Martin both date from Charles' final decade, and I consider them here as important and highly stressful features of his final years.

## Contexts: attitudes towards education and child-rearing

Despite a large amount of concentrated and detailed attention over the last forty years or so, the history of childhood still remains a controversial subject, to the extent that there is little agreement even on the broadest outlines of how relationships between parents and children have changed over time.[6] Many historians, however, would identify a move in the late seventeenth century to a more liberal set of attitudes to children and their education from views that had been prevalent earlier. These new attitudes were articulated by John Locke in *Some Thoughts Concerning Education* (1693), a work of immense influence on thinking on education for much of the eighteenth century.[7] The dominant attitude of seventeenth-century parents to children had been, in the words of J. H. Plumb, 'autocratic, indeed ferocious':[8] unquestioning obedience was expected of children, and infringements of discipline were met by harsh punishments. The new, more liberal attitude stressed the importance of gentler approaches: a series of rewards and punishments appealing to children's developing reason, by which they would be brought up as useful and accomplished members of society. Although both approaches can be seen in eighteenth-century educational thought, the more modern approach became increasingly the dominant one.

The two approaches have separate religious and theological pedigrees. The earlier model is Calvinistic and stresses the essentially evil nature of the child, acquired through original sin: in the words of Richard Allestree in 1658, 'the new-born babe is full of the stains and pollutions of sin which it inherits from our first parents through our loins'.[9] By contrast, the later model stresses the essential goodness and innocence of the child and the belief that with appropriate education and parental guidance he or she will prevail over the forces of evil. Theological underpinning for this view, which likens the child to Adam before the Fall, can be found as early as 1628 in John Earle's *Microcosmographie*: 'A child is a man in a small letter, yet the best copy of Adam before he tasted of Eve or the apple . . . He is purely happy, because he knows no evil.'[10] This stress on the innocence of the child was to become more prominent in the eighteenth century, and was in one guise or another to be central to many Romantic attitudes to children and childhood.

The most striking feature of the new attitude to children is the emphasis laid on the rationality of the child, and indeed on the rationality of the whole enterprise of child-rearing. As Locke says, expressing a point of view clearly novel at the time:

It will perhaps be wondered that I mention *Reasoning* with Children: And yet I cannot but think that the true Way of dealing with them. They understand it as early as they do Language; and, if I mis-observe not, they love to be treated as Rational Creatures sooner than is imagined.[11]

However, it is the earlier, harsher, approach which is to be seen in the methods employed by Susanna Wesley, the mother of Charles and John, and set down in a celebrated letter of 24 July 1732 to John Wesley. Foremost among the 'principal rules' she observed was that of 'conquering the will' of her children:

> I insist upon conquering the will of children betimes, because this is the only strong and rational foundation of a religious education, without which both precept and example will be ineffectual. But when this is thoroughly done, then a child is capable of being governed by the reason and piety of its parents, till its own understanding comes to maturity, and the principles of religion have taken root in the mind.[12]

The necessity of breaking the will of children was to attain the force of dogma in Methodist theories of the upbringing of children. The usual theological justification was the one given by Susanna: that children should learn to subjugate their own desires to those of their parents in preparation for the adult Christian life, in which they would subjugate their desires to the will of God:

> As self-will is the root of all sin and misery, so whatever cherishes this in children ensures their after-wretchedness and irreligion; whatever checks and mortifies it promotes their future happiness and piety. This is still more evident if we farther consider that religion is nothing else than the doing the will of God, and not our own; that, the one grand impediment to our temporal and eternal happiness being this self-will, no indulgences of it can be trivial, no denial unprofitable. Heaven or hell depends on this alone. So that the parent who studies to subject it in his child works together with God in the renewing and saving a soul. The parent who indulges it does the devil's work, makes religion impracticable, salvation unattainable; and does all that in him lies to damn his child, soul and body, for ever.[13]

The influence of Susanna's views and the experience of his own upbringing is apparent in the educational thought of John Wesley.[14] In the curriculum and rules for Kingswood School (1749), he combines Susanna's principles with elements of the Moravian educational practice that he had observed at Herrnhut.[15] The resulting regime was one of monastic severity: the only activities in the curriculum were lessons, prayer, walking and working, either in the garden or indoors, and the children were under constant adult supervision. No provision was made for relaxation, and play was specifically excluded: 'As we have no play-days (the School being taught every day in the year but Sunday) so neither do we allow any time for play on any day. He that plays when he is a child, will play when he is a man.'[16]

John Wesley's views on education and the upbringing of children showed no signs of relaxation as he grew older, and essentially the same principles are reiterated in his sermons of the 1780s on the subject.[17]

## Charles Wesley and his family

In his views on child-rearing and education, as in so many other matters, Charles Wesley differed markedly from his elder brother. The more extreme attitudes of John are characterized by a failure to understand the psychology of the child, and are of a harshness and austerity which would find few supporters today; Charles, on the other hand, is a figure whom modern readers can understand and with whom they can identify more easily. Hymns, poems and letters all attest to his deep love for his children and his involvement with them: his anxiety when any of them were ill, his grief at the death of those who died in infancy, the care he took over their upbringing, his delight at their successes, and his disappointment when any of them failed to measure up to his high standards of behaviour.

Charles had come to marriage and fatherhood late: he was 41 when he married and 44 at the time of the birth of his firstborn John, who lived for only 18 months. At the time of the birth of Charles, the eldest child to survive to adulthood, he was 49; at the birth of Samuel, the youngest, he was 58. Nonetheless, he seems to have made every effort to understand his children, to enter into their world and to bring them up in the way most appropriate to their personalities and talents. Some aspects of his approach – notably his seriousness, his insistence on discipline and his tendency to assume adult understanding on the part of his children – reflect orthodox Methodist thinking. But in other respects he is far more liberal. As his nursery verse shows, he was not unremittingly serious with his children, and had a well-developed, if rather ponderous, sense of fun. He also recognized the important role of play in children's lives, and we know from family correspondence that Samuel, at least, was allowed to keep a small menagerie of pets and to indulge in kite-flying and other boyish activities.[18] But friendships with other children were not encouraged: an undated letter from Charles to Sarah warns against the children having friends of their own age on the grounds that 'children are corruptors of each other'.[19] Significantly, too, and presumably for the same reasons, Charles and Samuel were educated at home.

## Charles and Samuel: musical child prodigies

It is largely because of the fame of Charles junior and Samuel as musical child prodigies that we know so much about their early lives. From an account by Charles given to the lawyer and antiquary Daines Barrington we learn of the young Charles playing a tune on the harpsichord 'readily, and in just time' at the age of nearly three, after which he was able readily to reproduce what his mother sang or what he heard on the streets.[20] Samuel's musical gifts were apparent at almost the same age: according to his father he taught himself to read from Handel's oratorio *Samson*, and at the age of five 'had all the airs, recitatives, and choruses of *Samson* and the *Messiah*: both words and notes by heart'. At around the same time he was said to have composed in his head the airs of his oratorio *Ruth*, which he was not, however, able to write down until he was eight.

From these and many other similar anecdotes it is clear that as musical child prodigies Charles and Samuel were among the most precocious of all time. In consequence, their childhood and upbringing was very different from that of other children. As prodigies, they were the objects of widespread adult attention, and were frequently called on to display their accomplishments to visitors to the family home and on their own visits to family and friends, although Charles Wesley senior took care not to exhibit them in public. This early involvement with the adult world inevitably continued as they grew older and as their musical education progressed.

The attitude of Charles to his sons' musical talents was ambivalent. As a music-lover himself, he was naturally delighted that his children were gifted musicians, and keen that they should develop their talents to their full extent: a view that of course had scriptural backing. At the same time, he would have soon become aware of some less welcome consequences of his children's childhood celebrity: they received a degree of attention and adulation from adults that would not always have been welcome or desirable, and they inevitably missed out on many of the features of a more normal childhood.

Such problems, of course, face the parents of child prodigies in any age, and whatever their religious beliefs and backgrounds. In the case of the Wesleys, they were exacerbated by Charles' prominent position within Methodism and by some deep-seated Methodist suspicions about music, forcibly articulated by John Wesley in his treatise *On the Power of Music*.[21] While prepared to admit the value of certain narrowly defined types of music in the context of worship, John Wesley was deeply distrustful of its sensual appeal and its association with worldly pleasures, in particular with dancing and the theatre. For many Methodists, as for John, the profession of music was not consistent with a godly life. In addition, Charles would have been uncomfortably aware that there were many within the Methodist community who were already disposed to criticize him for what they saw as his worldly style of life. John Fletcher voiced what was presumably a widely felt concern when he wrote:

> You have your *enemies*, as well as your brother, they complain of your *love for musick, company, fine people, great folks*, and of the *want of your former zeal and frugality*. I need not put you in mind to cut off *sinful appearances*.[22]

To another critic, a Methodist lady who objected to the 11-year-old Charles junior playing in concerts, Charles replied with more than a hint of weary resignation as well as of defensiveness:

> I always designed my son for a clergyman. Nature has marked him for a musician: which appeared from his earliest infancy. My friends advised me not to cross his inclination. Indeed I could not if I would. There is no way of hindering his being a musician but cutting off his fingers.[23]

This went to the heart of the problem: as Charles stated, the musical development of Charles junior, and later of Samuel, had much of the character of a force of nature, and was well-nigh unstoppable. In the face of such outstanding musical talents, it would have been a doctrinaire father indeed who would not have wished to see them developed to their fullest extent. And there is no doubt that Charles, when he had overcome his initial bewilderment at finding himself the father of not one but two musical child prodigies, came to be inordinately proud of his sons' musical accomplishments. A turning point occurred in August 1769, when Charles and the 11-year-old Charles junior were taken by William Bromfield, a prominent surgeon and family friend, to see the famous harpsichordist Joseph Kelway (c. 1702–82). Kelway, who usually refused to take on pupils, was so impressed with Charles junior's playing that he offered on the spot to teach him free of charge, and did so for the next two years. The interest shown by a musician as distinguished as Kelway seems to have been enough to convince Charles of the truly extraordinary nature of Charles junior's talents, and to lay his doubts to rest. For the next 12 months, Charles kept a detailed journal of Charles junior's twice-weekly lessons, noting down Kelway's repeated expressions of delight at his son's accomplishments.[24] The following, written on 25 September 1769, is characteristic:

To me Mr K —— said, 'You must take great delight in this boy. I am sure he is of a sweet disposition. His very soul is harmony.' 'All that I can say of him', said I, 'is that you hear him uncorrupted.' 'Uncorrupted!' answered he, 'he is purity itself. He is a miracle!' To him, 'You will not be vain my dear, it is a divine gift; and I hope you will make a proper use of it.'

While he went on playing Mr K —— said, 'He teaches me my own music.' To him, 'My dear boy, I will do for you all in my power, first for Mr Bromfield's sake, then for your sake, and my own. I am better pleased to teach you for nothing than if I had ever so much money with you.'

Criticisms of Charles similar to those in the letter from John Fletcher quoted above were later expressed by such nineteenth-century writers as Thomas Jackson and George Stevenson, both of whom had their own reasons for voicing their retrospective concern. Writing long after the event, they were confronted with the fact that in their later lives both Samuel and Charles junior had departed far from Methodism. The behaviour of Samuel, in particular, was of an extravagant rebelliousness that was a considerable embarrassment to the Methodist community and was badly in need of interpretation and explanation. A convenient and plausible place in which to look was in the children's childhood and upbringing. In the opinion of Jackson, for example, much of Samuel's behaviour stemmed from his father's imprudent handling of his celebrity status as a child prodigy. Another factor was the supposedly malign influence of Samuel's godfather Martin Madan (1725–90), the chaplain of the Lock Hospital and himself an accomplished musician, with whom the young Samuel spent a good deal of time in his childhood:

When the boy displayed his early powers as a musician, this Clergyman carried him from place to place, among his friends, as a sort of prodigy. The child, though very young, was sensible and observant. He therefore felt that he was degraded, and conceived a prejudice against his father for suffering him to be thus exhibited as a boyish wonder. This to him was an essential injury, and the beginning of that downward course which he afterwards bitterly lamented. From this time he was indisposed to pay a just deference to his father's judgment; and he lost that tender filial affection which, had it been cherished in all its power, would have operated as a restraint upon his passions, and have kept him in the way of receiving spiritual good.[25]

It is impossible to adjudicate on the accuracy of Jackson's comments, but they are of value as being characteristic of explanations of Samuel's behaviour offered at the time and for some time afterwards. In the case of his identification of Madan as a bad influence on Samuel, his judgement was no doubt affected by hindsight, for Madan was later to achieve notoriety following the publication of his controversial treatise *Thelyphthora* in 1780.[26]

Comparatively little is known about the formal education of the three children, but it is clear that Charles took a strong personal interest in their education and general welfare. This was often from a distance, particularly early in the children's lives, when he spent a good deal of time in London, away from the family home in Bristol. In August 1766, for example, when Charles was eight, Sally seven, and Samuel six months, we find him writing from London to say that he was looking forward on his return home to seeing Samuel's first teeth, to hearing Sally and Charles read, and to hearing Charles' latest music lesson.[27] In early 1771 Charles acquired the house in Chesterfield Street, Marylebone, that was to remain the family home until well after his death. For a while, the rest of the family divided its time between Bristol and London, but in 1778 they gave up the Bristol house and lived full time in London.

In accordance with modern views on the rationality of children, Charles treated his own children as adults from an early age. In March 1773, for example, he wrote to the seven-year-old Samuel:

Come now, my good friend Samuel, and let us reason together. God made you for Himself, that is to be ever happy with Him. Ought you not, therefore, to serve and love Him? But you can do neither unless He gives you the power. Ask, (He says Himself) and it shall be given you. That is, pray Him to make you love Him: and pray for it every night and morning in your own words, as well as in those which have been taught you. You have been used to say your prayers in the sight of others. Henceforth, go into a corner by yourself, where no eye but God's may see you. There pray to your heavenly Father who seeth in secret: and be sure He hears every word you speak, and sees everything you do, at all times, and in all places.

You should now begin to live by reason and religion. There should be sense even in your play and diversions. Therefore I have furnished you with maps and books and harpsichord. Every day get something by heart: whatever your mother recommends. Every day read one or more chapters in the Bible. I suppose your mother will take you now in the place of your brother, to be her chaplain, to read the psalms and lessons, when your sister does not . . .

Foolish people are too apt to praise you. If they see anything good in you they should praise God, not you, for it. As for music, it is neither good nor bad in itself. You have a natural inclination to it: but God gave you that: therefore God only should be thanked and praised for it. Your brother has

the same love of music much more than you, yet he is not proud or vain of it. Neither, I trust, will you be. You will send me a long letter of answer, and always look on me both as your loving father, and your friend,
C. Wesley[28]

There can be no doubt that Charles combined his love for his children and concern for their welfare with an occasionally stern and severe manner that they may on occasion have found off-putting and even intimidating. As can be seen in the letter to Samuel above, he did not hesitate to take them to task for their behaviour when it fell short of his expectations. It is not known what piece of boyish misbehaviour occasioned this letter, but there are other examples of much the same tone in letters to Sally and Charles. In a letter to Sally of 1777, in connection with a fall that Sally had experienced, he states:

[I] rejoice that you have soon recovered your fall. If it was occasioned by the narrow fashionable heels, I think it will be a warning to you, and reduce you to reason. Providence saved you from a like accident at Guildford. Beware the third time![29]

Charles also took care to encourage his children's literary and scholarly activities, albeit in terms that may have done little to increase their self-confidence. For example, Samuel received a good grounding in Latin and Greek, and at one stage in his teens had aspirations to be a Classical scholar. Charles, however, pointed out to him that he was not prepared to put in the necessary effort to make this a reality. This may have been kindly meant and intended as a blunt piece of fatherly plain speaking, but it probably did nothing to encourage Samuel.[30] It seems likely that Charles was aware of this trait, however: in 1777 he offered to assist the 18-year-old Sally in her studies, stating:

I think you may avail yourself of my small knowledge of books and poetry. I am not yet too old to assist you a little in your reading, and perhaps improve your taste in versifying. You need not dread my severity. I have a laudable partiality for my own children. Witness your brothers, whom I do not love a jot better than you, only be you as ready to show me your verses as they their music.
The evenings I have set aside for reading with you and them. We should begin with history. A plan or order of study is absolutely necessary. Without that, the more you read, the more you are confused, and never rise above a smatterer in learning.[31]

## The family concerts, 1779–87

It is likely that a large part of Charles' decision to move from Bristol to London in 1771 stemmed from a desire to provide his children with the best possible educational and (in the case of Charles and Samuel) musical opportunities. In London, the two boys would have all the musical opportunities they needed; at the same time, Charles would be able to keep their activities under supervision and control, and make sure they did not fall into bad company and bad habits. One result was the celebrated series of private subscription concerts at the family home in Chesterfield Street, which ran for nine seasons from 1779 to 1787 and attracted fashionable audiences and a good deal of publicity.[32] Predictably, the concerts gave rise to some controversy and strong criticism from within the Methodist community, including the following from Thomas Coke:

> I looked upon the Concerts which he allows his sons to have in his own house, to be highly dishonourable to God; and himself to be criminal, by reason of his situation in the Church of Christ: but on mature consideration of all the circumstances appertaining to them, I cannot now blame him.[33]

In the face of such remarks, Charles Wesley felt obliged to give a justification of his actions, and in early 1779 set out his 'reasons for letting my sons have a concert at home':

1. To keep them out of harm's way: the way (I mean) of bad music and bad musicians who by a free communication with them might corrupt both their taste and their morals.
2. That my sons may have a safe and honourable opportunity of availing themselves of their musical abilities, which have cost me several hundred pounds.
3. That they may enjoy their full right of private judgment, and likewise their independency; both of which must be given up if they swim with the stream and follow the multitude.
4. To improve their play and their skill in composing: as they must themselves furnish the principal music of every concert, although they do not call their musical entertainment a concert. It is too great a word. They do not presume to rival the *present great masters* who excel in the variety of their accompaniments. All they aim at in their concert music is *exactness*.[34]

He subsequently declared in a letter to his brother John his conviction that he was 'clear without a doubt that my sons' Concert is after the will and order of Providence'. John disagreed, adding in a footnote when he published the letter in the *Arminian Magazine* that he was '"clear" of another mind'.[35]

## The family in the 1780s

It was during the period of the family concerts that the first signs of major problems in the Wesley family started to become apparent. By this time Charles junior and Sally were of adult years, although continuing to live at home (as indeed they did after their father's death). Jackson says nothing of Sally at this time, but he reports that Charles junior's worldliness and lack of spirituality were matters of concern both to his father and to his uncle, and quotes two letters from John Wesley to Charles senior on the subject.[36] In the light of the inoffensive dullness of Charles junior's later life it is difficult to see these letters as reflecting any serious or continuing problem.

The case of Samuel, however, was another matter. As early as September 1778, as we know from a letter from Charles to Sarah, some aspects of his behaviour seem to have been giving grounds for concern. What was more, he was becoming interested in Roman Catholicism:[37]

> Sam will have many more escapes. Great will be his trials; but the Lord will deliver him out of all . . . Sam wants more pains to be taken with him. If I should not live to help him, it will lie all upon you. Make him a living Christian, and he will never wish to be a dead Papist.[38]

Exactly what form Samuel's interest took is not clear from Charles' comment, but it probably indicates Samuel's attendance at Roman Catholic services at one of the London embassy chapels, which were at this time the only places where Catholic rites could legally be celebrated. It may well be true, as Samuel asserted many years later in his manuscript *Reminiscences*,[39] that it was the music rather than the doctrines that initially drew him to Roman Catholic services; nonetheless, the mere fact of his attendance would have been a severe test for the most liberal father, and it is hard to imagine that the reaction of Charles could have been anything other than dismay.

Most of the details of the beginnings of Samuel's interest in Roman Catholicism remain unclear. His first surviving dated Roman Catholic church music composition is dated November 1780, but Charles' letter suggests an interest and involvement dating back to at least two years earlier. Whenever it occurred, it was an inopportune time, given the strong anti-Catholic feeling that followed the passing of the First Catholic Relief Act of 1779 and erupted in the violence of the Gordon Riots of June 1780. Although Charles' comment quoted above is our only record of his reaction to Samuel's initial interest, we can readily imagine his displeasure and his anxieties, not only for Samuel's spiritual well-being, but also for his physical safety. The fact of Samuel's involvement with Roman Catholicism gives a personal significance to Charles' poems on the Gordon Riots, one of which was written on 8 June 1780 when the disturbances were at their height and when Samuel and his mother had had to be evacuated from the family home for their own safety.[40]

Although Charles may have tolerated Samuel's attendance at Roman Catholic worship, he can hardly have been welcomed it or viewed it with equanimity. No matter how much Samuel protested that his interest was purely musical, there must always have been the worry that he would in fact convert to Roman Catholicism, and in early 1784 he did precisely this. It is not known whether he received instruction, conditional baptism and formal reception into the Roman Catholic Church, but one tangible outcome of his conversion was that he composed an elaborate *Missa de Spiritu Sancto* for chorus, soloists, and orchestra which he dedicated to Pope Pius VI and despatched to Rome.[41] The whole episode of the conversion was chronicled in considerable detail first by Jackson and later by Stevenson, for both of whom it evidently had a dreadful fascination.[42] Both authors describe what must have been an occasion of acute embarrassment when the Duchess of Norfolk, in her capacity as the wife of the leading Roman Catholic layman in England, paid a formal visit on Charles to break to him the news of his son's conversion – a situation made the more poignant by the fact that the Duchess's own son had recently abandoned Roman Catholicism for the Church of England.[43] Samuel's conversion also occasioned on 19 August 1784 a long letter from John Wesley, which in its tolerance and eirenic approach contrasts strongly with the intemperate anti-Catholic remarks which he had made in the aftermath of the passing of the First Catholic Relief Act. After voicing his disquiet at Samuel's behaviour in general terms, he expresses himself unconcerned about the precise form, 'Protestant or Romish', that Samuel's religious observance takes, and expresses his greater concern for Samuel's spiritual health:

> Whether of this church or that, I care not: you may be saved in either, or damned in either, but I fear you are not born again; and except you be born again you cannot see the kingdom of God. You believe the Church of Rome is right. What then: If you are not born of God, *you* are of *no church*. Whether Bellarmine or Luther be right, you are certainly wrong, if you are not *born of the Spirit*; if you are not renewed in the spirit of your mind in the likeness of Him that created you . . .
>
> O Sammy, you are out of your way! You are out of God's way! You have not given him your heart. You have not found, nay, it is well if you have so much as sought, happiness in God! And poor zealots, while you are in this state of mind, would puzzle you about this or the other church! O fools, and blind! Such guides as these lead men by shoals to the bottomless pit. My dear Sammy, your first point is to repent and believe the Gospel. Know yourself a poor guilty helpless sinner! Then know Jesus Christ and him crucified! Let the Spirit of God bear witness with your spirit, that you are a child of God and let the love of God be shed abroad in your heart by the Holy Ghost, which is given unto you; and then, if you have no better work, I will talk with you of transubstantiation or purgatory.[44]

Charles expressed the intense pain he felt over the Roman Catholic incident in verse in a notebook now known as MS Samuel Wesley RC, later endorsed by Sally as containing 'verses on his Son Samuel on being made acquainted he had embraced the Roman Catholic religion'.[45] In the best-known poem of this collection he expresses his grief at what he inevitably saw as an act of betrayal, and likens his 'sacrifice' to that of Abraham:

> Farewell, my all of earthly hope,
> My nature's stay, my age's prop,
> Irrevocably gone!
> Submissive to the will divine
> I acquiesce, and make it mine;
> I offer up my Son!
>
> But give I God a sacrifice
> That costs me nought? My gushing eyes
> The answer sad express,

My gushing eyes and troubled heart
Which bleeds with its belov'd to part,
Which breaks thro' fond excess.[46]

Samuel's conversion to Roman Catholicism was not the only aspect of his behaviour to cause concern to Charles and the family. What was now at issue was a general unruliness and rebelliousness that seems to have informed Samuel's behaviour from his early adolescence, and may – as we have seen – have originated in his childhood. There are, unfortunately, few relevant contemporary family documents and letters to fill out a fairly sketchy picture of life in the Wesley family in the 1780s.[47] Retrospective references in later letters, chiefly from Sally to Samuel, supply many of the details: Samuel's behaviour at this time seems to have included drunkenness, staying out until the early hours of the morning, and striking and otherwise abusing servants. It is clear that Samuel was in open revolt from his father and his family and all that they stood for, and it is possible to interpret his behaviour as a particularly extreme form of adolescent rebellion. But it seems more likely that it was to some extent an early manifestation of a hypomanic phase of the bipolar or manic-depressive illness that was to affect him for the remainder of his life.[48]

Our knowledge of Samuel's wild behaviour gives precise context to passages such as the following, which might otherwise be dismissed as overwrought and hysterical in tone:

From drunken, riotous excess
From vice, and open wickedness
His giddy youth restrain,
While flattery sooths, and pleasure smiles,
And harlots spread their slighted toils,
And glory courts in vain.[49]

Perhaps the greatest cause of family tension in the 1780s was Samuel's relationship with Charlotte Louisa Martin, whom he was eventually to marry. They had first met as early as October 1782, when Samuel was 16 and Charlotte was 21 or 22. The relationship was violently opposed by the family, largely on the grounds of what was perceived – with what degree of justification it is impossible to tell – as Charlotte's unsuitability of character;[50] we can also assume that Samuel's youth and the difference of five years in age between him and Charlotte would also have come into the matter. Samuel, predictably, refused to accede to his parents' demand that he should break off the relationship, and it continued up to the time of Charles' death as a potent source of family conflict.

The subsequent history of the relationship, while not of direct relevance here, is worth sketching as an indication of Samuel's later actions and the extent to which he departed from the values and conventions of the family, and indeed of respectable society of the day. After more than ten years of opposition from the family, Samuel and Charlotte married in April 1793. For some time before the marriage they had lived together and considered themselves as man and wife, while refusing to go through any marriage ceremony and claiming theological justification for their stance.[51] The abandonment of this position was no doubt occasioned by Charlotte's pregnancy and their desire to avoid the stigma of illegitimacy for their child and any succeeding children.[52] After the marriage their relationship almost immediately started to deteriorate, and their subsequent life together was unhappy and stormy, with frequent quarrels, infidelity on Samuel's part and incidents of violence on both parts. They finally separated in early 1810. Samuel subsequently took up with his housekeeper Sarah Suter, 15 or 16 years old to his 43, and lived with her until his death in 1837, fathering no fewer than seven children to add to the three by Charlotte.[53] As divorce was not readily available at the time to those in the Wesleys' position, Samuel and Charlotte remained married, and all the children by Sarah Suter were illegitimate.

In the 1780s these later episodes in Samuel's life lay far in the future. But it is apparent from the events described earlier that these years must have been ones of almost incessant domestic stress and turmoil for Charles. We should not, first of all, underestimate the continuing disruption to domestic routine caused by the family concerts over a period of eight years, or the continuing strain they must have imposed on Charles at a time when he doubtless would have preferred to lead a quieter life. The major problem, however, beside which any shortcomings in the behaviour of Charles junior or Sally must have seemed insignificant indeed, was the behaviour of Samuel. Few today would share the confidence of nineteenth-century writers such as Jackson or Stevenson in explaining root causes and in apportioning blame for Samuel's behaviour, and modern explanations are far more likely to take into account the part that may have been played by his manic-depressive illness. Nonetheless, it is clear that – for whatever reason – every significant action in Samuel's life at this period was taken in direct or indirect defiance of his father. An important part of the story of Charles Wesley's final years must be the story of this badly failed relationship, and the pain and suffering that it undoubtedly caused him.

## Notes

1 An earlier version of this chapter appeared as 'The Wesleys at Home: Charles Wesley and his Children', *Methodist History*, 36 (1998), 139–52. Earlier drafts of some sections have also appeared in *Samuel Wesley: The man and his music* (Woodbridge: Boydell Press, 2003). The material is used here with permission.

2 For biographies of Charles Wesley, see Thomas Jackson, *The Life of the Rev. Charles Wesley, M.A.*, 2 vols (London: John Mason, 1841); John Telford, *The Life of the Rev. Charles Wesley* (London: Wesleyan Methodist Book Room, 1900); Frederick Luke Wiseman, *Charles Wesley, Evangelist and Poet* (London: Epworth Press, 1933); Frederick C. Gill, *Charles Wesley, the first Methodist* (New York: Abingdon Press and London: Lutterworth Press, 1964); Arnold Dallimore, *A Heart Set Free: The life of Charles Wesley* (Welwyn: Evangelical Press, 1988). See also the relevant chapter in George John Stevenson, *Memorials of the Wesley Family* (London: S. W. Partridge and Co., 1876). Newport, *Sermons*, 5–6 n. 7, provides further references.

3 In this paper 'Sarah' will be used for Wesley's wife, and 'Sally' for his daughter.

4 For nineteenth-century biographies of the children, inevitably coloured by the prevailing attitudes of the time, see the relevant chapters in Stevenson, *Memorials of the Wesley Family*; for more recent summaries of their lives, see the relevant articles in *The Oxford Dictionary of National Biography* (Oxford: Oxford University Press, 2004). For Sally, see Wilma J. Quantrille, 'Sarah Wesley: Woman of her Times', *Proceedings of the Charles Wesley Society*, 4 (1997), 41–52. For Charles, see Gareth Lloyd, 'Charles Wesley Junior: Prodigal Child, Unfulfilled Adult', *Proceedings of the Charles Wesley Society*, 5 (1997), 23–36. For the musical careers of Charles and Samuel, see *The New Grove Dictionary of Music and Musicians*, ed. Stanley Sadie, 2nd edn, 29 vols (London: Macmillan, 2001). For an extended study of Samuel, see Philip Olleson, *Samuel Wesley: The man and his music* (Woodbridge: Boydell Press, 2003); see also Michael Kassler and Philip Olleson, *Samuel Wesley (1766–1837): A sourcebook* (Aldershot: Ashgate, 2001). See also William Winters, *An Account of the Remarkable Musical Talents of Several Members of the Wesley Family, collected from Original Manuscripts, &c., with Memorial Introduction and Notes* (London: F. Davies, 1874); James T. Lightwood, *Samuel Wesley, Musician* (London: Epworth Press, 1937); Erik Routley, *The Musical Wesleys* (London: Herbert Jenkins, 1968).

5 In the absence of a complete edition of Charles Wesley's letters, see *The Journal of the Rev. Charles Wesley, M.A.; to which are appended Selections from his Correspondence and Poetry*, ed. Thomas Jackson, 2 vols (London: John Mason, 1849) and Frank Baker, *Charles Wesley as revealed by his Letters* (London: Epworth Press, 1948). See also Charles Wesley's letters of 1779–1784 to John Langshaw in *Wesley–Langshaw Correspondence: Charles Wesley, his Sons and the Lancaster Organists*, ed. Arthur Wainwright and Don E. Saliers (Atlanta, Georgia: Scholars Press, 1993). For Charles Wesley's poetry, see *PW* and *Unpublished Poetry*. See also *Representative Verse of Charles Wesley*, ed. Frank Baker (Nashville: Abingdon Press, 1962) and *Charles Wesley: A Reader*, ed. John R. Tyson (New York and London: Oxford University Press, 1989). The two most important collections of Wesley family papers, including large numbers of letters by Charles' wife Sarah and the three children, are those at Emory University, Atlanta, Georgia (henceforth Emory) and at the MARC.

6 For a brief summary of approaches to the history of the family and of childhood, see Michael Anderson, *Approaches to the History of the Western Family, 1500–1914* (London: Macmillan, 1980) and the Introduction to Mary Abbott, *Family Ties: English families 1540–1920* (London: Routledge, 1993). Some of the most influential studies are (in chronological order): Philippe Ariès, *Centuries of Childhood: A social history of family life* (London: Cape, 1962); Lawrence Stone, *The Family, Sex and Marriage in England, 1500–1800* (London: Weidenfeld and Nicolson, 1977; shorter edn, Harmondsworth: Penguin Books, 1979); Linda A. Pollock, *Forgotten Children: Parent–child relationships from 1500 to 1900* (Cambridge: Cambridge University Press, 1983). See also J. H. Plumb, 'The New World of Children in Eighteenth-Century England', *Past and Present*, 67 (May 1975), 64–95.

7 John Locke, *Some Thoughts Concerning Education* (London, 1693); paragraph 81; for a modern edition see *The Educational Writings of John Locke: A critical edition with introduction and notes*, ed. James L. Axtell (Cambridge: Cambridge University Press, 1968).

8 Plumb, 'The New World of Children', 65.

9 Richard Allestree, *The Whole Duty of Man* (London, 1658), 20, quoted in Plumb, 'The New World of Children', 65.

10 John Earle, *Micro-cosmographie* (London, 1628), 1–2, quoted in Plumb, 'The New World of Children', 68, n. 22.

11 *Some Thoughts Concerning Education*, paragraph 81.

12 Quoted by John Wesley in his journal entry of 1 August 1742 (*The Journal of the Rev. John Wesley, A.M.*, ed. Nehemiah Curnock, 8 vols, (London: Robert Culley, [1909–1916]), vol. 3, 36, and in his sermon *On Obedience to Parents* (1784), in *The Works of John Wesley Vol. 3: Sermons III*, ed. Albert C. Outler (Nashville: Abingdon Press, 1986), 361–72.

13 Ibid.

14 For an overall discussion of John Wesley's educational thought, see Alfred H. Body, *John Wesley and Education* (London: Epworth Press, 1936).

15 *The Works of John Wesley*, 3rd edn, ed. Thomas Jackson, 14 vols (London: John Mason, 1829–31), vol. 13, 249–54, reprinted in Rupert Davies, A. Raymond George and Gordon Rupp (eds), *A History of the Methodist Church in Great Britain* (London: Epworth Press, 1988), vol. 4, 104–6.

16 Ibid.

17 See the sermons 'On Family Religion, On the Education of Children' and 'On Obedience to Parents' in *The Works of John Wesley Vol. 3: Sermons III*, ed. Albert C. Outler, 333–72.

18 Lightwood, *Samuel Wesley, Musician*, 45, citing Samuel's letters of 1777.

19 *CWJ*, 2.246. The date of this letter is uncertain, but internal evidence suggests either August 1762 or August 1765 (based mainly on the references to John Wesley's being en route to Land's End and the fact that while both Charles junior and Sally are mentioned, Samuel is not (which suggests first part of the 1760s).

20 Charles' account was made available to Barrington and published together with Barrington's own observations in his *Miscellanies* (London, 1781), 291–310. Barrington (1727–1800) had a particular interest in musical child prodigies, and had earlier written an account of the young Mozart, whom he had met and examined in London in 1765.

21 Dated Inverness, 9 June 1779; printed in *Arminian Magazine*, 4 (1781), 104–7.

22 John Fletcher to Charles Wesley, 13 October 1771, quoted in Gill, *Charles Wesley: The First Methodist*, 190.

23 Charles Wesley to Eleanor Laroche, post 3 February 1769, (MARC, DDWES, 4/73), quoted in Baker, *Charles Wesley as Revealed in his Letters*, 110.

24 MARC, DDCW, 10/2.

25 Jackson, *Life*, 2.357.

26 Madan was from 1758 until his death the honorary chaplain of the Lock Hospital, a charitable establishment for those suffering from venereal diseases. In *Thelyphthora* he attempted by the use of passages drawn from the Bible to prove the acceptability of polygamy in biblical times and advocated its reintroduction as a means of alleviating the plight of women who had been seduced and abandoned, and of their children. The resulting furore rapidly led to his disgrace and ostracism. Madan's arguments were trivialized and misunderstood in his own day, and the bald statement in most present-day reference books that he advocated polygamy does not do justice to the complexity of his thought or his motivations in writing *Thelyphthora*. See Victor N. Paananen, 'Martin Madan and the Limits of Evangelical Philanthropy', *Proceedings of the Wesley Historical Society*, 40 (1975), 57–68.

27 Charles Wesley to Sarah Wesley, 25 August 1766, in *CWJ*, 2.262 (MARC, DDCW, 7/27).

28 Charles Wesley to Samuel Wesley, 6 March 1773 (MARC, DDWes, 4/70), quoted in Olleson, *Samuel Wesley: The Man and his Music*, 12–13.

29 Charles Wesley to Sally Wesley, undated, *CWJ*, 2.276–7.

30 Samuel Wesley to Charles Wesley, 22 August 1785 (MARC, DDWF, 15/2), summarized in Kassler and Olleson, *Samuel Wesley (1766–1837): A source book*, 129–30.

31 Charles Wesley to Sally Wesley, 11 October 1777, *CWJ*, 2.276.

32 Olleson, *Samuel Wesley: The man and his music*, 20–4; Alyson McLamore, '"By the Will and Order of Providence": The Wesley Family Concerts, 1779–1787', *Royal Musical Association Research Chronicle*, 37 (2004), 71–220.

33 Thomas Coke to John Wesley, 15 December 1779, in *Arminian Magazine*, 13 (1790), 50–1.

34 Charles Wesley, memorandum, *c.* 14 January 1779 (MARC, DDWES, 14/65), quoted in Olleson, *Samuel Wesley: The man and his music*, 20.

35 Charles Wesley to John Wesley, 23 April 1779, printed in *Arminian Magazine*, 12 (1789), 386–8; quoted in Olleson, *Samuel Wesley: The man and his music*, 21.

36 Jackson, *Life*, 2.354–55, quoting letters of 4 August and 8 September 1781.

37 On Charles' interaction with Roman Catholicism and for other insights into Charles' reaction to the conversion of his son Samuel to that tradition, see further below, Chapter 9

38 Charles Wesley to Sarah Wesley, 5–7 September 1778 (MARC, DDCW, 7/36), in *CWJ*, 2.269–70.

39 London, British Library, Add. MS 27593.

40 See also Charles' eye-witness account of the Gordon riots in his letter to John Wesley of 8 June 1780, quoted in Jackson, *Life*, 2.320–1. For the Gordon Riots, see Christopher Hibbert, *King Mob: The story of Lord George Gordon and the riots of 1780* (London: Longmans, Green, 1958).

41 Autograph dated 22 May 1784 at London, British Library, Add. MS 35000; revised version at Cambridge, Fitzwilliam Museum, MS 730.

42 Jackson, *Life*, 2.359–60; Stevenson, *Memorials of the Wesley Family*, 505.

43 Stevenson mistakenly describes this incident as having taken place in 1785.

44 John Wesley to Samuel Wesley, 19 August 1784, in *The Letters of the Rev. John Wesley, A.M.*, ed. John Telford, 8 vols (London: Epworth Press, 1931), vol. 7, 230–1; see also his letter of 2 May 1784 to his nephew Charles (ibid., 216–17). For John Wesley and Roman Catholicism, see David Butler, *Methodists and Papists: John Wesley and the Catholic Church in the eighteenth century* (London: Darton, Longman Todd, 1995).

45 *Unpublished Poetry*, 1.303–16.

46 *Unpublished Poetry*, 1.304. The poem of which these stanzas form part is also printed by Jackson, *Life*, 2.361–4, and Stevenson, *Memorials of the Wesley Family*, 505–6.

47 Not surprisingly, Charles' letters to John Langshaw Sr in *Wesley–Langshaw Correspondence* contain no hint of family problems.

48 Samuel's extended periods of depression throughout his life have long been acknowledged by his biographers, but in the light of current knowledge of the condition a diagnosis of manic-depressive illness seems inescapable. It is borne out by the events of Samuel's life, his pattern of creativity and his letters. See Frederick K. Goodwin and Kay Redfield Jamison, *Manic-Depressive Illness* (New York and Oxford: Oxford University Press, 1990); Kay Redfield Jamison, *Touched with Fire: Manic-depressive illness and the artistic temperament* (New York: Free Press, 1993).

49 *Unpublished Poetry*, 1.305.

50 See, for example, Samuel's letter to his mother of 7 November 1792 (MARC, DDWF/15/5), in which he defends Charlotte against accusations of extravagance and the possession of a 'fickle and wanton nature'.

51 This stance derived in part from one of the arguments of Madan's *Thelyphthora*. Following Madan, Samuel claimed that there was no evidence for the existence of any sort of religious marriage ceremony in biblical times, and that marriage was constituted solely by sexual intercourse. By this criterion, as he declared in a defiant letter to his mother of 7 November 1792, he and Charlotte were by this time incontestably man and wife: 'She is truly and properly my wife by all the laws of God and Nature. She never can be made more so, by the mercenary tricks of divine jugglers.' For Samuel's views on marriage, see Olleson, *Samuel Wesley: The Man and his Music*, 40–5.

52 Their first-born child was Charles, who according to Stevenson (*Memorials of the Wesley Family*, 539) was born on 25 September 1793. Parish records reveal that he was baptized on 20 October of that year.

53 In addition, one child by Charlotte and two children by Sarah Suter died in infancy or early childhood.

# 9. Charles Wesley, Catholicism and Anti-Catholicism

## PETER NOCKLES

John Wesley's friend, the Irish Anglican layman Alexander Knox (1757–1831), who was the recipient of a series of letters of spiritual advice from Wesley between 1776 and 1785, maintained that an undue fear of 'Popery' had deprived the Church of England of great treasures of spiritual devotion. Among other things, he singled out a lack of attention to the interior effects of religion resulting from the formal neglect of auricular confession. Alexander Knox was not alone in ascribing an eighteenth-century Anglican recoil from movements of piety and 'vital religion' to an exaggerated fear of what were too often regarded as the twin and interconnected dangers of 'Popery' and 'enthusiasm'.[1] The Methodist movement under John Wesley's leadership has sometimes been regarded as one of the more notable of a series of internal reactions within the Church of England against an apparent spiritual vacuum at the heart of the Protestant tradition. According to this interpretation, John Wesley (and by implication also his brother Charles) sought to bring the Church of England back into the 'great Catholic tradition' of practical spirituality.[2] Some of the early negative response to Wesley and Methodism might be explained by fear of and hostility towards this aspect of his controversial evangelistic endeavour.

The type of eighteenth-century 'rational' Anglican reaction to Methodism exemplified by Bishop George Lavington's *Enthusiasm of Methodists and Papists Compared* (1749–51), with its comparisons of aspects of Methodist and Catholic spirituality, devotional practice, and above all supernatural awareness (as witnessed in visionary and ecstatic phenomena), and criticism of John Wesley for 'recommending Popish Books', was a classic of the genre.[3] The apparent religious affinities were enough to prompt the Catholic Bishop Richard Challoner to issue his *Caveat Against the Methodists* (1760), warning Catholics, who might be susceptible, against Methodist proselytizing by arguing that the Methodists were not the people of God, not the true gospel Christians and that their society was not part of the Church of Christ.[4] John Henry Newman later accused the Anglican authorities of Bishop Lavington's day of being counter-productive and myopic in their response to Wesley and Methodism by effectively checking the safety valve of religious feeling and thereby only further encouraging individuals either to turn Wesleyan in a sectarian way or Papist.[5] Moreover, as John Walsh has demonstrated, the *canard* that early

Methodists were really Papists and Jacobites, if not Jesuits, in disguise, and in 1743–5 actually in league with the 'Young Pretender', took deep root in the popular consciousness and became a rallying cry of anti-Methodist mobs.[6] In the early years of Methodism, John Wesley was frequently accused of being a Papist and of promoting 'Jesuitism'.[7] Many of the anti-Methodist prints and caricatures of the eighteenth century portrayed John and Charles Wesley and George Whitefield as crypto-Papists. A classic of the genre, William Hogarth's *Enthusiasm Delineated* (1764) includes a howling dog whose collar is labelled 'Whitefield'. As Robert Glen comments: 'the dog is mimicking the crypto-Catholic preacher (note the tonsure) who has abandoned reason in favour of an emotional, 'enthusiastic' style of preaching'.[8]

At the intellectual level, the Lavingtonian equation of Methodists and papists as fanatics from the same stable even became something of a staple of the anti-priestcraft literary genre of the Age of Reason. Clearly, John Wesley's authoritarian and organizing instincts had done nothing to dispel the charge. As late as 1779 one author was comparing the system of Methodism to 'the system of Loyola' and contending that the two were 'indistinguishable from each other'.[9]

It should not be surprising that the Wesley brothers took strong steps to strip away any grounds for such associations, however much they lacked foundation. Furthermore, the true theological perspective of the Wesley brothers was for a long time at the mercy of Victorian Nonconformist and Evangelical historians for whom any apparent approximation towards Roman Catholic doctrine and devotion had to be explained or airbrushed away. Certainly from the late eighteenth century onwards, and especially in the wake of the Oxford Movement (when the Church of England's formal Protestant credentials came under strain), nothing is more ubiquitous in the pages of Methodist literature than anti-Catholicism.[10] Was it ever thus?

The relationship of Charles Wesley towards Roman Catholicism needs to be viewed in these historiographical contexts and, above all, to the dominant sway of that long and vibrant tradition of British anti-Catholicism which Linda Colley (in *Britons: Forging the nation*), Colin Haydon and others have identified as a powerful determinant of national identity in the 'long' eighteenth century and which was always liable to be revived at times of national crisis such as the Jacobite risings of 1715 and 1745 and the French invasion scare of 1758–9.[11] Although the early Methodists were themselves obvious victims of this anti-Catholic paranoia, how far did they also share in it? How far was Charles Wesley's attitude to Roman Catholicism then typical of Methodism as a whole and how far was it shaped by wider trends? Was it inseparable from the firm Protestantism which was already part of the high church tradition in which he had been reared, as Henry Rack has suggested in the case of John?[12] On the other hand, eighteenth-century sentiments of toleration gradually helped mitigate in practice, at least in educated circles, an inherited 'Black Legend' tradition of anti-Catholicism. Did such 'reasonable' sentiments influence the 'enthusiast' Charles Wesley? Was the supposed tendency towards a dilution of elite anti-Catholicism in the later decades of the eighteenth century, as identified by James Sack, Nigel Aston and others,[13] reflected in Charles Wesley's own attitudes towards Roman Catholicism?

There is a substantial body of literature on John Wesley's attitude to and relationship with Roman Catholicism, the most recent of which, the late David Butler's *Methodists and Papists* (1995), sheds new light on the eirenical and ecumenical strand in John Wesley's thought and practice, while not ignoring Wesley's more polemical anti-Catholic side (highlighted in a work by the late Oliver Beckerlegge).[14] Furthermore, as David Hempton has recently put it, Wesley may have had controversial battles with Roman Catholicism but his real theological wars were with Calvinism.[15] Hitherto, however, as Kenneth Rowe has observed, historians had long been at the mercy of Victorian Nonconformists and Anglican Evangelicals who tended to give a somewhat one-dimensional portrait of him.[16] Even political and social historians of the stature of J. H. Hexter and Elie Halévy declared Wesley's anti-Catholicism as axiomatic, assuming that the undoubted anti-Catholicism of later generations of Methodists (especially in the era prior to Catholic Emancipation and of the Oxford Movement and after) was inherited from the Wesley brothers. Recent Catholic historiography, in contrast, has demonstrated a surprising amount of 'Roman' spirituality incorporated by John Wesley into his 'practical divinity' as part of Wesley's conscious attempt to reinvigorate the Protestantism of his day with modified and 'purified' forms of traditional Catholic spirituality. Scholars such as Maximin Piette (*John Wesley in the Evolution of Protestantism*, 1937) and more especially John Todd (*John Wesley and the Catholic Church*, 1958) and Jean Orcibal sought to show how far Wesley's 'evangelical' doctrines might be harmonized with Roman Catholic teaching.[17] Orcibal even argued that John Wesley's key doctrine of perfectionism was rooted in his reading of continental Roman Catholic sources.

David Butler's work has built on the insights of these scholars and fruitfully compared various spiritual points of affinity between Richard Challoner and John Wesley, though another scholar, Mark Massa, prefers to regard John Wesley's new synthesis of Catholic spirituality as transcending 'old Reformation polarities'.[18] Nonetheless, there is no doubt that various elements of Roman Catholic 'interior' spirituality abandoned at the Reformation, such as auricular confession, were reclaimed in modified form by John Wesley's creative evangelistic strategies as in the case of the Class and Band meetings (one of the points on which Bishop Lavington indicted Wesley for favouring 'Popery'). In fact, the Methodist historian Henry Bett even claimed that the seventeenth-century French Catholic nobleman, Gaston de Renty, was 'the real founder of the Class Meeting in Methodism'.[19] Moreover, there is no shortage of literature on the influence of the French Catholic authors Fénelon, Pascal and Bossuet on John and Charles' father, Samuel Wesley senior, and their influential mother, Susanna. It has been even argued that Susanna Wesley owed many of her ideas of religious and moral truth and their discernment to her reading of Pascal. She also introduced her children to Castaniza's *Spiritual Combat*, while Samuel Wesley's debt to Pascal is shown in his *Letters to a Curate*.[20] As Eamon Duffy has concluded, John Wesley inherited his active interest in Counter-Reformation spirituality, and 'a willingness to find even in Popery examples of heroic virtue and true devotion'.[21] What applied to John Wesley can be extended to his brother Charles.

There have been surprisingly few attempts, however, apart from the work of Fr Francis Frost,[22] to focus on Charles Wesley's attitude and relationship to Roman Catholicism. Indeed, a study of Charles Wesley related directly to Roman Catholicism might not seem an immediately fruitful line of enquiry, especially given the paucity of evidence that the early Methodists in Britain knew much about or had any contact with the Roman Catholic Church or individual Roman Catholics. However, it was different in Ireland where Methodists inevitably gained more knowledge and had more contact. We will focus on the main elements in Charles Wesley's contact with Roman Catholicism, one of which was through his preaching tours and evangelistic work in Ireland, noting the importance of the Cork riots of 1749. The other key elements to be considered will include: his spiritual writings and devotional literary output (was he as wedded to continental Catholic devotional writers such as Gaston de Renty and Gregory Lopez as was his brother John, or such an admirer of Pascal, Fénelon and Bossuet as was his father Samuel?); his evolving ecclesiology and attitude to church order (did the relative looseness or latitude of post-1738 Methodist ecclesiology help soften his anti-Catholic instincts?); the evidence from his sermons, such as on Acts 20.7;[23] his eucharistic theology and hymnody, such as his influential *Hymns on the Lord's Supper* (1745) which drew heavily on the sacramental–liturgical inheritance of the Caroline Divines, notably Lancelot Andrewes, John Cosin and Daniel Brevint (though because this aspect has been well treated elsewhere, it will only lightly be touched upon here); his eschatology and prophetical interpretation of scripture and consequent attitude to the 'Romish Antichrist', notably as revealed in a remarkable letter dated 25 April 1754, the original of which is in the Methodist Archives and Research Centre in the John Rylands University Library (DDCW 1/51) and which has been the subject of a close exegetical reading by Newport;[24] his response to seismic episodes such as the Gordon riots of 1780; and finally, in the context of his family life and relations and how far this shaped or modified his inherited attitudes, we will examine his reaction to the conversion to the Roman Catholic Church of his talented composer and organist son Samuel Wesley (1766–1837) in 1784, especially in the light of Philip Olleson's recent scholarly analysis of this subject in his biography of Samuel and his edition of his correspondence.[25] In particular, a possible tension between his eighteenth-century concern for freedom of conscience and the conventional anti-Catholicism of the Protestant eschatological tradition which he made his own, is worthy of exploration.

    The nature of Charles Wesley's perception of Roman Catholicism and the extent to which he evinced anti-Catholic attitudes or not should first be considered against the background of the character of the early Methodist movement. As is well known, both Wesley brothers, while active members of the so-called 'Holy Club' at Oxford in the early 1730s, were the strictest of high churchmen with a high view of the binding force of apostolical tradition and primitive Christianity which had affinities with that of the so-called 'usager' element among contemporary Nonjurors. Although the Nonjurors could be as anti-Catholic on occasion as any mainstream Protestant polemicist, the strict adherence of the 'usagers' to the so-called *Apostolical Constitutions* meant that they could not escape charges of crypto-Popery on account of their sacramental liturgical preoccupations (which amounted to a growing dissatisfaction with aspects of the existing Book of Common Prayer and a preference for the first Edwardine Prayer Book of 1549). It was the Wesley brothers' similarly strict adherence to various primitive practices and points of discipline, combined with their having 'most unmercifully damned all Dissenters of whatever denomination', which attracted charges of aiding and abetting 'Popery' among the Georgia colonists in North America in 1736–7. The Georgia landowners who made formal complaints about John Wesley and which led to an indictment from the Grand Jury of Savannah, declared that 'persons suspected to be Roman Catholics were received and caressed by him as his First-rate Saints'. They concluded that 'at last all persons of any consideration came to look upon him as a Roman Catholic'. Their main evidence for Wesley's supposed 'Popery', however,

arose from his endeavors to establish confession, penance, mortifications, mixing wine with water in the Sacrament, and suppressing the explanation adjoined to the Words of communicating by the Church of England, to show that they mean a Feeding on Christ by Faith, saying no more 'The Body of Christ; The Blood of Christ;' by appointing Deaconesses, with sundry other innovations, which he called Apostolic Constitutions.[26]

Nonetheless, it was the Wesley brothers' abandonment of stricter notions of churchmanship in the wake of their conversion experiences of May 1738 which, perhaps ironically, triggered the first sustained charges of crypto- or closet 'Popery' from that strand of anti-Methodism later associated with Bishop Lavington's notorious polemic. Early Methodist critics perceived that it was the very looseness and denominational amorphousness of the Methodist movement in the wake of 1738, with its declared mission to encompass individuals from all denominations (Roman Catholics included) anxious to escape 'the wrath to come', which made it potentially as lax in relation to Roman Catholicism as to other denominations such as the Quakers. For as Bishop Lavington famously argued in 1749 in respect of John Wesley (but which he could also have applied to Charles Wesley),

We may see in Mr. Wesley's writings that he was once a strict churchman, has gradually relaxed, put on a more Catholic spirit, tending at length to Roman Catholic. People of every communion are among his disciples, and he somewhere rejects with indignation any design to convert others from any communion, and consequently not from Popery. On the contrary, we find no small tendency to it.[27]

It was certainly true that early Methodists were regarded as blurring denominational boundaries, rendering them vulnerable to charges of being either pro-Dissenter or pro-Catholic. The Wesley brothers, certainly John, sometimes consciously encouraged this perception. Henry Rack has argued that John Wesley tended 'to welcome what he took to be evidence of a common Christianity defined as love of God and of neighbor, to be recognized and accepted as such whatever a person's denominational label'.[28]

In both his eirenic *Letter to a Roman Catholic* (1749) and in his sermon on the *Catholic Spirit* (1755, but composed in 1749), John Wesley sought to establish common ground with Roman Catholics, arguing that 'true religion' did not consist in forms of worship or modes of baptism but in a 'right heart' to be found in a person who knew Christ and Him crucified.[29] In similar vein, while visiting Kinsale in September 1748, Charles Wesley discovered that people thought he was 'of every religion', and noted in his journal: 'The Presbyterians say I am a Presbyterian; the church-goers that I am a minister of theirs; and the Catholics are sure I am a good Catholic in my heart.'[30]

It was probably to check the sources of friction and tension that arose from the fact that early Methodism was forged from such a melting pot of diverse and sometimes conflicting theological and spiritual traditions, that John Wesley published *A Preservative Against Unsettled Notions in Religion* (1758). There was certainly to emerge a harder edge of anti-Catholicism in John Wesley's writings and practice, along with that of his followers. Once moral and doctrinal weaknesses in Roman Catholic teaching came to be explicitly identified, it could be argued that those belonging to that faith would find it more difficult to attain salvation than Protestants. Once this was granted, it became the specific duty of Methodists to frustrate Catholic proselytizing by any means. John Wesley was capable of taking a lead in this respect. In sharp contrast to the eirenic tone of his sermon on the 'Catholic Spirit', with its emphasis on 'union in affection' based on a mutual pursuit of holiness, in more polemical works such as his acerbic response in the *London Chronicle* in 1761 to Challoner's *Caveat* he could even deny that the generality of Catholics were any holier than Turks or heathens. How far did Charles Wesley's attitudes fit this pattern of a developing anti-Catholic posture?

## Charles Wesley's early Roman Catholic contacts: Georgia and Ireland

For a long time Charles Wesley had very little or no personal contact with Roman Catholics, and his attitudes and assumptions tended to be shaped by a standard and inherited Protestant rhetoric of antipathy to Rome as a religious system. This rhetoric was infused by a Protestant prophetical and eschatological tradition, promulgated by writers such as Joseph Mede and reinvigorated by Thomas Newton in his *Dissertation on the Prophecies* (1762), by which Rome was portrayed as the Antichrist commonly thought at the time to be foreseen in the Books of Daniel, 2 Thessalonians and Revelation. Contemporary political events such as the Jacobite rising of 1745, along with the fact of Britain being at war with Catholic Powers in the 1740s, engendered a nightmare spectre of a return of Popery with the Pretender. This scenario, in which Methodists themselves were tarnished and implicated by their critics, triggered an early example of powerful anti-Catholic eschatological rhetoric from Charles (a rhetoric that was to find fuller expression in the letter of 25 April 1754 cited above, and discussed below). Charles was probably especially sensitive on the subject of dynastic allegiance because he and John were often unfairly accused not only of praying for but of being in league with the Pretender. An example of this was the way in which he reacted when preaching in Bristol to the news of the Jacobite capture of Edinburgh in September 1745:

Tidings came that General Cope was cut off with all his army. The room was crowded in the evening. I warned them [the Society], with all authority, to flee to the mountains, escape to the strong tower, even the name of Jesus. We seemed to have strong faith, that the Romish Antichrist shall never finally prevail in this kingdom.[31]

The Jacobite scare of 1745–6 certainly triggered anti-Catholic sentiments in Charles Wesley's 'Hymns for Times of Trouble' and 'Hymns in Time of Persecution'.[32] In his Thanksgiving Day hymn for the defeat of Charles Edward Stuart at Culloden there are vituperative references to 'bloodthirsty Rome' and the 'Romish wolf'. The standard eighteenth-century Protestant emphasis on the supposed political and religious tyranny and yoke found full expression in the following stanzas:

The scheme is Satan's conclave laid,
Improved by Rome's unerring hand,

To gall us with their yoke abhorred,
And plant their faith with fire and sword.[33]

Charles composed further hymns of similar anti-Catholic tenor in the wake of the French invasion scare of 1758–9, a scare which also had a Jacobite tinge. However, he also confided privately that he tried hard to quieten his wife Sarah's great fears of a resurgent Roman Catholicism at this time.[34]

Yet the circumstances associated with the gradual increase in his personal contact with individual Roman Catholics in new evangelistic situations often left Charles Wesley with little choice but to adopt a much more open-minded attitude. He first appears to have encountered individual Roman Catholics in his congregation while ministering in Georgia in 1736. This was in spite of the fact that the Trustees of the Georgia Colony, due partly to the proximity to Florida and the Society for the Propagation of the Gospel's fears of a Spanish threat from there, went to great lengths to prevent Catholics from going to Georgia, and severe restrictions were put on Catholics owning land.[35] There is no direct evidence that Charles shared his brother's exasperation at the amount of advice 'to beware of the increase of popery' which he had received from the Society for Promoting Christian Knowledge, the Georgia Trustees and others, 'but not one (that I remember) to beware of the increase of infidelity'.[36] One can only conjecture, however, as to whether Charles would have made his own the following avowal from John in relation to the one-sidedness of the advice he had received on going to Georgia, as recorded in John's manuscript Georgia journal for 25 May 1737 (which differs from the printed edition of the journal for this date):

Now this overgrown zeal for Protestantism, quite swallowing up zeal for our common Christianity, I can't term anything better than infatuation, for these very plain reasons: (1) Because as bad a religion as popery is, no religion at all is still worse, a baptized infidel being twofold more a child of hell than the fiercest Papist in Christendom; (2) Because as dangerous a state as a Papist is in with regard to eternity, a Deist is in a yet more dangerous state, if he be not (without repentance) an assured heir of damnation; and (3) Because as difficult as it is to recover a Papist, 'tis far more difficult to recover an infidel. This I speak from the strongest of all proofs, experience. I never yet knew one Deist re-converted; whereas, even in this place, I do not know of more than one Papist remaining, except an Italian or two, whom I cannot yet speak to.[37]

In 1739, there is evidence for Charles encountering two Catholics in Newgate Gaol. During the 1740s several adherents to the Methodist societies proved to be former or lapsed Catholics, though they remained statistically insignificant in relation to Methodist numerical growth as a whole. This provoked acrimony and indignation from Roman Catholic clergy, but Charles Wesley sought to be emollient and conciliatory in such personal situations. Typical of his approach is the following entry from his journal for 16 March 1745, written from the Foundery in London:

I spoke with one of the Society, lately a Papist, who is much haunted by her old friends, especially her confessor, who thunders out anathemas against her; and threatens to burn me, – if he would catch me at home. I sent my respects to the gentleman, and offered to talk with him before her, at my own lodgings, or wherever he pleased; but received no answer.[38]

However, it was only when he embarked on his preaching tours of Ireland from 1747 onwards that he came into regular personal contact with Roman Catholics. From this time onwards, the references to 'Papists' and his response to situations involving them become much frequent in the journal and elsewhere.

No sooner had Charles Wesley arrived in Dublin in September 1747 when he was confronted with reports of 'a mixed rabble of Papists and Protestants' attacking and breaking open the rooms of the Methodist Society in the city. As he recorded on 9 September 1747, 'The Popish mob, encouraged and assisted by the Protestant, are so insolent and outrageous, that, whatever street we pass through, it is up in arms.'[39]

On 17 September Charles reported in his journal another major mob assault by both Papists and Protestants on 'the house, where the Society was met after evening service'.[40] Charles' response was emollient. He sought to disarm Catholic opposition by reference to a Catholic devotional authority whom he evidently valued, no less than his brother John. Thus, he invoked not only a medieval Catholic spiritual master, Thomas à Kempis, but by implication the devotional riches of the Roman Breviary. As he recorded on 20 September:

I spoke with great freedom to the poor Papists, urging them to repentance and the love of Christ, from the authority of their own Kempis, and their

own Liturgy. None lifted up his voice or hand. All listened with strange
attention. Many were in tears. I advised them to go to their respective places
of worship. They expressed general satisfaction, especially the Papists.[41]

A week later, he similarly recorded: 'The Papists stood like lambs. I quoted
Kempis, which makes some of them confident I am a good Catholic.'[42] Charles
may have been less than happy at being taken for a Papist, if such really was
the case. However, such admissions served a useful rhetorical effect in creating an impression of disarming moderation and meekness in the face of hostility and contempt.

Charles, however, could also strike a less eirenical note when he was under
less evident pressure to adopt a conciliatory pose. Thus, on 23 September he
approvingly recorded the view of a Mr Aggit (in whose house he and his
friends were forced to take shelter) who 'was scandalized at such treatment
of a minister of the established Church' and asserted that 'a Popish Priest,
so used, would be succored by the Magistrate'.[43] Nonetheless, in his journal
account Charles' emphasis was on his gospel message acting as a solvent or
healer of denominational differences, suggesting that it was this that most
offended intolerant Papists. Thus, on 11 October he recorded the rage of a
Papist who cried: 'I ought to be stabbed for lumping them all [Protestant
and Papist] together, and telling them they might all be saved, of whatever
church or party, if they would return, like the prodigal, to their heavenly
Father.'[44] On another occasion, Charles similarly recorded: 'I exhorted all
alike to repentance toward God, and faith in Jesus Christ; and staked my
own salvation upon it, that he who believes, whether Papist or Protestant,
shall be saved.'[45]

Such eirenicism was very much in the spirit of his brother's *Letter to a Roman
Catholic* wherein he had stated: 'My dear friend, I am not persuading you to
change your religion, but to follow after that fear and love of God without
which all religion is in vain.'[46] However, his tone differed when reference was
made to the activities of Roman Catholic priests. In February 1748 Charles was
happy to suggest that Papists in the Athlone area had formed a 'scheme for
murdering us at the instigation of their Priest, Father Ferril, who had sounded
the alarm last Sunday and raised his crusade against us'.[47] In an entry for 5
September 1748 he noted that 'Romish Priests go secretly to work, deterring
their flock by the penalty of a curse. Yet some venture to hear us by stealth.'[48]
Such descriptions served the rhetorical effect of suggesting that he and his
cohorts were innocent victims or martyrs to the gospel. The intended implication was clear: far from promoting intolerance or persecution of Papists, it
was he and his brothers who passively suffered intolerance and persecution
at their hands. However, in an earlier journal entry (11 February 1748) personal contact with a 'sensible Roman' who 'seemed satisfied with my answers
to his objections; and not far from the kingdom of heaven',[49] had induced a
more conciliatory tone.

Charles Wesley was an emotional man, his mood and judgement sensitive
to the very varying circumstances and contexts in which his contact with
Roman Catholics and Roman Catholicism were made. While he might express
satisfaction if a Roman Catholic abandoned his communion after hearing a

Methodist preacher, his characteristic position (at least in his earlier years of active evangelistic ministry) was that 'coming over to the power of godliness' was more important than 'coming over to the Church of England'. The emphasis seemed to be to urge Roman Catholics 'to repentance and the obedience of faith' without a specific call to abjure the Roman Catholic Church. If only the 'Romish priests' ceased to intimidate their flock, the implication was that all would be well.

Yet Charles Wesley was able to strike a quite contradictory tone. He was capable of rejoicing that Papists were being 'reconciled to the church', but not so much to the Church of England as a visible branch of the Church Catholic as high church Anglican ecclesiology might have dictated but in a very low church evangelical Protestant sense of 'the true, invisible church, or communion of saints, with whom is forgiveness of sins'.[50] Similarly, on 25 September 1748 he noted that he had been invited to dine with 'Mr R, a gentleman of the Romish persuasion till he heard my brother; since which, both he and his house, with several others, are come over to the Church of England, and, what is far better, to the power of godliness.'[51]

Charles' reticence in broadcasting converts from the 'lost sheep' of Roman Catholicism appears to have been primarily tactical. As he explained, 'we . . . seldom speak of it', lest the Papists were stirred up 'to tear us in pieces'.[52] Charles' true feelings were perhaps best summed up in his poetry in which he intimated that Roman Catholics, far from being allowed to remain as they were, needed to be released from bondage and ensnarement by the forces of the Evil One. In the entry for 5 September 1748 he set out the words of a hymn he had composed for the Roman Catholics of Ireland while on the road to Bandon, the first verse of which ran:

Shepherd of souls, the great, the good,
Thy helpless sheep behold,
Those other sheep dispersed abroad,
Who are not of this fold.
By Satan and his factors bound
In ignorance and sin,
Recall them through the Gospel sound,
And bring the outcasts in.

A later verse referred to Roman Catholic hierarchical system and clergy in distinctly unflattering terms as agencies of Antichrist and sorcerers:

The hinderer of thy word restrain,
The Babylonish Beast,
The men who sell poor souls for gain,
Or curse whom thou hast bless'd;

Those blinded leaders of the blind,
Who frighten them from thee,
And still bewitch the people's mind
With hellish sorcery . . . [53]

As with his brother John, one can conclude that Charles could be eirenic and open-minded when dealing with individual Roman Catholics or, when in a corner, appealing for peace. Self-interested motives of self-preservation and tactical advantage played their part here, especially in the evangelistic context of predominantly Catholic Ireland. It was quite otherwise, however, when Charles, like his brother, faced up to Roman Catholic doctrine and practice from a less vulnerable vantage-point. In such cases, inherited prejudices and conventional anti-Catholic polemic readily resurfaced in their rhetoric and writings. The classic distinction was made between innocent 'deluded' Catholics and a 'corrupt', if not anti-Christian, system of Catholicism, the supposed evil of which was manifest in the machinations of priests. However, for all the many references to 'poor Papists' or 'poor Romans' in his journal during his two extended stays in Ireland, from September 1747 until March 1748 and again from August until October 1748, Teresa Berger has concluded that there was little evidence for Charles Wesley 'having confronted the Roman Catholic tradition in any depth'.[54]

One can conclude that the pressures and needs of the mission in Ireland played a part in determining Charles Wesley's attitude to Roman Catholicism, as they did those of his brother John. Rack has suggested that John Wesley probably 'shared the usual English beliefs about the Irish, being ready to cut Protestant throats as in the 1640s, and believing that Irish poverty was due to Popery'.[55] Charles Wesley almost certainly shared those stereotypical concerns. In both cases, however, it can be argued that their more hostile comments were as much anti-Irish as anti-Catholic *per se*. However, in the longer term, it was the anti-Catholic attitude of the Methodist preachers, especially those who originated from Ireland, which played the key part in hardening the Methodist movement as a whole against Roman Catholicism.

## Charles Wesley's eschatology and his prophetical interpretation of scripture as a vehicle of anti-Catholicism

The Protestant tradition of interest in eschatology and apocalypticism had a strongly anti-Catholic bias. As is well known, there was an almost universal Protestant view that the Pope and/or the Roman Catholic Church was the Antichrist depicted in the prophetic books of scripture. A rich source of a pronounced anti-Catholic strand in Charles Wesley's thought is to be found here in his eschatology. Newport has argued that Charles Wesley's interest in a form of eschatology that bore the hallmarks of pre-millennialism was discernible from an early stage and ran throughout the course of his documented career. However, there appears to have been a heightening of interest from at least the early 1740s onwards (Newport cites the example of Charles' 1742 sermon, 'Awake, thou that Sleepest'), culminating in the apocalyptic atmosphere triggered by the London earthquakes of 1750.[56] In the letter of 25 April 1754 to an unknown correspondent already cited above, Charles Wesley stated that he first began to study scriptural prophecies and chronology in depth at around that time, reading Joseph Mede's commentary *Clavis Apocalyptica* (1627) on the Book of Revelation and Bishop Thomas Newton's books on Daniel and Revelation:

> The first time I began to attempt the scripture calculations relating to the conversion of the Jews, the fall of Antichrist and the introduction of the fullness of the Gentiles was in the year 1746. And having made myself master of an ancient chronology, I did then make such calculations as happened to become pretty near to what I now find to be the truth.[57]

The poem composed during his experiences of Irish Catholicism, cited above, bore traces of the influence of this study. In the April 1754 letter itself, Charles Wesley gives vent to an apocalyptic anti-Catholicism which portrayed Rome as Antichrist and which belonged firmly in the tradition of Mede, Newton and others. He informed his correspondent that the scripture prophecies would be fulfilled within one man's lifetime, with 'ye destruction of the Romish AntiChrist' to be accomplished by the year 1794. As he bloodcurdlingly put it in the letter: 'Babylon will be finally destroyed, although first she will be given power to persecute the Protestants.' In fact, compared to the confident expectation among many Anglican divines in the second half of the eighteenth century that the power and influence of Roman Catholicism was ebbing away, Charles Wesley struck a profoundly pessimistic tone, claiming that Rome had as yet (1754) 'gained but a small increase in comparison of what it has yet to gain', and that while the destruction of the Romish Antichrist was certain, yet: 'before she shall be brought to her final ruin, power shall be given her to distress the Protestant Churches by wars and persecutions, and many of Christ's faithful ones in those days shall be tried and purified and made white'.[58]

Newport has concluded that, when it came to eschatology, Charles Wesley was much more confident that he could decipher the imagery of the Book of Revelation than was his brother John.[59] It might be inferred, therefore, that to this limited extent at least his anti-Catholicism was arguably keener and more theologically grounded, though John himself uncritically accepted Johannes Bengel's prediction of the death of the Papacy in 1836. John lifted the prediction into his *Explanatory Notes on the New Testament*, an embarrassing move given that those *Notes* were meant to be a standard of preaching and belief within the Methodist movement.[60]

## Charles Wesley and the Roman Catholic devotional tradition

John Wesley's debt to continental Roman Catholic devotional sources, edited versions of which found a prominent place in his own *Christian Library* (1749–55), has been exhaustively analysed.[61] Much less attention has been accorded to the influence of such devotional sources on Charles Wesley's spirituality. In 1737 there is evidence of Charles having read Pascal's *Prayer for Conversion*. Moreover, it has been suggested that his account of his own 'conversion' experience in 1738 bore strong echoes of Pascal's thought. He also appears to have read Thomas à Kempis and Lorenzo Scupoli's *Spiritual Combat* in the version by Castaniza at an early age.[62] There is also evidence of his reading de Renty's life if he was the author of the poem 'On reading Monsieur de Renty'.[63] Nonetheless, Butler has concluded that Charles Wesley came to be more critical of the Catholic spiritual writers as time passed, and probably more critical than his brother ever was. He cites as evidence Charles Wesley's preface to his *Hymns and Sacred Poems* of 1739:

> Some verses, it may be observed, in the following Collection, were wrote upon the Scheme of the Mystick Divines. And these, 'tis owned, we had once in great Veneration, as the best Explainers of the Gospel of CHRIST. But we are now convinced that we therein greatly err'd: not knowing the Scriptures, neither the Power of GOD.[64]

In the wake of his own conversion, Charles had become critical of Catholic mystical writers for using their inward righteousness as the basis of acceptance by God, and for choosing the path of solitude rather than congregation or community as the path to reach God.

Moreover, selective use of Roman Catholic devotional aids was one thing, but any approximation to Roman Catholic doctrine quite another. John Wesley was accused by Bishop Lavington of advocating prayers for the dead,[65] but Wesley cited the Book of Common Prayer's burial service and claimed not to have departed from what he regarded as scriptural practice – he insisted on only praying for those in heaven and not in Purgatory. There is no evidence that Charles Wesley went further. Charles Wesley certainly observed All Saints' Day, to which there are many references in his journal. However, it has been noted that throughout his vast poetical corpus there are no poems devoted to Saints' Days as such and little mention of the Blessed Virgin Mary, 'except the conventional Christmas reference to Jesus as Mary's son, and offspring of the Virgin's womb'.[66] There is no equivalent in Charles Wesley's poetical *oeuvre*, for example, of the Anglican John Henry Newman's sermons and discourses on the Virgin Mary.

Lines of theological convergence, however, between the eucharistic theology of Charles Wesley's *Hymns on the Lord's Supper* and that of the modern *Catechism of the Catholic Church*, have been fruitfully explored by Teresa Berger. She notes that they both emphasize the notion of sacrifice and both have strongly Trinitarian emphases. She cites several stanzas from Charles' *Hymns on the Lord's Supper*, notably Hymn 122, 3, and concludes that they can be characterized by the term a 'Protestant Crucifix', owing to their emphasis on the details and instruments of Christ's Passion typical of Roman Catholic devotion.[67]

Nonetheless, Charles was careful not to sacrifice Protestant doctrine out of any qualified empathy for a certain strand of Roman Catholic devotional literature. Admiration for such literature coexisted with a deep-rooted horror of supposed Roman Catholic 'corruptions' in both doctrine and practice.

## Charles Wesley and Roman Catholic doctrine

Charles Wesley's anti-Catholicism was not restricted to issues of political allegiance or eschatological fulfilment but had clear doctrinal roots. It was

also linked to his enduring loyalty to what he affectionately called 'our desolate Mother', the Church of England and his desire to see her restored to full
life and vigour. One of the doctrinal issues that emerged more clearly in his
thought in the wake of his conversion experience of 1738 was a heightened
understanding of the doctrine of Justification by Faith Alone. He complained
that many members of the Church of England no longer accepted or understood the doctrine, but that rather it had become 'a popish jumble of faith and
works'.[68] In a sermon preached before the University of Oxford on 1 July 1739,
he lamented that the Reformation doctrine of Justification by Faith Alone as
enshrined in the Articles and Homilies of the Church of England had been
diluted or abandoned by large numbers of Anglican clergy 'from the time
of the Grand Rebellion', as part of an over-excessive reaction against Puritan
doctrine which had come to be identified with political anarchy. Against this
perceived trend, Charles called for a clearer demarcation line between the
Church of England and Roman Catholicism on this doctrinal point:

> Let not those therefore who deny this doctrine any longer call themselves of
> the Church of England. They may be of the Church of Rome, but cannot be of
> ours, who allow works any share in our justification with God. Papists indeed
> they are, though they may not know it, for they lay the wood, hay, stubble
> of their own works, not as the superstructure, but as the very foundation, of
> their acceptance with God . . . This is our Church's censure of all that bring
> any other doctrine than justification by faith only; she calls them antichrists
> who presume to say they can by their own works justify themselves.[69]

For Charles Wesley, the 'worst error of Popery' was 'Justification by Works'.[70]
Berger has noted the irony of this accusation being made by Charles Wesley
given the similar charges made against the Wesley brothers themselves by
Calvinist contemporaries.[71] These charges can be dated from at least as early
as George Whitefield's and Howel Harris' (representatives of the Calvinist
wing of the early Methodist movement) breach with John and Charles Wesley
in 1740–1.

George Whitefield's *A Letter to the Rev. John Wesley in answer to his sermon
entitled 'Free Grace'* (1741) was a response to John Wesley's criticisms of the
doctrines of election and predestination. Whitefield's *Letter* seemed to
mark a doctrinal parting of the ways between the two factions within early
Methodism. As David Ceri Jones has shown in a recent article, the apparent rift was exacerbated by the arrival in England at this time of the leader
of the revival in Wales, Howel Harris. Harris became locked in controversy
with Charles Wesley over the doctrine of predestination. For Howel Harris,
Charles Wesley's belief in freewill and a universal atonement bordered on
Popery. He accused Charles of having, at root, strong sympathies with the
Roman Catholic Church, partly because of his recommending 'Papist Saints',
and declared that as a consequence he would have to separate from Charles
and his brother. As Harris recorded in his diary in June 1740:

> had freedom to tell all – how I did suspect them Popishly inclined – 1st as
> recommending papist Sts – 2 having their Doctrine etc – 3 not being simple

and open but he sd that all had or have or shall have freewill – I sd I must then divide from him & declare agt him on that acct.[72]

However, it seems that sensitivity to Protestant charges (primarily from Calvinists) that they were allowing too much space for 'Works' in the economy of salvation and that their doctrine of Christian Perfection was 'Popish', actually made the Wesley brothers more anxious to demonstrate their orthodox Protestant credentials. They could most easily achieve this by emphasizing Justification by Faith Alone and castigating Roman Catholicism for allowing a place for Works where they felt that there should be none – in the act of a sinner being justified.

The subject of Charles Wesley's high eucharistic doctrine as evident in his *Hymns on the Lord's Supper* is also relevant to perceptions of his attitude to Roman Catholicism. While the eucharistic theology of his hymns was in accord with or derived from high church Anglican doctrine as set forth by Caroline Divines (notably John Cosin and Daniel Brevint), it was evidently a source of potential embarrassment to the Protestant sensitivities of later generations of Methodists in the era of the Oxford Movement and a resurgent Roman Catholicism. It is probably for this reason that passages or stanzas open to a 'Popish' interpretation were edited out or excised by George Osborn, President of the Wesleyan Methodist Conferences of 1863 and 1881 and an editor of the *Hymns* in 13 volumes (published 1868–72). As the author of a series of polemical *Wesleyan Tracts for the Times*, Osborn's writings on the subject, but still more more those of J. H. Rigg, were coloured by the vigorous anti-Catholicism and anti-Tractarianism characteristic of nineteenth-century Methodism.[73]

Another apparent doctrinal aberration with which Charles Wesley charged Roman Catholicism was what he regarded as its having added 'legendary tales' as well as doctrines to the Faith once Delivered to the Saints – a conventional high church Anglican ground of critique of Roman Catholicism.

## Charles Wesley and the episode of the Gordon riots (1780)

John Wesley's reputation for eirenicism has certainly suffered from the ambivalent role he seemed to play at the time of the so-called Gordon riots in London in 1780 when anti-Catholic mobs laid waste not only to Catholic property but to large swathes of the City of London under the inspiration of a firebrand anti-Catholic rabble-rouser Lord George Gordon, leader of the so-called Protestant Association. His *Popery Calmly Considered* (1779) was much reported in the press and was even blamed for the Gordon riots. Although he eventually distanced himself from the agitation, John Wesley controversially defended the Protestant Association in print by reawakening old anti-Catholic fears. He recycled conventional anti-Catholic rhetoric and raised the old bugbears of 'bloody Mary' and the 'fires of Smithfield':

It is sincerely to be lamented that Protestants in general, are not more apprehensive of the danger. Have they forgot the reign of bloody queen

Mary? Have they forgot the fires of Smithfield, and can they behold the place without emotion where their fathers died? Will it ever be believed in future times, that persons of eminent and distinguished rank among the Protestants, and persons of high and exalted religious character, refused to petition against Popery . . . ?[74]

Not surprisingly, Wesley was accused of fanning the flames of anti-Catholic discontent and he was heavily criticized by Catholic apologists as a result. In a published letter to John Wesley, the Irish Capuchin friar Arthur O'Leary chided him for turning into an advocate of persecution, even though he had himself been the victim of persecution from established authority and been a religious innovator. For O'Leary, Wesley was:

> a MISSIONARY, *who has reformed the very reformation; separated* from all the Protestant churches, and in trimming the vessel of religion, which he has brought into a new ark, has suffered as much for the sake of conscience, as Ludovic Muggleton or James Nailer could register in their martyrology. Remark that same gentleman inflaming the rabble, and throwing the gauntlet to people who never provoked him.[75]

In response, an embarrassed Wesley distinguished between physical persecution which he rejected, and civil toleration for Catholics which he rejected on the conventional Anglican grounds of fears for the safety of the constitution and not on the theological ground of the truth or error of Roman Catholicism as a system of faith:

> With persecution I have nothing to do: I persecute no man for his religious principles. I consider not whether the Romish religion be true or false. I build nothing on one or the other supposition . . . Suppose every word of Pope Pius's creed to be true, – suppose the Council of Trent to have been infallible, – yet I insist upon it, that no government, not Roman Catholic, ought to tolerate men of the Roman Catholic persuasion.[76]

In contrast, Charles Wesley seems to have played an ameliorating and conciliatory role throughout the episode. He refrained from signing the petition drawn up for the repeal of the Catholic Relief Act of 1778 (which had granted the right of Roman Catholics to own property and ended life imprisonment for convicted Roman Catholic priests) and the petition against Popery which his brother recommended, and did not lend his voice in support of his brother's *Popery Calmly Considered*. He even identified with the besieged Catholics of London during the course of the Gordon riots. For a time it seemed that even City Road chapel, the nerve centre of London Methodism, was under threat from the mob who were not always discerning in the objects of their fury. In a letter to his brother John written at the height of the riots when he himself was at City Road, Charles declared:

> Imagine the terror of the poor papists. I prayed with the preachers at the chapel, and urged them to keep the peace. I preached peace and charity,

the one true religion, and prayed earnestly for the trembling persecuted Catholics. Never have I found such love for them as on this occasion.[77]

At the same time, in a letter to his daughter Sally, Charles wryly observed: 'No wonder your mother was terrified, when I was prescribed as a Popish person, for I never signed the Petition or ranked among the Patriots.'[78] Charles even wrote a satire on Lord George Gordon's Protestant Association, entitled *The Protestant Association in the Midst of Tumults.*[79]

## Charles Wesley's response to his son Samuel's conversion to Roman Catholicism (1784)[80]

As early as 1778 Charles was becoming concerned at the attendance of his son Samuel at Roman Catholic services, probably those at the embassy chapels which were the main centres of worship for Roman Catholics in London. As he confided to his wife Sarah: 'Sam wants more pains to be taken with him. If I should not live to help him, it will all lie upon you. Make him a living Christian, and he will never wish to be a dead Papist.'[81] Charles felt that the influence of a Monsieur Choquet was responsible for leading Samuel junior astray, informing Sarah in September 1778 that he thought that Choquet's agreeable conversation and company 'have given Sam his unhappy turn to Popery. Tis time to shut the stable door.'[82] At a slightly later date, the formative influence on Samuel in the direction of Roman Catholicism appears to have been Mary Freeman Shepherd, a Roman Catholic intellectual with Methodist sympathies who befriended him and became his self-appointed spiritual adviser and mentor.[83] When Samuel finally joined the Catholic Church in 1784, the news was broken to his father by the Duchess of Norfolk in a formal and embarrassing interview.

It might be asked if there was anything in Samuel Wesley junior's education and upbringing and being the son of Charles Wesley that might have predisposed him towards his youthful attraction towards Roman Catholicism and eventual conversion to Rome. Phillip Olleson, the most authoritative contemporary scholarly authority on Samuel Wesley junior and a contributor to this volume, has rightly highlighted the untypical nature of Samuel's path to Rome, concluding 'that what initially drew him to Roman Catholicism was its music rather than its doctrines',[84] while cautioning also that allowance should be made for Samuel's later violent opposition to Catholicism and anxiety to play down the extent and nature of his early involvement. Thus, perhaps inspired by his later rejection of Roman Catholic doctrines, Samuel later insisted that 'although the Gregorian music had seduced him to their chapels, the tenets of the Romanists never obtained any influence over his mind'.[85] This could have represented a convenient rewriting of history, and it was one which may have suited later Methodist historians embarrassed by the whole episode. Samuel's unusual combination of enduring fascination for Roman Catholic liturgy and music, alongside an apparent growing post-conversion distaste for its teachings and doctrines, has prompted it to be described as 'one of the oddest conversions to that church of which record has been preserved'.[86]

Whatever the extent of Samuel's commitment to Catholicism, Olleson points out that it was enough to test the tolerance of the most indulgent father and was bound to provoke dismay and alarm in Charles Wesley, especially coming as it did in the period of the first Catholic Relief Act of 1778 and subsequent Gordon riots of 1780.[87] The first hymn which Charles composed in the wake of his son's joining the Roman Catholic Church was infused with anti-Catholic invective:

Surely Thou hast in Babylon,
Where Satan fills his favourite throne,
Thy worshippers sincere

Who pure as Lot in Sodom live,
Glory to their Redeemer give
And love the God they fear.

To These my murder'd son unite,
Give him with these to walk in light,
Where hellish darkness reigns.[88]

In another hymn, Charles' anti-Catholic rhetoric was no less marked:

That poison of the Romish sect,
O let it not his soul infect,
With close serpentine art,
With bitter persecuting zeal;
But from those mysteries of hell
Preserve his simple heart.[89]

In the earlier hymn, we find a recurrence of the eschatological 'Babylonish Beast' language in Charles Wesley's writing, noted earlier. Nonetheless, as Berger observes, there was at least a clear recognition here that there could be 'sincere worshippers', 'walking in the light', in the Roman Catholic Church to which his son Samuel had recently joined.[90] The same poem also returned to doctrinal grounds of offence for which Charles held Roman Catholicism accountable, as is clear from this stanza:

Preserve, that he may never know
Those doctrines of the hellish foe
Which contradict thy word.[91]

Nonetheless, it was the personal note of sacrifice of a sin, with echoes of the sacrifice of Isaac by Abraham, that was the dominant theme of the poem which he wrote immediately in the wake of Samuel's conversion:

Farewell, my all of earthly hope,
My nature's stay, my age's prop,
Irrevocably gone!
Submissive to the will divine

I acquiesce, and make it mine;
I offer up my Son.[92]

In contrast to his anti-Catholic diatribes at the time of the Catholic Relief Act, however, John Wesley was relatively conciliatory (though as Samuel's uncle he was somewhat less emotionally involved than Charles), professing to be unconcerned as to the precise form, 'Protestant or Romish', that Samuel's religious observance took:

Whether of this church or that, I care not: you may be saved in either, or damned in either, but I fear you are not born again; and except you be born again you cannot see the kingdom of god. You believe the Church of Rome is right. What then. If you are not born of God, you are of no church.[93]

John insisted that he was unconcerned about which church it was to which Samuel belonged, as long as he was Christian, though he regarded it as a great loss that he had turned away from Methodist preaching. Here was a recurrence of the way in which John Wesley's (and, at other times, Charles') insistence on the primacy of 'godliness' and 'new birth' in Christ took precedence over denominational boundaries and allowed in practice a certain eirenicism even towards Rome. Samuel Wesley, according to his uncle, might have become a 'real scriptural Christian' if he had remained true to Methodism, but he could not deny that as a Roman Catholic convert he was still a Christian. Yet even at this troubled time, Charles was capable of matching the more catholic spirit of his brother. As one stanza of one of his poems written at the time put it:

Against the instrument of ill
O may I no resentment find,
No wrong, vindictive temper feel,
Unfriendly wish, or thought unkind;
But put the yearning bowels on,
The tender mercies of Thy Son.[94]

## Conclusions

It has been suggested that the very lack of scholarly attention to the subject of Charles Wesley and Roman Catholicism might be interpreted as a tribute to Charles Wesley's relative moderation and reservation on the issue.[95] David Hempton has argued that is difficult to establish what was typical of John Wesley's views on Roman Catholicism, because so much of the evidence comes from his journal which is 'a series of random comments occasioned by particular historical circumstances'.[96] The same difficulty applies in relation to Charles Wesley's views, and for the same reason. However, the evidence which does exist points to an essential ambivalence and ambiguity in Charles Wesley's attitudes towards Roman Catholicism. On the one hand, the demands of evangelistic mission in Catholic Ireland could induce conciliation and open-mindedness, but this was an essentially tactical and often short-lived response in the face of hard confessional realities and was often offset by a hostile attitude to Catholicism in an Irish context. On the other hand, when anxious to allay Protestant oppositions from outside, or Calvinist suspicions from within the Methodist movement, Charles Wesley was as capable as his brother of striking an anti-Catholic position, while his eschatological concerns could push him into an even more stridently anti-Catholic posture with highly coloured apocalyptic rhetoric about Rome being 'drunk with the blood of the Saints' (cf. Revelation 17.6). Moreover, Charles was probably more critical in his use of Catholic mystical writers than his brother ever was, and he remained ever alive to what he regarded as the doctrinal 'corruptions' of Popery.

It also needs to be recognized that both John and Charles' attitudes could have been hardened by their own contacts with continental Protestants, such as those expelled from Salzburg in 1731, whose encounters with Catholicism had been very different from their own and from whom they absorbed much in theological terms. Nonetheless, if a trend can be discerned in Charles Wesley's outlook it was in the direction of a certain mellowing and broadening of attitude towards Catholicism in his later years. For example, in 1771 after he had distanced himself from an earlier *rapprochement* with that 'Archbishop in Petticoats', Selina, Countess of Huntingdon, he appeared to make a favourable comparison of Roman Catholicism with Calvinism: in a letter to his daughter Sally, he observed that a 'sensible Roman Catholic' was more than a match for a Calvinist and that 'her Ladyship', the Countess, was too close to the 'Antinomian extreme' for his liking.[97] This mellowing was evidenced in his response to the Catholic Relief Act and Gordon riots (which contrasted with that of his brother), though the emotion of the paternal relationship partly explains his anguished reaction to his son's conversion. Charles Wesley's anti-Catholicism was essentially that of a conventional orthodox Protestant churchman, but as a child of the eighteenth century it could be and was offset and softened by tolerationist instincts and, above all, by an enduring belief that genuine godliness and holiness could not be confined within denomin--ational boundaries. In this way, Charles Wesley's very 'evangelicalism' served to moderate an often dormant or latent anti-Catholicism.

## Notes

1 A. Knox, 'On the Situation and Prospects of the Established Church' (4 June 1816), *Remains of Alexander Knox*, 2 vols (2nd edn, London, 1836), vol. 1, 58.
2 M. Piette, *John Wesley and the Evolution of Protestantism . . . Translated by the Rev. J. B. Howard* (London: Sheed & Ward, 1937), 15–19.
3 [G. Lavington], *The Enthusiasm of Methodists and Papists Compared*, 3rd edn (London, 1752), 172.
4 [R. Challoner], *A Caveat Against the Methodists: Showing how unsafe it is for any Christian to join himself to their society, or to adhere to their teachers* (London: M. Cooper, 1760), 5–6.
5 J. H. Newman, 'Memoir of the Countess of Huntingdon', *British Critic*, vol. xxviii (October, 1840).

6 J. Walsh, 'Methodism and the Mob', *Popular Belief and Practice* (Studies in Church History, vol. 8, ed. G. J. Cuming and Derek Baker) (Cambridge: Cambridge University Press, 1972), 214.

7 See his comment in his journal for 27 August 1739: 'The report now current in Bristol was that I was a Papist, if not a Jesuit. I can by no means approve the scurrility and contempt with which the Papists have been treated.' J. Wesley, 'An Answer to the Rev. Mr Church's Remarks', *The Works of John Wesley*, ed. J. Emory (New York edn, 1871), v, 267.

8 R. Glen, 'Man or Beast? English Methodists as Animals in 18th Century Satiric Prints', *Connecticut Review*, xv, 2 (Fall, 1993), p. 83.

9 *Methodism and Popery Dissected and Compared; and the doctrines of both proved to be derived from a Pagan origin: including an impartial and candid enquiry into the writings of St Paul* (London, 1779), 27.

10 See M. Selen, *The Oxford Movement and Wesleyan Methodism in England 1833–1882: A study in religious conflict* (Lund: Lund University Press, 1992), esp. chapter 3.

11 C. Haydon, *Anti-Catholicism in Eighteenth-century England, c. 1714–80: A political and social study* (Manchester: Manchester University Press, 1993), esp. introduction.

12 Rack, *Reasonable Enthusiast*, 310.

13 J. Sack, *From Jacobite to Conservative: Reaction and orthodoxy in Britain c. 1760–1832* (Cambridge: Cambridge University Press, 1993), chapter 9; N. Aston, *Christianity and Revolutionary Europe c. 1750–1830* (Cambridge: Cambridge University Press, 2002), 202.

14 D. Butler, *Methodists and Papists: John Wesley and the Catholic Church in the eighteenth century* (London: Darton, Longman & Todd, 1995). Cf. Oliver A. Beckerlegge, *John Wesley's Writings on Roman Catholicism* (London: Protestant Truth Society, 1993).

15 D. Hempton, 'John Wesley and the Rise of Methodism', *John Wesley Tercentenary Essays: Proceedings of a Conference held at the University of Manchester, June 2003*, ed. Jeremy Gregory, *Bulletin of the John Rylands University Library of Manchester*, 85, 2 & 3 (Summer and Autumn 2003), 38.

16 K. Rowe, 'The Search for the Historical Wesley', in *The Place of Wesley in the Christian Tradition*, ed. K. Rowe (Metuchen: Scarecrow Press, 1976), 1–3.

17 M. Massa, 'The Catholic Wesley: A Revisionist Prolegomenon', *Methodist History* xxii, no. I (October 1983), 38–53. See J. Orcibal, 'The Theological Originality of John Wesley and Continental Spirituality', *A History of the Methodist Church in Great Britain*, eds. R. Davies and G. Rupp (London: Epworth Press, 1965), vol. 1, especially 83–111; J. Orcibal, 'The Theological Originality of John Wesley and Continental Spirituality', *A History of the Methodist Church in Great Britain*, eds. R. Davies and G. Rupp (London: Epworth Press, 1965), vol. I, 83–111. See also J. Todd, *John Wesley and the Catholic Church* (London: Hodder & Stoughton, 1958).

18 Massa, 'The Catholic Wesley', 52.

19 H. Bett, 'A French Marquis and the Class Meeting', *PWHS*, 18 (1931–2), 43–5.

20 T. Bridgen, 'Pascal and the Wesleys', *Proceedings of the Wesley Historical Society*, 7 (1910), 61; J. Barber, *Strange Contrarieties: Pascal in England during the Age of Reason* (London: McGill-Queen's University Press, 1975), 181–2.

21 E. Duffy, 'Wesley and the Counter Reformation', *Revival and Religion Since 1700: Essays for John Walsh*, eds J. Garnett and C. Matthew (London: Hambledon, 1993), 5.

22  F. Frost, 'Biblical Imagery and Religious Experience in the Hymns of the Wesleys', *Proceedings of the Wesley Historical Society*, 42 (1980), 158–66. See also Fr Frost's exposition of the high sacramental themes in Charles Wesley's hymns in F. Frost, 'The Veiled Unveiling of the Glory of God in the Eucharistic Hymns of Charles Wesley: The Self-Emptying Glory of God', *Proceedings of the Charles Wesley Society*, vol. 2, ed. S T Kimbrough (1995), 87–99.

23  See Newport, *Sermons*, 277–86.

24  Kenneth G. C. Newport, 'Charles Wesley and the End of the World', *Proceedings of the Charles Wesley Society*, vol. 3, ed. S T Kimbrough (1996), 33–62.

25  On which see further above, Chapter 8.

26  *A True and Historical Narrative of the Colony of Georgia in America from the first settlement thereof until this present period* (Charles-Town, 1741), 41–2. Significantly, John Wesley even aroused the suspicions of leading members of the SPCK such as Sir John Phillips on account of a supposed too great leniency towards Popery. See *The Diaries of Thomas Wilson*, ed. C. L. S. Linnell (London: SPCK, 1964), 128–9. Partly on account of his abstemiousness and regime of fasting, Charles Wesley was accused of being 'an emissary, a Jesuit, a devil' by a fellow passenger on the return voyage from Georgia in 1736; CWJ, 1.41.

27  [Lavington], *Enthusiasm of Methodists and Papists Compared*, 166.

28  Rack, *Reasonable Enthusiast*, 310.

29  BE, 2.79ff.

30  CWJ, 1.31.

31  CWJ, 1.408.

32  PW, 4:3–90, especially 89: 'The waster of *Rome* Is now on his way, The Lion is come To scatter and slay: Beyond his fierce power We run to the Lamb, And rest in the tower Of Jesus's name.'

33  PW, 4.95.

34  Charles Wesley to Sarah Wesley, [9 July] 1759, MARC, DDCW, 7/18.

35  R. C. Strickland, *Religion and the State in Georgia in the Eighteenth Century* (New York: AMS Press, 1939), 79–82; *Diary of Viscount Percival, Afterwards First Earl of Egmont*, 2 vols (London: HMC, 1920), i, 299.

36  BE, 18.182.

37  BE, 18.511; but cf. 18.182 for the printed version of the journal for this date.

38  CWJ, 1.394.

39  CWJ, 1.457.

40  CWJ, 1.460.

41  CWJ, 1.460.

42  CWJ, 1.461.

43  CWJ, 1.460.

44  CWJ, 1.462.

45  CWJ, 1.22.

46  J. Wesley, *Letter to a Roman Catholic* (1749), cited in Butler, *Methodists and Papists*, 213–14.

47  CWJ, 2.3.

48  CWJ, 1.27.

49  CWJ, 1.5.

50  CWJ, 1.34.

51  CWJ, 1.36.

52  CWJ, 1.34.

53  CWJ, 1.27.

54  Berger, 'Charles Wesley and Roman Catholicism', in *Charles Wesley: Poet and theologian*, 217.

55  Rack, *Reasonable Enthusiast*, 310.

56  Newport, 'Charles Wesley and the End of the World', especially 49–51.

57  Charles Wesley to UC, 25 April 1754, MARC, DDCW, 1/51. A transcription of this letter appears in Kenneth G. C. Newport, *Apocalypse and Millennium: Studies in biblical eisegesis* (Cambridge: Cambridge University Press, 2000), 144–9.

58  MARC, DDCW, 1/51.

59  Newport, 'Charles Wesley and the End of the World', especially 52–6.

60  Butler, *Methodists and Papists*, 130–4.

61  Butler, *Methodists and Papists*, 148–54. John Wesley's *Christian Library* included among his chosen 50 volumes the works of Pascal, Fénélon, the Letters of John of Avila, the Life of Gregory Lopez, and a Guide to Molinos – 'a heavy dose of Roman Catholic spirituality'. Orcibal, 'Theological Originality of John Wesley and Continental Spirituality', 93.

62  C. Wallace, '"Some Stated Employment of Your Mind": Reading, Writing and Religion in the Life of Susanna Wesley', *Church History*, 58 (1989), 354–66, especially 357; Berger, 'Charles Wesley and Roman Catholicism', 207; Barber, *Pascal in England*, 181–2.

63  Berger, 'Charles Wesley and Roman Catholicism', 247n.

64  *PW*, 1.xix.

65  [Lavington], *Enthusiasm of Methodists and Papists Compared*, 166–7.

66  L. Wiseman, *Charles Wesley: Evangelist and poet* (London, 1932), 131.

67  T. Berger, '"Finding Echoes": *The Catechism of the Catholic Church* and the Hymns on the Lord's Supper', *Proceedings of the Charles Wesley Society*, vol. 2, ed. S T Kimbrough (1995), 68.

68  Newport, *Sermons*, 205.

69  Newport, *Sermons*, 205.

70  Cited in J. R. Tyson, 'Charles Wesley, Evangelist: The Unpublished New Castle Journal', *Methodist History*, 25 (1986), 49.

71  Berger, 'Charles Wesley and Roman Catholicism', 215.

72  D. C. Jones, '"The Lord did give me a particular honour to make [me] a peacemaker": Howel Harris, John Wesley and Methodist infighting, 1739–1750', *John Wesley Tercentenary Essays*, 87.

73  J. E. Rattenbury, *The Eucharistic Hymns of John and Charles Wesley* (London, Epworth Press, 1948), 13–19, 87ff.; see also Selen, *Oxford Movement and Wesleyan Methodism in England*, 230–1.

74  J. Wesley, 'A Defence of the Protestant Association', *Miscellaneous Tracts by the Rev Arthur O'Leary*, 2nd edn (Dublin, 1781), 202.

75  A. O'Leary, 'Remarks on Mr Wesley's Letter', *Miscellaneous Tracts by the Rev. Arthur O'Leary*, 221.

76  'A Letter from the Rev John Wesley, M.A. to the printer', *Miscellaneous Tracts by the Rev. Arthur O'Leary*, 2nd edn (Dublin, 1781), 192.

77  Jackson, *Life*, 2.320.

78  C. Wesley to Sally Wesley, 14 June 1780, MARC, DDCW, 7/42.

79  *PW*, 8.449–78.

80  See also above, pp. 133–5.

81  C. Wesley to Sarah Gwynne Wesley, 7 September 1778, MARC, DDCW, 736.

82  C. Wesley to Sarah Gwynne Wesley, 22 September 1778, MARC, DDCW, 7/35.

83  Olleson, *Samuel Wesley*, 27.

84  Olleson, *Samuel Wesley*, 26.

85  Olleson, *Samuel Wesley*, 29n; see also *The Letters of Samuel Wesley: Professional and social correspondence, 1797–1837*, ed. Philip Olleson (Oxford, 2001), xxviii.

86  E. Routley, *The Musical Wesleys* (New York, 1968), 65.

87  See further above, pp.

88  *The Unpublished Poetry of Charles Wesley*, 3 vols, eds. S T Kimbrough and O. Beckerlegge (Nashville: Kingswood Books, 1988–91), 1.303.

89  *PW*, 8.424.

90  Berger, 'Charles Wesley and Roman Catholicism', 213.

91  *Unpublished Poetry*, 1.310.

92  *Unpublished Poetry*, 1.304.

93  John Wesley to Samuel Wesley, 19 August 1784, *Letters of John Wesley*, vol. 7, 230–1.

94  *Unpublished Poetry*, 1.315.

95  Berger, 'Charles and Roman Catholicism', 219.

96  D. Hempton, *Methodism and Politics in British Society 1750–1850* (London: Hutchinson, 1984), 36.

97  C. Wesley to Sally Wesley, 27 May 1771, MARC, DDWES, 4/30.

# 10. Charles Wesley and a Window to the East

## S T KIMBROUGH JR

It has long been maintained that there is a strong influence of the early Church Fathers reflected in the theology and writings of John Wesley.[1] There have already been a number of studies of such influence and it is not the purpose here to review that bibliography.[2] Until recently, however, far less attention has been paid to Charles Wesley in this regard and it is the purpose of this chapter to fill this gap and to explore the 'window to the East' that one discovers in his writings. As we shall see, the study is not an unimportant one, for, though the case can be made for the influence of the Church Fathers on John, Gordon Wakefield's suggestion that 'Charles . . . is even more with the East'[3] seems to stand critical evaluation.

This chapter begins with a brief survey of recent publications that, at least in broad terms, treat the question of Charles Wesley and the East. An important point to note in this context, though it cannot be addressed in any detail here, is that while a number of scholars have explored resonances with the Church Fathers in the writings of the Wesleys, such studies underscore the fact that no matter what doctrinal convergences one may find in the Orthodox and Wesleyan traditions, there is yet much to be done in working out the methodology by which one studies theological traditions which are centuries apart but which share sources of history, knowledge and theology.

The survey of recent publications relative to this area is followed by a study of Charles Wesley texts, many of which have not before been included in such discussions. While there are many common resonances of thought in Charles Wesley's writings and the Orthodox tradition, his poetical texts cited in this chapter address the following areas of thought: (1) The nature of God – [a] God as Mystery, [b] God as divine essence and energy; and (2) *Theosis* and the Trinity. The latter will not treat the nature of God as Trinity *per se*, rather participation in the life of the Trinity as reflected in Charles Wesley's *Hymns on the Trinity* (1767).

## Annotated bibliography

It is only in recent years that there have been a significant number of explorations of the channels of influence and common resonances in the works of

Charles Wesley and Orthodoxy. A brief survey of some noteworthy investigations follows.

Anglican scholar A. M. Allchin was one of the first to explore substantively the close affinity of Charles Wesley and the Church Fathers. Against the background of the influence of seventeenth-century Anglicans Richard Hooker and Lancelot Andrewes, Allchin explores the doctrines of deification (*theosis*), Trinity and Incarnation from within the works of the Wesleys, Williams Pantycelyn and some of the early Church Fathers. Early in his discussion Allchin notes, 'Hooker opens up the way for a reaffirmation of the patristic conviction that man can indeed become partaker of the divine nature, but only and always by gift and grace, never by right and nature.'[4] It is in Andrewes' affirmation of the mystery of the *incarnatio Dei*, the Incarnation of God, and a corresponding mystery, the *inspiratio hominis*, the inspiration of a human being, that Charles Wesley in particular finds affinity with Andrewes. Allchin is convinced that one of the reasons for John and Charles Wesley's disagreement about perfection/sanctification in this life and the next is that Charles adheres to an earlier pattern of *theosis* of the Church Fathers whereas John does not.

More specifically Nicholas Lossky, in his study 'Lancelot Andrewes: A Bridge between Orthodoxy and the Wesley Brothers on Prayer',[5] discusses the fact that Andrewes, who preceded the Wesleys by a century, was immersed in patristics, a not insignificant observation here since it is clear that the Wesleys were very much aware of Andrewes and indeed were influenced by him. This was not merely a matter of both Andrewes and the Wesleys being deeply rooted in the early Church Fathers. What they shared, according to Lossky, was 'the patristic experience of God, deeply rooted in the scriptures and the liturgy of the Church'.[6] Lossky draws from Andrewes' *Preces Privatae* and Charles Wesley's hymns to illustrate the closeness of their patristic experience of God, for they 'prayed privately in ecclesial, liturgical terms'.[7]

In a chapter entitled 'John Wesley: Christian Perfection as Faith Filled with the Energy of Love' in the volume *Partakers of the Divine Nature*,[8] Michael J. Christensen includes a section with the title 'Charles Wesley's Forgotten Strand'. He reviews Allchin's perspectives on Charles and *theosis* and concludes that the poet-priest brings into one cosmic vision the doctrines of Incarnation, sanctification, glorification and deification (*theosis*).

In an article '*Theosis* in the Writings of Charles Wesley',[9] I address Charles Wesley's understanding of *theosis* as revealed in the Incarnation and in the Eucharist. There is no attempt to compare Wesley's views with parallel understandings in the Church Fathers; rather, to garner the broad spectrum of his thought on deification in the light of Wesley's poems primarily from two collections, *Hymns for the Nativity of Our Lord* (1745) and *Hymns on the Lord's Supper* (1745). These poems make clear that one may approach 'being made divine' only in the context of the ultimate Mystery, which cannot be fully comprehended. How one is transformed into the divine nature remains a mystery for Wesley.

In addition to his work, *Participation in God, A Forgotten Strand in Anglican Tradition*, A. M. Allchin has written a fascinating article with the title, 'The Trinity in the Teaching of Charles Wesley: A Study in Eighteenth-Century

Orthodoxy?'[10] In this article the author focuses on Wesley's volume *Hymns on the Trinity* (1767), based largely on William Jones of Neyland's volume *The Catholic Doctrine of the Trinity* (1757), as a remarkably perceptive lyrical response to the trends of rationalism, anti-Trinitarian and anti-Incarnational currents of the eighteenth century. Allchin avers that John and Charles Wesley maintained in large measure 'the tradition of Trinitarian and incarnational faith which was articulated in the first five centuries of Christian history',[11] though Charles perhaps more so. His subsequent discussion effectively relates the Wesleys to eighteenth-century 'Orthodoxy' and 'orthodoxy.'

Allchin also examines a number of the Trinitarian hymns, which reflect Charles' struggle to balance intellectual ascent to doctrine and faith experience (particularly inner purification). In summarizing Wesley's response to the Trinity in one poem, the author succinctly states the poet-priest's Trinitarian life posture: 'Charles Wesley sees our human life wholly caught up in the circulation of life and love which moves among the Persons of the Trinity.'[12]

Another seminal discussion for the encounter of the Orthodox and Wesleyan traditions is Geoffrey Wainwright's 'Trinitarian Theology and Wesleyan Holiness'.[13] Belief in the Holy Trinity, who enables holiness, is essential to both traditions. Wainwright notes at the outset of his study what he considers to be an 'accurate systematization of the scriptural record' in St Basil's work, *On the Holy Spirit*, in which he avers 'that all works of God towards us start from the Father, proceed through the Son, and are completed in the Holy Spirit, and that our grateful response begins in the Spirit and ascends through the Son to the Father'.[14] From this perspective Wainwright examines corresponding ideas in the writings of John and Charles Wesley, beginning with John Wesley's discussion of the Creed in his *Letter to a Roman Catholic*. In this treatise Wesley emphasizes the multiple roles of the Holy Spirit in human life: enlightenment of understanding, rectification of wills and affections, renewal of human nature, unification with Christ, assurance of adoption as children of God, purification and sanctification of soul and body, and guidance in behaviour.

Wainwright has an extended section entitled 'Trinitarian Hymnology' which is devoted largely to Charles Wesley's volume *Hymns on the Trinity* (1767). He takes up numerous themes addressed by Wesley, for example soteriology, doxology, praise, restoration of the *imago Dei*, and the 'indwelling' of believers. In addition, Wainwright cites a few Trinitarian poems of Charles Wesley outside the 1767 collection.

Kenneth Carveley's study, 'From Glory to Glory: The Renewal of All Things in Christ: Maximus the Confessor and John Wesley',[15] explores congruences in theological ideas found in the writings of Maximus the Confessor (sixth and seventh centuries) and sermons of John Wesley. While there is no evidence that John or Charles Wesley had read any of the writings of Maximus the Confessor, Carveley successfully structures a conversation between them on the subject of the 'religion of the heart', which is central to the theology of both. He also punctuates various aspects of the conversation with eloquent quotations from Charles Wesley's hymns. In particular, Carveley's work shows that the theological ideas of deification (*theosis*) and the 'religion of the heart' find parallels in Maximus and the Wesleys. Carveley's study emphasizes that both traditions, Orthodox and Wesleyan, more than advocating a set of doctrines, emphasize a way of life, a way of dynamic living with, in and through the Triune God.

Peter C. Bouteneff has done similar research in 'All Creation in United Thanksgiving: Gregory of Nyssa and the Wesleys on Salvation'.[16] The author is careful not to draw unwarranted conclusions about John Wesley's reliance on the Church Fathers based merely on references to them in his writings. One question Bouteneff poses is extremely important for contemporary scholarship and ecumenism: 'What is the relationship between apostolic themes and the Wesleys?' He is careful to view Gregory of Nyssa and the Wesleys in the context of the times in which they lived.

One example of a theme, which finds convergence in Gregory of Nyssa and the Wesleys, is universal salvation. Nevertheless, Bouteneff also points out some differences on this subject. The author has illustrated how one may do serious research of parallels and differences in theological ideas with integrity and without overemphasizing the 'reliance' of the Wesleys on early church sources.

There is a fascinating examination of 'Charles Wesley and Orthodox Hesychastic Tradition',[17] by Ioann Ekonomtsev, who begins by setting the parameters of the tension which resulted between Barlaam, the Calabrian monk, who understood God as incomprehensible, and the monks of Aphon who averred that they were the recipients of grace from a personal God of the universe. Barlaam was opposed by the Archbishop of Thessalonica, St Gregory Palamas, who developed the teaching of God the Creator, through whose creative energy humankind can participate in and experience God. The Archbishop's perspective that God's grace is not dependent on human action is very near that of the Wesleys' idea of prevenient grace. It is here that one finds the emergence among the early Church Fathers of the concept of *synergia*, namely, interaction between God's grace and human freewill.

Ekonomtsev then compares eighteenth-century England of the Wesleys' time and fourteenth-century Byzantium and sees their response to rationalism and the search for authentic religious experience as a parallel to the quest for authentic religious experience among the Aphon monks. He also compares the content and spirit of Charles Wesley's poetry with that of St Symeon the New Theologian, finding striking similarities. Ekonomtsev finds another parallel in the emphasis on social holiness in the Wesleys' preaching and the Hesychastic teachings of the East. As does Allchin, Ekonomtsev points to 'participation in the divine creative energy', which is emphasized by the Wesleys, particularly Charles, as an important spiritual bridge between East and West. It is precisely from divine grace that creative inspiration issues, and Ekonomtsev views Charles Wesley's poetry as an excellent example of creative art emerging from God's grace.

The first significant examination of 'The Missiology of Charles Wesley and Its Links to the Eastern Church'[18] was made by the late Tore Meistad of Norway. Drawing heavily from sacred writings of St Simeon the New Theologian, other Eastern sources and the sacred poetry of Charles Wesley, Meistad explores the close parallels between the Orthodox and Wesleyan traditions in the theology of mission. Central to both is a theology of mission that emerges from faith in the Holy Trinity. One of the most important aspects of Meistad's study is his analysis of Charles Wesley's emphasis on the plurality of the Trinity, more so than its unity, which shows his high regard for the Byzantine concept of a multifaceted God of intervention.

While Meistad's research stresses much common theological ground shared by the Orthodox and Wesleyan traditions as regards universal redemption, eschatology, and love as the presence of God, one of the most significant aspects of his investigation examines both traditions' averment that mission is the essence of the Church issuing from a theology of salvation. Certainly Meistad's work is one of the most significant studies of ecclesiology and soteriology in the Orthodox and Wesleyan traditions, which makes extensive use of the sacred poetry of Charles Wesley and numerous Eastern sources.

In 'Kenosis in the Nativity Hymns of Ephrem the Syrian and Charles Wesley',[19] I studied a specific theme found in the sacred poetry of Ephrem the Syrian and Charles Wesley. Both wrote collections of Hymns on the Nativity (Ephrem) and Hymns for the Nativity of our Lord (Charles Wesley). Affinities and differences in the writing styles of both poets are examined. Ephrem's poems are filled with a highly developed typological exegesis, which is not characteristic of Wesley's texts. The strongest affinity lies in the liturgical nature of Ephrem's and Wesley's hymns. They are intended for worship, though for two different styles of worship, Eastern and Western rites respectively.

Theologically the nativity hymns of Ephrem and Wesley share in common a strong emphasis on kenosis, God's assumption of human nature, and theosis, humankind's assumption of God's nature. In the light of these two emphases, both writers view Christian spirituality as incarnational. In their nativity hymns one encounters the memory of an undivided Church, which is fully united in the Incarnation of Christ. One finds also common theological strands in both poets such as sanctification, hope, peace, the Church, sharing life with the poor, sharing in the life of Mary, and the contemplative life.

While Gordon Wakefield's article, 'John Wesley and Ephraem Syrus', cited above, addresses primarily John Wesley's relationship to the East, he does include a brief discussion of Charles Wesley. In the first paragraph he states, 'I would also like to say at the outset that this paper brings in John Wesley's brother, Charles, and that is somewhat speculative.'[20] This is a very puzzling statement, since later Wakefield says, 'It is above all in the hymns [Wesleyan] that theosis has its place in Methodism. And it is related to the Incarnation.'[21] He then quotes one of the most frequently cited Charles Wesley texts, which addresses theosis, from Hymns for the Nativity of our Lord (1745).

5. He deigns in flesh t'appear,
   Widest extremes to join,
   To bring our vileness near,
   And make us all divine;

And we the life of God shall know,
For God is manifest below.[22]

In another study by Kenneth Carveley, 'The Visitation of the Word',[23] the author focuses on what he refers to as an 'experiential trilogy' of the visitation of the Word, which emerges from encounters with Orthodoxy and his own Methodist background. The trilogy involves truth, the warmed heart and prayer. In addition, Carveley makes a strong case for *lectio divina* in Orthodoxy and Methodism as a mediator of Christ's presence. He punctuates his arguments with a number of references from the Church Fathers, John Wesley's journal, and Charles Wesley's poetry, for example:

When quiet in my house I sit,
Thy book be my companion still.

As this poem reveals – whether at rising, throughout the day, or at evening when one retires, God's Word is the source of life's sustenance. Carveley finds similar concepts of 'The Visitation of the Word' in St Bernard, Cassian and other streams of monastic tradition and in the Wesleys.

Karen Westerfield Tucker explores the commonalities and dissimilarities of liturgical singing in Orthodoxy and Methodism in chapter 18, 'The Liturgical Functioning of Orthodox Troparia and Wesleyan Hymns', of *Orthodox and Wesleyan Scriptural Understanding and Practice*.[24] She shows how both traditions move from simplicity to complexity in musical development, from monodic to polyphonic forms of singing. The similarities and differences of singing in the two traditions are illustrated with numerous examples from Orthodox *troparia* and hymns of Charles Wesley. The author finds common metaphors, images and biblical language, and a shared hermeneutical principle: both traditions read the story of the old covenant from the perspective of the new covenant.

Geoffrey Wainwright's discussion of 'The Transfiguration of Jesus in Wesleyan Exegesis and Application' contrasts the Orthodox understanding of the Transfiguration as a Trinitarian mystery with the Wesleyan understanding, which has a stronger Christological emphasis, sociological purpose and eschatological vision. The Wesleyan sources upon which Wainwright draws are John Wesley's *Explanatory Notes upon the New Testament* and Charles Wesley's poetry from three publications: *Short Hymns on Select Passages of the Holy Scriptures* (1762), *Hymns and Sacred Poems* (1740), and *The Unpublished Poetry of Charles Wesley*, vol. 2, edited by S T Kimbrough Jr and Oliver A. Beckerlegge (1990). These sources of Wesleyan thought reveal an encounter with the resurrected Christ, who can transform one as a new creation in the present moment in selfless humility.

In 'Wesley Hymns, the Icons of the Wesleyan Tradition'[25] I explore the world of visual and verbal icons. Icons and hymns are spiritual art which emerge in the Orthodox and Wesleyan traditions from fasting, prayer and sacrament. Contrasting visual art and verbal pictures painted with words, one finds amazing similarities between the Orthodox icon and the Wesleyan hymn. Just as the icons of the Eastern churches are windows to God and spirituality, so the Wesley hymns are windows through which to glimpse the way of holiness, to interpret faith and practice, to celebrate the saints, to explore the mystery of God, and to approach God. 'Both are visible art forms, have subjects, invite the worshipper to encounter and fellowship with the saints, and create visions that enrich spirituality.'[26]

This brief survey of some of the more notable research has explored Charles Wesley's relationship to Orthodoxy and revealed that in Charles Wesley and his writings the window to the East is open wide. His language, conceptualization of God, and spirituality resonate profoundly with the early Church Fathers and Orthodoxy.

In the works cited above the concepts of *theosis*, *kenosis*, Incarnation, holiness and Trinity in particular have been examined for convergence and common resonance in texts of the Church Fathers and Charles Wesley. Two apects of the nature of God, however, God as Mystery and God as divine essence and energy, have received lesser attention and will be addressed below. In addition, while the doctrine of *theosis* in the writings of Charles Wesley and of the early Church Fathers has been examined by a few writers, discussions have focused largely on Wesley's *Hymns for the Nativity of our Lord*.[27] Therefore, the concluding part of this chapter expands considerably the discussion of the importance of Wesley's Trinitarian poems for a theology of *theosis* – of life lived in and through the Trinity.

## The Nature of God

### God as Mystery

Just as many of the early Church Fathers emphasize God as Mystery, Charles Wesley also speaks of God and God's ways as a marvellous mystery. "Tis mystery all, the immortal dies', he writes in one of his most famous hymns, 'And can it be that I should gain'. There is an enduring tension between the unrevealed and the revealed mystery of God, the God who is so far removed from us that we cannot fully know all dimensions of the divine life, yet the God who is so near that we may be indwelled by the divine, resurrected Son of God, Jesus Christ.

> 2. 'Tis mystery all! the Immortal dies!
>     Who can explore the strange design?
>   In vain the first-born seraph tries
>     To sound the depths of love divine.
>   'Tis mercy all! Let earth adore;
>   Let angel minds enquire no more.[28]

In this stanza there is an essential element of the Wesleyan approach to God as mystery. One confesses faith and raises questions about faith in the same breath. "Tis mystery all! the Immortal dies!' is a powerful confession of faith in God's act in Christ on Calvary. 'The immortal dies', the divine Son endures death. But Wesley asks: Who can believe this paradox that the Immortal dies? At the very heart, the core, of the Christian faith is the affirmation that God gives of the divine self through the incarnate Son of God, Jesus Christ, who is both fully human and fully divine. Wesley raises the profound question about such an act: 'Who can explore this strange design?' Confession and questioning of the Mystery go together for Charles Wesley. Try as they may,

even the angels cannot fully grasp this mysterious reality: 'In vain the first-
born seraph tries/to sound the depths of love divine.' Neither human beings
nor angels can sound the depths and immensity of God.

There is a story in *The Sayings of the Desert Fathers* that resonates with what
Charles Wesley is saying about the unknowableness of God.

> One day some of the brethren came to see Abba Antony, and among them
> was Abba Joseph. Wishing to test them, the old man mentioned a text from
> Scripture, and starting with the youngest he asked them what it meant. Each
> explained it as best he could. But to each one the old man said, 'You have not
> yet found the answer.' Last of all he said to Abba Joseph, 'And what do you
> think the text means?' He replied, 'I do not know.' Then Abba Antony said,
> 'Truly, Abba Joseph has found the way, for he said, I do not know.'[29]

In the stanza of the hymn, 'And can it be that I should gain' cited above,
one comes to another important facet of the Wesleyan approach to God as
Mystery, namely: the life of the Christian is a life of doxology. "Tis mercy all!
Let earth adore', exclaims Charles. Realizing that all of life is imbued with
God's mercy, one sees life itself as an act of God's mercy. Therefore one spends
that life, with all creation, in adoration of the Creator.

In an English translation of a Gerhard Tersteegen hymn, John Wesley eloquently expresses the theology of mystery of God's love:

> Thou hidden love of God whose height,
>     Whose depth unfathomed no one knows,
> I see from far thy beauteous light
>     And inly sigh for thy repose;
> My heart is pained, nor can it be
> At rest till it find rest in thee.[30]

In these lines John Wesley maintains confidently that the height and depth of
God's love are unfathomed. 'No one knows' them! One gets only a glimpse of
this love from a distance and yet yearns inwardly for the peace and solace it
offers. The New Testament avers that 'God is love' (1 John 4.8). Therefore we may
understand Wesley's translation as affirming that one cannot fully know God,
who is love; one only sees the beauteous light of God from a distance. These
lines are in concert with Evagrius Pontus' statement: 'God cannot be grasped
by the mind. If he could be grasped, he would not be God.'[31] God is beyond our
knowing. No one knows the height and depth of God, who is love.

Reflecting on Deuteronomy 7.7–8, 'The Lord did not set his love upon you
because you were more in number than any people – but because the Lord
loved you', Charles Wesley also expresses his confidence in God's love as a
mystery.

> What angel can explain
> The love of God to man,
> The secret cause assign
> Of charity divine?

Nothing in us could move,
Deserve, or claim his love:
'Tis all a mystery,
And must for ever be![32]

God's love is 'all a mystery/And must for ever be!' says Charles.

In a poem based on Job 11.7, 'Canst thou by searching find out God? Canst thou find out the Almighty to perfection', Charles once again stresses God's 'incomprehensible . . . immensity'. Stanza 3 culminates in the averment that God's love is '*most* unsearchable'. The italics for the word 'most' are in the first edition of *Short Hymns on Select Passages of the Holy Scriptures* (1762) and are no doubt Charles'.

1. Shall foolish, weak, short-sighted man
    Beyond archangels go,
The great almighty God explain,
    Or to perfection know?
His attributes divinely soar
    Above the creatures' sight,
And prostrate *Seraphim* adore
    The glorious Infinite.

2. *Jehovah's* everlasting days
    They cannot numbered be,
Incomprehensible the space
    Of thine immensity;
Thy wisdom's depths by reason's line
    In vain we strive to sound,
Or stretch our labouring thought t'assign
    Omnipotence a bound.

3. The brightness of thy glories leaves
    Description far below;
Nor man, nor angels' heart conceives
    How deep thy mercies flow:
Thy love is *most* unsearchable,
    And dazzles all above;
They gaze, but cannot count or tell
    The treasures of thy love![33]

This poem captures the spirit of the statement of St Simeon the New Theologian: 'As a friend talking with his friend, man speaks with God, and drawing near in confidence he stands before the face of the One who dwells in light unapproachable.'[34] Charles Wesley says that 'The brightness of [God's] glory leaves/description far below.' So that 'Nor man, nor angels' heart conceives/ How deep [God's] mercies flow.' Just as St Simeon the New Theologian says that one stands in the midst of 'light unapproachable', Wesley says, '[God's] love is *most* unsearchable/And dazzles all above.' The brightness impedes the fullness of one's sight.

In stanza 2 of the poem, Wesley affirms that though humankind may seek through diverse and energetic thought processes to assign boundaries to God's immensity and omnipotence, all such effort is in vain and hopeless. The love of God is so vast that it is impossible to discern all of its treasures.

In the hymn, 'Let earth and heaven combine', Charles Wesley stresses the mystery of the Incarnation in these words:

> 3. See in that infant's face
>     The depths of Deity,
>    And labour while ye gaze,
>     To sound the mystery;
>    In vain: ye angels gaze no more,
>    But fail and silently adore.[35]

Even the angels are left only to doxology in the presence of the Incarnation.

The sense of awe before the mystery of the Incarnation effervesces time and again from Wesley's soul and sounds the depths of poetical eloquence:

> When he did our flesh assume
>     Thou everlasting Man,
> Mary held him in her womb
>     Whom heaven could not contain!
> Who the mystery can believe!
>     Incomprehensible thou art;
> Yet we still by faith conceive,
>     And bear thee in our heart.[36]

Who can explain God's assumption of human flesh in the form of Jesus? Who can explain Mary's conception of the Holy Child? These mysteries are incomprehensible to the human mind. Yet, like Mary, 'we still by faith conceive,/and bear thee in our heart.'

## God as divine essence and energy

In the two poems that follow, Charles Wesley makes a distinction, as does the Orthodox tradition, between God's essence, the nature of God, and God's energy, the activity of God. The essence is incomprehensible and indicates God's transcendence.

> Essence incomprehensible
>     Jehovah, who can know,
> Who was, and is, and comes to dwell
>     With all his saints below!
> Then the whole world shall be restored
>     And bow to Jesu's name,
> Filled with the knowledge of the Lord,
>     The infinite I AM.[37]

Wesley's lines are in concert with two Church Fathers in particular. St Athanasius writes, 'He [God] is outside all things according to his essence, but he is in all things through his acts of power.'[38] St Basil the Great avers, 'No one has ever seen the essence of God, but we believe in the essence because we experience the energy.'[39] Bishop Kallistos Ware summarizes the *essence/energy* distinction eloquently:

> Such, then, is our God: unknowable in his essence, yet known in his energies; beyond and above all that we can think or express, yet closer to us than our own heart. Through the apophatic way we smash in pieces all the idols or mental images that we form of him, for we know that all are unworthy of his surpassing greatness. Yet at the same time, through prayer and through our active service in the world, we discover at every moment his divine energies, his immediate presence in each person and each thing. Daily, hourly we touch him.[40]

Charles Wesley speaks of 'The energy divine' which can quicken and give new life. 'The energy divine' signifies God's omnipresence.

1.   Can these dry bones perceive
      The quick'ning power of grace,
     Or Christian infidels retrieve
      The life of righteousness?
      All-good, almighty Lord,
      Thou know'st thine own design,
     The virtue of thine own great world,
      The energy divine.

2.   Now for thy mercy's sake
      Let thy great word proceed,
     Dispensed by whom thou wilt, to wake
      The spiritually dead;
      Send forth to prophesy
      Thy chosen messenger,
     And thou the gospel-word apply,
      And force the world to hear.[41]

This 'energy divine' is God in action, God's self-revelation in creation. Wesley says, 'Thou know'st thine own design.' God knows the way of active engagement with humankind. Wesley understands 'the energy divine' as enabling the Word 'to wake the spiritually dead', and maintains that one experiences the divine energy.

After reading both of the above poems, one is reminded of St Gregory Palamas' distinction of God's essence and energy:

> Because both the divine essence and the divine energy are everywhere inseparably present, God's energy is accessible also to us creatures; . . . Therefore God's grace and energy are accessible to each one of us, since it is

divided indivisibly. But since God's essence is in every way indivisible, how could it be accessible to any created being?[42]

For Charles Wesley, God's essence is the fullness of God's nature, which cannot be fully grasped by human beings. 'The energy divine' indicates the fullness of divine activity. 'Thus the essence–energies distinction is a way of stating simultaneously that the *whole* God is inaccessible, and that the *whole* God in his outgoing love has rendered himself accessible . . .'[43]

## Participation in the Trinity

### Life in the Trinity/living the Trinity

According to the Orthodox tradition, and to Charles Wesley, it is through the Holy Trinity that participation in the life of God transpires. In Wesley's view, life in the Trinity should have a daily impact on our lives. We are made in the image of God, that means in the image of the Trinity. The dynamic of the love between the persons of the Trinity should also be reflected in our lives. Thus we live sacrificially for one another with a daily commitment to acts of mercy and compassion.

In Charles Wesley's *Hymns on the Trinity* (1767) there are important clues to the meaning of life in the Trinity and what it means to 'live the Trinity', or to participate in the life of the Trinity.

He responds to the famous verse, which is the fulcrum of a concept of *theosis* in the New Testament, 2 Peter 1.4, 'Exceeding great and precious promises, that by these you might be partakers of the divine nature' and to Hebrews 3.14, 'We are partakers of Christ, if we hold fast' with the following lines:

1. All who partake of Christ, partake
     The nature properly Divine
   Of Him, who humbled for our sake,
     Us with Himself vouchsafed to join;
   And in His single person showed
   The substance both of man and God.

2. The precious promises in Him
     Are all contained and verified;
   And fashioned like the God supreme,
     Whoe'er in Christ by faith abide,
   Th'essential holiness they share,
   The image of the heavenly bear.

3. Jesus the Lord, Thy nature pure
     To us, as capable, impart,
   And thus our hallowed hearts assure
     That Thou the true Jehovah art,
   And wilt through death our Leader be,
   Our God through all eternity.[44]

Wesley affirms: 'All who partake of Christ, partake/The nature properly Divine.' Though he prays in the third stanza specifically to Jesus – 'Jesus the Lord, thy nature pure/To us, as capable, impart' – he does not pray to him as an entity separate from the other persons of the Trinity. Father, Son and Holy Spirit are one essence. Hence, the imparting of the pure nature of Jesus is the imparting of the nature of the Trinity.

In the section 'The Divinity of the Holy Ghost' in *Hymns on the Trinity* Wesley emphasizes that faithful followers of God are to be a 'temple of the Triune God'. One is indwelled by the Trinity and has life in the Trinity.

1. The self-same act of grace Divine
     Which in our second birth we prove,
   Great God, is an effect of Thine,
     And of Thy Spirit from above:
   His constituted witnesses
     To whom He makes the mystery known,
   One nature we in Both confess:
     God and the Spirit are but One.

2. Come, Holy Ghost, Thou God most high,
     Thou everlasting Spirit, come,
   Our faithful hearts to certify,
     And consecrate Thine earthly home:
   When Thou hast sealed Thy blessed abode,
     Jehovah's mansion we shall be,
   A temple of the Triune God;
     For all the Godhead is in Thee.[45]

In the second stanza Wesley offers a prayer to the Holy Spirit. Again, this is not a prayer that isolates the Holy Spirit from the other persons of the Trinity. As he says at the end of the first stanza, 'God and the Spirit are but One.' A prayer to Father, Son, and/or Holy Spirit is a prayer to the *whole* Trinity. In this prayer Wesley bids the Holy Spirit confirm the faithful as God's dwelling, as 'Jehovah's mansion . . . a temple of the Triune God'. Here one sees the relation of Trinity and *theosis*. Participation in God means participation in the Trinity. Whatever we do, we do in the name of the Holy Trinity. In our daily living we are living the Trinity.

Wesley emphasizes this further in responding to John 14.17, 'He (the Spirit of truth) dwelleth in you, and shall be in you' and 1 Corinthians 14.25, 'God is in you of a truth':

1. The Holy Ghost in part we know,
     For *with* us He resides,
   Our whole of good to Him we owe
     Whom by His grace He guides:
   He doth our virtuous thoughts inspire,
     The evil He averts,
   And every seed of good desire
     He planted in our hearts.

2. He whom the world cannot receive,
  But fight against His power,
Will come, we steadfastly believe,
  In His appointed hour:
He now the future grace reveals,
  Bespeaks His mean abode;
And *in* us when the Spirit dwells,
  We all are filled with God.[46]

Though Wesley is speaking of the third person of the Trinity in these two stanzas, he ends by stating, 'And *in* us when the Spirit dwells,/We all are filled with God.' All good in our lives we owe to the Holy Spirit, who guides us by grace. Our virtuous thoughts are inspired by the Holy Spirit, who aids in the averting of evil, and plants 'every seed of good desire . . . in our hearts'. Thus, when we act out goodness, when we think virtuous thoughts, when we exhibit the good desires of our hearts, we are living the Trinity. We are participating in the life of God.

There is an assurance we have, which Wesley finds promised in 1 John 5.24, 'And hereby we know that He abideth in us, by the Spirit which He hath given us.' Thus, he writes:

1. God, who did the Spirit bestow
  That in our hearts resides,
God supreme, hereby we know,
  Himself in us abides;
God eternally adored
His Spirit in us is the most high,
  Glorious, universal Lord,
  That fills both earth and sky.

2. Who the Holy Ghost receive,
  Th'indwelling Comforter,
We His Deity believe,
  And we alone declare:
When He speaks the promise sealed
In saints His permanent abode,
  With Jehovah's Spirit filled,
  We all are filled with God.[47]

Wesley ends this poem with the identical line that concludes the poem previously cited: 'We all are filled with God.' In the first stanza he states the reality of *theosis* as clearly as anywhere in his poetry: 'God supreme, hereby we know,/Himself in us abides.' The saints become God's 'permanent abode'. This is life in the Trinity.

Though Charles Wesley addresses each person of the Trinity through his *Hymns on the Trinity*, one section is entitled 'The Trinity in Unity'. Three verses of scripture preface a powerful poem on the unity of the Trinity: Deuteronomy 30.20, 'Love the Lord thy God, for He is thy life'; Colossians 3.4, 'When Christ who is life shall appear'; Romans 8.10, 'The Spirit is life'. In responding to these affirmations of scripture, Wesley writes:

1. He is our life, the Lord our God:
   Our Father's love we find,
   Who being graciously bestowed
   On us, and all mankind:
   Jesus our Life alike we own,
   Our Life eternal here
   Concealed, and by the world unknown;
   But He shall soon appear.

2. The Spirit is Life, we know and feel
   Who life to us imparts;
   And God doth in three persons dwell
   For ever in our hearts:
   Our Life is One: a Trinity
   In Unity we love,
   And gladly die from earth, to see
   His face unveiled above.[48]

The Father is our life, Jesus is our life, and the Spirit is our life. 'And God doth in three persons dwell/For ever in our hearts.' The Trinity in the fullness of its essence, three in one, dwells within us. Wesley says unequivocally, therefore, our life is 'a Trinity'. The word for the divine defines who we are. 'We are as persons who are "embodied beings" and "ensouled beings" and "enspirited beings" in vital interpersonal relationships on the various integrated levels of human existence with the indwelling Trinity.'[49]

While one tends to speak of the indwelling Christ and of the indwelling Spirit of God, Wesley is clear that it is the 'mysterious Trinity' which inhabits our hearts. In the section 'Hymns and Prayers to the Trinity' from *Hymns on the Trinity* one finds two stanzas which superbly articulate life *in* the Trinity. Here he links intellect and heart, both of which are overwhelmed by 'The whole mysterious Trinity/Inhabiting my heart.' In the prayer of the sixth stanza, Wesley prays for the unknown Triune God to 'take full possession' of him that he may be 'a temple of the Lord, and filled/With all the life Divine.' Again, this is life lived *in* and *through* the Trinity. Charles' emphasis on the unknown Triune God resonates with Symeon the New Theologian's insistence on the unknowability of the Trinitarian Mystery.[50]

5. Furnished with intellectual light,
   In vain I speak of Thee aright,
   While unrevealed Thou art:
   That only can suffice for me,
   The whole mysterious Trinity
   Inhabiting my heart.

6. Come then, Thou Triune God unknown,
   Take full possession of Thine own,
   And keep me ever Thine,

An heir of bliss, for glory sealed,
A temple of the Lord, and filled
    With all the life Divine.[51]

According to Wesley, right doctrine properly conceived is no substitute for
the revelation of God: 'In vain I speak of Thee aright,/While unrevealed Thou
art.' Only when 'The whole mysterious Trinity' inhabits the heart can one
speak in an appropriate way of glory of the Triune God and witness to it
among the nations and all peoples.

Finally, we come to the last poetical text to be cited in this discussion from
*Hymns on the Trinity*. It is the fourth stanza of hymn 22 in the section 'Hymns
and Prayers to the Trinity'.

4.   While yet I am calling, appear
         The end of my trouble and pain:
     Assured of a Trinity here,
         I rise from my ruins again;
     I know my Redeemer, who gives
         A sinner His glory to see,
     And all the Divinity lives
         Eternally present in me.[52]

Because of the assurance of the Trinity in the present, Wesley is able to rise
from the ruins of trouble and pain. He lives the Trinity for 'all the Divinity
lives/eternally present in me.' 'God . . . has made the mystery of the Trinity
the beginning and end of all reality.'[53] The Trinity is the source of all life and
sustains it through eternity.


## Conclusion

Unequivocally with the concepts of God as Mystery, and as essence and
energy, Charles Wesley is very close to Eastern Christian thought and spirituality. This may also be said of his emphasis on life in the Trinity and living the
Trinity. His theological vocabulary and perceptions of these ideas resonate
in perhaps unanticipated ways with the early Church Fathers. While he was
writing in an eighteenth-century context in which rationalism had resulted
in strong anti-Trinitarian and anti-Incarnation trends, Wesley's message on
these themes provides not only convergence with the early Church, but across
denominational lines as an ecumenical bridge in the twenty-first century.


## Notes

1 Albert Outler's article 'John Wesley's Interests in the Early Fathers of the
Church' *Bulletin* of the Committee on Archives and History of the United Church
of Canada, 29 (1983 [actually 1980–2], 5.17) evoked much discussion on this
subject.

2 Ted Campbell, *John Wesley and Christian Antiquity: A study of religious vision and cultural change* (Nashville: Abingdon/Kingswood, 1991); idem, 'Back to the Future: The Wesleyan Quest for Ancient Roots: The 1980s' in *Wesleyan Theological Journal* 32. 1, Spring 1997, 5–16); idem, 'Wesley's Use of the Church Fathers' published in English in a special volume of the *Asbury Theological Journal* 50. 2 and 51. 1 (together, Fall 1995 and Spring 1996, 57–70) and in Italian as *La Santificazione nelle Tradizioni Benedettina e Metodista* (ed. Febe Cavazzutti Rossi; Verona: Gabrielle Editori, 53–71); Richard P. Heitzenrater, 'John Wesley's Reading of and References to the Early Church Fathers', in *Orthodox and Wesleyan Spirituality*, ed. S T Kimbrough Jr (Crestwood: St Vladmir's Seminary Press, 2002), 25–32; Geoffrey Wainwright, 'Trinitarian Theology and Wesleyan Holiness', in *Orthodox and Wesleyan Spirituality* (2002), 59–80. John Chryssavgis, 'The Practical Way of Holiness: Isaiah of Scetis and John Wesley', in *Orthodox and Wesleyan Spirituality* (2002), 81–99; Frances Young, 'Inner Struggle: Some Parallels between the Spirituality of John Wesley and the Greek Fathers', in *Orthodox and Wesleyan Spirituality* (2002), 157–72; Kenneth Carveley, 'From Glory to Glory: The Renewal of All Things in Christ: Maximus the Confessor and John Wesley', in *Orthodox and Wesleyan Spirituality* (2002), 173–88. Peter C. Bouteneff, 'All Creation in United Thanksgiving: Gregory of Nyssa and the Wesleys on Salvation', in *Orthodox and Wesleyan Spirituality* (2002), 189–201.

3 Gordon Wakefield, 'John Wesley and Ephraem Syrus', *Hygoye: Journal of Syriac Studies*, 1, no. 2 (July 1998), 8.

4 A. M. Allchin, *Participation in God: A forgotten strand in Anglican tradition* (Wilton: Morehouse-Barlow, 1988), 13.

5 Nicholas Lossky, 'Lancelot Andrewes: A Bridge between Orthodoxy and the Wesley Brothers on Prayer', in S T Kimbrough Jr, ed., *Orthodox and Wesleyan Scriptural Understanding and Practice* (Crestwood: St Vladimir's Seminary Press, 2005), chapter 9, 149ff.

6 Lossky, 'Lancelot Andrewes', 151.

7 Lossky, 'Lancelot Andrewes', 154.

8 Michael J. Christensen and Jeffery Wittung, eds (Madison: Fairleigh Dickinson University Press, 2006).

9 S T Kimbrough Jr, to be published in a forthcoming issue of the *Journal of St Vladimir's Orthodox Theological Seminary.*

10 A. M. Allchin, 'The Trinity in the Teaching of Charles Wesley: A Study in Eighteenth-Century Orthodoxy? *Proceedings of The Charles Wesley Society*, 4 (1997): 69–84. The article was originally delivered as a paper at the Annual Meeting of the Charles Wesley Society in Oxford, England in June 1993.

11 Allchin, 'The Trinity', 69.

12 Allchin, 'The Trinity', 83.

13 Geoffrey Wainwright, 'Trinitarian Theology and Wesleyan Holiness', in S T Kimbrough Jr, ed., *Orthodox and Wesleyan Spirituality* (Crestwood: St Vladimir's Seminary Press, 2002), chapter 2.

14 Wainwright, 'Trinitarian Theology', 60.

15 Kimbrough, ed., *Orthodox and Wesleyan Spirituality*, chapter 7.

16 Kimbrough, ed., *Orthodox and Wesleyan Spirituality*, chapter 8.

17 Kimbrough, ed., *Orthodox and Wesleyan Spirituality*, chapter 12.

18 Kimbrough, ed., *Orthodox and Wesleyan Spirituality*, chapter 11.

19 S T Kimbrough Jr, '*Kenosis* in the Nativity Hymns of Ephrem the Syrian and Charles Wesley', in Kimbrough, ed., *Orthodox and Wesleyan Spirituality*, chapter

12. To be clear, it is indeed Ephrem (or Ephraem) the Syrian whose works are considered in this article. In recent years Father Ephraem Lash has pointed out that the source John Wesley identified as 'Ephraem Syrus' was in fact a Greek author whose works were published in the seventeenth century and whom Lash proposes to name 'Ephraem Graecus'. But the subject with which this article is concerned is the Syrian Ephraem.

20  Wakefield, 'John Wesley and Ephraem Syrus', 1.

21  Wakefield, 'John Wesley and Ephraem Syrus', 7.

22  *Hymns for the Nativity of our Lord* (London: William Strahan, 1745), Hymn 5, 8.

23  *Orthodox and Wesleyan Scriptural Understanding and Practice*, chapter 12.

24  Kimbrough, ed., *Orthodox and Wesleyan Scriptural Understanding and Practice*, 293–304.

25  S T Kimbrough Jr, 'Wesley Hymns, the Icons of the Wesleyan Tradition', *Proceedings of the Charles Wesley Society*, 8 (2002), 24–40.

26  Kimbrough, 'Wesley Hymns, the Icons of Wesleyan Tradition', 40.

27  It should be noted, however, that A. M. Allchin has suggested the importance of Wesley's *Hymns on the Trinity* [1767] for a discussion of *theosis*, though this is not the central focus of his article, 'The Trinity in the Teaching of Charles Wesley', discussed above.

28  *Hymns and Sacred Poems* (London: Strahan, 1739), 118.

29  *The Sayings of the Desert Fathers: Alphabetical collection*, Antony 17, tr. Benedicta Ward (London and Oxford: Mowbray, 1975), 4.

30  *A Collection of Psalms and Hymns* (Charlestown [Charleston, SC], 1737), 51.

31  Evagrius of Pontus, Migne, *Patrologia Graeca*, 40: 1275C.

32  *Short Hymns on Select Passages of the Holy Scriptures*, 2 vols (Bristol: Felix Farley, 1762), 1. 93. These volumes are henceforth cited as *SH* (1762) followed by volume and page number(s).

33  *SH* (1762), 1. 231–2.

34  *Symeon the New Theologian: The practical and theological chapters and the three theological discourses*, Cistercian Studies Series, 41 (Kalamazoo: Cistercian Publications, 1982), 65.

35  *Hymns for the Nativity of our Lord*, 7.

36  *SH* (1762), 2. 32, based on Jeremiah 31.22, 'A woman shall compass a man.'

37  *SH* (1762), 2. 33, based on Jeremiah 31.34, 'They shall know me.'

38  St Athanasius, '*On the Incarnation* 17, trans. R. W. Thomson, *Athanasius: Contra Gentes and De Incarnatione* (Oxford: Early Christian Texts: Clarendon Press, 1971), p. 174.

39  St Basil, in *Doctrina Patrum de Incarnatione Verbi*, ed. Franz Diekamp (Münster: Aschendorff, 2nd edn, 1981), 88–9.

40  Bishop Kallistos Ware, *The Orthodox Way* (Crestwood: St Vladimir's Seminary Press, 1998), 23.

41  *SH* (1762), 2. 51, based on Ezekiel 37.3, 4: 'And he said unto me, Son of man, can these bones live?'

42  G. E. H. Palmer, Philip Sherrard and Kallistos Ware, trans., *The Philokalia: The complete text*, 4 vols (Boston: Faber and Faber, 1979–95), 4. 380.

43  *The Orthodox Way*, 22.

44  *Hymns on the Trinity* (Bristol: William Pine, 1767 [hereinafter *HT*]), Hymn 50, pp. 33–4; section: 'The Divinity of Christ'.

45  *HT*, Hymn 58, p. 39; section: 'The Divinity of the Holy Ghost'.

46  *HT*, Hymn 62, p. 41; section: 'The Divinity of the Holy Ghost'.
47  *HT*, Hymn 67, p. 44; section: 'The Divinity of the Holy Ghost'.
48  *HT*, Hymn 123, p. 79; section: 'The Trinity in Unity'.
49  George A. Maloney, *Gold, Frankincense, and Myrrh: An introduction to Eastern Christian Spirituality* (New York: Crossroads Publishing Co., 1997), 40.
50  *Traités théologiques et éthiques* (Introduction, texte critique, traduction et notes par Jean Darrouzés), Sources chrétiennes, 122 and 129 (1966, 1967), IX. 19ff.
51  *HT*, Hymn 19, p. 103, stanzas 5 and 6; section: 'Hymns and Prayers to the Trinity'.
52  *HT*, Hymn 22, p. 106, stanza 4; Section: 'Hymns and Prayers to the Trinity'.
53  *Gold, Frankincense, and Myrrh*, 29.

# 11. Charles Wesley and Calvinism

## GEOFFREY WAINWRIGHT

The eighteenth-century controversies and conflicts between Wesleyans and Calvinists are part of 'the great debate' running through Protestant history on its Reformed side.[1] The Calvinism in question was that canonized by the Synod of Dort in 1618–19. By the title of his own *Arminian Magazine* John Wesley honoured the name of Jacob Arminius (1560–1609), whose positions were summarized in the *Remonstrance* of 1610 and thus condemned by the internationally representative Synod of the Dutch Church a few years later. Indeed, the first issue of the Wesleyan publication (in 1778) contained a sympathetic life of the earlier Dutchman, and the editor's declared design was to 'publish some of the most remarkable tracts on the universal love of God, and his willingness to save all men from all sin, which have been wrote in this and the last century'; to which would be added 'original pieces, wrote either directly upon this subject, or on those which are equally opposed by the patrons of *particular redemption*'.[2]

In England, the perennial debate began to affect Methodism at the start of the Revival in 1739–41 and flared up again in the early 1770s, having in the meantime been somewhat quiescent thanks in part to a degree of personal reconciliation between the Wesley brothers and George Whitefield. Both John and Charles Wesley combatted Calvinism in their preaching and in their practical counsels. John's most sustained intellectual contribution to the campaign was his treatise *Predestination Calmly Considered* (1752), which in fact followed on several other pieces on the topic from earlier years. Charles more characteristically operated by way of hymns and occasional verse, although his emotional tone and rhetorical ploys did not exclude – any more than they did in John's case – his employment of Scripture, doctrinal premises, logical reasoning and pastoral experience in making the case for an 'Arminian' gospel.[3]

It may first be useful to recall in outline the Calvinist positions to which the Wesleys were opposed, in order to see by contrast the version of the gospel that the Wesleys themselves positively propounded. Then we shall begin with the Wesley brothers together at the first eruption of the controversy in and around Methodism, examining in particular detail the matching pair of polemical items from 1739: John's sermon 'Free Grace' and Charles' poem 'Universal Redemption'. Thereafter we shall look at Charles' homiletical and pastoral handling of the controversy, particularly in the West Country in 1740–1. Finally, we shall revert to Charles' poetry in the *Hymns on God's Everlasting Love* from 1741 to 1742. There would be little point in pursuing the controversy beyond the opening years, because all the characteristic notes had by then been struck.

Generations of English-speaking students have been helped to remember the 'five points' of Dort by the horticulturally appropriate acronym of 'tulip':

Total depravity.
Unconditional election.
Limited atonement.
Irresistible grace.
Perseverance of the saints.[4]

Sketched one by one, and accompanied by the Wesleys' understanding and rejection of them, they run thus. First, 'total depravity': the Wesleys were ready to approach 'the very edge of Calvinism' in 'denying all natural free-will, and all power antecedent to grace' (so the Conference of 1745),[5] but 'total depravity' was mitigated precisely by prevenient grace (which also, in the other direction, ruled out a semi-Pelagian view of the beginnings of faith). Second: 'unconditional election' implied, for the Wesleys, 'double predestination' ('election' and 'reprobation'), and this for them was (with a twist on Calvin's *decretum horribile*) the 'horrible decree':

By virtue of an eternal, unchangeable, irresistible decree of God, one part of mankind are infallibly saved, and the rest infallibly damned; it being impossible that any of the former should be damned, or that any of the latter should be saved.[6]

In face of this, the Wesleys set God's 'everlasting love' and 'universal grace'. For, third, a 'limited atonement' was countered not merely by the all-sufficiency of Christ's redemptive work but by its 'general' or 'world-wide' scope and purpose from the start. Nevertheless, this grace, though freely given and offered to all, needed to be freely received, the Wesleyans held. For Calvinists, on the other hand, the gift of saving faith was a case, fourth, of 'irresistible grace'. Otherwise human freewill might (unthinkably) thwart the purpose of God for those whom he had chosen. Fifth, the 'perseverance of the saints' was guaranteed in the Calvinist account (and the early Arminians hesitated to deny it), whereas the Wesleyans taught that final salvation was dependent upon actively abiding in justifying and sanctifying grace, while an unconditional security of election risked misleading its claimants into antinomianism.

The field of play thus marked out, we may describe the circumstances of the first scrimmages, from the rough and tumble of which emerged the shape and style of both John's and Charles' respective anti-Calvinistic literary productions. At the start of his open-air preaching around Bristol and Bath, John Wesley wrestled with the question of whether the offer of salvation far and wide required him to speak out against the predestinarian doctrine espoused by his friend George Whitefield, the very man under whose persuasion he had first 'submitted to "be more vile" [cf. 2 Samuel 6.22], and proclaimed in the highways the glad tidings of salvation'.[7] The *alfresco* evangelism began in the first days of April 1739, but by the 24th of the month, having received a letter accusing him of 'resisting and perverting the truth as it is in Jesus' through 'preaching against God's decree of predestination' (though he 'had not done so yet'), John asked himself whether he 'ought not now to declare the whole counsel of God'. On the 25th, he 'writ upon predestination'. On the 26th, he preached at Newgate at 10.30 in the morning on 'He that believeth hath everlasting life' [cf. John 3.36; 6.47]. He was 'led, without any previous design, to declare strongly and explicitly that God "willeth all men to be *thus* saved" [cf. 1 Timothy 2.4]', and to 'pray that if I spake not the truth of God, he would stay his hand, and work no more among us; if this was his truth, he would "not delay to confirm by signs following" [cf. Mark 16.20]. Immediately the power of God fell upon us. One, and another, and another, sunk to the earth. You might see them dropping on all sides as thunderstruck.' At noon on the same day, he 'appealed to God concerning predestination'. The appeal was by way of lots, and the answer came out as 'Preach and print.' On Sunday 30 April, John Wesley 'declared the *free* grace of God to about four thousand people, from those words "he that spared not his own Son, but delivered him up for us all, how shall he not with him freely give us all things?"'[8] Thus he 'preached', but it was not until the autumn of 1739 that he 'printed' – reluctant to 'oppose the sentiments of those whom I highly esteem for their works' sake', but 'indispensably obliged to declare this truth [as it is in Jesus] to all the world'. The sermon 'Free Grace', under that same text of Romans 8.32, was at that point published at Bristol. To it was appended, under the title 'Universal Redemption', a hymn or poem usually supposed to be by Charles, which was soon included also in a second collection of *Hymns and Sacred Poems* published under the brothers' joint names (London, 1740). Thus the pair rode in public tandem from the start of the 'Calvinist' controversies in and around the 'religious societies' and the evangelistic preaching of their leaders.

We should now, therefore, look bifocally at the message conveyed in the two genres: the prose of John's sermon 'Free Grace', and the verse of Charles' accompanying poem 'Universal Redemption'. The common themes will prove to be God's character and God's will, the scope of Jesus' ministry and atoning death, the operation of divine grace and the restored freedom of humankind, the propriety and the purpose of preaching. But the argumentative sequence, the rhetorical devices and the substantive emphases differ somewhat.

In 'Free Grace', John's thesis is that 'the grace or love of God, whence cometh our salvation, is free in all, and free for all' (2).[9] With regard to the 'in', God's grace 'is free in all to whom it is given', 'no way depending on any power or merit in man, but on God alone' (3). We may thus conclude – and the hymn will confirm this – that the Wesleyan position here agrees with the Calvinist in totally rejecting Pelagianism. But is God's grace 'free for all, as well as in all'? 'No,' say some: 'It is free only for those whom God hath ordained to life, and they are but a little flock. The greater part of mankind God hath ordained to death; and it is not free for them. Them God hateth; and therefore before they were born decreed they should die eternally' (4). This 'decree of predestination' Wesley will not allow any Calvinists to mitigate into 'the election of grace' only, whereby God would determine to save the chosen but leave the rest to themselves (5), for to be thus passed over amounts to being damned; 'preterition' is tantamount to 'reprobation' (8–9). Now, says Wesley, that renders 'all preaching vain': 'it is needless to them that are elected', for 'they, whether with preaching or without, will infallibly be saved'; and 'it is useless to them that are not elected', for 'they, whether with preaching or without, will infallibly be damned' (10). That, then, 'is a plain proof that the doctrine of predestination is not a doctrine of God because it makes void the ordinance of God; and God is not divided against himself' (11).

In fact, says Wesley, not only is preaching nullified, but the doctrine of pre-destination 'directly tends to destroy that holiness which is the end of all the ordinances of God'. As to 'holiness in general', the doctrine of predestination 'wholly takes away those first motives to follow after it, so frequently proposed in Scripture: the hope of future reward and fear of punishment, the hope of heaven and fear of hell'; there is 'no motive to struggle for life' or to 'take any physic at all', if one will in any case 'unavoidably recover' or 'unavoidably die' (11). As to the 'particular branches of holiness', and especially 'meekness and love: love, I mean, of our enemies, of the evil and unthankful': the doctrine of predestination 'tends to inspire or increase a sharpness or eagerness of tem-per which is quite contrary to the meekness of Christ' and 'contempt or cold-ness toward those whom we suppose outcasts from God' (12). And 'whatever lessens our love must so far lessen our desire to do them good', and not only 'all acts of bodily mercy' but 'the hope of saving their souls from death', which is the greatest of all good works (18). Moreover, what Calvinists think of as a 'comfortable' doctrine in fact 'tends to destroy the comfort of religion, the happiness of Christianity' – first, of course, for 'those who believe themselves to be reprobated, or who only suspect or fear it' (13); but those who believe themselves the elect of God might be staking their happiness on a 'speculative belief' rather than enjoying 'the full assurance of faith' that is 'wrought from hour to hour by the mighty power of God', the 'great work of the Holy Ghost' in those who abide in Christ (14–16). And sarcastically: the thought that 'thou-sands and millions of men, without any preceding offence or fault of theirs, were unchangeably doomed to everlasting burnings' must be far from com-fortable to 'those who have put on Christ' and could even 'wish themselves accursed for their brethren's sake [cf. Romans 9.3]' (17).

So far, Wesley's arguments have aimed at the anthropological consequences of the doctrine of predestination, but now he turns to its implications for the scriptural witness concerning God in his historical work of redemption and, more profoundly yet, in his character: 'This doctrine not only tends to destroy Christian holiness, happiness, and good works, but hath also a direct and manifest tendency to overthrow the whole Christian revelation' (19). If all were fixed beforehand, the revelation would be unnecessary, and the gos-pel untrue. The revelation would indeed be self-contradictory. The forced interpretation of certain scriptural texts cannot be allowed to overthrow 'all the other texts, and indeed the whole scope and tenor of Scripture' (20). For example, 'Jacob have I loved, but Esau have I hated' (Romans 9.13) cannot be taken as 'implying that God in a literal sense hated Esau and all the repro-bated from eternity', for that would contradict all those texts which 'expressly declare, "God is love"'; or a restrictive interpretation of 'I will have mercy on whom I will have mercy' (Romans 9.15) is excluded by the 'express declar-ation' that 'The Lord is loving unto *every* man, and his mercy is over *all* his

188 GEOFFREY WAINWRIGHT

works' (Psalm 145.9). 'Flatly contrary' (21) to the predestinarian interpretation of all such scriptures is 'the whole tenor of the New Testament', and all such particular texts that speak of Christ as 'the Saviour of the world' (John 4.42), 'the Lamb of God, that taketh away the sins of the world' (John 1.29), 'the propitiation, not for our sins only, but also for the sins of the whole world' (1 John 2.2), who 'gave himself a ransom for all' (1 Timothy 2.6) and 'tasted death for every man' (Hebrews 2.9). If the Calvinist asks 'why then are not all men saved' (22), 'the whole law and the testimony answer: first, not because of any decree of God, not because it is his pleasure they should die' (cf. Ezekiel 18.32); and second, it is rather that they refuse the call to repentance (2 Peter 3.9) and neglect the offer of healing (Luke 5.17) and life (John 5.40). It is their own will, *not* to be saved. The contrast between the divine and this human will is epitomized in Matthew 23.37, where Wesley goes so far as to cite the twofold use of the Greek verb *thelein*: 'O Jerusalem, Jerusalem, thou that killest the prophets, and stonest them that are sent unto thee, how often *would* I have gathered thy children together . . . and *ye would not.*' And how could Jesus be 'weeping crocodile's tears, weeping over the prey which he himself had doomed to destruction'? (24). To turn 'our Blessed Lord' – 'Jesus Christ the righteous' (1 John 2.1), 'the only-begotten Son of the Father, full of grace and truth' (John 1.14) – into 'an hypocrite, a deceiver of the people, a man devoid of common sincerity' is 'blasphemy'.

For 'just as it honours the Son, so does this doctrine honour the Father' (cf. John 5.23); the ironizing Wesley means, of course, *dis*-honours. The doctrine of predestination 'destroys all God's attributes at once'; very precisely, in view of the attributes of Christ just mentioned, it destroys God's 'justice, mercy, and truth' (25). Indeed, it 'represents the most Holy God as worse than the devil'; as 'more false, more cruel, and more unjust'. And in three extraordinary pages, John Wesley assembles a barrage of scriptural texts in order to construct a fanciful dialogue in which the Devil admits being outdone by a predestinarian God in falsity, cruelty and injustice (25–28).

The one divine decree that Wesley will acknowledge and affirm is this: '"I will set before" the sons of men "life and death, blessing and cursing" [cf. Deuteronomy 30.19]; and the soul that chooseth life shall live, as the soul that chooseth death shall die.' Thereby 'all who suffer Christ to make them alive' are 'elect', and indeed 'according to the foreknowledge of God' (cf. Romans 8.29; 1 Peter 1.2). It is not entirely clear what, according to Wesley, is entailed in this divine foreknowledge, yet it is not thought to impinge on human freedom – a freedom restored to fallen humankind, as the hymn will clarify, by 'prevenient grace'. In any case, it is the decree concisely stated above, says John Wesley, that 'yields the strongest encouragement to abound in all good works, and in all holiness; and it is a well-spring of joy, of happiness also, to our great and endless comfort. This is worthy of God. It is every way consistent with all the perfections of his nature. It gives us the noblest view both of his justice, mercy, and truth. To this agrees the whole scope of the Christian revelation, as well as all the parts thereof' (29). The sermon ends with a stirring call to those 'that forget God': Repent, and you shall live (30).

Taking the sermon as a whole, one might perhaps conclude that, *theologically*, John is concerned above all for the *character* of God; and *anthropologically*, for the *responsibility* of humans. These two come together when the gratuitous love of God for his human creature is freely requited by love towards God – and imitated by love towards the neighbour.

Charles' appended hymn is headlined 'Universal Redemption', and the words 'all' and 'every' redound through the 36 four-line stanzas that spell out the sufficiency of Christ's atoning work and envisage its application. Invoking aid from the Triune God, the poet first of all sings the 'darling attribute' of God, namely his 'boundless grace', his 'universal love'. This attribute takes the shape of 'mercy' for all the Creator's works, and especially humankind. Redemptively, it was mercy that removed 'the fatal bar' of divine justice, when

> Thy only Son it gave –
> To save a world so dearly loved,
> A sinful world to save.

And now it is

> Mercy, by every sinner found,
> Who takes what God hath given.

The call of the gospel is made to 'as many souls as breathe', and 'all may hear the call'. Moreover, God is already preveniently at work in all, at least in liberating their faculties of decision:

> A power to choose, a will to obey,
> Freely his grace restores;
> We all may find the Living Way,
> And call the Saviour ours.[10]

Then, however, three stanzas intervene, where it seems that the respondents may be 'few', and thus it may be that 'election' remains a little mysterious after all:

> Whom his eternal mind foreknew,
> That they the power would use,
> Ascribe to God the glory due,
> And not his grace refuse:

> Them, only them, his will decreed,
> Them did he choose alone,
> Ordained in Jesus' steps to tread,
> And to be like his Son.

> Them, the elect, consenting few,
> Who yield to proffered love,
> Justified here he forms anew,
> And glorifies above.

These three stanzas, in fact, take up the verses in Romans (8.28–30) that immediately precede the text of John Wesley's sermon; and while they certainly support Wesley's contention that God's grace is 'free *in* all to whom it is given' (as the Calvinists would agree), it is by no means certain that this passage in St Paul would support the contention that God's grace is 'free *for all*'.[11] As with John in his sermon, it must therefore be on the grounds of other particular texts and the general 'tenor of Scripture' that Charles now leaps to affirm again the universal *sufficiency* of Christ's atoning work, the universal *offer* of salvation, and the universal *capacity* – under grace – to accept the gift of eternal life:

> For as in Adam all have died,
> So all in Christ may live,[12]
> May (for the world is justified)
> His righteousness receive.
>
> Who'er to God for pardon fly,
> In Christ may be forgiven,
> He speaks to all, 'Why will ye die,
> And not accept my heaven?'
> . . . . . . . . . .
> He would that all his truths should own,[13]
> His gospel all embrace,
> Be freely justified by faith alone,
> And freely saved by grace.[14]
> . . . . . . . . . .
> Ho! every one that thirsteth, come![15]
> Choose life; obey the Word;[16]
> Open your hearts to make him room,
> And banquet with your Lord.[17]

Next, our poet turns to a direct offensive against the predestinarians, arguing (as his brother did in the sermon) that they would make God both a deceiver and actively cruel:

> Thou bidd'st; and would'st thou bid us choose,
> When purposed not to save?
> Command us all a power to use,
> Thy mercy never gave?
>
> Thou can'st not mock the sons of men,
> Invite us to draw nigh,
> Offer thy grace to all, and then
> Thy grace to most deny!
>
> Horror to think that God is hate!
> Fury in God can dwell,
> God could an helpless world create,
> To thrust them into hell!

To the contrary, 'Our God, we know, is love.' And to this God, as 'infinite love', Charles then prays precisely for the mistaken predestinarians:

> The *horrible decree* confound,
> Enlarge thy people's heart!
>
> Ah! Who is as thy servants blind,
> So to misjudge their God!
> Scatter the darkness of their mind,
> And shed thy love abroad.
>
> Give them conceptions worthy thee,
> Give them, in Jesu's face,
> Thy merciful design to see,
> Thy all-redeeming grace.

That, then, is the message to be proclaimed; and Charles – not wishing to withhold from others 'the grace that found out me' – begs to be numbered among the preachers:

> Stir up thy strength, and help us, Lord,
> The preachers multiply;
> Send forth thy light, and give the word,
> And let the shadows fly.
>
> Oh! if the Spirit send forth me,
> The meanest of the throng,
> I'll sing thy grace divinely free,
> And teach mankind the song.

The poem then ends with a Trinitarian invocation matching its beginning, making the plea that 'our eyes shall see/Thy promised kingdom come':

> Thee every tongue shall then confess,
> And every knee shall bow.[18]
> Come quickly, Lord, we wait thy grace,[19]
> We long to meet thee now.

Charles, in fact, reports confirmatory 'signs following' his own preaching, already in the summer of 1739 in London and then later in Bristol:

> Fri., June 22nd [1739]: To-night I asked in prayer, that if God would have all men to be saved, he would show some token for good upon us. Three were justified in immediate answer to that prayer. We prayed again; several fell down under the power of God, present to witness his universal love.
>
> Tues., July 29th [1740]: One, pestered with the Predestinarians, desired me to expound Rom.ix. I did, through Christ strengthening me, in an extra-ordinary manner . . . Many believed in their heart, and made confession

with their mouth, of Jesus Christ the Saviour of all men. I have not known a more triumphant night since I knew Bristol.

Tues., October 28th [1740]: I was led in the evening to preach universal redemption from those words, 'The Lord is not willing that any should perish, but that all should come to repentance' [2 Peter 3.9]. The Spirit mightily confirmed that irresistible truth.[20]

In December 1740, while in America, George Whitefield composed a belated 'Letter to the Rev. Mr. John Wesley, in Answer to his sermon, entitled "Free Grace"' – what Wesley himself would call 'a mere burlesque upon an answer'. By March 1741, Whitefield was back in England, first in London (where he would become the chief minister of a Dissenting Tabernacle in Moorfields) and then in Bristol.[21] The year would see 'a division of the Methodist societies'. The impact of the controversy was felt by Charles Wesley in his pastoral work in Bristol. He recounts Whitefield's preaching thus:

I met the bands in Kingswood. One, who, in fear of God, and mistrust of himself, had heard Mr. W——, assured me he had preached barefaced reprobation. The people fled before the reprobating lion. But again and again, as he observed them depart, the preacher of sad tidings called them back, with general offers of salvation. Vain and empty offers indeed! What availed his telling them that, for *aught he knew,* they be *all* elect. He did not believe them all elect; he could not; therefore he only mocked them with an empty word of invitation.[22]

The antinomian effects of 'unconditional election' could even include domestic violence:

A woman spoke to me of her husband. He was under strong conviction, while he attended the word; but the first time he heard the *other gospel,* came home elect, and, in proof of it, beat his wife. His seriousness was at an end. His work was done. God doth not behold iniquity in Jacob; therefore his iniquity and cruelty abound. He uses her worse than a Turk, (his predestinarian brother,) and tells her, if he killed her he could not be damned.[23]

The guaranteed 'perseverance of the saints' could have less dramatic but nevertheless baneful consequences, although in the case now reported they appear to have been reparable:

One serious youth I spake with today, who did run well: But from the time that he was persuaded to believe there was no falling after justification, he did begin to fall, as he now confesses, into carelessness, self-indulgence, and at last into known sins.[24]

Amid the dissensions in Bristol and Bath during the spring of 1741, we find Charles Wesley instructing the 'bands', debating with a 'Mr H', and preaching, for example, on John 17.9(–23):

Mon., April 13th [1741]: While I was in great love, warning the bands, the Spirit of power came down, the fountain was set open, my mouth and heart enlarged, and I spoke such words as I cannot repeat. Many sunk under the love of Christ crucified, and were constrained to break out, 'Christ died for all.' Some confessed, with tears of joy, they were going to leave us, but could now die for the truth of this doctrine.[25]

Tues., May 19th [1741]: I am more and more confirmed in the truth by its miserable opposers. I talked lately with Mr. H—— . . . I asked him, 'Why does God command all men everywhere to repent? Why does he call, and offer his grace to, reprobates? Why does his Spirit strive with every child of man for *some* time, though not always?' I could get no answer, and so I read him one of his friend Calvin's: 'God speaketh to them, that they may be the deafer; He giveth light to them, that they may be the blinder; He offers instruction to them, that they may be the more ignorant; and uses the remedy, that they may *not* be healed' [*Institutes* 3.24.13] Never did I meet a more pitiful advocate of a more pitiful cause. And yet I believe he could say as much for reprobation as another . . . .

. . . At Kingswood I preached on those much perverted words, 'I pray not for the world, but for them which thou hast given me' [John 17.9]; that is, his apostles. He does not take in believers of later ages till verse 20. Then in verse 21 he prays for the unbelieving world; that, to use Mr. [Richard] Baxter's words on the place, 'by *their* concord, the *world* may be won to Christianity.' . . . So far is our Lord from not praying for the world *at all* that in this very chapter he prays once for his first disciples, once for believers in after-ages, and *twice* for the *world* that lieth in wickedness, that the world may *believe* – that the world may *know*. He who prays for all men himself, and commands us to pray for all men, was with us, and showed us, with the demonstration of his Spirit, that he is not willing that any should perish, but that all should come to the knowledge of the truth, and be saved.[26]

Finally, we hear from Charles what transpired at the visit of Howel Harris, the Welsh Calvinist Revivalist preacher, to the society in Bristol on Saturday 27 June 1741:

Last night Howel Harris told me he would come to our Society. I bade him come in God's name. We were singing:

'Thee triumphantly we praise,
Vie with all thy hosts above;
Shout thine everlasting grace,
Thine everlasting love.'

when W. Hooper, by my order, brought him in. I prayed according to God; gave out a hymn that we all might join in. The hand of the Lord was upon me. I asked Howel whether he had a mind to speak, and sat by for half an hour, while he gave an account of his conversion by *irresistible grace*, mixing with his experience the impossibility of falling, God's unchangeableness, &c. I could not but observe the ungenerousness of my friend; and after hearing him long and patiently, was moved to rise up, and ask in the name of Jesus, 'Ye that are spiritual, doth the Spirit which is in you suffer me still to keep silence, and let my brother go on? Can I do it without bringing the blood of these souls upon me?' A woman first cried out, (Mrs Rawlins, I think), 'The wounds of Jesus answer, "No."' Then many others repeated, 'No, no, no'; and a whole cloud of witnesses arose, declaring, 'Christ died for all!'

I asked again, 'Would you have my brother Harris proceed, or would you not? If you would hear him, I will be silent all night.' Again they forbade me in strong words, upon which I gave out,

> 'Break forth into joy,
> Your Comforter sing,' &c

They did break forth as the voice of many waters, or mighty thunderings. O what a burst of joy was there in the midst of us! The God and Saviour of all men magnified his universal love.

Howel Harris would have entered into dispute, but was stopped. 'Then,' he said, 'you must thrust me out.' 'No,' said I, 'We do not: you are welcome to stay as long as you please. We acknowledge you a child of God.' Yet he began again, 'If you do not believe irresistible grace;' and I cut off the sentences of reprobation which I foresaw coming, with,

> 'Praise God, from whom pure blessings flow,
> Whose bowels yearn *on all* below;
> Who would not have one sinner lost;
> Praise Father, Son, and Holy Ghost.'[27]

The choral victory of Arminianism on this occasion was achieved by three texts figuring in the *Hymns on God's Everlasting Love* that would be published in two series under the names of the Wesley brothers in 1741 and 1741–2. And to these – after our swing through Charles as preacher and pastor in the earliest years of the Calvinist controversy – we now come, in order to look again at Charles as poet (assuming these texts, for all intents and purposes, to stem from his pen).

The first series of *Hymns on God's Everlasting Love* comprises 16 texts of varying length, and the second series a further 16, followed by 11 expansions on the Gloria Patri – all in all, a good 100 pages in the *Poetical Works*. Given our limited space, we may mostly omit the continuing negative polemics and highlight rather Charles' positive statements of the gospel. In particular, we can select a few texts that are important on account of their absorption into the Methodist *lex orandi* via the successive hymnals, especially among the British.

The opening hymn is particularly important, having figured in all British Methodist hymnals since 1808. Thus (in its liturgically abbreviated form, though with original italics):

Father, whose *everlasting love*
Thy only Son for sinners gave,
Whose grace to *all* did *freely* move,
And sent Him down a *world to save*:

Help us Thy mercy to extol,
Immense, unfathomed, unconfined;
To praise the Lamb who *died for all*,
The *general Saviour of mankind*.

Thy *undistinguishing regard*
Was cast on *Adam's* fallen race;
*For all* Thou hast in Christ prepared
*Sufficient, sovereign, saving* grace.

The *world* He suffered to redeem;
For *all* He hath the atonement made:
For those that will not come to Him
The ransom of His life was paid.

Arise, O God, maintain Thy cause!
The fulness of the *Gentiles* call:
Lift up the standard of Thy cross.
And *all* shall own Thou diedst for all.[28]

Note the universal scope of God's love and of the atoning work of Christ, here described as 'redemption' and 'ransom'. A willing response is called for. The prospect is finally universal, too.

From hymn 10 in the first series the liturgically perduring stanzas paint a graphic, medieval-style picture of Christ on the cross, with the poet at his feet. They are preceded by a rehearsal of Jesus in his kenotic, servant ministry, including a stanza in which Wesley deploys a characteristic move against Calvinistic 'preterition' by showing that 'the incarnate God' never 'passed by' the needy:

See where the lame, the halt, the blind,
The deaf, the dumb, the sick, the poor,
Flock to the Friend of human kind,
And freely all accept their cure:
To whom doth He His help deny?
Whom in His days of flesh *pass by*?
. . . . . . . . . . . .

Would Jesus have the sinner die?
Why hangs He then on yonder tree?
What means that strange expiring cry,
Sinners, He prays for you and me:
'Forgive them, Father, O forgive,
They know not that by Me they live!'

Dear, loving, all-atoning Lamb,
Thee by Thy painful agony,
Thy bloody sweat, Thy grief and shame,
Thy cross and passion on the tree,
Thy precious death, and life, I pray –
Take all, take all my sins away!

O let me kiss Thy bleeding feet,
And bathe, and wash them with my tears;
The story of Thy love repeat
In every drooping sinner's ears,
That all may hear the quickening sound:
If I, even I, have mercy found!

O let Thy love my heart constrain,
Thy love for every sinner free,
That every fallen soul of man
May taste the grace that found out me:
That all mankind, with me, may prove
Thy sovereign, everlasting love.[29]

The preacher's task and message is summarized in doxological mode in the lovely hymn 11 from the second series that was reprinted in the *Arminian Magazine* (1778, p. 191):

Let earth and heaven agree,
Angels and men be joined,
To celebrate with me
The Saviour of mankind;
To adore the all-atoning Lamb,
And bless the sound of Jesu's name.
. . . . . . . . . .

O for a trumpet voice
On all the world to call,
To bid their hearts rejoice
In Him who died for all!
For all my Lord was crucified;
For all, for all my Saviour died.[30]

In hymn 14, the Trinitarian God insistently asks the entire human race – 'Creatures capable of God', 'You, whom He ordained to be/Transcripts of the Trinity' – why they refuse the gracious divine offer of eternal life (cf. Ezekiel 18.31f.):

Sinners, turn; why will ye die?
God, your Maker, asks you why;
God, who did your being give,
Made you with Himself to live:

He the fatal cause demands,
Asks the work of His own hands,
Why, ye thankless creatures, why
Will ye cross His love, and die?

Sinners, turn; why will ye die?
God, your Saviour, asks you why;
God, who did your souls retrieve,
Died Himself that you might live:
Will you let Him die in vain?
Crucify your Lord again?
Why, ye ransomed sinners, why
Will you slight His grace and die?

Sinners, turn; why will ye die?
God, the Spirit, asks you why;
God, who all your lives hath strove,
Wooed you to embrace His love:
Will you not the grace receive?
Will you still refuse to live?
Why, ye long-sought sinners, why
Will ye grieve your God, and die?[31]

A final example may be taken from another source, *Hymns and Sacred Poems* of 1749. Here Charles Wesley explores the 'dimensions' of God's grace on the basis of Ephesians 3.14–19:

What shall I do my God to love?
My loving God to praise?
The length, and breadth, and height to prove,
And depth of sovereign grace?

Thy sovereign grace to all extends,
Immense and unconfined;
From age to age it never ends;
It reaches all mankind.

Throughout the world its breadth is known,
Wide as infinity!
So wide it never passed by one,
Or it had passed by me.

My trespass is grown up to heaven,
But far above the skies,
In Christ abundantly forgiven,
I see Thy mercies rise.

The depth of all-redeeming love
What angel tongue can tell?
O may I to the utmost prove
The gift unspeakable.

Deeper than hell, it plucked me thence;
Deeper than inbred sin,
Jesus's love my heart shall cleanse,
When Jesus enters in.

Come quickly then, my Lord, and take
Possession of Thine own;
My longing heart vouchsafe to make
Thine everlasting throne.

Assert Thy claim, receive Thy right,
Come quickly from above,
And *sink* me to perfection's height,
The *depth* of humble love.[32]

How, then, may we sum up the content and style of Charles Wesley's ministry and writings in confrontation with 'Calvinism', particularly on the fundamental and most neuralgic point of predestination? He insists on love as the very nature of God and on its everlasting and universal character towards humankind. He sees this freely displayed and enacted in the Incarnation and atoning work of Christ, which is not only sufficient but effective for the redemption of a 'fallen race'. The depravity of humankind is mitigated by a 'prevenient grace':

By nature only free to ill,
We never had one motion known
Of good, hadst Thou not given the will,
And wrought it by Thy grace alone.[33]

Granted in virtue of Christ's redemptive death, this grace sets the human will free to accept the offer of eternal life, which is God's plan for humankind from the beginning. Accepted in repentance and faith, this gift will overflow in love towards the needy neighbour. All this is argued to be in harmony with the general tenor of scripture (what Charles calls God's 'written Will')[34] and crystallized in a number of favourite passages. The preacher's business is to proclaim it with intellectual and emotive power. Where pastorally necessary, he must clear the way by deconstructing 'the horrible decree' and its alleged consequences for God and humans – using all available tools of exegesis, theo-logic and rhetoric (especially irony and rhyme).[35]

And what was the score, in this contest between 'Evangelical Arminianism' and 'Calvinism'? Later Methodists have tended to think that the Wesleys won hands-down. Thus, for instance, Henry Bett in 1913 and again in 1956:

Many of the hymns of Methodism reflect the life-long controversy of the Wesleys with the Calvinists. It was undoubtedly these great hymns that were largely accountable for the diffusion of Arminian doctrine throughout evangelical Christendom. In this respect they mark a theological epoch. For the work of the Wesleys was the death of Calvinism, or at least of its baser nature. The Calvinism that survives in the world today is a thing refined, rarefied. The baser sort of Calvinism is so utterly extinct in our days – thanks to Methodism – that it is difficult for us to realize that it ever existed.[36]

Or J. Ernest Rattenbury in 1941 and again in 1954: 'Nothing did so much to destroy popular Calvinism in England as Charles Wesley's hymns; they made it incredible to the reason, and repulsive to the heart of decent people.'[37]

Leaving aside the triumphalistic claims of Calvinism's *historical* defeat, we may wonder whether the *theological* victory was quite so clear cut. Exegetically, it is more difficult than the Wesleys thought to deal with the Pauline use of the 'Jacob/Esau' text (cf. Romans 9.13) or the 'hardening of heart' attributed to God in the case of a Pharaoh (cf. Romans 9.17f.) or God's darkening of the people's eyes and stopping of their ears (cf. Romans 11.7–10; Matthew 13.13–15); and canonically, such texts should not be removed from the Scriptures, Old or New Testament. Metaphysically, awkward questions remain concerning God's 'foreknowledge' and human freedom, and the relation between time and eternity. Nor can the spontaneous existential response of converts be taken as logically probative of the universal redemption that has been preached to them. On the existential level itself, Calvinists in turn can point to good fruit in the lives of many who believe themselves elect (as indeed the Wesleys admit), so that the ethical danger of antinomianism may have been exaggerated for polemical purposes. In return, a Calvinist might wonder – despite the Wesleys' recognition of the 'gravity of sin' – whether there is a line to be traced, at least existentially if not probatively, from the 'universality' of the proclaimed gospel to an easy-going 'universalism' where final salvation is assured for all ('*Dieu nous pardonnera, c'est son métier*'). And historically at least (to sneak back there), the continuing line of Dutch Remonstrants descended from 'Arminianism' figure among the groups that have most noticeably departed – via an association with Socinianism – from classic Christianity on the broader doctrinal plane.

A nicely nuanced account of the issues between 'Wesleyanism' and 'Calvinism' is found in the report 'Together in God's Grace' (1987) from the dialogue between the World Methodist Council and the World Alliance of Reformed Churches.[38] Since the report is not well known, the text may be quoted extensively. On the fundamental matter that has been occupying us:

Methodists who follow Wesley must face two objections in particular from Calvinists. First, Calvinists object that the necessary freedom to choose salvation was lost in the Fall, and that to claim otherwise is Pelagian. Wesley in response agreed that all are dead in sin by nature, but maintained that none is now in a mere state of nature. Prevenient grace, which he saw as the universal inheritance of Christ's atoning work, restores this lost freedom of choice, while not guaranteeing salvation. Calvinists then object that this dishonours God by denying his sovereignty, since it claims that human freedom to deny is greater than God's will to save. Wesley's reply was that in creating people with free will, God chose to limit his power at this point. Therefore the human capacity to say no to saving grace is, according to

Wesley, just as compatible with God's sovereignty as is the human capacity
to sin.

In their turn, the Reformed who follow Calvin must face two questions
in particular from Wesleyans. First, Wesleyans ask how the predestinarian
approach avoids understanding God's freedom as anything more than arbi-
trariness, and human freedom as anything other than illusion, if the eternal destiny of every creature is already determined. The Calvinist answer
is that since God as creator is the author of justice and his ways are not
our ways, it is a fundamental category mistake for us to judge him at the
bar of our human and limited reason. The second Wesleyan question is,
how can the missionary and evangelical imperative be maintained if, no
matter what, the saved will be saved and the lost lost? Calvinists affirm in
reply that obedience to the sovereign God commits the church to the proclamation of the gospel so that people may hear and believe, and thus God's
will to save be fulfilled. Consequently, impetus for, and result of, missionary and evangelistic outreach are evident no less in the Reformed than in
the Methodist tradition, although the motivation may be understood and
expressed somewhat differently.

These questions that we put to each other lie in the realm of theological
problems, and answers can be given which in each case are consistent with
the basic agreed affirmations [the places at which the Wesleyans, according to the Conference of 1745, 'come to the very edge of Calvinism'] and
find scriptural support. But for both Methodists and Calvinists there is a
question which cannot be answered, not because it is difficult, but because
to propose an answer would be to destroy the very terms of the problem.
Those who claim that prevenient grace gives to all the freedom to come
to faith cannot answer the question 'why do these choose salvation, and
not those?' without denying the very human freedom they wish to affirm.
Those who contend that only the elect may come to faith, and thus be saved
by grace, cannot answer the question 'why does God choose these and not
those?' without limiting God's sovereign freedom which above all they
wish to maintain. That these questions, which are unanswerable in principle, exist at all, points to the fundamental mystery underlying both the
theological problem and the answers. Both traditions have gone wrong
when they have claimed to know too much about this mystery of God's
electing grace and of human response.

Within that modest framework, another matter controversial between the
Wesleys and the Calvinists – and that we can only skirt here – can be more
eirenically tackled: perfection. The 1987 report itself proceeded thus:

Both Reformed and Methodist traditions affirm the real change which God
by the Spirit works in the minds and hearts and lives of believers. By the
sanctifying grace of God, penitent believers are being restored to God's
image and renewed in God's likeness. To imitate God, says Wesley, is the
best worship we can offer. What God is in heaven, says Calvin, he bids us
to be in this world: the loving kindness of God is to be reflected in the love
Christians bear toward their neighbours. Our traditions agree that, on the

human side, salvation consists in the perfect love of God and neighbour, which is to have the mind of Christ and fulfill his law. We are to love God with singleness of heart, and to seek God's glory with a single eye. We are to love without reserve the sisters and brothers for whom Christ died. The work which God has begun in us, says Calvin, he will surely complete. What God has promised, says Wesley, he is ready and willing to realize now. In the two traditions we are taught to strive and pray for entire sanctification. The Reformed stress on election and perseverance gives believers the confidence that God will keep them to the end. The Methodist preaching of perfection affirms that we may set no limit to the present power of God to make sinners into saints.

Methodists and Reformed agree that 'man's chief end is to glorify God and to enjoy him for ever.' The heavenly fellowship of praise and bliss is, by God's grace, to be anticipated now, as we 'with one heart and one voice glorify the God and Father of our Lord Jesus Christ' [Romans 15.5f.] and together share his benefits. We are saved into community; and, as Jesus prayed that his disciples might be 'perfected into one' [John 17.23], so the closer sharing of life between Christians in the Reformed and Methodist traditions will be evidence of growing participation in the communion of the Triune God.

And on that happy – and challenging – note, we may conclude this investigation into the relations between 'Charles Wesley and Calvinism'.[39]

## Notes

1 Alan P. F. Sell, *The Great Debate: Calvinism, Arminianism and salvation* (Worthing: H. E. Walter), 1982.

2 *The Arminian Magazine: Consisting of extracts and original treatises on universal redemption* (London: R. Hawes, vol. 1, 1778), v. Capitalization has been modernized in this transcription.

3 Charles 'preached against absolute predestination, and in defense of God's universal love, much oftener, and with far greater warmth, than his brother, and expressed himself in language much stronger than John ever employed in reference to this subject'. So Jackson, *Life*, 216. For the relevant period between 1739 and 1741, see chapters 8 and 9 of Jackson's *Life*, 152–258.

4 As indicated, this is a traditional English-language summary of the teachings of the Synod of Dort. For the full text of the Synod's canons, cf. Jaroslav Pelikan and Valerie Hotchkiss, eds, *Creeds and Confessions of Faith in the Christian Tradition* (3 vols, with an additional collection of source material in original languages on CD ROM; New Haven: Yale University Press, 2003), 2. 569–600.

5 'Minutes of Some Late Conversations' (the so-called 'Doctrinal Minutes'), 2 August 1745, in *Works*, 8. 285.

6 John Wesley, Sermon 110, 'Free Grace' (1739), 9 (*BE*, 3. 547).

7 John Wesley, *Journal* for 2 April 1739 (*BE*, 19. 46).

8 This composite account of those last days in April 1739 is assembled from John's journal and diary (*BE*, 19. 50–2, 386–7) and his letter of 30 April 1739 to James Hutton and the Fetter Lane Society (*BE*, 25. 639–40).

9  Sermon 110 is cited by paragraph numbers from *BE*, 3. 544–59. The appended poem or hymn on 'Universal Redemption' figures on pp. 559–63 and will be cited from there.

10  The first line of this stanza is reminiscent of Philippians 2.12f., where the apostle's language refers to *believers*: 'Work out your own salvation with fear and trembling, for God is at work in you, both to will and to work for his good pleasure.'

11  John coolly admits at one point that 'there are many Scriptures the true sense whereof neither you nor I shall know till death is swallowed up in victory' (26).

12  Cf. 1 Corinthians 15.22.

13  Cf. 1 Timothy 2.4.

14  Cf. Romans 3.21–8; Ephesians 2.8.

15  Cf. Isaiah 55.1; John 4.10–15; 7.37–9.

16  Cf. John 5.38–40

17  Cf. Revelation 3.20

18  Cf. Philippians 2.10f.

19  Cf. Revelation 22.20f.

20  Quotations from *CWJ*, 1.155, 247, 254 respectively. Note Charles' use of the word 'irresistible' in his own cause. The journal shows other texts for preaching during this period to have been notably 2 Corinthians 5.19, 'God was in Christ, reconciling the world unto himself' (KJV); Matthew 11.28, 'Come unto me, all ye that labour and are heavy laden' (KJV); John 3.16, 'God so loved the world, that he gave his only begotten Son' (KJV); Isaiah 55.1, 'Ho, every one that thirsteth, come ye to the waters' (KJV).

21  See Luke Tyerman, *The Life of the Rev. George Whitefield* (New York: Randolph, 1877), vol. 1, 462–84.

22  *CWJ*, 1.272 (4 May 1741).

23  *CWJ*, 1.280 (8 June 1741). The reference to Jacob alludes to the 'Calvinist' interpretation of Romans 9.13 ('Jacob have I loved, but Esau have I hated'). In stanzas 6–10 of his poem 'The Horrible Decree' (*PW*, 3.34–8), Charles makes fiercely ironic use of what he calls the 'other gospel' preached by the predestinarians (cf. Galatians 1.8).

24  *CWJ*, 1.291 (28 July 1741).

25  *CWJ*, 1.267.

26  *CWJ*, 1.276f. Other texts Charles preached on in the spring and summer of 1741: 1 Timothy 1.15, 'This is a faithful saying, and worthy of all acceptation, that Christ Jesus came into the world to save sinners' (KJV), 17 April, *CWJ*, 1.268; Isaiah 45.22, 'Look unto me, and be ye saved, all the ends of the earth' (KJV), 20 April, *CWJ*, 1.268; John 12.32, 'And I, if I be lifted up from the earth, will draw all men unto me' (KJV), 7 May, *CWJ*, 1.274; Ezekiel 18, 28 May, *CWJ*, 1.278f.: 'Our Lord owned me here also, and the hammer of his word broke the rock of absolute predestination in pieces'; Titus 2.11, 'For the grace of God that bringeth salvation hath appeared to all men' (KJV), 12 July, *CWJ*, 1.286; Isaiah 53, 28 August, when he was 'greatly assisted to purge out the leaven of Calvinism', *CWJ*, 1.295.

27  *CWJ*, 1.283f.

28  See *PW*, 3.3–5 (stanzas 1–3, 8, 17). The original stanza 8 began 'A world'. The hymn figured in the 1877 *Collection of Hymns* as No. 39; in the 1904 *Methodist Hymn-Book* as No. 65; in the 1933 *Methodist Hymn-Book* as No. 75; and in the 1983 *Hymns & Psalms* as No. 520.

29  See *PW*, 3.20–3 (stanzas 7, 12, 16, 17, 18). The last four stanzas figured in the

1877 book as No. 33 (where the original stanza 14 was also included); in the 1904 book as No. 159; in the 1933 book as No. 173; in the 1983 book as No. 185.

30 See *PW*, 3.71–3 (stanzas 1 and 9). Most of the original ten stanzas were included in the books of 1877 (No. 34), 1904 (No. 99), 1933 (No. 114) and 1983 (No. 226).

31 See *PW*, 3.84–89 (stanzas 1, 2 and 3 of 16). These stanzas figure in the books of 1877 (No. 6), 1904 (No. 274), 1933 (No. 327) – but not 1983.

32 See *PW*, 4.445–7 (stanzas 11–18). In the 1780 *Collection* these stanzas are preceded by one beginning 'Infinite, unexhausted Love' (No. 207); so also in the book of 1877 (No. 216). Since 1904 the successive books have begun at 'What shall I do my God to love' and have omitted the stanzas 'Deeper than hell' and 'Assert Thy claim'.

33 'Free Grace', hymn 16 in the second series of *Hymns on God's Everlasting Love* (1741–2), stanza 9 (*PW*, 3.94).

34 So Charles' poetic 'address to the Calvinists', probably an earlier poem that was first published in the *Arminian Magazine*, 1778 (383f.). See Frank Baker, *Representative Verse of Charles Wesley* (London: Epworth Press, 1962), 331f.

35 All the rhetorical devices are employed in the ferocious poem 'The Horrible Decree', appended to the first series of *Hymns on God's Everlasting Love* (1741); see *Poetical Works* 3.34–8. In a manuscript poem (see Baker, *Representative Verse*, 167), Charles Wesley ascribes the 'horrible decree' to the Devil, and prays to God:

Drive the Old Fatalist to Hell,
Nor longer let him Refuge take
In Kirk, or School, or Mosque, or Cell,
Not ev'n in his own Leman-Lake.

Marginalia conveniently identify the Kirk 'of Scotland', the School 'of Zeno, ye heathen Philosopher', the Mosque 'of Mahomet the Imposter', the Cell 'of Dominick the Popish Friar' – 'All Predestinarians' – and the Lake 'of Geneva'.

36 Henry Bett, *The Hymns of Methodism in Their Literary Relations* (London: Charles H. Kelly, 1913), 115; repeated in the third edition (London: Epworth Press), as late as 1956, 60f.

37 J. E. Rattenbury, *The Evangelical Doctrines of Charles Wesley's Hymns* (London: Epworth Press, 1954), 117–36, here p. 121. Lately, some have discerned a loss of 'decency' in British society (cf. Christie Davies, *The Strange Death of Moral Britain*, 2004), but there are few signs, whether in England or in Scotland, of a reversion to 'Calvinism'.

38 The report "Together in God's Grace" was published in *Reformed World*, 39 (1986–7), 821–9. It can also be found in Jeffrey Gros, Harding Meyer and William G. Rusch eds, *Growth in Agreement II: Reports and Agreed Statements of Ecumenical Conversations on a World Level, 1982–1998* (Geneva: WCC Publications, 2000), 269–74.

39 For more detail on some of the matters treated here, see Geoffrey Wainwright, *Methodists in Dialogue* (Nashville: Abingdon Press/Kingswood Books, 1995), 143–58 ('Perfect Salvation in the Teaching of Wesley and Calvin'), and my Cato Lecture of 1985 delivered to the Assembly of the Uniting Church in Australia: *Geoffrey Wainwright on Wesley and Calvin: Sources for theology, liturgy and spirituality* (Melbourne: Uniting Church Press, 1987). In most cases – though not always – 'Wesley' is there intended to serve as a collective noun for John and Charles.

# 12. 'I preached at the Cross, as usual': Charles Wesley and Redemption

## JOHN R. TYSON

On Sunday, 4 January 1747, Charles Wesley wrote this terse entry in his journal: 'I preached at the Cross, as usual.'[1] While Wesley's annotation, in this particular instance, might have referred to a geographic location (such as Nottingham Cross) the assertion contained in it was theologically accurate as well. It really did not matter much what scripture text Charles Wesley had before him as he began preaching or writing a hymn, his hermeneutical method and poetical imagination seems almost invariably to have brought him back to the cross of Jesus Christ.[2] This cross-centred approach to the Bible fits well with the work of the preacher-poet, who understood himself primarily as a Methodist evangelist. In this sense, then, Charles Wesley's theology of the cross describes more than his doctrine of the atonement; it addresses his entire theology of redemption (justification and sanctification), as well as his understanding of the Christian's life in the world. When paired with 'the crown', 'the cross' spans a Christian's life, death, and life to come. As Charles wrote:

> If His death we receive,
> His life we shall live;
> If His cross we sustain,
> His joy and His crown we in heaven shall gain.[3]

In this way, then, Charles Wesley's theology of the cross is a fundamental, integrating feature in his writings, life and thought.

### Preaching the cross

Charles Wesley's extant sermons offer us an interesting, but also difficult and diverse corpus of material to assess.[4] They stem from four sources:

1. a slim corpus of 13 sermons, seven of which were mistakenly attributed to Charles Wesley; these seven were composed by John Wesley, but transcribed and subsequently preached by Charles[5] and published posthumously;[6] manuscripts for most of those texts are extant;

2. six unquestionably authentic Charles Wesley sermons, which were written almost entirely in shorthand[7] and which have only relatively recently been transcribed;[8]

3. three further manuscript sermons located in the MARC, one of which Charles has copied from another source (what that source was he does not indicate), while the other two appear to be original compositions,[9] and

4. two 'Standard Sermons' which were composed and preached by Charles Wesley ('Awake Thou, That Sleepest', and 'The Cause and Cure of Earthquakes') and then published among the works of his brother John – often without proper identification.[10]

Even early, pre-conversion sermons evidence him preaching 'the merits of Christ'[11] and asking the rhetorical question: 'Now if it be so joyful a thing to believe that Christ died to save sinners, what must it be to add to our faith in hope? To be assured that he died to save us? If knowing that a ransom is paid for lost man . . . how does he rejoice, who feels within his own soul, that this ransom is paid for him?'[12] Yet, as Newport rightly suggests, one detects 'a distinct note of works-righteousness' in these early sermons;[13] and even when Charles preached 'the cross' in these early sermons (as above in the sermon based on Psalm 126.7), the emotional texture of the message sounds hypothetical. But several of Charles' post-conversion sermons (that is, those sermons composed after 21 May 1738)[14] evidence a clear change in his preaching of the cross.[15]

In the first (extant) sermon that was preached after his 'personal Pentecost', he declared: 'He only comprehends and lives it, who hath Christ's righteousness imputed to him; "for the just shall live by faith" and from the moment anyone believes with the heart, he can truly say, "I am crucified with Christ; nevertheless I live; yet not I, but Christ liveth in me."'[16] This development continues in his sermon based on Titus 3.8, in which Wesley exclaimed: 'If Christ be given for us, he is likewise given to us; he is formed in our hearts by faith, and lives and reigns in our souls.'[17] The atonement was no longer viewed merely as an historical event, to be mentioned in Wesley's sermons; rather, in the post-conversion proclamation, the 'atonement' (and its related themes and terms) described a cleansing, transforming event which impinges upon a person's inner life.

In Charles' sermon on Romans 3.23–4, which he first preached on 21 January 1739, he drew upon the Anglican 'Homily on Salvation' to establish the soteriological foundation of his message: '. . . God sent his only Son our saviour Christ into this world to fulfill the law for us, and by the shedding of his most precious blood, to make sacrifice and satisfaction or amends to his Father for our sins, and assuage his wrath and indignation conceived against us for the same.'[18] The language of the traditional, penal substitution theory of the atonement is quite prevalent in this sermon, which echoes clearly in the recurrent references to God's justice and Christ's satisfaction of the wrath of God and penalty of the law. For example, Wesley declared: '. . . it pleased our heavenly Father, of his infinite mercy, without any our deserving, to prepare for us the most precious jewels of Christ's body and blood, whereby our ransom might be fully paid, the law fulfilled, and his justice fully satisfied.'[19] In this sermon, the historical and theological foundations of the doctrine of the atonement are used as a basis for Wesley's proclamation of Justification by Faith Alone. As, at the end of the sermon, he asked his hearers pointedly: 'Do you now depend upon the blood of Christ as fully, entirely, and solely as you would do were you this sinner? Do you rely on his death as the one sufficient satisfaction, oblation and sacrifice for your sins, and on nothing else? On, nothing you either are, or have done?'[20] As Newport rightly reports: 'As one would expect of a revivalist preacher, this determined presentation of the efficacy of the sacrifice of Christ dominates the soteriology of the sermon.'[21] This homiletical development reaches its climax in the next sermon in the same corpus.

Sermon No. 7 (in Newport's volume), which is based on Romans 3.23–5, was preached 'before the University, with great boldness' on 1 July 1739. Charles' journal goes on to report, 'All were very attentive. One could not help weeping.'[22] What was missing in the previous sermon, or if not missing at least was not sounded very clearly, was Wesley's characteristic emphasis upon 'receiving the atonement'. For Charles Wesley, the atonement was not merely an historical event or a theological verity; in his preaching and, as we shall see below, in his hymns, the 'receiving the atonement' became a current event in the inner life of a person. Charles promised to make this matter plain at the outset of the sermon: '. . . I will show what that faith is through which we receive the atonement *applied to our soul in particular*; and finally, I shall conclude with a particular application.'[23] In this sermon the historical and the hypothetical merge with the particular and personal. Again, Wesley returned to the Anglican standards to show that Justification by Faith is 'not only a common belief of the Articles of our Creed, but it is also a true trust and confidence of the mercy of God through our Lord Jesus Christ'.[24] But he began that explanation by asking, once again, 'What the faith is, through which we thus *receive the atonement* and apply Christ and all his merits to our soul in particular . . .'[25]

For Charles Wesley, the atonement was not merely an historical truth to be believed, it was a transforming experience to be 'received' in the inner person. This theological development, which was based on the phraseology of Romans 5.11 (in the King James Version), was frequently attested in Charles Wesley's journal. Beginning with Charles' own personal Pentecost[26] and continuing throughout his subsequent ministry, the atonement was not only something to be believed; it also needed to be 'received'.[27] The historical truth of Good Friday was brought into the life experience of the contemporary hearers of Charles Wesley's proclamation, and 'receiving the atonement' became a euphemism for conversion and new birth as a person sought to 'apply Christ and all his merits our soul in particular . . .'[28]

On Sunday, 15 October 1738, Charles Wesley's journal reports that he 'preached [his sermon entitled] the one thing needful at Islington, and added much extempore . . .'[29] This entry marks the beginning of another important transition in Charles Wesley's preaching; he was gradually moving from relying upon written sermons toward preaching almost entirely without notes. Five days later, Wesley reported: 'Seeing so few present at a St. Antholin's, I thought of preaching extempore; afraid, yet ventured on the promise, "Lo, I am with you always;" and spake on justification from Rom. iii, for three quarters of an hour, without hesitation.'[30] On 11 February 1739 he '. . . read prayers, and preached without notes on Blind Bartimaeus . . .'[31]

On some occasions, Wesley simply opened the Bible to a familiar passage and preached on '. . . the first words I met . . .'[32] By 11 July 1750 this process seems to have become so common for him that Wesley's journal ceased to comment upon preaching extempore, and mentions instead the more unusual instance in which he '. . . preached a written sermon'.[33] In a similar fashion, Charles Wesley's descriptions of the event of his own preaching began to stress its spontaneous character; for example, in the journal he often describes himself as preaching with 'great freedom' or 'much freedom'[34]; on many other occasions he preached 'with great enlargement'.[35]

Unfortunately, Charles Wesley's adoption of a spontaneous homiletical style had the unintentional result of leaving us with almost no written sermons from the height of the Wesleyan revival. But his journal, which has sometimes been described as an annotated sermon log, gives ample evidence of the biblical texts he preached.[36] It also gives some interesting suggestions as to how he might have preached them. For example, in his journal entry for 28 November 1746, Wesley reported: 'I set before their eyes Christ crucified, and crying from the cross, "Is it nothing to you [who pass by]?" The rocks were melted into gracious tears.'[37] A similar instance is recorded in his entry for 21 June 1747; once again the biblical text of Lamentations 1.12 became the words of Jesus Christ, spoken from the cross.[38] In Wesley's presentation, the eighteenth-century British audience became contemporaries of Christ on the cross as Christ spoke to them and made intercession on their behalf. Charles preached this text, in this way, at least ten times, and often with remarkable results. While a written text for this sermon does not seem to be extant, Charles' hymn 'Invitation to Sinners' (which is framed upon the same Bible passage) gives some indication of how he may have preached the cross from Lamentations 1.12:

> All ye that pass by,
> To Jesus draw nigh,
> To you is it nothing that Jesus should die?
> Your Ransom and Peace,
> Your Surety He is,
> Come, see if there every was sorrow like His.
>
> For what you have done
> His blood must atone:
> The Father had punish'd for you His dear Son.
> The Lord in the day
> Of His anger lay
> Your sins on the Lamb; and he bore them away.[39]

Traditional atonement themes, like substitution, sacrifice and Christ bearing the penalty of human sin are sounded throughout this hymn; Jesus is named as Ransom, Peace, Lamb and Advocate.[40] When examining Christ's intercession, however, Wesley does not content himself with the merits of Christ's

death, he also viewed Jesus' words, 'My Father forgive!' as an intercessory
prayer from the cross:

> He dies to atone
> For sins not His own;
> Your debt He hath paid, and your work He hath done.
> Ye all may receive
> The peace He did leave,
> Who made intercession 'My Father forgive!'

> For you, and for me
> He pray'd on the tree,
> The prayer is accepted, the sinner is free.
> The sinner am I,
> Who on Jesus rely,
> And come for the pardon God cannot deny.[41]

For the eighteenth-century singer of this hymn, the atonement can be embraced
'now' because of the intercession of Jesus Christ, both through his sacrificial
death ('blood') and the advocacy of his prayer ('Father forgive'); indeed, the
two types of intercession become one as the blood of Christ takes voice to
'speak . . . for me':

> My pardon I claim,
> For a sinner I am,
> A sinner believing in Jesus' name.
> He purchased the grace,
> Which I now embrace:
> O Father, Thou know'st He hath died in my place.

> His death is my plea,
> My Advocate see,
> And hear the blood speak that hath answer'd for me.
> Acquitted I was,
> When He bled on the cross,
> And by losing His life He hath carried my cause.[42]

This same hermeneutical process is echoed in the journal's description
of Charles preaching other cross-centred sermon texts. His entry for 26
September 1756, for example, reports: 'I preached on those words "His blood
be upon us, and on our children". Our Lord turned the curse into a blessing.'[43]
The scripture text from Matthew 27.25 (KJV), which in its context described
the scene before Pilate's judgement seat as the mob rejected Jesus and handed
him over to crucifixion, became 'a blessing' through Charles Wesley's proclamation. On another occasion the same sermon text was described as 'that
best of prayers, if rightly used . . .'[44] Wesley concluded: 'All present, I believe,
received then some benefit from His passion.'[45] His 'Short Hymn' on this
scripture text expounds the soteriological themes that may have shaped his
(non-extant) sermon:

HORRIBLE wish! Thy murders dare
The blessing to a curse pervert:
*We* turn the curse into a prayer;
To cleanse our lives, and purge our heart,
In all its hallowing, blissful powers
Thy blood be, Lord, on us and ours!

On me, Thou bleeding Lamb, on me
Be pour'd the consecrating stream,
From all, from all inquity
My life, my nature to redeem,
To fill with purity Divine,
And sign my soul for ever Thine.[46]

While these tantalizing references to Charles Wesley's cross-centred evangelistic sermons do not provide us with much hard evidence about how he
preached the cross, they do point us to both the historical context and the
theological vocabulary requisite for investigating his theology of redemption. The extant medium for this investigation is Wesley's gigantic corpus of
hymns and sacred poems.

## The cross as a focal theme in Charles Wesley's hymns

Typically one can write of a 'theology of the cross' and that phrase becomes
a synonym for 'redemption' or 'reconciliation'; however, in Charles Wesley's
theology the cross becomes a central symbol or image around which many
important soteriological themes are collected. In this sense, then, the 'cross'
is used to refer to Good Friday, yet also moves beyond Good Friday to Easter,
Pentecost and the Christian's contemporary experience. J. Ernest Rattenbury
detected this fundamental dynamic at work in the tension he drew between the
finished and the unfinished work of Christ.[47] It was typical of Charles Wesley's
dramatic approach to the theology of the cross that a shift from the past (Good
Friday) to the present (the current experience) tense occurred in the same
poem, verse, or even in the same line. For example, when Wesley expounded
the biblical text from Job 23.3, 'O that I knew where I might find Him', his verse
immediately took on a Christological dimension and pointed the reader to the
finished–unfinished work of Christ's cross. 'Where shall I find Him?'

Where but on yonder tree?
Or if too rich thou art,
Sink into poverty,
And find Him in thine heart.[48]

Christ, according to Wesley, is best known in his death on the cross, but that
dying must be linked to Christ's rising in the human heart. Past and present
are held in tension by the living Christ, who both died to remove sin, and lives
within Christians to purge the effects of sin out of their lives.

The finished work of the cross was a victory over the tyrants of sin and death, hence Wesley pointed to the 'triumph of His cross'.[49] The implement of torture became, in Charles Wesley's poetical imagination, the sceptre of Christ's Kingly office:

The King of saints He meekly bears
The scepter of His cross,
Thus his royal power declares
And executes his law.[50]

The finished work of the cross was also an 'atonement': 'the blood an atonement hath made,/And the Lamb for His murders died.'[51] Sacrificial, substitutionary and purchase language was often woven together to describe the saving effects of Jesus' death:

Father, behold the Son
And me, even me in Him
Who doth for all my sins atone
And by His death redeem;
As fasten'd to the tree,
And cover'd with His blood
His purchase and His members see
For ever one with God.[52]

Christ's cross is also a contemporary event. It stands ever before us as a sign of God's love and the great cost of God's love. This theme (as we saw above with respect to 'All ye who pass by') was a prominent feature of Charles Wesley's preaching as well as his hymns. He often identified the cross as an emblem of God's love, and as such the cross was an event which had both past and present power.[53] On several occasions this symbolism was reinforced by Wesley's willingness to depict the arms of Christ, extended painfully on the cross of his death, as being simultaneously thrown open wide in a long and lovely embrace:

Jesus the crucified
Invites our sinful race,
And with those arms extended wide
Would all mankind embrace.[54]

In Charles Wesley's preaching, the contemporary event of the cross became a powerful tool for breaking the hardness of human hearts: 'We were all melted into tears by our dying Lord's expostulation, "Is it nothing to you, all ye that pass by?" and long continued mourning in sight of his cross.'[55] And similar sentiments were sounded in his hymns: 'Now I look on Thee and mourn,/Now I give Thee all my heart.'[56] Just as the cross could be 'received' in a person's contemporary experience, in a related (though opposite way) the rejection of Christ and new life could be called crucifying Christ again.[57]

## The school of the cross

For Charles Wesley the cross was not only God's decisive act in the history of redemption, it became the pattern for the Christian's life as well. Wesley saw the entire life of Jesus through the lens of his suffering:

> Quite from the manger to the cross
> Thy life one scene of suffering was,
> And all sustain'd for me:
> O strange excess of love Divine!
> Jesus, was there ever love like Thine!
> Answer me from the tree![58]

Furthermore, the Christian was called to be 'conform'd to an expiring God':

> Conform'd to an expiring God
> We who feel his sprinkled blood
> The same distress abide;
> And every soul that Jesus knows
> Partakes his bitterest pangs and woes
> Together crucified.[59]

By observing and participating in Christ's sufferings, Christians come to 'know Him', they begin to partake of his Spirit, and are thereby prepared for their own victory over death and for the life to come:

> (1) What eve'r we can of Jesus know
> His followers, here comprised we see,
> His life of pain and grief below,
> His bleeding passion on the tree,
> His sacrifice our souls to save,
> His rise and triumph o'er the grave.
>
> (2) We now who Jesus' spirit breathe
> The ills of life with patience bear,
> With joy receive the stroke of death,
> With faith expect His rise to share,
> His victory o'er the gaping tomb,
> And live His endless life to come.[60]

Thus, those who live by faith in Christ have been 'wash'd in His blood', and must also be received 'into His cross's school'.[61] Charles Wesley, therefore, considered the 'scandal of the cross' to be 'the mark of Jesus's witnesses'.[62] And the very same cross which marked out the way of suffering could be viewed as a sign of God's 'electing love', or 'the seal of election'.[63] In this regard, J. E. Rattenbury was certainly correct about Charles Wesley's use of the *imitatio Christi* theme: 'Rarely indeed does Charles inculcate the imitation of Christ the of the Galilean narrative. Generally he means by imitation, conformity with His sufferings.'[64] Often this conformity to the pattern of Christ's sufferings had as its explicit goal the further conformity to Christ's character:

(5) While I thus my Pattern view,
I shall bleed and suffer too,
With the man of sorrows join'd
One become in heart and mind.

(6) More and more like Jesus grow,
Till the Finisher I know,
Gain the final Victor's wreath,
Perfect love in perfect death.[65]

Charles Wesley was convinced that to follow Christ was to share in Christ's sufferings. He was certainly familiar with the application established in the biblical witness (as in 2 Corinthians 1.5, 1 Peter 4.13 etc.), and occasionally his applications seemed to go beyond those parameters. For example, the way of the cross was said to be 'inevitable' for the Christian.[66] Or said simply, 'Thy suffering, Lord, doth mine imply,/And binds me on thy cross to die.'[67] Commenting upon 1 Peter 2.21 ('For even here unto were ye called: because Christ also suffered for us, leaving us an example, that ye should follow in his steps . . .'), Charles Wesley blended the finished and unfinished work of the cross to describe how Christian discipleship leads directly to a life of suffering:

Thou didst not work, that I secure
In sloth might all the day remain,
Thou didst not unknown grief remain,
To supercede my needless pain:
Thy life requires my active zeal,
Thy death, that I SHOULD SUFFER STILL.[68]

John Wesley, in his role of editor of the published hymns, reacted to the portion of this hymn that is capitalized above. John added an asterisk and penned the word 'NO!' into the margin of Charles' manuscript. Charles' emphasis upon an 'active zeal' both in service and in suffering challenged John Wesley's more traditional theology of the cross.

Christ, in Charles Wesley's view, continues to suffer in his 'members' and so they do not suffer alone; in a similar way, persecuting them is the same as persecuting him:

Jesus on the celestial hill
Doth for His people care,
Doth suffer in His members still,
And all our sorrows bear;
If crush'd on earth the foot complain,
Feeling the injury
The Head above cries out in pain,
'Thou persecutest me.'[69]

The way of suffering, in Charles Wesley's formulation, had didactic significance, and we can see again how, for Wesley, the cross became a 'school' and its lessons formed the mind of Christ within the Christian who walked the way of the cross.[70] The following verse, cast in the imagery of John 10.27, epitomizes many others:

> The sheep with the simplicity
> Attend and taste and keep Thy word,
> They lead the life approved by Thee,
> Follow their active suffering Lord,
> Copy thy life of love and pain,
> And labour all thy mind to gain.[71]

An important part of Charles Wesley's theology of the cross is found in 'my cross', which bids the Christian to lose 'self' in Christ.[72] The 'self' that is crucified on the 'cross' is the fallen, sinful self, full of 'pride and lust'.[73] Thus, the singer of Wesley's hymns is often found 'dying on the Cross'.[74] This metaphorical 'dying' on the part of the Christian was a dying to self and a corresponding willingness to live for God and for one's neighbour; this transition was called 'the inward cross'.[75] The way of the cross is, then, simultaneously the way of abjection and the way of self-commitment; it means laying one's self aside in order to live 'entirely Thine'. As Wesley wrote:

> I would the precious time redeem,
> By counting all things loss,
> By offering up my life for Him
> Whose blood distain'd the cross,
> Thus would I live entirely thine,
> Who gav'st thy self for me;
> And then my spotless soul reign,
> A sacrifice to thee.[76]

Because of the commitment and Christian growth that one gains in the way of the cross, this 'school' became a leadership training clinic for mature disciples. The following hymn, written for 'A Preacher of the Gospel', views the way of suffering as a credentialling process for taking leadership in the Church:

> A faithful steward of my Lord,
> Give me to minister thy word,
> And in thy steps to tread,
> By sufferings fully qualified
> Thy ailing flock to lead.[77]

## The cross and the crown

The way of the 'cross' was a Wesleyan epigram for costly discipleship, an emblem for self-denial and suffering. But what of the 'crown'? The biblical application of the term 'crown' is rather variegated; it runs from 'reward' to 'authority'.[78] This breadth of meaning was not lost in Charles Wesley's application of the image. He termed 'the crown' an 'immortal crown', and though the exact phraseology does not appear in the King James Version of his day, on two occasions one reads of a 'crown of life' (James 1.12; Revelation 2.10), which the righteous inherit.[79]

Charles Wesley consistently emphasized the connection between costly Christian discipleship ('the cross') and the Christian's inheritance through faith ('the crown'). He expressed this connection in various ways: 'through Thy cross obtain Thy crown'.[80] Those who remained steadfast in suffering would receive an eternal inheritance: 'And all that to the End endure/The Cross, shall wear the crown.'[81] The way of the cross was not easily followed, in order to receive the crown: 'I find in weariness a cross/That lifts me to a crown.'[82] In many instances sharing in 'the cross' results in sharing in Christ's Kingdom:

Depress'd by the cross, He wonted the higher,
He left all his dross and tin in the fire;
He brought by his mourning the curtain down,
And Jesus returning presented the crown.

All praise to the Lord, all praise is due:
His merciful word is tried, and found true;
Who his dereliction on calvary bear,
And share His affliction, His Kingdom share.[83]

In this particular hymn 'the Kingdom' seems to be presented in terms of its eschatological consummation. Charles often emphasized the presence of the Kingdom of God as living in the power of perfect love. Hence, 'the crown' was also associated with 'perfect love:'

O might Thy powerful word
Inspire a feeble worm
To rush into Thy kingdom, Lord,
And take it as by storm!

O might we all improve
The grace already given,
To seize the crown of perfect love,
And scale the mount of heaven![84]

In other instances, the 'crown' was identified as 'Full Salvation', which was another Wesleyan description for entire sanctification, and, in Charles Wesley's view, this 'crown' was to be received by being 'partners' in the Lord's tribulation:

Partners now in tribulation,
Sharers of a moment's pain,

For the crown of full salvation,
Shall we not the cross sustain?
Light the pain and transitory;
But our Lord we soon shall meet,
Sink beneath a weight of glory,
Sink for ever at His feet![85]

Many of Charles Wesley's hymns, especially those which were written in the 1760s, evidence his reaction against those within the Methodist movement who too easily claimed Christian perfection. This polemical use of 'cross' and 'crown' terminology was evident in his poetical comment on Matthew 20.22 ('Ye know not what he ask'), in which 'blind' and 'ignorant' 'babes' in Christ ambitiously seek the crown of perfect love:

Such was our ignorant desire
Our zeal above the rest to' aspire,
While babes, the father's joy to prove!
Ambitious at Thy side to reign,
The rest without the toil to gain,
We ask'd the crown of perfect love!

Blindly we ask'd for pain and loss,
A deeper cup, an heavier cross;
And still we all Thy grace implore;
But humbly waiting to receive,
Manner and time to Thee we leave,
Thy will be done, we ask no more.[86]

The perfectionist claims of George Bell and Thomas Maxfield, who were among the leaders of the London Methodist Society, had reached extravagant levels. Charles Wesley wrote poetical polemics against the 'pretenders to perfection' in an effort to clarify his understanding of Christian perfection and to silence those (like Bell and Maxfield) who claimed to be 'perfect as angels'. An example of this polemical application of the 'cross' and 'crown' dialectic emerged in Charles' polemical commentary on 1 Samuel 13.13–14. The context of that biblical passage involved Samuel's rejection of Saul's kingship because the impatient king took upon himself the priestly function. Charles Wesley, no doubt, saw the contemporary conflict mirrored in this biblical narrative:

What lost the king his regal power?
The want of patience for an hour,
And who for Christ refuse to stay,
With patience cast their souls away,
The cross they hastily lay down,
And forfeit an immortal crown.

After we have endured a while,
The Lord rewards our patient toil,

Establishes our hearts with grace,
And perfects us in holiness;
But if impatiently we rise*
To offer SINLESS SACRIFICE
To power we shall not long maintain,
Or Kings without our Saviour reign.[87]

In Charles Wesley's poetical imagination the forfeiture of Saul's kingdom
became a parable on the importance of bearing the cross in order to inherit
the crown. He drew a line of connection between suffering under the cross
and the purging out of one's sin – and hence the crown of Christian perfection. For one to reject the cross was to reject the process that leads to perfect
love. This connection is stated rather directly in the verses above; those who
shun the 'cross' (costly discipleship and suffering) and yet 'impatiently rise
to offer sinless sacrifice' lose the Kingdom. The 'sinless sacrifice' seems to be
a veiled reference to those who claimed Christian perfection in this life, 'the
cross they hastily lay down'.

John Wesley inserted the asterisk in the text above, at the location indicated. Attached to his editorial note was the query: 'How?' It is clear, as I
have noted elsewhere, that at this time John Wesley was preaching a qualified conception of Christian perfection that was to be expected 'now', at any
time, and in an instant.[88] Whereas Charles Wesley, especially in his later
years, preached and wrote about an unqualified kind of Christian perfection
that was received gradually throughout one's life, and finally at the threshold
between life and death. Charles merged the elements of crisis and process to
form an understanding of Christian perfection that emphasized pilgrimage,
suffering and steadfastness in faith. Thus, the 'cross' and 'crown' imagery
was deeply drawn into Charles Wesley's soteriology, and in the later years
became part of his polemic against those who made unguarded claims of
perfection in this life.

### Life under the cross: Charles Wesley's theology of suffering

One of the distinctive aspects of Charles Wesley's theology of the cross was
his growing emphasis upon human suffering and the benefit it brings to those
who suffer. An emphasis upon the purgative power of suffering is evidenced
in early hymns, like the *Trial of Faith* (1740), and steadily increases throughout Wesley's literary corpus, reaching its pinnacle in *Short Hymns on Select
Passages of Scripture* (1762) and subsequent unpublished hymns. Thus, J. E.
Rattenbury suggested that Charles 'was really preaching the crucifix rather
than the cross'.[89] Or, said another way, 'Charles overstated suffering as a necessity of the imitation of Christ.'[90] Certainly a portion of the rationale for this
alleged exaggeration is to be located in Wesley's own life experience. His later
years were full of physical pain, suffering and melancholy. As Rattenbury
opined: 'What Charles at this period of his life, in days of heroic personal suffering and challenge, only saw imperfectly was that if one gave his body to be
burned and lacked love, it profited nothing.'[91]

It is also clear that numerous Bible passages could be marshalled in support of a theological connection between discipleship, suffering and inward spiritual improvement. The synoptic motifs of bearing the cross (Matthew 10.38, 16.24) and the cup of suffering (Matthew 26.42) are among these, as are passages like 2 Corinthians 1, Philippians 3.10, Colossians 1.24, and 1 Peter 4.13. Able student of Holy Writ that he was, Wesley was not unaware of these texts.

The metaphor of the 'cup' of suffering was a frequent one in the hymns of Charles Wesley, and it sounds a distinctive note in his theology.[92] This basis of the image is found in the Synoptic account of Jesus' prayer in the Garden of Gethsemane.[93] In that context the 'cup' was identified as an emblem of Jesus' suffering and death. A second passage, Matthew 20.22/Mark 10.38f., is also significant for our examination of this metaphor. In this setting, Jesus responded to a request for special privilege from James and John by asking them a question in return: 'Can ye drink of the cup that I drink . . . ?' When the disciples affirmed that they could, Jesus predicted that they would in fact, share his cup and baptism (Mark 10.39). In this passage one notes an obvious connection between the 'cup' or sufferings of Christ and that of those who follow him. This later aspect formed an important part of Charles Wesley's application of the metaphor. This is seen in one of his favourite pairings in which the 'cup' is joined to the theology of the cross by means of the Pauline phrase 'fill the Lord's afflictions up' (Colossians 1.24).[94] The final, foundational New Testament reference to the 'cup' is found in Matthew 26.27, where the eucharistic cup holds the 'blood of the new covenant which is pour out for many for the forgiveness of sins'.

It is difficult to ascertain exactly what Charles Wesley sought to communicate through his varied application of this 'cup' image. No small part of the connection between his use of it to describe the sufferings of Christ and those of Christians may be found in the handy rhyme of 'cup' and 'up'. Hence, one might share the 'cup' of Jesus' sufferings, and thereby 'fill the Lord's afflictions up'. But the prevalence of this rhyme pairing has theological significance as well. Generally, Charles used it to point to the way in which the Christian participates in suffering because of the way of the cross: 'I fill thy sore afflictions up,/I faint thy burden to sustain . . .'[95] Thus, he wrote that the Christian 'fill'd her Lord's afflictions up/And TASTED death with Him.'[96] What Wesley emphasized in this image was the point that Christian discipleship was patterned after the way of the cross (the suffering, self-denial and dying), but he was unwilling to suggest that the Christian in any way contributed to the efficacy of Christ' saving death.

The theology of suffering has long been a portion of the Christian spiritual tradition. It was not only prominent among mystics, monks and ascetics, it also held a formative position in the thought of the Protestant Reformers. Luther, Calvin and the early Anabaptists all had robust theologies of suffering.[97] The English mystic, William Law, who had been one of the Wesleys' early mentors, considered humility and a willingness to suffer for Christ to be a part of one's spiritual development. In his *Christian Perfection* Law wrote: 'Christians must be full of humility and willing to suffer for their sin; there is a reasonableness about our suffering for our sins, it is a form of our participation in Christ's sufferings.'[98] The argument here is not to suggest that William

Law, the Anabaptists, Martin Luther, John Calvin and Charles Wesley all spoke with one voice on the theology of the cross and human suffering, it is rather to indicate that the way of suffering (*via dolorosa*) has been a prominent theme in Christian spirituality.

Tracing the development of Charles Wesley's theology of suffering takes the inquirer to his early sermons, journal and, most emphatically, to Charles' hymns. His sermon on John 13.7, which was No. VI in the 1816 edition of Charles' *Sermons*, and which had been transcribed from John's manuscript in May 1736, shows some of this same proclivity. He wrote:

> Why God is pleased to bestow on these persons such a measure of virtue and happiness as we can no more tell than why he is pleased to bestow such a measure of suffering as he does on others. In the latter case we may, it is true, commonly trace the immediate reason of the suffering. We may commonly observe that [the] particular affliction under which a man labours either is pointed at the particular vice to which he naturally inclines, or is conducive to that virtue he particularly wants.[99]

The next sermon, from the 1816 collection, which was based on Psalm 126.7, 'He that goeth forth and weepeth, bearing precious seed, shall doubtless come again with rejoicing, bringing sheaves with him', investigates the inward value of human suffering:

> Experience shows us, that even they who are Christians indeed, who serve God with all their strength, may go on their way weeping, perhaps for many years, perhaps to the end of their lives. They are followers of him who was a man of sorrows and acquainted with grief. And if any man will come after him, he must deny himself and take up his cross. He must suffer with his master more or less; being, like him, to be made perfect through suffering.[100]

The spiritual reasons offered for the disciple's affliction are essentially twofold: 'They go on their way weeping, that the good seed they bear forth may yield them more fruit. And that good seed, even all those Christian virtues, which are perfected by affliction shall in due time grow up into a plentiful harvest of rest and joy and life eternal.'[101] Those who follow Christ and walk in his way must expect to endure affliction: 'They may, nay they must, endure affliction, for so did the captain of their salvation.'[102] Wesley opined that affliction teaches the Christian humility, which he described as 'a deep sense of our spiritual poverty, a feeling knowledge that we are knowing but sin and deserve nothing but shame'.[103] The realization of true humility, Charles believed, gives birth to real joy: 'And is such a virtue as this the seed of joy? Yea, as surely as it is the seed of all other virtues. As surely as it is contrary to pride which is the storm and tempest, but it says to that sea "Peace, be still," and there is a great calm.'[104] Wesley recognized that there was pain in the trials of affliction, but it was a pain that heals the soul even as it wounds: 'There is pain, 'tis true, in the entrance into it, but that very pain is full of pleasure. There is mourning joined with it; but even that mourning is blessedness; it is health to the soul, and marrow to the bones. It heals even while it wounds; it delights to the same degree wherein it softens the heart.'[105]

Charles' hymns of the early period continued to draw this line of connection between affliction and the renovation of the human heart. The hymn 'In affliction' (from the 1739 edition of *Hymns and Sacred Poems*), depicts the Christian disciple thankfully receiving 'the cup' of suffering from Jesus Christ. The third stanza reads:

Thankful I take the cup from Thee,
Prepared and mingled by Thy skill;
Though bitter to the taste it be,
Powerful the wounded soul to heal.[106]

The thought that affliction leads to spiritual poverty, through the breaking of the human heart, which was evidenced in the early sermons, was continued in Charles' hymns:

In restoring love again,
O Jesus, visit me,
Give me back that pleasing pain
That blessed misery:
Now thy tendering grace afford,
And make me thine afflicted one:
Turn, and look upon me Lord,
And break my heart of stone.[107]

In Charles' later hymns, especially his *Short Hymns on Select Passages of Scripture* (1762) and subsequent unpublished poems, his emphasis upon the therapeutic value of suffering became even more pronounced. His comment on Deuteronomy 9.7, for example, seemed a bit excessive, since in it Charles asked God to put an end to his sin, but NOT his pain:

A rebel to this present hour!
Yet now for all thy mercy's power
I ask with contrite sighs
To end my sin BUT NOT MY PAIN:
I would lament till death,* and then
Rejoice in paradise.[108]

At the asterisk Charles' editor, John Wesley, penned in an editorial note as he prepared the manuscript for publication. In this case John wrote an emphatic 'God forbid!' as a comment upon Charles' desire to 'lament till death'.[109] An undated letter, appended to Charles' journal, advises: 'My dearest friends – you will learn obedience by the things you suffer.'[110] An unpublished hymn on Acts 5.42 connected human sufferings with Christlikeness and spiritual improvement:

Made out of weakness strong,
By suffering fortified,

We preach Him all day long,
Who once for sinners died;
Tis double joy to make him known
And to suffer for his sake alone.[111]

Perhaps the most provocative connection in Charles Wesley's theology of suffering was the line he drew between human suffering and Christian perfection in love. This connection was evidenced in many places, but it was most evident in his *Short Hymns on Select Passages of Scripture*. The following hymn, based on Proverbs 24.16, explicitly views the way of suffering as a person's path to perfection:

The just man falls to rise again,
And sit enthroned with Christ above,
Saved in a way of grief and pain,
THROUGH SUFFERINGS PERFECTED IN LOVE,
He falls – into a sea of blood,
He falls – into the depths of God![112]

J. E. Rattenbury's general observation is an apt commentary on this verse: 'the characteristic longing of Charles Wesley was for love. Even when he over-stressed suffering, it was for love that he was really seeking'.[113] It must be said, however, that the love which Charles Wesley sought through suffering was the perfect love of Christian perfection, and this connection was established in his thinking and his hymns from the early years of the Revival. It is evidenced, for example, in this verse from *Moral and Sacred Poems* of 1744:

Not long for all here heaven she stayed;
Her soul, THROUGH SUFFERING PERFECT MADE,
With joy forsook the earthly clod,
And sprang into the arms of God.[114]

This same emphasis continued throughout Charles' hymns of the middle years, 1749 to 1762. The following verse is representative of many others:

Gladly I drink Thy mercy's cup,
I fill my Lord's affliction's up,
I now am truly great;
Exalted by Thy kind command,
By sufferings placed at Thy right hand,
I in Thy kingdom sit . . .

As sure as now Thy cross I bear,
I shall Thy heavenly kingdom share,
And take my seat above;
Celestial joy is in this pain,
It tells me, I with Thee shall reign,
In everlasting love.

The more my sufferings here increase,
The greater is my future bliss;
And Thou my griefs dost tell:
They in Thy book are noted down;
A jewel added to my crown
Is every pain I feel.[115]

Charles' *Short Hymns on Select Passages of Scripture* continued this connection between suffering and inner cleansing, and the emphasis became increasingly exaggerated. The Book of Job lends itself well to reflection upon human suffering, and Charles Wesley's poetical comments on passages from Job are replete with reflection upon the 'sanctified use of woe' or similar phraseology which suggested that suffering prepares the Christian for heavenly glories while being renewed inwardly:

O Father of mercies, on me,
On me in affliction bestow,
A power of applying to Thee,
A sanctified use of my woe:
I would, in a spirit of prayer,
To all Thy appointments submit,
The pledge of my happiness bear,
And joyfully die at Thy feet.

Then, Father and never till then,
I all the felicity prove
Of living a moment in pain,
Of dying in Jesus's love.
A sufferer here with my Lord,
With Jesus above I sit down,
Receive an eternal reward,
And glory obtain in a crown.[116]

Perfection by love through suffering was a constant theme throughout Charles Wesley's poetical commentary on the Bible. Often this theme was linked to a second distinctive emphasis – Charles' unqualified conception of Christian perfection as an event that was to be more naturally expected at the moment of death:

Better for me to live, if thou
My tempted soul with strength supply,
And THEN my hoary head to bow,
And perfected in sufferings die.[117]

It was for this very reason that John Wesley wrote to Charles urging him to 'Go on, in your own way, what God has peculiarly called you to. Press the instantaneous blessing; the I shall have more time for my peculiar calling, enforcing the gradual work.' [118] Charles was not preaching the 'instantaneous work' of Christian perfection, at least insofar as we can ascertain from his hymns, hence John could not find time to preach the gradual work; he felt he had to make up for what he considered to be Charles' deficiency in this matter.[119]

Charles developed various poetical images to make the connection between suffering and Christian perfection more concrete; sometimes he described it as 'passing through tribulation'.[120] In other instances the process of 'purging' became a way of describing how the Christian's sufferings were to be viewed as chastisements that purified the inner person and prepared the way for Christian perfection. His poetical comment on John 15.2, 'Every branch in me that beareth no fruit he taketh away; and every branch that beareth fruit he purgeth it, that it may bring forth more fruit', was an example of this development:

Kindly thou dost chastise, reprove,
The objects of thy choicest love,
That this we may thy mind express,
Partakers of thy holiness,
May meekly all thy sufferings share,
And fruit unto perfection bear.[121]

John Wesley's displeasure with his brother's phraseology about the purifying benefits of suffering increased with Charles' increased application of these themes. The following hymn, which was based on Hebrew 12.8, 'Chastisement whereof all are partakers', showed John's persistent editorial reaction to Charles Wesley's theology of suffering:

To none of the believing race
This mark their Father's love denies:
But when he sees the light of grace
The babe in Christ that moment cries,*
And of the heavenly Spirit born
Begins at once to breathe, and morn.

In sorrow, as in grace, we grow,
With closer fellowship in pain,
Our Lord more intimately know,
Till coming to a perfect man
His sharpest agonies we share,*
And all His marks of passion bear.

Partakers of His bitterest cup,
And burden'd with His heaviest load,
We fill His suffering up,
Conform'd to an expiring God;
And only such our Father owns,*
And seat on our appointed thrones.[122]

Each location in which there is an asterisk in the text above, John Wesley penned an emphatic 'No!' into the manuscript. George Osborn, editor of the massive *Poetical Works of John and Charles Wesley*, offered an editorial opinion of his own on this matter: '[John] Wesley's repeated "No," will be echoed by every judicious reader in regard not only to the time and degree, but also to the universal necessity of such suffering as is here and several other places, spoken of.'[123]

Charles Wesley's sentiments about the purifying effects of suffering seemed to be born in his strong emphasis on the necessity of the Christian to live under the cross. Kinship with Christ in his suffering developed steadfastness, and from that theme Wesley moved steadily toward sanctification or Christian perfection. Most often the purifying effects of suffering emerge in passing; they are drawn out by reflection upon a particular passage of scripture or a life event. Suffering was certainly a part of Charles Wesley's life experience, and this experiential dimension may offer an explanation for the increase of this emphasis in his later hymns. When Charles sat down to address the question of human suffering, however, it seemed his theology was more traditional than the excesses we meet in *Short Hymns on Select Passages of Scripture*. This conservativism is even evidenced in his *Hymns for Families* (1767) which stemmed from roughly the same period as the *Short Hymns*. More circumspect reflection upon the theology of suffering appeared in verses like these:

Not that the suffering I endure,
His Father's favour can procure,
Or for my sin atone;
Jesus alone the wine-press trod,
Answered the just demands of God,
And paid my debt alone.

Nor can my utmost griefs or pains,
Purge out the 'original remains,'
Or kill the root of sin:
That blood which did my pardon buy,
That only blood must sanctify,
And wash my nature clean.[124]

But verses like these do not represent a repudiation of Charles Wesley's theology of suffering. They simply represent careful clarification of its proper parameters. Wesley did not think of human suffering as bearing reconciling prevalence with God; human suffering was seen as being incapable of paying the debt of sin, or purging it out of the human soul. The later aspect was occasionally voiced in Charles' hymns on trials and chastisement; as we saw above, he did sometimes link suffering with the purification on the inner person. But one might argue, that it was the attitude with which a Christian embraced suffering that was transformative, rather than the suffering itself. This distinction, which was sometimes lost in Charles' poetical renditions of his theology of suffering, was evidenced in his early sermon on Psalm 126.7. In that instance, the Christian was properly said to learn humility through suffering, and humility was lauded as a virtue that lead to perfect love. This same reply can be found in Charles' *Short Hymns on Select Passages of Scripture*. Sufferings or trials are said to produce patience and steadfastness (as in James 1.2–4, and 1 Peter 1.3–8); patience and steadfastness are virtues that contribute to inward renewal. But it is Christ, and not suffering – in the final analysis – who renews the Christian through the inner work of the Holy Spirit:

> Can suffering purge my inbred sin?
> No more than it can heaven procure:
> But He, Who brought the fire within,
> By patience makes my nature pure,
> But He, Who with suffering comes,
> My dross in His own way consumes.[125]

Charles Wesley's theology of suffering was a natural out-growth of his theology of the cross. It was part and parcel of his willingness to understand Christian discipleship as bearing the cross. In some instances his language is out of balance and unguarded; there are extant Charles Wesley hymns that seem to teach purification through suffering. Yet when Charles sought to give direct exposition to his theology of the cross and suffering, he remained well within the mainstream of Christian spirituality. It is also clear that Charles Wesley took the theology of the cross much more seriously than most modern people do, and perhaps more seriously than many of his own contemporaries.

In its broadest strokes Wesley's theology of the cross is graphic, grasping and demanding – daring the reader or singer to 'receive the atonement' and follow the costly way of Christian discipleship. The way of the cross led to the 'crown' of Christian perfection and the glories of heaven. Yet there are also a few verses in which Charles' own mysticism, his personal pain and his longing for Christian perfection coalesced into a theology that sought to make sense out of suffering by viewing it as a purifying chastisement from God. Daringly stated, the disciple was called to partake of Jesus' 'cup' and to 'fill our Lord's afflictions up'. It seemed as though Wesley's life experience demanded that he see some benefit in the painful maladies of life, and that this hope developed into a tacit reply in some of this later hymns.

# Notes

1 *CWJ*, 1.438.

2 On Charles Wesley's poetical hermeneutic, see John R. Tyson, 'The Transfiguration of Scripture: Charles Wesley's Poetical Hermeneutic', in *The Asbury Journal*, 47, 2 (Fall 1992), 17–42; and S T Kimbrough, 'Charles Wesley as Biblical Interpreter', in Kimbrough (ed.) *Charles Wesley: Poet and theologian*, 106–36.

3 John R. Tyson, ed., *Charles Wesley: A reader*, 284.

4 For a fuller discussion of the difficulties posed by these sermons, see my *Charles Wesley: A reader*, 13–20, and Newport, *Sermons*, 71–90.

5 Richard P. Heitzenrater, 'John Wesley's Earliest Sermons', *Proceedings of the Wesley Historical Society*, 36, 4 (February 1970), 112–13.

6 Charles Wesley, *Sermons by the Late Rev. Charles Wesley* (London: J. Baldwin, Caraddock and Joy, 1816). While these sermons 'were presented to the public by his widow' (xxxiv), they may have been edited and prepared for publication by a mysterious 'W.P.' – whose initials appear upon the manuscript. See Newport, *Sermons*, 78.

7 John Byrom, *The Universal Shorthand* (Manchester: John Hanop, 1767).

8 Thomas Albin and Oliver Beckerlegge, *Charles Wesley's Earliest Sermons: Six manuscript shorthand sermons now for the first time transcribed from the original* (Ilford: Wesley Historical Society, 1987), and subsequently in Newport, *Sermons*.

9 See Newport, *Sermons*, 85–8.

10 Thomas Jackson, ed., *The Works of John Wesley*, 14 vols (London: The Wesleyan Conference Office, 1872), properly ascribes 'Awake Thou, That Sleepest,' to Charles Wesley in 5.25, but fails to identify 'The Cause and Cure of Earthquakes' (VII. 386).

11 Newport, *Sermons*, 116, from Sermon #2, based on 1 Kings 18.21, which was first preached on 30 November 1735.

12 Newport, *Sermons*, 128, from Sermon #3, based on Psalm 126.7, which was preached in 1736 and 1737.

13 Newport, *Sermons*, 50–9, 108.

14 Cf. *CWJ*, 1.90–5, for description of the dramatic events surrounding Pentecost, 1738.

15 See Newport, *Sermons*, 60–7, for a fuller discussion on the theological contents of these sermons.

16 Newport, *Sermons*, Sermon #4, on 1 John 3.14, 140.

17 Newport, *Sermons*, Sermon #5. It was first preached on 21 December 1738, 164.

18 Newport, *Sermons*, Sermon #6, based on Romans 3.23–4, 171.

19 Newport, *Sermons*, 173.

20 Newport, *Sermons*, 179.

21 Newport, *Sermons*, 168.

22 *CWJ*, 1.156.

23 Newport, *Sermons*, Sermon #7, 187.

24 Newport, *Sermons*, 200.

25 Newport, *Sermons*, Sermon #7, 200, emphasis added. See also Sermon #12, 274.

26 *CWJ*, 1.86, 89.

27 *CWJ*, 1.90, 117. 122, 132, 135, 136, 148, 170, 226, 276, 307, 337, 397, 463; 2. 7, 15, 24, 91, 92.

28 Newport, *Sermons*, 200.

29 *CWJ*, 1.132.

30 *CWJ*, 1.133.

31 *CWJ*, 1.142.

32 *CWJ*, 1.307.

33 *CWJ*, 1.306.

34 *CWJ*, 1.145, 166, 171, 179, 183, 256, 257, 291, 421, 460; 2.45, 82, 86, 126, 138 etc.

35 *CWJ*, 1.145, 313, 392, 407; 2:17, 108,135 etc.

36 Cf. John R. Tyson, *Charles Wesley: A reader*, Appendix A: 'Charles Wesley's Favorite Sermon Texts', 487–90.

37 *CWJ*, 1.436.

38 *CWJ*, 1.452.

39 *PW*, 4.371–2; (reprinted from Charles Wesley's *Hymns and Sacred Poems*, 1749 edn).

40 *PW*, 4.371.

41 *PW*, 4.371.

42 *PW*, 4.372.

43 *CWJ*, 2.117.

44 *CWJ*, 1.410.

45 *CWJ*, 1.410.

46 *PW*, 10.422

47 J. Ernest Rattenbury, *The Evangelical Doctrines of Charles Wesley's Hymns*, 188–204.

48 *PW*, 9. #782, 257.

49 *PW*, 5. #139, 37–8.

50 MARC, ref. MS. John, 405–6, an unpublished poem.

51 *PW, 13* 'Sacramental Hymn', #2, 260.

52 *PW*, 9. #1568, 299.

53 *PW*, 9. #1095, 387–8; 7, 341–2, 9, 362–3.

54 PW, 13. #2252, 84. Cf. 7. #147, 177.

55 *CWJ*, II, 7.

56 *PW*, 10.1568, 122. cf. 5. #153, 61; 5, 153.

57 Ms. Luke, 235, based on Luke 16.13. Cf. Osborn, *Poetical Works*, VI, 37.

58 *PW*, 4.344.

59 Ms. Luke, 34, based on Luke 2.34.

60 *PW*, 10. #422, 301–2.

61 *PW*, 11. #1861, 125.

62 *PW*, 9. #715, 228.

63 *PW*, 5.181; 13.29–30.

64 Rattenbury, *Evangelical Doctrines*, 162.

65 *PW*, 13. #3313, 153–4. cf. 5. 147; X, 144; 13.154–5.

66 *PW*, 5. 'The Trial of Faith, #2, 144.

67 *PW*, 13. #3368, 181.

68 Ibid., emphasis added.

69 *PW*, 10. #1537, 112.

70 *PW*, 4.36; cf. 5, 15.

71 *PW*, 11.463.

72 *PW*, 13. #3176, 75.

73 *PW*, 3.318.

74 *PW*, 5.94; 104–5; 198; 7.25; 9.235; 10.305; 11.28, 491; 12.127.

75 *PW*, 5. 'The Inward Cross,' #12, 156.

76 Ibid.

77 *PW*, 5. #182, 'For a Preacher of the Gospel', #6, 96.

78 L. E. Tooms, 'Cross', in George Buttrick, ed., *Interpreters Dictionary of the Bible*, 5 vols (Nashville: Abingdon Press, 1962), vol. I, 745–6.

79 *PW*, 12. #2251, 84.

80 *PW*, 12. #2146, 37. Cf. Ibid., #2286, 102.

81 Ms. Luke, on Luke 6:11, 78. Cf. *PW*, 5.169; 12. 54.

82 *PW*, 5. #50, 209.

83 *PW*, 6. #43, 287.

84  *PW*, 10. #289 On Matthew 11.12, 249. Cf. #281, 250.

85  *PW*, 13. #3121, 47.

86  *PW*, 10.335–6.

87  *PW*, 9.158.

88  John R. Tyson, *Charles Wesley on Sanctification: A theological and biographical study* (Grand Rapids: Zondervan, 1986), 'A Brotherly Debate', 227–301.

89  Rattenbury, *Evangelical Doctrines*, 288–9.

90  Ibid., 290.

91  Ibid., 289.

92  Ms. John, unpublished hymn on John 16.31, 348; Osborn, *Poetical Works*, II, 71; IV, 394, 399; V, 15, 69, 157; VI, 265, 284, 285, 293, 340; VI, 354; VII, 100; IX, 144; XI, 297, 327–8; XIII, 154 and etc.

93  Matthew 26.42ff. = Mark 14.36ff. = Luke 22.42ff.

94  *PW*, 5.157, 6.265, 285, 293, 340, 354; 7.100; 11.327–8 etc.

95  *PW*, 5. #12, 157. cf. 7. #84, 100.

96  *PW*, 6. #28, 265.

97  Cf. Martin Luther, *Bondage of the Will* and *Galatians Commentary*, as well as Walther von Loewinch, *Luther's Theology of the Cross* (Minneapolis: Augsburg Press, 1976); John Calvin, *Institutes of the Christian Religion*, III, 8; and Wilhelm Niesel, *The Theology of Calvin* (Grand Rapids: Baker Book House, 1980), 142ff.; and Ethelbert Stauffer, 'The Anabaptist Theology of Martyrdom', in *The Mennonite Quarterly Review*, XIX, 3, 181–214.

98  William Law, *Christian Perfection*, in *The Pocket William Law*, A. W. Hopkins, ed. (London: Latimer Press, 1950), 48.

99  Newport, *Sermons of CW*, 331.

100  Newport, *Sermons of CW*, 125.

101  Ibid.

102  Ibid., 126.

103  Ibid., 127.

104  Ibid., 127.

105  Ibid.

106  *PW*, 1.128.

107  Ibid., 4. #14, 406. From *Hymns and Sacred Poems* (1749).

108  *PW*, 9. #319, 100.

109  Ibid.

110  *CWJ*, 2.217.

111  Ms. Acts, an unpublished hymn on Acts 5.42, 97.

112  *PW*, 9. #1009, emphasis added, 352–3.

113  Rattenbury, *Evangelical Doctrines*, 290.

114  *PW*, 3, emphasis added, 176.

115  *PW*, 5.70–1. Cf. Ibid., 233, 440; 6.325, 313.

116  *PW*, 9. #733, 234. The poem is based on Job 5.17, 'Happy is the man whom God correcteth.' Cf. Ibid., 233–4, 234, 236, 240, 241, 252, 259–60, 268 etc.

117  *PW*, 10. #1490, 96. Cf. 13.82–3, 164, 165–6.

118  John Telford, ed., *The Letters of John Wesley, A.M.*, 8 vols (London: Epworth Press, 1931), V.16.

119  Tyson, *Charles Wesley on Sanctification*, 284–301.

120  *PW*, 11. #1518, 278.

121  *PW*, 12. #2104, 18.

122  *PW*, 13. #3321, 157.

123  Ibid.
124  *PW*, 7. #34, 100.
125  *PW*, 13. #3262, 121.

# 13. Balsamic Virtue: Healing Imagery in Charles Wesley

## ROBERT WEBSTER

An old friend called to see me, under great apprehension that I was running mad. His fears were not a little increased by my telling him the prayer
of faith had healed me when sick at Oxford.[1]

Shall we forget His power to heal
Or doubt as unbelievers still?[2]

Upon their return from the American colonies in 1736 and 1737, John and
Charles Wesley found themselves disorientated.[3] They had originally set out
on their missionary journey with the intent of saving souls and working out
their own salvation. When they returned again to their British homeland,
they found instead their bodies spent, their spirits depressed and their souls
restless. The missionary venture that led them to America ended in failure
and the difficulties they faced while abroad only frustrated their abilities to
understand God's plan of redemption.

On 21 May 1738 Charles Wesley found himself bedridden with pleurisy
and imagined that a Mrs Musgrave had entered the house and uttered peculiar words which only troubled and confused him: 'In the name of Jesus of
Nazareth, arise, and believe, and thou shalt be healed of all thy infirmities.'
The full account of the incident for that Whitsunday was recorded in his
journal:

The words struck me to the heart. I sighed, and said within myself, 'O
that Christ would but speak thus to me!' I lay musing and trembling: then
thought, 'But what if it should be Him? I will send at least to see.' I rang, and
Mrs. Turner coming, I desired her to send up Mrs. Musgrave. She went down
and returning, said, 'Mrs. Musgrave had not been here.' My heart sunk
within me at the word, and I hoped it might be Christ indeed. However, I
sent her down again to inquire, and felt in the meantime a strange palpitation of heart. I said, yet feared to say, 'I believe, I believe!' She came up again
and said, 'It was I, a weak, and sinful creature, spoke; but the words were
Christ's: he commanded me to say them, and so constrained me that I could
not forbear.'[4]

For other Methodists in the eighteenth century, including John Wesley, healing was a category layered with many different meanings. Like Charles in the preceding quotation, many of the Methodists in the modern era found God's healing grace a support and corroboration of their belief in the supernatural and an indication of the importance of God's new created order that was breaking into a sinful world. Physical and spiritual healing often dovetailed in Methodist narratives of the eighteenth and nineteenth centuries, and provided sources of inspiration and instruction for Methodists in the eighteenth century.

## Methodism and healing: a new paradigm

It is certainly no secret that Charles was one of the most prolific poets in English history. His penning of more than nine thousand known poems, lyrics, and hymns position him as one of the leading poets of the modern world. By literary standards of any age, Wesley's literary production was nothing short of amazing. Frank Baker highlighted Wesley's literary acumen and reminded his readers that during his lifetime Charles wrote 27,000 stanzas and 180,000 lines – triple that of a Wordsworth or Browning. Additionally, during one five-year period (1762–6), Wesley wrote at least 6,248 scriptural hymns – an average of 1,250 hymns per year. Assessing the poet/evangelist for the contemporary student, Baker summarized: 'Taking the average – and it must be stressed that this is an average, not a description of normal practice – Charles Wesley wrote ten lines of verse every day for fifty years, completing an extant poem every other day.'[5]

What has remained untouched in the history of interpreting Charles Wesley's life and thought is the attention that he gave to supernatural healing. Certainly, as in other areas, this may be due in part to the towering significance of his older brother John and the popularity of his *Primitive Physic* in eighteenth-century popular piety.[6] Of the 38 editions in England and 24 in America during the eighteenth century, G. S. Rousseau has recounted that John Wesley's little book of therapies was second only to the Bible in the reading practices of the Enlightenment. 'It was found', wrote Rousseau, 'in almost every English household, especially in those of the poor, beside the Bible.'[7] Others have documented that John Wesley viewed healing as an integral part of the Methodist programme for wholeness that permeated both natural and supernatural dimensions.[8] On one particular occasion both John and Charles reprimanded James Wheatly and forbade him from preaching and 'practicing physic'.[9] As indicated, much information continues to surface about John and his healing ministry in the eighteenth century.[10] What has been virtually untouched, however, is Charles' concept of healing and the contribution that he made to the Methodist societies. This oversight in Methodist studies is somewhat surprising when one considers that on Whitsunday, in 1738, Charles encountered his 'palpitation of heart' experience on his sickbed. J. Ernest Rattenbury eloquently highlighted that this experience, for Wesley, was pivotal for a proper interpretation of the hymnist's life and thought. 'The experience of 21 May 1738', wrote Rattenbury, 'was decisive in his life; it meant faith, assurance, pardon, the Witness of the Spirit, adoption, and meant them all at once and perhaps indistinguishable.'[11] What is more, John Wesley's published journal revealed that on the same day he received the Holy Eucharist and recorded for the entry for 21 May 1738:

> The next day, being Whitsunday, after hearing Dr. Heylyn preach a truly Christian sermon (on 'They were all filled with the Holy Ghost' – and so, said he, may *all you* be, if it is not your own fault), and assisting him at the Holy Communion (his curate being taken ill in the church), I received the surprising news that my brother had found rest to his soul. His bodily strength returned also from that hour.[12]

Additionally, the belief in various forms of healing shows up in Charles' poetry where he used healing verbs over five hundred times, and to this could be added the fairly frequent mention of the theme in his journal, sermons and letters.[13]

Based on this evidence, then, the argument of this chapter is that Charles' understanding of healing is long overdue and that he indeed made an important contribution through his poetry and hymns to a particular understanding of God's healing ministry in the world. Furthermore, I will maintain that Charles' hymns are a unique deposit of theological formulation. Thomas Langford made a similar point several years ago when he wrote in his essay 'Charles Wesley as Theologian':

> To understand Charles Wesley's theology it is necessary to understand that it is theology-as-hymn, that is, it is theology expressed by, limited by, enlivened by its hymn form. Charles Wesley's theology is a 'theology one can sing'. In this sense it is a theology with which one can praise; it is a theology with which one can pray, a theology with which one can teach; it is a theology which one can use to initiate, to guide, and to envision the final hope of Christian existence.[14]

The healing message of Wesley's poetry and hymns, then, is not a marginal issue but an integral part of the design and destiny of Christian existence.

## Sin: the disease of the soul

Sickness and disease were serious problems in eighteenth-century England. Roy Porter noted that in 1750 the average citizen of England lived around thirty-six years. Porter stated: '. . . hardly any eighteenth-century scientific advance helped heal the sick directly. Therapeutics made Herculean efforts, but the net contribution of physicians to the relief and cure of the sick remained marginal.'[15] Because medical science was in a fledgling state many people initially treated themselves directly before consulting a physician for a cure of their ills. For persons living in the eighteenth century, it must be remembered, the oppression of suffering was an acute and problematical condition which sometimes called for desperate solutions; thus, the popular remedies

of air-bathing and blood-letting were not always seen as unrefined and super-
stitious. In his 1971 Yale dissertation, James McGee compared Anglican and
Puritan approaches to suffering and expressed the perspective of many in
the modern world: 'Pains', wrote McGee, 'now considered minor were made
excruciating when no painkillers were to be had.'[16]

During the seventeenth century both Anglicans and Puritans had taken the
reality of suffering as a point for theological debate. The Puritan Protestants,
on the one hand, made much of the 'physician of the soul' in their emphasis
for the need of God's grace to medicate the spirit of humanity. Anglicans, on
the other hand, tended to opt for a less pessimistic view of the human will in
their understanding of good works and salvation.[17] It is not surprising, then,
that when the Methodists emerged in the eighteenth century, they described
the world as a 'great infirmary'.[18] For the early Methodists, the reality of pain
and suffering was not merely a visible manifestation of the fragility of the
human body, but also a vivid reminder that the soul was sick and in need of a
cure. As Frank Baker noted, during Charles Wesley's lifetime the hymnist suffered from pleurisy, neuralgia, lumbago, dysentery, piles, rheumatism, gout
and scurvy.[19] On 1 July 1739, barely a year after his own 'palpitation of heart'
experience, Charles preached on justification at Oxford. Using Romans 3.23–5
for his text of exposition, Wesley proclaimed his view of human nature: 'The
whole head is sick, and the whole heart faint. From the sole of the foot even
unto the head there is no soundness in him, but wounds and bruises and
putrefying sores.'[20] In 1762, Charles Wesley published his *Short Hymns on Select
Passages of the Holy Scriptures*. In a hymn based on Isaiah 1.5–6 he wrote:

> Corrupt alas, in every part,
> Sick the head, and faint the heart
> Through sin's severe disease!
> From head to foot the fallen man
> Is full of leprosy and pain,
> And desperate wickedness.
>
> Selfish, and proud, in mind and will
> Nature's loathsomeness we feel
> Throughout our dying soul,
> Bruises, and wounds, and putrid sores,
> Till *Gilead's* bleeding balm restores,
> And Jesus speaks us whole.[21]

For Charles Wesley, Adam's fall has caused a spiritual infection that disrupted
the health and well-being of every man, woman and child. As a consequence,
in his mind, any attempt to sidestep the sinful nature of fallen humanity distorted the fundamental anthropological condition and thus prevented the
possibility of true healing. Even parental praise, for Charles, was conceived
as a poison that puts the soul in danger:

> Why should our parents call us good,
> And poison us with praise,

When born in sin, by nature proud,
And void we are of grace?


Who fancy righteousness in man,
Themselves they have not known;
Evil are all our thoughts and vain,
And God is good alone.[22]


Charles Wesley, then, left little doubt about the hope for self-improvement by the human subject apart from divine grace. The soul was infected with a disease that has caused a collapse in the fabric of the spiritual self. On 23–24 October 1740, he wrote to his older brother and partner in the evangelical revival: '. . . before I am in Christ a new creature I shall feel myself in Adam a fallen spirit'.[23] It was at this point of sin and its infection in the human soul where Charles' idea of sin became transparent. Donald Davie has suggested that Wesley used what he termed 'carnal language', which it must be noted at times offended his brother John, in order to push Christian tradition to its unavoidable conclusion. Davie wrote: '. . . the insistent physicality of his images and allusions . . . merely follows out the implications of what is an article of belief'.[24]

One of the predominant images that Wesley used in his poetry and hymns for the development of human sinfulness was blindness. The sinful heart was blind and could not see or apprehend the idea of sinful existence or the love of God which might be actualized in redemption. In 1742, during the height of Methodist persecutions, Wesley wrote a hymn based on Revelation 3.17:


How dark and dreary is my heart!
Dark as the chambers of the grave;
So blind, till Thou Thy light impart,
I cannot see Thy power to save;
Or know, till Thou the veil remove,
That I am sin, and God is love.[25]


The category of blindness was also a category that Charles Wesley used to describe the political and social disruptions which Methodism confronted throughout the eighteenth century. John Wesley had faced riotous mobs in London, Bristol and especially Wednesbury. On one visit to Cork, Ireland, John Wesley was confronted by Nicholas Butler who had organized a mob to attack the Methodists, slandering them with appellations like 'heretic bitches' and then assaulted them physically.[26] On another occasion, in May 1743, Charles Wesley came to meet with the Sheffield society where he was pelted with stones and then, under the instigation of the parish priest, the Methodist society house was torn down. Charles' courage and fortitude was revealed in his journal entry for 25 May of that year:


At six I went to the Society-house, next door to our brother Bennet's. Hell from beneath was moved to oppose us . . . The stones flew thick, hitting the desk and people. To save them and the house, I gave notice I should preach out, and look the enemy in the face. The whole army of the aliens followed me . . . After sermon I prayed for sinners, as servants of their master, the devil; upon which the Captain ran at me with great fury, threatening revenge for my abusing, as he called it, 'the King his master'. He forced his way through the brethren, drew his sword and presented it to my breast. My breast was immediately steeled. I threw it open, and fixing mine eye on his, smiled in his face, and calmly said, 'I fear God, and honour the King'. His countenance fell in a moment, he fetched a deep sigh, put up his sword, and quietly left the place.[27]

Certainly Wesley had the social dimensions of human depravity in mind when he wrote during the persecutions of the 1740s:

And make *us* think, there is no light,
Because *you* cannot see.[28]

The sinful condition was not merely a disease that effected one's individual state of being, but also one that deeply affected the societal structure which encompassed the life-forms of others as well. At the foundation of sin, for the reformer, was both God and neighbour. And at the core of this violence was the promotion of self-love. In a hymn based on Luke 6.31 – where Jesus commands his disciples to pray and bless those who persecute them – Wesley penned the following words which captivated the essence of the person controlled by sin:

SELF-LOVE which strikes us blind,
And makes us others wrong, . . .[29]

Left unchecked, self-love led to a deceptive blindness that is unable to distinguish good from evil in Charles' mind.[30] Stated simply but not simplistically: healing was impossible until the sinner realized and confessed the sinful condition of his or her human nature. Charles Wesley repeatedly reminded those with whom he came into contact that all attempts at self-healing are, in the end, a futility that generated despair and misery. In a poem written for Lady Huntingdon, for example, Wesley described sin as 'perfect misery'.[31] In *Hymns on Everlasting Love*, which was written in response to the Calvinist-Arminian controversy, Wesley displayed the sinfulness of humanity in autobiographical terms:

I know my soul is foul as hell;
The hottest hell my deeds require,
There only am I fit to dwell
With fiends in everlasting fire:
But why, Redeemer, didst Thou die?
O let Thy bowels answer why![32]

The despair of sin, though, was not a determined despair. It was not the case for Charles, nor for his brother John, that God determined some to eternal bliss while others to eternal damnation.[33] Instead, insisted the Wesleys, God's love extends itself to all who recognize their sinful condition and receive the healing of the great physician. So Charles Wesley could write:

Did He not all their sickness heal,
And satisfy their every need?
Did he reject His helpless clay,
Or send them sorrowful away?[34]

The doctrine of predestination was not a teaching that Charles Wesley could embrace because he was convinced that individuals wilfully participated and rejected the grace of God. Furthermore, double predestination was a heresy that cut at the root of the character of God and the healing grace which was offered through the cross of Christ.[35] It is to the 'balmy grace' of the cross that sin pointed for redemption and healing.

## The balmy blood and the cure of the soul

As was noted in the previous section, for the Methodists of the eighteenth century 'sin' was an infectious disease that made the head sick and the heart faint. Left alone, the infection spread into 'putrid sores' until the body was consumed by death. For Charles Wesley, the body was a visible reminder of the decay that was brought into the world by sin through Adam's disobedience in the Garden. The soul of natural man, then, was set against God. Because the Arminian Methodists rejected a determinist understanding of human nature they held strongly to a sense of hope for both soul and body. In a hymn based on Isaiah 40.31 entitled 'They that wait on the Lord shall renew their strength', Charles Wesley wrote:

The spirit of an healthful mind:
For this I wait in pain,
This precious pearl I long to find,
And to be born again.
Spare me till I my strength of soul,
Till I Thy love, retrieve;
Till faith shall make my spirit whole,
And perfect soundness give.[36]

The hope for healing in Charles Wesley, as for most eighteenth-century Methodists, was both physical and spiritual. Throughout his journal Wesley recorded both physical and spiritual healings, and at times the distinction between the two became blurred. Recorded for 21 September 1739, for example, was the following account: '. . . Richard Bourn, while I was speaking last Friday of the brazen serpent, looked up to the Antitype, and was healed. The devil raged exceedingly, and tore him with temptations; till Jesus about midnight got himself the victory, and filled his soul with love. All he desires now is to be with Christ.'[37] At other times the distinction was delineated clearly and

Charles commented on the sickness of his own body and the desire for God's healing grace. Just one month after he had recovered from an illness that had confined him to a sickbed, Wesley recorded another situation in his journal for 11 July 1738: 'The pain in my side was very violent; but I looked up to Christ and owned his healing power . . . No sooner did I enter the coach than the pain left me, and I preached faith in Christ to a vast congregation, with great boldness, adding much extempore.'[38] The Methodists, as these citations give evidence, found the link between body and spirit beneficial when they approached the topic of God's healing grace. The noted Methodist historian Henry Rack has commented, in his much-cited article 'Doctors, Demons and Early Methodist Healing', that the connection between body and spirit was a logical connection for many Methodists in the Enlightenment. Rack writes:

> In contrast with the ordinary religious outlook of the time, Methodists were convinced experimentally of the necessity for a 'new birth' as the mark of 'real' Christianity. If God could thus heal the soul by divine grace rather than by mere human effort, why not also the body? Primitive Christianity had after all appeared to experience spiritual healing along with the rest of the supernatural happenings which the Methodists believe they were experiencing in their own day.[39]

Rack's supposition, which has been corroborated by other historians, was that healing grace was a permeating presence in the life and faith of the people of God throughout history.[40] There was no dispensational chasm between God's healing power in the primitive Church and the miraculous demonstration of God's power in his own day. Even as Jesus was present to save and heal in ancient times, so he was present to save and heal in a contemporary setting too. So Charles could write:

> Jesus, the fame Of Thy great name
> My sin-sick soul allures:
> Still in every age the same,
> I hear, its virtue cures.

> In complicate Distress I wait
> My plague no more concealing:
> Pity my forlorn estate,
> And show Thy power of healing.

> Now then exert Thy gracious art
> To finish my distresses,
> Drive the legion from my heart
> Of devils and diseases.[41]

The primary image which Charles used to convey God's healing grace in his poetry was the phrase 'balmy grace'. Commenting on this metaphor, John Tyson notes: 'Terms such as virtue and balm in Wesley's hymns described the medicinal effects of God's love.'[42] Charles Wesley found in this biblical metaphor a powerful image that conveyed aspects of divine character that would be sufficient for both the physical and spiritual needs of his readers. On 12 February 1745 he recorded in his journal an incident at chapel: 'In asking, at the chapel, "Is there no balm in Gilead?" I found, with many others, that there was; and a good Physician too, whose power was ever present to heal.'[43] The 'balmy grace', for him, was imbued with a power that had the ability to overcome any disease of the body or disruption of the soul. For the infirm, this meant that God's power was not overcome by human sin and disease but, on the contrary, was capable of encountering every situation with health and wholeness, so that Wesley could confidently assert:

> Thy hand medicinal extend,
> To make my sins and sufferings end
> Apply Thy sovereign grace:
> Dry up in me corruption's flood
> And all my lust of creature good,
> And all my thirst of praise.
> Faith to be heal'd even now I feel,
> I trust that balm infallible
> Which Thy own Spirit applies:
> Thy love omnipotent display,
> And send me throughly heal'd away
> From earth to paradise.[44]

Theologically speaking, the reason that humanity had progressed toward health and wholeness in a fallen and sinful world was because the presence of Christ was incarnated in the medicines and techniques of humanity.[45] In 'For One That Is Sick, Before Using The Means of Recovery', Wesley reminded his readers:

> Health in Thine only name we find,
> Thy name doth in the medicine heal.[46]

The primary locus of God's healing presence for the Methodists was the cross of Calvary. The cross was not merely a sentimental symbolism of communion between sinful humanity and a holy God; it was a demonstration of the hope that despairing souls cling to while in the midst of sin. Ernest Rattenbury correctly pointed out 60 years ago that Charles Wesley's theory of the atonement was not always clear. However, it was the case that, for the hymnist of the Evangelical Revival, the sin of humanity was the primary focus and reason for the cross of Christ.[47] In some gruesome detail Wesley recalled the nature of the cross in the *Hymns on the Lord's Supper*:

> See His body mangled, rent,
> Cover'd with a gore of blood!
> Sinful soul, what hast thou done?
> Murder'd God's eternal Son!
> Yes, our sins have done the deed,
> Drove the nails that fix Him here,

Crown'd with thorns His sacred head,
Pierced Him with a soldier's spear,
Made His soul a sacrifice;
For a sinful world He dies.[48]

At one level, what has happened at the cross of Calvary – at least from Charles Wesley's perspective – was that Christ stands in judgement for sinful human-ity. At one point, he wrote in verse: 'All the guilt's on Thee transferr'd'.[49] At another juncture, however, the cross represented the idea that humanity stood guiltless before the presence of a holy and righteous God. In the cross of Christ, then, Charles found redemption and healing for the wounds which sin had inflicted. In a hymn based on John 3.14, he wrote:

He hath been lifted up for me,
For me, when wallowing in my blood:
I saw Him hanging on the tree,
And virtue from His body flow'd,
The poison of my sins expell'd
And all my wounds that moment heal'd.[50]

God's concern for the salvation of body and soul was clearly portrayed in the cross. It was no accident that the Methodists were concerned about both the condition of the human soul but also maintained a sensitivity for the social well-being of society. The establishment of schools at Kingswood, prison ministries at Newgate, and caring for the poor throughout England was tightly linked to their understanding of God which incorporated healing grace for body, mind and soul.

For Charles Wesley the healing dimensions of the doctrine of justification was realized by faith and acceptance of God's mighty acts in Jesus Christ. In his *Hymns on the Lord's Supper* (1745), Charles prefaced the hymns with an edi-tion of Daniel Brevint's *The Christian Sacrament and Sacrifice*. Published origin-ally at Oxford in 1673, Brevint's work became a pivotal theological treatment that both John and Charles Wesley deemed appropriate for the Methodists to read and digest in their development of sacramental theology.[51] At the begin-ning of his theological essay, Brevint stated concerning the woman with the issue of blood: 'If I but *touch*, as I ought, *the hem of Thy garment*, the garment of Thy passion, virtue will proceed out of Thee; it shall be done according to my faith, and my poor soul shall be made whole.'[52]

Faith is the central point of connection that the infirm have with the healing physician in Charles' thought. Throughout his own life, he had many oppor-tunities for demonstrating the power of faith, and he was not reluctant to share those events in his journal and sermons. In the early modern period many considered the monarchy to be the central healing agent in England. Jane Shaw, in her work *The Miraculous Body and Other Rational Wonders: Religion in Enlightenment England*, notes that '. . . the monarch was the one figure who was legitimately allowed to perform healing miracles within the structures of the Anglican church'.[53] For Charles Wesley, however, every believer must reach out to Christ in faith and incorporate a healing presence and eradicate the power of sin. In a hymn based on Luke 17.5, Wesley composed:

Thus throughout our course below
For more and more we pray,
Fresh degrees of faith bestow,
Nor let the grace decay;
Strengthen us to persevere,
And walk unblamed with Thee in white,
Till our faith is perfect here,
And swallow'd up in sight.[54]

This hymn also demonstrated that prayer was important in making an application of the 'balmy grace' of blood for the healing of 'putrid sores'. In the
same hymn he wrote: 'Faith alone gives birth to prayer/And prayer doth faith
increase.' Charles Wesley and the Methodists during the eighteenth century
were active in their prayer lives. Charles Wesley saw in prayer a dynamic
struggle where the healing mercies of God were fleshed out in the warp and
woof of life. The retreat from prayer was an abandonment of the chief activity
that might be done only by faith. In his journal entry for 5 August 1754, he
recorded an instance where prayer had ushered in the healing powers of God
to the body of a sick person.

> My companion was taken ill of a fever. We prayed for him in strong faith,
> nothing doubting. Monday and Tuesday he grew worse and worse. On
> Wednesday the small-pox appeared: a favourable sort. Yet on Thursday
> evening we were much alarmed by the great pain and danger he was in.
> We had recourse to our never-failing remedy, and received a most remark-
> able, immediate answer to our prayer. The great means of his recovery was
> the prayer of faith.[55]

For the early Methodists, prayer became a channel by which human faith
and the healing presence of Christ were revealed for sinful humanity. Charles
Wesley had great confidence in the power of prayer to unlock the mystery and
power of divine grace. In verse he wrote:

O God, Thy truth, and power declare,
We wait the answer of our prayer,
We know it must be given:
The prayer of faith can never fail,
It enters now within the veil,
And shuts, and opens heaven.[56]

For Wesley, prayer's power was not dependent on some magical incantation
but was present wherever the pray-er casts his or her self upon the mercies of
God in faith. In a hymn based on Matthew 21.22, Wesley offered his theology
of prayer:

FAITH is the source of prayer,
And measures our success,
And prayer is faith's interpreter,
And doth its source increase:

By faithful prayer we gain
Whatever God can give,
And more than earth and heaven contain
In Jesus we receive.[57]


## The healing nature of suffering

Charles Wesley, though a firm believer in prayer and faith, was not isolated
from suffering in his life. The physical illnesses that plagued him also brought
times of depression and emotional turmoil. Along with his wife Sally, he lost
five of his children. It is not surprising, then, that Charles Wesley took great
comfort in the Eucharist that celebrated the suffering and death of Jesus. Most
Wesleyan scholars are in agreement that some of Wesley's most creative work
is found in the Eucharist hymns.[58]

It is no radical insight that the Methodists found great comfort and personal strength in the activity of the Lord's Supper. The journals of both
John and Charles Wesley, along with the autobiographical accounts of other
Methodists, are filled with testimonies to this end. It is in the suffering of
Christ which presented itself in the Eucharist that the believer might find a
strength that lay outside the natural world and gave a reference point for suffering acts throughout human history. For the Methodists suffering during
the persecutions of the 1740s, for example, Wesley could write in his *Hymns
for Times of Trouble and Persecution*:

We drink the consecrated cup
Our Saviour drank before,
And fill our Lord's afflictions up,
And triumph in His power.[59]

Remembrance of Eucharist realities not only brought solace for troubling
times, but also a conquering of sin and suffering:

Soon as I taste the liquid life,
Sorrow expires, and pain, and strife,
And suffering is no more;
My inmost soul refresh'd I feel,
And fill'd with joy unspeakable
The bleeding Lamb adore.[60]

'Suffering is no more', was not a flippant dismissal of the existence of suffering but a commingling of personal sufferings with the healing grace of God in
the suffering of Christ. Charles Wesley was an excellent student of scripture
and wove passages in and out of his hymns and poetry. Additionally, he was
all too aware that the sufferings of Christ in the Gospels were a prelude to the
glory of God that was demonstrated throughout the world. In his *Hymns on
Select Psalms*, Wesley confessed:

Good it is for me to' have known
The sad lesson of distress,
That I might my Teacher own,
That I might my Saviour bless.
Taught by Thine afflictive hand,
Now I know Thy law to' obey;
Now I clearly understand
Suffering is the perfect way.[61]

In Wesley's view, suffering could be embraced under the direction of divine will. Certainly, as has been shown above, Charles Wesley was not timid about asking for manifestations of miraculous gifts of healing in the midst of desperate situations. However, not all prayers were answered easily or simplistically. Perfection was a resignation to God's will for the believer. Teresa Berger writes: 'Christian perfection is not about human struggle for sanctification. Rather, Christian perfection is God-centred. It is focused on God's action with believers, on the creative prerogative of God, which the faithful passively receive.'[62] Surely Charles Wesley must have looked on with a smile when he received a letter from his older brother John on 20 October 1753: 'We have had several instances', wrote John to Charles, 'of music heard before or at the death of those that die in the Lord. May we conceive that this is literally the music of angels? Can that be heard by ears of flesh and blood?'[63] Maybe Charles could have responded to John's inquiry with a hymn he wrote on John 6.56:

God as He will His grace bestows
Through the external sign:
We touch His sacramental clothes,
And feel the power Divine:
Annex'd to water or to bread
His Spirit we receive,
And help'd by Christ, and heal'd, and fed,
The life of angels live.[64]

## Notes

1 *CWJ*, 1.93.

2 *PW*, 10.340.

3 Jackson, *Life*, 1.99: 'When the Wesleys returned from America their spiritual state was peculiar, and far from being satisfactory to themselves.'

4 *CWJ*, 1.90–1. Charles Wesley related in his journal account how Mrs Turner had a dream where Jesus was knocking at the door of the house the night that Charles Wesley had been stricken with illness. At Friday evening prayers the word of God came to her again, commanding her to go speak the healing message to Charles Wesley. Initially she ignored these promptings but after her brother reminded her of the repercussions of Jonah she visited Charles Wesley on Whitsunday and spoke the words that brought '. . . a strange palpitation of heart'. For commentary on this experience, see Jackson, *Life*, 1.99–127.

5 Frank Baker, *Charles Wesley's Verse: An introduction* (London, 1988), 9. Baker also points out that Charles Wesley used no fewer than 45 iambic metres in his poetry, 15 of which contained over 1,000 lines of poetry. Idem, 'Charles Wesley's Productivity as a Religious Poet', *Proceedings of the Wesley Historical Society*, 47 (1989), 1–12.

6 Baker, *Charles Wesley as Revealed by his Letters*, 1: 'The main reason for the comparative neglect of Charles Wesley is, of course, John Wesley.'

7 G. S. Rousseau, 'John Wesley's Primitive Physic (1747)', *Harvard Library Bulletin*, 169 (1979), 23.

8 E. Brooks Holifield, *Health and Medicine in the Methodist Tradition* (New York, 1986), 28: 'Healing, in Wesley's view, could be either natural or supernatural, and it could occur through both medication and prayer.' For an examination of John Wesley's view of the natural dimensions of healing, see Deborah Madden, *Pristine Purity: Primitivism and Practical Piety in John Wesley's Art of Physic* (DPhil thesis, University of Oxford, 2003). For an evaluation of the supernatural dimensions of healing in John Wesley's thought, see my *Methodism and the Miraculous: John Wesley's contribution to the Historia Miraculorum* (D.Phil. thesis, University of Oxford, 2006).

9 John Wesley, *The Letters of John Wesley*, John Telford (ed.) (London, 1931), iii, 69: 'The least and lowest proof of such repentance which we can receive is this: that, till our next Conference (which we hope will be in October), you will abstain both from preaching and from practicing physic. If you do not, we are clear; we cannot answer for the consequences.'

10 See Webster, *Methodism and the Miraculous*, 203–44.

11 J. Ernest Rattenbury, *The Evangelical Doctrines of Charles Wesley's Hymns* (London, 1948), 248.

12 *BE*, 18.241.

13 According to my reading of the Osborn and Kimbrough editions of the Wesleyan poetical corpus, 'heal' and its derivatives appear 549 times. In light of this evidence, it is interesting, to say the least, that the absence of material on this facet of Charles Wesley's life has been untouched. Even John Tyson's massive *Charles Wesley's Theology of the Cross: An Examination of the Theology and Method of Charles Wesley as Seen in his Doctrine of the Atonement* (PhD dissertation, Drew University, 1983), gives little space to Wesley's view of healing. While there are some indirect references, the closest direct treatment comes in Tyson's 12-page treatment of 'Christ the Physician'.

14 Thomas Langford, 'Charles Wesley as Theologian', in S T Kimbrough Jr (ed.), *Charles Wesley: Poet and theologian* (Nashville, 1992), 97.

15 Roy Porter, *The Greatest Benefit to Mankind: A medical history of humanity* (New York, 1997), 266.

16 James McGee, *The Rhetoric of Suffering in England, 1630–1670: An inquiry into fundamental Anglican–Puritan differences* (PhD dissertation, Yale University, 1971), 2–3.

17 James McGee, ibid., 72–90 offers a treatment of this facet of the Anglican–Puritan debate.

18 The phrase is John Wesley's in the first sermon that he preached before embarking on his journey to Georgia. It is found in the collection originally attributed to Charles Wesley and simply titled *Sermons* (London, 1816), 228. Richard Heitzenrater has shown that these sermons were John Wesley's. Cf. Richard Heitzenrater, *Mirror and Memory: Reflections on early Methodism* (Nashville, 1989), 150–61.

19 Baker, *Charles Wesley as Revealed by his Letters*, 104.

20 Newport, *Sermons*, 188. See Teresa Berger, *Theology in Hymns? A study of the relationship of doxology and theology according to A Collection of Hymns for the Use of the People Called Methodists (1780)*, trans. Timothy E. Kimbrough (Nashville, 1995), 148: 'Charles Wesley rarely thinks in terms of individual sins but rather concentrates, almost exclusively, on the sinful condition of humankind, its predisposition and will to sin.'

21 *PW*, 9.369–370.

22 *PW*, 6.425–426.

23 *BE*, 26.xxvi, 42.

24 Donald Davie, *The Eighteenth-Century Hymn in England* (Cambridge, 1993), 67.

25 *PW*, 2.90.

26 Richard P. Heitzenrater, *Wesley and the People Called Methodists* (Nashville, 1995), 171–6. For an evaluation of the term 'heretic bitches' and the anti-Methodist rhetoric in the eighteenth century, see my '*Methodist Bitches': The Anti-Methodist Representations of Bishop George Lavington, William Hogarth, and Richard Graves* (unpublished MA thesis, University of the South, 2001).

27 *CWJ*, 1.309. Cf. Richard P. Heitzenrater, *Wesley and the People Called Methodists*, 128–34. For an examination of the social dynamics of anti-Methodist movements in the eighteenth century, Michael Francis Snape's 'Anti-Methodism in Eighteenth-Century England: The Pendle Forest Riots of 1748', *Journal of Ecclesiastical History*, 49 (1998), 257–81.

28 *PW*, 5.367.

29 *PW*, 11.154.

30 Richard P. Heitzenrater, *Mirror and Memory*, 134: 'The disease of sin results in the person's being effectively dead unto God. And being thus dead in sin, natural man has not "senses exercised to discern spiritual and evil" (Hebrews 5.14) – having eyes, yet he sees not; he hath ears, and hears not (Mark 8.18); he has no spiritual senses, no inlets of spiritual knowledge.'

31 Charles Wesley, *The Unpublished Poetry of Charles Wesley: Hymns and poems for Church and world*, S T Kimbrough Jr and Oliver A. Beckerlegge (eds) (Nashville, 1992), iii, 407.

32 *PW*, 3.28.

33 Rattenbury, *Evangelical Doctrines*, 117–21. Cf. Dale Johnson, 'Is This the Lord's Song? Pedagogy and Polemic in Modern English Hymns', *Historical Magazine of the Protestant Episcopal Church*, 48 (1979), 195–218.

34 *PW*, 2.281.

35 Charles Wesley's satire emerges often in his confrontation with the Calvinists. For Charles Wesley's use of satire, see James Dale, *The Theological and Literary Qualities of the Poetry of Charles Wesley in Relation the Standards of His Age* (PhD thesis, Cambridge University, 1961), 155–74.

36 *PW*, 2.281.

37 *CWJ*, 1.177.

38 *CWJ*, 1.120.

39 Henry Rack, 'Doctors, Demons, and Early Methodist Healing', in W. J. Shields (ed.), *The Church and Healing*, Studies in Church History (Oxford, 1982), xix, 150–1.

40 See, for example, Morton T. Kelsey's *Healing and Christianity in Ancient Thought and Modern Times* (New York, 1973) and more recently Amanda Porterfields's *Healing in the History of Christianity* (Oxford, 2005).

41 *PW*, 7.186–7.

42 Tyson, *Charles Wesley on Sanctification*, 225.

43 *CWJ*, 1.393–4.

44 *PW*, 11.224. Cf. 'A Prayer Against the Power of Sin', Ibid., i, 270, where Charles Wesley wrote: 'Balm of my grief and care/A medicine for every wound/All, all I want is there'.

45 Charles Wesley, 'The Physician's Hymn', *PW*, 5.391–3, especially 392: 'Medicinal derives its power/From Jesu's balmy name'.

46 *PW*, 5.65

47 Rattenbury, *Evangelical Doctrines*, 188–214.

48 *PW*, 3. 232–3.

49 *PW*, 2.275.

50 *PW*, 11.345.

51 See Henry Robert McAdoo, 'A Theology of the Eucharist: Brevint and the Wesleys', *Theology*, 97 (1994), 245–55.

52 Daniel Brevint, *The Christian Sacrament and Sacrifice*, in Charles Wesley, *PW*, 7.190.

53 Jane Alison Shaw, *The Miraculous Body and Other Rational Wonders: Religion in Enlightenment England* (PhD dissertation, University of California at Berkley, 1994), 74.

54 *PW*, 11.249.

55 *CWJ*, 1.432.

56 *PW*, 5.76.

57 *PW*, 10.343.

58 Rattenbury, *Evangelical Doctrines*, 227: 'Perhaps nowhere is it more easy to discern the difference evangelical faith made to inherited belief than in the Communion hymns.'

59 *PW*, 4.39.

60 *PW*, 3.169.

61 *PW*, 8.219.

62 Teresa Berger, *Theology in Hymns?*, 146.

63 John Wesley, *Letters*, iii, 111.

64 *PW*, 10.502.

# 14. 'The suffering members sympathise': Constructing the Sympathetic Self in the Hymns of Charles Wesley

## JOANNA CRUICKSHANK

In a letter to Sarah Gwynne, written in 1747, Charles Wesley declared: 'Those strong expressions of sin & misery which you repeated came from my heart and not my happy brother's. I am peculiarly called to weep with you that weep: and those who suffer most I find as near me as my own soul.'[1] Charles' portrayal of himself in these terms is, as he implies, in contrast to contemporary descriptions of his brother John. In 1750, the Methodist layman William Briggs wrote John a letter in which he criticized John for certain spiritual failings. 'You have the knowledge of all experience', Briggs wrote, 'but not the experience of all you know.' As evidence of John's lack of deep spiritual experience, Briggs pointed to '. . . the want of sympathy in your discourses and conversations. Those who attend to an inward work more than to an outward, pass through many weighty and grievous conflicts . . . When do you feelingly and with tears address yourself unto such?'[2]

These two descriptions may be used to illuminate the differences between Charles' and John's characters. They contribute to a fairly common portrayal of the two brothers as profoundly different: John as stable, cheerful, unsympathetic; Charles as melancholic, erratic, sensitive to the suffering of others. A closer reading of these descriptions is equally revealing, however, of certain assumptions about the qualities of the ideal Christian. In particular, both Charles' and Briggs' letters reveal assumptions about the quality of sympathy, the ability to 'weep with you that weep' or to respond 'feelingly and with tears' to those who suffer. Both writers assume that such sympathy is a spiritual quality: in Charles' letter it is a 'calling'; in Briggs' letter it is essential evidence of the work of the Spirit.

In this essay I explore the significance of sympathy in the hymns of Charles Wesley. I argue that in Charles' hymns, as in the descriptions above, the ideal Christian is constructed as one characterized by sympathetic responses towards the suffering. This ideal is constructed through portrayals of individual Christians, as well as through depictions of Jesus and the Christian community. Recognizing this element within the hymns is a reminder that Charles' hymns were important not just in encouraging particular theological convictions among early Methodists, but in constructing broader notions of self and community. I argue that understanding the construction of the sympathetic self within Charles' hymns illuminates significant aspects of early Methodist culture that have been the subject of historical debate, including the intensity of early Methodist community and the responsiveness of English Methodists to the reform movements of the late eighteenth and nineteenth centuries.

Charles Wesley's hymns were not, of course, written in a vacuum. In giving a central place to sympathy, his hymns reflected a broader trend within English culture. Many historians of eighteenth-century England have pointed to the growing value during this period of 'a new set of attitudes and emotional conventions at the heart of which was a sympathetic concern for the pain and suffering of other sentient beings'.[3] The value of sympathy was explored in a wide variety of texts and contexts, along with a number of related concepts such as 'sentiment', 'sensibility', 'pity' and 'benevolence'. These terms are at times difficult to distinguish from one another in their eighteenth-century usage.[4]

Perhaps the most extensive philosophical exploration of the idea and value of sympathy is found in Adam Smith's *Theory of Moral Sentiments*. Smith argued that however selfish people might be, they all possessed certain qualities that made them concerned with the needs and happiness of others.

> Of this kind is pity or compassion, the emotion which we feel for the misery of others, when we either see it, or are made to conceive it in a very lively manner. That we often derive sorrow from the sorrow of others, is a matter of fact too obvious to require any instances to prove it; for this sentiment, like all the other original passions of human nature, is by no means confined to the virtuous and the humane, though they may feel it with the most exquisite sensibility. The greatest ruffian, the most hardened violator of the laws of society, is not altogether without it.[5]

For Smith, such empathetic pity for the sufferings of another was one example of sympathy, which he defined broadly as 'fellow feeling with any passion whatsoever'.[6] The ability to sympathize with another's experiences was, in Smith's philosophy, a potential 'moral sense' and could thus form the foundation for the moral society. Smith's conviction that people shared a common propensity towards sympathy with each other's sufferings, and that virtue was reflected in a more 'exquisite' or heightened sensibility, can be seen throughout eighteenth-century England. Smith was not the only philosopher to suggest that sympathy could be the basis of a new morality – he was deeply influenced by David Hume, who had earlier affirmed the value of sympathy for society in his *Treatise of Human Nature* (1740). Prior to Hume, the essentially sympathetic nature of human beings had been suggested by Latitudinarian divines of the late seventeenth and early eighteenth centuries.[7]

These philosophical developments echoed ideas within contemporary medical treatises, which explored the 'sympathetic' relationship between organs. Ellis points out that during the eighteenth century, the key terms related to the 'culture of sensibility' – terms such as 'sentiment', 'sympathy' and 'delicacy' – can also be found throughout 'accounts of nerve function, models of the nervous system, accounts of the "circulation" of the blood and theories of the physiological organisation of the body as a whole'.[8]

The 'culture of sensibility' was perhaps most clearly demonstrated within literary fiction. Novelists such as Henry Mackenzie, Laurence Sterne and Samuel Richardson portrayed heroes and heroines who were men and women of intense feeling.[9] These novels relied on emotive language and heart-rending stories to move the reader to sympathy with these intense characters. Janet Todd describes this 'sentimental literature' as 'exemplary of emotion, teaching its consumers to produce a response equivalent to the one presented in its episodes'.[10] This sentimental literature constructed the ideal person as feeling deeply and sympathizing readily, even involuntarily, with those who suffered. These ideals were explicitly proffered to the reader as models for their own character and responses. In such novels, intense emotion was expressed in an entire 'sentimental rhetoric of the body' that included weeping, groaning, blushing, sighing, fainting and an inability to speak.[11]

Outside the world of fiction, moral reformers used similar literary techniques to portray the suffering of slaves or prisoners or factory workers to attract supporters to their causes. Reformers gave detailed descriptions of physical and emotional suffering to evoke sympathy among readers that would cause them to respond.[12] An example of this kind of writing from within Methodism is found in John Wesley's 1774 essay, 'Thoughts Upon Slavery'. Addressing English slave traders, John wrote:

Are you a man? Then you should have a human heart. But have you indeed? What is your heart made of? Is there no such principle as compassion there? Do you never feel another's pain? Have you no sympathy, no sense of human woe, no pity for the miserable? When you saw the flowing eyes, the heaving breasts, or the bleeding sides and tortured limbs of your fellow-creatures, was you a stone, or a brute?[13]

As Brycchan Carey has pointed out, the language and style of address that John uses here are typical of contemporary sentimental writing.[14] John's powerful evocation of sympathy suggests (in spite of Briggs' criticism of John as unsympathetic) a relationship between the 'culture of sensibility' and the culture of early Methodism.

The exact nature of this relationship is complex and contested.[15] Evangelicals, including Methodists, used the language of sensibility in preaching salvation and encouraging reform. For example, in a sermon on the woman caught in adultery, Charles employed many of the techniques of sentimental literature. Calling upon his listeners to consider the woman, he questioned them:

What says your holiness to an adulteress, a notorious, open sinner? Is pity the first emotion you feel at the sight of her, and do your eyes gush out with water, because she hath not kept God's law? Do you see yourself in her? . . . Are you thus affected towards her, thus full of pity, sorrow and love, and duly humbled under a sense of your own like sinfulness? Or do you not find the contrary tempers?[16]

Charles argues that the ability to respond to the adulteress with sympathy is the distinguishing characteristic of true holiness. While he elsewhere includes many other evidences of holiness, the emphasis here on tearful pity at the sight of the sinner is striking.

Early Methodist culture thus displayed many of the characteristics of the contemporary culture of sensibility. There were, however, underlying philosophical tensions between the suggestion that sympathy provided human beings with a natural moral sense and the evangelical claim that all people were inherently sinful and required conversion and transformation. Furthermore, both evangelicals and others had to grapple with the question of how sympathy related to charitable action. The evangelical reformer Hannah More, after defending sensibility in her early writings, went on in later life to condemn it. Sensibility could reduce suffering to an aesthetic experience, and 'a feeling heart could justify inaction and excuse error'.[17]

The hymns of Charles Wesley provide one context for exploring the relationship between early Methodism and broader cultural trends in relation to sympathy. In their perceptive study of eighteenth-century English hymnody, Janet Todd and Madeleine Forell Marshall have noted the similarities between Charles Wesley's poetic style and that of the 'literature of sensibility'.[18] Little attention has been paid, however, to the ways in which sympathy itself is treated in the hymns. A closer reading of the hymns reveals that sympathetic responses to suffering are a central aspect of many, in portrayals of individual Christians as well as representations of Jesus and the Christian community.

A valuable but neglected source for considering Charles' portrayal of individual Christians is a group of three collections of hymns that Charles Wesley and then George Osborn published under the title *Funeral Hymns*.[19] Charles composed a large number of hymns to commemorate deceased believers. While some of these hymns were written so as to apply to the death of any believer, many of them eulogize individual Christians, providing lengthy descriptions of the exemplary lives and deaths of the deceased. While the hymns do include specific details of the lives and experiences of these individuals, they also repeatedly emphasize certain key virtues as characterizing the deceased individuals they commemorate. Those who read and sang the hymns were encouraged to appreciate and develop these characteristics. These individual funeral hymns are thus a useful indication of how Charles wanted to construct the ideal Christian.

For the purposes of this chapter, it is significant that Charles repeatedly describes the sympathetic character of the individuals he portrays. A typical example is found in a hymn entitled 'On the death of Mrs Mary Naylor, March 21, 1757 (Part III)'.

1. Mercy, that heaven-descending guest,
Resided in her gentle breast,
And full possession kept;
While listening to the orphan's moan,
And echoing back the widow's groan,
She wept with them that wept.

2. Affliction, poverty, disease,
Drew out her soul in soft distress
The wretched to relieve:
In all the works of love employ'd,
Her sympathising soul enjoy'd
The blessedness to give.

3. Her Saviour in His members seen,
A stranger she received Him in,
An hungry Jesus fed,
Tended her sick imprison'd Lord,
And flew in all His wants to' afford
Her ministerial aid.

4. A nursing mother to the poor,
For them she husbanded her store,
Her life, her all bestow'd:
For them she labour'd day and night,
In doing good her whole delight,
In copying after God.

5. But did she then herself conceal
From her own flesh? or kindly feel
Their every want and woe?
*'Tis Corban this,* she never said,
But dealt alike her sacred bread
To feed both friend and foe.[20]

Wesley identifies Naylor as possessing (or rather, being possessed by) the quality of mercy. The practical aspect of this virtue – the exercise of charity – is, of course, a standard Christian virtue. Charles' description of Naylor's charitable acts echoes traditional formulations of charity as the service of Christ in the poor.[21] He also, however, emphasizes Naylor's emotional response to the suffering, a response that is clearly sympathetic. As the first verse concludes: 'She wept with those who wept.' Exposure to the suffering of others 'Drew out her soul in soft distress/The wretched to relieve.' The imagery of her soul being 'drawn out' implies the almost involuntary reaction of emotion to the sight of suffering that characterized eighteenth-century descriptions of sympathy.[22] In the final verse, Wesley emphasizes that her response to the suffering of her own family was similarly sympathetic, as she 'kindly' felt 'Their every want and woe.'

Sympathy is depicted here as closely connected to Christian virtue. It is an aspect of mercy, 'that heaven-descending guest', and it is described in specifically biblical terms, as a matter of weeping with those who weep (Romans 12.15). This portrayal of Naylor also echoes eighteenth-century formulations of the person of 'feeling' or 'sensibility'. Her 'gentle breast' and 'soft distress'; her empathetic response to the 'moan' and 'groan' of the suffering orphan and widow; her willingness to 'kindly feel' the 'woe' of her family: all are reminiscent of the characters described in the literature of sensibility.

Similar portrayals of individuals as deeply sympathetic can be found throughout the funeral hymns.[23] Historians have convincingly argued for the gendering of sensibility during the eighteenth century, but Charles portrays men and women in very similar terms.[24] For example, Charles writes of Mr Thomas Lewis:

6. His heart, as tender as sincere,
Melted for every sufferer,
And bled for the distress'd.
(Where'er he heard the grieved complain.)
And pity for the sons of pain
Resided in his breast.[25]

Like Naylor, Lewis is portrayed as deeply sympathetic, and his sympathy is described in physical (though metaphorical) terms. His heart was 'tender'; it 'melted' and 'bled' for those who suffered; pity '[r]esided in his breast'.

In eulogizing deceased believers in these terms, Charles constructs the ideal Methodist as one who feels deeply and sympathizes readily. The public singing or private reading of these hymns encouraged early Methodist readers or singers to adopt a similar ideal for themselves and others. The descriptions of John and Charles quoted at the beginning of this chapter both, in different ways, reflect this ideal. Without claiming that Charles' hymns simply made Methodists sympathetic, there is significant evidence to suggest that sympathy became an intrinsic part of Methodist identity. Consider, for example, the Methodist response to the campaign for the abolition of slavery. Methodist support for anti-slavery campaigns was extremely high throughout the late eighteenth and early nineteenth century.[26] Most Methodists had never been to the West Indies, or seen slaves at work on a plantation, or watched slaves being packed into a slave ship for transport. Their knowledge of this suffering came from its literary evocation in the writings of anti-slavery reformers, writings that conformed to the conventions of the literature of sensibility by seeking to evoke sympathetic responses from 'persons of feeling'. The powerful response among Methodists to this literature makes sense, I would suggest, in light of the repeated affirmation of sympathy found in Charles Wesley's hymns.

Clearly, Charles' construction of the ideal Methodist echoes contemporary affirmations of the value of sympathy, particularly as expressed in depictions of the 'person of feeling'. While these parallels are significant, however, they may also be misleading. Charles' hymns emphasize sympathy within a particular theological framework and for particular spiritual purposes. Without attention to this framework and these purposes, the distinctive nature of Charles' understanding of sympathy will be missed.

As the funeral hymn for Mary Naylor demonstrates, Charles emphasizes sympathy in the context of a traditional Christian motivation for charity. Sympathy towards the suffering is portrayed in this hymn as one aspect of serving Jesus in the poor.[27] In other funeral hymns, human sympathy is also portrayed as a quality that appropriately imitates the sympathy of Jesus. In a funeral hymn for Mrs Mary Horton, Charles writes:

1. Say, ye companions of her youth,
With what sincerity and truth,
How free from fear or shame,
Christ and His members she confess'd,
And through a blameless life express'd
The tempers of the Lamb.

2. How did she put His bowels on,
And answer every plaintive groan
Of poverty and pain!
In sad variety of grief
The wretched sought from her relief,
Nor ever sought in vain.[28]

The first way in which Horton 'express'd/The tempers of the Lamb' was to sympathize like Jesus, to 'put His bowels on' in responding compassionately to the needy. The phrase 'bowels of Christ' is here as elsewhere used as a metaphor for Jesus' emotions, in particular his sympathy and pity. This hymn thus makes clear Charles' conviction that Christian charity should involve an emotional, sympathetic response to suffering as well as practical action. More significantly, in portraying sympathy as a quality by which the believer imitates Jesus, this hymn points to Charles' broader representation of Jesus as a deeply sympathetic person.

The significance given to sympathy in depictions of Jesus can be seen in a lengthy early hymn entitled 'Written in stress of temptation'. While this hymn does not contain the word 'sympathy', a close reading demonstrates that the narrative focuses throughout on sympathetic responses.

1. I am the man who long have known
The fierceness of temptation's rage!
And still to God for help I groan:
When shall my groans His help engage?

2. Out of the deep on Jesus I call,
In bitterness of spirit cry;
Broken upon that Stone I fall,
I fall, – the chief of sinners I.

3. Saviour of me, my sad complaint
Let me into Thy bosom pour;
Beneath my load of sin I faint,
And hell is ready to devour.

4. A devil to myself I am,
Yet cannot 'scape the flesh I tear;
Beast, fiend, and legion is my name,
My lot the blackness of despair.
. . .

7. My Lord, (I still will call Thee mine,
Till sentenced to eternal pain,)
Thou wouldest not Thy cup decline,
Thy vengeance due to guilty man.

8. My sufferings all to Thee are known,
Tempted at every point like me:
Regard my griefs, regard Thine own:
Jesu! remember *Calvary!*

9. O, call to mind Thy earnest prayers,
Thine agony and sweat of blood,
Thy strong and bitter cries and tears,
Thy mortal groan, 'MY GOD! MY GOD!'

10. For whom didst Thou the cross endure?
Who nail'd Thy body to the tree?
Did not Thy death my life procure?
O, let Thy bowels answer me!

11. Art Thou not touch'd with human woe?
Hath pity left the Son of Man?
Dost Thou not all our sorrow know,
And claim a share in all our pain?

12. Canst Thou forget Thy days of flesh?
Canst Thou *my* miseries not feel?
Thy tender heart – it bleeds afresh!
It bleeds! – and Thou art Jesus still!

13. I feel, I feel Thee now the same,
Kindled Thy kind relentings are;
These meltings from Thy bowels came,
Thy Spirit groan'd this inward prayer.

14. Thy prayer is heard, Thy will is done!
Light in Thy light at length I see;
Thou wilt preserve my soul Thine own,
And show forth all Thy power in me.[29]

This hymn draws its readers or singers into a dramatic experience of temptation and salvation.[30] The first six verses of this hymn introduce the narrator
as one overwhelmed by long temptation but continuing to cry out to God. In
verses one and two, he describes his plight in biblical phrases that recall the
psalmists and the prophets, thus investing his own suffering with profound
theological meaning.[31] The narrator describes his emotional pain at length
and in detail – his 'groans', his 'bitterness of spirit', his 'sad complaint', the
'load of sin' he carries, 'the blackness of despair' he feels. His inner struggle

against temptation is compared to the struggle of the Gadarene demoniac, possessed by a legion of demons (Luke 8.26–39).

If the early verses of the hymn describe the suffering of the narrator, verse 7 shifts to a direct and desperate appeal to Jesus. The narrator appeals to the compassion of Jesus towards 'guilty man', as demonstrated in his Passion: 'Thou wouldest not Thy cup decline,/Thy vengeance due to guilty man.' As verse eight makes clear, Jesus' own sufferings make him able to empathize with human pain:

8. My sufferings all to Thee are known,
Tempted at every point like me:
Regard my griefs, regard Thine own:
Jesu! remember *Calvary!*

In appealing to this empathetic connection, the narrator makes use of biblical precedent. The writer to the Hebrews affirmed that 'we have not an high priest which cannot be touched with the feeling of our infirmities; but was in all points tempted like as we are, yet without sin' (Hebrews 4.15). Jesus' experience of temptation means that the narrator can present his own sufferings as Jesus' own: 'Regard my griefs, regard Thine own.' To prompt Jesus' memory with regard to his suffering on Calvary, the narrator launches into a vivid description of those sufferings.

Verses 9 to 12 contain a string of emotive references to Jesus' suffering.[32] Jesus' 'agony', his 'strong and bitter cries and tears', his 'mortal groan', his body 'nail'd' to 'the tree' – each is urgently brought to Jesus' attention. The purpose of this description is clearly to produce a powerful emotional response. In verse 10, for example, Jesus is confronted with a series of almost hysterical questions: 'For whom didst Thou the cross endure?/Who nail'd Thy body to the tree?/Did not Thy death my life procure?' The response that Wesley requires from Jesus is not verbal, but emotional: 'O, let Thy bowels answer me!' Jesus' own experience of suffering is posited as the basis by which he is able to 'feel' the sufferings of the narrator. 'Canst Thou forget Thy days of flesh?/Canst Thou *my* miseries not feel?' asks the narrator.

The emotive descriptions of these first twelve verses are clearly designed to evoke a sympathetic response from Jesus. Both the narrator's suffering and Jesus' own suffering are described in an attempt to create this response. Verse 12 marks the climax to this emotional crescendo, as Jesus' capacity to sympathize is identified as essential to his nature: 'Thy tender heart – it bleeds afresh!/It bleeds! – and Thou art Jesus still!' For Jesus to fail to be sympathetic, these lines imply, would be for him no to longer be himself. It is on the basis of this sympathetic response that Jesus is moved to act. His action involves the transformation of the heart of the narrator and thus his relief from temptation. This transformation is, as the narrator emphasizes, sensible: 'I feel, I feel Thee now the same!' As a result of this perceived transformation, the hymn ends on a note of confident rejoicing.

The portrayal of Jesus in 'Written in stress of temptation' is striking but not unusual. Similar depictions of Jesus as sympathetic fellow-sufferer appear throughout Charles' hymns.[33] These hymns emphasize pity or compassion as integral to Jesus' character and the basis on which he can be appealed to for help. In such hymns the concepts of love and sympathy are almost entirely interchangeable. For example, in one of the 'Hymns for Love', Charles writes:

1. When shall my grief and pain
Thy kind compassion move?
Thou know'st I languish still to' attain
The happiness of love:
If Thou my suit deny,
Out of Thy presence cast,
Excluded from Thy love, I die,
I die unsaved at last.

2. How shall I plead with Thee,
Saviour of sinful men?
Let Thy own dying love for me
Thy pitying heart constrain:
The universal load,
The cross Thou didst endure
With all the vengeful wrath of God,
To make my pardon sure.[34]

As in the previous hymn, Jesus' pity is here seen as central. Jesus is constrained by his 'pitying heart' to help the distressed penitent. Once again, the memory of the cross is evoked to move Jesus to act. Jesus' sacrificial death on the cross is that which most clearly demonstrates his compassionate nature. Reminding Jesus of the sacrifice he made is thus both a prompt to him identifying with the suffering of the believer and a way of urging him to be true to his nature. Again, the goal of this hymn is the transformation of the narrator, who 'languish[es] still to' attain/The happiness of love.'

In portrayals such as these Jesus has much in common with the 'man of feeling'.[35] Like the 'man of feeling', Jesus is deeply emotionally responsive to the troubles of others. Like the 'man of feeling' too, Jesus expresses this response through physical displays. This can be seen in the references within the hymns to Jesus' tears. For example, Charles interprets the famous verse 'Jesus wept' as evidence of Jesus' inherently sympathetic nature.

1. Jesus weeps, our tears to see!
Feels the soft infirmity;
Feels, whene'er a friend we mourn,
From our bleeding bosom torn:
Let Him still in spirit groan,
Make our every grief His own,
Till we all triumphant rise,
Call'd to meet Him in the skies.

2. Jesus weeps for sinners blind,
Mourns the death of all mankind;

Blesses us with sacred showers,
Sheds His tears to hallow ours:
Weeps to make our case His own,
For our guilty joys to' atone,
Wipes at last the mourner's eyes,
Sorrow's source for ever dries.[36]

In its context, this verse refers to Jesus' response at the death of Lazarus. Historically, Jesus' tears in this account have been interpreted in a myriad of ways. Margery Lange's study of early modern English sermons on this passage shows Jesus' tears understood as demonstrating, variously: grief at Lazarus' death, grief at human doubt, grief at the sin of the world and compassion for Mary and Martha.[37] In this hymn, though Jesus' tears are ascribed multiple meanings, they are first and foremost a sign of his sympathy for human beings. Jesus weeps in response to human tears. This portrayal is typical of Charles' treatment of Jesus' tears, which he repeatedly interprets as evidence of Jesus' pity or sympathy.[38]

The portrayal of Jesus in these terms clearly resonates with eighteenth-century ideas about sympathy and sensibility. In assuming that because Jesus loves, he sympathizes – and that these concepts are almost interchangeable – Charles is reflecting the assumptions of the 'culture of sensibility'. Again, however, Charles' understanding of Jesus' ability to sympathize is also connected to broader theological themes in the hymns. In particular, Charles draws direct and indirect connections between his Arminian theology and the sympathy of Jesus. In the hymn above, for example, the lines 'Jesus weeps for sinners blind,/Mourns the death of *all* mankind' clearly contain a typical swipe at limited atonement. More explicitly, in one of the anti-Calvinist 'Hymns on God's Everlasting Love', published in 1741, Charles writes:

6. Sinners, believe the gospel word;
Jesus is come, your souls to save!
Jesus is come, your common Lord!
Pardon ye all in Him may have;
May now be saved, whoever will;
This Man receiveth sinners still.

7. See where the lame, the halt, the blind,
The deaf, the dumb, the sick, the poor,
Flock to the Friend of human kind,
And freely all accept their cure:
To whom doth He His help deny?
Whom in His days of flesh *pass by*!

8. Did not His word the fiends expel,
The lepers cleanse, and raise the dead?
Did He not all their sickness heal,
And satisfy their every need?
Did He reject His helpless clay,
Or send them sorrowful away?

9. Nay, but His bowels yearn'd to see
The people hungry, scatter'd, faint;
Nay, but He utter'd over thee
*Jerusalem*, a true complaint;
*Jerusalem*, who shedd'st His blood,
That, with His tears, for thee hath flow'd.

10. How oft for thy hard-heartedness
Did Jesus in his Spirit groan!
The things belonging to thy peace,
Hadst thou, O bloody city, known,
Thee, turning in thy gracious day,
He never would have cast away.

11. He wept, because thou *wouldst* not see
The grace which sure salvation brings:
How oft would He have gather'd thee,
And cherish'd underneath His wings;
But thou *wouldst not* – unhappy thou!
And justly art thou harden'd now.[39]

Here Jesus' sympathy and compassion towards all those he encountered on earth – his 'tears', his 'groan', the yearning of his 'bowels' – are taken as evidence of his willingness to save anyone who repents. It is this conviction that also underlies the pleading of such hymns as 'Written in the stress of temptation', which seek to appeal to that sympathetic nature.

The implication that the divine nature is inherently sympathetic is significant in terms of broader theological developments during the late eighteenth and nineteenth centuries. David Bebbington has described the growing evangelical emphasis on the Fatherhood of God during the nineteenth century, in which ideas of the eternal 'paternal pity' of God gained ascendancy over ideas of God's just wrath against sin.[40] While Charles' hymns emphasize the 'vengeful wrath' of God the Father, Jesus is portrayed throughout as compassionate and sympathetic. This emphasis on sympathy as a divine quality seems to prefigure later evangelical portrayals of God as a sympathetic father.

Jesus' sympathy is also closely connected in the hymns to his relationship with believers. Specifically, Charles develops the biblical idea of 'the body of Christ' as a basis for shared sympathy. Several biblical passages describe the Church as the body of Christ – and individual Christians as 'members' of this body. A detailed exploration of this concept is found in 1 Corinthians 12.12–27:

For as the body is one, and hath many members, and all the members of that one body, being many, are one body: so also is Christ . . . For the body is not one member, but many . . . And whether one member suffer, all the members suffer with it; or one member be honoured, all the members rejoice with it.

Other biblical passages explore the concept of the Church as Christ's body, though elsewhere the connection between shared membership of this body and shared suffering is not emphasized.[41] In Charles' hymns, however, this connection is repeatedly stressed. Jesus' sympathy is seen to derive at least in part from his role as 'Head' of the body.[42] For example, Wesley writes:

> 1. The members here and Head above,
> United in the Spirit of love
> One mystic body make.
> And Jesus, once a Man of woe
> The sufferings of His saints below
> Doth still in heaven partake.[43]

And, similarly:

> Jesus on the celestial hill
> Doth for his people care,
> Doth suffer in His members still,
> And all our sorrows bear:
> If crush'd on earth the foot complain,
> Feeling the injury
> The Head above cries out in pain,
> 'Thou persecutest Me.'[44]

The idea of spiritual unity or 'membership' of Jesus' 'body' seems in Wesley's thought to be almost inseparable from the experience of suffering. Jesus is portrayed here as continuing to partake in the suffering of believers: he 'suffers in His members still'. The boundary between sympathy and unity is here blurred: Jesus actually enters into the pain of his suffering people.

Not surprisingly, this emphasis upon the sympathetic nature of the 'body of Christ' has great significance for Charles' portrayal of the Christian community. Sympathy becomes a central element in the ideal Christian community, as can be seen in a lengthy poem on 'The Communion of Saints', where Charles writes:

> 4. Sweetly now we all agree,
> Touch'd with softest sympathy,
> Kindly for each other care:
> Every member feels its share:
> Wounded by the grief of one,
> All the suffering members groan;
> Honour'd if one member is,
> All partake the common bliss.[45]

Here 'membership' of Jesus' body is again portrayed as the basis of a profound sympathetic connection. In this portrayal, the community's responses to each other's pains are given far more prominence than their responses to each other's pleasures. This emphasis on the sympathetic nature of the Christian community is repeated in many of Charles' hymns.[46]

Sympathy, rising out of the spiritual reality of shared membership of Jesus' body, is portrayed as a quality that distinguishes the Christian community from all others. A hymn on 'Desiring to Love' expresses this clearly:

1. O Saviour, cast a pitying eye,
A sinner at Thy feet I lie,
And will not hence depart,
Till Thou regard my ceaseless moan;
O speak, and take away the stone,
The unbelieving heart:

2. Till Thou the mountain load remove,
I groan beneath my want of love;
O hear my bitter cry:
Without Thy love I cannot live,
Give, Jesus, Friend of sinners, give
Me love, or else I die.

3. Dost Thou not all my sufferings know,
Dost Thou not see mine eye o'erflow,
My labouring bosom move?
Why do I all this burden bear?
Need I to Thee the cause declare?
Thou know'st, I cannot love.

4. This is my sin and misery,
I always find Thy love to me,
Seal'd by Thy precious blood;
And yet I make Thee no return,
I only for my baseness mourn,
I cannot love my God.

5. The world admire my mystic grief,
And torture me with vain relief,
And cruel kindness show;
They bid me give my wailings o'er,
And weep and vex myself no more
For One they never knew.

6. My Father's children feel my care,
With kind concern my cross they bear,
And in my sorrows join;
The suffering members sympathise,
And grieve my griefs, and sigh my sighs.
And mix their tears with mine.

7. But all in vain for me they grieve,
Their sufferings cannot mine relieve,
Or mitigate my pain:
No answer to their prayers they see,
And prevalent with God for me
They seem to pray in vain.

8. Thou then, O God, Thine hand lay to,
And let me all the means look through,
And trust to Thee alone,
To Thee alone for all things trust,
And say to Thee, who sav'st the lost,
Thine only will be done.[47]

This hymn again presents Jesus as deeply sympathetic towards the suffering believer. This sympathy is mirrored here by the sympathy of the supplicant's fellow-believers. These fellow-believers enter into the suffering of the one desiring to love: they 'bear' 'my cross', they 'feel my care'. Again, the 'body of Christ' provides the theological framework for these sympathetic responses: 'The suffering members sympathise,/And grieve my griefs, and sigh my sighs.' This sympathetic behaviour is contrasted starkly to the attitude of those in 'the world', who 'admire' the supplicant's grief but cannot sympathize with it. Sympathy thus unites, but it also divides.

This hymn also identifies, however, the potential limits of sympathy in Charles' understanding. As verse 7 makes clear, the sympathy of the supplicant's fellow-believers is ultimately 'all in vain'. Their empathetic 'sufferings' and even the prayers that they are moved to pray are ineffective. The solution to the deep need of the narrator can only be provided by God. The repeated use of the words 'alone' and 'only' in the final verse emphasizes that it is God's intervention that ultimately makes a difference, not the 'means' of the community's sympathy and prayers. This final verse seems to imply a warning that the sympathy of other Christians, while comforting, must not be relied upon for that which only God can provide. This hymn and others caution that the sympathetic fellowship offered by the Christian community could become idolatrous.[48]

While for Charles the shared membership of Jesus' body means that Christians are particularly sympathetic towards each other, the hymns also emphasize the importance of sympathy towards all who suffer. So, for example, in a 'Hymn for the National Fast', written in 1782, Charles writes:

3. With every sufferer,
We drop the generous tear,
(Whom Thy tendering Spirit leads,)
Pity no distinction knows,
Love for all the wounded bleeds,
Love embraces friends and foes.[49]

As this hymn makes clear, the 'tendering Spirit' leads Christians into an all-embracing sympathy. Even those American rebels whom Charles identifies as 'foes' are included in this embrace. Sympathy here becomes not only the means by which believers express love for each other, but also the means by which believers relate to those across boundaries of belief, race and nationality.[50]

As has been noted, the promotion of sympathy as a particular virtue existed within the broader culture of eighteenth-century England, but in Charles' hymns it is given a particular, Christological interpretation. Jesus is presented as inherently sympathetic, and the Passion is presented as both source and expression of this sympathy. Believers, individually and as a community, suffer and sympathize in imitation of a suffering and sympathetic Lord. This Christological framework also places limits on sympathy within the hymns. The broader uneasiness within evangelicalism about the power of sympathy is mirrored in Charles' insistence that human sympathy must not be relied on to provide that spiritual good which only God can provide. Sympathy in the hymns could be humanitarian, but it could never be humanist. Charles' portrayal of sympathy thus both reflected and resisted common contemporary constructions of the sympathetic person.

The construction of the ideal Methodist in these terms has real significance for illuminating certain distinctive aspects of early Methodist culture. It is a commonplace that Methodism was concerned with individual experience, but as D. Bruce Hindmarsh has argued in his recent book on evangelical conversion narratives, 'if the converts in the early Evangelical Revival appear as individualists of a sort, they were also communitarians of a sort'.[51] The Methodist conversion narratives he examines reveal that many individuals were drawn to the intense experience of community that early Methodism offered.[52] The writers of these narratives repeatedly draw attention to the value of the fellowship they experienced in the intimate settings of band and society meetings. These meetings provided a context within which those who were seeking salvation or greater holiness could share their experiences, comfort, challenge and pray for one another. Such shared practices were explicitly identified as 'means of grace'.[53]

Like many aspects of early Methodism, this intense community can be seen in part as a response to the particular social and cultural conditions in which eighteenth-century English people lived. As David Hempton and others have argued convincingly, early English Methodism thrived in areas where old ties to squire and parson had been loosened or disrupted, often because of broader social changes involving population growth and mobility.[54] Methodism offered an alternative community, based on alternative loyalties. This community was based not on shared family, social status or denomination, but on the perception of a shared experience of conversion.

Charles' emphasis on sympathy grows out of this context and affirms it. In a community gathered around the shared (and often painful) experience of conviction, conversion and the struggle for sanctification, the practice of sympathy provided a powerful cohesive force. The expression of sympathy in this context affirmed the shared nature of these experiences and so their validity. Charles' letters are full of his appreciation for the intensity of Methodist fellowship, and his hymns encourage Methodists to develop the quality of sympathy that contributed to this intensity.[55] Through hymns that depicted Jesus as profoundly sympathetic, Methodists were encouraged to associate divine love with the practice of sympathy. Through funeral hymns that lauded the sympathetic nature of deceased believers, they were provided with exemplars of the sympathetic 'person of feeling'. Through the emphasis on shared membership of Christ's body, they were assured that they could truly sympathize with each other's sufferings because these sufferings were ultimately part of a shared spiritual story and identity.

To 'weep with you that weep' was, for Charles Wesley, not only a personal calling, but also a mark of true Christian character and community. In constructing the ideal Methodist as deeply sympathetic, Charles' hymns resonate powerfully with broader cultural trends within eighteenth-century England. They also encourage the formation of a new, distinctively Methodist self, one that would follow a sympathetic Lord in weeping 'for all mankind'.

## Notes

1 Charles Wesley to Sarah Gwynne, Dublin, 17 November 1747, MARC, DDCW, 5/3.

2 William Briggs to John Wesley, 5 April 1750. MARC, Colman Box.

3 Karen Halttunen, 'Humanitarianism and the Pornography of Pain in Anglo-American Culture', *The American Historical Review*, 100, No. 2 (April 1995), 303.

4 Markman Ellis has discussed the difficulty of defining the term 'sensibility' as it was used in eighteenth-century England – he suggests that writings on sensibility from the period are 'a philosophical nightmare of muddled ideas, weak logic and bad writing'. Markman Ellis, *The Politics of Sensibility: Race, gender and commerce in the sentimental novel* (New York: Cambridge University Press, 1996), 7.

5 Adam Smith, *The Theory of Moral Sentiments*, ed. D. D. Raphael and A. L. Macfie (Indianapolis: Liberty Fund, 1982 reprint edition (Oxford: Oxford University Press, 1976), 9.

6 Smith, *The Theory of Moral Sentiments*, 10.

7 Karen Halttunnen quotes a number of examples. 'Humanitarianism and the Pornography of Pain', 304–5.

8 Ellis, *The Politics of Sensibility*, 18–19.

9 For example, Henry Mackenzie, *The Man of Feeling* (London, 1771); Laurence Sterne, *A Sentimental Journey through France and Italy* (London, 1768) and Samuel Richardson, *Pamela: or Virtue Rewarded* (London, 1740).

10 Janet Todd, *Sensibility: An introduction* (London; New York: Methuen, 1986), 4.

11 Markman Ellis, *The Politics of Sensibility*, 19.

12 The use of the literary techniques of 'sensibility' by moral reformers has been discussed in a number of places. Useful analyses include Karen Halttunen, 'Humanitarianism and the Pornography of Pain'; Marcus Wood, *Slavery, Empathy and Pornography* (Oxford: Oxford University Press, 2002); Carolyn Sorisio, 'The Spectacle of the Body: Torture in the Antislavery Writing of Lydia Maria Child and Frances E. W. Harper', *Modern Language Studies*, 30, No. 1 (Spring 2000), 45–66.

13 John Wesley, 'Thoughts upon Slavery', *Political Writings of John Wesley*, ed. Graham Maddox (Bristol: Thoemmes Press, 1998), 103.

14  Brycchan Carey, 'John Wesley's *Thoughts upon slavery* and the language of the heart', *Bulletin of the John Rylands University Library of Manchester*, 85, Nos. 2 and 3 (Summer and Autumn 2003), 278–84.

15  Different arguments in regard to this relationship are put forward by Todd, *Sensibility*; Wood, *Slavery, Empathy and Pornography*; and G. J. Barker-Benfield, *The Culture of Sensibility: Sex and society in eighteenth-century Britain* (Chicago: University of Chicago Press, 1992).

16  Newport, *Sermons*, 254–5.

17  Janet Todd, *Sensibility*, 64, 137. Hannah More criticized 'sentiment' in 'On the Danger of Sentimental or Romantic Connexions' (1778).

18  Madeleine Forell Marshall and Janet Todd, *English Congregational Hymns in the Eighteenth Century* (Lexington: University Press of Kentucky, 1982), 11.

19  Charles himself published two collections: one in 1746 and a subsequent one in 1759. Osborn apparently collected together another substantial group of funeral hymns, 'most of which were not published during the author's life' (the entire collection is in *PW*, 6.188–366; the quotation is from 6.289).

20  *PW*, 6.270–1.

21  For traditional views of charity in England, and the way these views changed during the eighteenth century, see Deborah Valenze, 'Charity, Custom and Humanity: Changing Attitudes towards the Poor in Eighteenth-Century England', in Jane Garnett and Colin Matthew, eds, *Revival and Religion Since 1700: Essays for John Walsh* (London and Rio Grande: Hambledon Press, 1993), 59–78.

22  See Norman S. Fiering, 'Irresistible Compassion: An Aspect of Eighteenth-Century Sympathy and Humanitarianism', *Journal of the History of Ideas*, 37, No. 2 (April–June 1976), 195–218.

23  Funeral hymns that portray the deceased as sympathetic include 'On the Death of Mr Thomas Hogg, June 29, 1750', *PW*, 6.290–1; 'On the Death of Lady Hotham, June 30, 1756. (Part III)' *PW*, 6.296; 'On the Death of Mr John Matthews, December 28, 1764' *PW*, 6.308–13; 'On the Death of Mrs Hannah Dewal' *PW*, 6.318–23; 'On the Death of Mrs Elizabeth Blackwell, March 27, 1772' *PW*, 6.323–31; 'On the Death of Mr Thomas Waller, In his Thirtieth Year, May 11, 1781' *PW*, 6.345–6 and 'On the Death of Mr Ebenezer Blackwell, April 21, 1782', *PW*, 6.353–5.

24  For the gendering of sensibility, see Barker-Benfield, *The Culture of Sensibility*. For a discussion of differences between sentimental literature authored by men and women, see Patricia Meyer Spacks, 'Oscillations of Sensibility', *New Literary History*, 25, No. 3 (Summer 1994), 505–20.

25  'On the Death of Mr. Thomas Lewis, April, 1782', *PW*, 6.350.

26  For the involvement of Methodists (and other evangelicals) in the anti-slavery campaigns, see Adam Hochschild, *Bury the Chains: Prophets and rebels in the fight to free an empire's slaves* (Boston: Houghton Mifflin, 2005), especially chapters 9 and 22.

27  Other hymns that communicate this understanding of charity include 'Before any work of charity' and 'In the work', *PW*, 5.18–21.

28  'On the Death of Mrs. Mary Horton, May 4, 1786, Aged Thirty-four. (Part III)' *PW*, 6.359–60. There are eight verses.

29  *PW*, 1.273–6.

30  I refer to the central figure of this narrative as 'the narrator'. As this figure is firstly identified with Charles himself (and because Charles writes 'I am the *man* . . .') I have used masculine pronouns in referring to him. This is not to suggest that Methodist women could not make use of such a hymn, but it does raise

interesting questions about the place of gender in the process of appropriating such a narrative.

31 Lamentations 3.1; Psalm 130.1–2; Isaiah 28.16 (the latter verse is also quoted in 1 Peter 2.6–8, and Wesley is obviously following this Christological interpretation).

32 There are a number of sources for this description. The Anglican Litany contains references to 'Thy agony, Thy bloody sweat'. Wesley also seems to be referring again to Hebrews. Hebrews 5.7 – 'Who in the days of his flesh, when he had offered up prayers and supplications with strong crying and tears unto him that was able to save him from death, and was heard in that he feared.'

33 A small selection of examples from many hymns that portray Jesus in these terms include *PW*, 1.83–5; 2.156–8; 4.250; 5.231–2; 9.34; 11.118; 11.223; 12.104.

34 Hymn IX, 'Hymns for Love', *PW*, 8.363. There are two more verses.

35 Janet Todd makes this point in *Sensibility: An introduction* (London and New York: Methuen, 1986), 50.

36 'Jesus wept' (John 9.35), *PW*, 11.475–6.

37 Marjory E. Lange, '"And Jesus Wept": Preaching Tears and Jesus', in *Telling Tears in the English Renaissance* (Leiden: E. J. Brill, 1996), 157–86.

38 See *PW*, 1.330 2; 11.223; 11. 233; 11.268–9.

39 *PW*, 3.20–3.

40 David Bebbington, *The Dominance of Evangelicalism: The age of Spurgeon and Moody* (Downers Grove, Illinois: InterVarsity Press, 2005), 166–9.

41 For example, see Romans 12.4–5 and Ephesians 4.15–16.

42 A selection of examples of Wesley's use of the idea of membership of the body of Jesus in relation to suffering includes *PW*, 1.362; 2.216; 4.339; 5.78; 5.232–3; 253–4; 10.112, 301, 425; 11.85, 308; 12.140.

43 *PW*, 12.234. This hymn is written in reference to Acts 9.4, 'Saul, Saul, why persecutest thou Me?' There are two more verses.

44 *PW*, 10.112. This hymn is written in reference to Zechariah 2.8, 'He that toucheth you toucheth the apple of His eye.'

45 *PW*, 1.362.

46 For example, *PW*, 1.298–9; 2.164–6; 3.173–4; 4.473–4; 5.78.

47 'Hymn 3' in a series on 'Desiring to Love', *PW*, 4.338–9.

48 See, for example, 'Upon Parting with His Friends (Part II)', *PW*, 1.245–6.

49 *PW*, 8.324.

50 Other examples of sympathy for enemies include *PW*, 4.28; 8.335.

51 D. Bruce Hindmarsh, *The Evangelical Conversion Narrative: Spiritual Autobiography in Early Modern England* (New York: Oxford University Press, 2005), 150.

52 Hindmarsh, *The Evangelical Conversion Narrative*, 150–6.

53 Hindmarsh, *The Evangelical Conversion Narrative*, 151.

54 David Hempton, *Methodism: Empire of the Spirit* (New Haven and London: Yale University Press, 2004), 17–30.

55 For examples of Charles' description of intense times of fellowship, see letter to Sarah Gwynne, 5/6 February, [1749], MARC, DDCW, 5/25; letter to Sarah Gwynne Wesley, 26 September, [1757], MARC, DDCW, 5/75, letter to Sarah Gwynne Wesley, 8 September, [1757], MARC, DDCW, 5/104.

# 15. Charles Wesley, *Theologos*

## TED A. CAMPBELL

Ah, Lord! enlarge our scanty thought
To know the wonders thou hast wrought!
Unloose our stamm'ring tongue, to tell
Thy love immense, unsearchable![1]

## Introduction

Among the many legacies of Charles Wesley is his contribution as a Christian theologian. But identifying either John or Charles Wesley straightforwardly as a 'theologian' has proven difficult. This is perhaps due to the fact that since at least the time of Schleiermacher, the term 'theologian' has been consistently associated with those who write prose works that reflect critically on religious teachings. Albert Outler suggested that we might think of John Wesley as a 'folk theologian', and Randy Maddox and others have identified John Wesley as a 'practical theologian'.[2] J. Ernest Rattenbury's foundational study, *The Evangelical Doctrines of Charles Wesley's Hymns* (originally published in 1941), struggled with this same issue in regard to Charles Wesley:

> It must be admitted that in the conventional sense of the term [Charles Wesley] was not a formal theologian. He cannot be classified as of the same calibre as Augustine, Anselm, Aquinas, Calvin, or Schleiermacher. As a formal theologian, some would even prefer his brother.[3]

Rattenbury went on to claim Charles Wesley as an 'experimental' theologian; that is, one whose focus was the experience of the divine. 'Is it not an exaggeration', Rattenbury asked, 'to claim that he was the prince of experimental theologians of modern times?'[4] S T Kimbrough Jr has written of Charles Wesley's 'lyrical theology'.[5]

There is no doubt, then, that we can find a definition of 'theologian' that suits Charles (and John) Wesley. However, it is also clear that the term 'theologian' has such overtones or connotations of systematic theology that the term will always have to be qualified as applied to the Wesleys. In this chapter, then, I propose to consider Charles Wesley as *theologos*, in the sense in which the term is used in Eastern Christian churches which speak of the author of the Fourth

Gospel as 'St John Theologos'. A *theologos* is one who gives us words (*logoi*) about God (*theos*). While this may indeed be the original meaning of the term 'theologian', using the term *theologos* here seems more appropriate since by doing so we will avoid the connotations that the word 'theologian' now has, namely one who is associated with the second-order work (*theologia secunda*) of critical reflection on religious teachings or religious practices. *Theologos* allows us to claim more explicitly Charles Wesley's first-order work (*theologia prima*) of giving us words by which we can speak of God and indeed by which we can speak to God.[6]

Charles Wesley's work as *theologos* has been thought of in the Methodist and Wesleyan traditions as the work of giving voice to Christian experience, hence Rattenbury's claim that Charles was 'the prince of experimental theologians'. What I suggest here, however, is that this reflects an authorized reading of Charles given shape most forcibly in John Wesley's *Collection of Hymns for the Use of the People Called Methodists* (1780), which served as the basis for subsequent Methodist hymnals.[7] It is not an incorrect reading of Charles Wesley: his hymns and other poems do indeed explore the depth of Christian experience, and John's arrangement of them faithfully exposits the range of Christian experience. But the 1780 hymnal was a small selection of Charles Wesley's hymns out of a much larger corpus of hymns and other poetry.

Within the broader range of Charles Wesley's verse, we can see not only the exposition of the 'way of salvation' and the 'evangelical doctrines' associated with it, but also the exposition of other Christian teachings, the ecumenical inheritance of Christian faith that was transmitted in the creeds and reflected in the liturgical year. The Charles Wesley Society's publications of Charles Wesley's many volumes of poetry celebrating specific moments in the Christian liturgical year (e.g. *Hymns for our Lord's Resurrection*, 1746) or on specific Christian teachings (e.g. his *Hymns on the Trinity*, 1767) show the vast range of Charles Wesley's poetry that celebrated not only the out-working of salvation in Christian experience but also the common inheritance of ancient (and Reformation) Christian teachings. So here I shall consider Charles Wesley as *theologos* in two senses: first, as *theologos* of historic Christian teachings; and then as *theologos* of the Wesleyan understanding of the 'way of salvation'.

## Charles Wesley, *theologos* of historic Christian teachings

In the first place, let us consider Charles Wesley as *theologos* of common or ecumenical Christian teachings. Like his brother John, Charles Wesley had been formed in an environment where he was exposed to the riches of historic Christian doctrinal and liturgical traditions. Both were formed in a particular culture – the inherited culture of Caroline Anglicanism – that had stressed the inheritance of doctrine and liturgy from the earliest Christian centuries.[8] Their mother, Susanna Wesley, had written a commentary on the Apostles' Creed, following the exposition of that creed by Anglican Bishop

John Pearson.[9] The doctrinal orthodoxy of their father, Samuel Wesley, is represented in the inscription on Samuel's tomb at Epworth:

As he liv'd so he died,
in the true Catholick Faith
of the Holy Trinity in Unity,
And that JESUS CHRIST is God
incarnate: and the only
Saviour of Mankind[10]

With this strong familial and cultural emphasis on consistency with the faith of the early Church, and with his own extensive study in Christian doctrine, Charles Wesley applied his poetic gifts to the exposition of historic Christian teachings.

While elsewhere in this book Charles' trinitarianism is dealt with in some detail,[11] it is worth noting here also, at least briefly, that it is with regard to this doctrine that we may find a clear example of Charles' role as *theologos* of historic Christian teachings. This can be seen, for example, in his collection of *Hymns on the Trinity* (1767).[12] This collection of 188 hymns was inspired by Charles' reading of William Jones' *The Catholic Doctrine of the Trinity* (1756) and, as did Jones' prose work, so also Charles Wesley's volume of hymns explicated historic trinitarian orthodoxy under four general headings:

1. The Divinity of Christ (hymns 1–57, nearly a third of the whole book).
2. The Divinity of the Holy Ghost (hymns 58–86).
3. The Plurality and Trinity of Persons (hymns 87–109).
4. The Trinity in Unity (hymns 110–36).

To these four main sections there is added a further group of 'Hymns and Prayers to the Trinity' (52 hymns numbered in a separate sequence). As Wilma Quantrille points out in her introduction to the Charles Wesley Society edition of *Hymns on the Trinity*, all of the hymns in this collection were written 'in doxological style'; that is, they were written as words to be sung to God in praise of the divine Trinity, and their intent was not primarily pedagogical or polemical (as William Jones' *Catholic Doctrine of the Trinity* had been).[13] Indeed, Charles writes explicitly in this collection that

Knowledge acquired by books or creeds
My learn'd self-righteous pride it feeds;
'Tis love that edifies.[14]

And yet, despite the warning that the knowledge acquired through books or creeds might feed one's pride, Charles does not hesitate to utilize the precise, technical language of the creeds and of historic doctrinal statements in his poetic explication of the mystery of the divine Trinity. So he utilizes technical terminology and historically defined doctrines in singing of the divine Trinity:

Hail Father, Son, and Spirit, great
before the birth of time,

Inthron'd in everlasting state
  Jehovah Eʟᴏʜɪᴍ!
A mystical plurality
  We in the Godhead own,
Adoring One in Persons Three
And Three in Nature One.[15]

Not only does this one verse utilize the technical terms 'Nature' (or 'substance', rendering *ousia*) and 'Persons' (*hypostaseis* or *prosopa*) that had been hammered out in the trinitarian controversies of the fourth century, it also utilizes Hebrew names of God (the plural ending evident in the word 'Elohim' suggesting the plurality of divine persons) and refers to the teaching of the co-eternality of the divine persons, the teaching that distinguished the orthodoxy of the first Councils of Nicaea (ᴀᴅ 325) and Constantinople (ᴀᴅ 381) from Arianism. All of this is accomplished within the space of eight short lines, 35 words, of poetry.

Another instance of Charles' acting in the role of *theologos* can be seen in his transmission of the Western Church's insistence on the *filioque* clause attached to the third article of the Nicene Creed, which holds that the Spirit proceeds 'from the Father *and the Son*'. Contemporary ecumenically minded Christians might prefer that he had known that the *filioque* had been added to the Creed subsequent to the Council of Constantinople, but Charles held this teaching to be part of the ancient inheritance of Christian faith and gives voice to it in the following words:

Our hearts are then convinc'd indeed
  That Christ is with the Father one;
The Spirit that doth from Both proceed.
  Attests the Co-eternal Son;[16]

Again in this case he has utilized the technical terminology of the Spirit's 'proceeding' from the Father and the Son ('that doth from Both proceed'), but this teaching is cast in the language of doxology, of worship.

Perhaps the most surprising instance of Charles' transmission of rather technical trinitarian teaching is a specific reference to the doctrine of *perichoresis* or circumincession, the teaching that all actions of the Godhead *ad extra*, that is, to the world apart from the Godhead, are performed by all the persons of the divine Trinity together. This teaching was not defined in the creeds or councils of the early Church but was part of the way in which Christian theologians explained the doctrine of the Trinity. The teaching of *perichoresis* became popular in late-twentieth-century systematic theology, and when Wesleyans looked for this teaching in the corpus of works of John and Charles Wesley, the only specific reference they could find was in Charles Wesley's *Hymns on the Trinity*:

God from hence, the God supreme
  We one and many know:
Every act that flows from Him
  Doth from Three Persons flow:[17]

Again, a very specific historic teaching is explicated, but in the form of direct address to the deity.

It is not only with reference to the teaching of the divine Trinity that Charles Wesley's verse utilizes precise language of historic Christian teachings. Consider the following verse that refers to the divine presence in the Eucharist:

> Let the wisest mortal show
>   How we the grace receive,
> Feeble elements bestow
>   A power not theirs to give.
> Who explains the wondrous way,
>   How through these the virtue came?
> These the virtue did convey,
>   Yet still remain the same.[18]

The term 'virtue' repeated twice in these verses might strike a reader as being out of place unless one realizes that 'virtue' was a crucial technical term in the debates over the manner of Christ's presence in the Eucharist. Steering a course between the Lutheran affirmation of bodily or corporeal presence on the one hand, and the Zwinglian belief that the presence of Christ in the Eucharist was simply that presence 'wherever two or more are gathered' (that is, a form of presence not distinctive of the eucharistic celebration), John Calvin and the main stream of the Reformed tradition had maintained that although Christ's literal body could not be present (since it had ascended to heaven), there is nevertheless a distinct spiritual 'power' available to those who receive the Eucharist with true faith. This spiritual power could not be identified with the literal body and blood of Christ (and so differs from the Lutheran view), but is distinctive, i.e., not simply the general form of Christ's presence apart from the Eucharist, and the term they used to describe this spiritual power was the Latin term *virtus* (which means 'power' or 'strength').[19] Understood in this way, the two references to 'virtue' as divine power or strength in the lines quoted above from Charles Wesley's hymn make perfectly good sense (in fact, one can see that 'virtue' is used in both cases as an appositive for 'power', which appears in one of the earlier lines cited), and these references to 'virtue' reveal again Charles' use of technical language to describe historic Christian teachings.

Charles Wesley's *Hymns on the Lord's Supper* (1745) and his *Hymns on the Trinity* (1767) serve as examples of hymns that exposit historic Christian teachings. It should be noted that, in addition to these collections of hymns on doctrinal subjects, in 1745 and 1746 Charles Wesley also issued a series of books containing collections of hymns for specific celebrations in the Christian liturgical year, including *Hymns on the Nativity* (1745), *Hymns for Our Lord's Resurrection* (1746), *Hymns for Ascension-Day* (1746), and *Hymns of Petition and Thanksgiving for the Promise of the Father*, subtitled *Hymns for Whitsunday* (1746). John R. Tyson has examined in detail the *Hymns for Our Lord's Resurrection* and has shown how this collection of hymns inculcates both traditional Christological doctrine and its implications for the life of a believer, focusing on the power of Christ's resurrection as empowering the believer in the quest for sancti-fication.[20] The entire sequence of Charles Wesley's hymns for the Christian festivals from 1745 to 1746 explicates the fullness of Christological teaching by way of the sequence of the liturgical year. In these cases, Charles does indeed weave together or 'synthesize' (as Tyson says) the themes of human redemp-tion and the out-working of the way of salvation with Christological material, but Charles' organizing principle in this sequence was the liturgical celebra-tion of the life of Christ, not the process of the way of salvation, which John Wesley would take as the organizing principle for his 1780 *Collection of Hymns for the Use of the People Called Methodists*. In this regard, it might be noted that the two most popular hymns of Charles Wesley, both within and outside of Methodist circles, are 'Hark, the herald angels sing' (1734, as altered subse-quently by George Whitefield and others) and 'Christ the Lord is risen today' (1739),[21] both of which celebrate Christological themes appropriate to the great Christian festivals of Christmas and Easter respectively, and neither of which appeared in the 1780 *Collection*. My point is that Charles Wesley's verse served theological ends far beyond the explication of the way of salvation, but one can argue that in the 1780 *Collection*, John Wesley gave a particular arrange-ment to Charles' verse in a way that led most subsequent interpreters, espe-cially those of the Wesleyan family, to see his contribution as lying chiefly in the area of the experience of the way of salvation (and on this, see the conclu-sion below). Even in the 1780 *Collection*, before the sections on sinners and believers and the way of salvation, John Wesley included a selection of hymns 'Describing the Goodness of God' as the presupposition of the theology of the way of salvation.[22]

There can be no doubt of Charles Wesley's creative abilities to express tradi-tional teachings. But his creativity stood beside his use of traditional doctrines and the traditional language that had been used to express those doctrines or teachings. That is to say, Charles Wesley not only sought to put historic teachings (about the divine Trinity, or the presence of Christ in the Eucharist) in contemporary terms, he also insisted on bringing believers into the rich-ness of the Christian Church's distinctive language for speaking of the divine mysteries. In this way he functioned as *theologos*, as one who gives us 'words' about 'God', words by which our tongues could confess the divine mysteries in the company of the historic Christian community and its teachings.

## Charles Wesley, *theologos* of the Wesleyan 'way of salvation'

Having said this about Charles Wesley's role as *theologos* of the broader Christian tradition, one must also affirm that he also served as a *theologos* of the distinctly Methodist teaching about the way of salvation. But if the back-ground to his role as *theologos* of the broader tradition lay in the traditions of Caroline Anglicanism which he and John had inherited, the background for his role of *theologos* of the way of salvation lay in the traditions of Puritan and Reformed theology and hymnody. J. R. Watson's study, *The English Hymn* (1997), has shown the critical role played by Puritans and then by Isaac Watts in the evolution of English hymns from the Reformed tradition's use of metrical English Psalms, including their use of the image of pilgrimage to Zion and their dramatic use of the first-person singular in addressing God.[23] A central focus in Puritan theology had been on the 'order of salvation' (*ordo salutis*) as the out-working of salvation in such typical stages as 'effectual calling', justification, sanctification and glorification.[24] At the same time as Charles Wesley was composing his verses, a Reformed hymn tradition was developing in the Welsh and English languages, explicating this understanding of the 'order of salvation'.[25] Charles, then, found himself the immediate heir of the tradition of Reformed spirituality expressed in the earlier hymn tradition and he became a participant in the flowering of the hymn tradition that was happening in his time as he explicated the Wesleyan understanding of the way of salvation.

The web of connections between Charles and John Wesley's interpretation of the 'way of salvation' and the Puritan and Reformed reading of the 'order of salvation' can be seen in treatments of 1 Corinthians 1.30: 'He is the source of your life in Christ Jesus, who became for us wisdom from God, and righteousness and sanctification and redemption' (NRSV). George Whitefield represented the Reformed understanding of this passage as reflecting the order of salvation: 'wisdom' is 'the fear of the Lord' and so implies repentance, 'righteousness' is justification, and 'redemption' is glorification, so that the Puritan understanding of the *ordo salutis* as effectual calling, justification, sanctification, and redemption can be seen in the verse.[26] John Wesley preached frequently on the same text and gave it his own understanding of the 'way of salvation'. Charles Wesley wrote a group of four hymns explicating this passage, published in the 1740 collection of *Hymns and Sacred Poems*. Although he did not explicitly take 'wisdom' to denote evangelical repentance in the hymn on 'Christ our wisdom', he did take 'Christ our righteousness' to refer to Christ as the ground of our pardon or justification, he took 'Christ our sanctification' to refer to Christ as the ground of the believer's sanctification, and he took 'Christ our redemption' to refer to the promise of redemption beyond death.[27] In this respect. Charles can be understood as voicing a Wesleyan interpretation of the common Wesleyan and Reformed theme of the way of the believer's spiritual pilgrimage. As early as 1740, his brother John was at work organizing and explicating his hymns as they interpreted the way of salvation.[28]

Despite the connection between the Reformed tradition and hymns celebrating the way of the Christian life, however, Charles Wesley showed himself consistently the advocate of a Wesleyan and Arminian understanding of human nature and salvation, especially celebrating the free gift of salvation available to all persons. This appears frequently in his addresses to sinners: 'harlots', 'thieves', 'ruffians' and the like:

Outcasts of men, to you I call,
Harlots and publicans and thieves!
He spreads his arms t'embrace you all,
Sinners alone his grace receives:
No need of him the righteous have,
He came the lost to seek and save.

Come all ye Magdalens in lust,
Ye ruffians fell in murders old;
Repent and live: despair and trust!
Jesus for you to death was sold;
Tho' hell protest and earth repine;
He died for crimes like yours – and mine![29]

The same image of Christ as the friend of all sinners appears in the hymn that was shortened by John Wesley and became 'O for a thousand tongues to sing':

Harlots, and publicans, and thieves,
In holy triumph join!
Sav'd is the sinner that believes
From crimes as great as mine!

Murtherers and all ye hellish crew,
Ye sons of lust and pride,
Believe the Saviour died for you;
For me the Saviour died.[30]

In other places Charles Wesley makes clear the universal scope of salvation in direct opposition to claims of limited atonement, implying that the latter view impugns the goodness of God:

Was there a single soul *decreed*
Thy unrelenting hate to know,
Then I were he – and well might dread
The horrors of eternal woe . . .

Whoe'er admits; my soul disowns
the image of a tort'ring God,
Well pleased with human shrieks and groans,
A fiend, a Molock gorg'd with blood!

Good God! That any child of thine,
So horribly should think of thee!
Lo, all my hopes I here resign,
If all may not find grace with me.[31]

Charles Wesley also emphasized the Wesleyan teaching of entire sanctification as he explicated the way of salvation. This can be seen in the hymn on 'Christ our sanctification' from the sequence on 1 Corinthians 1.30 in the 1740 *Hymns and Sacred Poems*:

Reign in me, Lord, thy foes control,
Who would not own thy sway;
Diffuse thine image thro' my soul,
Shine to the perfect day . . .

My inward holiness thou art,
For faith hath made thee mine:
With all thy fulness fill my heart,
Till all I am is thine.[32]

But it is a very frequent theme in Charles Wesley's verse:

Breathe, O breathe the loving Spirit
Into every troubled breast,
Let us all in thee inherit,
Let us find that second rest:
Take away our power of sinning,
Alpha and omega be,
End of faith as its beginning,
Set our hearts at liberty.[33]

In one respect, Charles Wesley's verse dealing with the 'way of salvation' shows a parallel tendency to his verse explicating historic Christian doctrine, and that is in his utilization of technical vocabulary. In the case of the Methodist and evangelical understanding of the way of salvation, the vocabulary itself was still emerging, but Charles' verse offers plenty of instances of such key terms as 'repentance', 'awakened', 'justified' and 'sanctified'. Consider the following verse, which John included in the 1780 *Collection* under the heading 'For Mourners Brought to the Birth':

Plenteous he is in truth and grace,
He wills that all the fallen race
    Should turn, repent, and live;
His pardoning grace for all is free;
Transgression, sin, iniquity
    He freely doth forgive.[34]

This verse refers explicitly both to the universal call to repentance and to the universal availability of 'pardoning grace', which John Wesley would elsewhere identify with justifying grace. Printed editions of Charles Wesley's hymns often have titles utilizing more technical theological vocabulary (for example, 'Gratitude for our conversion' or 'Justified, but not sanctified') although at some points it is not clear whether Charles himself entitled the poems or whether the titles were the work of John Wesley.[35] In some cases, Charles Wesley entitled whole collections of hymns utilizing the distinct language of the Wesleyan way of salvation: the title of his 1747 *Hymns for Those that Seek, and Those that Have Redemption in the Blood of Jesus Christ* has categories (seeking or 'groaning for redemption') that John Wesley would later utilize in organizing the 1780 *Collection of Hymns*.[36]

John Wesley's arrangement of the Charles Wesley hymn corpus in the 1780 *Collection* did a faithful job of communicating the content of Charles' hymns as respects the teaching about the way of salvation. But even as respects the spiritual pilgrimage, the schema given by John Wesley had a tendency to reduce some of Charles Wesley's more complex hymns to one or another point in the 'way of salvation', where Charles' own texts were multivalent and dealt (sometimes simultaneously) with different stages of the Christian journey. One suspects that John's arrangement also had the tendency not to include Charles' texts that were in fact more ambiguous as to where they might fit in the schematized 'way of salvation'. Perhaps most notably in this regard, 'Wrestling Jacob' ('Come, O thou traveler unknown') was first published by Charles Wesley in 1742 and so had been in use for 38 years when John compiled the 1780 *Collection*. Why this notable omission? The reason, I suspect, is that the poem progresses from recognition of sin (repentance) through justification and the assurance of pardon:

'Tis Love, 'tis love, thou diedst for me,
I hear thy whisper in my heart.
The morning breaks, the shadows flee:
Pure UNIVERSAL LOVE thou art.[37]

It would be difficult to include it either in the schematized section that includes 'praying for repentance' ('Part Third' of the 1780 *Collection*) or in the section that includes 'believers rejoicing' ('Part Fourth' of the 1780 *Collection*). When Methodists subsequently included the poem in their hymnals, they found it difficult to decide into which section of 'The Christian Life' it should be fitted. Given John's own admission in his funeral address for Charles that this was his brother's poetic masterpiece, it would appear that John's selections for the 1780 *Collection* were grounded more in didactic considerations than in considerations of the poetic qualities or even the broader spiritual values of Charles' verse.

Perhaps it was Charles Wesley's poetic mindset that enabled him to explore the depths of Christian experience in ways that were more complex and in some ways more nuanced than his brother's analytical schemes would allow, but this was his great contribution as *theologos* of the way of salvation, and it is in this respect that Rattenbury was justified in calling Charles 'the prince of experimental theologians'. Charles Wesley gave us profound words that express the depth and the complexity of the Christian pilgrimage empowered by divine grace.

## Conclusion

John Wesley's introduction to the 1780 *Collection of Hymns* stated that the collection 'is large enough to contain all the important truths of our most holy religion'.[38] This might be true in the sense that one could delve into the 1780 *Collection* and find references to all of the most central Christian teachings. But we might have to protest to John that his organization of the *Collection* highlights the 'evangelical' doctrines associated with the Christian experience of the 'way of salvation'. As John himself stated it, the hymns are 'carefully ranged under proper heads, according to the experience of real Christians'.[39] Thus the organization of these hymns does not highlight Charles Wesley's work as *theologos* of the broader Christian tradition, and sets in place the view of Charles Wesley consistently represented in Methodist tradition according to which he is pre-eminently the hymnist of religious experience.

There is a sense in which each of these poles of Charles Wesley's work as *theologos* came to be represented structurally in the organization of subsequent Methodist hymnals. The 'evangelical doctrines' were enshrined in sections in Methodist hymnals entitled 'The Sinner' and 'The Christian', or simply, 'The Christian Life', a consistent mark of Methodist hymnals from the time of the 1780 *Collection*.[40] From the time of the first Methodist hymnals subsequent to the 1780 *Collection*, Methodist hymnals consistently begin with a section of hymns in praise of the divine Trinity, with separate sections on God (typically, very seldom 'The Father'), Jesus Christ, and the Holy Spirit. One could argue that explicit and sustained material on the Trinity was missing from the 1780 *Collection* only because that collection was intended for a religious society within the Church of England, and it presupposed the trinitarian devotion of the Book of Common Prayer. The appearance of the initial section in praise of the Trinity (from 1846 in Methodist hymnals in the USA) does reflect the ecumenical side of the hymn tradition inherited from Charles Wesley, although by the time Methodists began adding material on the divine Trinity to their hymnals, they had also begun to utilize a wide range of hymn writers in addition to Charles Wesley.[41]

Methodist hymnals are only the most outward and visible expression of a theological and spiritual tradition that was initiated with John and Charles Wesley. Hymnals were complemented by catechisms, tracts and pamphlets, and eventually by full-fledged works of systematic theology explicating a Wesleyan understanding of the Christian faith and, in particular, of the way of the Christian life.[42] With respect to this developing Methodist theological and spiritual tradition, both John and Charles Wesley were *theologoi* insofar as they gave us words about God to which this theological and spiritual tradition has consistently turned. Their relevance to the theological tradition lies not only in their own contributions but in their giving birth to this distinctive theological and spiritual tradition.

And yet again, it is not to a single spiritual and theological tradition to which Charles Wesley made his theological and spiritual contributions. John Wesley's sermons and his other writings might indeed be studied today primarily by Methodists, but Charles Wesley's verse has become part of the ecumenical Christian inheritance, with his verses sung by Presbyterians, Baptists, Pentecostals, Lutherans, Catholics and others, as well as Anglicans and Methodists. John and Charles Wesley are today celebrated on 2 March (the date of John Wesley's death) in the sanctoral calendar of the Evangelical Lutheran Church in America, and they are celebrated on 3 March in the sanctoral calendar of the Episcopal Church in the US and in the calendars of other Anglican churches through the world.[43] Charles Wesley himself might be amazed or embarrassed at this fact, and at the title of a hymnal supplement in current use in the Episcopal Church in the USA that borrows a line from one of his hymns, *Wonder, Love and Praise*.[44] But however Charles himself might be amazed at these witnesses to his influence on the continuing life of the Church, they are appropriate, and on the occasion of the 300th anniversary of his birth we acknowledge his role in giving words to the people of God by which they may express their 'wonder, love, and praise'. We give thanks for Charles Wesley's role as *theologos* of the Wesleyan tradition and of the Christian faith.

Finish then thy new creation,
Pure and sinless let us be,
Let us see thy great salvation,
Perfectly restor'd in thee;
Chang'd from glory into glory,
Till in heaven we take our place,
Till we cast our crowns before thee
Lost in wonder, love, and praise![45]

## Notes

1 Charles Wesley hymn in *BE*, 7.112.

2 Albert C. Outler, 'John Wesley: Folk-Theologian', *Theology Today*, 34 [July 1977], 150–60; Randy Maddox, *Responsible Grace: John Wesley's Practical Theology* (Nashville: Kingswood Books imprint of Abingdon Press, 1994), 15–18.

3 Rattenbury, *Evangelical Doctrines*, 85.

4 Rattenbury, *Evangelical Doctrines*, 85.

5 S T Kimbrough Jr, 'Lyrical Theology', *Journal of Theology*, 98 [1994], 18–43.

6 Cf. Aidan Kavanagh, *On Liturgical Theology* (New York: Pueblo Publishing, 1984), 74–5; and cf. Maddox, *Responsible Grace*, 15–18.

7 Cf. the introduction that Franz Hildebrandt wrote for the critical edition of the 1780 *Hymnal*; *BE*, 7.3–4.

8 Ted A. Campbell, *John Wesley and Christian Antiquity: Religious vision and cultural change* (Nashville: Kingswood Books imprint of the Abingdon Press, 1991), 9–21.

9 In Wallace, *Susanna*, 377–407.

10 Quoted in Adam Clarke, *Memoirs of the Wesley Family* (New York: Lane and Tippett, 2nd edn, 1848), 281.

11 See below, Chapter 16.

12 Charles Wesley, *Hymns on the Trinity* (Bristol: Felix Farley, 1767; reprint edn, Madison: The Charles Wesley Society, 1998).

13 Wilma Quantrille, introduction to the *Hymns on the Trinity* in the reprint edition of the Charles Wesley Society (1998) cited above, vii–ix.

14 Charles Wesley, *Hymns on the Trinity*, No. 19 in the separate sequence of 'Hymns and Prayers to the Trinity' (p. 102).

15 Charles Wesley, *Hymns on the Trinity*, No. 87 in the initial sequence (p. 58); this is the initial verse of the first hymn in the section on 'The Plurality and Trinity of Persons'.

16 Charles Wesley, *Hymns on the Trinity*, No. 63 in the initial sequence (p. 42); cf. Quantrille's introductory comments on this, x–xi.

17 Charles Wesley, *Hymns on the Trinity*, No. 99 in the initial sequence (p. 64); cf. Wilma J. Quantrille, *The Triune God in the Hymns of Charles Wesley* (PhD dissertation, Drew University, 1989), 119.

18 Charles Wesley, hymn from *Hymns on the Lord's Supper* (1745), No. 57, in Rattenbury, *Eucharistic Hymns*, 213.

19 Cf. John Calvin, *Institutes* IV.17.10–12 (in John T. McNeill, ed., *Calvin: Institutes of the Christian Religion* [2 vols, Library of Christian Classics series; Philadelphia: The Westminster Press, 1960], 2.1370–3). McNeill used the term 'virtualism' to describe Calvin's sacramental views in this edition of Calvin's *Institutes* (2.1370, n. 27); cf. Ted A. Campbell, *Christian Confessions* (Louisville: Westminster John Knox Press, 1996), 181–3.

20 John R. Tyson, 'The Lord of Life is Risen: Theological Reflections on *Hymns for our Lord's Resurrection* (1746)', *Proceedings of the Charles Wesley Society*, 7 (2001), 81–99.

21 Charles Yrigoyen Jr, *Praising the God of Grace: The theology of Charles Wesley's hymns* (Nashville: Abingdon Press, 2005), xi.

22 In the *Collection of Hymns for the Use of the People Called Methodists*, hymns 22–38 (in *BE*, 7.107–28).

23 J. R. Watson, *The English Hymn: A critical and historical study* (Oxford: Oxford University Press, 1997), 110–32 (the emphasis on Christian experience in earlier Puritan hymns), 136–7 (Watt's use of the image of the pilgrimage to Zion), and 160–70 (the dramatic use of the first-person singular in Watts' 'When I survey the wondrous cross').

24 Cf. Ted A. Campbell, *The Religion of the Heart* (Columbia: University of South Carolina Press, 1991), 44–53. [William Perkins,] *A Golden Chaine, or The Description of Theologie, Containing the Order of the Causes of Salvation and Damnation, according to God's Word*, 2nd edn (Cambridge: John Legate, 1597); the four 'degrees' of salvation are specifically outlined on pages 138, 145, 149 [mislabelled as '145'] and 168; on these stages, more broadly, cf. William Haller, *The Rise of Puritanism, Or, The Way to the New Jerusalem as Set Forth in Pulpit and Press from Thomas Cartwright to John Lilburne and John Milton, 1570–1643* (New York: Columbia University Press, 1938), 86–92. William Ames, *The Marrow of Theology* (tr. John Dykstra Eusden; The United Church Press, 1968; reprint edn, Durham, NC: The Labyrinth Press, 1983), 157–74.

25 Ted A. Campbell, '"Guide Me, O Thou Great Jehovah": Contributions of Welsh and English Calvinists to Worship in Eighteenth-Century England', *Proceedings of the Charles Wesley Society*, 1994, 67–84.

26 George Whitefield, sermon on 'Christ the Believer's Wisdom, Righteousness, Sanctification, and Redemption', in *Sermons on Important Subjects: With a memoir of the author, by Samuel Drew, and a dissertation on his character, preaching, &c., by the Rev. Joseph Smith* (London: H. Fisher, Son, and P. Jackson, 1828), 500–18.

27 Charles Wesley, hymns on 'Christ Our Wisdom', 'Christ Our Righteousness', 'Christ Our Sanctification', and 'Christ Our Redemption', in John and Charles Wesley, *Hymns and Sacred Poems* (London: W. Strahan, 1740), hereafter cited as '*Hymns and Sacred Poems* (1740)', 94–9.

28 See the introduction to *Hymns and Sacred Poems* (1740), presumably by John Wesley, which explicates the 'way of salvation' in serial order (iii–xi).

29 Charles Wesley, hymn 'Christ, the Friend of Sinners'; in John and Charles Wesley, *Hymns and Sacred Poems* (London: William Strahan, 1739), 102. In this and the following quotations from original publications of Charles Wesley hymns, I have utilized the original spelling and punctuation, but I have modernized the capitalization of words and have generally left out Charles Wesley's italicized words except as noted.

30 Hymn 'For the Anniversary Day of One's Conversion', in *Hymns and Sacred Poems* (1740), 122. The hymn appears in the 1780 *Collection* as hymn No. 1 (in *BE*, 7.79–80), although these verses were not included.

31 Charles Wesley, hymn entitled 'Another' (following a hymn on 'Universal Redemption'), stanzas 5, 7, and 8, in *Hymns and Sacred Poems* (1740), 134 and 135. This is part of a series of three hymns on 'Universal Redemption' in this collection, 132–42.

32 Charles Wesley, hymn on 'Christ Our Sanctification', in *Hymns and Sacred Poems* (1740), 97 and 98.

33 Charles Wesley, hymn ix, 'To – Jesus, show us thy Salvation', in Charles Wesley, *Hymns for Those that Seek, and Those that Have Redemption in the Blood of Jesus Christ* (London: Felix Farley, 1747), 13.

34 In the *Collection of Hymns for the Use of the People Called Methodists*, hymn 138 (in *BE*, 7.255). I have retained Charles Wesley's italicized 'decreed' in this case, since it serves to contrast his views with the doctrine of limited atonement.

35 The titles quoted in parentheses are from *Hymns and Sacred Poems* (1739), 150 and 198.

36 See the bibliographical reference above for *Hymns for Those that Seek, and Those that Have Redemption in the Blood of Jesus Christ* (1747).

37 Charles Wesley, poem entitled 'Wrestling Jacob', in John and Charles Wesley, *Hymns and Sacred Poems* (Bristol: Felix Farley, 1742), 117.

38 John Wesley, introduction to the *Collection of Hymns for the Use of the People Called Methodists*, in *BE*, 7.73–5, pp. 73–4.

39 *BE*, 7.74.

40 Cf. Carlton R. Young, *An Introduction to the New Methodist Hymnal* (Nashville: Methodist Publishing House/Graded Press, 1966), 7. In the current British Methodist hymnal, *Hymns and Psalms* (1983), this is represented in the hymnal section on 'The Christian Life', comprising hymns 661–751. In the current *United Methodist Hymnal* (1989), this is is represented in the sections on 'Prevenient Grace' (hymns 337–60), 'Justifying Grace' (hymns 361–81) and 'Sanctifying and Perfecting Grace' (hymns 382–536).

41 In the current British Methodist hymnal, *Hymns and Psalms* (1983), this is represented in the hymnal sections on 'The Eternal Father (hymns 21–73), 'The Eternal Word' (hymns 74–278) and 'The Eternal Spirit' (hymns 279–328). In the current *United Methodist Hymnal* (1989), this is is represented in the sections on 'The Glory of the Triune God' (hymns 57–152), 'The Grace of Jesus Christ' (hymns 153–327) and 'The Power of the Holy Spirit' (hymns 328–36).

42 Cf. Ted A. Campbell, 'John Wesley and the Legacy of Methodist Theology', *Bulletin of the John Rylands University Library of Manchester*, 85, 2–3), 405–20.

43 On 3 March in Anglican calendars rather than 2 March, because the feast of St Chad of Lichfield falls on 2 March in Anglican calendars, and so 'John and Charles Wesley, Priests' are commemorated on the next day.

44 *Wonder, Love, and Praise: A supplement to the Hymnal 1982* (New York: Church Publishing, 1997).

45 Charles Wesley, in *Hymns for Those that Seek, and Those that Have Redemption in the Blood of Jesus Christ* (1747), 14.

# 16. Charles Wesley and the Revival of the Doctrine of the Trinity: A Methodist Contribution to Modern Theology

## JASON E. VICKERS

> If anything is wanting, it is the application, lest it should appear to be a mere speculative doctrine, which has no influence on our hearts and lives; but this is abundantly supplied by my brother's *Hymns*. (John Wesley on the Trinity, in a letter to Mary Bishop, 17 April 1776)

This chapter is about two things. First and foremost, it is about Charles Wesley's efforts to revive trinitarian doctrine and piety in eighteenth-century England. On this front, I will show the uniqueness of Charles' approach to the Trinity by comparing and contrasting it with other attempts to defend the Trinity in late seventeenth- and eighteenth-century England. More specifically, I will show that, whereas the majority of theologians in this period were preoccupied with defending the immanent Trinity as compatible with or confirmable by reason, Charles sought to ground a revival of trinitarian piety and worship in the saving activities of the Triune God, that is, in the divine economy. I will suggest that, in doing so, Charles recovered an approach to the Trinity that was in keeping with the origins of trinitarian doctrine and piety, i.e., with the approach to the Trinity that stresses the bond between the doctrine of God on the one hand, and the doctrine of salvation on the other.[1] Second, this essay is intended to aid in a much-needed reassessment of the place of both Charles Wesley and early Methodism in the history of Christian doctrine and theology. Early Methodism continues to be regarded by many as making little or no contribution in the history of doctrine and theology.[2] The reason for this has to do with a particular conception of what theology is and upon what it depends; namely, according to some, epistemology or speculative metaphysics.[3] On this conception, the theologian is primarily concerned with demonstrating the rationality or justification of Christian beliefs, or with the fit between Christian beliefs and a favoured speculative metaphysics. As much as any other factor, it is this conception of theology that leads to the loss of trinitarian piety and doctrine in late seventeenth- and eighteenth-century England and, subsequently, in modern theology. By contrast, Charles and John Wesley understood the theological task as primarily catechetical and doxological in nature.[4] John and Charles Wesley emphasized the therapeutic or healing power of theology (what they termed 'divinity') long before it was fashionable to do so.[5] Thus I will conclude this essay by suggesting that, in the light of the increasingly widespread emphasis on recovering both the therapeutic nature of the theological task and the economic ground for the doctrine of the Trinity, the time is ripe for a reappraisal of Charles Wesley's place in the history of theology.

## The Trinity and rational theology in seventeenth- and early-eighteenth century England

In order truly to appreciate Charles Wesley's efforts to revive trinitarian doctrine and piety, we must first come to grips with both the approach to theology and the understanding of the Trinity that prevailed among Protestant theologians in seventeenth- and early eighteenth-century England. First and foremost, it is important to recall that, in that period, there was no more heavily contested doctrine than that of the Trinity. From 1680 to 1730 an intense controversy over the Trinity was carried out in dozens, if not hundreds, of treatises, sermons, pamphlets and other propaganda materials. Virtually all of the leading figures in English Protestant theology were involved in the controversy, including Edward Stillingfleet (1635–99), John Locke (1632–1704), John Tillotson (1630–94), William Sherlock (1641–1707), Robert South (1634–1716), Samuel Clarke (1675–1729) and Daniel Waterland (1683–1740), to name but a few. The sheer volume of this material raises an obvious question: how did a doctrine that was secured originally and reaffirmed repeatedly by ecumenical church councils and, most recently, by its inclusion in the Church of England's 'Thirty-Nine Articles of Religion' become a matter of such deep controversy and disagreement?

The story of the trinitarian controversy in late seventeenth- and early eighteenth-century England is both long and complex, and we cannot go into it at any length here.[6] For our purposes, two crucial features of the debates are worth noticing, however. First, virtually everyone involved was concerned almost exclusively with the *immanent* Trinity. Otherwise put, they were utterly preoccupied with giving a rational account of the divine nature rather than with reflection on what God had done in and through God's personal dealings with human persons in creation, in the Incarnation, and in the coming of the Holy Spirit, i.e., with the so-called *economic* Trinity. Their overriding concern was to provide an account of the concept of personhood on which belief in three divine persons did not entail belief in three distinct gods or tri-theism.

Second, everyone involved in the controversy, including persons attacking as well as persons defending the Trinity, assumed that the primary task of theology was to demonstrate the rationality of Christian beliefs. Thus defenders of the Trinity set out to show that the immanent Trinity was compatible not only with various accounts of personhood, but also with the conceptions of reason and rationality in which the accounts of personhood were embedded. For example, William Sherlock attempted to show that the immanent Trinity was compatible with a Cartesian account of personhood, a proposal that invariably involved an appeal to a Cartesian conception of reason.[7] By contrast, Edward Stillingfleet tried to demonstrate that the immanent Trinity was compatible with a Lockean view of personhood and the related Lockean account of reason.[8] Stephen Nye, an ordained priest in the Church of England and one of the chief Socinian antagonists, astutely observed that there were Platonist, Aristotelian, Ciceronian and Cartesian doctrines of the Trinity, depending on the origins of the concept of personhood and reason with which the Trinity was purportedly compatible.[9]

At this stage, we do not need to go into further detail concerning the various proposals that emerged. Rather, we need to say a little more about what gave rise to the preoccupation with the reasonableness or intelligibility of the immanent Trinity in the first place. Once again, there is a long story to be told, and we do not have space to present the full range of developments in anything approximating their complexity.[10]

Two crucial developments in seventeenth-century English Protestant theology stand out in the background to the trinitarian controversy: on the one hand is Archbishop Laud (1573–1645) and William Chillingworth's (1602–44) linking of an Arminian doctrine of faith-as-*assensus* to a doctrine of assurance; and on the other is the emergence and spread of Polish Socinianism, the English variant of which would come to be known as Unitarianism. It is important that we take these developments in this order.

By the early seventeenth century, the Reformed doctrine of divine inscrutability had led to a growing crisis of assurance in England.[11] On the Reformed scheme, the Holy Spirit enabled people to discern that scripture was the word of God, but the Spirit did not shed light on whether people were among the elect. Indeed, many felt that it was impossible for people to know their standing with God.

Taking their cues from an emerging Arminianism, Archbishop Laud and Chillingworth sought to persuade English Protestants that humans had a role in their salvation. Rather than appeal to the Holy Spirit, they argued that people could discern by natural or unaided human reason that scripture was the word of God. For example, Archbishop Laud says:

> For though this truth, That Scripture is the word of God, is not so demonstratively evident *a priori*, as to enforce assent; yet it is strengthened so abundantly with probable arguments, both from the light of nature itself and human testimony, that he must be very wilful and self-conceited that shall dare to suspect it.[12]

Having argued that by natural reason human persons could recognize divine revelation in scripture, Archbishop Laud went on to argue that they could also comprehend the contents of scripture by reason. In fact, Laud argued that God gave reason to human persons precisely so that they could have access to salvation, saying,

> And certainly God did not give this admirable faculty of reasoning to the soul of man for any cause more prime than this, to discover, or to judge and allow, within the sphere of its own activity . . . of the way to Himself, when and howsoever it should be discovered.[13]

Finally, Laud made clear that, through the use of natural reason, people could be assured of their salvation. Upon discerning that scripture is the word of God, the most important thing that we must do is to give our 'full and firm assent' to those things contained in or deduced from scripture. 'This assent', said Laud, 'is called faith.'[14] Thus Laud introduced into English Protestant theology a critical transition in the understanding of faith. Rather than thinking of faith primarily as *fiducia* or personal trust in God, seventeenth- and eighteenth-century English Protestant theologians came increasingly to conceive of faith primarily as *assensus* or rational assent to intelligible propositions.[15]

After Laud laid the initial groundwork, Chillingworth finished setting the stage by insisting that those things that are necessary to be believed for salvation are contained in clear and intelligible propositions in scripture. Chillingworth says,

> [Scripture is] sufficiently perfect and sufficiently intelligible in things necessary, to all that have understanding, whether learned or unlearned. And my reason hereof is convincing and demonstrative, because nothing is necessary to be believed but what is plainly revealed. *For to say, that when a place of Scripture, by reason of ambiguous terms, lies indifferent between divers senses, whereof one is true and the other false, that God obliges men, under pain of damnation, not to mistake through error and human frailty, is to make God a tyrant;* and to say, that he requires us certainly to attain that end, for the attaining whereof we have no certain means; which is to say, that, like Pharaoh, he gives no straw, and requires brick, that he reaps where he sows not; that he gathers where he strews not . . . that he will not accept of us according to that which we have, but requireth of us what we have not.[16]

Like Laud and Chillingworth, most seventeenth-century English Protestant theologians simply assumed that the classical doctrines of the Christian faith – for example, those doctrines contained in the 'Thirty-Nine Articles of Religion' – were in fact contained in clear and intelligible propositions in scripture. Yet it is precisely here that the second background development – the spread of Polish Socinianism – comes on to the stage. Put simply, the Socinians maintained that many of the doctrines contained in the 'Thirty-Nine Articles' were unintelligible to reason, and none more so than the doctrine of the Trinity.[17]

What made the Socinian assertion that the Trinity is unintelligible so problematic was that clear and intelligible propositions were supposed to be readily understandable by anyone endowed with reason. This approach to theology had been attractive in the first place because the propositions necessary to be believed for salvation were said to be so clear and obvious that the 'man on the street' could recognize them and, upon giving his assent, be assured of salvation.[18] Presumably, propositions this clear would not be the sort of thing over which one could expect any significant disagreement.[19] When Socinian sympathizers in England challenged the intelligibility of the Trinity, English Protestant theologians had little choice but to assume the burden of proof, demonstrating that the Trinity was in fact among the things contained in clear and intelligible propositions in scripture and therefore necessary to be believed for salvation.

Repeated attempts to show the Trinity intelligible on Aristotelian, Cartesian and Lockean conceptions of personhood and reason made one thing painfully obvious. If persons had to comprehend Aristotelian, Cartesian or Lockean philosophy in order to see that the Trinity was intelligible, then the Trinity was not the sort of thing that was clear and intelligible to the 'man on the street'. Not surprisingly, by the turn of the eighteenth century, an increasing number of people reached the conclusion that, even if the Trinity turned out to be intelligible on, say, a Lockean conception of reason, it was surely not among the things necessary to be believed for salvation. For example, after declaring that he believed in the Trinity, Philipp van Limborch, the Dutch theologian and close personal friend of John Locke, hastened to add, 'Yet we dare not say 'tis necessary to be believed in order to Salvation.'[20]

Working backwards through these developments, we can now see that Charles Wesley and the early Methodists inhabited a world of theological sensibilities in which three critical transitions had taken place. First, there was a transition in and around the doctrine of divine revelation away from the Holy Spirit and toward human reason. This transition was intimately related to a second transition in which the prevailing understanding of faith migrated from *fiducia*, or personal trust in God, to *assensus*, or rational assent to intelligible propositions. Finally, the emphasis on reason and the view of faith as having primarily to do with rational assent to intelligible propositions combined to produce a third transition, namely the capacity to separate in theological reflection the immanent Trinity from the economic Trinity. This capacity was eventually realized in the subsequent quests for a concept of personhood and reason on which the doctrine of the immanent Trinity would appear intelligible.[21]

## The revival of the *economic* Trinity in Charles Wesley's sermons

While many of his English Protestant theological predecessors and contemporaries were preoccupied with showing that the propositional content of the doctrine of the immanent Trinity is compatible with reason, Charles Wesley's approach to and understanding of the Trinity was concerned primarily with the economic Trinity. More specifically, while other theologians were trying, unsuccessfully, to demonstrate the intelligibility of the immanent Trinity, Charles was gradually recovering a doctrine of the Trinity through extended reflection on the work of the Holy Spirit in bringing persons to God. As we will see, there is a major difference between Charles' approach to theology and the prevailing approach to theology in post-Restoration England, for whereas many of Charles' predecessors and contemporaries were primarily concerned with epistemological questions, Charles was primarily concerned with ontological matters, for example, with our encounter with God in the Incarnation, with the coming of the Holy Spirit to dwell in us at our baptism, with our meeting and coming to know God in worship, and the like.

Before we turn to Charles' doctrine of the economic Trinity, we should take a moment to say a word about recent scholarship on Charles' doctrine of the Trinity. When scholars have sought to get at Charles' understanding of the Trinity, they have turned primarily, if not exclusively, to two sources, namely, the 1746 collection of hymns entitled *Gloria Patri, &c., or Hymns to the Trinity*, and to the 1767 collection simply entitled *Hymns on the Trinity*.[22] To be sure, Charles is best known for his hymns, so this tendency in scholarship is understandable. An exclusive reliance on Charles' hymns, however, obscures a crucial component in his overall development as a trinitarian theologian, namely, the marked increase in his interest in the presence and work of the Holy Spirit beginning in 1738-9.[23] In order to view this development, the best place to look is Charles' sermons.[24]

Charles' interest in the Holy Spirit undergoes two important transitions in the sermons.[25] First, there was a transition from an early binitarian period, in which there are not any clear references to the Holy Spirit, to an initial period of interest in and reflection upon the work of the Holy Spirit (1738-9). In this period, however, Charles does not integrate his emerging doctrine of the Holy Spirit into a wider trinitarian framework in any meaningful way. Second, there is a transition from the period of initial interest in the Holy Spirit to a period in which Charles' sermons are virtually saturated with talk of the Holy Spirit (1740-2). In this period, he integrates his reflections on the Holy Spirit into a robust theology of the economic Trinity.

We now turn to a more detailed analysis of these transitions in Charles' theology.

In the three sermons dated before 1738 which are clearly Charles' own compositions, and not ones copied from John (Sermons 1-3 in Newport's edition), one looks in vain for clear references to the Holy Spirit. This is especially startling in light of the fact that these sermons are largely about the pursuit of holiness or Christian perfection and the need for singleness of focus. For example, in the second undisputed sermon, Charles declares, 'We say then that a state of voluntary imperfection, a half *course* of piety, a life divided between God and the world, is a state which God has nowhere promised to accept nor yet assured us of a reward for it.'[26] Similarly, in the third undisputed sermon, Charles reflects on the way in which Christian virtues stem from the graces of humility, faith, hope and love. Yet his theological outlook was, implicitly at least, binitarian, as references to the work of the Holy Spirit are noticeably absent.

The first clear references to the Holy Spirit occur in the sermons preached in the period 1738-9, or what is commonly viewed as the period of Charles' evangelical conversion.[27] There is some evidence that his interest in the presence and work of the Holy Spirit first emerges sometime after his evangelical conversion, as all three candidates for the so-called 'conversion hymn' are binitarian in content.[28] Where the conversion hymns are silent, however, the sermons in this period are not. In the fourth undisputed sermon – a sermon that Charles preached at least 21 times between 1738 and 1739 – he depicts the Spirit at work convicting persons of sin and ultimately rescuing them from sin. Moreover, Charles refers to the activity of the Spirit in fulfilling the promises of scripture to a soul 'thus disposed for Christ', giving special attention to the activity of comforting and bringing assurance of salvation.[29]

Despite this initial interest in the activity of the Holy Spirit in the fourth undisputed sermon, Charles had yet fully to integrate the activity of the Holy Spirit into his theology. This is true of the sixth and seventh undisputed sermons as well. Thus, while Charles stresses that the Spirit convicts persons of sin and frees them from it, he does not connect the work of the Spirit with Christ or with the Father in any significant way. The real flowering of Charles' trinitarian theology was, however, just around the corner.

Beginning with the seventh undisputed sermon, Charles deliberately integrates his reflections on the presence and work of the Holy Spirit into a wider doctrine of the economic Trinity. Once again, Charles begins by noting the Spirit's work in convicting persons of and rescuing them from sin. He then reflects on the Spirit's role in divine revelation, saying,

> So our Lord assures us no man can come unto the Son except the Father draw him. No man cometh to Father, but by the Son. They only believe, to whom it is given to know the mind of Christ. Eye hath not seen, nor ear heard, neither have entered into the heart of man, the things which God hath prepared for them that love him. But God hath revealed them unto us by his Spirit, for the Spirit searcheth all things, yea, the deep things of God. For what man knoweth the things of a man but the spirit of man which is in him? Even so the things of God knoweth no man but the Spirit of God. But the natural man receiveth not the things of the Spirit of God, for they are foolishness unto him; neither can he know them because they are spiritually discerned. God hath hid these things from the wise and prudent, and revealed them unto babes. No man knoweth the Son but the Father, neither knoweth any man the Father save the Son, and he to whomsoever the Son will reveal him.[30]

Here, Charles' theology is beginning to move in the direction of a robust doctrine of the economic Trinity. Thus the Spirit makes known to us the Son who in turn reveals the Father. Unlike many of his seventeenth-century English Protestant predecessors, Charles emphasizes the role of the Spirit and not the role of unaided or natural reason in discerning divine revelation. Indeed, Charles virtually excludes the possibility of identifying or comprehending divine revelation by reason alone, saying:

> These and numberless other Scriptures demonstrate the impossibility of believing God hath given us the spirit of revelation. We can never know the things of God till he hath revealed them by his Spirit, till we have received the Son of God that we should know the things which are freely given us of God. For this cause Jesus is called the author of our faith, because we receive in one and the same moment, power to believe and the Holy Ghost, who is therefore called the Spirit of faith. *And a true faith we cannot have till God gives us the Holy Ghost purifying our hearts by faith.*[31]

Next, Charles attributes the shedding abroad of God's love in believers' hearts to the presence and work of the Holy Spirit. By extension, he develops a doctrine of divine empowerment by the Spirit, saying that the Spirit enables all believers to keep Christ's commandments in love by delivering them 'not only from the guilt of sin but also from the power of sin'.[32] Here we can see Charles hard at work filling out his understanding of the work of the Spirit. It is, however, Charles' next move that is most crucial.

Having stressed the Spirit's role in conviction, pardon, divine revelation and divine empowerment, Charles moves his understanding of the presence and work of the Spirit in a decidedly trinitarian direction by developing and deploying a doctrine of divine indwelling. For Charles, the end or purpose of divine indwelling is nothing less than the hallmark of the patristic doctrine of the economic Trinity, namely, that human persons might become 'partakers of the divine nature' (2 Peter 1.4). He writes:

> This is the greatest and most glorious privilege of the true believer: whosoever shall confess that Jesus is the Son of God, God dwelleth in him and he in God: and hereby knoweth he that God abideth in him, by the Spirit which he hath given him. He that believeth hath the witness in himself, even the Spirit of God bearing witness with his Spirit that he is a child of God. Christ is formed in his heart by faith. *He is one with Christ and Christ with him. He is a real partaker of the divine nature. Truly his fellowship is with the Father and the Son. The Father and the Son are come unto him and make their abode with him, and his very body is the temple of the Holy Ghost.*[33]

Here, Charles recovers the heart of the fourth-century fathers' approach to theology and understanding of the Trinity, placing the emphasis squarely on what God has done and is doing to bring about the elevation of the human to the divine. He concludes the seventh undisputed sermon by reiterating the major themes that he has been developing with the following powerful trinitarian benediction:

> Now to God the Father, who first loved us and made us accepted in the Beloved; to the Son who loved us and washed us from our sins in his own blood, to God the Holy Ghost who sheddeth abroad the love of God in our hearts, be all praise and all glory in time and in eternity.[34]

If any doubts remained concerning the centrality of the doctrine of divine indwelling in his theology, Charles put them to rest once and for all in the eighth undisputed sermon – a sermon Charles preached in 1742 before the University of Oxford. In this sermon, Charles works backwards from our becoming partakers of the divine nature to the doctrine of the indwelling of the Holy Spirit via a series of powerful rhetorical questions. He asks,

> *Are thou 'partaker of the divine nature'?* Knowest thou not that Christ is in thee, except thou be reprobate? Knowest thou that 'God dwelleth in thee, and thou in God, by his Spirit which he hath given thee'? Knowest thou not that 'thy body is the temple of the Holy Ghost, which thou hast of God'? Hast thou the 'witness in thyself', 'the earnest of thine inheritance'? Are thou 'sealed by that Spirit of promise unto the day of redemption'? Hast thou received the Holy Ghost? Or dost thou start at the question, not knowing whether there be any Holy Ghost?[35]

Following this flurry of rhetorical questions, Charles asserts that our reception of the Holy Spirit and our partaking of the divine nature are both the
criterion of Christian identity and the marker of 'true religion'. Thus he says,

> Yet on the authority of God's Word and our own Church I must repeat
> the question, 'Hast thou received the Holy Ghost?' If thou hast not thou
> art not yet a Christian; for a Christian is a man that is 'anointed with the
> Holy Ghost and with power'. Thou art yet made a partaker of pure religion
> and undefiled. *Dost thou know what religion is? That it is a participation in
> the divine nature, the life of God in the soul of man*: Christ in thee, the hope of
> glory'; 'Christ formed in thy heart', happiness and holiness; heaven begun
> on earth; a 'kingdom of God within thee', 'not meat and drink', no outward
> thing, 'but righteousness, and peace, and joy in the Holy Ghost'.[36]

Finally, Charles reiterates that he regards the indwelling of the Spirit as the
criterion of Christian identity, saying, 'He is a Christian who hath received
the Spirit of Christ. He is not a Christian who hath not received him.'[37] He then
concludes by labelling those persons who deny the indwelling of the Holy
Spirit 'Antichrist' and by repeating for a third time that the divine indwelling
is 'the criterion of a real Christian'.

> He is Antichrist whoever denies the inspiration of the Holy Ghost, or that
> the indwelling Spirit of God is the common privilege of all believers, the
> blessing of the gospel, the unspeakable gift, the universal promise, *the
> criterion of a real Christian*.[38]

The time has come to step back and take stock of the terrain that we have
covered so far. In the seventh and eighth undisputed sermons, Charles develops the doctrine of the Holy Spirit into a robust doctrine of the economic
Trinity. This stands in stark contrast with the predominant orientation of trinitarian theology in late seventeenth- and early eighteenth-century England.

As we saw in the first section above, the overriding concern of many of
Charles' predecessors and contemporaries was to show that the doctrine of the
immanent Trinity (often without any reference to the economic Trinity) consisted of clear and intelligible propositions, i.e. propositions compatible with
and confirmable by various accounts of reason and rationality. By contrast,
Charles' understanding of and approach to the Trinity is highly similar to
the understanding of and approach to the Trinity that prevailed in the fourth
century. For example, in a statement that parallels much of what Charles says
about the Trinity in the seventh undisputed sermon, Basil of Caesarea says,

> 'No one knows the Father except the Son,' and no one can say 'Jesus is Lord'
> except in the Holy Spirit'. Notice that it does not say *through* the Spirit but *in*
> the Spirit . . . [The Spirit] reveals the glory of the Only-Begotten in Himself,
> and He gives true worshippers the knowledge of God in Himself. The way
> to divine knowledge ascends from one Spirit through the one Son to the
> one Father. Likewise, natural goodness, inherent holiness and royal dignity
> reaches from the Father through the Only-Begotten to the Spirit.[39]

At this point, it might be tempting to think that there is not so great a difference between Charles' and Basil's understanding of the Trinity on the one hand, and the understanding of many late seventeenth- and early eighteenth-century English Protestant theologians on the other. After all, Charles and Basil both speak of the Spirit bringing about knowledge of God. Presumably, such knowledge has propositional content and therefore is either intelligible or unintelligible; it is either compatible or incompatible with human reason.

Despite the initial appearances, however, the knowledge of which Charles and Basil speak is a vastly different type of knowledge than the knowledge sought by late seventeenth- and early eighteenth-century English Protestant theologians. One way to capture this difference is to say that, for Charles and Basil alike, we come to know God 'personally', and through coming to know God personally, our natures are healed and restored, even transformed, so that we really do become 'partakers of the divine nature'. Put another way, Charles and Basil are concerned with ontology rather than epistemology. Everything here hinges on taking the coming of God in the Incarnation and in the presence and work of the Holy Spirit in revelation and in divine indwelling with absolute seriousness. As Basil puts it, '[The Spirit] does not reveal [knowledge] to them from outside sources, but *leads them to knowledge personally* . . .'[40]

Finally, it needs to be said that the robust doctrine of the economic Trinity in Charles' sermons is mirrored in some of his hymns from the same period. For example, in 1740, he penned the following hymn inviting the Holy Spirit to dwell in human persons.

> I want the spirit of power within,
> Of love, and of a healthful mind:
> Of power to conquer inbred sin,
> Of love to thee and all mankind,
> Of health, that pain and death defies,
> Most vig'rous when the body dies.
>
> When shall I hear the inward voice
> Which only faithful souls can hear?
> Pardon and peace, and heavenly joys
> Attend the promised Comforter.
> O come, and righteousness divine,
> And Christ, and all with Christ is mine!
>
> *O that the Comforter would come!*
> *Nor visit as a transient guest,*
> *But fix in me his constant home*
> *And take possession of my breast;*
> *And fix in me his loved abode,*
> *The temple of indwelling God!*
>
> Come, Holy Ghost, my heart inspire!
> Attest that I am born again!
> Come, and baptize me with fire,
> Nor let thy former gifts be vain.

I cannot rest in sins forgiven;
  Where is the earnest of my heaven?

Where the indubitable seal
  That ascertains the kingdom mine?
The powerful stamp I long to feel,
  The signature of love divine!
O shed it in my heart abroad,
  Fullness of love – of heaven – of God![41]

## The economic and immanent Trinity in Charles Wesley's hymns

In the previous section, I suggested that Charles' understanding of the Trinity emerges out of his theological reflections on the presence and work of the Holy Spirit. I maintained that Charles' doctrine of the Trinity is primarily, if not exclusively, concerned with the divine economy, i.e. with the Holy Spirit's coming to dwell in us so that we might become 'partakers of the divine nature', and not with demonstrating that a doctrine of the immanent Trinity was compatible with or confirmable by unaided human reason. This does not mean that Charles did not have anything to say about the immanent Trinity. On the contrary, he goes on to reflect on the doctrine of the immanent Trinity as well. What makes his reflections on the immanent Trinity stand out, however, is that they presuppose at every turn what he has already said regarding the economic Trinity. Even when reflecting on the immanent Trinity, his outlook is primarily ontological and not epistemological or speculative. Put simply, Charles refuses to separate the immanent Trinity from the economic Trinity.

The first thing to observe about Charles' doctrine of the immanent Trinity is that, while his doctrine of the economic Trinity can be seen in both sermons and hymns, his reflections on the immanent Trinity are largely, if not entirely, located in hymns. By locating his reflections on the immanent Trinity in hymns, Charles brilliantly extends – whether by intention, intuition, or otherwise – the logic of early patristic arguments concerning the full divinity of the second and third persons of the Trinity. The reader will here recall that a major premise in patristic Trinitarian reasoning and argumentation is that the church worships, sings hymns and offers prayers to the Son and to the Spirit (*lex orandi, lex credendi*). Such activities, they observed, only make sense if the Son and the Spirit are regarded as fully divine.

In some respects, the hymn-setting of Charles' reflections on the immanent Trinity does more than simply extend the logic of patristic trinitarian reasoning; it embodies it. The effect of the hymn-setting is to situate theological reflection on the immanent Trinity in doxology. When we recall the nature of late seventeenth- and early eighteenth-century approaches to the Trinity, this is truly extraordinary. Rather than submitting the propositional contents related to the immanent Trinity to human reason, the doxological context invites persons to submit themselves in praise and thanksgiving to the Triune God.

Nor was the basic ontological orientation of Charles' trinitarian hymns lost on early Methodists. Thus in the advertisement for his *Hymns on the Trinity*, we find the following statement:

> And he has never lost sight of the experimental and practical bearings of that doctrine. Mr. Jones has an excellent paragraph at the conclusion of his argument, warning his readers that a sound belief without a holy life will not profit them. But our poet, true to the mission of Methodism, makes experience the connecting link between knowledge and practice, and devotes an entire section of his work to 'Hymns and Prayers to the Trinity,' in which the doctrine is presented in most intimate connection with his own spiritual interests, and those of his readers. *Such a mode of treating it is the best answer to those who represent it as a mere metaphysical speculation devoid of practical interest.*[42]

With regard to the content of the hymns themselves, three aspects are especially important. First, whether Charles is reflecting on the divinity of Christ, the divinity of the Spirit, the plurality of persons, or the unity of the Trinity, he never loses sight of the economic Trinity.[43] This is also true of the additional section entitled 'Hymns and Prayers to the Trinity'.[44] We can call this the *soteriological* aspect of the hymns. It is also the aspect that reveals the persistent ontological orientation of Charles' theology. The following are examples of this aspect of the hymns taken from each of the four major sections.

In Hymn VIII, Charles emphasizes Christ's role in the saving economy of God:

> The voice of God the Father sounds
>     Salvation to our sinful race:
> His grace above our sin abounds,
>     His glory shines in Jesus face,
> And by the Person of the Son
>     The Father makes Salvation known.
>
> Saved by the Son, the Lord our God,
>     Jehovah's Fellow we proclaim,
> Who washes us in his own blood,
>     To us declares his Father's name
> His nature pure, his love imparts,
>     With all his fullness to our hearts.[45]

In Hymn LXII, Charles highlights the Spirit's role in the divine economy:

> The Holy Ghost in part we know,
>     For with us He resides,
> Our whole of good to Him we owe
>     Whom by his grace he guides:
> He doth our virtuous thoughts inspire,
>     The evil he averts,
> And every seed of good desire
>     He planted in our hearts.

He, whom the world cannot receive,
    But fight against his power,
Will come, we steadfastly believe,
    In his appointed hour:
He now the future grace reveals,
    Bespeaks his mean abode;
And in us when the Spirit dwells,
    We all are filled with God.[46]

Turning to 'The Plurality and Trinity of Persons', Charles refers specifically
to the 'economy of grace' in Hymn CII:

Jehovah is but One
    Eternal God and true:
The Father sent the Son,
    His Spirit sent him too,
The everlasting Spirit filled,
And Jesus our Salvation sealed.

    Senders and Sent we praise,
        With equal thanks approve
    *The economy of grace.*
        The Triune God of love,
And humbly prostrated before
The One thrice holy God, adore![47]

When Charles turns to 'The Trinity in Unity', i.e. to the topic that was at
the centre of the trinitarian controversy – he juxtaposes his ontological orientation (first stanza) with the epistemological orientation of the rationalist
theologians (second stanza). Thus, in Hymn CXXIV, he writes:

By the Father, and the Son,
    And blessed Spirit made,
God in Persons Three we own,
    *And hang upon his aid*:

    *Reason asks, how can it be?*
But who by simple faith embrace,
    We shall know the mystery,
        And see Him face to face.[48]

In Hymn CXXIX, Charles returns to that most crucial component of the
saving economy, namely, the indwelling by which we have knowledge of God
and by which we are made divine. He says:

The Father, Son, and Spirit dwell
    By faith in all his saints below,
And then in love unspeakable
    The glorious Trinity we know

Created after God to shine,
Filled with the Plentitude Divine.[49]

Finally, in 'Hymns and Prayers to the Trinity', Charles gives thanks for 'Thy divine economy' in Hymn L, saying,

Triune God of pardoning love,
    Thy divine economy
All our thankful hearts approve,
    Thee adore in Persons Three;
Each our canceled sin reveals,
    Each confirms the babes forgiven,
Each the heirs of glory seals,
    Each conducts our souls to heaven.[50]

A second aspect of the hymns that is especially important is the way in which Charles captures the element of mystery or ineffability that is appropriate to divine transcendence. We might call this the *apophatic* aspect of the hymns. It is also an *eschatological* aspect of the hymns, as Charles often contrasts the limited knowledge of God that we have now with the knowledge that we will have when we behold God in the fullness of God's glory. Here are a few examples of this aspect of *The Hymns on the Trinity*.[51]
From Hymn LXXI:

The things invisible, Divine,
    Searched out by none but God can be:
Too short man's or angel's line
    To sound the depths of Deity:
The Spirit which in our God doth dwell,
    Which is our God, alone can tell.

None of a different nature can
    A far superior nature know:
Incomprehensible to man
    Is God, unless Himself he show,
Unless his heavenly Spirit impart
    His light to man's infernal heart.[52]

From Hymn XIX:

My notions true are notions vain;
By them I cannot grace obtain,
    Or saved from sin arise:
Knowledge acquired by books or creeds
My learned self-righteous pride it feeds;
    'Tis love that edifies

Furnished with intellectual light,
In vain I speak of Thee aright,

While unrevealed Thou art:
That only can suffice for me,
The whole mysterious Trinity
  Inhabiting my heart.[53]

Finally, from Hymn XL:

  He hath to us made known
    The awful mystery,
  The Trinity in One,
    And Unity in Three,
And taught the ransom'd sons of men
What angels never could explain.

  Beyond our utmost thought,
    And reason's proudest flight,
  We comprehend Him not,
    Nor grasp the Infinite,
But worship in the Mystic Three
One God to all eternity.[54]

A third and final aspect worth noting is that, throughout *Hymns on the Trinity*, Charles summons his readers to praise, adoration, thanksgiving and love for God. Let us call this the *doxological* aspect of the hymns. This is, of course, precisely what we would expect. On the one hand, Charles calls us to praise or to adore God because of what God has done in Christ and in the Holy Spirit to restore us to communion with God. Thus the soteriological aspect evokes doxology. On the other hand, Charles urges us to praise and to adore the Trinity in mystery. Thus even the *apophatic* or eschatological dimension is intended to elicit praise and thanksgiving. Of course, the hymns are doxological throughout. They are, one might say, theology in the form of direct address to God. A good example is found in Hymn CIX:

Hail holy, holy, holy Lord,
  Whom One in Three we know,
By all thy heavenly host ador'd,
  By all thy church below!

One undivided Trinity
  With triumph we proclaim:
The universe is full of Thee,
  And speaks thy glorious name.

Thee, holy Father, we confess,
  Thee, holy Son adore,
Thee, Spirit of true holiness,
  We worship evermore:

Thine incommunicable right,
  Almighty God, receive,

Which angel-quires and saints in light
   And saints embodied give.

Three Persons equally Divine
   We magnify and love:
And both the quires erelong shall join
   To sing the praise above:

Hail holy, holy, holy Lord,
   (Our heavenly song shall be)
Supreme, Essential One ador'd
   In co-eternal Three.[55]

## Charles Wesley's sermons and *Hymns on the Trinity*: a Methodist contribution to modern theology

Summarizing the dominant approach to theology in late seventeenth- and early eighteenth-century England, Mark Pattison once quipped: 'Christianity appeared made for nothing else but to be "proved"; what use to make of it when it was proved was not much thought about.'[56] While this certainly applies to the way that many English Protestants approached theology in this period and well beyond it, it applies in a special way to the doctrine of the Trinity. Indeed, were we to attempt to summarize much trinitarian discourse in the modern period, we could do worse than to paraphrase Pattison as follows: the Trinity appeared made for nothing else but to be proved; how it relates to our life with God and with one another was not much thought about.

I have suggested that two things are chiefly responsible for this development in modern theology. First, there is a gradual and subtle shift in and around the doctrine of divine revelation from the Holy Spirit to reason. While this shift has a great deal to do with the interpretation of scripture, it also reflects and furthers a much deeper shift already underway from ontology to epistemology. Second, in a parallel move, there is a tendency to reflect on the doctrine of the immanent Trinity in isolation from the divine economy.

By contrast, Charles Wesley maintained an ontological orientation in his approach to theology. For Charles, the principal aim of theology is to reflect on our encounter with God, beginning with the revelatory and convicting activities of the Holy Spirit and continuing all the way to the Spirit's making us 'partakers of the divine nature'. Further, Charles' ontological orientation expresses itself materially in his doctrine of the Trinity. Put simply, his onto-logical orientation does not allow him to think about the immanent Trinity apart from the economic Trinity. Thus, even in those sections of the *Hymns on the Trinity* having to do with the immanent Trinity, Charles persistently redirects the reader's attention to the divine economy.

In the late twentieth and early twenty-first centuries, theologians from many traditions are struggling to overcome the modern preoccupation with epistemology and speculative metaphysics.[57] Some theologians are even beginning to move in a decidedly ontological direction.[58] At the same time,

many theologians are hard at work stressing the indispensability of the economic Trinity for reflection on the immanent Trinity. To this end, the work
of Karl Barth, Karl Rahner and Catherine M. LaCugna has been extremely
important.[59] Generally speaking, these developments are often foregrounded
by a story that depicts the story of Trinity in modern theology in terms of
almost total loss. In the modern period, so the story goes, the Trinity is rele-
gated to a mere appendix in theology.

Amid these well-rehearsed stories of the loss of trinitarian doctrine and
devotion in modern theology (and especially in modern Protestant theology),
there is a new development on the horizon. Recently, a few theologians and
historians of doctrine have begun to call into question the narrative of total
loss.[60] This development is fuelled largely by one simple idea. You can find the
Trinity in modern (Protestant) theology if you look in the right places.[61]

In conclusion, the time is ripe to reappraise Charles Wesley's contribution
not only to the evangelical revival but also to modern theology. To be sure, he
did not write a major work in systematic theology or even a technical treatise
on the Trinity. This does not mean, however, that he did not help to revive
trinitarian doctrine and piety in English Protestant theology. On the contrary,
by engaging in theological reflection almost entirely in sermons and hymns,
Charles may have done more to preserve the Trinity than he would have by
writing the kind of technical treatises on the Trinity that were so common in
his day. Indeed, his contribution to modern theology may lie precisely here:
he reminds us that theology's true home is in worship and prayer, its true task
the work of praise and thanksgiving to God.


## Notes

1 For an analysis of the connection between the Trinity and soteriology in
patristic theology, see Catherine LaCugna, *God For Us: The Trinity and Christian
Life* (San Francisco: HarperSanFrancisco, 1993). For the importance of this connec-
tion in the work of John and Charles Wesley, see Samuel M. Powell, 'A Trinitarian
Alternative to Process Theism', in *Thy Nature and Thy Name is Love: Wesleyan and
process theologies in dialogue*, ed. Bryan P. Stone and Thomas Jay Oord (Nashville:
Kingswood Books, 2001), 143–67. Specifically of John's theology, Powell says,
'Wesley's doctrine of salvation is a Trinitarian doctrine' (152).

2 To see this, one only need look at recent histories of Christian doctrine and
theology. Methodism is associated in standard histories of Christianity with
revivals and awakenings of piety, but it is rarely associated with the renewal of
doctrine. For example, see Jonathan Hill, *The History of Christian Thought* (Downers
Grove: InterVarsity Press, 2003); see also William C. Placher, *A History of Christian
Theology: An introduction* (Philadelphia: The Westminster Press, 1983). For a text
that limits John Wesley and early Methodism's contribution to modern theology
to the doctrine of Christian life without connecting this in any meaningful way
to the doctrine of the Trinity, see Roger E. Olson, *The Story of Christian Theology:
Twenty centuries of tradition and reform* (Downers Grove: InterVarsity Press, 1999),
chapter 30. In what follows, I will maintain that Charles Wesley contributed to
the revival of the doctrine of the Trinity precisely because he refused to separate
trinitarian doctrine from trinitarian piety.

3 For an elegant history of this way of conceiving the theological task, see William J. Abraham, *Canon and Criterion in Christian Theology: From the Fathers to feminism* (Oxford: Oxford University Press, 1998).

4 On the catechetical or formative nature of John Wesley's approach to theology, see Randy L. Maddox, *Responsible Grace: John Wesley's Practical Theology* (Nashville: Kingswood Books, 1994).

5 For the recent emphasis on theology's therapeutic or healing power, see Ellen Charry, *By the Renewing of Your Minds: The Pastoral Function of Doctrine* (New York: Oxford University Press, 1997). Also see Vigen Guorion, 'Divine Therapy', in *Theology Today*, 61:3 (October 2004), 309–21. Finally, the recent revival of interest in the work of Yves Congar is contributing to the renewal of a therapeutic vision of theology. For example, see Elizabeth T. Groppe, *Yves Congar's Theology of the Holy Spirit* (New York: Oxford University Press, 2004).

6 For a more comprehensive analysis of the trinitarian controversy in seventeenth-century England, see Philip Dixon, *'Nice and Hot Disputes': The doctrine of the Trinity in the seventeenth century* (London: T&T Clark, 2003); William S. Babcock, 'A Changing of the Christian God,' *Interpretation* 45 (1991), 133–46; and William Placher, *The Domestication of Transcendence: How modern thinking about God went wrong* (Louisville: Westminster Press, 1996), chapter 10.

7 See William Sherlock, *A Vindication of the Doctrine of the Holy and Ever Blessed Trinity, and the Incarnation of the Son of God, Occasioned by the Brief Notes on the Creed of St. Athanasius, and the Brief History of the Unitarians, or Socinians; and Containing an Answer to both* (London, 1690). For a helpful essay on Sherlock's approach, see Udo Thiel, 'The Trinity and human personal identity', in *English Philosophy in the Age of Locke*, ed. M. A. Stewart (Oxford: Clarendon Press, 2000), 217–44.

8 See Edward Stillingfleet, *A Discourse in Vindication of the Doctrine of the Trinity: With an answer to the late Socinian objections against it from Scripture, antiquity and reason. And a Preface concerning the different explications of the Trinity, and the tendency of the present Socinian Controversy* (London, 1697). For a helpful essay on Stillingfleet's approach, see M. A. Stewart, 'Stillingfleet and the way of Ideas', in *English Philosophy in the Age of Locke*, ed. M. A. Stewart (Oxford: Clarendon Press, 2000), 245–80.

9 See Stephen Nye, *Considerations on the Explications of the Doctrine of the Trinity, by Dr. Wallis, Dr. Sherlock, Dr. S----h, Dr. Cudworth, and Mr. Hooker; as also on the account given by those that say, the Trinity is an unconceivable and inexplicable mystery* (London, 1693).

10 For various aspects of the story, see Peter Harrison, *'Religion' and the Religions in the English Enlightenment* (New York: Cambridge University Press, 1990); Frederick Beiser, *The Sovereignty of Reason: The defense of rationality in the early English Enlightenment* (Princeton: Princeton University Press, 1996); and Gerard Reedy, *The Bible and Reason: Anglicans and Scripture in Late Seventeenth Century England* (Philadelphia: The University of Pennsylvania Press, 1985).

11 For a classic, albeit somewhat later, example of the anxiety that the doctrine of divine inscrutability could produce, see James Hogg, *The Private Memoirs and Confessions of a Justified Sinner* (Oxford: Oxford University Press, 1969).

12 *A Relation of the Conference between William Laud and Mr. Fisher the Jesuit* (London: Macmillan and Co., 1901), p. 88.

13 *A Relation of the Conference*, 90.

14 *A Relation of the Conference*, 121.

15 One can see this development in John Wesley's struggle for assurance.

For the transition in John Wesley's understanding of faith from *assensus* to *fiducia*, see Maddox, *Responsible Grace*, 124–7. Also see Richard P. Heitzenrater, 'Great Expectations: Aldersgate and the Evidences of Genuine Christianity', in *Aldersgate Reconsidered*, ed. Randy L. Maddox (Nashville: Kingswood Books, 1990), 49–91.

16 William Chillingworth, *Religion of the Protestants: A Safe Way to Salvation*, 2 vols (London, 1638), 2.104 (emphasis added).

17 For the classical statement of Socinian theology, see the Rakovian Catechism, trans. Thomas Rees (reprint, Lexington: The American Theological Association, 1962). Also see H. John McLachlan, *Socinianism in Seventeenth-Century England* (London: Oxford University Press, 1951).

18 This is precisely the notion that Locke defends and popularizes in *The Reasonableness of Christianity* (Oxford: Clarendon Press, 1999). For Locke, there is only one clear and intelligible proposition in scripture that is necessary to be believed for salvation; namely, that Jesus is the Messiah. See Locke, *Reasonableness*, para. 229.

19 It is crucial to note that Chillingworth himself did not draw this conclusion. On the contrary, Chillingworth retained enough of the Calvinist notion of the epistemic consequences of sin that he actually anticipated that persons would disagree with one another over religious matters. For this aspect of Chillingworth's argument, see Robert Orr, *Reason and Authority: The thought of William Chillingworth* (Oxford: Clarendon Press, 1967), 152.

20 See Philipp van Limborch, *A Compleat System, or Body of Divinity*, 2 vols (London: 1702), 1.103. John Marshall has aptly named this emerging position 'irenic trinitarianism'. See John Marshall, 'Locke, Socinianism, 'Socinianism', Unitarianism', in *English Philosophy in the Age of Locke*, ed. M. A. Stewart (Oxford: Clarendon Press, 2000), 117.

21 On the inseparability of the economic and immanent Trinities, see Karl Rahner, *The Trinity* (New York: Crossroad, 1997).

22 For example, see Laura A. Bartels, 'Hymns of the Status Quo: Charles Wesley on the Trinity', *Methodist History*, 41:2 (January 2003), 25–32. Also see Barry E. Bryant, 'Trinity and Hymnody: The Doctrine of the Trinity in the Hymns of Charles Wesley,' *Wesleyan Theological Journal* (Fall 1990), 64–73. For more information on Charles' sources for these hymn collections, see Wilma J. Quantrille, 'Introduction', in Charles Wesley, *Hymns on the Trinity*, ed. S T Kimbrough Jr (Madison: The Charles Wesley Society, 1988), vii-xiii (hereafter *HT*).

23 One can see the impact of ignoring the sermons in Laura Bartels' criticism of Barry Bryant. Bartels criticizes Bryant for focusing only on 'the practical implication of Trinitarian theology for the individual' (p. 30). Similarly, she criticizes Bryant for analyzing Charles' view of the Trinity primarily 'from the perspective of the Revival' (p. 30). By contrast, Bartels contends that Charles' doctrine of the Trinity was a symbol of his ecclesiastical and political loyalties. While there may be some merit to Bartels' critique, she merely asserts rather than demonstrates that Charles' *Hymns on the Trinity* reflect his position as an advocate for the Anglican Church. When the evidence from the sermon corpus is taken into consideration, Bryant's position that Charles' doctrine of the Trinity has primarily to do with salvation and worship is largely substantiated. To put the matter bluntly, Charles' doctrine of the Trinity has more to do with piety than with polity.

24 For this study I have used Newport, *Sermons*, and I will cite both the relevant sermon number and the page number.

25  For more on Charles' doctrine of the Holy Spirit, see Jason E. Vickers, 'Charles Wesley's Doctrine of the Holy Spirit: A vital resource for the renewal of Methodism today', *Asbury Journal* 61:1 (Spring 2006), 47–60.

26  Newport, *Sermons*, Sermon 2, p.116. According to Newport, this sermon was preached at least four times in 1736. I have limited this research to what Newport identified as the 'undisputed sermons', i.e., to those sermons about which there are no doubts that Charles was the author.

27  For Charles' evangelical conversion, see Arnold Dallimore, *A Heart Set Free: The life of Charles Wesley* (Westchester: Crossway Books, 1988); and T. Crichton Mitchell, *Charles Wesley: Man with the dancing heart* (Kansas City: Beacon Press, 1994).

28  For the three 'conversion hymns', see John Tyson, ed., *Charles Wesley: A reader* (Oxford: Oxford University Press, 1989), 101–4. See also Dallimore, *A Heart Set Free*, 61–3; and Mitchell, *Man with the Dancing Heart*, 70–1.

29  Newport, *Sermons*, Sermon 4, 145. It is worth noting that the source for Charles' understanding of the Holy Spirit in this sermon is John Norris' *Practical Discourses on Several Divine Subjects* (1690).

30  Newport, *Sermons*, Sermon 7, 201.

31  Newport, *Sermons*, Sermon 7, 202 (emphasis added).

32  Newport, *Sermons*, Sermon 7, 202.

33  Newport, *Sermons*, Sermon 7, 203 (emphasis added). Charles paraphrases the following scripture texts: 1 John 4.15; 1 John 3.24; 1 John 4.13; 1 John 5.10; Galatians 4.19; 2 Peter 1.4; 1 John 1.3; John 14.23; 1 Corinthians 6:19.

34  Newport, *Sermons*, Sermon 7, 210.

35  Newport, *Sermons*, Sermon 7, 218 (emphasis added). Charles here paraphrases the following scriptural texts: 2 Peter 1:4; 2 Corinthians 13.5; 1 John 3.24; 4.12–13; 5.10; 1 Corinthians 6.19; Ephesians 1.13–14; 4.30; Acts 19.2.

36  Newport, *Sermons*, Sermon 7, 218 (emphasis added). Scripture paraphrases include: Acts 10.38, James 1.27, 2 Peter 1.4, Colossians 1.27, Galatians 4.19, Luke 17.21, Romans 14.17, Philippians 4.7; 1 Peter 1.8.

37  Newport, *Sermons*, Sermon 7, 221.

38  Newport, *Sermons*, Sermon 7, 222 (emphasis added).

39  St Basil the Great, *On the Holy Spirit*, trans. David Anderson (Crestwood: St Vladimir's Seminary Press, 1980), 74–5.

40  St Basil the Great, *On the Holy Spirit*, 74–5.

41  Hymn 365 in *BE*, 7.534–5 (emphasis added).

42  *Hymns on the Trinity*, 'Advertisement', xv (emphasis added). 'Mr. Jones' refers to William Jones, whose 1756 treatise, *The Catholic Doctrine of the Trinity, proved by above an hundred short and clear arguments, expressed in terms of the Holy Scripture*, was the inspiration and pattern for Charles' 1767 *Hymns on the Trinity*. The 'Advertisement' appeared in George Osborn's volume 7 of *The Poetical Works of John and Charles Wesley*, 13 vols (London: Wesleyan-Methodist Conference Office, 1870), 203–4. Also see the quotation from John at the outset of this chapter.

43  The four main sections of *Hymns on the Trinity* are derived directly from William Jones' *The Catholic Doctrine of the Trinity*.

44  This section is not found in Jones' work. Thus many feel that it is most representative of Charles' personal reflections on the Trinity.

45  *HT*, 8. Other hymns on the divinity of Christ that accentuate Christ's role in the divine economy include III, XII, XIII, XXXII, XXXIII, XXXV, L, LIV and LV.

46  *HT*, 41–2. Other hymns on the divinity of the Holy Spirit that accentuate the

298						JASON E. VICKERS

Spirit's role in the divine economy include LVIII, LXI, LXIII, LXV, LXVII, LXVIII, LXXX, LXXXIII and LXXXVI.

47 *HT*, 66 (emphasis added). Other hymns on the plurality of persons that emphasize the divine economy include XCI, XCV, XCVIII, CI, CV, CVI and CVII.

48 *HT*, 79–80 (emphasis added). For the divine economy in the section 'The Trinity in Unity', see Hymns CX, CXVI, CXVII, CXXXIV and CXXXV.

49 *HT*, 82.

50 *HT*, 130.

51 *PW*, 7.201–98.

52 *HT*, 47.

53 *HT*, 102–3.

54 *HT*, 124.

55 *HT*, 69–70.

56 See Mark Pattison, 'Tendencies of Religious Thought in England, 1688–1750', *Essays*, 2 vols (Oxford: Clarendon Press, 1889), 2:48.

57 Within the Methodist tradition, see Geoffrey Wainwright, *Doxology: The praise of God in worship, doctrine and life* (Oxford: Oxford University Press, 1984).

58 An early example of this can be seen in the work of Yves Congar and other Catholic *ressourcement* theologians. Examples in the Eastern Orthodox tradition are prevalent, but the work of Alexander Schmemann and Vladimir Lossky is exemplary in this respect.

59 For a mostly reliable introduction to the work of Barth, Rahner and LaCugna (among others) on the Trinity, see Stanley Grenz, *Rediscovering the Triune God: The Trinity in contemporary theology* (Minneapolis: Augsburg Fortress Press, 2004).

60 For example, see Amy Plantinga Pauw, *The Supreme Harmony of All: The trinitarian theology of Jonathan Edwards* (Grand Rapids: Eerdmans, 2002).

61 Thus theologians and historians of doctrine have begun to give the kind of attention to sermons that has traditionally been given to major works in systematic or dogmatic theology. For example, see Dawn DeVries, *Jesus Christ in the Preaching of Calvin and Schleiermacher* (Louisville: Westminster John Knox Press, 2002).

# 17. Charles Wesley and the Language of Faith

## PAUL WESLEY CHILCOTE

Charles Wesley preached, wrote and sang about faith. Christian faith defined his life and ministry. On 31 August 1748, an unnamed woman surrendered to God's grace under the influence of this Anglican priest/lyrical theologian who recorded her testimony in his journal:

> 'I seem', said she, 'to be laying hold on Christ continually. I am so light, so happy, as I never was before. I waked, two nights ago, in such rapture of joy, that I thought, "Surely this is the peace they preach." It has continued ever since. My eyes are opened. I see all things in a new light. I rejoice always.' Is not this *the language of faith*, the cry of a new-born soul?[1]

While many themes pervade Wesley's literary corpus, perhaps none stands out quite so dramatically as faith. In the following hymn about the 'Author of faith', Wesley describes the origins and nature of faith. He affirms the fact that faith is a gift, something related to the burning presence of the Spirit in the lives of the faith-ful. It is a source of knowledge concerning God and the way in which God offers salvation, hope and healing to humanity. Faith illumines the child of God and enables spiritual vision. In short, for Charles, faith is a complex reality in the lives of people, rich in meaning and central to the Christian vision of life.

Author of faith, eternal Word,
    Whose Spirit breathes the active flame,
Faith, like its finisher and Lord,
    Today as yesterday the same;

To thee our humble hearts aspire,
    And ask the gift unspeakable:
Increase in us the kindled fire,
    In us the work of faith fulfil.

By faith we know thee strong to save
    (Save us, a present Saviour thou!)
Whate'er we hope, by faith we have,
    Future and past subsisting now.

Faith lends its realizing light,
  The clouds disperse, the shadows fly;
Th'Invisible appears in sight,
  And God is seen by mortal eye.[2]

For the student of Charles Wesley, of course, none of this is news. To assert that the concept of faith figures prominently in his poetic and prose works is tantamount to saying that Christianity exerted a profound influence on his life. It simply states the obvious. But the way in which Wesley employs the language of faith reveals, I believe, some of the most important insights with regard to the Wesleyan vision of Christianity. What I propose here, therefore, is a detailed analysis of 'Charles Wesley and the language of faith' as a lens through which to focus attention on the essence of the Methodist movement and to contemplate anew the meaning of faith.[3]

The parameters of this study need to be set out at this early point. The Wesleyan corpus, as may be deduced from other contributions to this book, is immense. An exhaustive analysis of Wesley's 'concept of faith' in a brief essay such as this is hardly possible. Some rather serious limits on the study are hence imposed. First, I am examining Charles' use of the term 'faith' in order to delineate his 'concept of faith', rather than attempting to unearth the ideas that are reflected throughout his works. Second, I have restricted myself in this task to two primary sources: the 1780 *Collection of Hymns for the Use of the People Called Methodists* and the published journal. My methodology with regard to these sources has involved the identification of every instance of the term 'faith' in this restricted corpus of material. Third, I have made important use of Wesley's *Sermons*[4] (a rich source hardly to be neglected in such a study), but have made no effort to survey this material in an exhaustive fashion with regard to language. Rather, I have focused my attention on those sermons in which Charles deals with the 'subject of faith' and expounds his understanding in a definitive manner, for the benefit of the corroborative evidence and further interpretive insight this provides.[5] While I fully recognize the limitations and dangers of this design, I am convinced that its benefits are great. The portrait of faith that emerges, I trust, is both authentic and compelling.

I

Despite the fact that we are not able here to discuss at any length the mass of detail that is, to be sure, relevant to this study, but are concerned rather with the big picture it provides, simply looking at the data does provide some interesting conclusions and confirmations. For example, an examination of the Jackson edition of the journal reveals that Charles uses the term 'faith' 406 times between March 1736 and November 1756.[6] Despite the fact that the published journal material is uneven at best and deficient at worst, over the course of these years the extraordinary nature of the year 1738 stands out dramatically. Wesley's struggle with faith, his conversations about faith, and his discovery and experience of living faith dominate his narrative account of this year. His record of 1738 reflects a veritable explosion of faith in his life.

The language of faith permeates this narrative in particular (153 instances), representing more than one-third of the uses of the term in the published journal. In the context of that year itself, the fact that more than two-thirds of these references come from his account of the summer months, May–July, demonstrates the crucial significance of the 'faith changes' Charles was undergoing in that period.

During the previous two years (1736–7) he only refers to faith nine times. The afterglow of Wesley's discoveries about faith in 1738 are reflected in the immediately subsequent years, 1739 with 63, and 1740 with 37 references. But his use of the term tapers off in the following decade (1741–51) with an average of only about 13 references per year. Simply on the basis of his use of the term 'faith', it is clear that 1738 represents a critical turning point with regard to Charles' engagement with the concept of and existential appropriation of faith.

The 1780 *Collection*, of course, represents a Wesleyan *summa pietatis* in that it is 'A Little Body of Experimental and Practical Divinity'. While it is impossible to examine Charles' use of the term 'faith' in the hymns with reference to chronology, the dating and attribution of this poetic corpus being highly controverted issues, a detailed examination of the *Collection* reveals some interesting facts as well, leading to a broad but significant generalization. Wesley refers explicitly to faith in roughly one out of every four of the 525 hymns in the collection.[7] The vast majority of these uses of the term are singular, but a number of hymns function as commentaries on faith, as it were, with multiple references. Four hymns, in particular, might be designated as 'hymns on faith' by virtue of Charles' pervasive use and interpretation of the term throughout.[8]

As might well be expected, more than half of the hymns that reference faith (76 in all) are located in the major section of the collection 'For Believers' (Part 4). The largest concentration of these hymns (17) falls under the category 'For Believers Groaning for Full Redemption'. This provides tacit evidence at least for the fact that Charles places strong emphasis upon *sanctification* (as well as justification) *by faith*. The foundational Pauline/Reformation doctrine of justification by grace through faith is represented with nearly equal strength by hymns 'For Believers Rejoicing' (16). Next in order of frequency, Wesley refers to faith in 13 hymns related to 'Praying for Mourners brought to Birth', in the separate Part 3 of the collection, also stressing the concept of salvation by faith. The next highest concentration of hymns featuring the language of faith comes from the final section of the collection (Part 5), 'For the Society, Praying' (11).

Despite the fact that the heaviest concentration of these hymns comes from the sections where one might well expect 'faith' to be found, namely in those crucial sections related to the Wesleyan *via salutis*, there is amazing balance throughout the entire collection in terms of proportional distribution.[9] The 'hymns on faith', as I have described them, reflect this pervasive utilization of the language of faith, located, as it were, in four different major parts of the collection: 'Describing Inward Religion' (Part 1, Hymn 92), 'Praying for Mourners brought to Birth' (Part 3, Hymn 142), 'For Believers Groaning for Full Redemption' (Part 4, Hymn 350), and 'For the Society, Praying' (Part 5,

Hymn 507). This detailed analysis of Charles' use of faith language simply confirms in rather dramatic fashion just how central the concept of faith was in the hymns and the experience of the early Methodist people. If the hymns of Charles Wesley communicated the essential doctrine of the movement, as many have argued persuasively,[10] then faith stood at the heart and core of the Wesleyan way.

These are some of the conclusions we can draw from the raw data, the minute detail, related to the presence of faith language in the journal and hymns, but of even greater significance are the major themes and powerful images that revolve around the language of faith in Charles Wesley's prose and poetic writings.

II

Three particular themes – distinct but inseparable from one another – characterize Charles Wesley's understanding of faith and demonstrate the essential Anglican orientation of his lyrical theology and doctrinal language: the concept of true and lively faith, the doctrine of justification by faith, and the vision of faith working by love.

## The concept of true and lively faith

Charles Wesley distinguishes sharply between 'dead faith' and 'living faith'. Both he and his brother, John, were well aware of the debates related to faith that led to the important definitions and distinctions of the Protestant scholastics. Philip Melanchthon, for example, differentiated between historical faith (which the devils also possess) and saving faith in Christ (defined as trust or assurance).[11] In his sermon on Romans 3.23–5, Wesley echoes the language of Augsburg:

> The faith which justifies is not purely an assent to things credible as known; it is not that speculative, notional, airy shadow which floats in the heads of some learned men; it is not a lifeless, cold, historical faith, common to devils and nominal Christians; it is not learnt of books or men; it is not a human thing, but a divine energy.[12]

On several occasions in his journal, he refers to this shadow of a true faith, or faith improperly so-called, as the 'faith of adherence'. All of these references are pejorative. 'I spoke closely to those who trusted to their faith of adherence', he wrote concerning a confrontation in May 1740, 'and insisted on that *lowest mark* of Christianity, forgiveness of sins.'[13] On other occasions he identifies this sub-species of faith with the view of certain Dissenters, half persuading one out of her aberrant view[14] and expressing triumph over another when his preaching 'stripped her all at once of her self-righteousness, faith of adherence, and good works'.[15] Wesley's attempt to disabuse some Baptists of their misconception of faith elicited a fairly concise definition of living faith and its consequences:

I passed two hours with M. Powel, and another Baptist, whom I almost persuaded to give up their faith of adherence, so called, for the faith of the Gospel, which works by love, and is connected with peace, joy, power, and the testimony of the Spirit.[16]

In explicating this distinction, Wesley simply defended the conception of 'true and lively faith' articulated by his Church in the Anglican *Articles of Religion* and *Homilies*.[17] The English reformer and author of the Book of Common Prayer, Thomas Cranmer, embedded the same dynamic conception of faith in his *Homilies*, a rich theological reservoir in which Charles immersed himself and upon which he drew repeatedly as a source for his sermons and hymns.[18] In one of his most significant sermons on Christian faith, based upon Titus 3.8, Charles defines both dead and living faith by simply quoting at length from Homily 4:

Faith is taken in scripture two ways. There is one faith which is called a dead faith, which bringeth not forth good works, but is dead, barren, and unfruitful. And this faith is a persuasion in man's heart whereby he knoweth there is a God, and agreeth to all truths maintained in holy scripture. And this is not properly called faith . . .

Another faith there is in scripture which is not idle, unfruitful, and dead, but worketh by love; and as the other vain faith is called dead, so may this be called a quick and lively faith. And this is not only the common belief of the Articles of our faith, but it is also a sure trust and confidence of the mercy of God through our Lord Jesus Christ, and a steadfast hope of all good things to be received at God's hand. This is a true, lively, and unfeigned Christian faith, and is not in the mouth and outward profession only, but it liveth and stirreth inwardly in the heart'.[19]

That this faith must be stirred up and realized in fallen humanity by an external power Wesley make abundantly clear in the prayer of a spiritual pilgrim to the 'hidden God':

An unregenerate child of man,
  To thee for faith I call;
Pity thy fallen creature's pain,
  And raise me from my fall.

The darkness which through thee I feel
  Thou only canst remove;
Thy own eternal power reveal,
  Thy Deity of love.

Thou hast in unbelief shut up,
  That grace may let me go;
In hope believing against hope
  I wait the truth to know.[20]

God must transform a dead faith into something that is living and vital. 'The power of living faith impart', prays the lost child, 'And breathe thy love into my heart'.[21] 'My want of living faith I feel', a tormented soul cries out, 'Show me in Christ thy smiling face'.[22] Reflecting on the meaning of John 5.24 and the transition from spiritual death to life, Wesley affirms that this change 'belongs only to them that believe with a living, saving, justifying faith'.[23] His overriding concern was for people to 'know that we have passed from death to life' (1 John 3.14).

Before defining this living faith more fully and demonstrating its connection to justification, it is important to note a second, related distinction with regard to Wesley's concept of faith, associating it with belief. Nowhere in his writings does he distinguish explicitly between faith and belief, but the distinction is implied throughout his corpus. While failing to employ the classical terminology, Charles differentiates between the 'faith in which one believes' (*fides quae creditur*) and the 'faith by which one believes' (*fides qua creditur*). The contrast here is not so much between a dead and a living faith as it is between an objective faith (what might be described as *the* faith, or a system of belief) and a subjective faith (what Wesley describes as a living or saving faith).[24]

St Augustine articulated the same distinction concisely in his monumental work *On the Trinity*: 'For faith is not *that which is believed*, but *that by which it is believed*; and the former is *believed*, the latter is *seen*.'[25] A true and lively faith enables spiritual perception, and it is not surprising, as we shall see later, that one of Charles' favourite images is 'the eye of faith'. Ancient Christian sources, upon which the Wesleys were highly dependent, frequently point to the heart as that locus of this spiritual vision.[26] And so Wesley concludes the hymn quoted in part above:

Speak, Jesu, speak into my heart
    What thou for me hast done!
One grain of living faith impart,
    And God is all my own![27]

As important as it is to believe in certain things (the fundamental substance of faith), Wesley pointed to the act of faith, or that living faith by which one believes, as the foundation of the Christian life. While faith and belief are integral – never to be separated from one another – in the Wesleyan tradition, the 'enpersonalization' of faith remains the key to authentic life in Christ; *the* faith must become, at some point and in a dynamic way, *my* faith.[28]

## The doctrine of justification by faith

Charles Wesley's essential discovery concerning life in Christ, and the dominating theme of faith in his writings, revolves around the classic Pauline text, Romans 3.23–4: 'Since all have sinned and fall short of the glory of God; they are now justified by his grace as a gift, through the redemption that is in Christ Jesus.' It should be no surprise to us that his discoveries with regard to justification by grace through faith were profoundly autobiographical. The doctrine and Wesley's own experience both bear close scrutiny.

With regard to the later sermons of Charles Wesley – i.e. the post-Pentecost 1738 collection, subsequent to his 'evangelical conversion' – Newport maintains that 'the one overriding concern is salvation and how it is achieved, and the one consistent answer given is that it is by faith in Christ, who has paid the price of human sin'.[29] Of the several sermons in which Wesley explores the nature of faith, one of his two sermons from this period on the Romans 3.23–5 text, the longest of all his sermons to have survived, provides a vigorous account of his doctrine of justification by faith.[30] In his explication of justification, Wesley adheres closely to the language of the *Homilies* and *Articles*.[31] After having described the corrupt and fallen condition of the human creature, Wesley quotes nine paragraphs from Homily 3 'Of Salvation', describing justification by faith as the remedy for this sickness, and tersely summarizes his position by quoting Article XI 'Of the Justification of Man':

> We are accounted righteous before God, only for the merit of our Lord Jesus Christ through faith, and not for our own works or deservings. Wherefore, that we are justified by faith only, is a most wholesome doctrine, and very full of comfort.[32]

Likewise, he imports the language of Homily 4 'On Faith' in order to define faith in this regard:

> The true, lively and converting faith, the sure and substantial faith which saveth sinners . . . is also a true trust and confidence of the mercy of God through our Lord Jesus Christ, and a steadfast hope of all good things to be received at God's hand. It is not in the mouth and outward profession only, but liveth and stirreth inwardly in the heart.[33]

That, in 1738, all of this was a discovery for Charles is a point that does not need belabouring. Attempts to interpret his awakening of faith on the Day of Pentecost and his poetical account of the experience in that year abound.[34] Suffice it to say that, on the threshold of that transformative experience, he was pondering the spiritual insight of his Anglican heritage, as is clear from his journal account:

> Who would believe our Church had been founded on this important article of justification by faith alone? I am astonished I should ever think this a new doctrine; especially while our Articles and Homilies stand unrepealed, and the key of knowledge is not yet taken away.
>
> From this time I endeavoured to ground as many of our friends as came in this fundamental truth, salvation by faith alone, not an idle, dead faith, but a faith which works by love, and is necessarily productive of all good works and all holiness.[35]

Having been convinced about the truth of this doctrine, God soon transformed his intellectual assent into a vital experience by virtue of which he could claim: 'I saw that by faith I stood; by the continual support of faith, which kept me from falling, though of myself I am ever sinking into sin.'[36] One hears autobiographical echoes of this experience, particularly in his hymns for those groaning for full redemption.

I hold thee with a trembling hand,
    But will not let thee go
Till steadfastly by faith I stand,
    And all thy goodness know.[37]

'By faith I every moment stand', sings Wesley, 'Strangely upheld by thy right hand'.[38]

He explicitly refers to 'justification by faith' nearly twenty times in his journal, primarily in his record of 1738 and 1739. More often than not, however, the term 'faith' simply functions as a shorthand reference to the doctrine of justification by grace through faith. Whether described as the 'doctrine of faith', the 'experience of faith', 'faith of the gospel', 'life in the faith', 'faith in the blood of Christ', or 'spirit of faith', these expressions, and the term 'faith' itself, connote the experience of having been accepted and pardoned by God through faith in Christ alone. The foundation of this concept, of course, is trust (*fiducia*). Faith is the gift of trust; the Spirit enabling the child of God to entrust his or her life into the care of the God of love. The centre around which all else revolved for the Methodists was the shared experience of faith-as-trust and salvation by grace. Originally written to help distinguish the Wesleyan way from that of the Moravians, one of Wesley's 'Hymns for One Convinced of Unbelief' celebrates this theme:

Author of faith, to thee I cry,
To thee, who wouldst not have me die,
    But know the truth and live;
Open mine eyes to see thy face,
Work in my heart the saving grace,
    The life eternal give.

I know the work is only thine –
The gift of faith is all divine;
    But, if on thee we call
Thou wilt the benefit bestow,
And give us hearts to feel and know
    That thou hast died for all.

Be it according to thy word!
Now let me find my pard'ning Lord,
    Let what I ask be given;
The bar of unbelief remove,
Open the door of faith and love,
    And take me into heaven![39]

## The vision of faith working by love

In framing the Anglican *Articles of Religion*, and particularly the *Homilies*, Thomas Cranmer exemplified a twin concern. Not only did he seek to establish the nature of salvation as God's free gift of grace received through faith, but he also demonstrated that salvation by faith alone need not lead to anti-nomianism and the abandonment of morality. Rather, he viewed good works, still, as an essential part of the Christian life. These entwined goals frame Homily 3 'Of Salvation', which, as we have already seen, figured prominently in Wesley's own sermons. The subsequent homilies 'Of Faith' and 'Of Good Works' further elaborate the connection of faith and works in the Christian life.[40]

When Charles uses expressions like 'practical faith' or the 'full assurance of faith', or admonishes the believer to press on toward the 'obedience', 'triumph' or 'righteousness of faith', he refers to the process by which faith is made effective in love. Standing squarely in his Anglican heritage, he affirms that faith – God's restoration of the capacity to entrust one's life to God – is the foundation of the abundant life, but also claims that faith is but a means to love's end. This dynamic conception of the interrelation of faith and love, or faith and works, is one of the primary contributions of the Wesleyan theological tradition. Charles explicates this vision of authentic Christianity repeatedly in all of his writings.

Joseph Williams offers a rare first-hand glimpse of Charles' synthesis of faith and works in his journal account of a sermon Wesley preached on 2 Corinthians 5.17–21 in 1739. After stressing the importance of justification by faith alone, according to Williams' report:

> Nor did he fail to inform them thoroughly, how ineffectual their faith would be to justify them in the sight of God, unless it wrought by love, purified their hearts, and reformed their lives: for though he cautioned them with the utmost care not to attribute any merit to their own performances, nor in the least degree rest on any works of their own, yet at the same time he thoroughly apprized them, that their faith is but a dead faith if it be not operative, and productive of good works, even all the good in their power.[41]

In all of his preaching Wesley defends his conviction that works come after faith and are the consequence and not the cause of divine acceptance. This, in fact, is the principal theme of his sermon on Titus 3.8.[42] In his exposition of this text, among the marks or effects of true faith, he includes inward peace of conscience; joy; liberty not only from the guilt, but from the power of sin; and love, for 'faith works by love, and he that loveth not knoweth not God, for God is love'.[43] He enforces this point in characteristic fashion at the conclusion of his sermon on 1 John 3.14 in a fifth word of advice:

> . . . show your faith in good works. Without these all pretensions to faith are false. These are the necessary effects or fruits or signs of a living faith. Necessary they are, not to justify us before God, but to justify us before man; or rather, not to make, but to show us acceptable; not as the cause but as the evidence of our new birth; not as conditions, but consequences and tokens of our salvation. The faith which worketh not by love, is an idle, barren, dead faith; that is, no faith at all.[44]

The biblical locus for this critical theme for both Wesley brothers is Galatians 5.6, 'The only thing that counts is faith working through love.' Charles frequently alludes to this text in his sacred verse:

> Happy the man that finds the grace,
> The blessing of God's chosen race,
> The wisdom coming from above,
> The faith that sweetly works by love.[45]

Or again:

> O might we through thy grace attain
>   The faith thou never wilt reprove,
> The faith that purges every stain,
>   The faith that always works by love.[46]

While Wesleyan soteriology affirms the importance of justification by faith (the forensic dimension of salvation), it emphasizes the restorative process of salvation, the goal of which is the fullest possible love of God and neighbour (the therapeutic dimension of salvation). One of Wesley's 'Hymns for Christian Friends' captures this dynamic movement of faith to love, elevates the eucharistic and eschatological dimensions of the journey, and celebrates the trilogy of faith, hope, and love:

> Come, let us ascend,
>   My companion and friend,
> To a taste of the banquet above;
>   If thy heart be as mine
>   If for Jesus it pine
> Come up into the chariot of love.
>
> By faith we are come
>   To our permanent home;
> By hope we the rapture improve;
>   By love we still rise,
>   And look down on the skies,
> For the heaven of heavens is love.[47]

This journey toward love, as Charles describes it in the hymn, requires a community of faithful companions. It takes a fellowship of believers, shaped by God's grace, to teach the children of God how to love. Wholeness means conformity to Christ in all things – holiness of heart and life. Faith is a means to the realization of this lofty goal. 'Lord, I believe, and not in vain –', claims Wesley, 'My faith shall make me whole'. And that faith makes it possible to prove, with all the saints, 'What is the length, and breadth, and height,/And depth of perfect love'.[48] He captures the essence of this quest in a one stanza reflection on Psalm 81.10:

Give me the enlarged desire,
  And open, Lord, my soul,
Thy own fullness to require,
  And comprehend the whole;
Stretch my faith's capacity
  Wider and yet wider still;
Then, with all that is in thee,
  My soul forever fill![49]

Wesley's poetic reflections on Ephesians 2.8–10 provide the most memorable lyrical expression of this central theme. As S T Kimbrough has observed: 'Unlike many of his other hymns, this text is not a prayer. It is an exhortation, an urging, an encouragement for all to plead for faith alone.' But this 'faith "forms the Saviour in the soul". The form of the Saviour, Jesus Christ, within us shapes our personalities, characters, attitudes, and demeanor. The essence of the Saviour is love and his love becomes the very essence of our being.'[50] The hymn describes faith as an ongoing, life-transforming experience, something for which the child of God yearns and stretches forward to receive as a gift:

Plead we thus for faith alone,
Faith which by our works is shown;
God it is who justifies,
Only faith the grace applies,
Active faith that lives within,
Conquers earth, and hell, and sin,
Sanctifies, and makes us whole,
Forms the Saviour in the soul.

Let us for this faith contend,
Sure salvation is its end;
Heaven already is begun,
Everlasting life is won.
Only let us persevere
Till we see our Lord appear;
Never from the rock remove,
Saved by faith which works by love.[51]

### III

A whole constellation of images, as can be easily seen, revolves around these three primary conceptions of faith. Wesley employs many other images, however, leaving us with a richly textured portrait of faith in his lyrical theology. Faith sustains, empowers, increases, assures; it is yearned for, called upon, and, though a gift, possessed; the arms of faith embrace, the unconquerable shield of faith guards and protects, the household of faith rejoices; faith leads the believer home. Of the many images Wesley uses to explore, illuminate and communicate the mystery of faith, several call for particular attention because of their pervasiveness in his writings and their enduring significance. These include the image of faith as the door opening into a new world of spiritual vitality, faith as power (and its close relationship to prayer and healing), and faith as the source of spiritual vision (the eye of faith) and light.

## The door of faith

The Wesleyan way of salvation consists essentially in three dynamic movements, summarized by John Wesley in an important piece of correspondence to Thomas Church: 'Our main doctrines, which include all the rest, are three – that of repentance, of faith, and of holiness. The first of these we account as it were, the porch of religion; the next, the door; and third, religion itself.'[52] Faith – or more precisely the experience of justification by grace through faith – is the door through which one enters the domain of true religion. The immediate biblical allusion upon which Charles draws is the apostles' report of their evangelistic labours upon return to Antioch and their celebration of the way in which God 'opened a door of faith for the Gentiles' (Acts 14.27). The Spirit elicited faith among these Gentile converts when the followers of Jesus offered Christ to them through the preaching of the Word.

Indeed, one of the most pervasive expressions in Charles' journal is the simple entry: 'I preached repentance towards God and faith in Jesus Christ.'[53] 'Fountain of unexhausted love, Of infinite compassions, hear', he prays, 'Repentance, faith and pardon give; O let me turn again and live!'[54] He pleads for the Spirit to remove all barriers to genuine reconciliation:

Still let the publicans draw near;
  Open the door of faith and heaven,
And grant their hearts thy word to hear,
  And witness all their sins forgiven.[55]

## The power of faith

Of greater mystery is the connection between faith and power, especially as this power is linked to prayer and to healing. One of Charles' favourite biblical images in this regard is the mustard seed faith that possesses the ability to move mountains:

That mighty faith on me bestow
  Which cannot ask in vain,
Which holds, and will not let thee go
  Till I my suit obtain.

On me that faith divine bestow
  Which doth the mountain move;
And all my spotless life shall show
  Th'omnipotence of love.[56]

'Give me the faith which can remove', he prays, 'And sink the mountain to a plain!'[57] The prayer of faith provides access to this capacity, this strength, as Charles makes clear in a lyrical reflection upon the whole armour of God:

> In fellowship, alone,
> To God with faith draw near;
> Approach his courts, besiege his throne
> With all the powers of prayer.[58]

The early Methodist people viewed their life as a journey with Christ in which, as in John Bunyan's classic account of the Christian pilgrim, progress is made only through struggle and even battle. And so, faith provides the resources for 'believers fighting':

> That bloody banner see,
> And in your Captain's sight
> Fight the good fight of faith with me,
> My fellow-soldiers, fight.

Tremendous impediments stand in the way of faith's journey toward love, but the 'ancient conqueror' arms the faithful followers who shout in triumph in the end:

> This is the victory!
> Before our faith they fall;
> Jesus hath died for you and me!
> Believe, and conquer all![59]

Convinced of the necessity of total dependence upon Christ in the Church's quest for righteousness and truth, Charles, along with the gathered community of faith, intercedes on behalf of the church in the life of the world:

> Jesu, from thy heavenly place,
> Thy dwelling in the sky,
> Fill our Church with righteousness,
> Our want of faith supply;
> Faith our strong protection be,
> And godliness with all its power
> 'Stablish our posterity
> Till time shall be no more.[60]

Not only is the prayer of faith a personal discipline, it is a corporate action. Faith requires a community. 'O let us stir each other up, Our faith by works to approve', Wesley admonishes, for only through this corporate act of obedience in love can we hope to 'Stretch out the arms of faith and prayer' and 'reach' God 'now!'[61] The prayer of faith is 'incessant;'[62] 'effectual and fervent' prayer brings spiritual healing and liberation.[63] While 'Faith to be healed thou know'st I have', claims Wesley before God, 'For thou that faith hast given',[64] the working of God's grace is a mystery, the depths of which can never to be fully plumbed. Not infrequently, therefore, prayer breaks forth into praise and faith takes on the wings of flight:

> Angels and archangels all
>   Praise the mystic Three in One,
> Sing, and stop, and gaze, and fall
>   O'erwhelmed before thy throne.

> Vying with that happy choir
>   Who chant thy praise above,
> We on eagles' wings aspire,
>   The wings of faith and love.[65]

## The eye of faith

Nearly twenty of Charles' hymns in the 1780 *Collection* refer explicitly to 'the eye(s) of faith' or to the connection between faith and spiritual vision. It is not too much to claim that this is another of Charles' favourite expressions. His first use of this language in the journal comes in the rather moving entry of 25 May as he stands before the Sacrament and continues to linger in the spiritual awakening of his Pentecost experience of 1738 and that of his brother from the previous day:

> I had no particular attention to the prayers: but in the prayer of consecration I saw, by the eye of faith, or rather, had a glimpse of, Christ's broken, mangled body, as taking [sic] down from the cross. Still I could not observe the prayer, but only repeat with tears, 'O love, love!'[66]

The primary object of this vision is the crucified Lord, whose remembrance not only fixes the image of the crucifix in the mind's eye but transforms the heart and soul:

> Vouchsafe us eyes of faith to see
> The Man transfixed on Calvary,
>   To know thee, who thou art –
> The one eternal God and true;
> And let the sight affect, subdue,
>   And break my stubborn heart.[67]

'Before my eyes of faith confessed', Charles sings, 'Stand forth a slaughtered Lamb'.[68]

The restoration of sight makes spiritual knowledge possible. Charles demonstrates great concern throughout his life for the intimacy involved in knowing God as God has known us. It should be no surprise, therefore, that the immediate consequence of the wrestler's discovery of God's 'Pure Universal Love' in Wesley's famous hymn, 'Come, O thou traveller unknown', is the unimpeded vision of God:

My prayer hath power with God; the grace
   Unspeakable I now receive;
Through faith I see thee face to face;
   I see thee face to face, and live!
In vain I have not wept and strove –
Thy nature, and thy name, is LOVE.[69]

His hymn on 'Moses' wish' articulates the same essential theme:

Before my faith's enlightened eyes
   Make all thy goodness pass!
Thy goodness is the sight I prize –
   O may I see thy smiling face!
Thy nature in my soul proclaim!
Reveal thy love, thy glorious name![70]

There is an interesting trajectory in the hymns of Charles Wesley that leads from faith to vision, from vision to knowledge, and from knowledge to the ultimate beatific vision of the God of love.[71] For Charles, as for John, as we have seen, faith always moves towards love.[72] So despite the fact that 'By faith we already behold/That lovely Jerusalem here',[73] the community of the faithful yearn for that day 'When faith in sight shall end', at the great marriage banquet of the Lamb and God brings 'strength, life, and rest' to ultimate fruition in Jesus.[74] The vision of Moses, once again, springs immediately into Wesley's mind, and he plays with the image of his theophany in a hymn on the nature of prayer:

The spirit of interceding grace
   Give us in faith to claim,
To wrestle till we see thy face,
   And know thy hidden name.

Then let me on the mountain top
   Behold thy open face,
Where faith in sight is swallowed up,
   And prayer [is] endless praise.[75]

God illuminates the soul with the gift of faith. God restores sight to the blind and rescues those who dwell in darkness. Those who entrust their lives to God through Christ by faith pray for all the fullness of God in their lives. One of Charles Wesley's 'redemption hymns' celebrates the language of faith and draws us ever upward to the amazing gift of faith working through love:

Father of Jesus Christ, the just,
   My Friend and Advocate with thee,
Pity a soul that fain would trust
   In him who lived and died for me.
But only thou canst make him known,
And in my heart reveal thy Son.

If drawn by thine alluring grace
  My want of living faith I feel,
Show me in Christ thy smiling face;
  What flesh and blood can ne'er reveal,
Thy coeternal Son display,
And call my darkness into day.

The gift unspeakable impart:
  Command the light of faith to shine,
To shine in my dark, drooping heart,
  And fill me with the life divine;
Now bid the new creation be!
O God, let there be faith in me!

Thee without faith I cannot please,
  Faith without thee I cannot have;
But thou hast sent the Prince of peace
  To seek my wandering soul, and save;
O Father, glorify thy Son,
And save me for his sake alone!

Save me through faith in Jesu's blood,
  That blood which he for all did shed;
For me, for me, thou know'st it flowed,
  For me, for me, thou hear'st it plead;
Assure me now my soul is thine,
And all thou art in Christ is mine![76]

## Notes

1 *CWJ*, 2.23–4.

2 *BE*, 7.194–5 (Hymn 92.1–3, 6).

3 It is important for me to note at the outset, perhaps, that it is not my intention in this brief chapter to examine the differences between and debate about dogmatic speech and the language of faith, although there may be important implications the theologian wishes to draw from this study. For a helpful discussion of this debate, primarily in Protestant theology, see Teresa Berger, *Theology in Hymns?*, 41–7. I use the phrase 'language of faith' throughout in a much more literal sense as the way in which Charles Wesley employs the term 'faith' and what we learn from his usage.

4 Newport, *Sermons*.

5 The principal sermons include Sermon 4 on 1 John 3.14 (particularly the second part of the sermon dealing with advices), Sermon 5 on 'Faith and Good Works' (Titus 3.8), Sermon 6 on Romans 3.23–4, Sermon 7 on Romans 3.23–5, and Sermon 8 on Ephesians 5.14.

6 A detailed analysis of the journal reveals the following usage of the term faith: 1736 (8), 1737 (1), 1738 (153), 1739 (63), 1740 (37), 1741 (15), 1743 (28), 1744 (18), 1745 (14), 1746 (13), 1747 (14), 1748 (20), 1749 (2), 1750 (2), 1751 (5), 1753 (2), 1756 (11).

7 Despite the fact that the vast majority of these hymns are from Charles' pen, it must be acknowledged that not all of these texts can be attributed directly to him. See *BE*, 7.31–8, 'The Sources of the *Collection*', for a discussion of attribution. Regardless, Charles (and John as well) 'owned' these hymns and their language. In the analysis of the hymns that follows I draw no conclusions with regard to the meaning of 'faith' from hymns other than those attributed incontrovertibly to Charles. Those hymns which directly reference faith are 1, 3, 4, 12, 14, 26, 37 (George Herbert), 50, 56, 58, 63, 71, 72, 73, 74, 77, 80, 81, 83, 86, 92, 107, 114, 116, 117, 118, 123, 124, 127, 129 (trans. of German hymn), 132, 134, 136, 137, 138, 142, 144, 146, 148, 158, 163, 166, 173, 176, 182 (trans. of German hymn), 184, 185, 186, 188 (trans. of German hymn), 192, 203, 208, 212, 219, 220, 226 (attrib. John Wesley), 231 (trans. of German hymn), 240, 249, 254, 259, 260, 264 (attrib. John Wesley?), 268, 269, 272, 274, 275, 277, 288, 289, 294, 297, 298, 303, 305, 314, 316, 318, 320, 324, 333, 337, 341 (attrib. John Wesley?), 343 (trans. of German hymn), 346, 347, 349, 350, 351, 354, 355, 357, 361, 364, 376, 378, 381, 382, 385, 386, 388, 391, 394, 402, 403, 408, 409, 419 (trans. of German hymn), 421, 433, 437, 442, 443, 444 (Henry More), 445 (Henry More), 446, 452, 453, 468, 471, 476, 477, 480, 484, 486, 489, 493, 497, 501, 505, 506, 507, 508, 509, 512, 515, 521, 523 and 525. I have provided parenthetical identifications for those 12 hymns that include references to 'faith' but cannot be attributed indisputably to Charles Wesley. It can be assumed that all of the remaining hymns are of his composition.

8 See Hymns 92, 'Author of faith'; 142, 'Father of Jesus Christ the just'; 350, 'Father of Jesus Christ my Lord'; and 507, 'Let us plead for faith alone'. In each of these 'signature hymns', Wesley refers to faith five or more times.

9 In other words, regardless of the section in the collection, Wesley explicitly refers to faith in one out of four hymns, with the exception of the very brief second section (only eight hymns), as demonstrated by the data from each section: Part 1 (20 out of 87 hymns or 23 per cent), Part 2 (1/8 or 12.5 per cent), Part 3 (23/86 or 27 per cent), Part 4 (76/283 or 27 per cent), Part 5 (21/61 or 34.5 per cent).

10 The Methodist authority on the Wesleys, Richard P. Heitzenrater, observes: 'It has long been a truism that the theology of the Wesleyan revival was carried on the wings of the Wesleys' hymns perhaps more readily than on the words of their sermons' (S T Kimbrough Jr, *A Heart to Praise My God: Wesley hymns for today* [Nashville: Abingdon Press, 1996], 5); cf. *BE*, 7.1–22 and Berger, *Theology in Hymns*, especially Parts II & III.

11 See Article 20 of the Augsburg Confession, in particular, in which this distinction is articulated clearly: '. . . the term "faith" does not signify only historical knowledge – the kind of faith that the ungodly and the devil have – but that it signifies faith which believes . . . Augustine also reminds his readers in this way about the word "faith" and teaches that in the Scriptures the word "faith" is understood not as knowledge, such as the ungodly have, but as trust that consoles and encourages terrified minds' (Robert Kolb and Timothy J. Wengert, eds, *The Book of Concord: The Confessions of the Evangelical Lutheran Church* (Minneapolis: Fortress Press, 2000), 57).

12 *Sermons*, 201. In his sermon on Romans 3.23–4, Wesley quotes Homily 3, 'Of Salvation', extensively, including the statement: 'Yet that faith which bringeth forth either evil works, or no good works, is not a right, pure and lively faith, but a dead, devilish counterfeit, and feigned faith. For even the devils know and believe all the Articles of our creed, and yet, for all this, they be but devils, remaining still in their damnable estate' (Newport, *Sermons*, 176).

13 *CWJ*, 1.228 (10 May 1740).

14 *CWJ*, 1.236 (2 June 1740).

15 *CWJ*, 2.10 (14 March 1748).

16 *CWJ*, 1.462 (2 October 1747).

17 The language 'true and lively faith' comes from both sources, from Article XII 'Of Good Works' and from Homily 4, entitled 'A Short Declaration of the True, Lively, and Christian Faith' ('Of Faith'). The edition of the *Homilies* upon which both Charles and John Wesley drew was undoubtedly the final reprint authorized by Charles II in 1683: *Certain Sermons or Homilies Appointed to be Read in Churches in the Time of the late Queen Elizabeth of Famous Memory; and now Thought fit to be Reprinted by Authority from the King's Most Excellent Majesty* (Oxford: Thomas Guy, 1683). The 1662 Book of Common Prayer, which included the '39 Articles of Religion', shaped the Wesleys' lives and theology in innumerable ways.

18 See Robin A. Leaver, 'Charles Wesley and Anglicanism', in Kimbrough, ed., *Charles Wesley: Poet and Theologian*, 157–75; and John Lawson, 'Charles Wesley: A Man of the Prayer-Book', *Proceedings of The Charles Wesley Society* 1 (1994), 85–118.

19 Newport, *Sermons*, 155.

20 *BE*, 7.261 (Hymn 144.3–5).

21 *BE*, 7.226 (Hymn 116.1).

22 *BE*, 7.259 (Hymn 142.2).

23 Newport, *Sermons*, 147.

24 I am indebted to Professor Timothy J. Wengert, Ministerium of Pennsylvania Professor of Christian History at the Lutheran Theological Seminary at Philadelphia, for documenting the development of this distinction in the Lutheran tradition. One of the late-seventeenth-century scholastics, Johann Wilhelm Baier (1647–95), distinguishes between 'subjective' faith, 'that by which one believes (faith, properly so-called, which dwells in a believer as a subject)' and 'objective faith, or that which is believed (which is the doctrine of faith, and which is figuratively called faith, because it is the object of faith)'. He used these terms in his major writings from which they were later taken over into common theological parlance. There is no evidence that either of the Wesleys had any knowledge of Baier's works.

25 *De Trinitate*, XIV.8.11. Italics mine.

26 As Robert Cushman observed: 'What is *fides*? It is acknowledgment (*agnitio*) of the Word in the form of the Servant. Preeminently, it is love awakened by the lowly form of the historical. It is fundamentally "a motion of the heart"'. Robert E. Cushman, *Faith Seeking Understanding* (Durham, North Carolina: Duke University Press, 1981), 20.

27 *BE*, 7.261 (Hymn 144.10).

28 In his discussion of 'the faithful life', Craig Dykstra observes: 'To many people, faith means belief. Faith is, indeed, closely related to belief, but the relations between the two are complex . . . Faith involves more than believing *that* something is true, it also involves believing *in*, having confidence in, trusting. Trust and confidence in God and in God's promises have been classical Protestant emphases in describing faith' (*Growing in the Life of Faith: Education and Christian Practices*, 2nd edn [Louisville: Westminster John Knox Press, 2005], 19–20). I explore these issues more fully in the next section on the doctrine of justification.

29 Newport, *Sermons*, 62.

30 Newport, *Sermons*, 183–210. Wesley's less protracted sermon on this text (Sermon 6 in *Sermons*, 167–82) obviously addresses the same subject, the preacher

taking pains to demonstrate that all have sinned and fall short of the glory of God and that the cure of humanity's diseased condition is faith in the blood of Christ. When he preached this more lengthy sermon before Oxford University in July 1739, he observed that 'all were very attentive. One could not help weeping' (John Telford, ed., *The Journal of the Rev. Charles Wesley* [London: Robert Culley, 1910], 241).

31 Indeed, 40 per cent of the shorter version of this sermon (Sermon 6) consists in direct quotations from this source (Newport, *Sermons*, 68). It is not too much to say that he was rediscovering the established doctrine of his church and explaining it to his hearers through these sermons.

32 Newport, *Sermons*, 199.

33 Newport, *Sermons*, 200.

34 See J. Ernest Rattenbury, *The Conversion of the Wesleys* (London: Epworth Press, 1938); Bernard Holland, 'The Conversions of John and Charles Wesley', *Proceedings of the Wesley Historical Society* 38 (1971–2), 46–53, 51–65; John Tyson, *Charles Wesley: A Reader*, 92–111; Neil Dixon, 'The Wesleys' Conversion Hymn', *Proceedings of the Wesley Historical Society*, 37 (February 1967), 43–7.

35 *BE*, 1.88 (17 May 1738).

36 *BE*, 1.92 (21 May 1738). In this brief chapter it is impossible to discuss one of the principal questions that consumed much of the Wesleys' time and apologetic energy in the months subsequent to these discoveries related to faith, namely, whether God can give faith instantaneously. On the basis of the scriptural evidence, the doctrine of their church, the witness of others, and their own experience, the brothers had become convinced of the validity of this claim. The fact that faith is God's gift, in fact, demanded the possibility. When Mrs Delamotte accused John Wesley of 'preaching an instantaneous faith', Charles sprang to his defence: 'As to that,' I replied, 'we cannot but speak the things which we have seen and heard' (*CWJ*, 1.110 [26 June 1738]). A parallel concern that troubled many of the Wesleyan antagonists had to do with what they considered to be the 'enthusiastic' claims of the Methodists with regard to assurance that accompanied the experience of justification by faith, an issue the Wesleys revisited on a number of occasions throughout their lifetimes and adapted accordingly. The close connection between justification and assurance in Charles Wesley's theology is explained, in part, by J. Ernest Rattenbury: 'Saving faith is, as [John Wesley's] early sermon ('Salvation by Faith') shows, a trust in Christ as a Saviour; in this sense it is difficult to distinguish it either from Assurance or the Witness of the Spirit. Charles makes this clear in the hymn "How can a sinner know." In point of fact, if the two notions are kept in mind that faith is a gift of God and also an evidence of things unseen, it necessarily follows that the distinction between it and Assurance and the Witness of the Spirit is so tenuous as hardly to be worth making' (*Evangelical Doctrines*, 265).

37 *BE*, 7.517 (Hymn 351.2). One also hears the echoes here of what might be claimed the greatest of all Charles Wesley's hymns, 'Wrestling Jacob'.

38 *BE*, 7.524 (Hymn 355.6). If asked how this experience is mediated to the would-be believer, Wesley would most certainly have quoted Romans 10.17, 'faith comes by hearing'. He uses this phrase repeatedly in his journal. While 'preaching faith' was essential to the appropriation of God's grace in the lives of the people to whom he ministered, Wesley also affirmed the mystery of faith and recognized the myriad ways in which his followers experienced God's love and grace through faith.

39  *BE*, 7.224–5 (Hymn 114.1, 3, 5).

40  It is worth noting that Charles' brother, John, abridged these three homilies, the pamphlet extract of which he published in 1738. The value of this publication can hardly be overemphasized. For the definitive text of *The Doctrine of Salvation, Faith, and Good Works* and discussion of this critical publication, consult Paul W. Chilcote and Randy L. Maddox, eds, *BE*, 12 (forthcoming); cf. Albert C. Outler, ed., *John Wesley* (New York: Oxford University Press, 1964), 121–33. For an excellent discussion of 'faith working by love' in the theology of John Wesley, see Randy L. Maddox, *Responsible Grace: John Wesley's Practical Theology* (Nashville: Kingswood Books, 1994), 174–6.

41  Quoted in Newport, *Sermons*, 30–1.

42  See Newport, *Sermons*, 152–66.

43  Newport, *Sermons*, 160–1.

44  Newport, *Sermons*, 150–1.

45  *BE*, 7.96 (Hymn 14.1).

46  *BE*, 7.623 (Hymn 443.2).

47  *BE*, 7.673 (Hymn 486.1, 3).

48  *BE*, 7.244–5 (Hymn 132.10–11).

49  *BE*, 7.529 (Hymn 361).

50  Kimbrough, *A Heart to Praise*, 128.

51  *BE*, 7.698–9 (Hymn 507.3–4). These two stanzas of 'The Love-feast' hymn were actually published separately in their original form as four four-line (7.7.7.7) stanzas in *Hymns and Sacred Poems* (London: Strahan, 1740), 183–4. They appear in the 1780 compilation as two eight-line stanzas, concluding the second section of a monumental 16-stanza poem divided into four parts of four stanzas each. The original version has been restored in many subsequent collections, including *The United Methodist Hymnal*, 385.

52  John Telford, ed., The *Letters of the Rev. John Wesley, A.M.* (London: Epworth Press, 1931), 2:268.

53  Cf. *CWJ*, 1.158 (7 August, 1739), 1.244 (30 June, 1740), 1.375 (2 August, 1744); and 1.406 (8 October, 1745).

54  *BE*, 7.286 (Hymn 163.3).

55  *BE*, 7.180 (Hymn 80.8).

56  *BE*, 7.489–90 (Hymn 333.3, 6).

57  *BE*, 7.596 (Hymn 412.1).

58  *BE*, 7.402 (Hymn 260.1).

59  *BE*, 7.412–3 (Hymn 268.3, 6).

60  *BE*, 7.631–2 (Hymn 452.1).

61  *BE*, 7.721 (Hymn 525.3).

62  *BE*, 7.613 (Hymn 437.2).

63  *BE*, 7.690 (Hymn 501.1).

64  *BE*, 7.249 (Hymn 135.3).

65  *BE*, 7.346 (Hymn 212.2, 3).

66  *CWJ*, 1.95–6 (25 May, 1738).

67  *BE*, 7.228 (Hymn 118.2).

68  *BE*, 7.235 (Hymn 124.6).

69  *BE*, 7.252 (Hymn 136.8).

70  *BE*, 7.422 (Hymn 274.2).

71  The parallels with the thought of Clement of Alexandria are rather startling: 'There seems to me to be a first kind of saving change from heathenism to faith, a

second from faith to knowledge, and this latter, as it passes on into love, begins at once to establish a mutual friendship between that which knows and that which is known' (Quoting *Stromateis*, VII.10.57.4, in J. Stevenson, ed., *A New Eusebius* [London: SPCK, 1957], 199–200). The incisive analysis of Rex Matthews with regard to faith in the development of John Wesley's thought may be of particular interest here. He demonstrates three distinct conceptions of faith in Wesley's works, namely, faith as assent, faith as trust, and faith as an actual spiritual experience, his emphasis moving sequentially toward the latter understanding in the mature Wesley. While it is not possible to chart Charles Wesley's developing conception of faith with such precision, there may be parallels, and the concept of the 'eye of faith' may point to this experiential dimension, grounded, as it is, in a spiritual sense. See the distillation of Rex Matthews' analysis in '"With the Eyes of Faith": Spiritual Experience and the Knowledge of God in the Theology of John Wesley', in *Wesleyan Theology Today*, ed. Theodore Runyon (Nashville: Kingswood Books, 1985), 406–15; cf. Maddox, *Responsible Grace*, 127–8.

72  In light of this movement from faith to love, Gordon Wakefield once claimed that the Wesleyan spirituality is more 'Catholic' than 'Protestant', a claim borne out by a close study of Charles' hymns and prose writings. See Gordon Wakefield, *Methodist Spirituality* (Peterborough: Epworth Press, 1999), where he maintains that Wesley's 'spiritual theology was based more on 'love of God' than the 'faith in Christ' of continental and Puritan Protestantism. The Christian must aim for nothing less than perfect love' (p. 24).

73  *BE*, 7.170 (Hymn 71.3).

74  *BE*, 7.340 (Hymn 208.5).

75  *BE*, 7.440–1 (Hymn 288.3, 6).

76  Wesley published the first three verses of this hymn as cited in *BE*, 7.259 (Hymn 142). The final two verses, restored here from the original *Hymns for those that seek, and those that have Redemption in the Blood of Jesus Christ* (London: Strahan, 1747), Hymn XIV, verses 4–5, are also restored in many of the subsequent hymnals.

# 18. Charles Wesley's Sermons

## KENNETH G. C. NEWPORT

As the many essays in this book so clearly demonstrate, Charles Wesley was a man of many and varied talents.[1] The one for which he is remembered today, of course, and almost exclusively so, is that of hymn writing; but there were others. Indeed, his own brother John once described Charles' poetic ability as the 'least' of those he possessed.[2] Few perhaps would agree with John here, and perhaps in saying that Charles Wesley's 'least' talent was that which he possessed in the poetic arena, and might argue that John may simply have been seeking here to extol longed-for virtues at the expense of an actual one. That is a possibility. Perhaps we should not be so quick to brush aside John's comments, however; at least not before considering the evidence.

In this chapter an attempt is made to address this issue with regard to Charles' preaching abilities. As we shall see, the mass of evidence suggests that Charles was a preacher of great power whose homiletic work, perhaps even more than his hymns, contributed much to the spread of Methodism, and indeed to its content, especially in the early years.

That preaching was at the very heart of Charles' life work is attested to extensively in the primary sources available to the researcher. Indeed, Charles' own journal is replete with references to this aspect of his work, so much so that at times the journal becomes little more than an annotated preaching log. The following extract from 1739 is not untypical.

> **Saturday, February 10.** I expounded to many hundreds at a Society in Beech Lane. **Sunday, February 11.** We prayed for utterance this day . . . I read prayers, and preached without notes on blind Bartimeus, the Lord being greatly my helper. Let him have all the glory. Returned to pray at Mr Stonehouse's. Miss Crisp asked to be admitted. We had close searching talk, before I expounded to the Society . . . **Tuesday, February 13.** Read a letter from Sarah Hurst, pressing me to Oxford, and Cowley (which is now vacant). Quite resigned, I offered myself; opened the book upon those words, 'With stammering lips, and with another tongue will he speak to this people' [Isaiah 28.11]. Thought it a prohibition, yet continued without a will. With Captain Flatman at the Marshalsea; read prayers, and preached from Luke 7.36, the woman washing Christ's feet. The word was with power; all attentive and thankful. Visited Zouberbouler, removed the Fleet. **Wednesday, February 14.** Read prayers at Newgate, and preached the law first, and then the gospel. Sang, 'Invitation to sinners.' All were affected.

**Thursday, February 15.** Preached again at the Marshalsea. Sent for by an harlot (supposed to be dying), and preached Christ, the friend of sinners, I trust to her heart.[3]

This entry in the journal is from a young, energetic Charles who has only relatively recently experienced his 'strange palpitation of heart'.[4] However, as a reading of the journal and other relevant primary material quickly shows, it is plain that Charles kept up this level of preaching for many years, and even towards the end of his life was still going strong. Thus, for example, James Sutcliff describes hearing Charles preach at a very advanced age. He wrote

The preacher was an aged gentleman in a plain coat and wig. His voice was clear, his aspect venerable and his manner devout. In his introductory sentences he was very deliberate, and presently made a pause of some moments. This I attributed to his age and infirmities, but in a while he made a second pause, twice as long as before. This to me was painful, but the people took no notice of it. However he helped himself out by quoting three verses of the hymn: 'Five bleeding wounds He bears, Received on Calvary'. And when I was most affected with sympathy for his infirmities, as I then thought, he quoted his text in Greek with remarkable fluency. Coming then to the great salvation, he was on his high horse, age and infirmities were left behind. It was a torrent of doctrine, of exhortation and eloquence bearing down all before him.[5]

Sutcliffe's views are those of a sympathetic admirer and must be seen as such. However, he does not stand alone in the view that Charles Wesley was an able and effective preacher. More than thirty years before Sutcliff, another early Methodist, John Nelson (1707–74), referred to Charles' preaching and again indicated that it was powerful indeed. In his diary, Nelson reports that Charles had passed briefly through Birstall, six miles outside Wakefield, around Michaelmas (29 September) 1742.[6] Charles pressed on quickly to Newcastle, but was later to return, and 'when Mr. Charles Wesley came back from Newcastle', wrote Nelson

the Lord was with him in such a manner that the pillars of hell seemed to tremble; many that were famous for supporting the devil's kingdom fell to the ground while he was preaching, as if they had been thunderstruck.[7]

Another interesting account of Charles' eloquence and ability comes from Joseph Williams of Kidderminster, who was a Congregationalist and not a Methodist. On 17 October 1739, Williams wrote to Charles asking him to look over a letter which he (Williams) intended to send to the editor of the *Gentleman's Magazine*.[8] The letter was designed as a defence of the Methodists who, states Williams, had been the object of 'the loud, the ignorant, and malignant clamours' which had been raised up against them. Williams himself had heard many rumours concerning Methodist belief and practice, but it was only after he had read Whitefield's *Discourse upon Generation, or the New Birth* that he had begun to get a clearer view of what the Methodists were really about. Some time later he had visited Bristol on business and had heard that Charles Wesley was to preach in the afternoon. Williams got a guide and went to hear him. There then follows a lengthy account of what he found which gives a detailed first-hand glimpse of Charles Wesley the preacher in action. It is worth quoting here in full.

I found him standing upon a table, in an erect posture, with his hands and eyes lifted up to heaven in prayer, surrounded with (I guess) more than a thousand people; some few of them persons of fashion, both men and women, but most of them of the lower rank of mankind. I know not how long he had been engaged in the duty before I came, but he continued therein, after my coming, scarce a quarter of an hour; during which time he prayed with uncommon fervency, fluency, and variety of proper expression. He then preached about an hour from the five last verses of the fifth chapter of the second Epistle to the Corinthians, in such a manner as I have seldom, if ever, heard any minister preach: i.e. though I have heard many a finer sermon, according to the common taste, or acceptation of sermons, yet I scarce ever heard any minister discover such evident signs of a most vehement desire, or labour so earnestly, to convince his hearers that they were all by nature in a state of enmity against God, consequently in a damnable state, and needed reconciliation to God; that God is willing to be reconciled to all, even the worst of sinners, and for that end laid all our guilt on Christ, hath imputed it to him, and Christ hath fulfilled all righteousness and punishment due to our sins in our nature and stead; that on the other hand the righteousness and merits of Christ are, and shall be, imputed to as many as believe on him; that it is faith alone, exclusive entirely of any works of ours, which applys to us the righteousness of Christ, and justifies us in the light of God; that none are excluded but those who refuse to come to him, as lost, undone, yea as damned sinners, and trust in him alone, i.e. his meritorious righteousness, and atoning sacrifice, for pardon and salvation. These points he backed all along as he went on with a great many texts of scripture, which he explained, and illustrated; and then freely invited all, even the chief of sinners, and used a great variety of the most moving arguments, and expositions, in order to persuade, allure, instigate and, if possible, compel them all to come to Christ, and believe in him for pardon and salvation. Nor did he fail to inform them thoroughly, how ineffectual their faith would be to justify them in the sight of God, unless it be wrought by love, purified their hearts, and reformed their lives: for though he cautioned them with the utmost care not to attribute any merit to their own performances, nor in the least degree rest on any works of their own, yet at the same time he thoroughly apprized them, that their faith is but a dead faith if it be not operative, and productive of good works, even all the good in their power.[9]

There is, then, ample evidence to suggest also that the craft of sermon construction, like the writing of hymns and other poetic compositions, was a form of literary activity to which Charles was able to give full and vibrant expression. Indeed, it was probably in the context of Charles' preaching abilities that John wrote to his brother 'In connexion I beat you; but in strong, pointed sentences, you beat me'.[10]

This last point is worth following up. John Wesley is of course known as one of the great preachers of the Christian Church, as indeed he was. However, according to John Whitehead (1740–1804), John Wesley's first official biographer, and an individual who had heard both John and Charles preach, Charles' sermons were the better. They were, said Whitehead, more 'awakening and useful' than John's.[11] This is high praise indeed when seen in the context of John's own not insignificant preaching abilities; and the testimony must be taken seriously as it is from one who, we might think, would be more likely to promote John than Charles. The evidence suggests, then, that Charles was indeed an exceptional preacher.

Seeking to assess the actual quality and content of Charles' preaching is not easy. The main problem by far is with the paucity of evidence. This is frustrating. Over the course of his life Charles must have preached many hundreds, indeed thousands, of sermons, but only a small handful have survived. Indeed, after a very extensive search of Methodist library catalogues in archives throughout the world, only 23 surviving sermon texts have been located.[12] Twenty of these survive in manuscript form, and all are held in the Methodist Archives at the John Rylands University Library of Manchester. This compares with John's sermons, texts for 151 of which have survived.[13]

One reason for the lack of surviving manuscripts for so many of Charles' sermons seems obvious: they never existed in the first place. This is so since Charles early developed the method of preaching without notes, that is, *ex tempore*, and the fact that he preached in this way means that little written material ever came into existence.

Quite when Charles adopted this policy of *ex tempore* preaching is not absolutely clear. It is Tyson's suggestion (the same basic point was made by Doughty in 1957)[14] that Charles began to develop the method on or about 15 October 1738 when, he writes, 'Preached the one thing needful at Islington, and added much extempore.'[15] Five days later Charles wrote

Seeing so few present at St. Antholin's, I thought of preaching extempore: afraid; yet ventured on the promise, 'Lo, I am with you always;' and spake on justification from Rom. 3 for three quarters of an hour, without hesitation. Glory be to God, who keepeth his promise forever.[16]

After this date, argues Tyson, Charles began increasingly to preach *ex tempore* and depended less upon written material.

As far as can be judged from the very limited evidence available, Tyson's basic point seems correct, though he probably overestimates the extent to which 15 October 1738 was the turning point. Charles had been 'adding much extempore' at least since 11 July of that year, when he 'preached faith in Christ to a vast congregation, with great boldness, adding much extempore'.[17] What we do know is that Charles had clearly developed the method of preaching totally without notes (as opposed to 'adding' extempore to a written text during the delivery) by the time Williams went to hear him preach, presumably

in late 1739. One of the things that impressed Williams with Charles' ability
as a preacher seems to have been that

> [a]lthough he [Charles] used no Notes, nor had anything in his Hand but a
> Bible, yet he delivered his Thoughts in a rich, copious Variety of Expressions,
> & with so much Propriety, that I could not observe anything incoherent, or
> inaccurate thro' the whole Performance.[18]

Already by 1739, then, according to Williams and the testimony of Charles'
own journal, he seems to have been preaching fairly regularly without notes,
or, it seems, even mental preparation. By March 1740 the method seems to be
well ingrained, so much so that Charles can describe the act of 'premeditating
what to preach' as 'unusual'. He wrote

> I was greatly distracted by an unusual unnecessary premeditating what
> to preach upon. My late discourses had worked different effects. Some
> were wounded, some hardened and scandalized above measure. I hear no
> neuters. The Word had turned them upside down. In the pulpit, I opened
> the book and found the place where it is written, 'the Spirit of the Lord is
> upon me, because He hath anointed me to preach the gospel to the poor, &c.'
> I explained our Lord's prophetic office, and described the persons on whom
> alone He could perform it. I found as did others that he owned me.[19]

It is true, as Baker notes,[20] that few knew the Bible as well as Charles, and
his knowledge of the scriptures made the business of *ex tempore* preaching
less of a hazardous occupation for him than it might have been for many.
However, he did encourage others to adopt the practice. This can be seen in a
letter written to him by Walter Shirley (1726–86), an evangelical Anglican who
became rector of Loughrea in Ireland.[21] In January 1760 Shirley wrote, 'I have
upon my late coming here assumed that resolution which your council [sic]
inspired, and no longer making use of a formal written discourse, I only plan
out the heads, and so trust to the Lord for the rest.'[22]

Shirley then goes on to discuss in greater detail what he considered to be
the chief benefits of this method of preaching. In December of the same year,
in another letter to Charles, Shirley thanks God for his gift of 'enabling me to
preach *ex tempore*' since it is a great blessing in his time of sickness not to have
to spend time preparing material before hand.[23]

Even where we do have texts for the sermons, they may well represent only
a portion of what Charles actually preached.[24] This is so since in the one case
mentioned that can be checked, a sermon on Ephesians 5.14 ('Awake thou that
Sleepest'), there is an obvious discrepancy between the written text and what
others said about how long it took Charles to preach it. It was claimed by a
critic that the orally delivered form of this sermon lasted two hours, though
Charles argued that it was in fact 'within one'.[25] Even on Charles' defensive
reckoning, however, it is plain that a substantial portion of what he said did
not make it into the published form, which takes about half an hour to read
aloud at a modest pace. Thus Charles must have expanded considerably upon
his written text, perhaps by adding, as did John, stories to illustrate par-

ticular points that were being made while keeping to the main topic under discussion.[26]

The true spirit and content of Charles' preaching, then, cannot be recaptured simply examining the few surviving texts of his sermons. The vast majority have not survived in any form, and even those for which there are written texts need to be treated with caution, for the written text and the spoken words seem often to have diverged. That 'much' which Charles 'added *ex tempore*' has gone for ever, but the references to it in the primary sources, i.e. the accounts of Charles' preaching that have survived, indicate that his work was held in very high regard.

## The texts

We turn now to an account of the texts themselves. Elsewhere I have described at some considerable length the nature of the evidence relative to the surviving Charles Wesley sermon corpus and argued that, even given some serious problems and doubts, the total number of confirmed sermons, standing at 23, is rather larger than has been previously stated.[27] That material need be only summarized briefly here.

Two of Charles Wesley's sermons were published during his lifetime, and both were eventually to find their way into editions of John Wesley's works. Both of these sermons carry the name of Charles as the author. The manuscript for neither has survived. These sermons are 'Awake thou that sleepest'[28] and 'The Cause and Cure of Earthquakes'.[29] No dispute surrounds the authorship of either text.[30]

In 1987 a major step was taken towards bringing to publication Charles' sermon material when six sermons, transcribed by Oliver Beckerlegge and Thomas Albin, were published as an occasional publication of the Wesley Historical Society.[31] Charles' authorship of these texts is certain and they have a real claim to being the heart of the surviving Charles Wesley homiletic corpus.

The texts of these sermons are in Byrom's shorthand, and the difficulty of transcribing the material does present something of a problem.[32] Albin and Beckerlegge did a first-rate job, and since then every single stroke of those at times infuriating shorthand texts has been examined again and, where it seems proper, alterations (or in some cases completions and additions) have been made to the deciphered form. As a result of this process most of the ambiguities that confront the reader of the Albin and Beckerlegge edition have now been ironed out.

The sermons in this category are:

1. Sermon on 1 John 3.14  1738  (16 July)
2. Sermon on Titus 3.8  1738  (21 December)
3. Sermon on Romans 3.23–4  1739  (1 January)
4. Sermon on Romans 3.23–5  1739  (1 July)
5. Sermon on John 8.1–11[33]  1739
6. Sermon on Luke 18.9–14[34]  No date

Nearly all the sermons in this category, then, are clearly dated from the period after Charles' 'strange palpitation of heart' that took place on 21 May 1738,[35] and the one undated manuscript seems also to come from this period. They exude a confidence in the salvation that comes in Christ.

In 1816 a small volume of sermons appeared under the title *Sermons by the Late Charles Wesley A.M. Student of Christ-Church, Oxford. With a Memoir of the Author by the Editor.* This volume poses major problems, which again have been dealt with more fully elsewhere, though a summary is required at this point.[36] The first problem to be negotiated is that of editorial emendation. Of the 12 sermons in the 1816 edition, manuscripts have survived for 11, and in each case comparison with the originals reveals marked divergence. That problem can of course be easily overcome by reference to those original manuscripts. New transcriptions of all these texts are now available.[37] The second and more major problem is that several of the sermons in the 1816 edition appear to be copies of sermons made by Charles from his brother's manuscripts. Indeed, Charles says as much (in shorthand) in the case of seven of the sermons. This fact was first noted by Richard Heitzenrater in 1969 and his remarks seem entirely accurate.[38] This does not mean, however, that the texts ought be excluded when examining Charles' homiletic work, for both common sense and indeed hard textual evidence suggests that Charles did not copy his brother's sermons without making editorial changes.[39] Similarly, the fact that Charles preached these sermons, some of them several times, means that they were in at least this sense 'his'.[40]

The other five sermons in the 1816 edition all stand at least a chance of being original Charles Wesley compositions. In three cases this looks more or less certain (sermons on 1 Kings 18.21; Psalm 126.6;[41] Philippians 3.13–14).

There are two further texts that need to be considered at this point: Charles' sermons on John 4.41 and Acts 20.7. Both sermons look secure as original Charles Wesley compositions. The sermon on John 4.41 appears to have been written as a first draft and there are lots of crossings-out and changes evident. The sermon on Acts 20.7, however (which would appear to be the first part of a three-part series), is in a much more polished form. It begins with a lengthy section in Greek, not just from the New Testament but from other early church sources too.[42]

These then are the 23 Charles Wesley sermon texts that are available to the researcher, and they are revealing. From them we can gain a glimpse of Charles' development as a preacher and also of his developing confidence in his quest for salvation.[43] However, as was noted above, what has survived is but a tiny fraction of what Charles preached and hence the full picture of Charles' homiletic work cannot now be reconstructed. The sample, however, backed up by the other primary materials such as Charles' own journal and contemporary reflections on Charles written by others, surely gives us an insight into this area of his ministry, an area at which he seemed to excel and may have been one of those other talents that his brother John had in mind when seeking to place Charles' poetic gift in wider context.

## Style

What has been said above provides some insight into the centrality of preaching to Charles' ministerial work and its importance in early Methodism, and it is the context of grass-roots Methodism that Charles' work needs primarily to be seen. It is true that Charles did preach before the University of Oxford (and we know also from Sutcliff and from the sermon on Acts 20.7 that he sometimes used Greek in his sermons); however, this was not the primary focus of his preaching activity. Neither, it seems, did Charles write many sermons for publication. He was, rather, an evangelical preacher whose interest was in conversion and the sustaining of faith as it was practised in the early Methodist societies.

This given, Charles was a child of his age and something needs to be said here briefly regarding the nature of preaching in the eighteenth century more generally and Charles' place within it. This is an area in which there has been a fair degree of work already, both in general histories[44] and more specific studies.[45] Indeed, Outler deals with the question in the very specific context of John Wesley's preaching, and much of what he says with respect to John is applicable also to Charles.[46]

In outline, Charles' sermons reflect the 'plain style' of preaching that had by the eighteenth century become fairly widespread. This 'plain style', as Outler observes, was argued for by John Wesley in the preface to the very first edition of his *Sermons on Several Occasions* (1746),[47] a volume which in fact contained Charles' own sermon 'Awake Thou that Sleepest'. This 'plain style' in the English homiletic tradition was more than just a Wesleyan whim, and, as Outler again notes,[48] in employing it the Wesleys were taking a particular stand on an issue that was widely debated in eighteenth-century England. On the other side of the divide stood those who followed in the tradition of Lancelot Andrewes (1555–1626), John Donne (1573–1631) and others.[49] The style of this latter school was ornate, depending for its power upon the exquisite use of language and exhibiting a carefully constructed web of conceits and images, internal rhymes and assonances. Dargan summed up Andrewes' sermons as

> at times artificial and stilted in tone, and often overloaded with learning and Latin quotations, not free from the whimsical fancies of the age, but weighty in thought, exhaustive in treatment and much occupied with the careful exposition of scripture: but his exposition is sometimes vitiated, both by polemical bias and the play of fancy.[50]

Charles, it must be said, could display some of the same characteristics. In addition to his use of Greek noted above, he can pick up also on nuances in the English language, as for example he does in a sermon on Luke 16.8 where he plays on various meanings of the word 'wiser' ('the children of this age are wiser than the children of light'). Similarly, some of the prose he uses in the sermons is quite elegant and he is often at pains to tie in what he has to say with the homilies[51] and the articles of the Church of England from which he again quotes at some length. Anyone listening to Charles would hence probably have to conclude that this was a man of considerable learning and mastery of the English language.

That said, much of what Charles had to say he said in a very direct and uncomplicated manner. Like his brother, he was aware that his design was to speak 'ad populum' and, it seems, he tailored his style to meet that end. His sermon on John 8.1–11, for example, is straightforward enough. The language is direct and uncomplicated and it is a sermon clearly designed to appeal to as wide an audience as possible.

The tradition of 'plain style' preaching in England was not new even in the eighteenth century, though quite when it began to emerge as a self-conscious reaction to other forms of the homiletic art is a matter of some dispute. Outler traces it back as far as Joseph Mede (1586–1638) and especially (with Smyth)[52] to the work of John Wilkins (1614–72), Bishop of Chester, who put forward a reasoned argument in favour of the style in his *Ecclesiastes: Or, A discourse concerning the gift of preaching as it falls under the rules of art* (1646).[53] Others have argued that the style is already in evidence in the preaching of Bishop Lloyd (1627–1717)[54] and, even earlier, that of Archbishop James Ussher (1581–1656).[55] It was arguably with John Tillotson (1630–94),[56] however, that the style came to fruition and it is perhaps significant that Charles had at least one volume of Tillotson's sermons in his personal library, suggesting that he had some interest in his work.[57] Tillotson, who became Archbishop of Canterbury in 1691, used a plain style, and exhibited simplicity in both language and plan. His style was to make a lasting impact on the English homiletic tradition. The 'three point rule' which he espoused, for example, is still influential today.[58] Its influence can be seen also in a number of Charles' sermons. In one of the earliest, sermon 2 on 1 Kings 18.21, he states that

> In discoursing upon which words I shall first show who they are that come under this censure of halting between two opinions. Secondly, I shall consider the folly and danger of such a state. And thirdly, conclude with an earnest exhortation to an entire devotion of ourselves to God.

A somewhat lesser figure than Tillotson, but perhaps of particular importance in the present context, is Robert South (1634–1716). South, an Anglican clergyman, sometime Canon of Christchurch and chaplain to Charles II, similarly employed the 'plain style' of preaching. Charles had three volumes of South's sermons in his own library.[59] Again, then, a potential direct link is hence established between Charles and his 'plain style' predecessors and contemporaries.

## Content

No full analysis of the content of Charles' sermon corpus can be attempted here. However, in this book much of Charles' theology has been brought to the surface by others and in this context it is a particular pleasure for me as an editor of this volume and an editor of the sermons to note that the latter has been used fairly extensively by others working on the life, legacy and literature of Charles Wesley. The sermons do help in assessing the theology of Charles, of that there can be no doubt, though we must remember the sorts of limitations and problems that the sermons present that have been noted above.

The sermons can, for example, give a fairly clear insight at least into the very broad framework of Charles' doctrine of salvation, and it makes an interesting study to read the sermons in the order in which they were composed. Charles can be seen to go from a very soteriologically uncertain position when he is preaching in America to a position of great assurance in the shorthand texts and others that stem from the post-1738 period. This is in fact quite noticeable when one reads the sermons through. The early material, some of it adapted from John but preached by Charles, is characterized by a fundamental uncertainty that salvation will be achieved. There are images of races and long roads and the inadvisability of stopping to rest, for if one does one will find the road is even longer when the journey is restarted than it was when it was left off. Christ appears predominantly as a demanding judge and not the 'friend of sinners' that Charles would later claim him to be. Indeed, in some of the sermons Christ barely appears at all. With 1738, however, a turning point did come. It is not complete and it would probably be unwise to seek to pinpoint an exact day, but the sermons that come after Charles' 'Day of Pentecost' are much lighter and we see a Charles who is now fully confident in the love of God and in the power of God to save, and to do so instantaneously. [60]

The new confidence and total dependence upon the power of God to save rather than the persistence of the sinner to see the race to its conclusion is reflected also in the journal where, following his experience (whatever that was), we frequently read of Charles' offer in his sermons of full, instantaneous salvation and the response that seems to have been the result. The following from 31 August, 1738 is typical:

At the Society read my sermon, 'The Scripture hath concluded all under sin', and urged upon each my usual question, 'Do you deserve to be damned?' Mrs Platt with the utmost vehemence cried out, 'Yes; I do, I do!' Prayed that if God saw there any contrite soul, he would fulfil his promise of coming and making his abode with it. 'If thou hast sent thy Spirit to reprove any sinner of sin, in the name of Jesus Christ, I claim salvation for that sinner!' Again she broke out into strong cries, but of joy, not sorrow, being quite overpowered with the love of Christ. I asked her if she believed in Jesus. She answered in full assurance of faith. We sang and rejoiced over her (she still continued kneeling), joined in thanksgiving; but her voice was heard above ours.

There is one aspect of Charles' preaching, however, that is perhaps not all that well reflected in other discussions of his theology but which in the context of a discussion of his preaching does need mention. This is Charles' fairly raw apocalypticism and his apparent conviction that Jesus would soon return to this earth and that his coming would be visible, glorious, cataclysmic and premillennial. An examination of the surviving texts fails to bring this adequately to the surface (the sermon on the 'Cause and Cure of Earthquakes' is a dramatic exception to this rule), but a reading of the journal and the letters makes it plain that belief in the soon-coming end of the present age was something with which Charles was intensely concerned, at least in the 1740s and 1750s.

The journal entry for 1 February 1745 is fairly typical. Here Charles wrote, 'At our watchnight I described the new Jerusalem, Rev. 21, and great was our rejoicing before the Lord.'[61] The wider context of this statement makes it clear that the New Jerusalem was something that Charles was anticipating coming to replace the present age rather than, as Augustine had said, a symbol of the Christian Church. Further, on 31 October 1747 he preached on 'These are they that came out of great tribulation, and washed their robes, and made them white in the blood of the Lamb [Revelation 7.14]' and recorded that 'It was a time of solemn rejoicing in hope of His coming to wipe away all tears from our eyes.' Here Charles is again clearly preaching from the book of Revelation; the allusions are to Revelation 7.14 and 21.4. Charles was working with the text preached again when on 16 July, 1751. He wrote 'At two rejoiced to meet some of our dear children in Sheffield. I encouraged them by that *most* glorious promise, "Behold, he cometh with clouds, and every eye shall see him" [Revelation 1.7]'. It would be easy to multiply such references, but such seems hardly necessary. The situation already looks plain enough: Charles, in addition to preaching repentance and the love of God, warned of the impending end of the age. This was no passing fad: it was a matter with which he was very concerned and which, as the journal makes plain enough, he preached on fairly frequently.[62]

## Conclusion

In this chapter it has been shown that preaching was central to Charles' ministerial career: the evidence is that he was good at it and that he did it a lot. While some of what has survived indicates that Charles could at times use a style of preaching that was rather ornate, making use of Greek and in other ways making apparent his not inconsiderable learning, a reading of the corpus as a whole, and even more so a study of the journal, locates him as a preacher *ad populum*. The preaching from the years following Charles' ordination in 1735 to 1738 appears to have been rather austere, while the texts dated after his 1738 experience reflect a much more confident, much less morose, Charles; a Charles who is now convinced that God will bring him to salvation and is who desperate to communicate this 'good news' to others. By accessing the primary sources relevant to this part of Charles work, we can catch a glimpse of the early Methodist preacher at work.

Perhaps, then, John's tongue was not entirely in his cheek when he described Charles' 'least' talent as his poetic. We will never know. At the very least, however, the evidence is that Charles surely deserves to be remembered as a quite exceptional preacher as well as a virtually unrivalled writer of hymns.

## Notes

1 Some of the material in this chapter was originally published in Newport, *Sermons*, and I am grateful to the Press for permission to use that material here.

2 See *Minutes of the Methodist Conferences, from the First, Held in London, by the Late Rev. John Wesley, A.M. in the Year 1744*, 4 vols [1812–18], 1.201.

3 References to the journal here are from the manuscript journal (MARC, DDCW, 10/2) and not from *CWJ*. The full text of DDCW, 10/2 has been prepared for publication by S T Kimbrough and Kenneth G. C. Newport and will appear in 2007 as *The Journal of Charles Wesley* (Nashville: Abingdon).

4 See journal entry for 21 May 1738.

5 As quoted in Flint, *Charles Wesley and His Colleagues*, 148. Flint also notes that 'Mr Wright' the plumber (Charles' brother-in-law) and the one for whom Wright worked went to hear Charles preach. Mr Wright's employer wrote: 'I find his business is only with the heart and the affections; as to the understanding, that must shift for itself . . . most of the clergy are in the contrary extreme, and apply themselves only to the head' (147).

6 Charles' journal from 22 September 1741 to 2 January 1743 is missing and so this cannot be checked against it.

7 John Nelson *et al.*, *Wesley's Veterans*, 7 vols. (London. Charles A. Kelly, 1912) 3.65. The quotation continues: 'One day he had preached four times; and one that had been amongst the people all day said at night twenty-two had received forgiveness of their sins that day.' Nelson then goes on to claim that about 'fourscore' of individuals were added to the number of 'true believers' as a result of Charles' and Mr Graves' labours. See further, W. L. Doughty, 'Charles Wesley, Preacher', *LQHR*, 182 (1957); 263–7, 267.

8 The letter which Williams intended to send and the covering letter to Charles Wesley are now held in the MARC, DDPr, 1/92. It was never published in the *Gentleman's Magazine*, but it did appear in *Wesleyan Methodist Magazine* (vol. 57 [1828], 383–5). The letter is an extract made by Williams of part of his own diary, the MS of which is held in Dr Williams' Library, London. (ref. If 6). A slightly more substantial extract from the diary, which includes the account of Williams' meeting with Charles, was published by Geoffrey F. Nuttall in 1980 ('Charles Wesley in 1739. By Joseph Williams of Kidderminster', *Proceedings of the Wesley Historical Society* 42 [1980], 181–5).

9 MARC, DDPr, 1/92, 2–3.

10 John Wesley to Charles Wesley, 27 June 1766 (*WJW*, 12.130–1).

11 John Whitehead, *Life of the Rev. John Wesley*, 2 vols (1793–6), 1.292. I owe this reference to *BE*, 1.2, n. 6.

12 In addition to these 23 full sermon texts there is also a very brief sermon outline located at Queen's College, University of Melbourne, Australia, ref. WF4, and a transcript of a Charles Wesley sermon found in the manuscript notebook of Samuel Robert. The notebook is in the personal possession of Dr John Walsh, Jesus College, Oxford.

13 There is an overlap in the numbers since eight of the texts contained in the Outler edition of John Wesley's sermons (*BE*, 1–4) are included also in the edition of Charles' sermons (Newport, *Sermons*, nos 16–23). The reasons for this overlap are made plain below.

14 Doughty, 'Charles Wesley, Preacher', 264.

15  DDCW, 10/2, *in loc.*

16  DDCW, 10/2, *in loc.*

17  DDCW, 10/2, *in loc.*

18  Nuttall, 'Charles Wesley', 184.

19  Charles Wesley to John Wesley, March 1740, as quoted in Baker, *Charles Wesley as Revealed by his Letters*, 38.

20  Baker, *Charles Wesley as Revealed by his Letters*, 38–9.

21  Harmon, ed., *Encyclopedia*, 2.2146.

22  Walter Shirley to Charles Wesley, 12 January 1760. MARC, DDPr, 1/69.

23  Walter Shirley to Charles Wesley [10 December 1760]. MARC, DDPr, 1/99. The date is taken from a note which Charles has himself made on the letter, which was presumably the date upon which it was received.

24  The length of Charles' sermons is far from uniform; among those for which manuscripts have survived there is considerable variety. The sermon on Romans 3.23–5, for example, is c. 10,000 words; the shorter of the two on 1 Kings 18.21 only c. 3,500. The journal and letters have much to say on the length of Charles' preaching. Note for example the journal entry for 10 September 1739 which records that at 'Gloucester-lane' he 'discoursed two hours on John 3' (DDCW, 10/2, *in loc.*). The letter which he wrote to his wife in June 1764 included a reference to 'Mr Venn' whom Charles had apparently chastized for preaching a 'long sermon' and then goes on to note that Charles himself preached at the Foundery 'near an hour and a half long' – see Charles Wesley to Sarah Wesley, 7 June [1764]. MARC, DDCW, 7/10 which is quoted in Baker, *Charles Wesley as Revealed by his Letters*, 37. Charles often spoke for more than an hour – see, for example, MARC, DDCW, 7/16, Letter of Charles Wesley to Sarah Wesley, 18 June [1763] in which he notes that his sermon on Psalm 23 lasted more than an hour, and then reports that 'I was near two hours speaking of blessed Mr Grimshaw', who had died in April 1763. Charles spoke for at least a hour on 'holiness' – see DDCW 7/31, Letter of Charles Wesley to Sarah Wesley. n.d. He refers also to 'the old days, at the Foundery, where I exhorted the society for above an hour to humility and love' – see DDCW, 7/20, Letter of Charles Wesley to Sarah Wesley, n.d.

25  See Charles' journal for 15 April 1750 where he reports that he read 'Mr. Salmon's *"Foreigner's Companion through the Universities of Cambridge and Oxford"* printed in 1748' and extracted Salmon's remark that: 'The times of the day the University go to this church, are ten in the morning, and two in the afternoon, on Sundays and holidays, the sermon usually lasting about half an hour. But when I happened to be ~~there~~ at Oxford, in 1742, Mr W[esley], the Methodist, of Christ-Church, entertained his audience two hours, and, having insulted and abused all degrees, from the highest to the lowest, was in a manner hissed out of the pulpit by the lads.' Charles rejected this claim and stated that the sermon 'was within the hour' and that he was not 'hissed out of the pulpit' as charged.

26  See further, Heitzenrater, *Mirror and Memory*, 162–73.

27  Newport, *Sermons of Charles Wesley*, chapter 4.

28  'A Sermon preached on Sunday, April 4th, 1742, before the University of Oxford. By Charles Wesley, M.A., Student of Christ Church' (London, n.d.). The second edition indicates that it was printed by W. Strahan in 1742. The sermon is included in Outler's edition of John Wesley's sermons (*BE*, 1.142–58).

29  *The Cause and Cure of Earthquakes: A sermon preached from Psalm xlvi. 8. occasioned by the earthquake on March 8th, 1750* (London, 1750). The second edition (1756) gives the name of the author as Charles Wesley. The sermon is not included by

Outler, but it is found in the conference edition of John Wesley's works (7.386–99).

30 See Newport, *Sermons*, 71–2.

31 Beckerlegge and Albin, eds, *Charles Wesley's Earliest Evangelical Sermons*.

32 On which see further Chapter 20 below.

33 Two different manuscripts for this sermon have survived, though one is very short indeed.

34 Two somewhat different manuscripts for this sermon have survived.

35 DDCW, 10/2, *in loc.*

36 See Newport, *Sermons*, 77–85.

37 See Newport, *Sermons*, sermons nos 1–3, 15–16, 18–23.

38 See Richard P. Heitzenrater, 'John Wesley's Earliest Sermons', *Proceedings of the Wesley Historical Society*, 37 (1969–70), 112–13.

39 See Newport, *Sermons*, 78–81.

40 See Newport, *Sermons*, chapter 4.

41 Charles actually gives the reference as '126.7' which is the verse reference in the *BCP*.

42 See Newport, *Sermons*, No. 13.

43 On this latter point see especially Newport, *Sermons*, chapter 3.

44 See, for examples, Charles Smyth, *The Art of Preaching: A practical survey of preaching in the Church of England 1747–1939* (London: SPCK, 1940), 99–166; Edwin Charles Dargan, *A History of Preaching*, 2 vols (London: Hodder and Stoughton, 1905–12), 2.186–349.

45 Among the more useful works in this area are James Downey, *The Eighteenth-Century Pulpit: A study of the sermons of Butler, Berkeley, Secker, Sterne, Whitefield and Wesley* (Oxford: Clarendon, 1969). A sample collection of some of the relevant texts is found in C. H. Sisson, *The English Sermon Volume II: 1650–1750* (Cheadle Hulme, Cheshire: Carcanet Press Ltd, 1976) and Robert Nye, ed., *The English Sermon Volume III: 1750–1850* (Cheadle Hulme, Cheshire: Carcanet Press Ltd, 1976); William Fraser Mitchell, *English Pulpit Oratory from Andrewes to Tillotson*, 2nd edn (London: Macmillan, 1962).

46 Outler, *Sermons*, 4.13–29.

47 Thus Wesley wrote concerning the sermons presented in that volume: 'But I am thoroughly sensible, these are not proposed, in such a manner as some may expect. Nothing here appears, in an elaborate, elegant, or oratorical dress. If it had been my desire or design to write thus, my leisure would not permit. But in truth I, at present, designed nothing less; for I now write (as I generally speak) *ad populum*: to the bulk of mankind, to those who neither relish nor understand the art of speaking: but who, notwithstanding, are competent judges of those truths, which are necessary to present and future happiness. I mention this, that curious readers may spare themselves the labor, of seeking for what they will not find. I design plain truth for plain people. Therefore of set purpose I abstain from all nice and philosophical speculations, from all perplexed and intricate reasonings; and as far as possible, from even the show of learning, unless in sometimes citing the original Scriptures. I labor to avoid all words which are not easy to be understood, all which are not used in common life: and in particular those kinds of technical terms, that so frequently occur in bodies of divinity, those modes of speaking which men of reading are intimately acquainted with, but which to common people are an unknown tongue.' (*Sermons on Several Occasions* [1746], iv–v).

48 Outler, *Sermons*, 1.21.

49 See further Outler, *Sermons*, 1.21.

50  Dargan, *History of Preaching*, 2.150.

51  As a clergyman Charles was well acquainted with the Homilies of the Church of England and indeed uses them fairly extensively in several of the sermons. The production and publication of these Homilies was first agreed in 1542, though they did not appear until 1547. There were originally 12, but to these were added 21 more in *c.* 1563, and the collection reached its final form in 1571. See further F. W. Cross and E. A. Livingstone, eds, *Oxford Dictionary of the Christian Church*, 3rd edn (Oxford: Oxford University Press, 1997), 785–6. The form known to Charles would have been one very similar to the 1766 edition held at the John Rylands University Library of Manchester entitled *Certain Sermons or Homilies Appointed to be Read in the Churches in the Time of Queen Elizabeth of Famous Memory. Together with The Thirty-Nine Articles of Religion.*

52  Smyth, *The Art of Preaching*, 99.

53  See further, *BE*, 1.23.

54  Smyth, *The Art of Preaching*, 99.

55  Smyth, *The Art of Preaching*, 99.

56  On Tillotson, see especially Smyth, *The Art of Preaching*, 99–166. A sample sermon is found in Nye, *The English Sermon*, 193–204.

57  John Tillotson, *Of Sincerity and Constancy in the Faith and Profession of True Religion, in Several Sermons* (1695), MARC, MAW.CW25. The 'MAW.CW' collection at the MARC is Charles Wesley's own library which, rather helpfully, has survived intact as a separate unit with the collection. This material is fairly well catalogued, but to date little research on it has been conducted. This volume from Tillotson carries Charles' signature inside the front cover.

58  See W. E. Sangster, *The Craft of Sermon Construction*, reprint ed. (London: Marshall Pickering, 1978), 100ff. Sangster is actually arguing against what he considers to be a slavish following of the 'three decker' rule. The fact that he here is concerned to argue for departure from it suggests that it is still very much a part of the norm.

59  Robert South, *Twelve Sermons upon Several Subjects and Occasions* (1698) MARC MAW.CW26; *Twelve Sermons Preached at Several Times, and upon Several Occasions* (1715) MARC, MAW.CW27; *Twelve Sermons and Discourses on Several Subjects and Occasions* (1717) MARC, MAW.CW28. The first and third volumes contain the annotation, in Charles' hand, 'Cha. Wesley X$^t$. Ch. Oxon'.

60  See Newport, *Sermons*, 54–66 for a fuller account.

61  DDCW, 10/2, *in loc.*

62  See further, Kenneth G. C. Newport, *Apocalypse and Millennium: Studies in biblical eisegesis* (Cambridge: Cambridge University Press, 2000), 119–49.

# 19. The Letters of Charles Wesley

## GARETH LLOYD

The correspondence of Charles Wesley represents one of the great documentary treasures of the Evangelical Revival, an event that had an enduring influence across a number of areas of early modern history, from popular religion to the fight against slavery and the rise of trade unions. The case for the collection's significance stands on a number of solid foundations. In the first place there is the importance of Charles Wesley himself. Regarded as one of the greatest hymn writers that the Christian Church has produced, Charles was also an important figure in the development of two of the world's major denominational families. As a life-long Anglican, Charles' ministry contributed to the birth of the evangelical wing of the Church of England and he was also co-founder of the Methodist churches, a family of denominations that in 2001 had a world membership of over fifty million. The pivotal role played by his brother John Wesley in Methodism's birth has received considerable attention, but Charles too made a vital contribution across a number of areas unrelated to hymnody.

The archive is important also because of its size and expansive date coverage. There are approximately 750 letters written by Charles Wesley dispersed in archive institutions around the world, with more than three-quarters deposited as a discrete collection in the Methodist Archives in the John Rylands University Library at the University of Manchester.[1] The earliest letter is dated 1727 when Charles was barely out of his teens, and the last was written shortly before he died at the age of 81. The 60 years between those dates witnessed a radical transformation not just in Charles Wesley's life but also in the society and the Church in which he was raised. The letters document in vivid detail the many twists and turns of one man's contribution to a momentous period in church history. Their importance is enhanced by the fact that Charles' journal terminates in 1756 and we are therefore dependent on the correspondence for documentation of the last 30 years of his life.

Attention should also be drawn to the existence of the many hundreds of letters written to Charles Wesley. This material has never received the attention given to items bearing a Wesley autograph, but it does represent a rich source in its own right. At the Rylands Library alone, there are approximately six hundred such letters. They include correspondence to Charles from other evangelical leaders including 60 letters from John Fletcher and 22 from members of the family of Vincent Perronet. There are also several hundred letters sent to Charles by a diverse number of preachers and lay members of the societies including more than one hundred and fifty conversion testimonies written during the decade commencing 1738. These represent a rare opportunity to study early evangelical spirituality at its grassroots.

One might expect that the Charles Wesley correspondence collection would be well known in church historical circles, but it is in fact surprisingly underused. In part this is a product of the general neglect afforded to Charles' place in evangelical history. He has been a controversial figure, one whose opinions and ministry in later life was a source of acute discomfort to Methodist historians. The fact that there have been very few biographical works written about Charles Wesley means that the evidence provided by his correspondence has not been fully employed in the most obvious area of study that one would expect.[2] This situation is exacerbated by the fact that comparatively few of the letters are in print, and these have not in many cases been accurately transcribed.

The first attempt to make the letters available for research came with the publication in 1841 of extracts in Thomas Jackson's two-volume life of Charles Wesley.[3] This was followed eight years later by Jackson's edition of Charles' journal to which was added an appendix containing transcripts of 106 letters,[4] consisting mainly of correspondence written to his wife Sarah. In his introduction to the journal Jackson states that his selection was based on the material's value as illustrations of Charles' ministerial excellence and happy family life.[5] He also made the important point that the letters compensate for the fact that the journal terminates in 1756.[6] In the context of Jackson's work therefore, the correspondence represented an opportunity to continue the narration of his subject's life.

Jackson's transcripts and quotations from the primary sources are extremely unreliable and should not be used as the basis for research. The clear evidence is that Jackson tampered with the original text in ways that went far beyond correction of grammar or punctuation.[7] Jackson's aim appears to have been the removal of anything that did not fit the accepted iconic picture of early Methodist history. Comments critical of John Wesley or the brothers' itinerant preachers were routinely excised or watered down, and more domestic matters were also removed as somehow unworthy of the great hymn writer. The following letter, written from London in 1766 to Sarah Wesley, stands as an example of Jackson's abuse of the primary material. Words and passages set in italic are missing from the journal edition and have never been published:

My Beloved Friend,

Yesterday I dined at M. Heritage's, with Miss Darby and Billy Ley. Ask Mr. Brown, Mr. Rouquet, and whom else you meet, if they can get him a curacy at or near Bristol.

[I] walked with him to the Lock, where Mr. Madan sincerely desired and pressed me to preach, but in vain. If I cannot do the poor rich people good, I would not hinder him from doing it. I attended an hour to the singers, and heard Mr. Madan for another hour or more, on searching the Scriptures. His chapel is always crowded, and many souls will doubtless be saved through his ministry. He showed me a young woman lately acquitted of murdering her child, though the fact was undeniable. She seems now under deep convictions.

I got a good deal of rest last night; breakfasted this morning with M. Gumley, who made me an offer of Drayton living, in Oxfordshire, the drunken Incumbent being near death. I neither refused nor accepted it; for I had not consulted you.

*Lord Robert [Manners], whom I visited begs and entreats you to continue phys-icking [unreadable word] and Sammi [Samuel Wesley junior] once a week for at least a month after the doctors, pothecaries, and nurses have done physicking them.*

I dined at Miss Gideon's. We spent half an hour before dinner in the best way. She is setting out for Brighthelmstone, weak in body as weak can be; but strong in faith working by love. The Gospel Ministers have thrown away upon her much pains to alienate her from my [brother] and me. She is too humble to imbibe their envious spirit.

*Drank tea with your hearty friend Miss Hardy and rode to Islington to bespeak with Beck's help, a lodging for her. Slept at my host Evans's.*

*Sunday July 27. Mr Lewis did not speak truth. All the stewards did not forbid Isaac for W. Hopkins did not but we have had enough of it. Insult is added to ingratitude, yet they cannot hurt us unless we choose it. I hope neither you nor I shall think any more of them.*

Comfort poor S. Pownal. My brother writes, he will give her £5 till she can provide for herself. A poor recompence! It is pity our friends could not find out something for her.

Sunday Afternoon. I preached in the morning on, 'I will bring the third part through the fire;' and many rejoiced for the consolation. We had a vast number of communicants, and the spirit of supplications abundantly poured out. *I carried Mr Stokes to dinner at M. Bird's: Mr and Mrs Judd present as usual. My friend was much delighted with them all and observed of what a differ-ent spirit they are from the good people of Bristol. We drank tea at Brother Kemp's, another great favourite of Mr Stokes's. He sets out on Tuesday for Bristol, but to make sure I send this by the post. Ask him how he likes M. Boult from the glimpse I have him of her.*[8]

Jackson's censorship, which also extended to the text of the journal, represents a significant obstacle to scholarship. Charles' social circle and his children's health may have seemed mundane matters to Jackson, but they represented important parts of his subject's life. It is impossible to arrive at a true picture of Charles Wesley or the times in which he lived without taking them into consideration. The fact that Jackson's published versions of the letters remain uncorrected, if not exactly unchallenged, has helped to perpetuate a distorted image of the man and his ministry.

Since Jackson, attempts to publish Charles Wesley's correspondence, either in whole or as extracts, have been few and sporadic. In 1948 appeared *Charles Wesley as Revealed by his Letters*, in which Frank Baker used the collection as the basis for a fresh biographical study, quoting from over two hundred docu-ments, more than half of which had not appeared previously in published form.[9] In his introduction Baker, the foremost Methodist historian of his day, attested to the low profile that Charles' letters enjoyed compared with those of his brother John.[10] Unfortunately, Baker did not provide full bibliographical information concerning his sources and this seriously limited the value of his work as a means of access to the collection. Baker transcribed about six hundred of the letters,[11] but his intended full-text edition of the correspondence was never completed.

It was not until 1989 that the next major academic work to make use of the letters appeared. This was a collection of transcriptions and extracts from Charles Wesley's sermons, poetry, journal and correspondence, edited by John Tyson.[12] Like Baker and Jackson before him, Tyson confirmed in his introduction that the correspondence represented a 'virtually unutilized source for examining the man and his ministry'.[13] Tyson's use of the correspondence is, however, disappointing – only 33 letters were included in his selection of 302 documents and just seven of the letters were based on original manuscripts. The rest were taken from Jackson's biography of Charles or his edition of the journal,[14] both of which were published over one hundred and fifty years ago, and, as we have seen, do not meet the kinds of standards of scholarship that would be expected today.

In 1993 Emory University published the correspondence between the Wesley and Langshaw families as a volume in the Texts and Studies in Ecclesiastical Life series.[15] This included 24 letters written by Charles and two sent to him by John Langshaw, organist of Lancaster Parish Church, dated between 1778 and 1784.[16] The collection benefits from a well-written introduction and extensive annotations. It is to be regretted therefore that the edition covers only a very small part of the overall Charles Wesley archive and that the focus is very much restricted to musical matters.

Outside of the major collections, individual letters have appeared in print both in books and serial publications. The proceedings of the Wesley Historical Society contain several examples, such as the letter written to Sally Kirkham under her pen name 'Varanese' in February 1736.[17] Such publications, especially from the early period, have been invaluable in the preservation of material that would otherwise have been lost. For example, in 1791 Joseph Priestley published a collection of letters that included two written by Charles Wesley,[18] the originals of which have since vanished. Unfortunately, such publications tend to be little known and copies are accessible only in special collection libraries. It is only in recent years that an accurate and comprehensive list has been compiled of surviving correspondence, both in manuscript and printed form, together with their locations.[19]

The sum of the above is this: of the approximately seven hundred and fifty extant letters written by Charles Wesley, less than a third have been published in anything like a complete version and a considerable percentage of those printed transcripts cannot be regarded as accurate. As with many other areas of early Methodist scholarship, there has been an unhealthy reliance on nineteenth-century secondary sources and insufficient attention devoted to working with the primary material in order to achieve textual accuracy. The situation is even more pessimistic when one considers letters written to Charles Wesley, as, with the exception of family correspondence, very few of these have aroused any scholarly interest at all.

One of the reasons why the correspondence has not received more than cursory attention, is, perhaps, Charles' letter-writing style, which was idiosyncratic at best and could even be described as eccentric. Charles was not writing for publication or posterity and this is reflected in important features of the collection. Many of the letters are undated and unsigned, especially those written to his wife. In 1948 Baker stated that 'of about 250 [letters] so far transcribed . . . there is not one signed, and only five initialled whilst only 36 are adequately dated'.[20] The fact that many of the letters do not bear a signature has probably resulted in failure to identify Charles as the author and it should be assumed that papers have been destroyed as a result or lie unrecognized in archive institutions. When one places Charles' undated and unsigned manuscripts alongside those of his brother John, the fact that historians have shown a marked preference for studying early Methodism through the older man's papers is understandable. John was more systematic and careful in his record-keeping and gives the impression that he was very aware of future generations looking over his shoulder.

The absence of dates and signatures does not in fact present insuperable difficulties. Many of the letters can be easily dated enough through internal evidence, and, for papers written before 1756, cross-checking against the journal often leads to fairly firm conclusions. Similarly, Charles' handwriting is easily recognizable and he makes regular use of characteristic salutations such as 'farewell',[21] 'Adieu',[22] or a more spiritual closing reflection such as 'The Lord be your strength and peace!'[23] The association of such unusual concluding lines with the absence of a following signature becomes in itself a clear identification. This does, however, require the development of a deeper acquaintance with the collection than most scholars have been willing to acquire.

There are other features of Charles' letter-writing habits that have not helped in the process of making the material more accessible. His handwriting, while clear enough on most occasions, can vary drastically in quality and legibility, and often words are missing or placed out of context as his brain moved faster than his pen. One can trace the ups and downs of Charles' volatile nature by the appearance of his letters just as much as through their content. This is a particular feature of correspondence written during Charles' courtship of Sarah Gwynne in 1748 and 1749, as negotiations over the marriage contract did not always proceed smoothly. His habit of using initials in preference to proper names is also frustrating; often these are easily identified, such as George Whitefield for 'GW',[24] but more lowly members of the societies are likely to go unrecognized by the historian.

Charles' occasional use of shorthand presents another problem.[25] Knowledge of the Byrom system even in Wesley's time was restricted to a small number of people and it quickly vanished entirely except in specialist circles.[26] Furthermore, Charles' use of abbreviations within the shorthand sometimes renders its interpretation virtually impossible except to scholars who have an intimate knowledge of Wesley's life[27] – for example, Charles often used the letters 'TMB' as the abbreviation for 'to my brother'. In addition to shorthand transcriptions of entire documents, Charles also used the shorthand in passages of plain text to disguise the names of those who he wished to criticize.[28] It is true that this is more a feature of the manuscript journal than the correspondence, but it has certainly contributed to the difficult reputation of Charles' non-poetic corpus.

There are, however, many attractive aspects of Charles Wesley as a letter-writer and these contribute greatly to the value of the collection. His brother John, who was not one for giving praise lightly or often, stated that 'I am very sensible that writing letters is my brother's talent not mine.'[29] Charles Wesley's prose style is characterized by vigour and eloquence; his personality leaps from the page, expressed in language that reflects both his prodigious talent for poetry and flair for narrative.[30] The following description of a winter journey in 1748 evokes the harsh reality of eighteenth-century travel as well as the uncompromising Wesley character:

Friday morning, soon after 4 I set out in the thick darkness and rain. We had only one shower but it lasted from morning to night. By half hour past eight we got in sad plight to Calne; set out in an hour as wet as we came in somewhat against my companion's will, who did not understand me when I told him I never slack my pace for wind or weather. In a quarter of an hour I was again wet to the skin; the wind driving the rain in our faces so violently we could scarce sit on the horses. It grew stronger and stronger the nearer we came to the Downs. I foresaw the trial approaching and prepared for a storm. It was the fiercest I ever knew either by land or by sea. Before we had rode half a mile on the Downs, the wind took my horse off his legs and blew me off his back. I dared not mount again the beast was blown down so often. Forty times, I believe, I was overturned and born to the ground. Never had I such a combat with the wind. It was labour indeed to bear up against it . . .

Many times it stopped me as if caught in a man's arms. Once it blew me over a bank and drove me many yards out of the road before I could turn. For a mile and a half I struggled on, till my strength was quite spent when I came to mount my weary beast. How we got 16 miles farther I cannot tell; for when we came to Hungerford, there was scarce any sense or life in us. My fellow traveller was only less wet and battered than me. We would have shifted our clothes, but our linen in the bags was in the same condition with ourselves. However we dried it in some time and changed. I almost lost the use of my right arm. It cost me all my rhetoric to get my companion out again. He rode on groaning as far as Newbury, ten miles from Hungerford, and then refused to stir a step farther. I was forced to drop him and ride alone to Woolhampton 6 miles farther. My last hour was calm. From 4 to 5 I had spent at the Throne of Grace with my dearest friends of G. [Garth] offering up each particularly to the Father of Mercies through Jesus the righteous and wrestling for the blessing. Yea and they shall be blessed, I cannot doubt both in this world and the world to come. By 7 the moon lit me to my inn. I lay down from 9 to 3 and rested better than I expected.

Saturday December 17. Took horse at 4 in a bright star-light morning. Such cheerfulness of heart, such a spirit of joy and thanksgiving I have not felt for some years. Five hours passed away imperceptibly; and I forgot my body till I came to Maidenhead . . .[31]

One of the most interesting and valuable features of Charles' correspondence is the contrast that it illustrates between the characters of the Wesley brothers. They were, in many respects, strikingly different personalities, and this is reflected in their personal papers. John was not one for displaying his innermost thoughts and although he left a huge collection of extant letters, it is surprisingly difficult to gain an intimate picture of the man from them. His correspondence tells us infinitely more about the movement that he created than the personality of the man who created it.[32] This is particularly the case with documents written after the birth of Methodism in 1739 and these form the bulk of the John Wesley collection. Correspondence became the principal tool by which Charles' brother administered the far-flung societies and although there is inevitably some personal reflection, John's public face as the supreme leader of the Methodists was never far from view. In a letter written to the layman Thomas Bigg at the time of the collapse of John's engagement to Grace Murray, he revealed an habitual concern with keeping his deepest thoughts to himself, even in private communications: 'To you therefore I can freely speak my mind as knowing it will go no further.'[33] Such occasions when John Wesley allowed his mask to slip were very rare.

Charles Wesley, by way of contrast, found it difficult to conceal his true state of mind, and he probably had little interest in trying. His letters are intensely personal, reflecting a nature that was by turn openly affectionate, fiercely abrupt, exuberant and prone to depression. Unlike his brother, Charles' personal life tends to be fully exposed in the pages of his correspondence; letters written from London during his lengthy visits in the 1750s and 1760s contain touching glimpses of a husband and father anxiously counting the days until he could be reunited with his family.[34] His loving and slightly fretful concern is shown in such passages as the following, from a letter of 1766 to his wife:

> I am looking towards Bristol and counting the hours till we meet. By your next, I expect news of Sammy's first teeth appearing; of Charles and Sally's continued health and progress in their respective learning. He is a long time learning one [musical] solo and wants me to hear him more diligently . . . The Lord bless you all.[35]

This experience of being a devoted family man, one that came to Charles relatively late in life, gave him an understanding of other people's domestic situations. His empathy is shown in such passages as the following from a letter written to the London layman Thomas Marriott after the death of Marriott's son:

> Jesus wept to see his creatures weeping. He does not disapprove your feeling your loss; neither do you offer to God a sacrifice which costs you naught . . . My partner sympathizes with yours. We lost our only son by the smallpox.[36]

More than fifty years after Charles Wesley's death, aged members of the London society could still recall him as someone who was 'singularly tender and affectionate in his manner, when addressing those that were afflicted in mind, body, or estate'.[37] By contrast, John Wesley sometimes displayed remarkable insensitivity to the grief of others. In November 1742 his letter to his sister Martha upon the death of her last surviving child contained this shocking sentiment:

> I believe the death of your children is a great instance of the goodness of God towards you. You have often mentioned to me how much of your time they took up. Now that time is restored to you, and you have nothing to do but to serve our Lord without carefulness and without distraction.[38]

Advancing age did not temper this aspect of John Wesley's character. In 1791, he told the young preacher Adam Clarke that his voicing pain over his son's death represented 'inordinate affection'.[39]

Charles' openness with regard to sharing aspects of his own experience extended to spirituality. His letters contain many descriptions of public worship and the impact of his ministry as Charles not only exercised spiritual direction but also engaged in a personal fellowship that was a source of mutual inspiration to minister and people.[40] This generosity of spirit, which was not always shared by his brother,[41] is exemplified by a letter of December 1748:

> Found an unexpected opportunity of once more visiting Alex White triumphant on his deathbed. He had told those about him that I should come this morning and accosted me with 'O! I am glad you are come. The Lord has kept me in my senses that we may rejoice together once more. I have had such a conflict with Satan! I want words to describe it.' 'Did he try' (I asked) 'to make you doubt your saviour's love or your interest in him?' 'No' (he answered) 'that he could not do: But he showed me all the glory of the world and strove to influence my heart to desire it. But I have conquered him at last.' 'Then' (said I) 'he is departed from you.' 'No' he replied 'I *see him* now, but he is under my foot.' I asked 'Were you not troubled while the conflict lasted?' His reply was 'Nay, but rejoiced with great joy – exceedingly great.' I believed him for I was partaker while he spoke and we encouraged one another with the same hope shortly of sitting down with Jesus Christ and judging angels. 'I am just on the wing' he said 'ready to depart. The chariot is come and I wish you might now go with me.' In a flood of tears I told him 'I wish so too.' But why should I desire it he added, 'Pass but a moment and *you* shall be with me. You all shall follow me to paradise . . . I tell you, you shall soon come after me.' Then he called each of us by name assuring us we should quickly meet above . . .'
>
> I never felt more piercing words, no, not from my dying daughter Richardson. The shortness of life which he again and again insisted on gave me the strongest consolation and though he warned *me* in a more particular manner 'You all will follow soon but you sooner than the rest!' This may be because several in the room were younger than me, but I cannot help hoping his words had something prophetical.
>
> I earnestly bade his prayers, especially when his soul should be on the brink of its departure. I told him I had many friends in paradise as well as a

father and mother and desired him to tell them (if permitted) that I should soon be with them. 'We shall expect you', he answered, 'and all our brethren in tribulation and may the spirit of glory rest upon you now.' He then solemnly blessed us, kissed me and said 'I shall see you no more till we meet in paradise. But wait only for one moment and the days of mourning shall be ended . . .'[42]

Charles' willingness freely to voice an unguarded opinion was exercised not just in letters, but also in conversation and public discourse, and was not always an endearing characteristic. He held strong views and it was well known that John Wesley's brother was not one to pull his punches in an argument. This can be seen to particular effect when looking at the controversies that plagued the Wesleyan movement during the second half of the eighteenth century. Charles was a fervent supporter of Methodism remaining within the Church of England and, in this, ran counter to the views of a number of lay preachers, who believed that the brighter future lay in independence from the established church. The resulting conflict dominated Wesleyan polity during the last 30 years of Charles Wesley's life and cast a shadow over his posthumous reputation. Charles' letters and those of his correspondents constitute one of the best sources of information that we have concerning this fundamental issue and one that has never received the attention that they deserve.

Charles Wesley's blunt and often aggressive nature was increasingly in evidence as the gulf between Methodism and the Church of England widened. This extract critical of separatist preachers is from a public letter sent to the Leeds society in October 1756:

> I knew beforehand that the Sanballats and Tobiahs would be grieved when they heard there was a man come to seek the welfare of the Church of England. I expected they would prevent my words as if I should say '*The Church could save you*', so indeed you and they thought till I and my brethren taught you better and sent you in and through all the means to Jesus Christ. But let not their slanders move you. Continue in the old ship . . .[43]

John Wesley could be equally forthright in his comments when defending a point of principle, but his controversial writings lack the sharp personal edge displayed by his brother, who was memorably described by Thomas Jackson as 'generally happy in the application of epithets. Whether he intends to praise or blame . . .'[44] Even people who respected Charles were exasperated by his refusal to curb either his tongue or his pen, as shown by the following letter sent to him by the preacher John Valton:

> Was it likely to do good to the cause of God to tell a friend of mine, that Mr J. Wesley had a hard matter to keep us [the preachers] together, *pride had got such a* footing among us, and that as soon as your brother's head was laid, you *forsaw what would be the consequence*? Did you not speak stronger things in your sermon at the fast day? Dear Sir *what good can such unhappy* prophecies *do the preachers* or *the cause of God*? It will irritate the men of little grace, and *distress* the sincere preachers of the Word.[45]

Charles Wesley's outspoken and bitter opposition to men whom he described in public shortly before he died as 'grievous wolves' who would 'rend and tear the flock'[46] contributed to keeping many of his personal papers out of the public eye. It is ironic therefore that it is this very feature of his correspondence that renders them so valuable to the historian. Charles' bluntness encouraged others to be equally open in their replies and his concern for the future of the Methodist movement struck a chord with many of the brothers' followers. In 1760 the Irish itinerant John Johnson expressed to Charles his own misgivings about separation from the Anglicans – 'I have often thought that desire in the hearts of some of the preachers to give the sacrament, would be the means of destroying the work.'[47] The traditional opinion within Methodist scholarship has long been that the majority of the Wesleys' followers were in favour of Methodist separation as the eighteenth century approached its close. The correspondence of Charles Wesley acts as a partial corrective to that view; many people were in fact vehemently opposed to any parting of ways with the Church of England and were able to influence events in ways rarely acknowledged by denominational historians. Letters between Charles Wesley and Henry Durbin of Bristol written in 1784 at the time of the famous ordinations for North America illustrate this point very well.[48]

Durbin was a wealthy layman and was representative of a party that remained devoted to the Church of England as well as to Methodism. Men and women like Durbin were to be found in towns and cities across the country;[49] they emerged principally from within the rising commercial and professional class that was being enriched by rapid industrialization and growth in trade. Durbin and his friends frequently underwrote the costs of building chapels and occupied prominent lay administrative positions within societies. At the same time they remained staunch members of the Church of England and represented a considerable brake on any attempt to break away from the mother Church. The many surviving letters written between Charles Wesley and these so-called 'Church Methodists' provide an invaluable insight into the many-faceted world of evangelical opinion.

The separation question is only one of many areas of Methodist history that can be illuminated by Charles Wesley's letters. It is enlightening, for example, to consider what they tell us of the different ways in which people responded to the Wesleys on a personal level. John was of course held in tremendous regard. His influence was such that one contemporary observed that the societies considered their 'sovereign pastor as a sovereign good'.[50] However, he paid a personal price for this central place, experiencing difficulty in relating to the lives of ordinary people.[51] John Wesley always had to be the dominant partner in any relationship,[52] and his sense of personal mission seems at times inhuman in its intensity. It is hardly surprising that some Methodists felt that Charles was more accessible and understanding of their worries. In August 1776, Ann Chapman wrote of the people's concern about the quality of the Bristol preachers. She asked Charles to approach his brother on their behalf for 'the people here are discouraged and say its no use for them to speak: I believe they think of Mr [John Wesley] as some do of our [King] that he will not hearken to any remonstrance'.[53] Charles was regularly made aware of people's fears about aspects of Methodism; this was in part a response to his own requests for information,[54] but is also a reflection of his approachability compared with a supreme leader who did not like to be contradicted.[55] The preacher John Pawson remarked in 1789 that even at the age of 85, John Wesley 'loves to have his own way and he must have it'.[56] For people like Ann Chapman and John Johnson, Charles provided a sympathetic ear and a channel through which they could express their hopes and fears.

The correspondence of Charles Wesley represents an excellent opportunity to study the Revival and early Methodism specifically from a perspective that is different from the John Wesley-centred view that has held sway for so long. Historians have concentrated so much on the life and ministry of that one remarkable man that the contribution made by others has often been overshadowed.[57] Methodism was more than the Wesley brothers or their preachers. It also encompassed thousands of ordinary people, who had their own ideas about the evangelical movement of which they were part. No single manuscript collection can comprehensively document all such viewpoints, but the Charles Wesley letters are invaluable in that they reflect the open, confrontational character of their creator and the equally frank reactions that he provoked. By contrast, John Wesley, whose papers have provided the major building blocks of early Wesleyan scholarship, was in many respects a politician, with all a politician's need for circumspection and focused propagation of a party line. In 1791, the prominent preacher John Pawson had this to say about his recently deceased leader:

> In a very great variety of affairs . . . he acted as a politician, and one could not help seeking something that looked artful and designing and there was a manifest want of that simplicity, sincerity and uprightness, which are so amiable both in the sight of God and man.[58]

Charles Wesley was very different in character. He was once described in a letter sent to him by the preacher Michael Fenwick as like a 'wild bull in a net . . . raising a very great dust . . . as for evil speaking together with tittle tattle this nation Sir cannot compare with you'.[59]

The brothers' correspondence collections reflect these stark differences in personality and are wonderfully complementary as a result, allowing for varied perspectives on the Methodist movement and the wider revival. On the one hand we have the papers of John Wesley charting in disciplined detail the early institutional development of what became the Methodist Church: on the other, we have his brother and close associate writing from a different angle and presenting an alternative view of the Methodist story. It is ironic that the very qualities that rendered Charles Wesley's letters rather embarrassing to previous generations of scholars are the very attributes that greatly enhance their modern research value. Three hundred years after his birth, it is time that Charles Wesley, his friends and his adversaries, were allowed the opportunity to speak through their own words.

## Notes

1 The precise number of extant letters is extremely difficult even to estimate. The figure of 750 given here is a conservative estimate. As part of the Charles Wesley Letters project (eds Newport and Lloyd and being prepared for publication in two volumes by Oxford University Press), a very extensive search for extant letters has been conducted; the current estimated total figure stands at over 1,000, though it is extremely likely that this will need to be reduced significantly.

2 The most complete biography of Charles Wesley remains the two-volume life written by Thomas Jackson and published in 1841.

3 Jackson, *Life*.

4 *CWJ*, 2.167–286.

5 *CWJ*, 2.xli–xliii.

6 *CWJ*, 2.xli.

7 See Chapter 1 above.

8 CW to Sarah Wesley, ALS, 25/27 July [1766], MARC, DDCW, 5/99 and *MSJ*, 2.212.

9 Baker, *Charles Wesley as Revealed by his Letters*, 5.

10 Baker, *Charles Wesley as Revealed by his Letters*, 2.

11 Baker, *Charles Wesley as Revealed by his Letters*, 4.

12 *Charles Wesley: A reader*, ed. Tyson.

13 Tyson, *A Reader*, 12.

14 Two letters are based on transcripts found in Jackson's biography of Charles and the rest, 24 in number, are from Jackson's edition of the journal.

15 *Wesley/Langshaw Correspondence: Charles Wesley, his sons, and the Lancaster organists*, ed. Arthur W. Wainwright in collaboration with Don E. Saliers (Atlanta: Scholars Press for Emery University, 1993).

16 The collection also includes letters by Charles' sons Charles junior and Samuel.

17 WHS proceedings, vol. 25 (1945–6), 17–23 and 97–104.

18 Joseph Priestley, *Original Letters by the Rev. John Wesley and his Friends* (Birmingham: Pearson, 1791).

19 See above, note 1.

20 Baker, *Charles Wesley as Revealed by his Letters*, 3.

21 CW to Sarah Wesley, ALS, 4 October [1753], MARC, DDCW, 7/99.

22 CW to Sarah Wesley, ALS, 18/19 February [1753], MARC, DDCW, 5/98.

23 CW to Sarah Wesley, ALS, 22 May 1760, MARC, DDCW, 7/7.

24 For example, CW to Sarah Wesley, ALS, [14 April] 1752, MARC, DDCW, 5–92.

25 For example, Charles' draft reply written on the reverse of the letter of Henry Durbin to CW, ALS, 3 December 1784, MARC reference 'Letters Chiefly to the Wesleys', 2.76.

26 For example, Jackson does not appear to have known the shorthand as he did not include it in his edition of the journal or appended letters.

27 In recent years, only a small number of people have been able to combine mastery of the Byrom system with knowledge of Charles Wesley to the extent that they have been able to decipher the script.

28 Baker, *Charles Wesley as Revealed by his Letters*, 5.

29 Quoted by Baker, *Charles Wesley as Revealed by his Letters*, 6.

30 Many of Charles' letters contain substantial poems that he appears to have

composed on the spur of the moment. See for example, CW to Sarah Gwynne junior, ALS, 1 March [1749], MARC, DDCW, 5/30.

31 CW to Sarah Gwynne junior, ALS, 17 December 1748, MARC, DDWES, 4/1.

32 'Increasingly Methodism, its doctrines and its experimental practices, form the focal point of the correspondence.' BE 26.10.

33 JW to Thomas Bigg, 7 October 1749, BE, 26.388–9.

34 For example, 'I count the days between us and look toward Charles Street, sleeping and waking', CW to Sarah Wesley, ALS, 31 May [1755], MARC, DDCW, 7/53.

35 CW to Sarah Wesley, ALS, 13 August [1766], MARC, DDCW, 7/23.

36 Quoted by Jackson, Life, 2.435.

37 Jackson, Life, 2.433.

38 JW to Martha Hall, 17 November 1742, BE, 26.90–1.

39 Quoted by Rack, Reasonable Enthusiast, 543.

40 See for example, CW to Sarah Wesley, ALS, 22 September [1755], MARC, DDCW, 5/73.

41 John was often reluctant to reveal details of his own spiritual condition, despite the fact that he required such disclosures from others.

42 CW to Sarah Wesley, ALS, 30 December [1748], MARC, DDCW, 5/11.

43 Letter transcribed in Charles Wesley's journal for 28 October 1756. MARC, DDCW, 10/2.

44 Jackson, Life, 2.75.

45 John Valton to CW, ALS, 13 November 1779, MARC, DDPr, 2/55.

46 John Pawson to [Charles Atmore], 8 August 1787, Letters of John Pawson, ed. Vickers and Bowmer, 1.46.

47 John Johnson to CW, ALS, 2 June 1763, MARC, EMV 92.

48 For example, Henry Durbin to CW, ALS, 4 November 1784, reference 'Letters Chiefly to the Wesleys', MARC, 2.74.

49 Their number included William Marriott and Edward Allen in London, William Pine in Bristol, William Hey in Leeds, John Ryle in Macclesfield and James Walker in Sheffield.

50 Charles Wesley, Sermons [1816 edition], xxxi.

51 'If Wesley showed a grim disregard of the hardships of himself and his men, he was even less sensitive about their wives and families', Rupp, Religion in England, 394.

52 Rack, Reasonable Enthusiast, 538.

53 Ann Chapman to CW, ALS, 21 August 1776, MARC, DDCW, 2/13.

54 See, for example, William Ellis to CW, ALS, 23 December 1762, MARC, EMV, 56.

55 'I have often heard you do not take those persons to be real friends who reprove you or tell you what they think wrong: but cleave to those who give you praise and respect.' Sarah Ryan to JW, March 1764, quoted by Gordon Rupp, Religion in England, 397.

56 John Pawson to Charles Atmore, 19 March 1789, Letters of John Pawson, ed. Bowmer and Vickers, 1.78.

57 'Too little work has yet been done on the Methodists as distinct from Wesley', Rack, Reasonable Enthusiast, 558.

58 Henry Rack, 'Wesley Observed', Proceedings of the Wesley Historical Society 49.1 (February 1993), 17.

59 Michael Fenwick to CW, ALS, undated, MARC, DDPr, 2/22.

# 20. Charles Wesley's Shorthand[1]

## OLIVER A. BECKERLEGGE
## (with Kenneth G. C. Newport)

When I entered Richmond College in September 1946, it was in a bad state. Towards the end of the war a flying bomb had fallen in the grounds and its explosion had blown in windows and window frames, fetched down the plaster from the walls and ceilings, and shattered the glass in a number of bookcases. Three or four of these bookcases were located in Dr Harold Roberts' large lecture room. Upon inspection it became apparent that these contained a number of eighteenth-century, calf-bound documents. Greatly daring, I took out one or two of these volumes smothered in broken glass and plaster and was horrified to find they were from John Wesley's own library. The College had been so recently reopened that the authorities had not yet had time, in the midst of many more pressing needs, to tidy up these books. Receiving permission to clean and dust and rearrange, I finally found among the books not only printed works, but one or two volumes in manuscript of Charles Wesley's poems and hymns. That led to correspondence with Frank Baker who told me of the existence of many more Charles Wesley manuscripts, at which I worked over the next 20 years, and it was in doing so that I first came across some manuscripts written in Byrom's shorthand.[2]

How was I to begin to learn to decipher it? It occurred to me that somewhere in the Methodist Archives, then at City Road, London, there might be Byrom's work expounding his system, and in enquiring of Dr J. C. Bowmer, then connexional archivist, I found that this was indeed the case, and he sent me a photocopy of the one-page 'Table containing the Alphabet, the common words which the letters stand for, the Prepositions and Terminations' (Figure 20.1) – in other words, the key to Byrom – explaining that that was all I should need. In point of fact, I might have found it far from sufficient had I not discovered that one long poem existed both in longhand and shorthand versions, and the comparison of the two with one another and with the key enabled me to get the drift of Byrom's system in the course of time.

## Charles Wesley's use of shorthand

For what purposes, and on what occasions, did Charles Wesley use the shorthand? There were several main reasons for its use. First, as its name implies, it is a shorthand – and therefore takes up much less room than longhand, so

**Figure 20.1: Table of symbols from John Byrom's *Universal Shorthand* (1767)**

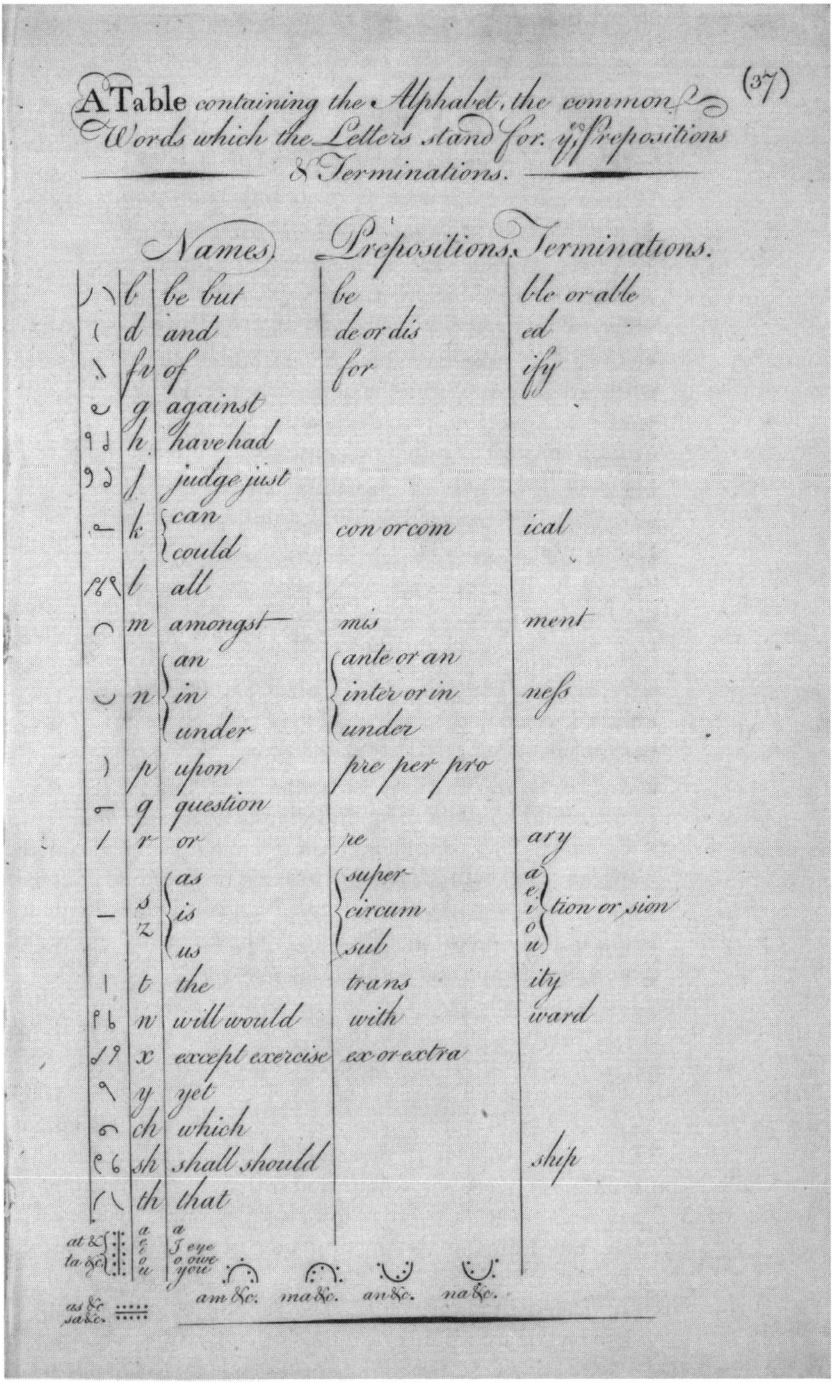

(37)

A Table containing the Alphabet, the common Words which the Letters stand for. ye Prepositions & Terminations.

| | Names | Prepositions | Terminations |
|---|---|---|---|
| b | be but | be | ble or able |
| d | and | de or dis | ed |
| fv | of | for | ify |
| g | against | | |
| h | have had | | |
| j | judge just | | |
| k | can could | con or com | ical |
| l | all | | |
| m | amongst | mis | ment |
| n | an in under | ante or an, inter or in, under | ness |
| p | upon | pre per pro | |
| q | question | | |
| r | or | re | ary |
| s z | as is us | super circum sub | a e i o u tion or sion |
| t | the | trans | ity |
| w | will would | with | ward |
| x | except exercise | ex or extra | |
| y | yet | | |
| ch | which | | |
| sh | shall should | | ship |
| th | that | | |
| a e o u | a I eye o owe you | | |

at &c. ta &c.

am &c. ma &c. an &c. na &c.

as &c. sa &c.

that on many occasions it was used for that reason only. One can see a very practical example of this in Charles' sermon on John 4.41 where Charles evidently runs out of physical space towards the end of a page and switches from longhand into shorthand in order to complete his sermon without having to begin a new page.[3] The practical desire to save space may also have been the reason for Charles copying out all four Gospels into a very small booklet, perhaps with the intention of making a copy of the sacred texts that could be carried very easily by him on his travels. That booklet has survived and is also of great value to anyone attempting to learn Charles' use of the shorthand script.[4] Second, Charles Wesley also sometimes used shorthand in order to make a correction to, or more often write an alternative line or so of, verse, when he had only a very narrow margin in his manuscript in which to do so; again shorthand was the obvious answer to the problem. Third, on other occasions Charles used shorthand to make brief notes. For example, there are a number of letters to Charles Wesley which have Charles' shorthand script on them. What is recorded in those brief notes is sometimes simply a date and/or the name of the person from whom the letter has come. On occasion, however, there is more, since Charles would sometimes write on the back of the letter either a note or two regarding its content or else a shorthand summary of his reply. These shorthand summaries can be particularly useful, especially so when the original longhand version that Charles sent to his correspondent is now lost.[5]

Fourth, and perhaps the most important feature of shorthand (at least to Charles Wesley), was the fact that few people could read it (it would indeed be interesting to know just how many people in Wesley's lifetime had in fact learned the script, but such information is not available). The shorthand was hence for Charles Wesley a secret code by which he could record thoughts not intended for unauthorized eyes, and verses that were very personal in nature. This aspect of Charles' use of shorthand is particularly evident in his journal, i.e. the manuscript now catalogued in the John Rylands University Library of Manchester as DDCW 10/2. This is a thick volume made up of a number of apparently once separate sections that appear to have been bound together (or re-bound) at some point in the nineteenth century.[6] Even a cursory glance at the manuscript will quickly reveal that Charles frequently used shorthand script – not for reasons of space or revision, but for privacy.

Charles' journal was published by Thomas Jackson in 1849. That edition is defective. Not only was Jackson limited to the portions of the journal that had survived,[7] but also to the portions that he could read and transcribe. Charles' journal, in the nature of the case, was a private affair meant for his eyes only – it was never a public *apologia* as was his brother's; consequently whole passages that were especially private, whether a few words only, or a whole paragraph or so, were set down in shorthand (see Figure 20.2). These shorthand passages cover a variety of topics, for example the very real problems that Charles faced during his time in America and the accusations made against him by Mrs Welch and Mrs Hawkins, and the extent to which Olgethorpe was implicated in the scandal. The section below is a small part of that story. The words underlined are those that Charles recorded in shorthand:

Figure 20.2: Example of shorthand from Charles Wesley's journal

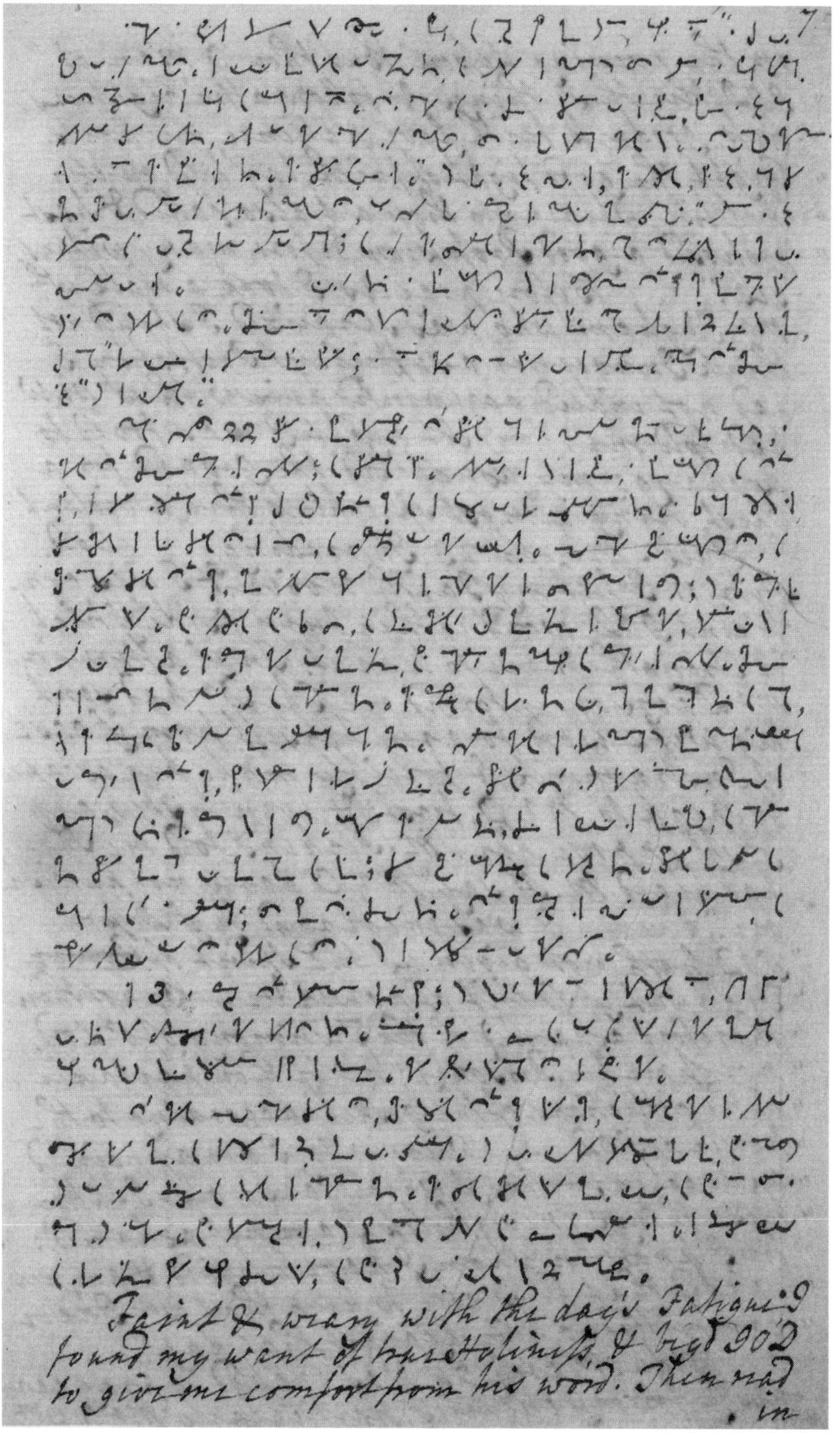

**Thursday, 18 March [1736].** Today Mr O[glethorpe] set out with the Indians, to hunt the buffalo upon the main, and to see the utmost limits of what they claimed. In the afternoon Mrs W[elch] discovered[8] to me the whole mystery of iniquity. What she said was as follows:

'Mr Oglethorpe is a wicked man and a perfect stranger to righteousness. He kept a mistress in England to my knowledge; and even solicited me there. He forebore while I was sick, pretending he had laid aside all such designs, but resumed them upon my recovery. He persuaded me, religion is all a myth. Mrs Hawkins persuaded me he has the same designs; I fear, with better hopes of success so greatly laboured to set him against your brother. In regard to this, she has told him, your brother was in love with her, has kissed her a thousand times and wept bitterly in the ship at the thought of parting from you. Mr Oglethorpe refused a long time to believe it. She is exceedingly jealous of me; fell upon me lately with "Must I have the character of Mr Oglethorpe's whore to seize on you?" She has also used him with the utmost insolence.

He is extremely jealous of you; having done all he could to persuade me you have the same design upon me which he has. He contrived your going on the other boat without answers to hinder your speaking to me.' She further said that she loved him and was much grieved at the thought of losing his love. Besides she dreaded the consequence of its being changed into hatred as she would then be exposed to the mercy of a woman with absolute power. I encouraged her to trust in God and only then pressed her to seek for satisfaction [?][9] in the means of grace.[10]

There are also passages that outline disagreements with his brother, for example on the issue of whether Charles should receive some sort of 'provision' for his work with the Methodist societies.

**Wednesday, 16 November [1747].** At the hour of intercession the Lord looked upon us, and we lay a long time at his feet weeping. Talked with my brother about a provision, in case I married, and he said [that] the church could not afford it. Then I thought, the church did not deserve a gospel minister.[11]

There are passages too which record some of the more intimate and private details of Charles' life, such as the point at which he proposed to his future wife Sarah Gwynne:

**Sunday, 3 April [1748].** Through the divine blessing on the tender care of my friends, I recovered so much strength that I read prayers, and gave the Sacrament to the family. At night my dearest Sally, like my guardian angel, attended me. In the loving openness of my heart, without premeditation I asked her 'if she could trust herself with me for life',[12] and with a noble simplicity she readily answered me [that] she could.[13]
**Monday, 4 April** Frightened at what I had said last night, I condemned my own rashness and almost wished I had never discovered myself.[14]

None of these shorthand sections were transcribed by Jackson, though some were subsequently deciphered by Nehemiah Curnock and published in the section of Charles' journal (1736–9) that was published by John Telford.[15] Transcriptions of the remainder can be found in the 2007 edition of the journal brought to publication by Kimbrough and Newport.[16] They tell an interesting story and one which to date has remained largely inaccessible to the scholarly guild.

The fifth use to which Charles Wesley put the shorthand was in writing whole poems. One manuscript at the Rylands, known simply as 'MS Shorthand', contains four long poems, one of which, as I have said, exists also in longhand, 'An Epistle to a friend, July 1743'. The others are all in some measure personal and autobiographical: 'Come then, my soul, thou restless exile, come', 'Stillness, written for Lady Huntingdon' and 'With humble, meek, submissive fear', an early poem expressing his own desire for celibacy – written before he had met Sally Gwynne. The volume originally contained some 100 leaves and the majority of those torn out, together with those that remain, were (from the evidence of the stubs) in shorthand. From the nature of these poems it is not surprising that Charles Wesley did not commit them to longhand or to later publication; they were too private. All have now been published in *The Unpublished Poetry of Charles Wesley*.[17]

A final use of shorthand is found in Charles' composition of a group of early sermons. There are six such sermons, though eight manuscripts, since for two of the sermons there are two separate manuscripts (i.e. earlier drafts of more polished completed forms). All of these sermons are written in a very clear and large shorthand. It would appear, then, that Charles Wesley could easily read his own shorthand and used these manuscripts as his material to take into the pulpit. Here the reason for the shorthand is clearly to save space and time.[18]

It is hence clear that Charles used the shorthand system fairly extensively and for a variety of reasons. An understanding of that script is important. This is particularly so since, as we have seen, it was the form of writing to which Charles resorted for some of the more sensitive parts of his work, be those places where he was in dispute with John or where he was engaged in more personal reflection. Wesley scholars will be at a disadvantage if they cannot read this script, for although the amount of shorthand may be comparatively small, its significance is entirely disproportionate to its extent.

## Byrom's shorthand symbols

In Byrom's shorthand the principle (as, I suppose, in all systems of shorthand) is to represent consonants by a symbol, vowels being indicated by appropriately placed dots (see Figure 20.1). However, it is important to note that Byrom's system is fundamentally phonetic and hence it is not simply the case that an English letter is represented by an equivalent shorthand sign. For example, in three cases one symbol covers two letters of the English alphabet (or better two 'spoken sounds'); thus *f* and v share the same symbol, as do s and z, and c (where it is 'hard' as in 'clock') and *k*. In several cases a symbol can take two possible forms (three in the case of the symbol for *l*; for ease in connected writing), conversely, some English sounds requiring two letters are reduced to one symbol by Byrom – such instances are *ch, sh, th* (though in practice the symbol for *t* is often used for *th*). There are further modifications in that the symbols can be used to represent prepositions (which sometimes therefore function as prefixes in words such as '*under*stand') and suffixes (in words such as 'sacra*ment*'). This is complicated further in that any letter can be used to represent single common words, so that the symbol for *d* is often used for 'and', the symbol for *t* is used for 'the', and the symbol for *ch* is used for 'which'. Examination of Figure 20.1 will explain all this more fully.

## Deciphering Charles Wesley's shorthand

This title may appear to some to be an ignorant misnomer, especially in the light of what has so far been said in this chapter: should it not read 'Deciphering Byrom's shorthand'? To be sure, both the Wesleys used Byrom's system, and the symbols used are certainly of Byrom's devising; but Charles Wesley so adapted the system to suit his own needs that it became almost a different shorthand. Hence, even for the one who has made a careful study of Byrom's system, Charles' idiosyncratic form of the script presents numerous additional challenges. For example, Charles will often abbreviate even the abbreviated shorthand form, sometimes contracting an entire word to one single letter. *H* in Wesley's script sometimes means 'holy' or 'holiness' or even 'happy'; similarly *R* fairly frequently means 'righteousness'. And it is not just single words that are so contracted: *gg* may be 'glory of God' while *hg* can be 'Holy Ghost'. Some such composite abbreviations (such as those to which reference has just been made) are fairly obvious. Others are identifiable only through context. While the meaning of the passage may have been clear to Charles Wesley who had written it, the intended reading can be much more elusive for the one coming to the passage afresh some two and a half centuries later. To take a couple of examples: *fb* puzzled me for some time. This could presumably stand for 'fab', 'feb', 'fib', 'fob', or something else along those lines with the possibly a vowel before or after the *fb* part of the (presumed) word. Nothing fitted. Most of what I considered are not even words. In the end it was the context that suggested the *almost* obvious interpretation; *fb* was not one word at all, but two: 'flesh and blood'. Similarly, the shorthand *md* (in one of Charles' shorthand sermons) proved completely baffling for a long time until suddenly 'music and dancing' (from the story of the Prodigal Son) was seen to fit the context perfectly. *HR* also proved elusive, though remembering that the system is fundamentally phonetic, the reading is almost certainly 'holy writ'.[19] Consequently, when working with Charles' shorthand one must not assume that any 'word' in the shorthand is a single word in longhand: it may be several words or even a phrase. And there is another temptation, which is the inclination to fill in a difficult gap in transcription at any cost, even that of using contemporary English (whether English or American). The truth is of course that Charles was writing in eighteenth-century English, and that must be kept clearly in mind as one works with these texts. The temptation to solve the problem using contemporary English must be fiercely rejected! Better to leave a blank, allowing the reader to make his or her own interpretation than to suggest words that may inhibit more lateral thinking.

All this is not an insurmountable problem, however. It is true that Charles' shorthand prose is more of a challenge, but we have real helps when transcribing verse. Charles Wesley was a very skilful and competent poet. He wrote in recognizable metre and verse forms; his octosyllabic lines *are* of eight syllables, his six-syllable lines *did* contain six syllables, and his lines *did* rhyme, whether precisely or by making use of accepted half-rhymes or eye-rhymes. Hence, when puzzled by a word or so in his shorthand verse, we know how many syllables we need, and where the stress falls; and if the baffling word lies at the end of a line of verse, we know its rhyming vowel from the word at the end of the line with which it rhymes.

As has been said above, I learned the shorthand with the aid of one manuscript hymn which was extant both in longhand and shorthand. However, I quickly found I could easily be led astray. One particular problem was that the two texts turned out not to be identical, though on reflection this is hardly surprising. Charles Wesley constantly revised his yet unpublished work, and this was just another example of that process. It quickly became evident that there were a few examples of changes of individual words between the longhand and the shorthand versions of the hymn. More substantially, on a number of occasions there were passages in shorthand which did not appear in the longhand version at all, and indeed the same was true vice versa. Similarly, in deciphering the sermons,[20] I discovered that while in some of them Charles quoted from the *Homilies of the Church of England* at length, I could not simply copy out from the text of earlier printed editions, for where Cranmer (who composed most of the *Homilies*) used typical sixteenth-century phraseology, involving a measure of tautology, Charles Wesley would omit the superfluous phrase. Hence the potential 'help' in the form of the longhand version or printed homily could easily be as much of a trap as a help. The price of even approximate accuracy is, like the price of liberty, eternal vigilance.

## Charles Wesley's shorthand prose

A good example of some of the issues just mentioned comes in the text of the sermon on Romans 3.23–5.[21] This is of course a prose composition, but the frustrations, as those found in Charles' shorthand verse, apply – indeed they are perhaps even more acute. At one point in the sermon Charles is quoting his biblical text, and, since it is a quotation, the full expansion of the shorthand seems reasonably clear. It provides an excellent example of how Charles could abbreviate whole words and even phrases into just one single shorthand stroke or a composite sign. Simply transcribed stroke-for-letter the actual shorthand reads: '*l h snd d cm sh. f gg; bing jd frl bsg tr t r. ths n jc: wm gd hth st frt tb a pr. tr. fth ns bld*'.

In this passage we find the recognized symbols for 'have', 'and', 'of', 'the' and 'that'. The obvious vowels to supply give us the words 'all', 'sinned', 'come', 'freely', 'in whom', 'God hath set forth' (we must remember that *t* often represents *th* in the symbol for 'through' (twice). But in three cases we find a single letter, the initial letters of the words *sh*(ort), *j*(ustified), *r*(edemption), and in another case we have the initial two letters: *pr.*(opitiation). Finally we find – what in any other context than in a biblical quotation would cause problems – the use of one shorthand 'word' to represent a phrase: so, as already indicated, *gg* represents the glory of God; *bsg* represents 'by his grace'; *JC* clearly stands for 'Jesus Christ' (unless Charles Wesley found it easier to write the shorthand *JC*, rather than *CJ*, and would actually have said 'Christ Jesus' as in the AV); *tb* stands for 'to be', and *ns* for 'in his'. One ought to add that the little oblique detached stroke after the symbol for *b* gives us 'be*ing*' – it is the common abbreviation of the present participle. And so we have:

| *l* | *h* | *snd* | *d* | *cm* | *sh.* | *f* | *gg* | *bing* | *jd* |
|-----|-----|-------|-----|------|-------|-----|------|--------|------|
| all | have | sinned | and | come | short | of | [the] Glory of God | being | justified |

| *frl* | *bsg* | *tr* | *t* | *r.* | *ths* | *n* | *jc* | *wm* |
|-------|-------|------|-----|------|-------|-----|------|------|
| freely | by his grace | through | the | righteousness | that is | in | Jesus Christ | whom |

| *gd* | *hth* | *st* | *frt* | *tb* | *a* | *pr.* | *tr.* | *fth* | *ns* | *bld* |
|------|-------|------|-------|------|-----|-------|-------|-------|------|-------|
| God | hath | set | forth | To be | a | propitiation | through | faith | in his | blood |

This sort of treatment of the shorthand is fairly simple for us today when, as here, it is a matter of a familiar quotation, and it would be even more simple for Charles Wesley who had written it and in any case knew the Bible extremely well. The shorthand functioned as it ought: it served as an *aide mémoire* to an already familiar bit of scripture. Charles did not abbreviate to the same extent when writing words that were not already in his memory. But even in these cases words and phrases that were part of a preacher's natural vocabulary were subjected to drastic abbreviation. For example, when writing the shorthand of the opening sentence of this sermon, Charles was able to trust himself to read and interpret the shorthand: '*n ts ep. sg b t mth fs ap. frst cnvnss t w f sn, d tn f r.*' What he was writing here is: 'In this epistle [the] spirit of God by the mouth of his apostle first convinces the world of sin and then of righteousness.' Some of the required simplification is obvious, but even here Charles reduces familiar words to the opening consonant (preceded in two cases by differentiating vowels): 'epistle', 'apostle', 'world', 'righteousness'. He indicates the fact of abbreviations of words down to one letter by the use of a dot underneath the symbol. But he again conflates two words into one: *sg* signifies '[the] Spirit of God',[22] and *fs* signifies 'of his'. In the next sentence of the sermon, Charles is quoting once more from the AV so he can afford again to abbreviate severely: '*hrn s t rt of gd rvld frm h. g l ng and nrtsn of mn . . .*' and so on. It reads (quoting Romans 1.18): 'Herein is the righteousness of God revealed from heaven against all ungodliness and unrighteousness of men . . .' It will be noticed that 'righteousness' is reduced to *rt*, 'ungodliness' to *ng*, and 'heaven' to its initial *h*; the *g* is used for the word 'against' (as in Byrom's key; see Figure 20.1).

It is worth commenting that these sermons are written in a fairly large hand, a much larger hand in fact than the one Charles normally employed. This is probably because he was going to preach from them and needed to be sure that he was able to read what he had written. But even so, the vowel 'pointing' (as Hebraists would say) is often missing and is normally utilized only when there might otherwise be confusion. Anyone seeking to transcribe such texts will therefore often find that, even when all the strokes of the script have been identified, he or she is left with (at best) only a consonantal skeleton of what Charles had in his mind as he wrote. Deciphering this script is emphatically not an exact science.

This brief study of a few lines of Charles' sermon on Romans 3.23–5 illustrates some of the difficulties and some of the principles in deciphering his shorthand script. One must approach the task with a real mixture of caution and imagination, and a readiness to suspend judgement and at times to admit defeat.

## Insoluble problems?

At times, as one may imagine, the transcriber is finally left with apparently insoluble problems. There are, of course, cases where the abbreviation baffles because a symbol has been less well formed than might ideally be the case. For example, one is sometimes unsure whether a slightly slanting stroke is a *t*, *b*, or *r*; or whether a slightly curved stroke is intended to be a curve or a straight line. There can even be confusion over the strokes for *t* (a straight vertical line) and *f/v* (a diagonal line). In Byrom's printed manual these two are clearly quite different. When Charles is writing with pen and ink, however, the distinction can be blurred. Then, of course, we can be seriously led astray, as when an abbreviated word has no final full stop to indicate its abbreviation, and so on. Often, and especially in quotations, the context is sufficient to solve the problem. But these single initial letters can give rise to other problems. Charles Wesley is fond of the single initial *h*. As noted above, this has a variety of possible expansions. It may represent 'holy', 'happy', 'heavenly' or 'heaven', and further confusion may arise if the suffix '-ness' (the shorthand stroke for *n*, giving 'holiness' or 'happiness') is not present. Now the context tells us whether the word is a noun or an adjective; but how can we be sure that, in a non-biblical phrase, it is 'holy' rather than 'heavenly' or 'happy'? As Martin Schmidt has pointed out,[23] for the Wesleys (as for their mother) holiness and happiness were virtually synonymous terms. So while one cannot, in such cases, always be sure one has transliterated Wesley correctly, one can nonetheless be sure that one is not far from his thought.

There are occasions when one is completely beaten: and one must graciously accept defeat. Better to leave a gap of a word or so, and leave the reader to solve the problem, than to make an inaccurate wild guess, and lead them astray. To leave a problem for a few weeks sometimes enables one to come back to it with a fresh mind that sometimes resolves the difficulty. The example of *md* noted above is one such case. When Thomas Albin and I were deciphering the manuscript sermons this *md* presented us with a particular problem, and even after repeated reading and (it was to be hoped) intelligent guessing, we failed to find an interpretation. It was only when reading the proofs (we had hitherto left the space blank) that it suddenly dawned on me that the abbreviation represented, without any doubt at all, 'music and dancing' (quoting the conclusion of the parable of the Good Samaritan – Luke 15.25).

But Charles Wesley can be more obscure. In his desire to ensure secrecy he has another trick up his sleeve. Occasionally (happily only occasionally) he will change the first consonant of a name for the preceding consonant of the alphabet, and the problem is heightened by the fact that in such cases only the single letter is used. Thus in the autobiographical poem 'Come, then, my soul, thou restless exile, come',[24] we find the line:

And, weeping, kissed the lov'd r's name.

Here *r* in fact represents *s* – and, with a vowel before it, and the required three syllables to fit in with the decasyllabic metre of the poem, its expansion is obvious: 'Aspasia's' is clearly intended.

## Conclusion

One final word should be emphasized again. Wesley was an eighteenth-century Englishman, not a twentieth-century Englishman or American. And he wrote most of his shorthand, apart from small corrections in the margins of later poetical manuscripts, in the first half of his life. So his English is the English of over two hundred and fifty years ago. Charles was also a man well versed in the literature of his own day, and not ours. When transcribing Charles' script, then, care must be taken not to coin a phrase or passage that would be quite alien to his vocabulary. In days when we, broadly speaking, no longer read the Authorized Version nor pray in the language of Cranmer, it is essential that we learn to write in another language than that of our own day; in Wesley's language, in other words, uneasy though we may feel in using it. The scriptures Wesley knew and quoted were the scriptures in the Authorized Version or the version of the Psalms in the Book of Common Prayer. And even there we need to be aware, since very occasionally the AV was updated after Wesley's day. For example, the symbols *trl* can represent 'truly' and 'thoroughly' – only the context can tell (and sometimes either would be satisfactory); but Wesley would not, normally, write or read 'thoroughly' but 'throughly' as we find in the AV form of Psalm 51. It is only by reading Wesley and his sources and immersing our minds, as it were, in his language and vocabulary, that we can hope to reproduce his shorthand in its true form. And that is the least debt we owe him.

## Notes

1 This chapter is based upon Oliver A. Beckerlegge, *The Shorthand of Charles Wesley* (Madison: Charles Wesley Society, 2002). That publication is itself comprised of two separate studies: a general article on Charles' use of shorthand

(which was first published as 'Charles Wesley's Shorthand' in *Methodist History* . . . 29 [1991], 225–34), and a short manual which acts as a guide to reading Charles' shorthand. There is some overlap between those two pieces and not all of the material in that publication has been included here. Dr Beckerlegge, who died in 2003, led the way in deciphering Charles' shorthand script and must take much of the credit for opening up that section of the Charles Wesley literary corpus. This chapter has been prepared for publication here by Kenneth G. C. Newport, who has also spent considerable time working with Charles' shorthand texts (principally the sermons and sections of the manuscript journal).

2 John Byrom (1692–1763) was born in Manchester and educated at Cambridge, being elected fellow of Trinity in 1714. In the early 1720s he began teaching a method of shorthand which he had earlier devised. Although he issued proposals for publishing his system as early as 1723, his work *The Universal English Short-Hand* was not in fact published until 1767. A copy of that work is located in the John Rylands University of Manchester, ref. MAB M68.

3 See further, Newport, *Sermons*, 259

4 MARC, DDCW, 9/1.

5 One such example is found on the letter from John Fletcher to Charles Wesley dated 26 May 1771. The letter is held at Duke University Library, Frank Baker Collection, Wesley Family Box, 8.

6 For a more detailed account of the physical state of DDCW, 10/2 see the introduction of Kimbrough and Newport, *The Journal of Charles Wesley*.

7 DDCW, 10/2 begins in March 1736 and ends in November 1756. Even within those dates, however, the coverage is far from complete. There is nothing at all for the year 1743 and after 1751 the material is very thin indeed. Some of the gaps may be filled from other sources. For more detail see the introduction of Kimbrough and Newport, *The Journal of Charles Wesley*.

8 'Discovered' here has the eighteenth-century meaning of 'un-covered', i.e. 'disclosed'.

9 The shorthand stroke here expanded to 'satisfaction' could equally be 'strength'.

10 Transcription of Richard P. Heitzenrater.

11 Transcription of Kenneth G. C. Newport.

12 The shorthand here is 'lf' or 'lv' (the sign for 'f' and 'v' being the same). One might therefore read 'love' in place of 'life'.

13 Transcription of Kenneth G. C. Newport

14 Transcription of Kenneth G. C. Newport

15 John Telford, *The Journal of the Rev. Charles Wesley* (London: Robert Culley, [1910]).

16 Kimbrough and Newport, eds, *The Journal of Charles Wesley*.

17 Edited by S T Kimbrough Jr and Oliver A. Beckerlegge, 3 vols (Nashville: Abingdon/Kingswood, 1988, 1990, 1991).

18 See Newport, *Sermons*, 73–6 for an introduction to these sermons. The transcribed sermons themselves are also found in that volume.

19 See Newport, *Sermons*, 209, n. 362.

20 See Oliver A. Beckerlegge and Thomas R. Albin, *Charles Wesley's Earliest Evangelical Sermons: Six shorthand manuscript sermons now for the first time transcribed from the original* (Ilford: Wesley Historical Society, 1987).

21 For the full text of this sermon and discussion of its content and custodial history see Newport, *Sermons*, 183–210.

22  This could be '[the] Son of God', though given the possible echo of John 16.8, 'Spirit of God' seems more probable.

23  Martin Schmidt, *John Wesley: a theological biography*, translated by N. P. Goldhawk (London: Epworth, 1962), I, 101, 114, etc.

24  See Kimbrough and Beckerlegge, *The Unpublished Poetry of Charles Wesley*, vol. 3.

# 21. The Hymns of Charles Wesley and the Poetic Tradition

## J. R. WATSON

Books speak to other books; they are always in dialogue.
(Jeanette Winterson)[1]

Charles Wesley's hymns are written with a genius for the placing of words in
a line, and lines in a verse; they carry a theology of salvation for all and do so
with precision and confidence; they are full of psychological insight and an
awareness of human problems; and they are allusive and complex. It is the
last of these on which this essay is concentrated: the allusiveness and complexity that comes from Charles' wide reading and allows him to articulate
his ideas with such confidence and economy. His hymns are a form of communication that resonates with meaning, a form that is dense with multiple
signification, if only because it works in at least three ways: it calls up the past;
it speaks to Wesley's own time; and it speaks to the human condition outwith
the constraints of history. Wesley is thus three things: a student of the past; a
prophet for his own time; and our contemporary.

The sheer weight of a Wesley hymn comes from his use of words in a particular way, with a strong sense of their multiple possibilities. Each hymn is
a word-performance, often brilliant, always dense with meaning. But it is a
word-performance that exists in relation to other similar word artefacts, and
responds to them; the words that are used are spoken or written in response
to the same words in other situations and contexts. The word communicates
in two ways with the reader or singer in a Wesley hymn: it calls up words
from the reader or singer in response, and it is itself a response to earlier uses
of that word. It is a spectacular example of what the Russian theorist Mikhail
Bakhtin called 'dialogue'. Dialogue is, of course, communication between two
persons, but also 'verbal communication of any type whatsoever'. A book,
says Bakhtin, is an example of this verbal communication. It is what he calls 'a
verbal performance in print . . . it is calculated for active perception, involving
attentive reading and inner responsiveness'.

For Bakhtin's 'book' we could substitute 'hymn', as we could in the discourse that follows:

Moreover, a verbal performance of this kind also inevitably orients itself
with respect to previous performances in the same sphere, both those by

the same author and those of other authors. It inevitably takes its point of departure from some particular state of affairs involving a scientific problem or a literary style. Thus the printed verbal performance engages, as it were, in ideological colloquy of large scale: it responds to something, objects to something, affirms something, anticipates possible responses and objections, seeks support, and so on.

Any utterance, no matter how weighty and complete in and of itself, is only a moment in the continuous process of verbal communication. But that continuous verbal communication is, in turn, itself only a moment in the continuous, all-inclusive, generative process of a given social collective.[2]

Bakhtin's dialogic theory is useful for an understanding of what happens when we read or sing a Charles Wesley hymn. We encounter a verbal performance in print (which, in reading or singing, becomes a verbal performance again), and we recognize the way in which that performance exists in relation to others in the past and future of historical time. The hymns depend on the Bible, on Latin and English poetry (especially on Milton), on the Book of Common Prayer; and their language is echoed in the work of Fred Pratt Green and Timothy Dudley-Smith, so that our perspective on Charles Wesley's hymns changes as we sing the modern hymns that are derived from them. The words of these hymns – by Wesley, Pratt Green, Dudley-Smith – respond to something, object to something, affirm something, anticipate responses. They are part of a continuous process of revisiting and reassessing the texts in the continuity in which they stand.

They also stand, as Bakhtin saw, in relation to the 'given social collective'. They engage in dialogue with the world in which they were written: 'verbal communication can never be understood and explained outside of this connection with a concrete situation'.[3] Bakhtin's recognition demands that we should connect Wesley's hymns with the personal and public needs of his own age, and with the psychological and societal promptings of our own. Wesley's specific verbal performances on such topics as the rebellious 'Times of Trouble' of 1745 or the Lisbon earthquake of 1755 are part of a never-ceasing response to the world around him, from the appeal to 'harlots, and publicans, and thieves' in 1738 to the general invitation to sinners in *Hymns for those that Seek and Those that Have Redemption in the Blood of Jesus Christ* of 1747, and then onward. In writing about these things, however, Wesley's use of words responds to other words, supplementing them, re-apportioning them, sending them out in search of support or a new response. They are his inheritance and his bequest: they come to him from what Roland Barthes called 'the innumerable centres of culture' that a writer draws upon: indeed Barthes goes so far as to say that 'the text is . . . a multi-dimensional space in which a variety of writings, none of them original, blend and clash. The text is a tissue of quotations drawn from the innumerable centres of culture.'[4]

The idea of the text as a tissue of quotations has an obvious application to Charles Wesley's hymns. His choice of culture-centres comes from his education, his reading, his memory, his understanding and appreciation, his critical sense, his personal needs. He takes them in to his hymns, and then sends them out, filled with their accumulated meaning, for the readers and singers to take in to themselves: the words come down to us from Charles Wesley's many sources, but enriched by him. They are from different places – the Bible, the Prayer Book, other poets, such as Herbert, Matthew Prior, Elizabeth Singer Rowe, Samuel Wesley – but the very fact that Charles Wesley has used them gives them a new lustre. His hymns shine with the words he has transformed.

A good example is the use of Daniel Brevint's *The Christian Sacrifice and Sacrament* of 1673 as the inspiration for some of the hymns in *Hymns on the Lord's Supper* (1745). John Wesley printed an abridgement of Brevint's book as an introduction to the 1745 book, and the hymns then followed. Poetry and prose, the seventeenth and the eighteenth centuries, interact and intertwine; words reappear in new contexts; some things are left out, others brought in. The hymns do not fear the comparison with the writings of an eminent Anglican divine: they are in dialogue with them. 'Charles Wesley', said J. Ernest Rattenbury, 'gives Brevint wings . . . he turns the devotional theology of a High-Church Caroline divine into the flaming Methodist Evangel'.[5] This is neatly and persuasively said, and I think it is true; but as I have tried to show on another occasion,[6] the transformation owes everything to what Wesley brought to the dialogue with Brevint – his literary inheritance and his liturgical understanding.

Rattenbury was responsible for another famous saying about Charles Wesley: that 'a skilful man, if the Bible were lost, might extract much of it from Charles Wesley's hymns'.[7] He was rightly drawing attention to Wesley's encyclopaedic knowledge of the Bible, and his detailed use of it. Episodes, images, phrases, all enter the discourse of the hymns and enrich them. They are the most important of the many tissues of culture that are found in the hymns: but they are in a relationship to the world of Wesley's own time and to his individual needs. Similarly, they are in dialogue with the many other originating impulses of his work, from the classical authors, through Milton, to Brevint and to Wesley's contemporaries.

Every word that Wesley utters is necessarily bearing a burden. It brings with it accumulated meanings and instances, other contexts, other times. For as Bakhtin points out elsewhere, all writers and speakers have their predecessors, except one:

> Only the mythical and totally alone Adam, approaching a virgin and still unspoken world with the very first discourse, could really avoid altogether this mutual reorientation with respect to the discourse of the other, that occurs on the way to the object.[8]

An example from Charles Wesley might be his Nativity hymn, 'Hark, how all the welkin rings/"Glory to the king of kings"'. In writing those lines he was 'on the way to the object', the celebration of the great mystery of the Incarnation. He chose to speak of the welkin ringing as a way of suggesting that the whole sky was alive with sound, as Luke's Gospel tells it: 'And suddenly there was with the angel a multitude of the heavenly host, praising God, and saying, Glory to God in the highest, and on earth peace, good will toward men' (Luke 2.13–14). But why use a word such as 'welkin'? The answer, I suggest, lies in a little-known poem by William Somerville called 'The Chase', published in 1735. We can imagine Wesley in 1736, newly returned from Georgia, reading the newest poetry in a London bookshop. This poem is about fox-hunting. At Book II, lines 157–8, we read:

> The welkin rings, Men, Dogs, Hills, Rock and Woods
> In the full Consort join.

'The welkin rings' seems to have become something a cliché for the noise made by fox-hunters.[9] In Wesley's hymn we have a deliberate appropriation of the phrase, as though he is taking a secular usage and taking it over, 'converting it' we might say, for Christ. If such a noise can be made over such a trivial matter as fox-hunting, how much more wonderful would be the song of the angels at the Nativity: 'Hark, how all the welkin rings/Glory to the King of kings'. I suspect, though of course I cannot prove, that the couplet later in the hymn has its origins in Somerville's lines too: the 'Men, Dogs, Hills, Rock and Woods' which join in consort become Wesley's 'Universal Nature say/ Christ the Lord is born today'. Similarly, we notice that Somerville's poem continues:

> Now, my brave Youths
> Stripp'd for the Chace, give all your Souls to Joy! (II.158–9)

'Give all your Souls to Joy' is suitable as an instruction to young men eager to begin the day's sport, and Somerville's poem is satisfactory enough as an example of eighteenth-century minor poetry. But 'souls' and 'joy' might, to a Christian writer, suggest something else. To have joy in the soul would be an apt response to the birth of the Saviour: 'Joy to the world, the Lord is come', Isaac Watts had written, in words that Wesley would have known.

Wesley has appropriated Somerville's lines and phrases and used them for his own purpose. His 'dialogue' with Somerville would run something like this: 'all the joy, which you say should fill the souls of the young men, would be far better as a response to the birth of the Incarnate God, which began the process of salvation for mankind'. It is a dialogue, in the Bakhtinian sense, between secular and sacred. The words, the phrases, the concepts themselves, are wrenched from their initial meaning by being taken from the context for which they were written: it is as though Charles Wesley was saying, 'These are now *my* words: I take them from you in the name of Christ, and use them in his service.'

The process of assimilation of the innumerable centres of culture must have begun at school, with the reading of Greek and Latin authors. Henry Bett's admirable chapter on 'The Hymns and the Poets' in the third edition of *The Hymns of Methodism*, which enlarges the findings of his earlier editions, begins by reminding us that 'judging by their quotations, Virgil was [Charles's] favourite Latin poet, as Horace was his brother John's'.[10] Bett goes on to point out some remarkable debts to both poets, while entering the qualification that one can never be sure whether the borrowing was direct from the Latin text or from an English poet who was echoing the classics. His caution is appropriate, and (for the present purpose) significant: it reminds us that Charles Wesley's hymns are part of a complex process of dialogism with both the original writers or their translators – it is probably impossible to say which, and it does not matter. The hymns create a space wherein (to return to Barthes) 'a variety of writings, none of them original, blend and clash'. Bett's examples demonstrate this, although they are confined to individual echoes. 'Any reminiscences of the Latin poets in the hymns', he writes, 'must be almost entirely confined to single phrases.'[11]

Modern critical practice suggests that this is too exclusive: that Charles Wesley's hymns demonstrate that there was a pervasive influence upon him from Greek and Latin writers. It could not have been otherwise for a school-boy and an undergraduate brought up as he was. He would have learned the craft of verse from reading and writing Greek and Latin verses; he would have assimilated the values of heroism, tragic fortitude and human love; he would have been fascinated by myths and legends (Bett cites some telling evidence for this).[12] It all points to a poetic mind that sometimes remembered specific phrases and instances, but which was fundamentally shaped by the techniques and themes of classical poetry.

The habit of beginning a hymn with 'And', for example – there are five in the 1780 *Collection of Hymns*, including 'And can it be, that I should gain' and 'And are we yet alive' – may have come from the Greek way of beginning a sentence with a connective.[13] Equally, the reading of Homer could have given Charles Wesley an early example of the 'pitying tenderness divine' which is so important in his hymnology: the final book of the *Iliad* describes Priam's visit to the tent of Achilles to beg the body of Hector, their encounter bringing forth the most unexpected demonstrations of human feeling. There are plenty of other places where this pitying tenderness could have been found, most notably in the Gospel according to St Luke;[14] but the fundamental humanity that makes Homer so great must have been one of the innumerable contributing centres of culture that made up the thought and feeling of Charles Wesley's hymns. Similarly, Greek tragedy was concerned, as the psalms were, with justice (*dike*) and its relationship to mercy: and there are plenty of examples in Greek tragedy of what Wesley called 'the sin-sick soul'.

The argument, therefore, is not only that Wesley borrowed specific phrases, myths and incidents, but that the whole shaping of his mind came from his multifarious reading. Turning from Greek to Latin, for example, we find the example of Ovid (Ovid is not mentioned by Bett, who concentrates on Virgil and Horace). Ovid was very popular during the Renaissance, and although his influence was waning by the mid-eighteenth century, it was still considerable. *Metamorphoses* is about change, as the first sentence makes clear:

*In nova fert animus mutatas dicere formas corpora.*[15]

The legends of change that are recounted in Ovid's great poem are more than stories about changing shapes. They are emblems of changing identities and selves, demonstrations of possibility. As Herman Frankel has written of the *Metamorphoses*: 'The theme gave ample scope for displaying the phenomena of insecure and fleeting identity, of a self divided in itself or spilling over into another self.'[16] To an evangelical Christian, bodily change is a metaphor: it presents an emblematic view of the salvific process, of the sinner cleansed, saved, redeemed, made whole; and Charles Wesley wrote of it in one of the poems in *Hymns on the Lord's Supper* (No. 87):

> To thy foul and helpless Creature,
> Come, and cleanse
> All my sins,
> Come and change my Nature.

'Change my nature' is a phrase at the centre of Charles Wesley's evangelical hymnody. The Christian soul is no longer locked in the prison of a self that is conditioned by heredity or upbringing: Wesley's gospel teaches that the chains can fall off and the heart can be free. 'And can it be that I should gain' is a sustained expression of wonder at his own changed self:

> No condemnation now I dread;
> Jesus, and all in Him, is mine!
> Alive in Him, my living Head,
> And clothed in righteousness divine . . .

This comes from the wonderful transition in the Epistle to the Romans from chapter 7 to chapter 8, from the perplexed bafflement of the follower of the law to the radiant assurance of 'There is therefore no condemnation to them which are in Christ Jesus, who walk not after the flesh, but after the Spirit.' It is Pauline, certainly, quintessentially; but Ovid and the *Metamorphoses* are also present. If this seems doubtful, consider this verse from 'God of almighty love', which ends with a spectacular metamorphosis:

> Spirit of faith, inspire
> My consecrated heart;
> Fill me with pure, celestial fire,
> With all thou hast and art.
> My feeble mind transform,
> And, perfectly renewed,
> Into a saint exalt a worm,
> A worm exalt to God!

The most remarkable example of Ovidian influence is in 'Love divine, all loves excelling'.[17] That hymn demonstrates particularly clearly the many-stranded influences described by Barthes, for it has long been recognized that the opening lines parody Dryden's libretto for *King Arthur*, Purcell's opera of 1691:

> Fairest Isle, all isles excelling,
> Seat of pleasures and of loves;
> Venus here will choose her dwelling,
> And forsake her Cyprian groves.

As with Somerville's *The Chase*, Wesley here snatches back the poetry and gives it to Christ. His subject is not sexual love, and its pleasures, but divine love. The sexual *topos* lies there beside (or beneath) the new lines, discarded and worthless beside the new glory of:

> Love divine, all loves excelling,
> Joy of heaven, to earth come down . . .

But the hymn becomes much richer when we understand that it has its origins also in Charles Wesley's memories of *Metamorphoses* VIII, in which Baucis and Philemon are turned into trees. They were poor and old, living in a wretched house. To the house came Jupiter and Mercury in disguise, after having been turned away from many richer dwellings. Baucis and Philemon made them welcome, and gave them their simple food – cabbage and bacon, olives, endives and radishes, cheese and eggs. They even tried to kill their only goose (which kept escaping). Eventually the gods reveal themselves, and ask the old couple what they would wish as a boon. Their reply is that they would like to become guardians of the temple, and to die together: the wish was granted, and in extreme old age they were turned into trees. As they were standing in front of the temple, Baucis saw Philemon putting forth leaves, and Philemon saw Baucis doing the same. They just had time to cry 'Farewell, dear mate' before taking root as trees in front of the temple.

The story, told by Ovid with many delightful and amusing details, has features that engage with the Christian gospel. In particular, the welcome of strangers by the poor, after the rich and privileged had refused them, has parallels in the story of the Good Samaritan, and the reminder in Hebrews 13.2 that we should not be forgetful to entertain strangers, 'for thereby some have entertained angels unawares'. But the parallels go deeper than the morality of the tale. The story is of gods 'to earth come down' and visiting the 'humble dwelling'. It is of the openness of human beings to the gods, and of the revelation of gods to human beings, both of which are fundamental to Wesley's verse. It is particularly clear in the magnificent *Hymns on the Lord's Supper* of 1745. In 'Jesu, we thus obey', Christ enters our world in the moment of the sacrament:

> Our hearts we open wide
> To make the Saviour room:
> And lo! The Lamb, the Crucified,
> The Sinner's Friend is come! (Hymn 81)

To see this, human beings need to be open to the revelation of the Godhead:

> Unseal the Volume of thy Grace,
> Apply the Gospel-word,
> Open our Eyes to see thy Face,
> Our Hearts to know the Lord.

> Of Thee we commune still, and mourn
> Till Thou the Veil remove,
> Talk with us, and our Hearts shall burn
> With Flames of fervent Love.

Wesley is remembering the story of the road to Emmaus here, but the idea that the gods can visit mortals is Ovidian. The greatest example is the Nativity itself, in which (as the Advent Collect puts it) 'thy Son Jesus Christ came to visit us in great humility'. Like Jupiter in the story of Baucis and Philemon, he comes *'specie mortali'*, in the guise of a mortal, and he and Mercury are refused entry to a thousand homes ('there was no room for them in the inn'), only to be allowed into one house *'parva quidem'*, poor indeed.

I am not suggesting that Ovid should replace the Bible as a source for Wesley's hymns. The Bible was of paramount importance. The account in Luke's Gospel, for example, was fundamental to Wesley's apprehension of what the Incarnation means: it was a part of his special interest in that Gospel as one which was particularly rich in human understanding. In the 1919 edition of *Peake's Commentary on the Bible* it was described as the Gospel of a physician, 'a *religio medici* in its pity for frail and suffering humanity, and in its sympathy with the triumph of the Divine healing art upon the bodies and souls of men'.[18] The compassion of Luke was deeply important to Wesley as a part of his understanding of the processes of salvation. But it enters his system as one of many accumulations of experience: as he strove to express his wonder at the gospel of grace for all humankind, his imagination drew on his whole self, on what Coleridge was to describe as 'the whole soul':

The poet, described in *ideal* perfection, brings the whole soul of man into activity, with the subordination of its faculties to each other, according to their relative worth and dignity. He diffuses a tone and spirit of unity, that blends, and (as it were) *fuses*, each into each, by that synthetic and magical power, to which we have exclusively appropriated the name of imagination.[19]

Wesley's hymns bring 'the whole soul of man into activity' in their synthesizing of religious and literary elements, drawn from many sources and all periods: in this he was following Milton, who took a classical form, the epic, and made a Christian epic from it.

The influence of Milton on Wesley has often been remarked. Henry Bett thought that 'his influence upon the poetic style of the Wesleys is greater, perhaps, than that of any other writer'.[20] James Dale's perceptive essay on 'The Literary Setting of Wesley's Hymns' in the modern edition of *A Collection of Hymns for the Use of the People Called Methodists* is more precise: what he rightly calls the 'immersion in Milton' produces results that are apparent, 'though largely because of the allusive use of words and concepts rather than the imitation of verse-form'.[21] In what follows, I wish to try to expand on Dale's argument.

'Paradise Lost' gestured to Homer and Virgil, only to claim that it was based on superior values. Its description of the Fall was:

Sad task, yet argument
Not less but more Heroic than the wrauth
Of stern Achilles on his Foe pursu'd
Thrice Fugitive about Troy Wall; or rage

Of Turnus for Lavinia disespous'd
Or Neptun's ire or Juno's, that so long
Perplex'd the Greek and Cytherea's Son; (IX. 13–19)

Milton takes the *Iliad*, the *Aeneid*, and the *Odyssey* here, to claim that the Christian story of Fall and Redemption was 'not less but more heroic': all the wars and battles of traditional epic had left

The better fortitude
Of Patience and Heroic Martyrdom
Unsung; (IX.31–3)

Milton was part of a distinguished tradition of Christian humanism that Wesley inherited. It was a Renaissance synthesis of Christian and classical, described by Douglas Bush as 'the result of the long effort, which began with some of the Church Fathers, to reconcile and fuse the natural wisdom of the pagans with the supernatural illumination of Christianity'.[22]

'Paradise Lost' would have confirmed Charles Wesley's sense of the accumulated wisdom of earlier literature, now modified by Milton's passionate sensibility into the greatest of all Christian poems. But it would have done much more than this. It would have been for Wesley, as it was for other eighteenth-century poets, a towering work of genius, in whose shadow they wrote and thought. Many eighteenth-century poems, such as Sir Richard Blackmore's 'Creation', are pale imitations of Milton; and all poets of the age struggled with what Harold Bloom called 'the anxiety of influence', the need to fight against the domination of a great predecessor. Weak poets, in Bloom's reading, produce imitations of their forebears; strong poets wrestle with their forebears and often deliberately misread them in order to create something new (Blake is an example of a strong poet misreading Milton for his own purposes).[23] Wesley, who is a strong poet, takes Milton, as he takes Somerville, and appropriates his work for the infant Methodist societies. It was a remarkable, even a bold, gesture: even more remarkable than John Wesley's abridgement of the classics for his 'Christian Library'. Both brothers were conscious of the riches that should be made available to their followers: but Charles took Miltonic ideas and phrases and forged them into something new.

The debt to Milton, however, was more complex even that this. Because epic was the greatest of all poetic forms, the one into which all branches of learning should be pressed into service, 'Paradise Lost' carried with it a huge weight of accumulated knowledge – biblical, poetical, theological and philosophical. Milton showed how the Bible could be used in poetry, how classical legends could be incorporated, how theological speculation could be treated. Wesley would have found in Milton a justification for bringing *everything* to God in his poetry:

My talents, gifts, and graces, Lord,
Into thy blessed hands receive;
And let me live to preach thy word;
And let me to thy glory live:

My every sacred moment spend
In publishing the sinner's friend.

This hymn, 'Give me the faith which can remove' is No. 421 in the 1780 *Collection of Hymns for the Use of the People Called Methodists*, one of those in the section 'For Believers, Saved'. Hymn after hymn in this section emphasizes the dedication to Christ, the devotion of the whole soul to the service of God. It is what Milton himself had done, as a student, as a poet, and as Latin Secretary to the Commonwealth, in which post he worked his eyes so hard that he became blind. 'Paradise Lost' has a deeply moving account of the poet's blindness at the beginning of Book III, which itself is a reminder that Milton was writing at a time when he had seen the collapse of the Commonwealth and the return of Charles II, and with it the return of all the old tyrannies and corruptions that he had spent his life fighting. The loss of political power was as real to Milton as the loss of his sight: both were vivid reminders of the fact that paradise was lost: this was a world in which hopes were ruined and the wicked prospered, while the good were old, blind, neglected (and even, at one time, in mortal danger). It is into this situation that Milton places the redemption of the world.

The force of his imagination carries a lifetime's study into the poem and shapes it to a great expression of human failure and divine purpose:

That to the highth of this great Argument
I may assert Eternal Providence,
And justifie the wayes of God to men. (I.24–6)

One way of seeing Wesley's hymns would be as springing from this, as being a continuous and endlessly incomplete justifying the ways of God: of recording God's saving acts and care for sinners, in particular by celebrating the anti-Calvinist 'undistinguishing regard' that was 'cast on Adam's fallen race'. The 1741 *Hymns on God's Everlasting Love*, from which this comes (in the first hymn, 'Father, whose everlasting love') might be seen as Wesley's adaptation of Milton's subject, as stated in the first lines of 'Paradise Lost':

Of Mans First Disobedience, and the Fruit
Of that Forbidden Tree, whose mortal tast
Brought Death into the World, and all our woe,
Restore us, and regain the blissful Seat,
Sing Heav'nly Muse, . . . (I.1–6)

Milton's great epic does not flinch from depicting wickedness (in the figures of Satan and his associates) or human folly (in the actions of Adam and Eve). But these first lines are a reminder of what the poem is all about, which is the regaining of the blissful seat *after* the Fall. Milton follows tradition in seeing the Fall as a *felix culpa*, a fortunate Fall: the poem is about a paradise that is lost, but also about a Redemption by 'one greater Man'. The events of Genesis 3 are seen through New Testament eyes: an example may be found in Book X, where the Lord God who was 'walking in the garden in the cool of the day' (Genesis 3.8) is the God who intercedes for humanity by his death on the Cross:

> When he from wrauth more coole
> Came the mild Judge and Intercessor both
> To sentence Man: the voice of God they hear
> Now walking in the Garden . . . (X.95–8)

God is both Judge and Intercessor, and Mary is the 'second Eve', beginning the world over again. So Adam reflects in the final book of the poem, after he has been told the story of the Redemption by the Archangel Michael:

> O goodness infinite, goodness immense!
> That all this good of evil shall produce,
> And evil turn to good; more wonderful
> Then that by which creation first brought forth
> Light out of darkness! (XII.469–73)

This is Charles Wesley's 'sovereign grace' that extends to all, 'immense, unfathomed, unconfined'; it is also the traditional evangelical view of the redemptive act as greater than the creative act. Wesley would have found it in Isaac Watts' *Hymns and Spiritual Songs* of 1707:

> Nature with open volume stands
> To spread her Maker's name abroad.
> And ev'ry labour of his hands
> Shows something worthy of a God.
>
> But in the grace that rescu'd man
> His brightest form of glory shines; . . .

This is the grace which Wesley, following Milton, sees as 'infinite':

> He left his Father's throne above,
> So free, so infinite his grace,
> Emptied himself of all but love,
> And bled for Adam's helpless race . . .

'Paradise Lost' brings the failure of Adam and Eve, and thus of humanity, into sharp perspective. But the poem is not only about the great myth of Eden, which explains the fallen state of humanity. It is also about human behaviour in a fallen world: it describes envy, hatred and revenge, in the person of Satan, and goodness, loyalty and love in the angels and in the archangels Raphael and Michael. Above all, of course, it describes love, in the person and work of Jesus Christ, who came into that world in order to transform it.

The poem describes the ideal and the actual. It gives an idea of perfection, in the Garden of Eden and the uninhibited sexuality of Adam and Eve (Milton explicitly rejects one medieval teaching that sexual desire was a consequence of the Fall). It gives an account of the terrible events that are part of the fallen world: Cain and Abel, the Tower of Babel, wars, diseases. Human beings live in this world, as Milton and Charles Wesley knew. Milton describes the beginning of it in the final lines of the poem, as Adam and Eve look back at their old home before going out to begin the unpredictable process of human history:

> They looking back, all th'Eastern side beheld
> Of Paradise, so late thir happie seat,
> Wav'd over by that flaming Brand, the Gate
> With dreadful Faces throng'd and fiery Armes:
> Some natural tears they drop'd, but wip'd them soon;
> The World was all before them, where to choose
> Thir place of rest, and Providence thir guide:
> They hand in hand with wandring steps and slow,
> Through Eden took thir solitarie way. (XII.641–9)

The portrayal of these two figures, going into the world outside Eden with only each other for comfort, is one of the supreme moments of religious verse. Wesley follows it, picking up Milton's 'hand in hand', in one of his hymns from *Hymns for Those that Seek and Those that Have Redemption in the Blood of Jesus Christ* of 1747:

> All praise to our redeeming Lord,
> Who joins us by his grace,
> And bids us, each to each restored,
> Together seek his face.

> He bids us build each other up;
> And, gathered into one,
> To our high calling's glorious hope
> We hand in hand go on.

In this hymn the believers press on together through the world, the world that Wesley knew so well and portrayed so vividly, the world of 'harlots, and publicans, and thieves'. Like Adam and Eve, they have an awareness of something else, a better world: in the case of Adam and Eve they have just lost it, but they remember it, 'so late thir happie seat'; in the early Methodist societies they set themselves the task of travelling through the world in such a way that they would one day attain to the ideal:

> And if our fellowship below
> In Jesus be so sweet,
> What heights of rapture shall we know
> When round his throne we meet!

This is the conclusion of the journey of life. Meanwhile, the pilgrimage has to be made, and this is where Charles Wesley follows Milton in the astonishing acuity of his psychological insight. In 'On a journey' from *Hymns and Sacred*

*Poems* of 1740, he reflects on the relationship to God 'while here on earth I rove':

> Saviour, who ready art to hear,
> (Readier than I to pray,)
> Answer my scarcely utter'd prayer,
> And meet me on the way.
>
> Talk with me, Lord: thyself reveal,
> While here on earth I rove;
> Speak to my heart, and let it feel
> The kindling of thy love.
>
> With thee conversing, I forget
> All time, and toil, and care,
> Labour is rest, and pain is sweet,
> If Thou, my God, art there.

The third verse begins with a neat rewriting of 'Paradise Lost' IV.639–40, in which Eve is speaking to Adam:

> With thee conversing I forget all time,
> All seasons and thir change, all please alike.

The whole hymn (still in Methodist books as 'Talk with us Lord, thyself reveal') is concerned with the presence of God in the heart of the individual believer on the journey through life. As Milton portrays the delight of conversation in Eden before the Fall, so Wesley seeks a daily 'conversation' with God:

> To attend the whispers of thy grace,
> And hear thee inly speak.

In such attention to the whispers of grace, Wesley can recapture the 'speaking with God' that was lost at the Fall, and by employing Milton's line he registers the goodness of the moment: this is the ideal as opposed to the actual.

Wesley's hymnody, like 'Paradise Lost', presents the reader with the good without ignoring evil. If Milton's Satan is spectacular in his pride and envy, Wesley also knows 'the pride that lurks within'. The depth of human depravity is so great that it is hard to bear, and Wesley prays for divine gentleness and tact in enabling him to contemplate it:

> Show me, as my soul can bear,
> The depth of inbred sin;
> All the unbelief declare,
> The pride that lurks within;
> Take me, whom thyself hast bought,
> Bring into captivity
> Every high aspiring thought
> That would not stoop to thee.

The 'high aspiring thought' is an apt summary of the behaviour of Satan when he rebels against God's decree in Book V of 'Paradise Lost' and draws a third of the heavenly host after him (V.654 ff.). Against that pride and envy there is the central doctrine of 'Paradise Lost', that of obedience to God and the consequences of neglecting to obey. The disobedience of Eve and then Adam is a disaster which leads to their unhappiness, their penitence, and their expulsion from Eden: they enter the world that Milton and Charles Wesley knew, the world of the corruption of the 1660s and the 'harlots, publicans and thieves' of the 1730s. But the loving purposes of God lead to the redemption of the world through Jesus Christ, and thus to a new hope.

To express this, Wesley creates a variant of Watts' 'But in the grace that rescued man/His brightest form of glory shines'. With a certain wit he declares that the depths of love divine in the redemption are so fathomless that 'In vain the first-born seraph tries/To sound the depths of love divine'. The first-born seraph is the seraph of light, as the magnificent opening of 'Paradise Lost' Book III declares:

Hail, holy light, ofspring of Heav'n first-born
Or of th' Eternal Coeternal beam
May I express thee unblam'd? since God is light,
And never but in unapproached light
Dwelt from Eternitie, dwelt then in thee,
Bright effluence of bright essence increate. (III.1–6)

Wesley would have found it either in Milton or in Elizabeth Singer Rowe's *Poems on Several Occasions* (1696),[24] in which her 'Soliloquy XVII' describes God as

Still rising in superior excellence
To all the lovely things thy hands have made:
Ev'n seraphim in their immortal bloom
Those morning stars, the first-born smiles of heav'n
If once compar'd with thee, their brightest charms
Would fade away, and wither in thy sight. (21–6)

Both Rowe and Wesley describe God as superior to the first-born seraph, the former in superior excellence, the latter in redeeming love. So in 'Father of everlasting grace' Wesley celebrates the gift of the Holy Spirit, which is also 'the Spirit of thy Son' that makes 'the depth of Godhead known', which enables him to pray, and praise, and serve:

Till, added to that heavenly choir,
We raise our songs of triumph higher,
And praise thee in a nobler strain,
Out-soar the first-born seraph's flight,
And sing, with all thy sons in light,
Thy everlasting love to man.

Redeemed humanity can out-soar even the first-born seraph. It is this aston-ishing and sublime hope that Wesley's hymns express again and again. And although he knows 'the depths of inbred sin', his hope is in the name of Jesus that calms our fears and sets the prisoner free. In the same way, Milton acknowledged his blindness, even as Wesley acknowledged his sin. Nature's works were to Milton 'expung'd and ras'd/And wisdom at one entrance quite shut out':

> So much the rather thou Celestial light
> Shine inward, and the mind through all her powers
> Irradiate, there plant eyes, all mist from thence
> Purge and disperse, that I may see and tell
> Of things invisible to mortal sight. (III.51–5)

This is part-source of one of Wesley's greatest hymns, 'Christ, whose glory fills the skies'. As so often it depends on the Bible, in this case on Luke 1.78–9, where 'the day-spring from on high hath visited us/To give light to them that sit in darkness, and in the shadow of death'. But there is also the dialogue with Milton:

> Dark and cheerless is the morn
> Unaccompanied by thee:
> Joyless is the day's return,
> Till thy mercies beams I see,
> Till they inward light impart,
> Glad my eyes, and cheer my heart.

The 'inward light' echoes 'Paradise Lost' but the opening – 'dark and cheer-less' – comes from Samson's lament in 'Samson Agonistes' – 'O dark, dark, dark, amid the blaze of noon', and the first speech of the Chorus:

> Thou art become (O worst imprisonment!)
> The Dungeon of thy self; thy Soul
> (Which Men enjoying sight oft without cause complain)
> Imprison'd now indeed,
> In real darkness of the body dwells,
> Shut up from outward light
> To incorporate with gloomy night;
> For inward light alas
> Puts forth no visual beam. (155–63)

The darkness is 'incorporate with gloomy night', unrelieved by the inward light of grace: for Samson is imprisoned in his own despair. Wesley's third verse, which echoes this, goes *through* it to pray for the 'radiancy divine':

> Visit then this soul of mine;
> Pierce the gloom of sin and grief;

Fill me, radiancy divine;
Scatter all my unbelief;
More and more thyself display,
Shining to the perfect day.

The verse moves with a measured assurance from darkness to light: but its greatness comes also from its acknowledgement of the dark places of the soul. And as Samson was imprisoned in the dungeon of the self, so Wesley recognizes his own state before his conversion:

Long my imprisoned spirit lay,
Fast bound in sin and nature's night.
Thine eye diffused a quick'ning ray;
I woke; the dungeon flamed with light.
My chains fell off, my heart was free,
I rose, went forth, and followed thee.

I am not suggesting that Wesley was deliberately or consciously echoing 'Samson Agonistes' here. But the processes of his poetic mind were such, and the influence of Milton so dominant, that the great drama was one of the 'innumerable tissues of culture'. Wesley was perpetually in dialogue with his predecessors, and when we note the borrowings, as Bett and Dale and others have done, we are only part-way into his work. We need to appreciate the way in which the vast wealth of literary experience is taken into Wesley's work, because that is the way he thought and felt. He was striving to express what were for him the great truths of human existence: that people can be changed, that they can come out of the prison of the self, that sin can be forgiven. He knew that we live in a fallen world, shut out from paradise, for he saw it all around him in the Britain of his own time. He was in perpetual dialogue with that world, and with his poetic predecessors, in ways that make his hymnody incomparably rich.

## Notes

1 'From Innocence to Experience: Louise Tucker talks to Jeanette Winterson', printed at the end of Winterson's *Lighthousekeeping* (London, New York, Toronto and Sydney: Harper Perennial, 2005), 2.

2 From V. N. Voloshinov/M. Bakhtin, *Marxism and the Philosophy of Language*, 1929, trans. L. Matejka and I. R. Titanic (Cambridge, MA: Harvard University Press, 1973), reprinted in Pam Morris, ed., *The Bakhtin Reader* (London: Edward Arnold, 1994), 58–9. The authorship is uncertain. The book was published under the name of Voloshinov when Bakhtin was under arrest, but the ideas are thought to be Bakhtin's.

3 Morris, *Bakhtin Reader*, 59.

4 Roland Barthes, 'The Death of the Author', from *Image – Music – Text*, reprinted in David Lodge, ed., *Modern Criticism and Theory* (London: Longman, 1988), 170.

5  Rattenbury, *Eucharistic Hymns*, 13.

6  J. R. Watson, 'Hymns on the Lord's Supper, 1745, and Some Literary and Liturgical Sources', *Proceedings of the Charles Wesley Society*, 2 (1995), 17–33.

7  Rattenbury, *Evangelical Doctrines*, 48.

8  M. Bakhtin, 'Discourse in the Novel', quoted in Tzvetan Todorov, *Mikhail Bakhtin: The dialogical principle* (Minneapolis: University of Minnesota Press, 1984), 62.

9  It occurs, for example, in Robert S. Surtees's hunting novel, *Handley Cross* (1854): 'the pack forward, and away they go full cry, making the welkin ring'.

10  Henry Bett, *The Hymns of Methodism* (London: Epworth Press, 1945), 124.

11  Bett, *Hymns of Methodism*, 125.

12  Bett, *Hymns of Methodism*, 128–9.

13  Richard Jenkyns, *The Victorians and Ancient Greece* (Oxford: Basil Blackwell, 1980), 37: 'It is a Greek habit to begin each sentence with a connective; at the same time the repetitions of "and" sound vaguely biblical.'

14  See J. R. Watson, 'Pitying Tenderness and Tenderest Pity: The Hymns of Charles Wesley and the Writings of St Luke', The A. S. Peake Memorial Lecture, The Methodist Conference, 2005.

15  'My mind/spirit intends to tell of shapes changed into new bodies.'

16  Herman Frankel, *Ovid, a Poet between Two Worlds* (Los Angeles, 1945), 99.

17  The discussion of this hymn follows an argument which is made in greater detail in my article 'An Ovidian Source for Charles Wesley?', *Bulletin of the Hymn Society of Great Britain and Ireland*, 209, October 1996, 271–5.

18  A. J. Grieve, quoting J. V. Bartlet, in *Peake's Commentary on the Bible*, ed. Arthur S. Peake, with the assistance for the New Testament of A. J. Grieve (London: Thomas Nelson, 1919), 725. See also J. R. Watson, 'Pitying tenderness and tenderest pity'.

19  Samuel Taylor Coleridge, *Biographia Literaria*, chapter xiv.

20  Bett, *Hymns of Methodism*, 132.

21  *BE*, 7.40.

22  Douglas Bush, *Prefaces to Renaissance Literature* (Cambridge, MA: Harvard University Press, 1965), 37.

23  Harold Bloom, *The Anxiety of Influence: A theory of poetry* (New York: Oxford University Press, 1973).

24  For Elizabeth Singer Rowe, see James Dale, 'Charles Wesley and the Line of Piety: Antecedents of the Hymns in English Devotional Verse', *Proceedings of the Charles Wesley Society*, vol. 8, 2002, 52–64.

# 22. The Metamorphosis of Charles Wesley's Christmas Hymns, 1739–88[1]

## FRANK BAKER

John and Charles Wesley hold a remarkable record as collaborating hymn writers. Some five hundred hymns were published under their joint names between 1739 and 1746, forming the 'classic hymns' of Methodism.[2] This has led to one of the major literary problems of the eighteenth century, the attempt to distinguish between the verse of the two brothers: John or Charles?[3] The last but one of these jointly produced volumes was the epochal *Hymns on the Lord's Supper*, printed in the spring of 1745. The last was known familiarly by its sub-title as *Hymns for Whitsunday* rather than by its ponderous title, *Hymns of Petition and Thanksgiving for the Promise of the Father*. This appeared in May 1746. Intervening between these two hymn-pamphlets was *Hymns for the Nativity of Our Lord*, published in December 1745. But why, it should be asked, was this pamphlet, which passed through three times as many editions as *Whitsunday Hymns*, not an 'official' joint publication of the two brothers? We can offer no concrete proof, but it seems likely that Charles was cooling to the discipline of collaboration, especially if it involved joint *composition* as well as publication.[4] On the other hand, John Wesley was nothing like as enthusiastic as his younger brother about publishing Christmas hymns, in spite of Charles' strong emphasis on the theological significance of the Nativity. The Incarnation of our Lord Jesus Christ in human flesh was a miracle upon which Charles never ceased to dwell, often in unforgettable phraseology: 'Being's Source *begins to be*,/And God Himself is *born*' – 'The Incarnate Deity,/ Our God contracted to a span,/Incomprehensively made man'.[5]

Charles Wesley, far more than his brother John, was a devotee of the Church's Year, and almost all their verse celebrations of its anniversaries were owing to him, including the *Whitsunday Hymns* of 1746 – though here a few may in fact have been written by John. Charles' first major collaboration with his brother John, *Hymns and Sacred Poems* of 1739, contained a handful of hymns dedicated to the Incarnation. One of these he commissioned William Strahan of London to reprint for him at Christmas 1743, under the title which it bore in the 1739 volume, 'A hymn for Christmas Day'.[6] The following Christmas (20 December 1745) Strahan printed for Charles Wesley a penny collection of *Hymns for the Nativity of Our Lord*, which again was so thumbed to pieces that not a copy now remains. And then at Christmas 1745 Charles commissioned from Strahan a completely independent collection of 18 hymns under the same title – though Strahan's ledger refers to it simply as *Hymns for Christmas*. This work contained some of Charles' best compositions, from which the quotations above have been taken, though also (according to his brother John) some of his weakest: the best emphasizing the mystery and marvel of the Incarnation, the less successful ones the more sentimental side of Christmas.

The 1739 Christmas hymns and its 1743 reprint seem to have represented the larval stage of what Charles Wesley was planning, the penny pamphlet of Christmas hymns the pupal stage. Charles longed for the culmination, the metamorphosis into a creative winged song to the glory of God in Christ. He pulled out almost all the stops for this little book, his third attempt to give a personal hymnodic salute to the Incarnation. Two earlier ones had disappeared or were rapidly disappearing. This new one, however, could hardly be classed as the 'definitive' collection of his Christmas hymns, for it lacked 'Hark, how all the welkin rings', still on sale in its penny predecessor.[7] Almost from the outset, however, the two-penny *Nativity Hymns* was dogged by misfortune. A very peculiar publishing mishap spread its gravely unsettling results over no fewer than 16 years, and led to a quarter of the 28 known editions being seriously defective. It may have been due, however unlikely this seems, to Charles' extreme carelessness in handling his manuscripts for the 1745 *Nativity Hymns* that these errors came about. Certainly he could not match his brother John in meticulous administration, and some momentary lapse may well have brought upon him endless and fruitless labours in trying to stem the flow of faulty editions. Whether by way of atonement or out of true zeal, however, he continued to tinker at the text for 40 years. Almost every edition through which it passed saw changes of some kind or another. The final edition in his lifetime (1788) was different in dozens of deliberate details from the first – as well as introducing one obvious short-lived error in Hymn 15, line 19, the omission of 'thy' from 'Didst thou not in thy person join' – surely due to a faulty printer rather than to a failing Charles.

This was probably Charles' favourite small collection of hymns, which went through many more editions than any other. Yet in spite of its great merits, after two centuries it is hardly known outside Methodism, and very little within. Here an attempt is made to reconstruct the strange story of these four embodiments of Christmas hymns, and dozens of editions. First we will look at the constant revision to which Charles subjected his work, and then briefly examine each of the 18 hymns of 1745 in turn.

We find no earlier manuscript or printed form of these 18 hymns, any such items apparently having already been incorporated in the doomed tiny 1744 collection. From Charles' standpoint it was a newly created religious work of art. It was typically varied in language, in imagery and in versificiation – 14 different metrical patterns in 18 hymns, including four rollicking anapaestics. On 17 December 1745, Strahan charged him for a large London edition – 3,000 copies.

Charles was apparently anxious to have it appear almost immediately in good numbers in Bristol also in time for Christmas 1745, the date which it bears on a much more elaborate title-page describing it as 'The Second Edition'. That Christmas, however, both John and Charles Wesley remained together in London for much longer than Charles intended. The reason for the delay may well have been pastoral anxiety over the London Methodist Society, for although Bonnie Prince Charlie turned north from his march on London on 6 December, the city continued in something near panic, and the Wesleys were also anxious about their brother-in-law, Westley Hall, who was dithering in his loyalty. From whatever combination of circumstances, Charles did not leave London for Bristol until a week into the New Year, John two weeks later still.

Charles seems to have prepared another manuscript, including several revisions of the text, and probably sent it off to Felix Farley for printing in Bristol shortly after he had handed his original text to William Strahan in London. (The assumption made here is that this manuscript for Strahan had indeed included all the original 18 hymns, though it is just possible that the eighteenth was added at the last moment, and therefore not inserted in the manuscript already on its way to Farley.) Nor did Charles add to the Strahan manuscript the revisions later inserted in the second edition for Bristol. However it actually happened, something went sadly awry, and for its first two Christmas appearances in 1745 there was a London edition with 18 hymns and a Bristol one with 17, some of which were slightly revised.

This defective Bristol edition was in turn reproduced by Samuel Powell in Dublin (as the third edition) in 1747, and again in 1751 as the fourth in Dublin. This 17-hymn edition was again reprinted in Bristol as late as 1756 (fifth) by the deceased Farley's widow, and by Powell again in Dublin (as the sixth) in 1761.[8]

Charles had apparently discovered the absence of Hymn 18 from the Bristol edition soon after returning there in January 1746. Speedily he sought to set things at least partially straight by reprinting several of Strahan's original copies, which he carried around with him – though he does not seem immediately to have transcribed into these the revisions which he had earlier made to his first Bristol manuscript. Nor was he able to keep track of or to amend the continuing series of faulty 17-hymn reprints, which led a life of their own, though some cross-fertilization seems to have taken place at various points. One of these Strahan copies he almost certainly utilized to secure the printing of a Newcastle edition in 1746 when he spent some months there later that year,[9] probably another for a Cork edition in 1748,[10] and a fully correct third Bristol edition in 1749, for the housewarming of his bride in their new home in Charles Street, Bristol.[11] The third Bristol edition has completely disappeared, but surely upon this would be based the fourth Bristol edition of 1750, to a copy of which John added his own editorial comments. It was apparently earlier in the same year of 1750 that Charles supervised the preparation of the tenth edition, by Henry Cock in London.

It was not until a decade later, however, as they were nearing Christmas 1761, that John Wesley had any inkling of the publishing tribulations through which Charles had been passing. John had just seen the sixth of the 17-hymn editions, printed by William Pine of Bristol in 1761. On 26 December he wrote somewhat caustically to Charles in Bristol: 'Pray tell R. Sheen I am hugely displeased at his reprinting the *Nativity Hymns*, and omitting the very best hymn in the Collection, "All glory to God in the sky, etc." I beg they never more may be printed without it. Omit one or two and I will thank you. They are *Namby-*

*Pambical.'* (It should be pointed out that Ambrose Philips [1675?–1749] was a minor poet who was satirized as 'Namby-Pamby' because of a child's poem of his beginning 'Dimply damsel, sweetly smiling'). John Wesley's own copy of the fourth Bristol edition of the *Nativity Hymns* marks the passages which he particularly disliked, in Hymns 6, 12 and especially 16. It seems fairly clear that Charles Wesley was not *directly* responsible for this curtailed Bristol sixth edition, but he was at least indirectly responsible for the confusions which had bred it. And it spurred him to even more feverish activity to remove the stain from his reputation.

We, in this very different age, may well be amazed at the numbers – and the numbering – of these editions of which we hear, and by the temerity of a textual researcher who can demonstrate that severely flawed editions may continue to circulate for a decade and a half after publication of the original; and also that such a researcher is prepared to accept as correctly numbered a purported tenth edition while being unable to point to editions numbered seventh, eighth or ninth. What was really going on in those days? Is it possible to unravel the convoluted history of the text of Charles Wesley's *Hymns for the Nativity of Our Lord*? Was the printer's devil employed by Felix Farley and other printers only as an innocent if grubby errand-boy? Or were some dark imps secretly concocting this grand confusion of editions, aptly termed Pan-Demonism?

First we must understand that the pamphlets of John and Charles Wesley – and of other pamphleteers of their day – were subject to horrendous wear and tear, and that instead of being surprised at how many items have completely disappeared we should be surprised at how many have survived, if only in their ones and twos and threes. One thousand copies of Charles Wesley's 1743 *Hymns for Christmas Day* were printed by William Strahan in London. None have survived. Strahan printed 1,500 copies in 1744 of the penny *Nativity Hymns*. Not one has survived. Of the first edition of the two-penny *Nativity Hymns* of 1745 Strahan prepared no fewer than 3,000 copies. In this instance we are more fortunate: 18 are listed in libraries throughout the world, and probably there are a few others which will eventually surface, perhaps enough to make the total 30 – a survival rate of one per cent. Of no other edition during the lifetime of the Wesleys can we record any more than eight extant copies. We have actual copies of 26 editions of the *Nativity Hymns* issued between 1745 and 1791, good evidence of the actual publication of at least two other early editions, and the likelihood that Charles Wesley himself informed Henry Cock in 1750 that the London edition which he was then printing should be described as the tenth – though the probability is that not even Charles himself could have confidently identified its nine supposed predecessors.

The printing ledgers of William Strahan are invaluable in listing several hymn pamphlets which he had printed for Charles Wesley, but of which no copy now remains; on the other hand, not even those records are infallible; some Wesley publications bearing Strahan's imprint fail to appear in his ledgers. The many printers who worked for Wesley in other cities left no record at all. Yet in spite of many gaps in our knowledge of the reprints of this rare bundle of 18 hymns, so zealously preserved by Charles Wesley, in spite of the impossibility of being absolutely sure about the links between each edition and its predecessors, we can deduce with some certainty Charles Wesley's later activities during the 40 years that he was revising and printing them, constantly striving not only to keep them in print and free from error, but also to ensure that the latest edition was always an improvement on its predecessor, and that the last was incomparably better than the first.

## The text

The text of the 1745 *Nativity Hymns* underwent a host of minor transformations during Charles Wesley's lifetime. Some changes were normal reactions against poor writing, but most were in response to Charles' revising zeal as new editions were needed. What about the influence of John Wesley? It seems clear that he had very little direct influence on the text, though he did voice some critical comments. John's pencil notes in his copy of the 1750 Bristol edition may possibly have been mentioned occasionally in private conversation or letters, and in some instances may have surfaced years later as 'spontaneous' revisions by Charles himself. In Hymn 18, stanza 5, line 1 (18:5.1) the anapaestic rhythm clearly indicated a metrical fault in 'no horrid alarm of war', which John quickly correctly altered to 'no horrid *alarum* of war'; this Charles had apparently spotted for himself, and incorporated in the London 1750 edition.[12] In the last hymn (18:1.7), in 'Once more to thy creature return', John suggested reading the plural, 'Once more to thy creatures return', which Charles quickly accepted – in 1755. But in 10:1.3, Charles had written 'From our fears and sins relieve us', which John's note altered to 'release us' rhyming with 'Jesus'; this Charles accepted eventually – 25 years later, incorporating it into the text from 1777 onwards.

Charles would flatly turn down, however, two other corrections offered by his brother in two other hymns: in 14:4.4, 'His nature is sinless perfection below', which John wanted to change to 'spotless perfection', and in 15:8.1, where John would discard his pet hatred, 'dearest Lord', in favour of 'gracious Lord'. Nor was Charles ready to expunge even one of the ten stanzas from the 'namby-pamby' hymns which John had struck through. He had laboriously brought them to birth, and felt unable to sacrifice them, even on the altar of his older brother's taste, however discerning. It seems likely, however, that John's criticism did arouse Charles to a more assiduous polishing than might otherwise have been given. This detailed revision continued through 40 fruitful years, though the differences were in nuance rather than in radical innovation.

All 18 hymns underwent change. More than fifty lines were altered, usually in small points, but often undergoing major revision – altogether some ten per cent of the book. Thirty-four lines were demonstrably different in 1788 (the year of Charles' death) from the urgency of their first creation in 1745. One incidental result of this host of variants and their ramifications is that it is possible, albeit with some hesitancy on occasion, to construct a relatively reliable stemma of the known editions, which itself offers its own graphic demonstration of the spread of editions across the British Isles and even across the Atlantic to Philadelphia.

Some of the normal touching up of spelling and even of vocabulary may well have been the modernizing work of printers or copy editors, such as the alteration of 'hath' to 'has', 'thine' to 'thy', or 'quite' to 'choir'.[13] Other verbal changes, however, were turning the clock backward rather than forward, surely to make the lines more euphonious, as in changing 'swaths' to 'swathes', 'burden' to 'burthen', then especially 'chant' to 'chaunt'.[14] Undoubtedly the reason that John Wesley wished to remove stanza 3 from Hymn 12 was the unfamiliar dialect word 'cratch' – 'a rack or crib to hold fodder', otherwise a manger; eventually in 1761 Charles forsook this for a word which completely altered his original meaning – 'church': 'Cast we off our needless fear,/Boldly to his *church* draw nigh'.[15]

Eventually Charles Wesley also came to terms with one of his major metrical problems, the presentation of the Holy Spirit in one syllable, truncated to 'Sp'rit'. This he used regularly in 'That we his Sp'rit may gain' (9:3.6) from 1745 until 1777, when he left his metrically educated congregations to fend for themselves in 'That we his Spirit may gain'.

Many improvements were quite minor, some even doubtful. Others come as sudden revelations. The collection opens with the angel appearing to the shepherds:

Ye simple men of heart sincere,
    Shepherds who watch your flocks by night,
Start not to see an angel near,
    Nor tremble at this glorious light.

It was not until 1762 that the angel himself was revealed as the source of the radiance, 'the glory of the Lord' concentrated in the messenger: '*this* glorious light' (1:1.4) was transformed to '*his* glorious light'. One of Wesley's most pleasing changes appeared in the accident-prone second edition. Strahan's first and only edition read: 'Infant of days he here became,/And bore the *loved* Immanuel's Name'. This remained the text for four later editions, apparently based mainly on the copy of Strahan carried about by Charles Wesley. Eventually, however, Charles rescued from the 17-hymn edition his original 1745 revision, 'the *mild* Immanuel's Name' – a conscious return to the euphonious adjective employed in his first Christmas hymn, 'Hark how all the welkin rings', as part of the angel's song, 'peace on earth, and mercy mild', and in his own heralding of the Saviour's self-emptying purpose:

Mild he lays his glory by,
Born – that man no more may die,
Born – to raise the sons of earth,
Born – to give them second birth.[16]

The edition which may be regarded as the standard line divider between the old and the new text was that which brought a close to 13 variously numbered editions from the five different cities, an end also to the six 17-hymn editions, and the beginning of Charles' most careful attempts to appease his brother John. This edition, Pine, 1762, reveals the introduction of more variants than most, though not all are of major importance. Pine 1761 ['M' in the stemma on page 393] had rescued 'the mild Immanuel's Name' from Wesley's 1745 revisions; 'N' marks a similar rescue: 'thine all-*restoring* merit' instead of 'all-redeeming merit' – a prayer for individual salvation altered to search for general restoration.[17] Another change was quite new, the preference for a more active ending: 'Come, thou desire of nations, come,/And take us all to God' becomes 'And take us *up* to God!'[18] Another subtle revision occurs when ' Bring peace to us poor worms of earth,/And take us *up* to God!' is altered to 'Bring peace to us poor worms *on* earth!'[19]

For both Wesley brothers Robert Hawes was a favourite London printer, and one of the last to print for them before they were able to set up their own publishing house there. (It was Hawes who economized in the production of the *Nativity Hymns* by removing the running headlines, and thus reducing the number of pages from 24 to 23). Charles handed over three editions of the *Nativity Hymns* to Hawes in the 1770s, and each of them displayed tasteful 'modern' printing, and revealed that Charles Wesley was becoming if anything more subtle about his punctuation and the careful articulation of his verse. If we seek – as surely we must – to discover what Charles really sought in the structure of his punctuation, we must be happy to find the sensitive response of little-known printers like Hawes and the Paramores. Another subtle and faintly theological revision took place in 15:5.1–6.

In my weak flesh appear,
O God, be manifest here,
    Peace, righteousness, and joy:
Thy kingdom, Lord, set up within
My faithful heart; and all sin
    The devil's works destroy.

This faithfully reproduced the running on of the sense between lines 4 and 5, which was first made clear in Pine's edition of 1762; Hawes' first edition (*c.* 1774) also printed for the first time a deliberately abridged closing line, 'The devil's *work* [singular] destroy'.

Other revisions appear in the same hymn. Stanza 6 dealt with the hope of Christian perfection at the Second Coming of Christ.

I long thy coming to confess,
The mystic power of godliness,
    The life divine to prove;
The fullness of thy life to know,
Redeemed from all my sins below,
    And perfected in love. (15:6.1–6)

This was apparently strengthened by the change from 'all my *sins* below' (in all the 17-hymn editions) to 'all my *sin* below', but in preparing Pine's 1762 edition Wesley returned to his original 'sins', and retained this to the end. In stanza 7 his original had read:

O Christ, my hope, make known *in* me
The great, the glorious mystery,
   The hidden life impart:

A decade later, however, in Hawes' first edition, Charles altered the opening line to read 'make known *to* me', and retained this more modest expectation to the end (15:7:1).

Somewhat startling was the transformation brought about by the punctuation and alteration of a word in the closing stanza of Hymn 17 on the Magi's search for Christ. Until Pine's 1770 edition it began thus:

Lord, we receive thy grace and thee,
   With joy unspeakable receive, . . . (17:10.1–4)

In 1772 this was subtly transformed by a run-on line to an ascending double gift:

Lord, we receive thy grace, and thee
   With joy unspeakable receive,
And rise thine open face to see,
   And one with God for ever live.

John Wesley's favourite Nativity hymn, as we have seen, was No. 18, 'All glory to God in the sky'. In this Charles introduced very few revisions. There was John's own suggestion of praying for Christ's return to his creatures rather than to his creature (18:1.7); a miscalculated alteration claiming that 'heaven was open on earth' (rather than 'opened'), which was restored after lasting for over a decade (18:2.4); a couple of corrected printing errors ('nation' for nations' [stz. 3] and 'alarm' for 'alarum' [stz. 5]; and the removal from 1750 onwards of the italics in, 'The world was *united* to bless' [18:2.6]).

So far we have emphasized the lengthy and careful processing of Charles Wesley's revisions. It is important also to visualize his collection as a collection, with its varying themes and versification and pace, and an occasional emphasis upon some special points. First, perhaps, we should mention that the *Nativity Hymns* remained on continuous sale at the Methodist Book-Room until John Wesley's death in 1791, when the inventory showed on hand a total of 1,200 copies, as well as 450 'in sheets'.[20]

## The hymns of the collection

**No. 1.** The first hymn in the collection, 'Ye simple men of heart sincere', is a simple paraphrase of the herald angels addressing the shepherds, four verses in a steady iambic long meter, 8.8.8.8.

**No. 2.** The second, 'Ye heavenly choir', announces that we must echo the angels' song, in two stanzas of lilting anapaestics, 5.5.5.5.6.5.6.5.

**No. 3.** 'Angels speak, let me give ear', is set to music in Charles Wesley's *Hymns on the Great Festivals* (1746, see *A Union Catalogue of the Publications of*

*John and Charles Wesley*, No. 124), with rather florid tunes by Handel's friend, John Frederick Lampe (1703?–51), entitled 'The Shepherd's Song'. It is an unusual staccato metre, 8.3.3.6, whose ten stanzas are presented by *Hymns on the Great Festivals* in five pairs, of which the last is:

9. Sing we with the host of heaven ,
    Reconciled
    By a child
  Who to us is given.

10. Glory be to God the giver,
    Peace and love
    From above
  Reign on earth for ever.

The emphasis of **No. 4**, 'Glory to God on high', is the self-emptying of Christ, the *kenosis* (Philippians 2.7), expressed in a rich assortment of paradoxes in mixed iambic and trochaic verse (7.6.7.6.7.7.7.7.6.):

2. Him the angels all adored,
    Their maker and their king:
  Tidings of their humbled Lord
    They now to mortals bring:
  Emptied of his majesty,
    Of his dazzling glories shorn,
  Being's source *begins to be,*
    And God himself is BORN.

3. See th'eternal Son of God
    A mortal son of man,
  Dwelling in an earthly clod
    Whom heaven cannot contain!
  Stand amazed, ye heavens, at this!
    See the Lord of earth and skies!
  Humbled to the dust he is,
    And in a manger lies!

**No. 5**, 'Let earth and heaven combine', echoes the same marvel of Immanuel, the Hebrew for 'God with us', which is Wesley's constant awed refrain noted earlier, and here in the second stanza of this iambic metre (6.6.6.6.8.8):

1. He laid his glory by,
    He wrapped him in our clay,
  Unmarked by human eye
    The latent Godhead lay;
  Infant of days he here became,
  And bore mild Immanuel's name.

In the opening paragraph of this study three things of the unforgettable opening lines of this hymn were quoted, but perhaps it is well to remember that its central phrase is a fruitful borrowing from George Herbert's 'The Pulley':

> When God at first made man,
> Having a glasse of blessings standing by;
> Let us (said he) poure on him all we can:
> Let the worlds riches, which dispersed lie,
>     Contract into a span.

About Hymn **No. 6**, 'Join all ye joyful nations', John Wesley was doubtful. Its unusual iambic verse-form (7.7.4. 4.7.7.7.4 4.7) was apparently originated by Charles himself (and hardly ever imitated), in his robust celebration of Christian martyrs, 'Head of the Church triumphant'. For this J. F. Lampe wrote a tune in *Hymns on the Great Festivals* (No. 20), which has continued in the 1983 British *Hymns and Psalms* (No. 818, with Lampe's tune named 'DYING STEPHEN'). Although John Wesley wished to discard the third and the fourth of the six stanzas of 'Join all ye joyful nations', on a more generous day he would probably have raised no more quibble than he did with the first, of which the closing lines may well furnish a worthy title:

> 1. Join all ye joyful nations
>    Th'acclaiming hosts of heaven!
>      This happy morn
>      A child is born
>    To us a son is given;
>    The messenger and token
>    Of God's eternal favour,
>      God hath sent down
>      To us his Son
>    An universal Saviour.

Hymn **No. 7**, 'All glory to God, and peace upon earth', is another lilting anapaestic (5.5.5.5.6.5.6.5) emphasizing the fulfilment of biblical promises. The second of the five stanzas rejoices thus:

> 2. There let us behold Messias the Lord,
>    By prophets foretold, by angels adored,
>    Our God's incarnation with angels proclaim,
>    And publish salvation in Jesus's name.

Also in joyful iambic-anapaestic is **No. 8** (5.5.5.5.11), which tells in eight varied images the old story of God's reconciliation with sinful man.

> 1. Away with our fears!
>      The Godhead appears
>      In Christ reconciled,
>    The Father of mercies in Jesus the child . . .

4. The Ancient of days
   To redeem a lost race,
   From his glory comes down
Self-humbled to carry us up to a crown.

5. Made flesh for our sake,
   That we might partake
   The nature divine,
And again in his image, his holiness shine.

In **No. 9**, 'Father, our hearts we lift', Charles moves to a double short metre (6.6.8.6.6.6.8.6), a simple universal song of praise for the peace and love brought by 'the precious gift of thine incarnate Son:

4.     His kingdom from above
       He doth to us impart,
And pure benevolence and love
       O'erflow with faithful heart:
       Changed in a moment, we
       The sweet attraction find,
With open arms of charity
       Embracing all mankind.

The two trochaic stanzas of **No. 10** (8.7.8.7.8.7.8.7) form one of the best known prayers for the universal birth of the Saviour, and one of the least subject to revision, the only major change being 'release us' for 'relieve us' in 1777.

1. Come thou long expected Jesus,
       Born to set thy people free,
From our fears and sins release us,
       Let us find our rest in thee:
Israel's strength and consolation,
       Hope of all the earth thou art,
Dear desire of every nation,
       Joy of every longing heart.

2. Born thy people to deliver,
       Born a child and yet a king,
Born to reign in us for ever,
       Now thy gracious kingdom bring:
By thy own eternal spirit
       Rule in all our hearts alone,
By thy all-sufficient merit
       Raise us to thy glorious throne.

**No. 11**, 'Light of those whose weary dwelling', in exactly the same trochaic verse as the previous one, forms a companion piece, a prayer for the spread of the gospel:

2.5–6  Come, thou universal Saviour,
Come, and bring the gospel grace.

**No. 12**, 'Sing, ye ransomed nations sing,/Praises to our new-born King', is a rapidly flowing hymn in nine relatively straightforward trochaic verses (7.7.7.7) intended for unsophisticated congregational song:

6. Will his majesty disdain
The poor shepherd's simple strain?
No; for Israel's Shepherd, he
Loves their artless melody.

**No. 13** is addressed to the angels, 'Let angels and archangels sing', in his favourite six-eight iambic metre (8.8.8.8.8.8):

3. Angels, behold that infant's face,
With rapt'rous awe the Godhead own:
'Tis all your heaven on him to gaze,
And cast your crowns before his throne;
Tho' now he on his footstool lies,
Ye know he built both earth and skies.

The awesome search for Christian perfection in God is the crowning theme of **No. 14**, 'O astonishing grace', in a breathless iambic-anapaestic measure (5.5.5.11), closing with a memorable epigram:

4. And shall we not hope,
After God to wake up,
His nature to know?
His nature is sinless perfection below.

5. To this heavenly prize
By faith let us rise,
To his image ascend,
Apprehended of God, let us God apprehend.

**No. 15**, 'All-wise, all-good, almighty Lord', is more steadily and theologically meditative, in eight stanzas of another favourite iambic metre (8.8.6.8.8.6). Again the *kenosis* of Philippians 2.7 is the predominant theme, but Wesley also explores the Being of God:

4. Didst thou not in thy person join
The natures human and divine,
That God and man might be
Henceforth inseparably one?
Haste then, and make thy nature known
Incarnated in me.

We now come to the most questionable of Charles Wesley's *Nativity Hymns*, **No. 16**, 'O mercy divine', 15 fully rhymed iambic-anapaestic stanzas (5.5.11). With such severely limited material Charles was doubtless tempting providence, but he was nothing if not dangerously innovative in his use of verse. To put the author of 'Gentle Jesus, meek and mild' to the test we will jettison some of the continuity, and quote only the seven verses rejected by John:

4.   Our God ever blest,
       With oxen doth rest,
     Is nursed by his creature and hangs at the breast.

5.   So heavenly mild
       His innocence smiled,
     No wonder the mother should worship the child.

6.   The angels, she knew
       Had worshipped him too,
     And still thy confess'd adoration is due . . .

10.  The wise men adore,
       And bring him their store,
     The rich are permitted to follow the poor.

11.  To the inn they repair
       To see the young heir:
     The inn is a palace; for Jesus is there . . .

13.  Like him I would be,
       My Master I see
     In a stable! – a stable shall satisfy me.

14.  With him I reside:
       The manger shall hide
     Mine honour; the manger shall bury my pride.

**No. 17** follows the travels of the Magi in the search of the baby, 'Where is the holy, heaven-born child?' There are ten long-metre stanzas (8.8.8.8) following the narrative of their study and enquiry step by step, until the staccato of discovery:

7.  See there! The new born Saviour see,
      By faith discern the great I AM;
    'Tis he! The eternal God! 'tis he
    That bears the mild Immanuel's name.

Wesley reminds us of the fulfilment of the prophecy of Isaiah 9.6:

8.  The Prince of peace on earth is found,
      The Child is born, the Son is given,

> Tell it to all the nations round,
> Jehovah is come down from heaven.

The last, **No. 18**, 'All glory to God in the sky', a much more sinewy ana-paestic (8.8.8.8.8.8.8.8), was claimed by John as indubitably the best of this collection. This was the only one which he welcomed into his classic 1780 *A Collection of Hymns for the Use of the People Called Methodists*, No. 211, in the section, 'For Believers Rejoicing'. This was the hymn he began to sing, after a restless night on 1 March 1791, his last full day on earth. The dying John Wesley could not quite struggle to the end of the five long stanzas, but we will conclude, in full, with this tribute to his brother and his Lord:

1.  All glory to God in the sky,
    And peace on earth be restored!
    O Jesus, exalted on high,
    Appear, our omnipotent Lord!
    Who meanly in Bethlehem born,
    Didst stoop to redeem a lost race,
    Once more to thy creatures return,
    And reign in thy kingdom of grace.

2.  When thou in our flesh didst appear
    All nature acknowledged thy birth;
    Arose the acceptable year,
    And heaven was open on earth;
    Receiving its Lord from above,
    The world was united to bless
    The giver of concord and love,
    The prince and the author of peace.

3.  O wouldst thou again be made known,
    Again in thy Spirit descend,
    And set up in each of thine own
    A kingdom that shall never end.
    Thou only art able to bless,
    And make the glad nation obey,
    And bid the dire enmity cease,
    And bow the whole world to thy sway.

4.  Come then to thy servants again,
    Who long thy appearing to know;
    Thy quiet and peaceable reign
    In mercy establish below;
    All sorrow before thee shall fly,
    And anger and hatred be o'er,
    And envy and malice shall die,
    And discord afflict us no more.

5. No horrid alarum of war
   Shall break our eternal repose,
   No sound of trumpet is there,
   Where Jesus's Spirit o'er flows:
   Appeased by the charms of thy grace,
   We all shall in amity join,
   And kindly each other embrace,
   And love with a passion like thine.

## Notes

1 This chapter was first published as an article in the *Proceedings of the Charles Wesley Society* 7, (2001), 43–59 and is reprinted here, with a few minor changes, by permission, including the table *'Hymns for the Nativity*: Stemma' on page 393.

2 See Frank Baker, 'Charles Wesley's Productivity as a Religious Poet', *Proceedings of the Wesley Historical Society*, 47 (February 1989), 1–12 (especially 1–2).

3 *BE*, 7.31–8; Baker, *Charles Wesley's Verse*, 105, 128.

4 For some clues to the overlapping of the brothers' writing, *cf.* Baker, *Charles Wesley's Verse*, 105, 128.

5 *Hymns for the Nativity of Our Lord* (Bristol: Felix Farley, 1745), Hymns 4 (2.7–8), 5 (1.4–6).

6 Baker, ed. *Representative Verse of Charles Wesley*, 12–14. Strahan's ledgers charged for the paper and printing on 23 December 1743, 1,000 copies. It used half a small sheet of paper for each copy. No copies have survived.

7 One of Strahan's catalogues of the Wesleys' publications, printed on 23 December, 1743, advertised both items together, and the same pairing appeared in Samuel Powell's Dublin list of 1748. (Frank Baker, *A Union Catalogue of the Publications of John and Charles Wesley* (Durham, NC: The Divinity School, Duke University, 1966), Nos. 94, 737, 741).

8 See stemma opposite.

9 Although Charles alone was surely responsible, this new edition was advertised in the *Newcastle Journal* for 20 December 1746, as to be published 'the beginning of next week . . . By the Rev Mr John and Charles Wesley'. No physical trace of it remains, though there is an oblique reference to the composer of three tunes for it. J. F. Lampe, in a letter by Charles Wesley dated 11 December from Newcastle to Ebenezer Blackwell in London.

10 Charles had answered an urgent call to lead a revival in Cork in 1748, was befriended by the Cork printer, George Harrison, and apparently basically left Strahan's text for him to reprint. See edition E.

11 Charles Wesley had married Sarah Gwynne of Garth on 8 April 1749, but he continued with his preaching itinerancy until their new home in Bristol was ready. He preached in the New Room, Bristol, on Sunday 24 December, and on Christmas Day conducted a special service from four to six, the theme being Isaiah 9.6 – see Hymn 17.

12 The 1748 Cork (?) edition [E] inserts 'u' in the manuscript within 'alarm'; it is difficult to accept that Charles himself was responsible for the makeshift alteration in the 1750 Bristol edition [G], 'No horrid alarm of dread war'.

13 6:4.7; 10:2.5, 7; 12:4.3.

## The Metamorphosis of Charles Wesley's Christmas Hymns, 1739–1788, *Hymns for the Nativity*: Stemma

| | | | | | |
|---|---|---|---|---|---|
| A | | London | [Strahan] | 1745 | – – – – – – – – ┬─A─┬ |
| B* | 2 | Bristol | Farley | 1745 | – – – – – – – B |
| C | | Newcastle | Gooding | 1746 | [no known copy]   C |
| D* | 3 | Dublin | Powell | 1747 | – – – – – – – – D |
| E | | [[Cork? | Harrison? | 1748?] | – – – – – – – E |
| F | 3? | Bristol | Farley | 1749 | [no known copy]   F |
| G | 4 | Bristol | Farley | 1750 | – – – – – G |
| H | 10 | London | Cock | 1750 | – – – – – – – – – – H |
| I* | 4 | Dublin | Powell | 1751 | – – – – – – – – – – |
| J | 11 | London | Foundry | 1755 | – – – – – – – – – – J |
| K* | 5 | Bristol | Farley | 1756 | – – – – – – – – – – K─┐ |
| L* | 6 | Dublin | Powell | 1760 | – – – – – – – – – – L |
| M* | 6 | Bristol | Pine | 1761 | – – – – – – – – – – M |
| N | | Bristol | Pine | 1762 | – – – – – – – – – – N─┐ |
| O | | Bristol | Pine | 1764 | – – – – – – – – – – O |
| P | | Bristol | Pine | 1766 | – – – – – – – – – – P |
| Q | | Bristol | Pine | 1768 | – – – – – – – – – – Q |
| R | | Philadelphia | Dunlap | 1769 | – – – – – – – – – – R |
| S | | Bristol | Pine | 1770 | – – – – – – – – – – S |
| T | | Bristol | Pine | 1772 | – – – – – – – – – – T |
| U | | London | Hawes | [*ca.* 1774] | – – – – – – – – – – U |
| V | | London | Hawes | 1777 | – – – – – – – – – – V |
| W | | London | Hawes | 1778 | – – – – – – – – – – W |
| X | | London | Paramore | 1782 | – – – – – – – – – – X |
| Y | | London | Paramore | 1784 | – – – – – – – – – – Y─┐ |
| Z | | London | Paramore | 1787 | – – – – – – – – – – Z |
| 2A | | London | New Chapel | 1788 | – – – – – – – – – – 2A |
| 2B | | London | Paramore | 1791 | – – – – – – – – – – 2B |

[* = 17 hymns]

N.B. The stemma provides a kind of genealogical table for multiple editions of works. The vertical lines indicate *probable*, though at times uncertain, links between editions. The horizontal lines indicate the more certain links between them. Clues to links between editions are also provided by repeated revisions and (more convincing still) repeated errors. Often, as here, the numbering of the editions is flimsy evidence, sometimes misleading, because the Wesleys used so many printing centres. Notable revisions are recorded in the descriptions of most of the editions. In addition to the two conjectural editions noted (C and F), there may well have been others.

(Reproduced from the *Proceedings of the Charles Wesley Society* 7, 2001.)

14 'Wrapped in swathes th'immortal Stranger' (3:5.1, 1772); 'Every hour bur-
thened soul release' (11:2.6, 1770); 'Humbly chaunt Immanuel's name' (12:8.2 in
[H], 1750).

15 This may have been the somewhat despairing acceptance of a copy-editor's
(R. Sheen's?) suggestion in the defective 1761 Bristol edition [M], 12:3:2.

16 Hymn 5:2.6.

17 11:3.5.

18 9:5.8.

19 15:3.1–3.

20 From 1793 onwards it was combined with another collection (listed as No.
176 in *A Union Catalogue of the Publications of John and Charles Wesley*) and appeared
as *A Collection of Hymns for the Nativity of our Lord; and New Year's Day*. This continued in print until 1816.

# 23. The Influence of Charles Wesley on Contemporary Hymnody

## ANDREW PRATT

Current discussions about the nature of authorized hymnody within British Methodism underline the importance of the continuing influence of Charles Wesley on the hymns which are sung within the denomination. The Report of the Board of the Methodist Publishing House to the Methodist Conference of 2004 stated that there have been authorized hymn books in Methodism since the earliest days. The report goes on to argue that 'if a hymn or song is included in an authorized collection, leaders of worship are entitled to assume that it is consistent with our doctrines and most congregations use authorized hymn books as their normal book'.[1] The report concludes that 'to dispense with authorized or recommended hymnody would be a major break with our tradition and should not be entertained without serious and lengthy consideration'.[2] If we believe exactly the same as other denominations then there is no problem, but if that were so we would not be Methodists. Therefore the particular nature of what we believe is important. So what was distinctive about the legacy which Charles Wesley left to hymn writers who came after him? This might be expected to be discerned in three ways: the style of writing; the use of scripture, and theological emphasis.

## Style of writing

The hymn-writing tradition in which Charles Wesley stood was one which had originated in the German Reformation. Martin Luther had written many hymns. John Wesley translated many texts of German origin. It was not Charles' way to translate, but to write in his own style according to his own sense of need and inspiration. English hymnody had been written before the time of Isaac Watts, though it was Watts who first produced any serviceable quantity of texts. For the most part Watts would follow a single scripture passage and use this as a basis for hymnic reflection. Hence 'O God our help in ages past' is a reflection on Psalm 90. At other times a wider biblical narrative might provide Watts with a source for reflection, as in 'When I survey the wondrous cross'. From this starting point Charles Wesley was to develop the form in a more complex, elegant and elaborate way than any who had come before him and, arguably, set the standard for those who were to follow.

The style that Charles Wesley used followed a pattern in which stanzas were regular, with a consistent rhyme scheme. The argument of the text was developed from stanza to stanza in a logical manner. Scripture and religious poetic allusion were interwoven in the texts.

## Use of scripture

In some instances Charles Wesley took a scriptural narrative as his starting point, as in 'Come, O thou traveller unknown' (cf. Genesis 32). What is different here is both the sheer scale of the text, reaching to 12 six-line stanzas, and the way in which it is personalized and interpreted. The author becomes Jacob and the wrestling is a metaphor for the struggle of the Christian in keeping faith and knowing God. The consequence of this interpretation is an allusion to other scripture references, and the chief examples of these have been indicated by Hildebrandt and Beckerlegge.[3] This is the essence of Wesley's genius, the capacity to move through scripture interpolating references one with another in such a way as to leave the reader feeling that they had always been associated in this way. Many texts are extant in which there is no clear, single scriptural source. Scripture passages are taken from various parts of the Bible and intermingled with allusions to other Christian verse or prose. These are woven together to provide an *aide-mémoire* of the gospel message or a particular doctrine. Isaac Watts had begun to do this, as 'Art thou afraid his power shall fail' shows. The text is based on Isaiah 40.28ff., but alludes to Exodus 33 – the rock of ages. Broadly, though, this hymn is a paraphrase with little inter-textual reference. Comparison with Charles Wesley's use of scriptural texts and allusions is illuminating: 24 lines of 'Behold the servant of the Lord' offer no fewer than 41 scriptural allusions or references.[4]

## Theological emphasis

Berger identified various theological themes in *A Collection of Hymns for the Use of the People Called Methodists*.[5] It is important to recognize that this was a collection edited by John Wesley and upon which John left his mark. However, the volume is a worthwhile place in which to start an analysis of those themes which occupied Charles Wesley and which we might seek to find in contemporary material influenced by him. Berger identifies four emphases: the Soteriological Emphasis; the Experience of Salvation and the Understanding of Revelation; the Experience of Salvation as Realized Eschatology; and the Struggle for Christian Perfection.

This is the base from which this study must begin, but the influence which is discerned today is one which has percolated down through the history of the Methodist Church, its ecumenical partners and the use of hymnody within this tradition.

## A thumbnail sketch of the evolution of Methodist tradition

A thumbnail sketch of the evolution of Methodist tradition does not simply re-examine history, which is dealt with in greater depth elsewhere in this book, but allows for an understanding of the influence that Charles Wesley has continued to exercise through the twentieth century and on into the twenty-first. While the actual usage of hymns from collections is always difficult to ascertain, the presence of such hymns indicates the value placed on them by editors working in the service of the Church.

Methodism has held together those who take a literary–critical view of scripture[6] and those who are conservative–evangelical; those who put into practice the priesthood of all believers and those who have a high-church view of ordination; those who are pre-eminently sacramentalist and those who are not. From the beginning, certain theological themes have permeated Methodism, giving the movement its own particular shape and character. It is these which will either be seen to determine the future of Methodist hymnody or to have been discarded already as outmoded or less than useful for the present age.

Before looking to such a future it is necessary first to determine the *status quo*. This requires an understanding of what might be regarded as the determining Methodist theological themes.

## The nature of god

God is revealed in scripture. John Wesley stated that 'the Scripture, therefore, of the Old and New Testament is a most solid and precious system of divine truth'. This is a statement with which Charles Wesley would most certainly have concurred (as might be expected given the historical context in which the brothers were working) and such a view remains central to the Methodist Church today. This is not to say that the Methodist understanding of scripture is, or ever has been, fundamentalist; it is not. It has, however, always been evangelical. John Wesley put it like this: 'faith and salvation, include the substance of all the Bible, the marrow, as it were, of the whole Scripture'.[7] Humankind is the recipient of God's revelation confided in scripture but that does not mean that God is perceived without a struggle.[8] Scripture is regarded as having been inspired by the Holy Spirit and the same Spirit is needed for right interpretation.

If, as John Wesley insisted, scripture contains that which is necessary for salvation, an affirmation that is still part of the ordination service for Methodist presbyters in the United Kingdom,[9] then its character is ageless.

The understanding of God espoused by the Methodist Church has been of a God of power and authority. This is an almighty God, a God who inspires awe. What has been lacking has been the sense of reprobation associated with Calvinism. John Wesley had been restrained in his critique of Calvinism, Charles less so.[10] What neither of them had accepted was double predestination.[11] Both brothers believed in universal grace, and such grace prevented the condemnation of those who accepted salvation through faith. While the

reality of judgement was never underestimated by the Wesleys, the potentially universal nature of salvation that could ensue led to what some would
regard as compromise when it came to this issue. Such a conclusion would be
an unfair assessment of the Wesley brothers but it has caused tension within
the Methodist Church over generations. The issue of popular Calvinism has,
however, long been put to rest.

God is, in summary, a creative and providential deity. God is trinitarian
working out, through the action of Jesus and the Holy Spirit, a salvific purpose in creation.

For Methodists, Jesus was the 'Son of thy sire's eternal love'[12] (found in the
British *Methodist Hymn Book*, 1933 and *Hymns & Psalms* as 'Eternal Son, eternal love'). The sense of mercy that was attributed to God continued with a
theology that required the love of God to be incarnate in Jesus. What was
anticipated was a 'philanthropy divine',[13] a sense of the overwhelming love
of the Godhead toward humanity finding expression in human form. John
Wesley, in commenting on John 1.14, had expressed it like this: '. . . in order to
raise us to this dignity and happiness, the eternal Word, by a most amazing
condescension, was made flesh, united Himself to our miserable nature, with
all its innocent infirmities.'[14] This is allied with an understanding of universal
grace. The theology of the Wesleys was unapologetically Arminian, so that
this person, Jesus, would become the saviour of all humankind. Incarnation,
redemption and salvation are bound up in one as part of the whole of salvation
history. The kenotic giving of God to the world is foundational, as Charles'
'And can it be' suggests: 'So free, so infinite His grace – [God] Emptied Himself
of all but love'. Redemption is dependent on the Incarnation. A single text
serves to underline this understanding. 'Glory be to God on high' provides
sound Wesleyan theology from beginning to end. The use of the name 'Jesus'
rather than Christ[15] serves to emphasize the concept of God's kenosis and
self-investment in humanity. The theme continues, for this is the King who
is 'Emptied of His majesty'. Charles Wesley recognized the immensity of the
subject on which he was exhorting people to reflect:

> Of His dazzling glories shorn,
> Being's source begins to be,
> And God Himself is born!

Language is almost insufficient to expound humanity's response to this act of
grace but it must be penned:

> We, the sons of men, rejoice,
> The Prince of Peace proclaim;
> With heaven's host lift up our voice,
> And shout Immanuel's name.

Wesley now moves to Philippians 2.10 to continue this peroration, this
catalogue of human amazement. The mix of sound theology and emotion,
together with the poetic balance of the text (the rhyme scheme is consistent
with only the rhyming of 'am' and 'name', and 'man' and 'contain' showing

any kind of strain to modern ears), makes for a hymn which must rate as one of the most elegant and profound within the compass of this subject.

The goal of Jesus' life, humanity and death might best be summarized by the opening verse of 'Lord, as to Thy dear cross we flee':[16]

> Lord, as to Thy dear cross we flee,
> And plead to be forgiven,
> So let Thy life our pattern be,
> And form our souls for heaven.

The pattern of Jesus' life rather than his teaching is the informing principle of Methodist theology as expressed by hymns in mid-twentieth-century Britain. What theological expression of the nature of atonement is afforded to Methodism? There is an underlying sense of personal responsibility for the death of Jesus, an awareness of sin. Within Methodism the authority for such an interpretation is deeply rooted: 'Died he for me, who caused His pain?/ For me who Him to death pursued?' asked Charles Wesley. This theme of dependence on the crucified Jesus is central. 'And can it be that I should gain/ An interest in the Saviour's blood' begins in a highly introspective manner, reflecting on what God has done for the author in the work of Christ. What has happened is impenetrable to rational, human understanding: "Tis mystery all! The Immortal dies:/Who can explore His strange design?' Even the heavenly beings only manage to stumble on the verge of comprehension for 'In vain the first-born seraph tries/To sound the depths of love divine', and ultimately the conclusion is reached that 'angel minds [should] enquire no more'. The next stanza is a straightforward exposition of the Incarnation, the reason for this wonderment. Only then does the hymn begin to express something of what is happening, this realization of the transformation of the slave of sin into the child of God. Only now can the vehicle for these words become a tune of triumphant, confident expectation and praise.

That Christ died in the place of the sinner was, for Charles Wesley, beyond question. In 'O Jesus, my hope' he pictures himself as the murderer in whose stead Jesus died. In the light of this revelation he pleads for his hardness of heart to be removed, to be 'vanquished . . . with the sense of Thy love'. The picture which is beginning to develop is one of a penal substitutionary theory of atonement. This is further underlined by Wesley's 'All ye that pass by' (188). The personal nature of this text is evident as the author directs the singer to the objective action that takes place on the cross, together with the image of Christ as intercessor, 'For you and me/He prayed on the tree'. He goes on to ask, 'How shall a sinner find/The Saviour of mankind?' (203). Through the process of this agonizing death, Charles Wesley believes that there is salvation and so he pleads:

> What hast Thou done for me?
> O think on Calvary!
> By thy mortal groans and sighs,
> By Thy precious death I pray,
> Hear my dying spirit's cries,
> Take, O take my sins away!

The need which this process meets is recognized as being universal. Jesus is depicted by Charles Wesley as the 'Friend of sinners' for, he marvels, 'Was never love like Thine!' Yet the love is equivalent to the sorrow that the Saviour demonstrated, and both found their source in the divine nature of the sufferer, for 'Faith cries out: 'Tis He, 'tis He,/My God, that suffers there'. Incarnation and soteriology are immutably linked.

For Methodists, salvation has always been a universal possibility.[17] Christ's work on the cross is available to all. This work is experienced at an individual level.[18] While the authority of God is maintained, the justice of God is tempered with mercy. This emphasis had always been central to Methodism. While a theology of predestination has survived in certain branches of Methodism, that of Charles Wesley was Arminian. He wrote with passionate horror with regard to the doctrine of Reprobation:

Whoe'er admits; my soul disowns
The image of a torturing God,
Well-pleased with human shrieks and groans,
A fiend, a Moloch gorged with blood.

Good God! That any child of Thine
So horribly should think of Thee!
Lo! All my hopes I here resign,
If all may not find grace with me.[19]

All can benefit from the work of God in Jesus. Calvinism was not an acceptable option. While the early Methodists had disputed this, those who followed the Wesley brothers were left in no doubt as to which course they were expected to adopt. The Arminianism of Methodism is clear: 'Love, like death hath all destroyed,/Rendered all distinctions void', 'He spreads his arms to embrace you all', 'The invitation is to all'. God's mercy is 'Immense, unfathomed, unconfined', for Jesus is 'The general Saviour of mankind'. Charles Wesley's majestic and scholarly 'Let earth and heaven agree' concludes with a polemic which would not have been lost on contemporary Calvinists: 'for all my Lord was crucified,/For all, for all my Saviour died'. This is a constant thread throughout Charles Wesley's hymns. Another text, 'Would Jesus have the sinner die?' develops the theme in an evangelistic manner. This is a God whose 'grace to all extends,/Immense and unconfined . . . wide as infinity'. Such grace had 'never passed by one,/Or it had passed by me'. The personal thrust of this text is evident, and the more so when it is understood that Charles recognized his need for continuing gracious forgiveness. Houghton notes that he had originally written, 'My trespass is grown up to heaven'.[20] His brother John produced the more confident, 'My trespass was grown up to heaven' that was followed by the British *Methodist Hymn Book* (1933).

Wesleyan theology expresses a dependence on God and a response of faith. Yet anyone who makes such a response will find God to be accepting of them. There are no exclusion clauses. Theologically, Methodists believe in salvation by faith, through grace. Charles Wesley's 'O God of God, in whom combine' relates the Godhead to personal salvation in which the author seeks to participate. The text recognizes, using imagery of the sea, our need of grace from day to day. Heaven is referred to as 'our soul's abode' where our life can be 'Hid . . . with Christ in God'. Charles Wesley looks forward to a time of perfect salvation, '. . . filled with Thee be all our thought,/Till in us Thy full likeness shine'.

The response to God's call is best illustrated by Charles Wesley's 'Where shall my wondering soul begin?' This starts, appropriately, at the point of conversion. The scriptural allusions within the text are diverse but they are also personal. For instance, 'A brand plucked from eternal fire' refers to Zechariah 3.2. The text relates to Joshua, and Charles Wesley adopts it as his own in two ways. First, this hymn and the text associated with it mark his own conversion. As Joshua was chosen by God, so was the author. Second, Charles and John had both been rescued from a fire at Epworth Rectory in their childhood. The experience left a vivid impression on them and they allied it to this text. The second stanza then provides a classical exposition of evangelical salvation. Understanding what God has done for him, Charles reflects that it would be to 'slight my Father's love' if this gem were hidden 'within my heart' and so the evangelical imperative is born and given expression in the fourth verse. Without the preceding stanzas this would be patronizing indeed, but Wesley has indicated his own need for redemption and can call effectively to others in similar circumstances.

Grace is freely offered and those who receive it do so by faith. While grace can be prevenient, its effects do not need to be evident in order for a person to be acceptable to God. Methodists believe that evangelism is a crucial task and no one needs to be excluded from its goal. The response to the gospel is, initially, one of repentance. No sin need stand in the way of God. 'Depth of mercy! Can there be' demonstrates that Jesus is persistent in calling even the most grievous sinner. 'Can God His wrath forbear?/Me the chief of sinners spare?' And we anticipate that the answer is in the affirmative. 'Ye neighbours and friends of Jesus draw near' shows that a confident response can be made to God's grace for 'His love condescends' to invite the sinner.

Dedication is regarded as something which is evangelical in its motivation, yet soundly rational. In this light it makes sense to sing, 'Let Him to whom we now belong/His sovereign right assert'. As Christ has 'bought us with a price', 'He justly claims us as His own'. Christians owe everything in life and death to Christ. To this end they should expire in God's cause, recognizing that they are God's 'to all eternity'.[21] This is not a sacrifice but a condition for which the believer longs. 'Being of beings, God of love' proceeds to a conclusion in which we sing, 'So shall we ever live, and move,/And be with Christ in God'. Dedication to God is ultimately understood as dedication through the Church. The Church in its interpretation of scripture then begins to mould the mind of the latent disciple. Methodist theology understands that, following conversion, the Holy Spirit works in the life of the individual to enable his or her regeneration. The response to the teaching of the Church is indicative of the reality of this process.

Methodism has valued the concept of the 'open [Communion] table' at which conversion can occur. By implication such Communion is open to those outside the Church and the scandal of this position is not avoided, as the text, 'Sinners, obey the gospel word/Haste to the supper of my Lord!' shows. In being addressed to the 'sinner', it lays to rest any suspicion that those who receive Communion have to be perfect. The response of faith involves struggle, as 'Come, O thou Traveller unknown', inspired by the account of Jacob's struggle with the stranger at Jabbok's well, demonstrates.

The question of whether the Christian can fall from grace is one which exercised John Wesley[22] and one which has continued to exercise Methodism. Charles Wesley addressed the question in 'O Jesus full of truth and grace'. Christ prays for us, and even if we fall through sin, we never fall from grace, for we may pray, 'freely of my backslidings heal':

> The stone to flesh again convert,
> The veil of sin again remove;
> Sprinkle thy blood upon my heart,
> And melt it by thy dying love;
> This rebel heart by love subdue,
> And make it soft, and make it new.
>
> Ah! give me, Lord, the tender heart
> That trembles at the approach of sin;
> A godly fear of sin impart,
> Implant, and root it deep within,
> That I may dread thy gracious power,
> And never dare to offend thee more.

The response of faith is not a guarantee against difficulty. Charles Wesley acknowledges 'From trials unexempted/Thy dearest children are'.

Belief in God is, for Methodists, dependent on the direct witness of the Holy Spirit.[23] The Spirit 'is especially connected with mediating Christ to believers'.[24] The Spirit works in convicting sinners, recalling Christ to remembrance, enabling the adoption of people as children of God and building up believers in holiness.[25] 'The Church is the organ of the Spirit . . . called into existence, created, shaped, animated, ensouled, actuated by the Spirit.'[26] The Spirit is the transforming gift of God to individuals and to the Church. The Spirit is seen as being present in every believer. There is a lack of elitism. The sole condition to the receipt of this gift of grace is contrition. The Spirit has a sanctifying purpose. The presence of the Spirit is evidenced by moral power and the developing holiness of the recipient. The Spirit can inspire our present life. The Spirit's influence is not other-worldly and the believer is expected to apply Christian principles to social evils. It is very much a power for the life lived now. Salvation and justification open the door to sanctification.

John Wesley's publication, *A Plain Account of Christian Perfection*,[27] has been seminal for Methodists. Both John and Charles Wesley felt compelled to maintain that an element of Christian perfection was the attainable goal of every believer.[28] Holiness has been a central tenet for Methodists and was doubly underlined by Charles Wesley in his sermons. The path to holiness is a path to purity. The people who have been redeemed, who have committed their lives to God, who rest in trustfulness and peace, are being 'perfected in holiness' through the vicissitudes of their lives. This is the life towards which the early Methodists aspired and it is a goal which, as Charles Wesley underlined, required commitment and action, for there is a need to

Still forget the things behind,
Follow Christ in heart and mind,
Toward the mark unwearied press,
Seize the crown of righteousness.

The early Methodists sought for Christian perfection, they aspired to be perfect in love and this is an aspiration that has not been lost in the twentieth century. John Wesley had written, 'Come, Saviour, Jesus, from above!/Assist me with Thy heavenly grace'. Such grace frees the believer from the ties of this world in order to obtain 'Thy pure love within [his] breast'. Charles Wesley understood that for this to happen a re-creation of the person was necessary, and this is the theme of 'The thing my God doth hate'.

The content of these hymns makes a doctrinal statement that might be summed up as follows:

1. The place of people before God ought to be one of humility.
2. In spite of sin, through the redemptive action of Christ's work on the cross, perfection is an attainable goal.
3. This goal is universally available.
4. People may approach God in confidence.
5. The ultimate end of the Christian is in paradise in unity with God.
6. This end is reached through the transforming work of the Spirit.
7. It is an end that we can both anticipate, and for which we can pray.

The right end of redemption for the Methodist theologian is perfect holiness. 'The mission of Methodism [is] to "spread Scriptural holiness through the land"', asserted the Bible Christians in line with John and Charles Wesley and the tenets of historical Methodism. The redemptive work of God elicits both humility and evangelistic zeal. This redemption is brought about by the soteriological work of Christ.

Realized as well as future eschatology have a place in Methodist theology. 'Jesus the conqueror, reigns' offers an understanding of the present reign of Christ, yet those who are taken up within God's love anticipate that they will 'cast their crowns before Thee,/Lost in wonder, love and praise'.[29] Jesus is 'the name high over all' before whom 'devils fear and fly'.

It is appropriate to look 'to things above', beyond this temporal realm. Believers will 'hand in hand go on' to their 'high calling's glorious hope'. There is an eschatological feel as Wesley ponders, 'What heights of rapture shall we know/When round His throne we meet'. The signs of the Kingdom are anticipated. Wesley grasps the vision and sings, 'Come, let us join our friends above'. The oneness of the Church and the communion of saints is acknowledged and, in words that have never been surpassed, the dynamic unity and continuity of this communion are pictured.

Close fellowship was one of the formative features of Methodism. Class Meetings and Bands allowed for organizational structure but also brought people together with the expectation that they would support one another. Fellowship was to involve study and prayer. Confidence in the group was such that the Band Meeting became the place for personal confession and reconciliation. Members were expected to look out for one another's spiritual well-being. If prayer binds people to God then the fellowship are bound to each other in equally powerful ways. Here was a pilgrim band:

> The little fellowship of Christian people was, as it were, the microcosm through which Charles Wesley understood and interpreted the deepest principles of the Church of God. Like his brother, he believed that Christianity was in its essence a social religion.[30]

While Charles Wesley's main emphasis was directed to another world for which God was the 'Captain of Israel's host, and Guide' his sense that it also involved a fellowship in which we 'build each other up' was inescapable.

The Lord's Supper is seen as the place of spiritual sustenance for the believer. Here are 'fresh supplies of love' which is 'our immortal food', 'The true and living bread' and 'Thy flesh is meat indeed'. Christ is the 'Victim divine' but lest it should be thought that this is the language of the Mass the text reminds us that he was '*Once*[31] offered up' for the atonement of 'all mankind'.[32]

Fellowship is presented as companionship on earth. This is recognized as a precursor to 'heaven's unutterable bliss' for here believers offer each other 'the right hand/Of fellowship' indicative of worldly trust and a spiritual bond. These are 'Brethren in Christ, and well beloved' who know that God's uniting love 'will not let us part', who 'join hearts and hands' in order to 'gain our calling's hope'. There is an expected mutuality of support. In spite of this the fellowship that is experienced finds its source in God. 'Jesus we look to Thee' affirms Charles Wesley's expectation that not only are the believers in fellowship one with another, but 'Thou in the midst of us shalt be'.

The distinctive connexionalism of Methodism can be traced to a Lutheran belief in the priesthood of all believers. Rattenbury, commenting on Luther, understood his emphasis to be 'on the priesthood of *each* believer rather than on the corporate priesthood of the whole church'. He goes on to state that 'The hymns of Wesley enlarge, develop, and enrich the Lutheran conception of the priesthood of each believer.'[33]

## How is this theology incorporated and reflected in Methodist hymnody?

Historically Methodist hymn books have followed one of three patterns. That used by John Wesley in *A Collection of Hymns for the Use of People Called Methodists*[34] was determined by the need to provide hymns for a group of people within a denomination who found their ecclesial roots within the Church of England. This denomination would provide for rites of passage and the sacraments during the lives of John and Charles Wesley. A second determining factor for this collection was that of evangelism.

As distinct Methodist denominations developed in England during the nineteenth century the hymnodic needs of the various connexions evolved. A second model of hymn book followed the outline of a traditional preaching service. God is adored, Jesus is worshipped, his life and work is described, the Holy Spirit is invoked, the gospel is proclaimed and the people respond. The goal of this progression is a future life that is accessed through death and judgement. The intent is practical. Worship as a subject, prayer, sacraments, mission, the place of children, social interaction and times and seasons are addressed in what is essentially an appendix.[35] This is a theology based on worship. There is a precedent, for Teresa Berger has identified a similar relationship between the theology of hymns and worship based on her study of *A Collection of Hymns for the Use of the People Called Methodists*.[36] Other Methodist denominations used idiosyncratic systems of ordering such as that adopted by the Primitive Methodists of grouping hymns according to metre in order to facilitate ease of use by musicians charged with finding appropriate tunes. Latterly there has been a move towards liturgically-based services and hymn-book editors have sought to meet this need by offering collections organized according to the seasons of the church year.[37]

The extent to which the definitive doctrines and practices of Methodism are maintained depends on the actual hymns included in any collection. The extent to which Charles Wesley's hymns and those which follow his example have been chosen are an indication of his continuing influence.

## The continued use of Charles Wesley's hymns

The clearest and most obvious influence of the hymns is demonstrated by their presence in present-day collections. The decline of inclusion of such texts in British hymnals has been more rapid than that in the USA. If a conservative estimate is taken of Charles Wesley's corpus as numbering some 4,000 hymns (estimates have gone as high as 7,000)[38] then an indication of the decline of inclusion can be ascertained by the number of texts included in a resource like *HymnQuest* which lists 530 first lines. This listing is taken from some 331 British hymn books.

In terms of Methodist hymnals the *Methodist Hymn Book* (1933) contained 243 texts of which one was a translation. *Hymns & Psalms* (1983) contained 156 (a lower number than the Methodist Conference had requested) of which, judiciously, the editors recognized that the authorship of eight was disputed.

*The Methodist Hymnal* (1932, 1935, 1939) had 56 texts, while *The United Methodist Hymnal* (1989) had 51 plus a further eight poems and six responses. The American books clearly had a lower baseline number of hymns but the total content of these books is also lower and the rate of the decline of the use of the Charles Wesley oeuvre noticeably less. In fact, if the additional texts are taken into account, it could be argued that there is an increasing influence.

## Charles Wesley's influence on other writers

More subtle is the influence that can be detected in the work of other writers. A hymn in the classic style of Charles Wesley in every respect is provided by Brian Wren. 'Lord God, your love has called us here'[39] uses the same metre and rhyme scheme as 'Behold the servant of the Lord'. The text is eclectic in its use of scriptural references, Gospels and Pauline epistles being prominent, but the Old Testament also features, '. . . you call our name,/and then receive us as your own' (Isaiah 43.1). The overall theme is that of sin and redemption, and the thrust of the text is clearly Arminian for it is the purpose of God in Christ to

> . . . show how grandly love intends
> To work till all creation sings,
> To fill all worlds, to crown all things.

Notice the repetition of the word 'all'. There is even an echo of 'And can it be' as Wren understands that we are '. . . half bound by inner chains' while Wesley has the subject of his text 'fast bound by sin and nature's night' and, within the same stanza announces, 'My chains fell off'. Ultimately Wren concludes that '. . . love is making all things new', a sentiment which is not far from that of Charles Wesley in 'Love divine, all loves excelling': 'Changed from glory into glory,/Till in heaven we take our place'.[40]

Timothy Dudley-Smith's 'Child of the stable's secret birth'[41] mirrors 'Let earth and heaven combine'. Both texts compare and contrast the human child Jesus with God the creator and Lord of all. In this there is nothing particularly unusual. Graham Kendrick's popular text, 'From heaven you came' ('The Servant King') does just this. For Dudley-Smith the 'Child of the stable's secret birth' is 'The Lord by right of the Lords of earth'. This is the same God who, Wesley says, 'Laid his glory by', 'Our God contracted to a span,/ Incomprehensibly made man'. Dudley-Smith puts it this way: the 'Voice that rang through the courts on high/contracted now to a wordless cry'. The only other use of the word 'contracted' in English hymnody in this sense is in Charles Wesley's older brother, Samuel's, 'Hymn to God the Son'. In a different context the words were used by George Herbert[42] and also Jeremy Taylor.[43]

In both these authors, Wren and Dudley-Smith, we recognize the debt which is owed to Charles Wesley in the use of scripture, the logic of form, the strictness of rhyme and the imperative to provide theological interpretation.

More subtle is the continued influence in terms of theological theme. Here it is useful to return to the four emphases identified by Berger.[44]

### The soteriological emphasis

The language of Martin E. Leckebusch's 'A crown of piercing thorns'[45] is characteristic of the realism that was beginning to show itself in much hymnody at the end of the twentieth century.[46] Yet the individual nature of the writing and the sense of salvation being with a purpose,

Your feet they firmly held
as nails were hammered through:
my feet are free – but how can I
not choose to follow you?

echoes Charles Wesley, 'Died he for me'? . . . 'I rose, went forth, and followed thee'.[47] What is lacking is the wider vision that drove Charles Wesley's imperative for evangelism. Hayward Osbourne's communion hymn takes a further step in stating that

As the bread is broken
Let each of us recall
The person who was broken
Because he loved us all.[48]

There is here a flavour of Arminianism that must be present in any soteriological text if it is to be identified as having been influenced by Charles Wesley. Carl Daw Junior's 'How shallow former shadows seem'[49] describes the reality of the cross and admits that 'with awe we glimpse its true import/and dare to call it good'. The text is inclusive in its tenor. The Arminian soteriology of Charles Wesley is prominent in Judy Davies' 'Put your hand in your neighbour's hand'. This is most clearly expressed in the last four lines of the final stanza:

for Christ on the cross is the bridge between
my Father and me and my friend across the sea,
and all God's people are one in him.
and all God's people are one.[50]

Yet the text lacks both elegance and power.

A step closer to Wesley is provided in Fred Pratt Green's 'Life has many rhythms, every heart its beat'.[51] The third stanza is particularly pertinent:

It was you who promised: *All who seek shall find.*
What we find lies deeper than our reach of mind;
What we found was you, Lord, you the God Above.
You had come as Victim to the world you love.

It is clear that the Victim is the Jesus of the cross, and the salvation inherent here is for all. The sense of being saved for a purpose is underlined by the last line of the hymn: 'ours the only victory we would serve and share'. Culturally speaking, the latter half of the twentieth century was a time of increasing individualism. Many of the hymns and spiritual songs of this time lack Wesley's understanding of fellowship and the inclusivity which he had promulgated. There was, nevertheless, a reaction against this mood. It is to Pratt Green again that we turn for words of simplicity and elegance. The cross is assumed and the acceptance of incorporation of the Church within the cross is stated. Amid change 'The Church of Christ in every age'[52] must 'keep on rising from the dead'. As the text develops it is clear that the gospel is something which is both practical and universal. It is to reach the victims of injustice around the world. The 'cure of souls' is found in the shed blood of Christ, and the role of the saved is to

> . . . have no mission but to serve
> In full obedience to our Lord:
> To care for all, without reserve,
> And spread his liberating Word.

The word 'all' is significant and provides a validation of the Wesleyan soteriological influence within the hymn.

It is clear from this brief summary that the combination of a soteriology with an Arminian theology is not as obvious in late-twentieth-century hymn writers as it had been in the texts of Charles Wesley. The influence can be detected in Methodist writers, but it is not their primary theme.

## The experience of salvation and the understanding of revelation

For Charles Wesley the means of salvation is disclosed in scripture. God enables that revelation to be understood and interpreted as well as being its source. 'Come, Holy Ghost, our hearts inspire' asks that the Holy Ghost should 'unseal the sacred book' while acknowledging that 'moved by thee/ The prophets wrote and spoke'.

George W. Briggs' 'God has spoken by his prophets' states that 'God is speaking by his spirit' . . . In the age-long word expounding/God's own message, now as then'. So while there is a rooting in history there is a new interpretation for every age.

Michael Forster in 'The Saviour of the nations' states unequivocally:

> The mystery of ages,
> the secret long-concealed,
> of full and free salvation,
> at last has been revealed.

And it is clear from the context that this revelation is in the birth of Christ.

Brian Wren takes it a step further. Salvation is seen as revealed in the love of God seen in Christ, clearly visible in scripture, but it is still working 'when a hungry child is fed'.[53]

This moves us towards a consideration of the experience of salvation as realized eschatology.

## The experience of salvation as realized eschatology

Salvation now is a theme which would be expected to be emphasized in an age when everything is instant. The constant search for opportunities in, and solutions for, the context in which we find ourselves as human beings is a common preoccupation. Such opportunities have to be a present reality or they are disregarded as irrelevant. We seek to 'serve the present age' but we also require our eschatological ends to be met within its compass.

Christopher Idle takes Romans 12 as a starting point for his text, 'Now in view of all God's mercies'. He begins with an interpretation of the scripture, recognising all that has gone before that has ensured the redemption of the Christian. It then becomes clear that in the light of this redemption the individual should be committed to service so that Christians might

> laugh and cry with one another
> through the joy or pain God sends;
> welcome neighbour, sister, brother,
> giving time and making friends.

The actions of God in which the believer shares are seen as being necessary and possible now. We do not need to wait for some future moment to bring in the reign of God. Through faith and action its reality can be experienced now:

> See the rule of Christ advancing,
> let his will be understood;
> praying, working, peace-enhancing,
> evil overcome with good.

## The struggle for Christian perfection

If any theme defined Charles Wesley's approach to religion it was the struggle for Christian perfection. Most recently this has been underlined by the publication of the definitive edition of Charles Wesley's sermons, commented on elsewhere in this book. Charles Wesley struggled to achieve perfection and saw this as the right activity for the Christian under God's grace in the power of the Spirit.

Brian Foley's text expresses in very simple language what Charles Wesley believed, that

> The Law of God is no mere list
> of things to do and not to do,
> but God's perfection – this alone –
> the yes and no of what we do!

In this perspective

> The Will of God must be our will,
> to wish, to want, to do, to be;
> and with the mind of God, to think,
> and through the eyes of God to see!

What is lacking here is the rigorous self-examination and introspection which was so characteristic of Charles Wesley's personal religion, the 'sensibility of sin, [the] pain to feel it near'. For David G. Preston, echoing Psalm 15, the righteous are those who are 'pure in heart, whose spotless lives/By word and deed obey your will'. This is nearer to Wesley, though it cannot claim to have been influenced by him.

'In judgment, Lord, arise', by Timothy Dudley-Smith, asks:

Discern my thoughts, I pray,
Discover all my mind
And keep me in the narrow way
To innocence inclined.

In these words, written in 1998, though sounding as though they come from an earlier phase in Dudley-Smith's writing, there is an echo of Psalm 26, yet it can be argued that here he is very near to that sense of introspection that we have observed in Charles Wesley.

## Conclusions

The 'four alls' of Methodism summarize Methodist belief but do not necessarily underline the priorities of Charles Wesley in relation to religious faith.

*All need to be saved* is a tenet he would have held comfortably. For many in the Church today this is still a valid presupposition. In the world thoroughgoing universalism is more in keeping with the ethos of the age. This tension has resulted in a diminution in the number of hymns being written which contain a classic 'gospel call'. In this instance the thematic influence of Charles Wesley on contemporary hymnody has diminished because what he once said is less in tune with the culture now prevailing.

The universalism mentioned above is far more in keeping with the idea that *all can be saved*. The emphasis is now on the 'all', the inclusivity of the call and care of God. This leads to an ethos that is open to those of other denominations that have a similarly inclusive view and, logically, to those of other faiths. In the realm of hymnody this is not an expression which is supported by all those in the Church. The *Bulletin of the Hymn Society of Great Britain and Ireland*[54] carried two articles presenting different perspectives on this issue. But hymns are being written by Methodists that seek a recognition of and dialogue with those of different faiths.[55]

A psychological affirmation of the value of the individual is consonant with the idea that *All may know themselves saved*. To know one's own salvation, to be sure of it, is to underline the premise that one is a uniquely loved child of God. So the way is open to provide such affirmation that the shepherd still brings us home with rejoicing, that even we can 'cast our crowns before thee,/ Lost in wonder, love and praise'. But the language can now be of the age, and sometimes is.

*All may be completely saved* is an assertion of the totality of God's love, that God's love reaches in all completeness with no limits, to everyone. It proclaims that sanctification, which in Methodist understanding follows on from conversion, can be complete. Perfect holiness can become a present reality.

Charles Wesley might have grasped that with his heart, but his head battled against it, such was his own sense of unworthiness. The struggle which he had, the need to come again and again in search of grace, is a counter to the certainty of the rightness of individual human action which derives from self-determination. It offers a basis for duty. Charles Wesley's text, 'A charge to keep I have', allows the interpretation that sanctification takes place while we are working out our time in faithfulness. Failure to be faithful to the charge leads to eternal death, an assertion too harsh for the editors of *Hymns & Psalms*.[56] Charles Wesley's Calvinist understanding of the priority of God's power is largely lost, not being sympathetic to the present age in which Methodists still seek to work out their calling. Such a rigorous interpretation of personal piety has been largely lost from modern mainstream hymnody.

The continuing influence of Charles Wesley on contemporary Methodism is clear, though this effect is subtly nuanced and the emphasis on particular themes has shifted. It cannot be doubted that the shape of twenty-first-century hymnody would be different were it not for the inspiration and craft of the 'sweet singer of Methodism'.

## Notes

1 Proposed Hymn Book Supplement, Methodist Conference Agenda, 2004, 441.

2 Proposed Hymn Book Supplement, 442.

3 *BE*, 7.250ff.

4 *BE*, 7.734f.

5 Berger, *Theology in Hymns?*, *passim*.

6 The Revd W. T. Davison had faced a heresy charge in 1890–1 for promoting the adoption of modern critical methods.

7 *BE*, 2.156.

8 Berger, *Theology in Hymns?*, 132f.

9 *Methodist Worship Book* (London: Trustees for Methodist Church Purposes, 1999), 303.

10 Rattenbury, *Evangelical Doctrines*, 120; and see further Chapter 11 above.

11 John Wesley presented predestination as a doctrine full of blasphemy: 'The grace or love of God, whence cometh our salvation, is free in all and free to all . . . The doctrine of predestination is not a doctrine of God . . . [it] tends to destroy the comfort of religion, the happiness of Christianity . . . this uncomfortable doctrine also destroys our zeal for good works . . . [the doctrine of predestination] hath also a direct and manifest tendency to overthrow the whole Christian revelation'. *BE*, 3.544–59.

12 Bett, *The Hymns of Methodism*, 86. Henry Bett, who wrote first prior to Methodist Union and then revised his work after the Union, underlined the centrality of the works of Wesley in any hymnody that deserved the name 'Methodist' and derived his theology as much from those hymns as from John Wesley's sermons or notes. His Wesleyan position was held even more tenaciously than that of F. Luke Wiseman, but he also valued the literary qualities of Wesley's hymns.

13 Bett, *The Hymns of Methodism*, 91.

14 J. Wesley, *Explanatory Notes upon the New Testament*, reprint edn (London, Epworth, 1976), 304.

15 Cf. 'Stupendous height of heavenly love' – 'God did in Christ Himself reveal', which is much less effective.

16 Included in the British *Methodist Hymn Book*, 1933.

17 Berger, *Theology in Hymns?*, 109.

18 Berger, *Theology in Hymns?*, 115.

19 Rattenbury, *Evangelical Doctrines*, 5.

20 H. Houghton, *The Handmaid of Piety* (The Wesley Fellowship, Quacks Books, 1992), 5.

21 This text is evidence of Charles Wesley's emphasis on the Christian exertion which is evident also in his sermons. See further, Newport, *Sermons*.

22 *BE*, 3, Sermon 86, 'A Call to Backsliders', *passim*.

23 Davies *et al.*, eds, *History of the Methodist Church*, 3.185.

24 Davies *et al.*, eds, *History of the Methodist Church*, 3.190.

25 Davies *et al.*, eds, *History of the Methodist Church*, 3.190.

26 Quoted in Davies *et al.*, eds, *History of the Methodist Church*, 3.191.

27 *A Plain Account of Christian Perfection as believed and taught by the Reverend Mr. John Wesley, from the year 1725, to the year 1777*, from *The Works of John Wesley* (1872, ed. Thomas Jackson), vol. 11, 366–446, further editing by George Lyons for the Wesley Center for Applied Theology at Northwest Nazarene College (Nampa, ID).

28 Berger, *Theology in Hymns?*, 143.

29 'Love divine, all loves excelling.'

30 Rattenbury, *Evangelical Doctrines*, 320.

31 My italics.

32 'O God of our forefathers, hear' (*Methodist Hymn Book*, No. 723) follows a similar theme with the lines:

With solemn faith we offer up,
And spread before Thy glorious eyes,
That only ground of all our hope,
That precious bleeding sacrifice.

33 Rattenbury, *Eucharistic Hymns*, 153.

34 *BE*, 7.

35 For example, *Wesleyan Methodist Hymn Book* (London: Wesleyan Conference Office, 1904).

36 Berger, *Theology in Hymns?*

37 *Hymns & Psalms* (Peterborough: Methodist Publishing House, 1983).

38 Charles' published poetical works near 9,000 compositions. Exactly how many of those were written specifically as hymns, however, is not clear.

39 *Hymns & Psalms*, No. 500.

40 'Love divine all loves excelling.'

41 *Hymns & Psalms*, No. 124.

42 F. Baker, *Charles Wesley's Verse*, 2nd edn (London: Epworth, 1988), 32f.

43 R. Watson and K. Trickett, *Companion to Hymns & Psalms* (Peterborough: Methodist Publishing House, 1988), 97.

44 Berger, *Theology in Hymns?*, 107–53.

45 M. E. Leckebusch, *More than words* (Stowmarket: Kevin Mayhew, 2000), No. 3.

46 See especially, 'These things did Thomas count as real', T. Troeger and C. Doran, *New Hymns for the Lectionary* (New York: Oxford University Press, 1986), 68.

47 *Hymns & Psalms*, No. 216.

48 H. Osbourne, in *Living Lord* (London: Joseph Weinberger, 1979).

49 C. P. Daw Jr, *A Year of Grace*, (Illinois: Hope Publishing Company Ltd, 1990).

50 J. Davies, from *Praise God Together*, (London: Scripture Union, 1985).

51 *Hymns & Songs* (London: Methodist Publishing House, 1969) No. 85.

52 F. Pratt Green, *Twenty-six Hymns* (London: Epworth/Methodist Publishing House, 1971).

53 'There's a spirit in the air', *Hymns & Psalms*, No. 326.

54 *The Bulletin of the Hymn Society of Great Britain and Ireland*, Vol. 18, No. 9, April 2005.

55 For example, 'Great God of many names', *Whatever Name or Creed* (London: Stainer & Bell Ltd, 2002), No. 39.

56 See *Hymns and Psalms*, No. 785.

# 24. The Musical Charles Wesley

## CARLTON R. YOUNG

Singing and music-making were salient features of the eighteenth-century British Methodist revival. Commentary on these qualities began with John Wesley's opinions in his journal, occasional works[1], and correspondence,[2] continued during Methodism's liturgical, musical and hymnic[3] developments in the nineteenth century, and was greatly expanded in the research and commentary by James T. Lightwood[4] and Maurice Frost.[5] Nelson F. Adams' unpublished doctoral thesis[6] carefully documents the sources of John Wesley's three tune books;[7] Nicholas Temperley[8] relates the music of the Wesleyan revival to other developments in eighteenth-century evangelical song; and Oliver A. Beckerlegge and Frank Baker trace the tunes in the 1786 edition of *Sacred Harmony* that Wesley suggested as appropriate for each hymn in the 1780 *Collection*.[9] These studies and others establish John Wesley as the revival's chief music critic, compiler and editor, but tend to overlook his brother's interests, influence and contributions.

Erik Routley's *The Musical Wesleys*[10] was the first to include in one volume the musical interests, proclivities and products of three Wesley generations. Routley's coverage tends to centre on Samuel and Samuel Sebastian, and, as others,[11] portrays Charles as Methodism's premier lyricist, father and guide to the musical training of his precocious sons, Charles junior and Samuel, and the sponsor-defender of their famous London house recitals. My own study in this area, *Music of the Heart*, affirms these earlier conclusions, while pointing also to Charles' contributions to the development of the repertory, performance practice and commentary on eighteenth-century British Wesleyan-style worship-song. The study presented here focuses on Charles' musicality, commentary on music and musicians, and his collaborative and parodistic works.

## Charles Wesley's musicality

Charles Wesley's own assessment of his musical gifts, compared to those of his precocious sons and his talented wife, is summarized in this poem that Frank Baker transcribed from the poet's shorthand, adding this assessment: 'Charles Wesley's musical urges undoubtedly outstripped his talents':

Who would not wish to have the skill
Of tuning instruments at will?

Ye powers who guide my actions, tell
Why I, in whom the seeds of music dwell,
Who most its power and excellence admire,
Whose very breast itself a lyre
Was never taught the happy art
Of modulating sounds
And can no more in concert share a part
Than the wild roe that o'er the mountains bounds[12]

Charles' earliest musical experiences were apparently singing metrical psalms in the Epworth rectory led by his disciplining mother, Susanna,[13] and during worship in the Epworth Parish Church of St Andrew[14] where his controversial father Samuel was priest. He was introduced to English cathedral musical–liturgical traditions while a student, from 1716 to 1726, at Westminster School, adjacent to Westminster Abbey where William Croft was organist from 1708 to 1727. The Abbey, along with the Chapel Royal and St Paul's, 'was the chief magnet for church musicians and the source of most new cathedral music of national importance'.[15]

Charles' early days at Oxford included trips with friends to London where, among other activities, they attended the theatre.[16] Charles also played the flute.[17] However, as Gill notes, 'there is no evidence of his talent with any other instrument, though his sweet-toned organ is preserved at City Road [Foundery] chapel and it is difficult not to think that he played on it'.[18]

Samuel Wesley adds these insights about his father's musical talents and interests:

My father . . . was partial to the old masters: Purcell, Corelli, Geminiani, Handel; and among the English Church composers, Croft, Blow, Boyce, Green, &c. were favourite authors with him. He had a most accurate ear for time, and in every piece which had repetitions, knew exactly which part was to be played or sung twice, which, when any one failed to do, he would immediately cry out, 'You have cheated me of a repeat.' He had not a vocal talent, but could join in a hymn or simple melody tolerable well in tune. I never heard that my grandfather had any particular partiality to music, nor the contrary . . . My father used to say of my brother and me, 'The boys have music by the mother's side,'[19] meaning that *he* had no claim to any of the talent which she certainly possessed.[20]

Early on in the Revival Charles used his untrained voice to good advantage, often spontaneously breaking into song.[21] W. L. Doughty comments:

[His] voice was also one of his great assets. He records how at Bristol he preached to a congregation that 'filled the valley and sides of a hill like grasshoppers for multitude. Yet my voice reached the most distant, as I perceived them bowing at the Holy name. God gave me the voice of a trumpet and sent the word home to many hearts.' He had also a fine singing voice, and occasionally, during his sermon, he sang verses that emphasized the message he was delivering.[22]

In his journal for 26 August 1739, from Runwick [apparently Ranwick, Gloucestershire], Charles writes: 'God enabled me to lift up my voice like a trumpet; so that all distinctly heard me. I concluded with singing an invitation to sinners.' This account prompted the following reflection by Frank Baker:

> We are reminded by [this] sentence that he had a fine voice for singing, as well as for preaching. It is good to think of him underlining his evangelical appeal by the singing of his own verses – 'O let me commend my Saviour to you'; 'O all that pass by, to Jesus draw near'; or, 'Would Jesus have a sinner die?'[23]

Two further examples about singing from Charles' journal are appropriate at this point.[24] On 30 July 1743, at St Just in Cornwall, Charles 'walked with our brother Shepherd to the Land's-end, and sang on the extremist point of the rocks . . .

> Come, Divine Immanuel, come,
> Take possession of thy home;
> Now thy mercy's wings expand,
> Stretch throughout the happy land.[25]

While on 25 October in Walsall, Charles comments that

> The accusers mentioned the only crime against [me] . . . He makes people rise at five in the morning to sing psalms . . . Never was I before in so primitive[26] an assembly. We sang praises lustily, and with good courage . . . We laid us down and slept, and rose up again; for the Lord sustained us. We assembled before day to sing hymns to Christ as God.[27]

Such references could be multiplied easily enough, but such is not necessary here. The simple point is that, although Charles was not accomplished as a singer or instrumentalist, it was the 'lusty' singing of hymns and not simply their composition as written texts that was of importance.

## Charles Wesley's commentary on music and musicians

Charles' views[28] on music and musicians are also included in his journal[29] and correspondence,[30] and in a number of poems and epigrams. His views concerning the purpose of music and music education in the church and societal contexts of his time came into focus as he attempted to balance the musical education and performances of his two precocious sons, with the explicit objections of some in the Methodist movement who looked askance at musicians[31] and the theatre. Philip Olleson comments,

> the attitude of Charles to his sons' musical talents was inevitably ambivalent. As a music-lover himself, he was delighted that his children were gifted musicians, and regarded their abilities as God-given talents, to be devel-

oped to their full potential. At the same time, he would have soon become aware of some less welcome consequences of their childhood celebrity.[32]

Criticism of Charles sons' public performances began while the family lived in Bristol. For example, the Methodist leader John Fletcher warned: 'You have your enemies, as well as your brother, they complain of your *love for musick, company, fine people, great folks*, and of the *want of your former zeal and frugality*. I need not put you in mind to cut off *sinful appearances*.'[33]

Criticism of Charles junior's music lessons came by way of his father's Watchnight hymn, 'Innocent Diversions,' st. 4, especially line 8, 'And chant in a grove to the harpers of Hell',

> The civiller croud,
> In theatres proud,
> Acknowledge his power,
> And *Satan* in Nightly Assemblies adore:
>
> The masque and the ball
> They fly at his call;
> Or in pleasures excel,
> And chaunt in a grove* to the harpers of Hell.

---

\* Ranelagh's Gardens, Vaux-Hall, &c.[34]

According to Baker, Charles 'faced the challenge boldly, and in February 1769 read out a public proclamation on the subject, containing the following passage:'[35] 'How can I call musicians harpers of hell, yet breed my Son a Musician? I answer, there are Heavenly as well as Hellish Harpers.'

In sts. 7 and 8 Charles contrasts these qualities with heavenly singing, dancing and harping.

> Our concert of praise
> To Jesus we raise,
> And all the night long
> Continue the new evangelical song:
>
> We dance to the fame
> Of Jesus's Name,
> The joy it imparts
> Is heaven begun in our musical hearts.
>
> Thus, thus we bestow
> Our moments below,
> And singing remove,
> With all the redeem'd to the *Sion* above:
>
> There, there shall we stand
> With our harps in our hand,
> Interrupted no more,
> And eternally sing, and rejoice, and adore.[36]

Charles and Sally attempted to contain the controversy by restricting their sons' performances to private recitals. An exception was the London concert on 20 May 1777, directed by J. C. Bach, where Samuel's participation, apparently on orders of his parents, was billed: 'End of Act II, a young Gentleman will perform extempore on the organ.'[37] Criticism intensified during the nine-season London home subscription concerts, 1779–87,[38] which attracted 'fashionable audiences and a good deal of publicity'.[39]

It was concerning such concerts that Thomas Coke reported to John Wesley:

> I looked upon the Concerts which he allows his sons to have in his own house, to be highly dishonorable to God; and himself to be criminal, by reason of his situation in the Church of Christ; but on mature consideration of all the circumstances appertaining to them, I cannot now blame him.[40]

To these and others' objections Charles responded in this poem:

> Men of true piety, they know not why,
> Music with all its sacred powers decry,
> Music itself (not its abuse) condemn,
> For good or bad is just the same to Them.
> But let them know, They quite mistake the Case,
> Defect of nature for excess of grace:
> and, while they reprobate th'harmonious Art,
> Blam'd we excuse, and candidly assert
>     The fault is in their ear, not in their upright heart.[41]

And in a letter to Garrett Wellesley[42] Charles gives his 'reasons for letting [his] sons have a concert at home'.

1. To keep them out of harm's way; the way, (I mean) of bad music and bad musicians, who by a free communication with them might corrupt both their taste and their morals.
2. That my sons may have a safe and honourable opportunity of availing themselves of their musical abilities, which have cost me several hundred pounds.
3. That they may enjoy their full right of private judgment, and likewise their independency, both of which must be given up if they swim with the stream and follow the multitude.
4. To improve their play and their skill in composing; as they must themselves furnish the principal music of every concert, although they do not call their musical entertainment a concert. It is too great a word. They do not presume to rival the *present great masters* who excel in the variety of their accompaniments. All they aim at in their concert music is *exactness*.

If they excel in any degree it is in composition and play. Here then they chiefly exert themselves, as sensible that 'many accompaniments may hide and cover bad play,' that the fewer the accompaniments are, good play is the more conspicuous.

I am clear, without a doubt, that my sons' concert is after the will and order of Providence. It has established them as musicians, and in a safe and honourable way. The Bishop (of London) has since sent us word that he has never heard any music he liked as well, and promises Charles five scholars next winter.

The foregoing responses succinctly summarize certain of Charles' views on music and the musical profession: parental oversight, affirming freedom of choice, defining musical excellence, claiming that the concerts are God's will and the sovereign's delight, and music is God's gift, to be nurtured, not denied.

With regard to the latter, Charles replied to the objections of a Methodist woman about Charles junior's public performances:

I always designed my son for a clergyman. Nature has marked him for a musician: which appeared from his earliest infancy. My friends advised me not to cross his inclination. Indeed I could not if I would. There is no way of hindering his being a musician but by cutting of his fingers.[43]

Charles affirmed music as God's gift that one should accept and give praise to God for, not boast in. Further, music in itself is neither good nor bad, its values formed and determined by the contexts in which it is used, and by the intent of the performer; premises that Charles six years earlier had included in an extended letter of advice to Samuel:

Foolish people are too apt to praise you. If they see anything good in you they should praise God, not you, for it. As for music, it is neither good nor bad in itself. You have a natural inclination to it: but God gave you that: therefore God only should be thanked and praised for it. Your brother has this same love of music much more than you, yet he is not proud or vain of it. Neither, I trust, will you be.[44]

Philip Olleson describes another aspect of Charles' balancing act which may have drawn additional criticism, including that of his brother John.[45] Charles', and presumably Sally's, educational theory and child-rearing style and practices affirmed the 'innocence of the child', and were the opposite of Charles' Epworth upbringing and home education which his mother Susanna stated was a matter of 'conquering the will'.[46]

Charles encouraged his wife Sally to continue singing[47] and playing the harpsichord.[48] Social singing together began during their courtship, 'Quite spent with examining the classes, I was much revived in singing with Miss Burdock and Sally' (28 June 1748). With regard to her continuing to play the harpsichord he wrote, 'How many of Lampe's tunes can you play? I am offered an exceeding fine harpsichord for sixteen guineas! What encouragement do you give me to purchase it for you?'[49]

Sally, who as a mother 'used to quiet and amuse [Charles junior] with the harpsichord',[50] continued to sing in the years of Charles' itinerancy, some-times with mixed reception.

She generally rode behind her husband. She had traveled thus with him from Manchester, through Macclesfied, Congleton, and Newcastle-under-Lyme, to Stone. It was a beautiful summer evening when they reached their resting-place. After their meal she walked into the garden of the inn. Some young ladies in an adjoining garden heard her singing. Her clear, sweet voice charmed them. Their father, who was a clergyman, was equally pleased, and invited her to sing in his church on the following Sunday. But when he found that the stranger was Mrs. Charles Wesley, and that she could not consent to sing in the church unless her husband was invited to preach, prejudice roved stronger than love of music.[51]

Sally continued to sing in the years following Charles' death, until her own passing. Comments on her enduring musical qualities are included in the manuscript journal of Revd Francis Fortescue Knottesford for 24 January 1797:

We were much delighted at hearing Mr. [Charles] Wesley play upon the harpsichord . . . Mrs. Wesley, his mother, who is upwards of eighty years of age, sung, to our great astonishment, two of Handel's songs most delight-fully – 'He shall feed His flock,' etc, and 'If God be with us,' etc.[52]

On 17 October 1822 Charles junior writes to John Langshaw junior, 'My aged mother returns her thanks for your kind enquiry, she is now 96, and sang an air, on her birthday last week.'[53]

## Charles Wesley's opinions on music and musicians in his poems and epigrams[54]

Charles' London residency increased his contacts with music-making and musicians of his day,[55] which served to increase the concert activity and visibility of his two sons. For example, his younger son Samuel became the protégé of Martin Madan, later chaplain at the Lock Hospital, and Charles junior, celebrated for his keyboard skills, began to attract private students. Charles expressed some of this interaction in poems composed for the moment. They afford valuable insight into his subtle and at times acerbic humor, and his impressive grasp of issues related to musical style and performance-practice. In this latter regard some poems reflect the resistance to the introduction of instruments from the continent by music patrons and performers in London's concert halls and theatres.

The audiences of the home concerts[56] reflect Charles' ability and three decades of practice,[57] unlike his brother John, to move and converse with ease among London's West End theatre patrons, musicians and composers. For example, the subscribers for the first two home concerts, 1779 and 1780, 'included the Bishops of London and Durham, the Earl of Dartmouth, the Hon. Daines Barrington[58] and Lord Mornington, the Lord Mayor and Lady Mayoress, Sir. W. W. Wynn, and General Oglethorpe . . . Many other distin-guished names appear from time to time, amongst them being Dr. Shepherd

(Dean of Windsor), Dr. Worgan, Dr. Arnold and Pascal Paoli.'[59] These attend-ees, and others, a mixture of musicians,[60] royalty, church and political figures, probably influenced and may have deepened Charles' essentially conserva-tive if not counter-cultural views on music and musicians as seen in his poems and epigrams.

Joseph Kelway, prominent London organist at St Martin-in-the-Fields, London, taught Charles junior for two years, apparently without being paid.[61] Both Kelway and Charles senior held conservative tastes and resented the incursions of German and Italian composers. The poem 'Modern Music'[62] was probably inspired by Kelway's comment to Charles junior on 21 September 1769: 'My dear, let not the world debauch you. Some decry music for being old. They may as well object to an antique statue, or painting. But B and A and G[63] have cut the throat of music: true music is lost.'[64]

### Modern Music

G, B, and all
Their followers, great and small,
Have cut Old Music's throat,
And mangled every Note;
Their superficial pains
have dash'd out all his brains:
And now we doat upon
A lifeless sceleton,
The empty sound at most,
The Squeak of Music's Ghost.

The following peevish poem on the encroachment of the pianoforte[65] on the harpsichord was composed 15 years after the former's introduction into England by J. C. Bach, who is credited with performing the first solo in public on the piano in 1768.[66] Samuel's greatest output in his early years was for the keyboard: his first published work, in 1777 or early 1778, was a set of sonatas for harpsichord or pianoforte. The poem reflects Charles' disagreements in matters of musical taste, tradition, personages and style.

### The Pianoforte
### Written in the Year 1783

Our Connoisseurs their plausive voices raise,
And dwell on the PIANO-FORTE'S praise.
More brilliant (if we simply take their word)
More sweet than any tinkling Harpsichord,
While soothing Softness and Expression meet
To make the Contrast, and the joy compleat.
To strike our fascinated ears and eyes
And take our Sense and Reason by surprise.

'Tis thus the men whose dictates we obey,
Their taste, and their Authority display,

Command us humbly in their steps to move,
Damn what they damn, & praise what they approve,
With Faith implicit, and with blind esteem,
To own – All Music is ingross'd by Them.

So the gay Nation whose capricious law
Keeps the whole fashionable world in awe,
Nor to Italian Airs their ear incline,
Nor to the noblest Harmony divine,
But as the Sum of Excellence propose
Their own sweet Sonnets – warbled thro' the Nose!

Yet skilful Masters of the tuneful string,
(Masters who teach the Harpsichord to – sing)
Tell us of Music's powers a different story,
And rob PIANO-FORTE of its glory;
Assuring us, if uncontroul'd by Fashion,
We hear, and judge without exaggeration,
The Merit of the favourite instrument,
And all its Use and musical intent,
By the discerning Few is understood
'To hide bad Players, & to spoil the Good.'

### Second Part

What cannot Fashion do? with magic ease
It makes the dull Piano-forte please,
Bids us a triffling Instrument admire,
As far superior to Apollo's Lyre:
Loud as a spanking Warming-pan its tone,
Delicious as the thrilling Bagpipe's Drone.
Organs and Harpsichords it sweeps away
And reigns alone, triumphant for a day:
The Great acknowledge its inchanting power
The echoing multitude of course adore:
Ev'n Those who real Music dared esteem
Caught for a while, are carried down the stream,
O'er all her slaves while Fashion domineers,
A Midas lends them his sagacious Ears!

Shou'd Fashion singling out (if that could be)
A poorer tool of modern harmony
The sanction of her approbation give;
The world polite her dictates wou'd receive,
The list'ning Herd wou'd fall with awe profound
And die transported at a JEWS-HARP'S Sound!

In this stunning satire,[67] traditional musical style combining sound and sense, which Kelway personified, is compared with the confusion caused by modern music.

### Written in Kelway's Sonatas

Kelway's Sonatas who can bear?
'They want both harmony and air;
Heavy they make the Player's hand
And who their tricks can understand?
Kelway to the profound G [Giardini]
Or B[J. C. Bach] compared, is but a Ninny,[68]
A Dotard old (the Moderns tell ye)
Mad after Handel and Corelli,
Spoilt by original disaster,
For Geminiani was his Master,
And taught him, in his nature's ground
To gape for Sense, as well as sound.'
'Tis thus the Leaders of our nation,
Smit with the Music now in fashion,

Their absolute decisions deal,
And from the chair Infallible,
And praise the fine, Italian Taste,
Too fine, too exquisite to last.

Let Midas judge, and what will follow?
A whis[t]ling Pan excels Apollo,
A Bag-pipe's sweeter than an Organ,
A Sowgelder* surpasses Worgan**
And Kelway at the foot appears
Of Connoisseurs – with Asses ears!

Another poem about the London music scene is entitled 'To Miss Davis', the English soprano, Cecilia Davies, *c.* 1756–1836, whose Italian nickname was L'Inglesina. She was trained in Vienna and became the first Englishwoman to appear on the Italian stage. Wesley's wry poem questions whether the young and acclaimed singer would be successfully received by the fickle and unpredictable London audiences and musicians.[69] It may have been composed in anticipation of, or at some point during, 1773–7, when she performed in Italian opera and public concerts with mixed reviews. Her performances in Handel oratorios in The Three Choir Festivals[70] were well received, as were her concerts in Oxford and elsewhere. The poem is included in manuscript, loose sheet, Lamplough Collection.[71]

### To Miss Davis

Gentle Inglesina, say
Can the smooth Italian Lay
Nature's ruggedness remove,
Soften Britons into love?

---

\*    A maker and master of Castratos.
\*\*  John Worgan, organist and composer, tutor to Charles junior.

Yes; the stocks & stones* draw near,
Thy inchanting Voice to hear
And all the Savages agree
In praise of harmony & Thee!

In this social context Charles also met John F. Lampe, a German associate
of Handel and a prominent operatic composer. Because of Charles' relationship with Lampe it is quite possible[72] that his poem 'The Musician's Hymn'[73]
was composed to celebrate the composer's conversion by John Wesley, who
entered in his journal for Friday 29 November 1745, 'I spent an hour with
Mr. Lampe, who had been a Deist for many years, till it pleased God, by the
Earnest Appeal [to Men of Reason and Religion, 1743] to bring him to a better
mind.'[74]

Wesley composed this poem to commemorate Lampe's death, 25 July 1751,.

## On the Death of Mr Lampe

1. 'Tis done! the Sovereign will's obey'd,
   The soul, by angel-guards convey'd,
       Has took its seat on high;
   The brother of my choice is gone
   To music sweeter than his own,
       And concerts in the sky.

2. His spirit, mounting on the wing,
   Rejoiced to hear the convoy sing,
       While harping at his side:
   With ease he caught their heavenly strain,
   And smiled and sung in mortal pain,
       He sung, and smiled, and died.

3. Enroll'd with that harmonious throng,
   He hears the'unutterable song,
       The'unutterable name:
   He sees the Master of the choir,
   He bows, and strikes the golden lyre,
       And hymns the glorious Lamb.

4. He hymns the glorious Lamb alone;
   No more constrain'd to make his moan
       In this sad wilderness,
   To toil for sublunary pay,
   And cast his sacred strains away,
       And stoop the world to please.

5. Redeem'd from earth, the tuneful soul,
   While everlasting ages roll,
       His triumph shall prolong;

---

*   Stocks and stones = gods of wood and stone.

His noblest faculties exert,
And all the music of his heart
    Shall warble on his tongue.

6. O that my mournful days were past!
O that I might o'ertake at last
    My happy friend above;
With him the church triumphant join,
And celebrate in strains divine
    The majesty of love!

7. Great God of love, prepare my heart,
And tune it now to bear a part
    In heavenly melody:
'I'll strive to sing as loud as they,
Who sit enthroned in brighter day,'
    And nearer the Most high.

8. O that the promised time were come!
O that we all were taken home
    Our Master's joy to share!
Draw, Lord, the living vocal stones,
Jesus, recall Thy banish'd ones,
    To chant Thy praises there.

9. Our number and our bliss complete,
And summon all the choir to meet
    Thy glorious throne around;
Thy whole musician-band bring in,
And give the signal to begin,
    And let the trumpet sound.[75]

Charles, more than his brother John came in contact with famous musicians, including Handel. This is apparent, for example, in Charles Wesley's account of the musical training of his two sons in his journal (Wesley 1849, 140–66) and also in the Wesley/Langshaw Correspondence.[76] Frank Baker includes two tributes to Handel in his *Representative Verse*.[77] The first is from MS Patriotism: Misc., p. 5, and second from MS E. T. Clark.

### Ode on Handel's Birthday
### S. Matthias Day Febr[uary] 24

Hail the bright auspicious Day
    That gave Immortal Handel birth.
Let every moment glide away
    In solemn joy and sacred mirth;
Let every soul like his aspire
And catch a glowing spark of pure etherial fire.

### Written in Handel's Lessons

Here all the mystic Powers of sound,
The soul of Harmony is found,
Its perfect Character receives,
And Handel dead for ever lives!

The poet described the beginning of Samuel's musical training for Daines Barrington who first heard him play in 1775, when the boy was nine years of age.

### On Samuel Wesley

Sam for his three first years the Secret kept,
While in his heart the Seed of Music slept,
Till Charles' Chissel by a carnal Stroke
Brought forth the Statue latent in the block:
Like Memnon then, he caught the Solar Fire,
And breath'd spontaneous to Apollo's lyre,
With nature's ease th'Harmonious Summit won
The envious, and the gazing Croud outrun,
Left all the rest behind, & seizd on – Barrington.[78]

In the early 1770s Charles petitioned William Boyce, the celebrated eighteenth-century English church musician, composer and compiler of the monumental and influential three-volume *Cathedral Music*[79] (1760, 1768, 1773), to take his son Samuel into his choir and to present him with the three-volume work as a gift. Evidently Charles had deep respect for Boyce, whom, he states, set some of his hymns.[80] Thus this hymn of tribute:

1. The humble Petition
   Of a rhiming Musician,
       (A Petition of Natural Right)
   Undeniably shews
   That, wherever he goes,
       Church-Music is all his delight:

2. That he never can rest,
   Till enrich'd with the best,
       His Talent aright he employs,
   And claims for his own,
   A True Harmony's Son,
       The Collection of good Doctor Boyce.

3. Three Volumes of yours,
   Which his Prayer procures,
       Will afford him Examples enough,
   And save Poet Sam

(Your petitioner's Name)
 From a Deluge of Musical Stuff.

4. So, good Doctor, if now
 His suit you allow,
  And make him as rich as a king,
 Taken into your Choir,
 To his Organ and Lyre,
  Your Petitioner ever shall – Sing![81]

Following the composer's death on 7 February 1779, Charles composed this lyrical remembrance

1. Father of harmony, farewell!
 Farewell for a few fleeting years!
 Translated from the mournful vale
 Jehovah's flaming ministers
 Have borne thee to thy place above,
 Where all is harmony and love.

2. Thy generous, good and upright heart,
 Which sigh'd for a celestial lyre,
 Was tuned on earth to bear a part
 Symphonious with the heavenly choir,
 Where Handel strikes the warbling strings,
 And plausive angels clap their wings.

3. Handel, and all the tuneful train,
 Who well employ'd their art divine
 To' announce the great Messiah's reign,
 In joyous acclamations join,
 And, springing from their azure seat,
 With shouts their new-born brother greet.

4. Thy brow a radiant circle wears,
 Thy hand a golden harp receives,
 And, singing with the morning stars,
 Thy soul in endless raptures lives,
 And hymns, on the eternal throne,
 Jehovah and His conquering Son.[82]

The following poem,[83] addressed to the Bristol surgeon Abraham Ludlow, was apparently composed by Charles on behalf of his sons as a commentary on the comic-like situation that developed when Samuel Wesley, who was to substitute for his brother Charles in a benefit performance in Bristol Cathedral on 31 March 1774, was set aside by the last-minute appearance of his older brother who apparently played the announced organ concerto – one of the evening's 7 performers.

**An Epistle to Dr Ludlow**

1. To you, dear Doctor, I appeal,
   To all the Tuneful City.
   Am I not used extremely ill
   By Musical Committee?

2. Why 'tis enough to make one wild –
   They court, and then refuse me,
   They Advertize and call me Child,
   And as a Child they use me.

3. Excusing their contempt, they say
   (Which more inflames my passion)
   I am not grave enough to play
   Before the Corporation.

4. To the sweet City-waits altho'
   I may not hold a candle,
   I question if their Worships know
   The Odds t'wixt me and Handel.

5. A Child of 8 years old I grant,
   Must be both light & giddy,
   The Solidness of Burgum* want
   The Steadiness of Liddy*:

6. Yet quick perhaps as other folks
   I can assign a reason,
   And keep my time as well as Stokes*
   And come as much in season.

7. With Bristol-Organists not yet
   I come in competition:
   But let them know I wou'd be great
   I do not want ambition.

8. Spirit I do not want, or will
   Upon a just occasion,
   To Make the rash Despisers feel
   My weight of indignation.

9. Tread on a worm, twill turn again:
   And shall not I resent it?
   Who gave the sore affront, in vain
   They wou'd with tears repent it.

---

\* Burgum, Liddy (Lediard) and Stokes were friends of Charles Wesley and patrons of the arts in Bristol.

10. Nothing shall, sir, appease my Rage
     At their uncouth demeanor,
     Unless they prudently assuage
     Mine anger with – A Steyner.*

## Charles Wesley as collaborator

John Wesley has been identified as the central figure in eighteenth-century British Methodist music; its chief compiler, editor and publisher of the Foundery *Collection* (1742), *Sacred Melody* (1761) and *Sacred Harmony* (1780). Charles' collaborative role, if any, in producing these publications has not been identified. Nor is there any evidence that he assisted in the preparation of *Harmonia Sacra*, *c.* 1754, compiled by Thomas Butts, the Wesleys' book-keeper and steward at the Foundery and sometime travelling companion, for a Methodist market, and widely used for two decades.[84] This collection contained 162 musical settings in a variety of styles, mostly set for three voices. Charles Wesley's hymns were featured, including those with Lampe's settings from *Hymns on the Great Festivals and Other Occasions*.[85] John Wesley chose many tunes from it for *Select Melody* (1761).[86] *Hymns on the Great Festivals and Other Occasions* (1746) may have been a collaborative work of Charles and Lampe. Frank Baker[87] thought it probable that Lampe published it at his own expense as a gesture of appreciation for the friendship of John and Charles Wesley, who were introduced to him by Mrs Rich, successful singer and spouse of the impresario John Rich, who entertained them in their home.

These excerpts from Charles' journal show the continuing friendship that Charles had with Lampe,[88] some of it by way of Mrs Rich, until Lampe's death on 25 July 1751.[89]

> Sat., Oct. 26, 1745. [London] I dined at Mrs. R's. Mr. R [ich] behaved with great civility. I foresee the storm my visit will bring upon him;
> Saturday March 29, 1746. 'I passed the afternoon at Mrs. Rich's, where we caught a Physician by the ear, through the help of Mr. Lampe and some of our sisters. This is the true use of music;
> Mon. April 27, 1747, That I might abstain from all appearance of evil, particularly of pride and resentment, I took up my cross, and went in Mrs. Rich's coach to Chelsea. I passed an hour or two at Lampe's, before I waited upon one who was once my friend.

Lampe's settings were entirely new engravings,[90] which necessitated an editorial and production process that probably lasted about one year. It probably began some time after 29 November 1745, when John Wesley states in his journal, 'I spent an hour with Mr. Lampe.' Frank Baker's careful review and comparison[91] of earlier versions of the texts with what appears in Lampe's collection, including the doubling of final lines of stanzas sometimes creating refrains, strengthens and elaborates his claim that the collection involved

---

* A Stainer violin made in Tyrol.

interaction and participation by the poet, and suggests this possible scenario: following their substantive conversations about a collection with hymns selected for their place in the Christian year, Charles selected 23 of his hymns, and one by his late brother Samuel, from existing collections and manuscripts,[92] each having 'a different scheme of rhythm and rhyme'[93] and the number of stanzas. Charles gave them directly to Lampe, or if away from London mailed them to Mrs Rich who may have been the go-between for this project, as suggested in this excerpt from her letter to Charles of 27 November, 1746, signed 'Your worthy daughter in Christ', regarding Lampe's response to reading 'The Musicians Hymn',

> I gave a copy of the hymn to Mr. Lampe, who at the reading, shed some tears, and said he would write to you for he loved you as well as if you were his own brother.[94]

Lampe made further alterations for lyrical-vocal reasons,[95] and he and/or his copyist prepared the first stanza of each hymn for interlining and the balance of the hymn into text blocks, and the music manuscripts[96] for the printer M. Cooper.[97] Lampe, who possibly had limited participation by Charles and/or John, proofed the collection and saw it through to publication in October 1746.[98] Charles' concerns for the success of the collaboration were expressed a month after publication when Mrs Rich responds to his request for a report on the sales of the collection, 'As to the sale of the hymns, he [Lampe] could give me no account as yet, not having received any himself; nor have I got my dear little girl's.'[99]

Lampe's settings for solo voice and continuo may have been first performed in John Rich's home in Chelsea. Not everyone affirmed Lampe's tunes, as seen in Charles' sharp defence written to his banker friend Ebenezer Blackwell[100, 101] a month after their publication:

> Tell Mrs. Dewal not to mind that envious gentleman who slandered Lampe. His tunes are universally admired here among the musical men, and have brought me into high favour with them. (Journal Appendix: Selections from Correspondence, 'To the Same' [My very dear Friend], Newcastle, December 11, 1746).[102]

Their subsequent use in Methodist Revival-style preaching and song services can only be speculated.

Charles' continuing promotion and presumed use of Lampe's theatre-style settings is seen in his identifying Lampe's tunes with the 11 texts in *Graces Before Meat*, c. 1746, and the 15 in *At or After Meat*, by giving the first line of each hymn and its number in *Festival Hymns*. All 24 tunes are named and numbered, two of them twice. He also referenced Lampe's tunes in the Dublin 1747 reprint of that collection. In *Hymns for Those that Seek and Those that Have Redemption in the Blood of Jesus Christ* (1747) (*Redemption Hymns*) Wesley's match of Lampe's tunes with his texts also promotes the 1746 volume with the footnote that the first hymn is 'The first of Mr. Lampe's Hymns on the Great Festivals.'[103] Lampe's 24 tunes were included in Butts' *Harmonia*

*Sacra, c.* 1754, and 13 in John Wesley's tune collections[104] *Sacred Melody* (1761) and its companion, *Sacred Harmony* (1780). A few of Lampe's tunes, shorn of their ornamentations, survived the avalanche of Victorian-style tunes. Two, Invitation and Dying Stephen are included in the British Methodist collection, *Hymns and Psalms* (1983).

Two additional noted composers, Handel and Jonathan Battishill,[105] set Charles Wesley's hymns, apparently without the poet's collaboration.[106] Between 1749 and 1752 Handel composed three settings for Charles Wesley's hymns for solo voice and figured bass: On the resurrection[107] for 'Rejoice! the Lord is King', The Invitation for 'Sinners, obey the gospel word'; and Desiring to Love for 'O Love divine, how sweet thou art'. The original one-page manuscript was discovered in 1826 in the Fitzwilliam Museum Library at Cambridge by the poet's son Samuel, who transcribed and published it as *The Fitzwilliam Music never before Published, Three Hymns, the Words by the late Rev. Charles Wesley . . . Set to Music by George Frideric Handel . . . 1826*. Samuel's edition was in two formats, two-stave realized Basso Continuo and melody and one stanza on a separate stave; and harmony and arrangement for SATB (soprano, alto, tenor and bass) voices, one stanza interlined in each voice, and keyboard reduction.[108]

Battishill was a theatre composer, conductor, leading church organist and composer of anthems, glees and songs who often attended the family home recitals. Lightwood comments, 'his friendship with the father [Charles] led him to set some of the poet's hymns to music',[109] and he and others taught the young Samuel oratorio performance style and repertory.[110] However, there is no evidence that the author and composer collaborated on the selection, publication, use or promotion.

## Charles Wesley, parodist

Five Charles Wesley texts have been identified as parodies of existing texts and/or tunes: 'Love divine, all loves excelling', 'The peaceful shade', 'Pastures green', 'He comes! he comes! the Judge severe', and 'Listed in the cause of sin'.

'Love divine, all loves excelling' first appeared in *Redemption Hymns* (1747). It is considered a spiritual parody, to use Baker's description,[111] of Venus' soprano aria 'Fairest isle, all isles excelling', Act 5: Scene 1, Henry Purcell's *King Arthur*, libretto by John Dryden (1691).

When the text of the aria and the first two stanzas of the hymn are compared, Wesley's parody appears to be primarily on the first four lines of the aria.

| | |
|---|---|
| Fairest isle, all isles excelling, | Love, divine, all loves excelling, |
| Seat of pleasure and of love; | Joy of heaven to earth come down, |
| Venus here will choose her dwelling, | Fix in us thy humble dwelling, |
| And forsake her Cyprian grove. | All thy faithful mercies crown; |
| Cupid from his fav'rite nation, | Jesu, thou art all compassion, |
| Care and envy will remove; | pure unbounded love thou art, |
| Jealousy that poisons passion, | Visit us with thy salvation, |
| And despair that dies for love. | Enter every trembling heart. |

Gentle murmurs, sweet complaining,     Breathe, O breathe thy loving Spirit,
    Sighs that blow the fire of love;          Into every troubled breast,
Soft repulses, Kind disdaining,          Let us all in thee inherit,
    Shall be all the pains you prove.        Let us find that second rest:
Ev'ry swain shall pay his duty,           take away our power of sinning,
    Grateful ev'ry nymph shall prove;     Alpha and Omega be,
And as these excel in beauty,           And of faith as its beginning,
    Those shall be renown'd for love.      Set our hearts at liberty.

Some also connect Purcell's melody with the writing of the parody, but this is ruled out by Charles' choice[112] of Lampe's tune for 'Jesu, shew us thy Salvation', No. 9 in *Festival Hymns*. Purcell's smooth and lilting 3/4 melody, put in a dotted rhythm and called Dublin, was included in *The Divine Musical Miscellany* (1754).[113] In that form, and named Westminster, it was matched for the first time with Wesley's text in Thomas Butts, *Harmonia Sacra*, c. 1754,[114] and from there into John Wesley's *Sacred Melody* (1761). A comparison of the first phrases of Lampe's solo with Purcell's aria adapted as a jingly evangelical hymn tune suggests why the latter became the accepted setting.

Lampe's tune, "On The Resurrection," Hymn IX in *Festival Hymns*, 1746,
the tune Charles Wesley initially preferred for "Love Divine, all loves excelling."

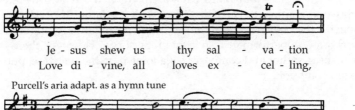

'The peaceful shade' (apparently unpublished), and 'Pastures green' (*Scripture Hymns*, 1762), are thought[115] to have been inspired by the words and the music of the popular 12/8 Siciliana-style tenor or soprano aria, 'Let me wander, not unseen', No. 19 in Handel's oratorio *L'Allegro, Il Penseroso, Ed Il Moderato*, 1740 ('Mirth, Melancholy and Moderation'), libretto by Charles Jennens, based on two poems by John Milton.

Let me wander, not unseen
By hedge-row elms, on hillocks green.
There the ploughman, near at hand,
Whistles over the furrow'd land,
And the milkmaid singeth blithe,
And the mower whets his scythe,
And every shepherd tells his tale
Under the hawthorn in the dale.
And every shepherd tells his tale
Under the hawthorn in the dale.

## The Peaceful Shade

Hide me in the peaceful shade
For lonely contemplation made,
Where the birds on every tree
Whistle artless melody,
Where the river glides so slow,
where the landscape swells below,
And every soul may muse its fill
Under the Side of St. Anne's Hill.

Bear me to the sacred scene,
The silent streams & pastures green.
There the chrystal waters shine,
Springing up with life divine,
There the flock of Israel feed;
Guided by their Shepherd's tread,
And every sheep delights to hide
Under the tree where Jesus died!

Wesley's parody is shown in this example where the first phrase of the D minor aria and the first lines of the poems are interlined.

Let me wan - der, not un - seen by hedgerow elms, on hil - locks green;
Hide me in the peace - ful shade for lone - ly con - tem - pla - tion made
Bear me to the sa - cred scene, the si - lent streams and pastures green.

The hymn 'He comes! he comes!' is based on the words and music of Henry Carey: 'He comes, he comes, the hero comes', *Britannia* (1734).[116] Carey's song was used to celebrate the capture of Porto Bello by Admiral Edward Vernon in 1739, at the beginning of the War of Jenkins' Ear, when England went wild with excitement.[117]

## Song in Britannia

He comes, he comes, the hero comes,
Sound your trumpets, beat your drums;
From port to port let cannons roar
His welcome to the British shore

Prepare, prepare, your songs prepare;
Loudly rend the echoing air;
From pole to pole your joys resound,
For virtue is with glory crown'd.

'He comes! he comes!' first appeared in *Intercession Hymns*. 'The words were probably written by Wesley especially to make use of the tune, and it may well have been written long before its first publication.'[118]

### Thy Kingdom Come

He comes! he comes! the Judge severe!
The seventh trumpet speaks him near;
His light'nings flash, his thunders roll;
How welcome to the faithful soul!

From heaven angelic voices sound,
See the almighty Jesus crowned!
Girt with omnipotence and grace,
And glory decks the Savior's face!
Descending on his azure throne,
He claims the kingdoms for his own;
The kingdoms all obey his word,
And hail him their triumphant lord!

Shout all the people of the sky,
And all the saints of the Most High;
Our Lord, who now his right obtains,
For ever and for ever reigns.

The hymn appeared in *Sacred Melody* (1761), set to Judgment, which is essentially Carey's tune composed for his 87.88 text. Following common practice in popular song of that time, the melody doubles the last line of Wesley's Long Meter (88.88) text to become 88.88.88. Originally in the key of 'G,' the tune is transposed down one step to 'F'.

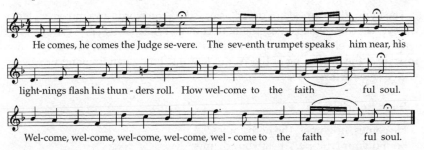

Wesley is thought to have composed 'Listed in the cause of sin' to a Scottish/Irish/English folk melody[119] that had been sung and/or danced by half-drunk sailors who had interrupted a hymn he was singing at an open-air preaching service in Plymouth in 1746.[120] Some accounts state that at the next service Wesley sang his newly composed hymn using the folk tune. The following is this present writer's guess as to how the poet may have accommodated his words to the dance tune.

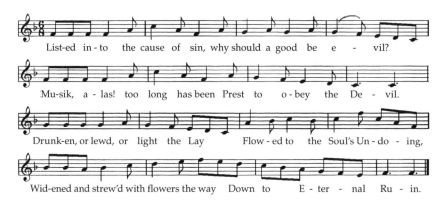

The text first appeared in four 87.87.87.87 stanzas in *Hymns and Sacred Poems* (1749), and in Thomas Butts's *Harmonia Sacra, c.* 1754 it was set to a sturdy minor tune Epworth. The poet later rewrote the hymn in 88.88.88.88, adding three stanzas. It appears that the folk melody, together with Wesley's original text, were never printed.

### The 1749 Version

1. Listed into the Cause of Sin,
     Why should a Good be Evil?
   Musick, alas! too long has been
     Prest to obey the Devil:[121]
   Drunken, or lewd, or light the Lay
     Flow'd to the Soul's Undoing,
   Widen'd, and strew'd with Flowers the Way
     Down to Eternal Ruin.

2. Who on the Part of God will rise,
     Innocent Sound recover,
   Fly on the Pray, and take the Prize,
     Plunder the Carnal Lover,
   Strip him of every moving Stain,
     Every melting Measure,
   Musick in Virtue's Cause retain,
     Rescue the Holy Pleasure?

3. Come let us try if JESU'S Love
     Will not as well inspire us:
   This is the Theme of Those above,
     This upon Earth shall fire us.
   Say, if your Hearts are tun'd to sing,
     Is there a Subject greater?
   Harmony all its Strains may bring,
     JESUS'S Name is sweeter.

4. JESUS the Soul of Musick is;
   His is the Noblest Passion:
JESUS'S Name is Joy and Peace,
   Happiness and Salvation:
JESUS'S Name the dead can raise,
   Shew us our Sins forgiven,
Fill us with all the Life of Grace,
   Carry us up to Heaven.[122]

Although it is a single instance (and others are not known), this may be the small grain of truth in the very widespread rumor that Charles Wesley set sacred texts to 'popular' or 'bar-room' tunes.

## Summary

This study has brought together much of the available evidence of Charles Wesley's musicality as seen in his commentary on music and musicians, and collaborative and parodistic works. His commentary shows a pragmatic approach to the musical education and the emerging professional careers of his sons, Charles Wesley junior and Samuel, and a remarkable acquaintance with the personages, repertory and conflicting claims of London's musical elite in the mid to late eighteenth century. All against the backdrop of his continuing responsibilities in the Methodist Revival in London and elsewhere.

Although Charles apparently shared his brother's flexible approach to appropriate musical settings of his poems, at the same time he lyrically expressed, not without humour and sarcasm, his leanings towards traditional church music, defending it against the claims of the new and invading generation of composers and performers.

While apparently invisible in the compilation and production of John's tune books, and perhaps those of others, nevertheless Charles' collaborative and parodistic works demonstrate a sure musical instinct, which, combined with his wife Sarah's inherited and demonstrated considerable musical talents and performance skills, are remarkably fulfilled and expressed in the musical careers of Charles junior, Samuel and Samuel Sebastian. Careers whose studies by the aforementioned Michael Kassler, Philip Olleson on Samuel, and in Peter Horton's[123] recent biography of Samuel Sebastian greatly expand our understandings of these musicians' remarkable careers, and their combined corpus of poetry, essays, commentary and correspondence.

Their musical careers in a great measure answer Charles' earlier plaintive questions,

Who would not wish to have the skill
Of tuning instruments at will?
Ye powers who guide my actions, tell
Why I, in whom the seeds of music dwell,
Who most its power and excellence admire,
Whose very breast itself a lyre

Was never taught the happy art
Of modulating sounds
   And can no more in concert share a part
Than the wild roe that o'er the mountains bounds.[124]

and bring maturity and fulfilment to his understanding of music as a heavenly and powerful art, 'the music of the heart':

Celebrate th'eternal God
   with harp and psaltery,
timbrels soft and cymbals loud
   in this high praise agree;
praise with every tuneful string;
   all the reach of heavenly art,
all the powers of music bring,
   the music of the heart.[125]

and a foretaste of the heavenly union:

1. Jesus, soft, harmonious name,
   Every faithful heart's desire;
See thy followers, O Lamb!
   All at once to thee aspire:
Drawn by thy uniting grace,
   After thee we swiftly run,
Hand in hand we seek thy face:
   Come, and perfect us in one.

2. Mollify our harsher will;
   Each to each our tempers suit,
By thy modulating skill,
   Heart to heart, as lute to lute:
Sweetly on our spirits move,
   Gently touch the trembling strings;
Make the harmony of love,
   Music for the King of kings.[126]

## Notes

1 For example, 'Thoughts on the Power of Music', completed at Inverness, 9 June 1779, and published in *Arminian Magazine*, 4 (February 1781), 103–07.

2 See Carlton R. Young, *Music of the Heart: John and Charles Wesley on Music and Musicians* (Carol Stream: Hope Publishing, 1995), 82–101.

3 For hymnic developments in the nineteenth century, see, R. E. Ker, 'The Sources of Methodist Hymnody', *The Hymn Society of Great Britain and Ireland Bulletin*, vol. 3, no. 7 (Summer 1953); 'Preface', iii–x to *Wesley's Hymns and New Supplement with Tunes*, 1877; and John Telford, *The Methodist Hymn Book Illustrated*, 1906, edn, 1929; 1–14.

4 James T. Lightwood's studies include: 'Notes on the Foundery Tune-Book', *PWHS* 1 (1900), 116–17; 'Notes on the Foundery Tune-Book,' 2nd Part, *PWHS* 6 (1900), 147–17; 'Tune Books of the Eighteenth Century', *PWHS* 4 (1905), 101–08; *Hymn-Tunes and Their Story* (London: Charles H. Kelly, 1905); *Methodist Music in the Eighteenth Century* (London: Epworth Press, 1927); *Stories of Methodist Music: Nineteenth century* (London: Epworth Press, 1928).

5 Maurice Frost's studies include: 'John Wesley's Hymn Tunes', *Bulletin: Hymn Society of Great Britain and Ireland*, 1 (1944), 5–7; 'Harmonia Sacra by Thomas Butts – I and II', *Bulletin: Hymn Society of Great Britain and Ireland*, 3 (1952), 66–79, 1952; 'The Tunes Associated with Hymn singing in the Lifetime of the Wesleys', *Bulletin: Hymn Society of Great Britain and Ireland*, 4 (1957–8), 118–26.

6 Nelson F. Adams, *The Musical Sources for John Wesley's Tunebooks: the Genealogy of 148 Tunes* (New York: unpublished DMA thesis, Union Theological Seminary School of Sacred Music, 1973).

7 John Wesley, *A Collection of Tunes, Set to Music, As They are commonly sung at the Foundery* (London, 1742); John Wesley, 'Sacred Melody or a Choice Collection of Psalm and Hymn Tunes, with a Short Introduction', in *Select Hymns with Tunes Annext: Designed chiefly for the use of the people called Methodists* (London, 1761); Lu Chen, instructor in music at the Methodist Seminary, Sibu, Malaysia, in an unpublished research paper, 'The Variety of Musical Styles in John Wesley's *Sacred Melody*, 1761' 2004, traces and comments on the sources and styles of 114 tunes in that collection and their variants in John Wesley's next collection; *Sacred Harmony, or A choice collection of psalm and hymn tunes in two or three parts for the voice, harpsichord & organ* (London, 1780)

8 Nicholas Temperley, 'Reform Movements, 1760–1830', *The Music of the English Parish Church*, 2 vols (Cambridge: Cambridge University Press, 1979), 1, 204–43.

9 *BE*, 7.770.

10 Erik Routley, *The Musical Wesleys* (London: Herbert Jenkins, 1968). The first study of the Wesley family (slight coverage of S. S. Wesley) and music was W. (William) Winter's (1835?–1893) *An Account of the Remarkable Musical Talents of Several members of the Wesley Family: Collected from original manuscripts, &c, / with memorial introduction and notes by W. Winters*, London, 1874.

11 For example, Frederick C. Gill, *Charles Wesley: The first Methodist* (London: Lutterworth Press, 1964), 37, 66–67, 72–73, 177, 205–6.

12 Frank Baker (ed.), *Representative Verse* (London: Epworth Press, 1962), 311.

13 Following the rectory fire in 1709, while the house was rebuilt the children were kept by several families, where, according to Susanna, 'they got knowledge of several songs and bad things, which before they had no notion of' (see Adam Clarke, *Memoirs of the Wesley Family*, 2 vols, [London: T. Tegg & Son, 1826], 2.13). Further, John Telford states that 'after the parsonage was rebuilt [following the 1709 fire], the custom of singing psalms was introduced at the opening and close of [Susanna's home] school'; see John Telford, *The Life of the Rev. Charles Wesley, MA* (London: Religious Tract Society, [1886]), 21.

14 In 1702 Samuel senior established a parish Religious Society, a high church movement founded in the late seventeenth century to encourage devotional life. According to Robin Leaver the societies' singing practice and repertoire of tunes influenced the development of eighteenth-century evangelical song (S T Kimbrough Jr and Charles A. Green (eds), *Hymns on the Great Festivals, and Other Occasions* (Madison: The Charles Wesley Society, 1996), 31, 36). Nicholas Temperley traces the societies' influence in the development of parish choirs. A

choir was already in place at Epworth when Wesley arrived in 1697 (Temperley, *The Music of the English Parish Church*, 1, 141, 143; see also Stevenson, *Memorials*, 100). Samuel senior articulated the importance of church music in his 1706 letter on 'public devotion' to his son Samuel junior who probably had 'musical abilities' (see Stevenson, *Memorials*, 104): 'music [is] a great help to our devotion, as it notably raises our affections towards heaven, which I believe has been the experience of all good men, unless they have been dunces or fanatics' (Stevenson, *Memorials*, 98).

15 Nicholas Temperley, 'Anglican and Episcopalian Church Music, No. 5, English Cathedral Music, 1660–1830', *Grove Music Online*, ed. L. Macy (accessed 11 July 2006) <http://www.grovemusic.com>

16 Gill, *First Methodist*, 35. His interest in the theatre, opera and oratorio may have begun while a student at Oxford.

17 Sally, when asked by King George III if her husband performed on any instrument, replied, 'A little, please your majesty, on the German flute when at college.' Stevenson, *Memorials*, 456.

18 See Gill, *First Methodist*, 192. Gumley's house in Chesterfield Street, Marylebone, which she leased to Charles in 1771, included 'a spacious music-room in which an organ was erected by the munificence of Mrs. Gumley' (see James Higgs, 'Samuel Wesley: His Life, Times, and Influence on Music', *Proceedings of The Musical Association*, 20th Session [1893–4], 132). Lightwood indicates that the room contained two organs and the harpsichord which had been given to the boys (James T. Lightwood, *Samuel Wesley, Musician: The story of his life etc.* (London: Epworth Press, 1937), 50). Due to the several restorations of presumably that organ (for example, one of the two ranks of pipes was changed at some point in the early twentieth century), it is only partially the one the Wesley sons played in their Marylebone house concerts, 1779–86 (National Pipe Organ Register D01993). There is no evidence that Charles senior played this or any other keyboard instrument.

19 'Sarah's [education was] . . . carefully superintended by private masters [and] was advanced to a maturity of accomplishments quite unusual in those days. Proficiency in music and singing then distinguished her . . .' (see Stevenson, *Memorials*, p. 428). However, after reviewing Samuel senior's interest in and knowledge of music, Stevenson states, 'It is reasonable to conclude that the marvelous musical genius of his two grandsons . . . was largely inherited from their grandfather, as well as from their own mother' (Stevenson, *Memorials*, 100).

20 Lightwood, *Samuel Wesley, Musician*, 14–15.

21 See, Young, *Music of the Heart*, 122–52, for 100 events and references to music, song and singing found in Charles Wesley's journal, for the years 1736–51. For example, Charles' conversion, Tuesday, May 23, 1738, was accompanied by song, including the singing of his first hymn, 'Where shall my wondering soul begin'.

22 W. L. Doughty, 'Charles Wesley Preacher', in *London Quarterly and Holborn Review*, 1958, 263–7.

23 Frank Baker, *Charles Wesley as Revealed by his Letters* (London: Epworth Press, 1948), 36.

24 *CWJ*, 1.329–30, 338–9.

25 The first of six stanzas included in *CWJ*, 1.330.

26 In context this would mean 'early Christian practice' and hence be, for Charles, a very positive remark.

27 *CWJ*, I.339. The ending words may refer to Pliny, a letter to Trajan of the 100s AD, where Pliny states that it was the Christians' custom, *carmen . . . Christo quasi*

*deo dicere*, 'to sing a hymn to Christ, as to a god.' See A. N. Sherwin-White, ed., *Fifty Letters of Pliny*, 2nd edn (Oxford: Oxford University Press, 1969), 69.

28 John Wesley's views are included in his journal and correspondence; see, 'John Wesley: Tune Book Editor and Music Critic', in Young, *Music of the Heart*, 33–113; 'Thoughts On The Power of Music', Inverness, 9 June 1779, included in *Arminian Magazine*, IV, 103–7 (February 1781). For text of and commentary on 'Thoughts on the Power of Music', see Routley, *The Musical Wesleys*, 14–26; *BE*, 7.766–9; Young, *Music of the Heart*, 84–93; and John Wesley, 'Directions for Singing', *Select Hymns: With tunes annext: designed chiefly for the use of the people called the Methodists* (London, [n.pbl.] 1761).

29 See, 'Charles Wesley: Lyrical Theologian and Music Critic', in Young, *Music of the Heart*, 118–52.

30 Letters in *CWJ*, 2.174, 181, 184, 208, 246, 256–7, 260, 262, 264–5, 274, 276; Arthur W. Wainwright & Don E. Saliers, eds, *Wesley-Langshaw Correspondence: Charles Wesley, his sons, and the Lancaster organists* (Emory: Scholars Press, 1993), *passim*, and Baker, *Charles Wesley as Revealed by his Letters*, 110–16.

31 There are two aspects of this objection: the immorality, perceived and real, of the theatre and its musicians; and 'The life of a professional musician was not one that a gentleman would in normal circumstances consider for his son, given the competing attractions of the three traditional "learned" professions of the church, medicine, and the law.' See Philip Olleson, *Samuel Wesley: The Man and His Music* (Woodbridge: Boydell, 2003), 14; and Deborah Rohr, *The Careers of British Musicians, 1750–1850: A Profession of Artisans* (Cambridge: Cambridge University Press, 2001).

32 For commentary on Samuel's declining relationships with his family, particularly his father, during the years of the home concerts, see further, Philip Olleson, 'The Wesleys at Home: Charles Wesley and His Children', *Methodist History*, 36, 3 (April 1998), 144.

33 Fletcher to Charles Wesley, 13 October 1771, quoted in Gill, *First Methodist*, 190.

34 Baker, *Representative Verse*, 115

35 Baker, *Representative Verse*, 115–16

36 *PW*, 5.284.

37 *The Public Advertiser*, 20 May 1777, quoted in *The Musical Times*, 1 September 1908. See commentary on this concert in Olleson, 2003, 19–20.

38 The most complete coverage is Alyson McLamore's article, '"By the Will and Order of Providence": The Wesley Family Concerts, 1779–1787', in *Royal Musical Association Research Chronicle*, 37 (2004), 71–220. William Cowper, in his poem 'Occiduus,' a fictitious name for Charles, accuses him of being a Sabbath-breaking clergyman for allowing his sons to perform song-tunes and religious music in Sunday evening concerts. Thomas Jackson, *The Life of the Rev. C. Wesley*, 2 vols (London: John Mason, 1841), 2.372. Others, including Olleson (see *Samuel Wesley [1766–1837], A Source Book*, 257), think 'Occiduus' is Martin Madan.

39 Olleson, 'The Wesleys at Home', 147 and see above, pp. 131–2.

40 Coke's letter to John Wesley, 15 December 1779, in *Arminian Magazine*, 13 (1790), 50–1.

41 MARC, *MS Patriotism: Misc.*, 11, see Baker, *Representative Verse*, 312.

42 14 January 1779, quoted in Lightwood, *Samuel Wesley, Musician*, 51–2.

43 Wesley to Eleanor Laroche, 3 February 1769 (Rylands, DDWES, 4/73), quoted in Baker, *Charles Wesley as Revealed by His Letters*, 190. See also, Olleson, 'The

Wesleys at Home', 145 and above pp. 128–30.

44 Lightwood, *Samuel Wesley, Musician*, 33–4.

45 See the sermons 'On Family Religion', 'On the Education of Children', and 'On Obedience to Parents', in *BE*, 3.333–72.

46 'I insist upon conquering the will of children betimes, because this is the only strong and rational foundation of a religious education, without which both precept and example will be ineffectual.' Stevenson, *Memorials*, 164.

47 'Mrs. Wesley was endowed with a voice of unusual compass and melody. This distinctive feature she possessed in common with every member of her own family, several of whom were musical geniuses of the highest order.' Stevenson, *Memorials*, 432. A review of Sarah Gwynne Wesley's musicality is included in Carlton R. Young's catalogue for the 2007 exhibit, 'Sacred Harmony: The Musical Wesleys', Bridwell Library, Perkins School of Theology, Southern Methodist University, Dallas, Texas.

48 Charles' Easter Day 1750 letter to Sally included: 'Do not neglect your short-hand; do not neglect your music; but, above all, do not neglect your prayers.' *CWJ*, 2.181.

49 Selections from Correspondence, letter to Sally Gwynne, 29 March [no year, presumed to be in early 1750s], *CWJ*, 2.184. See also Gill, *First Methodist*, 165.

50 *CWJ*, 2.140.

51 Telford, *The Life of the Rev. Charles Wesley, M.A.*, 193–5.

52 Telford, *The Life of the Rev. Charles Wesley, M.A.*, 316.

53 Wainwright and Saliers (eds), *Wesley/Langshaw Correspondence*, 74.

54 The following section is excerpted and expanded from 169–89 in Carlton R. Young, *Music of the Heart: John and Charles Wesley on music and musicians*, © 1995, 2007, Hope Publishing Co., Carol Stream IL, 60188. Used by permission. All rights reserved.

55 Philip Olleson comments, '. . . in the first section of Charles Wesley senior's long account [see Wesley vol. 2, 1849, 140–4] of his elder son's musical experiences. The names he gives make up a roll-call of many of the most prominent musicians in London at the time, and it is apparent that Charles Wesley was able to make contact with them quickly and easily, even though he was unlikely to have known them previously.' Olleson, *Samuel Wesley: The man and his music*, 5.

56 In nine seasons, 1779–87, there were 64 subscription home concerts for which 84 different performers were engaged (McLamore, 'The Wesley Family Concerts', 78). The management of these concerts, including invitations, promotion, book-keeping, refreshments, rehearsals and musicians' dinners, was no small task for Charles Wesley senior and his wife Sally.

57 Perhaps as early as 1744 the Wesleys furthered their ministry among wealthy theatre patrons by leasing 'a former Huguenot Chapel in West Street, [where they] Whitefield, the saintly Fletcher and other leaders ministered in crowded services, and the narrow street, now so unprepossessing, in the Drury Lane area lined regularly with the waiting coaches of their more fashionable followers . . . among its first worshippers, and a notable convert, was Mrs. [Priscilla] Rich, the wife of John Rich, the proprietor of Covent Garden Theatre.' (Gill, *First Methodist*, 120.) Mrs Rich probably introduced Charles to Lampe. Lampe in turn may have introduced the Wesleys to Handel. Charles' long association with Mrs Rich began with her attendance at the West Street Chapel, and is evidenced in his journal entries beginning 26 October 1745. '[London] I dined at Mrs. R's. Mr. R [ich] behaved with great civility. I foresee the storm my visit will bring upon him; 29 April, 1748.

[London] Mrs. Rich carried me [in her coach] to Dr. [Johann C.] Pepusch, whose music entertained us much, and his conversation more; 30 May, 1750. [London?] We had a long day's journey to St. Anne's. It was past nine before we got under shelter. Mrs. Rich was there, who, with our old friends, received us gladly. London, 13 August, 1770, Not finding Lady Huntingdon this morning, who was returned to Sussex, I rode on to M. Rich's and spent two more agreeable hours with her and M. White, &c.' Charles' 9 August 1770 letter to Sally indicating Mrs Rich's invitation to Charles junior to attend oratorio performances shows that his continued relationship with Mrs Rich assisted Charles junior's entry into London musical circles (*CWJ*, 2.260).

58 Barrington apparently requested Charles Wesley to write an account of Samuel, the first part of which appeared in Daines Barrington, *Miscellanies by the Honourable Daines Barrington* (London: J. Nichols, 1781), 291–8. The second part, his own observations and a song by Samuel, is in Barrington, *Miscellanies*, 298–310, and was issued separately. A copy of part two is in the Bridwell Library, Southern Methodist University, Dallas, Texas. Kassler and Olleson have traced Charles Wesley's manuscript and Barrington's essays. See Michael Kassler and Philip Olleson, *Samuel Wesley (1766–1837), A Source Book* (Aldershot: Ashgate, 2001), 733; and Olleson, *Samuel Wesley: The man and his music*, 4–5.

59 Lightwood, *Samuel Wesley, Musician*, 50–1.

60 Including Jonathan Battishill, 1738–1801.

61 Richard Heitzenrater has determined that Kelway expected payment and threatened to sue Wesley if not paid. (Correspondence with Carlton R. Young, 22 February 2006.)

62 MS Patriotism: Misc., 6–7, Baker, *Representative Verse*, 312.

63 B = Johann Christian Bach, 1735–82; A = Karl Friedrich Abel, 1723–87; and G = Felice de Giardini, 1716–96, were active and influential in London musical circles during the Wesley family's residency.

64 *CWJ*, 2.146.

65 Baker, *Representative Verse*, 312, from MS Patriotism: Misc., 13–15.

66 Christoph Wolff, 'J. C. Bach, 2. London, 1762–72', Grove Music Online, ed. L. Macy (accessed 21 February 2006) <http://www.grovemusic.com>

67 MS Patriotism: Misc., 6–7 in S T Kimbrough and Oliver A. Beckerlegge (eds), *The Unpublished Poetry of Charles Wesley*, 3 vols. (Nashville: Kingswood Books, 1992), 3.382.

68 J. Richard Watson comments in correspondence with Carlton R. Young, '"But a Ninny" is perhaps an echo from John Byrom's "On the Feuds between Handel and Bonnoncini".'

Some say, compar'd to Bonnoncini,
That Mynheer Handel's but a ninny;
Others aver that he to Handel
Is scarcely fit to hold a candle.
Strange all this difference should be
'Twixt Tweedledum and Tweedledee.

69 Wesley calls them 'the whole Tribe of Musicians, who neglect Sunday worship and were not punctual'. See letters 8 and 14, in Wainwright and Saliers (eds), *Wesley/Langshaw Correspondence*, 32–3, 44–5.

70 She performed in the Salisbury and Hereford festivals. For commentary,

excerpts from reviews and correspondence, see Betty Matthews, 'The Davies Sisters, J. C. Bach and The Glass harmonica', *Music & Letters*, vol. 56, 2 (April 1975), 150–69.

71  Text in Baker, *Representative Verse*, 327–8.

72  Dennis R. Martin, *The Operas and Operatic Style of John Frederick Lampe* (Detroit: Information Coordinators, 1985), 73.

73  John Wesley and Charles Wesley, *Hymns for those that seek and those that have Redemption in the Blood of Jesus Christ* (London, 1747), No. 25

74  *JWJ*, 3.226 n. 1.

75  *CWJ*, 2.408–9.

76  Wainwright and Saliers (eds), *Wesley/Langshaw Correspondence, passim.*

77  Baker, *Representative Verse*, 311.

78  Kimbrough and Beckerlegge, *Unpublished Poetry*, 3.384. n. 20. Beckerlegge comments that Memon, line 5, was king of the Ethiopians and conqueror of the East 'whose statue when struck by the first rays of the raising sun, was said to give forth a sound like the snapping asunder of a chord'.

79  Charles states that his son Charles received from his uncle, presumably John Wesley, the 'inestimable present of Dr. Boyce's Cathedral Music', *CWJ*, 2.144.

80  Nicholas Temperley has discovered: [A] Boyce setting in G Major of 'Servant of God, well done' that was published with a four-voice tune by Charles Wesley junior, about 1795, with the heading: 'Written by the Revd. Charles Wesley on the Death of the Revd. George Whitefield. Set to music by the late Dr. Boyce, Composer to His Majesty' (correspondence with Carlton R. Young, April 1994).

81  Kimbrough and Beckerlegge, *Unpublished Poetry*, 1.279.

82  *CWJ*, 2.410.

83  MARC, Nursery MS; Baker, *Representative Verse*, p. 325.

84  Hilderbrandt and Beckerlegge suggest that Lampe may have assisted Butts in its preparation, *BE*, 7.738, n. 2.

85  Charles Wesley, Samuel Wesley junior & John F. Lampe, *Hymns on the Great Festivals and Other Occasions* (London: M. Cooper, 1746).

86  John Wesley, in his preface to *Sacred Melody*, p. iv, praises the collection, but states that it is too expensive, and does not include 'the tunes which are in common use among [Methodists]'. Notwithstanding, as stated above, Wesley chose most of his tunes for *Sacred Melody* from *Harmonia Sacra*!

87  Baker states 'Most of the evidence seems to imply that the total expense of publishing, like the general format and much of the text and all of the engraved plates, were Lampe's responsibility alone.' Baker, *Representative Verse*, 82.

88  Samuel Wesley in his preface to *Original Hymn Tunes, Adapted to Every Metre in the Collection by the Rev. John Wesley . . . Newly Composed and Arranged for Four Voices* (London: Published for Samuel Wesley, [1828]), iii, states that his father 'had an extreme regard for him [Lampe, who] furnished an admirable Set of Tunes'.

89  See Charles' poem, 'On the death of Mr. Lampe', *CWJ*, 2.408–9 and above, p. 424.

90  The collection was printed on large sheets, with the single music pages formatted similarly to the single-sheet broadside ballad containing the melody and bass, with one stanza interlined and the balance in text blocks. It is an example of good quality London mid-eighteenth-century music and text engraving and printing.

91  Wesley, Wesley and Lampe, *Hymns on the Great Festivals* [facsimile of 1746 edn] (Madison: The Charles Wesley Society, 1996), 21–9.

92 For an inventory of the 24 texts with commentary, see Frank Baker's essay, 'The Texts of Hymns on the Great Festivals', in Wesley, Wesley and Lampe, *Hymns on the Great Festivals*, 21–9.

93 Wesley, Wesley and Lampe, *Hymns on the Great Festivals*, 21; a formidable task for composers even those with the abilities of Lampe. For comment on Lampe's compositions in binary and aria style, see Martin, *The Operas and Operatic Style of John Frederick Lampe*, 112–16.

94 The entire letter is included in Telford, *The Life of the Rev. Charles Wesley, M.A.*, 152.

95 See S T Kimbrough Jr, 'Lampe's Variant Readings and Vocal Performance', in Wesley, Wesley and Lampe, *Hymns on the Great Festivals*, 45–7.

96 Concurrent with his work on the collection, Lampe appears to have moved from theatre works to song collections 'for [his] Lyra Britannica finally was completed, and Lampe made important contributions to Walsh's multivolume work *The Vocal Musical Mask*', Martin, *The Operas and Operatic Style of John Frederick Lampe*, 71.

97 M. Cooper, London, published few titles with music, but specialized in mid-eighteenth-century literary essays, papers and treatises on foreign and domestic affairs.

98 Baker dates its publication from an advertisement on p. 560 in the October issue of *Gentlemen's Magazine*: *Hymns on the great festivals*, 1746, 26.

99 Telford, *The Life of the Rev. Charles Wesley, M.A.*, 152.

100 Wesley, Wesley & Lampe, *Hymns on the Great Festivals*, 26.

101 Telford, *The Life of the Rev. Charles Wesley, M.A.*, 15.

102 *CWJ*, 2.174

103 Wesley, Wesley and Lampe, *Hymns on the Great Festivals*, 26–7. The 24 hymns are included on pp. 88–108 in Charles Wesley, *Hymns on the Trinity* [facsimile of 1767 edn] (Madison: The Charles Wesley Society, 1998).

104 Robin Leaver traces into the early nineteenth century the appearance of Lampe's tunes in 15 tune books, in Wesley, Wesley and Lampe, *Hymns on the Great Festivals*, 39–44.

105 Battishill, 1738–1801, set 12 Wesley hymns, in Charles Wesley, *Hymns and Sacred Poems*, 2 vols (Bristol: Felix Farley, 1749), similar to Lampe's settings in strophic form, melody and figured bass, but even more ornamented. Jonathan Battishill, *Twelve Hymns, The Words by the Revd. Mr. Charles Wesley M.A. Late Student of Christ Church, Oxford. Set to Music by Mr. Jonathan Battishill* (London: printed for the author by C. and S. Thompson in St Paul's Church Yard, [*c.* 1770] Where may be had by the same Author The Favourite Songs in the Opera of Almena. Price 3S).

106 Sarah, in a letter to John Gaulter, 25 October 1826, suggests that Mrs Rich led Handel to write the tunes. Wainwright/Saliers 1992, 88. Sarah's, Charles' daughter's account: 'By the intimacy of Mr. and Mrs. Rich with Handel, he was doubtless led to set to music these hymns of my father.' Stevenson, *Memorials of The Wesley Family*, 527. Perhaps Mrs Rich gave Lampe's *Festival Hymns* to Handel, which includes the three texts Handel set.

107 Of the three tunes, this one has survived and is included in mainline denominational hymnals with the name GOPSAL.

108 See Kassler and Olleson 2001, 694; Donald Burrows, *George Frideric Handel, the Complete Hymns & Chorales*, facsimile edn (London: Novello, 1988); and John Wilson, 'Handel's Tunes for Charles Wesley's Hymns', The Hymn Society of Great Britain & Ireland, *Bulletin*, 163, vol. 11, no. 2 (May 1985).

109 Lightwood, *Methodist Music in the Eighteenth Century*, 52.

110 *CWJ*, 2.143.

111 Baker, *Representative Verse*, 94.

112 Baker, *Representative Verse*, 94. Wesley assigned Lampe's 24 tunes in *Festival Hymns* to texts in *Redemption Hymns*.

113 The tune book for George Whitefield's *Hymns for Social Worship, More Particularly Design'd for the use of the Tabernacle Congregation, in London* (London: William Strahan, 1753).

114 Butts may have consulted with Wesley, or vice versa, to bring the hymns and Purcell's melody together for the first time.

115 'In April 1751 . . . [Wesley] retired for a week to the home of Mrs. Colvil and Miss Degge on St. Anne' Hill, Chertsey. His *Journal*, under date 9 April, states that the time was spent chiefly in "reading, singing, and prayer". The singing seems to have included a number of contemporary ballads, to which Wesley wrote his own words, some of them simple appreciations of rural life, others more specifically religious in tone'; see Baker, *Representative Verse*, 275–6. Charles Wesley junior's entry in his notebook for 31 May 1824 is also worth noting: 'Wrote [composed?] out a pastoral Hymn of my late Dear Father's made at St. Anns hill Cottage for Mrs. G.' See further, Betty Matthews, 'Charles Wesley on Organs: 2', *Musical Times*, vol. 112, no. 1545 (November 1971), 1111.

116 A *c.* 1724 version of the song, too fragile to copy, is in the Folger Shakespeare Library: 'A Two Part Song in Britannia', shelfmark: M1497 C42 v.1 Cage, fol. 220r.

117 *BE*, 7.779.

118 *BE*, 7.779.

119 The melody is associated with texts including: 'Nancy Dawson', 'Here we go round the mulberry bush', 'I saw three ships come sailing in', and 'Piss on the grass'. The latter was published under this title in J. Walsh's *Caledonian Country Dances, c.* 1744. It was included in John Gay's ballad opera *The Beggar's Opera* (1729) labelled a hornpipe, although it must be noted that any step-dance at the time could be called a 'hornpipe'. Andrew Kuntz in *The Fiddlers Companion*, <http://www.ceolas.org/tunes/fc/> (accessed 17 July 2006).

120 For variants of the story, see Baker, *Representative Verse*, 117.

121 Perhaps presaging 'Why should the Devil have all the good tunes?', a saying variously attributed to Martin Luther and John Wesley, the source of which Nicholas Temperley and Frank Baker have narrowed to E. W. Broome's book published in 1881, on the Anglican clergyman Rowland Hill, 1744–1833, a critic of John Wesley. Broome says of Hill, 'He did not see any reason why the devil should have all the good tunes', Young, *Music of the Heart*, 104.

122 Baker, *Representative Verse*, 118.

123 Peter Horton, *Samuel Sebastian Wesley: A life* (Oxford: Oxford University Press, 2004).

124 Baker, *Representative Verse*, 311.

125 *PW*, 8.262.

126 *Hymns and Sacred Poems*, 1749, 2.329–30; No. 23 of 'Hymns for Christian friends'.

# 25. Charles Wesley's Spirituality

## MARTIN GROVES

Given the influence Charles Wesley must have had on the English-speaking spiritual tradition through the singing of his hymns, it is unfortunate that Martin Thornton in his work *English Spirituality: An outline of ascetical theology according to the English pastoral tradition* should maintain that the death of William Law in 1761 'was nearly, but not quite, the end of the development of spirituality within the English Church'.[1] Thornton did not like Law and does not spend much time on the spirituality of the eighteenth century. He does, however, set the scene for some of what follows in this present chapter by quoting from P. Pourrat's 1922 work on *Christian Spirituality* regarding the distinction between ascetic and mystical theology.

> The former treats of the exercises required of aspirants to perfection. Ordinarily the soul rises to perfection by passing through three stages. First of all, it gets free from sin, penance and mortification; then it forms inner virtues by prayer and the imitation of Christ; and, lastly, it advances in the love of God till it reaches habitual union with Him. It is for us to enter the path of perfection and to traverse its stages more or less quickly. God calls us to do this, and gives us the graces needed for corresponding with His call.
>
> It is otherwise with the extraordinary states dealt with in mystical theology – states such as mystical union with its concomitant manifestations – i.e., ecstasy, visions and revelations. The mark of these states is their independence of those who experience them. They are the privilege of the few to whom God unites Himself ineffably by flooding them with light and love. No one can effect these mystical phenomena within himself by any efforts or merits of his own. The soul of the ascetic with the help of grace makes an effort to rise towards God; but the soul of the mystic is suddenly and impetuously visited by God without exerting any activity beyond that of receiving and enjoying the Divine gift.[2]

The question then arises as to whether Charles is best understood as a mystical or ascetic spiritual theologian. Putting the question in this way will provide opportunity to explore apparently contradictory tendencies in his spirituality: in some ways Charles' concern with the self-conscious self might be thought to lead to the development of an ascetic spiritual theology; however, his view that the self is best lost in 'the other' might suggest a greater sympathy with aspects of the mystical tradition. It is as well to consider the case for both.

First then the case for locating Charles within the ascetic pastoral tradition. Here it is natural to begin at the beginning with his years in Oxford from 1726 to 1735. This is the period which gave birth to Charles' spiritual work, and Methodism was born in both name and substance. From the outset Charles conceived of the spiritual life as one of discipline and practice. Much later in life he wrote of this period:

> My first year at College I lost in diversions. The next I set myself to study. Diligence led me into serious thinking. I went to the weekly sacrament, and persuaded 2 or 3 young scholars to accompany me, and to observe the method of study prescribed by the statutes of the University. This gained me the harmless nickname of Methodist.[3]

The story of Charles Wesley in Oxford is the story of his commitment to spiritual, mental and sacramental discipline. The commitment was his own and the discipline was exercised with a handful of others who collectively became known as the 'Holy Club'. Here was one at work on his soul and on his relationship with God. Frank Baker writes of Charles' disposition in 1729: 'Gone now was his careless gaiety, and his introspection and anxious striving after the good life are almost oppressive. His finger was constantly on his spiritual pulse.' Charles wrote to his brother in that year, concerned about his spiritual coldness:

> What you say about coldness has put me upon considering whence mine can proceed, and how it may (be remedied?) I think I may truly esteem it the nature and just consequence of my past life. One who – has for almost thirteen years been utterly inattentive at public prayers can't expect to find there that warmth he has never known at his first seeking: he must knock oftener than once before 'tis opened to him . . . I resolve that my falling short of my duty in one particular shan't discourage me from vigorously prosecuting it in the rest. I look upon this coldness as a trial, and that when I sink under it 'twill in the end greatly contribute to my advantage. I must, I will, in spite of Nature and the Devil, take pains: while my strength lasts, I will put it to the utmost stretch, for a day's relaxing throws me back to my first setting out. I won't give myself leisure to relapse, for I'm assured, if I have no business of my own, the Devil will soon find me some.[4]

From 1728 Charles Wesley's life was marked by spiritual activism in pursuit of warmth (cf. the 'heart strangely warmed' experienced by his brother). From 1729 his spiritual exercises included prayer, reading the scriptures, fasting, attending the sacraments, keeping account of his time, keeping a journal, studying and in due course visiting the sick and prisoners. In his *Short History of the People Called Methodist* John Wesley was clear that these Oxford years marked the birth of Methodism. The marks of Charles Wesley's ascetic spirituality were established in this period and characterized the rest of his life and the subsequent life of the Methodist Church.

It is instructive (if mainly from an historiographical point of view) that the literature we know Charles to have been reading at this time are mainly manuals of spiritual direction: Thomas à Kempis' *The Imitation of Christ* and *Christian Pattern*, William Law's *Christian Perfection* and *A Serious Call to a Devout and Holy Life* and Jeremy Taylor's *Rules and Exercises of Holy Living* and *Rules and Exercises of Holy Dying*. Everything about this Oxford period speaks of Wesley's interest in, and commitment to, ascetic spiritual development. Further evidence of the ascetic character of this period is found in the document *A Scheme of Self-Examination Used by the First Methodists in Oxford*.[5] The reference in the title to 'Self-Examination' supplies further evidence of the importance of the self-conscious self, developed and exercised in the spiritual disciplines of the Oxford Methodists begun, if not finally led, by Charles Wesley.

The period after Oxford from 1735 to 1738 provides evidence which both supports and challenges the view of Charles as an ascetic. This period was dominated by the excursion to Georgia. The expedition was first thought of as a migration of the Holy Club with its spiritual endeavours and ascetic disciplines intact for the purposes of 'promoting the work of God among the heathen'.[6] From the outset Charles was less enthusiastic about the project than his brother, but still it bore all the hallmarks of self-conscious, disciplined, spiritual undertaking that characterized the Oxford Methodists. The disasters that befell the Wesley brothers at this time have tended to obscure their intention to maintain and develop their Oxford disciplines with the hope that they would be extended and bequeathed to both native Americans and colonists. But, and this is the point, the experience was not a happy one. Whaling describes it as a debacle, saying that (for John) it represented 'a period of bewilderment and spiritual seeking after the relative repose of his earlier discipline when he was able to explore more fully his own self and the will of God for his life.'[7] Charles gave strong expression to his unhappiness in a letter to Sally Kirkham, and this was when he had barely arrived and before things got really bad.

> God has brought an unhappy, unthankful wretch hither, through a thousand dangers, to renew his complaints, and loathe the life which has been preserved by a series of miracles. I take the moment of my arrival to inform you of it, because I know you will thank him, though I cannot, for I yet feel myself. In vain have I fled from myself to America; I still groan under the intolerable weight of inherent misery! If I have never yet repented of my undertaking, it is because I could hope for nothing better in England – or Paradise. Go where I will, I carry my Hell about me. Nor have I the least ease in anything, unless in thinking of S[elina] and you.[8]

The apparent failure and certain unhappiness of the Georgian excursion raised fundamental questions about the ascetic experiment being undertaken by Charles at this time. These questions lay behind the spiritual struggle he experienced on his return to England in late 1736. He was ill, unhappy and confused. His spiritual endeavours seemed to have born no fruit, no sense of well-being, no spiritual satisfaction. Charles' spiritual guides at this time were Moravian. He and his brother had their first close encounter with Moravian piety on board the *Simmonds*, the boat that took them to Georgia, and they remained close to the Moravian community in Savannah. At a time when Charles' life seemed seriously battered with storms of every kind he could hardly fail to be impressed with the Moravian calmness first demonstrated to him in the midst of the near shipwreck they had experienced on the voyage to America.

On his return to London and during the period marked by physical and spiritual distress, 1737–8, Charles was actively seeking spiritual direction. Ironically his spiritual activism repeatedly pointed him towards more passive and quietist solutions. At the end of August 1737 Charles went for spiritual direction to William Law. Charles reports in his journal 'The sum of his advice was "Renounce yourself; and be not impatient".'[9] These words raise the two questions at the centre of this investigation into Charles Wesley's spirituality: first, whether and to what extent Charles took the view that the self was best renounced; and second, whether and to what extent Charles' spirituality ought to be characterized by patience or activity.

It was, however, the Moravians, Nicholas Zinzendorf and Peter Böhler, who provided the most intensive direction at this time. The issue was about faith and works, activism or quietism, asceticism or mysticism. Although there was a certain predictability to the spiritual drama that was unfolding over the first six months of 1738, drama it most certainly was. The account of this period is well known but bears rehearsing in part. From his journal for 24 February Charles (on his sick-bed) reports his conversation with Böhler:

> . . . he took me by the hand, and calmly said, 'You will not die now.' I thought within myself, 'I cannot hold out in this pain until the morning. If it abates before, I believe I may recover.' He asked me, 'Do you hope to be saved?' 'Yes.' 'For what reason do you hope it?' 'Because I have used my best endeavours to serve God.' He shook his head and said no more. I thought him very uncharitable , saying in my heart, 'What, are not my endeavours a sufficient ground of my hope? Would he rob me of my endeavours? I have nothing else to trust to . . .'[10]

The narrative here, if not contrived, follows certain conventions. Perhaps it is nonetheless instructive for that.

It would not be entirely correct to represent this period as a time when an over-active semi-Pelagian ascetic, subdued by sickness of both body and soul, was guided by quietist Moravian mentors to a still and confident apprehension of the peace of God. There was nothing quiet, accidental, unintended or passive about the events that led Charles Wesley to have an experience of the peace of God at Pentecost in 1738. The journal account of the preceding months reads like the account of a fretted-over labour. Its result was as planned, managed and inevitable as any labour. The dramatic narrative has a host of spiritual midwives and nurses (Mr Bray, Mrs Bray, Mrs Turner, Mrs Musgrave) all popping in and out of Charles' bedroom offering predictions about the immediacy of his deliverance. However Moravian quietism is understood, Charles' spiritual experience of May 1738 was as much a result of ascetic discipline as mystical accident.

If asceticism is about the active structuring and ordering of the spiritual journey then Charles Wesley's spirituality can be characterized as ascetic to the end. Charles the activist poet articulated the question of his life:

What shall I do my God to love,
My loving God to praise?[11]

The hymn that he wrote in response to the sense of peace he experienced in 1738 is particularly interesting:

Where shall my wond'ring soul begin?
How shall I all to heaven aspire?
A slave redeemed from death and sin,
A brand plucked from eternal fire,
How shall I equal triumphs raise
Or sing my great Deliverer's praise?[12]

The spiritual activist was not quieted by his much sought-after experience.

In consideration of whether or not Charles' spirituality conforms to the English ascetic tradition, account has to be taken not only of the content but also the form and purposes of his hymnody. The 1780 *Collection* is particularly important in this respect and raises the technical question about the extent to which John's editorial structure can be said to belong also to Charles. There is no evidence that Charles dissented from John's view famously expressed in the Preface to the *Collection*: 'The hymns are not carelessly jumbled together, but carefully ranged under proper heads, according to the experience of real Christians. So that this book is in effect a little body of experimental and practical divinity.'[13]

The 1780 *Collection* can most naturally be said to be addressed to the individual soul who begins his or her journey conscious only of sin and who needs first to be introduced to the pleasantness of religion and the goodness of God, the certainty of death, judgement, the hope of heaven and the fear of hell. Such an individual soul, having been given a grand tour of the geography of the spiritual world, is then educated about the difference between formal and inward religion. The *Collection* then begins the work of providing this soul with the words to pray for repentance, to articulate a conviction of sin, and to announce and celebrate being brought to the new birth of life with Christ. Here the book thoughtfully pauses to enable backsliders to express their contrition and give thanks for their recovery. At this point (the sheep being safely in the fold) the ordinary work of the believing Christian soul is set out under ten headings. This is what the ordinary Christian soul will be doing throughout his or her Christian life: Rejoicing, Fighting, Praying, Watching, Working, Suffering, Seeking full redemption, Being brought to birth, Being saved, and, lastly, Interceding for the world. In the final section of the *Collection* such souls find themselves in a (Methodist) society meeting where they are given hymns to celebrate their meeting, their giving thanks, their praying together, their parting and their dispersal.[14]

Here is the work of an individual soul described and prescribed by John Wesley, and delivered by the verse of Charles. There are three main observations to be made about this spiritual manual. First, it is addressed to an individual self or soul. Second, it is about what that soul should do. Third, it is about how that soul stands in relation to God. To be sure, this self will be a busy soul doing all that is to be done on the spiritual journey. This is the architecture of an ascetic spiritual structure designed by John but furnished almost entirely by Charles.

There is more to be said about the spirituality of Charles' hymnody than is apparent from the 1780 *Collection*. This is because the *Collection* is designed for the use of Methodist societies prior to their formal separation from the Church of England. Charles' Eucharistic hymns and the hymns he wrote to celebrate the festivals of the Church are not found in this *Collection*; selections of such hymns were added as supplementary material to the 1830 and subsequent hymn books. Frank Whaling has commented on the quality and significance of the hymns for festivals,[15] but the importance of the eucharistic hymns for understanding Charles' spirituality can hardly be overstated. Rattenbury's classic study provides a very substantial starting point for anyone looking for secondary material on the eucharistic hymns.[16] The 166 hymns were first collected together in 1745 and published in *Hymns on the Lord's Supper*. Much has been made of Charles Wesley's use of Daniel Brevint's work on *The Christian Sacrament and Sacrifice*, an extract from which he published as a Preface to the 1745 *Collection* and the structure of which he reproduced in the ordering (and probably in the writing) of the hymns.

Regular eucharistic observance was a part (maybe even at the centre) of Charles' spiritual discipline all his life. It is present in all the spiritual instructions and directories with which he was associated. In his book on *Methodist Spirituality*, Gordon Wakefield observes:

> The Methodist revival was something of a sacramental revival in that the Wesleys presided over crowded communion services, unknown in the church at that time, and wished for more frequent communion than was customary when perhaps three or four times a year was the norm. They seemed to have believed that daily communion was the early church custom . . . The last of the Hymns on the Lord's Supper prays 'restore the daily Sacrifice' and implies that this will herald the coming of the kingdom.[17]

Whaling has noted that the eucharistic hymns 'were occasioned partly by Wesley's reaction against Moravian quietism'.[18] The point here is that participation in the sacraments and particularly at the Eucharist is an active state. Reading the 1745 hymn book is an exhausting business. Central to Wesley's understanding of the sacrament is that the participant, even the reader or singer of his hymns, is drawn in to the drama, the very work of Christ that is being represented and re-enacted in the sacramental action. This matter of the primacy of the participating self in the drama of God is characteristic of the whole of Charles' hymnody but is brought to an intense pitch in the eucharistic hymns 'On sacrifice' and 'Concerning the sacrifice of our persons'. Consider just one hymn:

Amazing love to mortals show'd!
The sinless body of our God
Was fasten'd to the tree.
And shall our sinful members live?
No, Lord, they shall not Thee survive,
They all shall die with Thee.

The feet which did to evil run,
The hands which violent acts have done,
The greedy heart and eyes,
Base weapons of iniquity,
We offer up to death with Thee,
A whole burnt sacrifice.

Our sins are on Thine altar laid,
We do not for their being plead,
Or circumscribe Thy power;
Bound on Thy cross Thou seest them lie:
Let all this cursed *Adam* die,
Die, and revive no more.

Root out the seeds of pride and lust,
That each may of Thy passion boast
Which doth the freedom give:
The world to me is crucified,
And I who on His cross have died
To God for ever live.[19]

The main purpose of Charles' hymns is to serve as a vehicle for the self to participate in the drama of salvation. Charles' spirituality almost always assumes the perspective of the participating self. This participation is active, conscious and self-conscious. All this is strikingly demonstrated in the eucharistic hymns and provides further support to the contention that Charles' spirituality belongs in the English ascetic pastoral tradition.

Thus far it has been loosely argued that there is a correspondence between the importance of the individual self or self-conscious soul in Charles Wesley's spirituality and his place in the English ascetic tradition. The other side of that coin (it may or may not be a contradictory and counter argument) is that Charles is representative of a mystical, spiritual tradition which has at its heart the apophatic and kenotic position that the self is saved only when entirely lost in the unsayable love of God.

Now let me gain perfection's height;
Now let me into nothing fall,
Be less than nothing in thy sight,
And feel that Christ is all in all.[20]

The section 'Concerning the Sacrifice of our Persons' in *Hymns on the Lord's Supper* provides much material in support of this position. Wesley's view is that the goal of the spiritual journey for all selves (seemingly sinful or not) is the death of self.

> Baptized into Thy death
> We sink into thy grave,
> Till Thou the quickening Spirit breathe,
> And to the utmost save.
>
> Thou said'st, 'Where'er I am
> There shall my servant be';
> Master, the welcome word we claim
> And die to live with Thee.[21]

or in a hymn which has survived through into the most recent generations of Methodist hymns books:

> Let Him to whom we now belong,
> His sovereign right assert,
> And take up every thankful song,
> And every loving heart.
>
> He justly claims us for his own,
> Who bought us with a price;
> The Christian lives to Christ alone,
> To Christ alone he dies.
>
> Jesus, thine own at last receive!
> Fulfil our heart's desire!
> And let us to thy glory live,
> And in thy cause expire.
>
> Our souls and bodies we resign:
> With joy we render thee
> Our all, no longer ours, but thine
> To all eternity.[22]

What is mystical about all this is that the goal of Charles' spirituality is an apophatic union with the divine Being. The purpose of life as Charles saw it is not to create a better society on earth (or even in heaven); it is not to cultivate knowledge or beauty (even of God); it is not (in any very normal sense) to receive the reward of being in heaven. For Charles, the end of the ascetic endeavour is not therapeutic, it is not undertaken to do oneself some good or even to make oneself a better person; rather it is to be crucified with Christ, to become not-self, 'lost in wonder, love and praise', to live only by virtue of incorporation into the life of God through dying with Christ.

> Jesus, did they crucify
> Thee, by highest heaven adored?
> Let us also go and die
> With our dearest dying Lord!

Lord, Thou seest our willing heart,
Knows't its uppermost desire
With our nature's life to part,
Meekly on Thy cross t'expire.

Fain we would be all like Thee,
Suffer with our Lord beneath:
Grant us full conformity,
Plunge us deep into Thy death.

Now inflict the mortal pain,
Now exert Thy passion's power,
Let the Man of Sin be slain;
Die the flesh, to live no more.[23]

About the apophatic union little can be said. That is why Charles writes mainly about the journey and the conditions that bring the soul to the edge of its lostness in God. After that, nothing can be said. It is an eschatological vision. Rattenbury and Newport have written on the significance of eschatology in Charles Wesley's spiritual theology. This is important. The overwhelming majority of Charles' hymns are aspirational, they look forward to a future condition. They are about the desire of the soul for that which may well be accomplished and even assured, but still is not yet. The theological debates that took place around these themes in the eighteenth century were to do with the doctrines of perfection and assurance. Charles and his brother were protagonists in both debates. Much of what they had to say about assurance and perfection was to clarify that here were ways of speaking of the overwhelming fullness of desire that the Christian soul can possess for the object of its love. Charles' ascetic spirituality fills the space between the present and the consummation of the soul's encounter with God.

Related to Charles Wesley's eschatological sense of the provisionality of his present spiritual condition is his characteristic use of the conditional tense. This communicates a sense of humility or even reserve in his poetic discourse. It is an attractive aspect of his spirituality that is not often noted:

Son of God if thy free grace
Again hath raised me up,
Called me still to seek thy face,
and given me back my hope;
Still thy timely help afford,
And all thy loving-kindness show;
Keep me, keep me, gracious Lord,
And never let me go[24]

So far this chapter has sought to draw attention to four main characteristics of Charles Wesley's spirituality: first, that it assumes the view point of the self-conscious self; second, that it holds that the self is best lost in the other; third, that it is almost exclusively concerned with encouraging, facilitating, enabling the self's journey to its spiritual destination; and fourth, that this destination may be best described as being a loss of self in a apophatic, mystical union with God. Many who have sung his hymns and who have reflected on them have believed that Charles gave sublime expression to these thoughts and to this spiritual work. But even the father of modern Wesley scholarship, Frank Baker, recognized that there is a problem, not so much with his poetry or even with his theology, but with the disconnectedness of his spiritual world to our own. The last paragraph of Baker's influential work *Charles Wesley as Revealed by His Letters* contains this thought:

> We turn from our study of Charles Wesley as revealed by his letters with a sense that we have been in a spiritual world quite foreign to many Christians of today, a world of the aching sorrows of sin, the throbbing joys of salvation and the utter renunciation of self. To some it may seem not only foreign, but unreal, a fantastic dream-world of the soul . . .[25]

Some scholars have drawn attention to the relationship between Wesleyan spiritual theology and eighteenth-century rationalism and empiricism. A case can be made for noting the apologetic security of locating the basis of theological endeavour in religious experience (cf. Schleiermacher) made the more secure by the agnosticism of its apophatic conclusions. But there is a price to be paid for this, and it is the price of a dangerous disconnectedness between the spiritual world of which Wesley is eloquent and the ordinary conditions of material life about which he is so often disgruntled. If that is true of the relationship between Charles Wesley and his own world, it is even more true about the relationship between Charles' spiritual world and the modern materialist world that we inhabit after Darwin, Marx and Freud. There are two main critical conversations that contemporary Christian ortho-doxy must have with Charles Wesley. The first conversation will be about what it means to be human, and in particular what it means to be a human individual in relation to other individuals. The second conversation is about God, and Charles Wesley's view of God, and in particular what it means for God to be God in relation to creation.

First, then, there is a conversation to be had with Charles about what it means to be an individual self and what it means for that individual self to be in relation to other selves. The question arises because it has been argued here that the first characteristic of Charles' spirituality is that it assumes and stresses the viewpoint of the self-conscious self. Any spiritual theology that can be so characterized will have to address the criticism that it is implic-itly and intrinsically prone to individualism. However, the proposition that Wesley's spirituality is essentially about the journey of an individual soul or self and is therefore vulnerable to the charge of individualism is contested. Methodists have usually claimed for themselves and for their founders a particular and distinctive commitment to various expressions of society and fellowship. The defence case for Charles Wesley against the charge of individ-ualism can and does produce a lot of evidence. His brother famously asserted that there is 'no holiness, but social holiness'.[26]

The defining theological characteristic of the Wesley brothers was their

Arminianism. In contrast to the more limited soteriology of Calvinism and the individualism of reformers and pietists, Arminianism articulated the socially inclusive scope of the work of God. It is possible to pile up verse after verse in which Charles expresses his characteristic belief in the universal scope of the love of God for all. The 1741 collection of hymns *On God's Everlasting Love* was designed for just this controversial purpose.

> O for a trumpet-voice
> On all the world to call,
> To bid their hearts rejoice
> In him who died for all!
> For all my Lord was crucified,
> For all, for all my Saviour died![27]

The case in defence of Charles and against the charge of individualism continues. Methodism simply would not have happened were it not for the Wesleys' commitment to the creation, maintenance and organization of religious societies, societies which they both considered absolutely vital to the spiritual work to which all Christians were called. This is what Methodism was. To speak of connexionalism is to speak about the Wesleys' commitment to the social character of their spiritual organization. It has already been noted that the 1780 hymn book significantly ends with a concluding section for the society. There is no doubt that Charles Wesley and Methodists ever since have prized and celebrated fellowship.

> All praise to our redeeming Lord,
> Who joins us by his grace,
> And bids us, each to each restored,
> Together seek His face.
>
> He bids us build each other up;
> And, gather'd into one,
> To our high calling's glorious hope
> We hand in hand go on.
>
> The gift which he on one bestows,
> We all delight to prove,
> The grace through every vessel flows,
> In purest streams of love.
>
> Even now we speak and think the same,
> And cordially agree,
> Concentred all, through Jesu's name,
> In perfect harmony.
>
> We all partake the joy of one,
> The common peace we feel,
> A peace to sensual minds unknown,
> A joy unspeakable.

And if our fellowship below
In Jesus be so sweet,
What heights of rapture shall we know
When round his throne we meet![28]

That Charles Wesley and his brother prized religious society, spiritual organization and Christian fellowship more than many in their generation is admitted. But they prized these things from the viewpoint of the individual soul seeking union with God, as a means of grace in the economy of salvation. As John wrote in *The Nature, Design and General Rules of the United Societies*, the purpose of a society (i.e. a religious or Methodist society) is to '... watch over one another in love, that they may help each other to work out their salvation ...'[29] Fellowship was understood in an instrumental way from the perspective of individuals seeking salvation. That Charles believed that God desired all people to be finally incorporated in his kingdom of love, definitely added a proleptic element to the significance of fellowship in the religious societies. Nevertheless the viewpoint remains that of the individual human self or soul seeking to be lost in the love of God (with the help of others).

The same case is to be made about the instrumentality of the Wesleys' view of doing good and engaging in social welfare. Again Methodists have made much of the practice of Charles and his brother visiting the poor, the sick and prisoners and of charitable works. Throughout its history the Methodist Church has (rightly) been characterized as a religious movement with a social conscience. The story is invariably begun with the account of the early Oxford Methodists visiting the condemned in Oxford jail. Interestingly it seems as though this practice was initiated not by Charles, nor even by John, but by another of their group, William Morgan. But even here the evidence is that this activity was undertaken primarily for the sake of the spiritual life of the members of the Holy Club. Gordon Wakefield was wrong when he wrote of John that the 'discipline he practised was not simply an ascetic attempt to save his soul, but in order that he might give to the poor ...'[30] The Wesleys' giving to the poor, like their use of money, was precisely part of the ascetic discipline undertaken primarily as part of their spiritual exercises. Wakefield quotes a hymn from the 1780 *Collection* without having read it carefully enough.[31] The last verse unashamedly asserts the instrumental significance of works for the poor as part of the ascetic quest for integrity and salvation.

Thy mind throughout my life be shown,
While listening to the wretch's cry,
The widow's and the orphan's groan,
On mercy's wings I swiftly fly
The poor and helpless to relieve,
My life, my all for them to give.

Thus may I show the Spirit within,
Which purges me from every stain,
Unspotted from the world and sin
My faith's integrity maintain,

The truth of my religion prove
By perfect purity and love.[32]

The strength of Charles Wesley's spirituality (at least for the eighteenth, nineteenth and some of the twentieth centuries) lay in its anthropocentrism. That it assumed the primacy of the viewpoint of the individual fitted it well to the theological, spiritual and cultural needs of the modern age. Whether such an individualistic humanism will serve the Church of the twenty-first century is less clear.

The second critical question to be had about Charles' spirituality concerns his view of God and how he understood the relationship that God has with creation. If Charles' spirituality is strikingly anthropocentric, then his spiritual theology is radically theocentric. If you were to believe what Charles Wesley wrote you would come to the view that the only real significance or value of life is to get to God, to die in God, to be utterly incorporated into the being of God. Charles Wesley doesn't really have much of a view about what God will be doing in heaven or, to put it more conventionally, what the kingdom of heaven will be like.[33] For Charles it is enough to say that heaven will be constituted by the incorporation of the self into the life of God. That is what it means to describe his theology as apophatic. The destination of the spiritual journey is the lover lost in his or her beloved.

Now this is all very well, and it is true to say that the anthropocentricity of the spiritual journey and the theocentrism of its destination provide a robust apologetic base for Charles' spiritual theology, should one be required. But the question that needs to be asked of Charles is about his understanding of the relationship between God and the material order. There is very little evidence that Charles believes God to have any real interest in the material order and in the ordinary stuff of life. Peace, justice, healing, order, liberty, beauty – all these things are mainly metaphors used by Charles to speak about the bliss of the soul lost in God. Charles does not use them in any very obvious sense to describe the material conditions of the Kingdom of God on earth.

One could say that behind Charles' spirituality is a weak theology of creation and Incarnation. And that would be true notwithstanding his most remarkable incarnational hymns.

Let earth and heaven combine,
Angels and men agree,
To praise in songs Divine
Th' incarnate Deity,
Our God contracted to a span,
Incomprehensibly made man.

He laid his glory by,
He wrapped Him in our clay;
Unmark'd by human eye,
The latent Godhead lay;
Infant of days He here became,
And bore the mild *Immanuel's* name.

Unsearchable the love
That hath the Saviour brought;
The grace is far above
Or man or angel's thought:
Suffice for us, that God we know,
Our God is manifest below.

He deigns in flesh to' appear,
Widest extremes to join,
To bring our vileness near,
And make us all Divine:
And we the life of God shall know,
For God is manifest below.

Made perfect first in love,
And sanctified by grace,
We shall from earth remove,
And see His glorious face;
His love shall then be fully show'd,
And man shall all be lost in God.[34]

Often and rightly cited as one of the greatest hymns on the Incarnation of any age, even this hymn demonstrates how Wesley's view of the Incarnation was subordinated to his doctrine of atonement. Unlike F. D. Maurice or the late nineteenth-century Anglo-Catholics, Charles did not use the Incarnation to speak of the divine significance of the natural and material order. Charles Wesley's God became incarnate almost exclusively for the purposes of rescuing human souls from the material order by clutching them to himself even in the embrace of death. For later English theologians the atonement was the consequence of the Incarnation. But for Charles (as indeed for all eighteenth-century theologians) the Incarnation was but the dramatic means that God chose to secure the atonement. Indeed, most of Charles' theology is woven around this view of the atonement. It is not a substitutionary or Anselmic view of the atonement. Instead it is a dramatic act of divine kenosis and self sacrifice to establish and secure the possibility of the union of the soul with its God. For what it is worth the death of God is central to Charles' sacrificial understanding of atonement and references to the death of God abound, especially in the eucharistic hymns.

All of this offers some suggestions as to how Incarnation and atonement are related in the context of Charles' mystical and still apophatic theology. They constitute central acts in the drama of a love affair between a (possibly lonely) human self-conscious self and his or her God whom otherwise would remain for ever on the other side of death. Charles' doctrines of Incarnation and atonement do surprisingly little to redeem the natural order. It is then not surprising that his spirituality seems dangerously dissociated from the ordinary stuff of life.

With this in mind it seems significant that the biographical material out of which a full account of Charles Wesley's spirituality has yet to be constructed is fragmentary and not sufficiently prepared for the task. Somehow the ordinary stuff of Charles' life wasn't treasured enough for it to have been preserved and studied in the way that his hymns have been treasured, preserved, studied and used. This state of affairs has persisted into twentieth-century and modern Methodist scholarship which has chosen not to prioritize the letters and the life in comparison to the attention it has given to the verse and other parts of the Charles Wesley legacy. This is no accident. There is a real and troublesome dissociation between Charles' spiritual theology and the ordinary stuff of life, and this is not unrelated to the concern expressed here about Charles Wesley's God and God's lack of interest in God's own creation. Here are some expressions or illustrations of the issue at hand.

While undertaking a reading of the largest and possibly determinative section of the 1780 *Collection*, 'For Believers Rejoicing', the reader is struck by a change of focus and emphasis in the hymns 215–17 beginning 'I'll praise my maker while I've breath . . .' The change has to do with this matter in question. The previous hymn 'When Israel out of Egypt came . . .' is about the exodus, but sees that event and its associated miracles as significant not for any improvement that might have been experienced in the temporal conditions of the Israelites but as an epiphany, a revelation of the might and power of God himself. Indeed the hymn concludes:

> And all things as they change proclaim
> The Lord eternally the same.[35]

The following hymn, 'I'll praise my maker while I've breath . . .', takes a quite different view of the purposes and work of Israel's God at that time:

> Happy the man whose hopes rely
> On Israel's God; he made the sky,
> And earth, and seas, with all their train;
> His truth for ever stands secure;
> He saves th'oppressed, he feeds the poor,
> And none shall find his promise vain.
>
> The Lord pours eyesight on the blind,
> The Lord supports the fainting mind;
> He sends the labouring conscience peace;
> He helps the stranger in distress,
> The widow and the fatherless,
> And grants the prisoner sweet release.[36]

This hymn clearly has an interest in the liberation of the people of Israel and in the improvement in the material conditions of their lives. It understands the liberation and salvation of the people of Israel to be something which happens in material history and not something merely illustrated on the stage of history as metaphor. Of course it turns out that the hymns 215–17 are not from Charles at all, but are John's adaptations of Isaac Watts' *Psalms of David* (Psalms 146 f.). Charles' spirituality, on the other hand, operates with a dissociated and essentially metaphorical view of the ordinary history of this world.

Reference has been made to the fragmentary and unsatisfactory nature of the sources of Charles' biography. There is, however, more than enough of the biography to supply material illustrative of the disjuncture between Charles' intensified and enraptured spiritual vision and the ordinary stuff of his life. As it happens, Charles is often compared favourably with his brother in this respect. His clearly happy marriage and successful domestic life are cited as evidence of his 'humanity'. The comparison with his brother may well be true. There is no doubt from the letters that Charles was much in love with his wife Sally and was not afraid to express his feelings for her in poetry and other ways. Still there seems to be a problem about the relationship between his enraptured spirituality and the rest of his life. It seems a very great distance from 'the dungeon flamed with light' to the arrangements he needed to make to move the family cat from Bristol to London in 1771.

A notorious though happily not typical illustration of this is found in Charles' correspondence with John immediately following his marriage to Sally. Charles was as usual sick, but what follows is not indicative of a happy and integrated spirituality. Charles protests to his brother that all is well because he still prefers death to life and ministry to marriage.

> More zeal, more life, more power, I have not felt for some years: . . . so that hitherto marriage has been no hindrance. You will hardly believe it sits so light upon me. I forgot my wife (can you think it?) as soon as I left her. Some farther proof I had of my heart on Saturday last, when the fever threatened most. I did not find, so far as I can say, any unwillingness to die on account of any I should leave behind. Neither did death appear less desirable than formerly; which I own gave me great pleasure, and made me shed tears of joy . . .[37]

Were a full-length critical study of Charles' spirituality to be undertaken, this is the point at which a psychoanalytic account would need to be given of Charles' inner world. The results of such an analysis would need to be interpreted carefully and not reductively in the context of a wider appreciation of Charles' spirituality. Were this to be undertaken it would be important to give further attention to a study of what Charles had to say in both verse and prose about the relationship between inward and outward religion, derived as it was from William Law and the German mystics. This material will need to be reconsidered in the light of the dissociation of sensibility to which this chapter has drawn attention. In the meantime it is only fair to note that this view of Christian spirituality which stresses the primacy of the individual soul's inner relationship with God is the one which has been largely adopted by contemporary movements in evangelical and charismatic spirituality, perhaps following Wesley in this respect. Nevertheless, it seems to fall considerably short of the non-dualist account that Christian orthodoxy wishes to give of itself and its spiritual endeavour.

This chapter has sought to offer a critical account of the main delineating characteristics of Charles Wesley's spirituality. It has found that spirituality to be both ascetic and mystical. In either and both cases it is intensely so. Charles Wesley's asceticism is the disciplined exercise of the desire for God. Charles Wesley's mysticism is the account he gives of the goal of that desire, the place where the self is lost in God. Wesley's spirituality is anthropocentric in that it takes the viewpoint of the human self and is highly conscious, self-conscious of that viewpoint. While being almost frighteningly innocent of any understanding of self that would later come with Freudian and post-Freudian psychology, it is possible that Charles Wesley's spirituality did much to develop the modern sense of self and establish the self as an object for analysis and study. Nevertheless, the connection between Charles' asceticism and his mysticism is that they both speak of the loss of self. The first speaks of the spiritual work to be undertaken in respect of the loosing of self. The second speaks of the hoped-for outcome, the lostness of self in the divine Other.

It has sometimes been noted that much Wesley and Methodist scholarship has been done by insiders and has tended towards hagiography. Partly as a corrective to this tendency, this study has drawn attention to two areas of critical weakness in Charles' spiritual theology. The first is the centrality of the self-conscious self in Charles' work which makes it vulnerable to the charge of individualism, and that notwithstanding the importance of fellowship and religious society in the life and work of Charles and his brother. The second area of critical weakness is the shadow side of his theocentric mystical theology. The spirituality that issues from this theocentric mystical theology is marked by a dissociated sensibility which values the material world only as a metaphorical stage on which the drama of salvation is acted out. The strength of Charles Wesley's spirituality is the intensity and clarity of his preoccupation with the human self and the divine Other. Its weakness is its underlying individualism and dissociated sensibility.

By way of a constructive conclusion, and notwithstanding these criticisms, it might be suggested that there is here an account of the dynamics of love that is of theological, spiritual and anthropological interest. The theological narrative behind Charles' spirituality asserts the absolute priority of God. The intrinsic otherness of God results in a certain apophaticism in Charles' spirituality. Not much can be said about this union with God. It will be what it will be. What can, however, be spoken about and indeed practised, are disciplines for the cultivation of selflessness. There is a logic to all of this. If what is most desired is union with God in God's otherness, all that can be spoken about in the meantime is the kenosis, the giving up and loosing of self. And that is what we find in Charles Wesley's spirituality. But if you want to know how it works, the answer in summary is that it is theocentric, apophatic, kenotic and ascetic. In Charles Wesley's spirituality each term implies the others.

If love may be understood as the movement from self to the Other then it may be that Charles is offering a description of its dynamics. This was Charles' view and he was not embarrassed to claim that the whole business of Christianity and the drama of salvation was the enactment of the drama of love:

Thy nature, and Thy name, is Love.[38]

It certainly is the case that there is more to be said about love and indeed about the love of God than is said by Charles Wesley. It is possible that he might even be wrong that the fundamental dynamic of love is the loosing of self in the other. It is also possible that he was right. Whether he was right or wrong, he gave the idea exquisite expression:

Love divine, all loves excelling,
Joy of heaven, to earth come down,
Fix in us thy humble dwelling,
All thy faithful mercies crown!
Jesu, thou art all compassion,
Pure, unbounded love thou art;
Visit us with thy salvation!
Enter every trembling heart.

Come, almighty to deliver,
Let us all thy grace receive;
Suddenly return, and never,
Never more thy temples leave.
Thee we would be always blessing,
Serve thee as thy hosts above,
Pray, and praise thee without ceasing,
Glory in thy perfect love.

Finish then thy new creation,
Pure and spotless let us be;
Let us see thy great salvation
Perfectly restored in thee;
Changed from glory into glory,
Till in heaven we take our place,
Till we cast our crowns before thee,
Lost in wonder, love, and praise.[39]

## Notes

1 M. Thornton, *English Spirituality: An outline of ascetical theology according to the English pastoral tradition* (Cambridge, MA: Cowley Publications, 1986), 282.

2 As quoted in Thornton, *English Spirituality*, 17.

3 Charles Wesley to Dr Chandler; quoted in Newport, *Sermons*, 14.

4 Baker, *Charles Wesley as Revealed by his Letters*, 13.

5 This fragment is attributed to John Wesley and reproduced in F. Whaling, ed., *John and Charles Wesley: Selected writings and hymns*, Classics of Western Spirituality (London: SPCK, 1981), 85–7.

6 Gill, *First Methodist*, 49.

7 Whaling, *John and Charles Wesley*, 16.

8 Baker, *Charles Wesley as Revealed by his Letters*, 22.

9 B. W. Tabraham, *Brother Charles* (Peterborough: Epworth, 2003), 34.

10 Tabraham, *Brother Charles*, 36.

11 *PW*, 4.446; cf. *Hymns and Psalms*, No. 46.

12 *BE*, 7.116.

13 *BE*, 7.74.

14 *BE*, 7.77f.

15 Whaling, *John and Charles Wesley*, 33.

16 J. Ernest Rattenbury, *The Eucharist Hymns of John and Charles Wesley* (London: Epworth Press, 1948).

17 G. S. Wakefield, *Methodist Spirituality* (Peterborough: Epworth, 1999), 26.

18 Whaling, *John and Charles Wesley*, 28.

19 *Hymns on the Lord's Supper*, No. 135 (in Rattenbury, 238).

20 *BE*, 7.555.

21 *Hymns on the Lord's Supper*, No. 130 (in Rattenbury, 237).

22 *BE*, 7.590–1; cf. *Hymns and Psalms*, No. 698.

23 *Hymns on the Lord's Supper*, No. 154 (in Rattenbury, 244).

24 *BE* 7.305

25 Baker, *Charles Wesley as Revealed by his Letters*, 149f.

26 This remark is found in the preface to the Wesley brothers' publication *Hymns and Sacred Poems* (London: William Strahan, 1739); cf. *PW*, 1.xxii.

27 *Op. cit.* and *BE*, 7.123.

28 This was not included in the 1780 text; cf. *PW*, 4.252 and *Hymns and Psalms*, No. 753.

29 *Op. cit.* in Whaling, *John and Charles Wesley*, 108.

30 Wakefield, 26.

31 Tabraham, *Brother Charles*, 17 is more correct on this point '. . . the main purpose of these "good works" was to contribute to their own moral and spiritual advancement'.

32 *BE*, 7.522 (incorrectly referenced in Wakefield, 27).

33 Cf. Revelation 21.4.

34 *PW*, 4.109–10; cf. *Hymns and Psalms*, No. 109.

35 *BE*, 7.349.

36 *BE*, 7.350.

37 Baker, *Charles Wesley as Revealed by his Letters*, 68. Some have come to Charles' defence here by suggesting that this letter may tell us more about John's pathology than that of Charles, but the letter implies a shared perspective on this matter.

38 *BE*, 7.251; cf. *PW*, 2.175.

39 *BE*, 7.545–7; cf. *PW*, 4.219.

# 26. 'A most solemn season of love': Charles Wesley and Marriage in Early Methodism

## ANNA M. LAWRENCE

The subject of Charles Wesley's marriage to Sarah Gwynne illustrates how Methodists in general, and Charles in particular, thought of marriage, sexual relationships and the connection between earthly and divine passions. As with most Methodists, Charles exhibited some ambivalence about the purpose of secular love. But unlike his brother, he resolved that his marriage to Sarah Gwynne was a divine act, unquestionably positive towards his spiritual development.

Inevitably, when discussing the subject of Charles Wesley, comparisons to John Wesley arise. This is especially true in works that deal with the subject of the brothers' attitudes towards marriage. Through the 1740s, prior to the brothers' respective marriages, Charles was as important as John in his early leadership of Methodist societies.[1] However, as Rack notes, John and Charles differed significantly in 'one important and perhaps fateful respect': their attitude towards marriage and their choice of marriage partners (though of course one could argue that there were many other significant and, in the end, fateful differences between the two brothers). Hence one of Charles Wesley's biographers, Frederick Gill, remarked, 'In nothing did the brothers differ more than in their approach to marriage. John sailed recklessly into it (after several near shipwrecks), but Charles came to it naturally. John was secretive, where Charles was open. John married a vixen, but Charles had the sense to choose a good wife.'[2]

A good part of their differences has been attributed to their dissimilar social proclivities. Gill notes that Charles was a social type at Oxford, 'never at a loss for friends . . . at the centre of a lively group'.[3] As Gill describes it, Charles 'indulged in a gay and innocent round of excitement.[4] It was a natural reaction after his strenuous years at Westminster and the spartan background of Epworth. When John, who was of a cooler and less impetuous nature, frowned on these diversions, as he called them, Charles retorted with spirit: "What, would you have me be a saint all at once?"'[5]

Charles had a passing interest in a young London actress, Molly Buchanan, and indeed had a brief involvement with this 'pretty creature'.[6] However, as Charles began to be serious about Methodism and reform his life along this system of self-discipline, his interest in stage beauties faded.[7] These dalliances now seemed to lack any real romantic conviction on Charles' part, and appeared insignificant compared to the work he would take up as he led a life of piety with his brother and began to form the Holy Club at Oxford. In analysing the Wesleys' bachelor years, Rack seems to agree with their friend and fellow Methodist James Hutton's assessment that Charles and John were 'in danger from emotional young women'. Rack underlines this point: 'The danger for men in his position in an emotional religious movement was indeed considerable.'[8] This seems to give too much credence to the idea that evangelical women would naturally have designs on the young preachers, but Rack does well to try to shift the blame of emotionality from the women (in Hutton's remarks) to the movement itself.

On one occasion, Charles did have to defend himself against charges that that he had been sexually inappropriate with a woman: in 1745, rumours reached the Bishop of London that a woman charged Wesley with 'committing or offering to commit lewdness with her'.[9] Wesley's side is the historical evidence we are left with, as he addressed the charges in a letter to the Bishop, Edmund Gibson. In February 1745, he wrote in his defence, 'It is now twenty years since I began working out my salvation, in all which time God, in whose presence I speak, has kept me from committing any act of adultery or fornication . . . I never did the action . . . I never harboured any such design in my heart.'[10] It would be difficult not to believe the sincerity of those words or doubt the transparency he claimed to possess. Still, it is impossible to say for certain whether there really was no compromising act or transgression of word or deed, no matter how slight.

The arena in which Charles first faced his trouble in relating to women was that of his time on the Georgia mission (1735–6). Both Rack and Gill delve into the case of the women who presumably foiled their mission there. In John's case, his affair with Sophy Hopkey makes her one of the 'Serpents in Eden', as Rack's chapter on Georgia is titled.[11] In addition, there were other women, Mrs Hawkins and Mrs Welch, who caused some trouble for the brothers. These two women led Charles to believe that they had had adulterous affairs with Oglethorpe. Charles then reported these accusations to Oglethorpe himself, while the women told Oglethorpe that Wesley was fabricating slander against them all.[12] In this case, as with the 'serpents in Eden', or the women in Georgia, Rack asserts Wesley's blamelessness in these machinations.[13] Gill writes of Charles Wesley's mission to Georgia: 'What strange fate had brought him to this? There was no "noble savage", not even a field ripe for harvest, only a rough living (and that he would not have minded), office chores, and a pack of angry women. Rarely was a man more pestered by malicious talk and petty intrigue, or less fitted to meet it.'[14] These squabbles over power were somewhat expected in a society as volatile as colonial Georgia. Rack does an admirable job of putting these scandals into perspective, as he lays out the dissonance between the idealized mission in the New World and the reality of disappointment that ensued for the brothers. Oglethorpe did nothing to make Charles' life easier, denying him any real comforts while in his house, and blaming him for unrest among the laity.[15] Another of Charles' biographers, Mabel Brailsford, emphasizes that he was not an effective clergyman in

Georgia, or even a good assistant to Oglethorpe, and this allowed the breach between them to develop. While Charles was seemingly unaware of these shortcomings, they did not make him blameless in his belief of the rumours and his reporting them to Oglethorpe.[16]

Part of the difficulty in assessing past narratives of the brothers' relations with women has to do with the language that biographers and contemporaries assigned to the women involved. If they were not 'Mothers in Israel', they might deserve titles such as 'the designing actress',[17] 'brace of ferrets',[18] 'shrew',[19] 'vixen',[20] 'serpents'[21] and 'pack of angry women'.[22] In each case, Charles was lucky to escape the designs/plots/schemes of these nefarious individuals.[23] In fact, of course, both the Wesley brothers possessed short-comings that made them ill-suited to the Georgia mission, in particular their rigidity in certain social and religious expectations. In addition, we cannot be sure that the women, who were 'scheming' romantically or otherwise, did not have legitimate expectations or disappointments in the men. It seems as if, in order to believe that these men were laudable, one needs to discredit the women around them. Fortunately, no such title has survived to blight the character of Sarah Gwynne, Charles' wife.

Charles was certainly more suited to marriage than his brother, and Oglethorpe may have been insightful in this regard, as he counselled Wesley to marry following the failed Georgia mission: 'On many accounts I should recommend to you marriage, rather than celibacy. You are of a social temper, and would find in a married state the difficulties of working out your salvation exceedingly lessened and your helps as much increased.'[24] Charles did not have the same wrestlings with human nature as did John; Charles left behind no parallel extended expositions on the pros and cons of marriage or whether holiness precluded sexuality. While John Wesley's well-known affairs with Sophy Hopkey and Grace Murray both ended disastrously, Charles only had one serious romance, and she became his wife. When he was preaching in Wales in August 1747, he met Sally Gwynne. Though she was 19 years his junior, their age difference seemed not to matter. Her father, Marmaduke Gwynne, was a convert of Howel Harris, so she had a good Methodist pedigree and there was no family opposition to their courtship on that count.[25] In a short time, their correspondence developed from a spiritual into a romantic one, though still largely concerned with spiritual development. Charles wrote a poem during this time:

> Two are better far than one
> For counsel or for fight
> How can one be warm alone
> Or serve his God aright?'[26]

Charles never seemed to question or doubt his path to courtship with Sarah, 'in telling contrast with John Wesley's hesitant and self-questioning love-affairs'.[27] During the courtship and protracted marriage settlement, Wesley never betrayed much doubt on the matter. He was meant to marry Sarah, he believed; God had willed it so.

John wrote about his own marriage that it had not altered his itinerancy 'one iota' – he was anxious to maintain that marriage had done no harm to his spiritual goals.[28] Charles was more balanced about his duties to marriage and fellow Methodists, and this balance is probably largely responsible for his successful union to Sarah. As most married Methodist preachers would have to concede, marriage almost certainly changed their commitment to itinerancy, particularly when children were involved. It became difficult for Charles and others to be constantly on the road, especially when illness and death of their children begged his presence at home. His own experience with the loss of children made him a sympathetic ear to fellow Methodists who struggled with the same tragedies.

Was matrimony responsible for Charles' giving up of itinerancy?[29] Anglican evangelical John Berridge commented in 1770 that '[m]atrimony has quite maimed poor Charles',[30] but there is good reason to doubt this theory. Charles' growing dissatisfaction with the moves in some quarters towards separation from the established church, and his well-documented disagreements with fellow preachers, made it difficult for him to be an effective leader or itinerant himself, at least after 1756.[31] However, the assessment that Rack eventually offers, 'in the end the traditional view that Charles's chief contribution to Methodism was in his hymns is probably correct', seems unwarranted.[32] This judgement hinges on his early abandonment of itinerancy and inability to mobilize or organize the preachers, but it ignores his significant contributions to organizing and mobilizing the laity. Charles was the human side of the Wesley brothers, and his marriage and commitment to social concourse counterbalanced John's sometimes chilly assessment of earthly commitments. This assessment is based upon a study of the voluminous letters between Charles Wesley and laity, particularly correspondence with important female laity.[33] Letters were a vital channel of communication in early Methodism, knitting disparate societies together and providing support for the laity between periodic visits by itinerant ministers. Additionally, Charles was always accessible and centrally located, whether in Bristol or London, to counsel Methodist laity in person.

Charles Wesley was certainly more supportive of marriage than his brother. As for the Methodist layperson, John Wesley was fairly divided about whether matrimony was the best state for those committed to Methodism, perhaps reflecting his own failures in that arena.[34] John tended to see marriage as a tortured puzzle, where the issue of how one would be able to carry on spiritual development and duties was compromised. In addition, sexuality and its place within spiritual development was a real question for him. Meanwhile, Charles was more positive regarding the prospect of Methodists marrying, and he wrote letters to married laity and preachers that reflected positively on the benefits of his partnership with Sarah.[35] Charles proclaimed that his wedding 'was a most solemn season of love! Never had I more of the divine presence at the sacrament.'[36] He stressed here his belief that marriage was a religious deed. His obvious enjoyment of marriage was a model to which other Methodists aspired. As John Johnson wrote to Charles: 'By the Happiness I have with my own Partner, I often, say, I know two Happy marriages at least; yours is one and my own is another; for this I desire to Praise the Lord also.'[37]

The danger in all deep attachments, including marriage, was that believers might value their temporal relationships more than their relationship to God. More than that, Wesleyan Methodists stressed unity of belief and social regularity. Methodism was more than a religion: it was a way of life. Private unions, especially between believers and non-believers, were troublesome to many Methodist preachers and lay persons alike. If marriages took individuals away from the unity of the Methodist religious culture, then they were certainly obstacles to the Methodist family.

The tendency of Methodists to de-emphasize their own desires in the case of marriage points to the fact that the arena of marriage, and sexual decisions more broadly, were seen as a potentially dangerous place for the true believer. The decision to marry had to be brought before God, and approved by divine will, or the believer ran the risk of being deluded by satanic or earthly snares. The result of such a mis-step could be catastrophic – it may indeed be a wandering from one's true religious path.

Charles Wesley had fewer quandaries about his own marriage. It was perhaps this and his certainty about the rightnesss of marriage in general that is reflected in the extent to which the laity felt comfortable with approaching him about issues within their own marriages and children. One can see evidence of this in the many letters from laity and preachers which raise issues regarding such matters as searching for the right mate, married life, and children.[38] For example, in striking contrast to John Wesley's chilly response to preacher John Valton's marriage in 1787, Valton felt free to write to Wesley about the positive aspects of marriage. Valton had declared:

With respect to domestic Affairs, I enjoy all the benefits that I expected from such a suitable Union. Our love increases, and we are, I believe, mutually helpful. I do not know where I could have met with such a safe and suitable Partner. I see, I own, I adore the kind indulgence of Heaven. She does not abate my zeal, nor lessen my love for GOD; but encourages and animates my Soul in the 'Wars of the Lord'. Thanks be to GOD for the precious Gift.[39]

Valton's description of his marriage underlined the holiness of matrimony and the idea that women were vital partners in individual spiritual development. In Valton's case, where his diary describes someone who was intensely insecure about the damage that errant sexual thoughts could bring to his soul, marriage was a salve.[40] Charles Wesley did not exhibit such a tendency towards despondency in his own writings, but his own description of the spiritual partnership of marriage is strikingly similar.

In his letters, Charles wrote that his imminent union with Sarah was a gift from God, the phrasing that Valton would echo back to him 40 years later. He wrote to Sarah in January of 1749:

My own Heart you have a Right to know even every thought thereof but I know not how to describe it. I dare not with any Degree of confidence expect so great a Blessing as – in this Life. Hope & I had long since shook hands & parted; & all my Expectation was to go softly all my Days, & be saved at last as by Fire. Providence (for I can ascribe it to Nothing else) has strangely *brought* me, the Best Gift Heaven cd bestow on Man in Paradise; at best it *seems*, as it were, within my Reach. Yet does my Soul *humble at* the Prospect & remains as a Weaned Child. What afflicts me most is that I cannot pray. My every Breath *ought* to be Prayer or Praise. Help me my beloved Friend to wrestle for The Blessing of Divine Love & now lift up your Heart with me . . .[41]

Interestingly, Charles Wesley here described his union with Sarah as part of his spiritual development. Before meeting her, he had seen that 'Hope & I had long since shook hands & parted'; he was only waiting for death and the salvation to follow. However, as he phrased it, providence had given him the 'Best Gift' that God could give in allowing him to have a partner such as Sarah Gwynne. Again, he phrases his love for Sarah as part and parcel of his love for God, and the goals of his spiritual life later in the same letter:

Who knoweth what a Month may bring forth? In half that Time One or Both of us may be secure of The great End we aim at in this Alliance, & meet our Lord in Paradise. How inexpressibly sure am I – that if this *is* it is Best. Full of this Hope I defy – Death's subtle seed within . . . For we are persuaded that wither Death, nor Life, nor Angels, nor Principalities, nor Powers, nor things present, nor things to come, nor Height nor Depth, nor any other Creature shall be able to separate us from ye Love of God in Christ Jesus, or from that Love wherewith, for His sake, we love each other.[42]

Charles was sure that his partnership with Sarah only strengthened his spiritual development and ministry. Sarah Gwynne was clearly a part of his mission, as he confirms in his letters to her. If she had concerns about being in his way, he was clear to state that he took her with him everywhere and she strengthened his ministry in every respect.[43]

It is clear in examining the couple's correspondence written during their courtship that there was a very romantic love growing between them. It would be untrue to the source to try to separate the romantic from the spiritual. A truer expression of the matter, for both Charles and Sarah, was that their spiritual and romantic lives were intertwined. They had begun corresponding on spiritual matters in September 1747, shortly after they met during Charles' visit to Methodists at Garth in Brecknockshire. Wesley had become acquainted with her family and stayed at their family home for five days. Their particular attachment to each other seems to have sprung up rather quickly. Wesley wrote on 17 September 1747 that his heart was 'deeply engaged' for Sarah, her sisters and cousin.[44] He had not yet let her know that he was singularly interested in her and thinking of proposing marriage to her. He wrote of the time: 'It was then a distant first thought, not likely to ever come to a proposal; as I had not given the least hint, either to Miss Gwynne or the family.'[45]

After leaving Wales, he began a long tour of preaching in Ireland, when he communicated his 'embryo intentions' to his brother John.[46] Charles noted then that John 'neither opposed, nor much encouraged' his interest in Sarah Gwynne.[47] Despite this lack of encouragement, the romance seemed to be an unstoppable course. They had reached a new level of intimacy in their relationship by late spring of 1748, after Charles spent some time being nursed back to health in Sarah's care. In his shorthand, he wrote in his journal that he had proposed to her on 3 April 1748.[48] He wrote, 'At night my dearest Sally, like my guardian angel, attended me . . . I asked her if she could trust herself with me for life and with a noble simplicity she readily answered me she could.'[49]

However, to his friends he maintained that this matter was still under deliberation. He wrote in his journal in April of 1748:

> To-day I rode over to Shoreham, and told Mr. Perronet all my heart. I have always had a fear, but no *thought,* of marrying, for many years past, even from my preaching of the Gospel. But within this twelvemonth that thought had forced itself in, 'How know I, whether it be best for me to marry, or no?' Certainly better now than later: and if not now, what security that I shall not then? It should be now, or not at all. Mr. Perronet encouraged me to pray, and wait for a providential opening. I expressed the various searching of my heart in many hymns on the important occasion.[50]

In his 'embryo' thoughts of marriage, Charles had stressed his caution on the subject. But he also expressed a certain conviction in his journal that this was the time to marry, or else he would never do so. Before he shared his feelings directly with Sarah or the rest of her family, he sought out the counsel of his brother. Charles seems somewhat disappointed in his brother's tepid response to his desire for marriage, but it could not have completely surprised him given the embryo state of his own relationship with Gwynne. Vincent Perronet was someone who would remain a trusted adviser for Charles, and he seemed cautious, though not disapproving of Charles' intentions, advising him to do what many Methodists did at the time, 'wait for a providential opening'. According to Gareth Lloyd's interpretation of his writings at this time, Charles was immediately cautious and fearful following his proposal to Sarah. Lloyd speculates that it was part of Wesley's nature to be cautious and pessimistic, but he also notes that their age difference, his lack of income and home, and perhaps also John Wesley's seeming disapproval may have been factors in his pessimism over the affair.[51]

With Perronet's advice in mind, Charles Wesley turned to writing hymns on the subject, looking for divine direction. These hymns ask God to 'Guide my wandering Footsteps right', asking God to be a 'faithful Pilot'.[52] Charles hopes and trusts that God will

> make thy Counsel plain,
> Thou shalt teach me what to do,
> Signify thy Love's Decree
> Shew me all thy Blessed Will –
> When, & how I leave to Thee.[53]

In his hymns, he emphasized the theme of submitting earthly loves and their passions to his love of God and Christ. Wesley was clear that this love could not overwhelm his love of the divine.

From all Earthly Expectation
Set me free
Seize for Thee
All my strength of Passion.
Into absolute subjection
Be it brought
Every thought,
Every fond Affection.
That which most my Soul requires
For thy sake
Hold it back
Purge my Best Desires.
Keep from me thy loveliest Creature,
Till I prove
Jesus' Love
Infinitely sweeter.[54]

By August 1748, Charles Wesley was assured of their imminent union; Wesley and Gwynne's correspondence had reached a new level of intimacy. He wrote to Sarah that he expected to hear that 'ye have met constantly every morning and evening to sing and pray together both for yourselves and your absent friends. I can hardly reckon myself in that number, so continually do I bear you upon my heart.'[55] A few months later, he wrote that she was always with him, wherever he went, that every spot in the road brought his 'dearest friend' to his mind.[56] By mid-December 1748, they have clearly confirmed their intent to marry. Charles writes, 'I need not, cannot tell you the Joy of our Meeting. It was a Fortaste of the Happiness we shall feel . . .'[57]

While their courtship seemed to be unstoppable and fated for a successful marriage, Charles Wesley still sought others' approval to confirm that this marriage was right for him. At first, he and Sarah were challenged in their courtship by friends, who doubted the suitability of this match. This clearly bothered Sarah in her letters to him, but Charles was steadfast in his response that they should be ignored altogether. As to his friends who feared that this marriage would hinder his ministry, he characterized these friends' doubts as 'groundless fears'; Sarah would never 'be given to us but as a blessing, both to me and all my spiritual children. I dare stake my soul upon it; *and I do.*'[58] Rather simplistically, Wesley saw his friends' support of Sarah Gwynne as a test of their true religiosity: 'My friends would not be mine, if they were not equally *yours*, if they did not love you as their own soul . . . Jesus loveth you; therefore his disciples do the same: And their love, like his, will increase towards you throughout eternity.'[59]

However, clearly some of their friends failed this test. Particularly, Molly Carteret had voiced her opposition to others in the Methodist circle and convinced a few to lend their own opposition as well. The stalwart friends, like Elizabeth Vigor and Sarah Perrin, would not be convinced that Wesley's choice of mate was anything but divinely willed and certainly suitable. However, one woman was convinced by Carteret's arguments and came forward with a divine revelation that she said showed the error of this match. Charles had 'in

10 words speaking . . . made her recant her revelation and entirely acquiesce'.[60] He also felt that Carteret had made a 'cat's paw' of his friend Edward Perronet, who had believed that Wesley should marry his [Perronet's] sister.[61] However, as Charles wrote in January 1748: 'Ned has since recanted and begged my pardon, being set right by his father.'[62] He underlined that only Molly Carteret stood strong in doubting that it was 'the will of God in this matter'; they waited only on her parents to confirm that the couple's consciences would be clear and open to the marriage.[63]

As for his own family, they were generally supportive of his marriage to Sarah Gwynne. His sister, Martha Hall, wrote to Wesley in April 1749:

> Surrounded as I am with distress on every side I find my heart can rejoice for you. I verily believe the Glory of the Lord is Risen upon you, and your Sun shall no more go down! . . . May the God of *our* Fathers bless you both, and enable you to Glorify him all your Days by showing forth to all Men that he Wills the Marriage State shou'd be.[64]

Of course, Martha Hall had more than her share of first-hand knowledge on how the marriage state should *not* be. Her description of being surrounded by distress could only refer to her own troubled marriage to Westley Hall. Still, she was optimistic for the sake of her brother, and believed that God had sanctified his marriage to Sarah. John Wesley seemed also supportive of Charles' and Sarah's union, after some initial hesitancy perhaps.

It has been argued by many of Charles' biographers, including Frederick Gill and Frank Baker, that his brother John was supportive of the match.[65] Gareth Lloyd takes a different perspective, in which he stresses John's ambivalence towards the marriage at key moments.[66] Certainly, Charles' marriage had the potential to cause a rift between the brothers, and there is evidence that while John was generally supportive at many times, he could also be passively and actively resistant to this wedding taking place.

On 11 November 1748, many months after Charles had proposed to Sarah, he did his fraternal duty and notified his brother of his intentions. He wrote:

> My brother and I having promised each other, (as soon as he came from Georgia,) that we would neither of us marry, or take any step towards it, and without the other's knowledge and consent, to-day I fairly and fully communicated every thought of my heart. He had proposed three persons to me, S.P., M.W., and S.G.; and entirely approved my choice of the last. We consulted together about every particular, and were of one heart and mind in all things.[67]

The Wesley brothers had seemed to work out an accord on the matter; John was frequently called upon to serve as a mediator in the settlement of the marriage, and Charles referred to his support in letters to Sarah Gwynne during their courtship. He gently chided her for her reluctance to write to John, 'Why at a loss to write to *my* brother? Because you are welcomed to own him for *your's*? One little child need not fear another. He knows every thought of my heart concerning you: for they are his own, and none upon earth loves you better, allowing me but one exception.'[68]

John's support of the marriage ended up being quite instrumental to the success of Charles' negotiations of the marriage settlement.[69] He wrote to Sarah about his brother's constant support of the marriage in the winter of 1748. John had urged him to go to Garth and to negotiate in person with Sarah's mother, Sarah Gwynne senior, in December of 1748. These negotiations were in fact the only thing standing in the way of their marriage, as the Gwynnes required proof that Sarah would be well provided for, especially if she outlived Charles. And this was a certain possibility, considering the age gap between them. Charles was certainly not offended by the suggestion that he would predecease his young wife: 'It is *not fair* for me, in the noon of life, to wish a friend only in the morning of hers, to accompany *me* to paradise. Many happy years may you labour in the vineyard after I am gone to my reward . . .'[70]

The Gwynnes' approval of the marriage hinged on the amount of the marriage settlement and allowing the publishing proceeds from some of Charles' and John's books to go to Sarah, in order for her to have a personal income that she could live on securely following Charles' death. Sarah conveyed these details to Charles, and reassured him that she knew his support of her would suffice ('I have not doubt your care of me, tho' very unworthy').[71] Sarah did not think it would be proper to talk directly of the matters under dispute, and there were direct correspondences and conversations between Charles and other members of the Gwynne family, predominantly Sarah Gwynne senior. Even when it seemed as though Mrs Gwynne's demands exceeded reason, Charles seemed unflappable in his words to Sarah on the subject: 'Infinitely obliged am I to your [mother] that she would give you to me on any terms. Those she lately proposed are not practicable, but if the thing be of God, I am sure she will recede from them'.[72]

Sarah Gwynne senior was adamant that the settlement be sufficient and would not consent to the marriage without it. Charles felt that the Gwynnes' approval of the marriage, even with these demands, was nothing short of a divine miracle. He wrote to Sarah:

Your dearest [mother's] *consent so far* is plainly miraculous, and what I never expected, although my friends insisted on it, as my duty to make the proposal. I cannot think providence would suffer the matter to proceed so far, were it to stop here. The hinge on which all turns, is not fortune, not even consent of friends (which will *follow* and fall in with the will of providence) but the glory of God and the good of souls (yours especially).[73]

By mid-January 1749, Sarah Gwynne senior was softening and allowing her husband to have the final word in this matter. This seemed to augur well that the wedding would take place.[74]

Charles Wesley's difficulty in getting the marriage settled economically reflected the real impoverished state of Methodist funds, as well as perhaps John Wesley's unwillingness to part with his brother as an itinerant, at any price.[75] A few days after he told his brother about his engagement to Gwynne, in November of 1748, Charles confided to his journal in shorthand, 'Talked with my brother about a provision in case I got married and he said the Church could not afford it. "Then" I thought, "the Church did not deserve a gospel minister".[76] The Gwynnes were prominent landowners, and Sarah was considered a 'gentlewoman'; their marriage would require that she be maintained in the manner to which she was accustomed. This would seem difficult for any itinerant preacher like Charles, who lacked a home and the income necessary for starting a family. The marriage settlement was a difficult one for Charles, John and perhaps Methodists as a whole. The terms of the settlement were that £2,500 be given from the profits on publications to an investment, which would give Sarah £100 annually. The combined publications that were part of this agreement included many of Charles' works, hymn books especially, but also works by John. Therefore, the outcome of this settlement meant diminished profits for the whole Methodist connexion, since much of this profit came out of the Methodist coffers.[77]

Charles saw the eventual resolution of parental opposition to the marriage as providential, an indication of how God supported and desired their marriage. He wrote in retrospect to Sally in 1756:

In reading over the passages of *our* history, you cannot think what love I feel towards every one of *our* family. Your mother, sister, father, cousins, nurse so behaved as to deserve my esteem and love during Life. I look back with delight on every step, every circumstance in that whole design of providential *love*. I rejoice with grateful joy at our blessed union and feel my obligations to every person instrumental therein. Above all I desire to thank my great benefactor for giving you to my bosom; and to fulfil his gracious end by leading you to the marriage of the Lamb.[78]

Generally, despite the fact that this marriage agreement took some time and the Gwynnes were, at times, making somewhat unreasonable demands on Charles, he never wrote an uncertain word to Sarah. His tone, throughout their letters, was one of peaceful resignation to God's will. Sarah had written in January 1749, while the outcome of their marriage settlement was still uncertain, that she accepted whatever the result might be, agreeing with him that it was best to be compliant in this matter. Sarah quoted Charles in a letter, when she responded to him,

My Dearest Friend's Letters comforted me *not a little* finding, such strong Confidence & Trust in the Lord had taken up its residence in your Heart, 'as that if a disappointmt happens (says you) it must be Best, for you, for me, for the whole Church' – those words check'd my fears, for all the future events in this matter.[79]

Sarah wrote later in the same letter,

On thee O Lord will I wait; 'I cannot chuse, Thou canst not Err'. And if we are permitted to *join Hands, as well as Hearts* (the latter we have done already) I shall I'm *firmly persuaded*, receive you as the *Greatest Blessing Heaven co'd bestow* this side the Grave . . .[80]

Charles looked to others for approval of the marriage, particularly the Gwynnes, as signs that this union was blessed by God. He wrote in December 1748, while the marriage was still being settled that any disapproval of the settlement from the Gwynnes, 'I should have received as an absolute prohibition from God. But hitherto it seems as if the way was opened by particular Providence.'[81]

In the final months before their wedding, Charles happily notes in his journal that all members of the Gwynne family seem resolved and supportive of their marriage. He noted, 'Mrs. Gwynne was extremely open and affectionate; has fought many battles against her own relations . . .'[82] These last blockades seemed easily removed during his time in Garth in February 1749.[83] His wedding to Sarah was planned for April 1749. However, as Charles got ready to go to meet his bride in Garth, he was shocked to hear some last-minute doubts from his brother: 'Just as we were setting out for Wales, my brother appeared full of scruples, and refused to go to Garth at all. I kept my temper, and promised, "if he could be satisfied there, to desist". I saw all was still in God's hands, and committed myself to Him.'[84] In fact, John had planned to be busy preaching through to the end of that week, during which they were supposed to have travelled and arrived in Garth for the nuptials.[85] Charles had attempted to be resigned to God's plan on this count, but he was also understandably annoyed with his brother's passive intransigence. After the brothers finally left for Wales, they travelled together, but their relationship was strained by this opposition.[86] By the time they reached Garth on 7 April and talked again with Mrs Gwynne, John was ready finally to sign the settlement, and according to Charles, 'my brother's fears were scattered'.[87] The next day, the couple would be married.

Their wedding day was clearly a religious occasion. On 8 April 1749, Charles, Sally and John arose at 4 a.m. to sing and pray together. At 8 a.m., Sally and Charles walked to the church together. A small group of friends and family were present. Charles notes in his journal that he and Sally remembered the struggle to arrive at this moment, as they approached the door of the church: 'I thought of a prophecy of a jealous friend, "that if we were even at the church-door to be married, she was sure, by revelation, that we could get no farther". We both smiled at the remembrance. We got farther.'[88] While the wedding day was solemn, they both had a sense of humour and triumph over getting to this moment. The approval of family was evident: Sally's father gave her away and John married them. In fact Charles noted, 'My brother seemed the happiest person among us.'[89] After a hymn and prayer, they all walked back to the house for more prayer: 'We were cheerful without mirth, serious without sadness.' This was a fine balance between noting the solemn nature of the event, but still letting the ceremony be lively and happy. A passer-by noted that 'It looked more like a funeral than a wedding.'[90]

Two weeks following their wedding, Charles left Sarah to do his 'Master's work'.[91] Charles continued to carry on his work as an itinerant minister for the first seven years of their marriage, until 1756 when he withdrew from itinerancy.[92] Yet he continued to be active in his ministry throughout their marriage, particularly in London and in areas surrounding his home in Bristol, and their letters during separations point to how involved he was in the domestic life of his family. Sarah had promised, in the months leading up to their marriage, that she would support his continuing to travel and his vegetarian diet, promises she had made with John Wesley present.[93] Still, it must have been difficult in times of particular distress, when children were being born, or were sick and dying, for Charles to be away. These were times that tested the itinerant demands of Methodist preachers and ministers.[94] Charles did not turn a blind eye to practical, domestic routines; indeed, he seemed to share them fully with his wife, even when he was distant from family. In one letter, Charles had written to Sarah, at the time she was pregnant, demonstrating his desire to be involved while away. While she was expecting in February 1759, he wrote to her from London: '"She shall be saved in Childbearing". Let my dear Companion take comfort from this Word; which she has experienced . . . and shall yet experience.' He also seconded her judgement that walking at night or going beyond their friend Elizabeth Vigor's house would be too much in her condition.[95]

In 1752, Charles had left the family in Bristol to attend his brother John's bedside in London, where he was struggling with a severe case of the consumption or flu. Many thought this was a fatal illness, and they warned Charles that he should hurry to see his brother alive.[96] After riding hard and sleeping little for three days, Charles reached his brother's bedside. It had been serious, and John had already written his own epitaph.[97] While he seemed to be recovering, there was still a fear that the sickness was too far gone.[98] Meanwhile, back in Bristol, Sarah had contracted smallpox, which she had caught from her sister.[99] Charles and others speculated that her sickness may have been hastened by the stress of hearing that her brother-in-law was dying.[100]

Only a few days after reaching John at the Foundery in London, Charles was again on the road to Bristol to see his wife:

I saw her alive; but, O, how changed! The whole head faint, and the whole heart sick! From the crown of the head to the soles of her feet there is no soundness. Yet, under her sorest burden, she blessed God that she had not been inoculated; receiving the disease as immediately sent from Him.[101]

Charles was forced to make a constant circuit between his severely ill brother and wife, and travelled back and forth between Bristol and London at this point. Sarah was mortally sick for three weeks, and the affliction left her disfigured for life, at the young age of 24. Charles believed that this made him love her even more for herself, and not the good looks that must have played some role in their early courtship.[102] After the recovery of his wife and brother were secure, Charles and Sarah were hit by the death of their beloved 16-month old son, John Wesley junior, from smallpox on 7 January 1754. This was their firstborn son and a difficult loss. Charles composed a poem:

Dead! dead! the child I loved so well!
   Transported to the world above!
I need no more my heart conceal:
   I never dared indulge my love:
But may I not indulge my grief,
And seek in tears a sad relief? . . .

Turn from him, turn, officious thought!
  Officious thought presents again
The thousand little acts he wrought
  Which wound my heart with soothing pain:
His looks, his winning gestures, rise,
His waving hands, and laughing eyes!

Those waving hands no more shall move,
  Those laughing eyes shall smile no more:
He cannot now engage our love
  With sweet insinuating power
Our weak, unguarded hearts ensnare,
And rival his Creator here . . .[103]

The poem expresses some of the same struggles that consumed other Methodists, namely how to admit to loving someone and not having that love overwhelm in any way their love for God. Charles expresses the relief of not having to guard that love now that his son is gone. Ironically, his death freed him to love his son without fear.[104]

This was not the only time that Charles would find himself away when their family was struggling with death and disease. In a particularly poignant letter from 1768, Sarah relayed the devastating news that their young child had just died, and she was now unsure of how the rest of the children would survive the spread of smallpox, which was close by. She wrote:

> This comes to acquaint you that our D[ea]r little Babe is no more, his agony is over, but it was a hard struggle before he cd depart, he was dying all yesterday from ten o'clock; & about 9 last [night] he departed; he scream'd three times about half an hour before he died that he cd be heard fm Nurse's Parlour to ye other side the street, not thro' Guilt, (That is my Comfort) but thor' extreme pain, perhaps were I of Calvin's opinion I might have attributed it To a different cause, but Glory be to a Redeemer's Love in declaring (for the consolation of distress'd Parents) 'that of such is the Kingdom of Heaven' . . . The rest of the Childn are well at present but know not how long it may be so, The small pox is next door but one to us, & I fear for my little Sammy. – I can do no more, than the united Love of many here attends you.[105]

The next day, Sarah would bury their child without Charles. And in this letter she writes, 'you can sympathize with me in the loss of my D[ea]r little Babe . . .', which seems to say that this baby was more hers than Charles' – perhaps, children who were that young were seen as more attached to their mothers, but also because Charles was away for a significant portion of the baby's life. She wrote of her understandable sadness, but also of her desire to resign herself to the idea that God 'orders all things for good to His children'. She again wrote of her dread that their son Samuel would also be threatened while smallpox was in the vicinity, and she wrote of various preventatives that she was trying. She was clearly unconvinced that much would help in the end, since these methods had all been used on their 'Dear Jacky . . . but to no purpose' before his death in 1752 (although 16 years earlier, she wrote of it as though it was much fresher for both of them). Sarah further wrote that she did not want these events to burden Charles or force him home. She wanted him there, but only 'when you think you can leave London with freedom, knowing ye can be spar'd: otherwise I wo[ul]d not wish ye to neglect the public on my acc[oun]t especially as your ministry is so much Bless'd in that place [London]'.[106]

In an earlier letter, Sarah Wesley had underlined this desire to stay out of his way, when he was on the road and involved in the ministry. She was sometimes ill, or the children were, but she never demanded his presence at home. She expressed that she would be happy to see Charles at home but that she was sure that people in London, especially, needed him and his work. This refutes the common complaint that marriage had undone his work, rendered him less useful or even neutralized his impact on early Methodism. Marriage did not seem to be the decisive factor in limiting Charles' impact on early Methodism. In fact his marriage strengthened his ministry, as his experiences with domestic life reflected in his communications to the laity.[107] He was frequently sympathetic and understanding on issues involving children. John Collinson wrote to Wesley on 11 September 1772, 'You can weep with those that weep. But I am too much affected to detain you with Ceremony. My Children are dead.'[108] Collinson further wrote about the spiritual fate of the two children he had lost simultaneously to smallpox and whooping cough.

Charles and Sarah Wesley tried as best as they could to conduct their marriage, their family and their romantic partnership, when frequent absences were required of someone in Charles' position. He demonstrated a constant involvement with Sarah's life through their letters. Their love and respect for one another is clearly evident in their correspondence. Charles wrote in 1757, 'My dearest of dear ones. Absence only increases Love for you and never absent from my heart – I go on heavily without you: & shrink . . . from the thought of losing you . . .'[109] His involvement in their family life is clear, not only in times of distress, but during the more mundane day-to-day involvements; he wrote letters that reflected his desire to be involved in decisions over child-rearing.[110] Their epistolary partnership reveals the fact that they were able to remain partners, even when they were required to be apart from each other.

## Conclusion

How does this examination of Charles Wesley's courtship and marriage change our view of him? Even through the deaths of his children and the sickness of his wife, he was able to continue an active ministry. This examination should render him human, and to remind ourselves that the Wesley brothers both had their own foibles and mis-steps. If it was one of John's faults that he tried to stay above the common humanity of his followers, Charles embodied humanity for other Methodists, exemplified through his love and his marriage. The marriage itself did not present any real challenges to his ministry;

on the contrary, his union to Sarah was remarkably stabilizing. A common
fault of Wesleyan scholarship is that it pits women against the brothers' aims
of religiosity, posing a split between domesticity and work, sexuality and
spirituality. However, as has been shown here, Charles Wesley's romantic life
and his spirituality were not divorced or at war.

Looking at Charles' decision to marry, one can see some similarities to how
other early Methodists approached this choice. Most eighteenth-century marriages were based on a careful weighing of parental control and the marrying individuals' self-will, while Methodist marriages seemed almost to do
away with considering the will of the marriage partners.[111] In most narratives, Methodists went to great lengths to emphasize the will of God and the
will of their parents. As John Wesley had advised another preacher who was
disappointed by his fiancée's parents ultimately voting the match down, 'I
hope you are able to say, "Lord, not as I will, but as Thou wilt" . . . I hope you
will think of it no more, but will be now more unreservedly devoted to God
than ever!'[112] If God had wanted this wedding to happen, Wesley claimed,
her parents would have approved. In Charles Wesley's courtship, we see his
quiet resignation to God's will. In his description of the wedding ceremony,
he tempered every celebratory note with a solemn one; divine approval was
everywhere, and his own will was unrepresented.

Even as Methodists emphasized the divine element of their decisions,
the decision of whom to marry was ultimately initiated and guided by the
intendeds themselves. Divine will was a prerequisite of these marriages, but
signs had to be selected and carefully portrayed by the prospective husbands
and wives. Charles Wesley looked for approval from the Gwynnes, selecting
this as the one insurmountable obstacle. If they approved the wedding, this
meant God's will was secured as well. As Charles looked back on the time
that brought him together with Sarah, he saw 'Delight on every step, every
Circumstance in that whole Design of Providential *Love.*'[113]

## Notes

1 Henry Rack, *Reasonable Enthusiast*, 252. Gareth Lloyd, 'Charles Wesley:
A New Evaluation of his Life and Ministry' (PhD dissertation, University of
Liverpool, 2002).

2 Gill, *Charles Wesley: The First Methodist*, 125.

3 Gill, *Charles Wesley: The First Methodist*, 35.

4 Gill, *Charles Wesley: The First Methodist*, 35.

5 Gill, *Charles Wesley: The First Methodist*, 35.

6 Gill, *Charles Wesley: The First Methodist*, 35.

7 Rack, *Reasonable Enthusiast*, 86. See also Frank Baker, *Charles Wesley as
Revealed by his Letters* (London: Epworth Press), 11–12.

8 Rack, *Reasonable Enthusiast*, 253.

9 Rack, *Reasonable Enthusiast*, 253. Baker, 54–5. The account is cut from Jackson,
*CWJ*, but see DDCW, 10/2 entry for Thursday 7 February 1745.

10 Quoted from Baker, *Charles Wesley as Revealed by his Letters*, 54–5.

11 Rack, *Reasonable Enthusiast*, 107–36.

12 Much of this story is concealed by Charles in extensive sections of short-hand in his journal. These have now been transcribed in full. See Kimbrough and Newport, *The Journal of Charles Wesley, in loc.*

13 Rack, *Reasonable Enthusiast*, 115–16.

14 Gill, *Charles Wesley: The First Methodist*, 53.

15 Gill, *Charles Wesley: The First Methodist*, 53–5.

16 Mabel Brailsford, *A Tale of Two Brothers* (New York: Oxford University Press, 1954), 91–2.

17 This refers to Molly Buchanan. Baker, *Charles Wesley As Revealed by His Letters*, 54.

18 This was originally uttered by James Hutton to describe Mrs George Whitefield and Mrs John Wesley, but it has been repeated by later Methodist historians. Rack does not completely dismiss the title in *Reasonable Enthusiast*: 'perhaps unfair to the former [Mrs Whitefield] though less so to the latter [Mrs Wesley]'. Rack, *Reasonable Enthusiast*, 253.

19 This refers to Mary Vazeille Wesley. Baker, *Charles Wesley as Revealed by his Letters*, 55.

20 This is in reference to Mary Vazeille Wesley. Gill, *Charles Wesley: The first Methodist*, 125.

21 Rack's chapter on Georgia is titled 'Serpents in Eden' in *Reasonable Enthusiast*, 107–36. This presumably refers to Hopkey, Hawkins and Welch, though Hopkey is singled out as 'the worst of all the serpents in [John Wesley's] Eden'. Rack, *Reasonable Enthusiast*, 123.

22 This refers to the women of Georgia. Gill, *Charles Wesley: The first Methodist*, 53.

23 John was less lucky than Charles on this count, since he married one such woman, Mary Vazeille, and had his reputation seriously compromised by his affair with another, Sophy Hopkey.

24 *CWJ*, 1.35

25 Rack, *Reasonable Enthusiast*, 253.

26 Quoted from Gill, *Charles Wesley: The first Methodist*, 130. See generally, Frank Baker, 'A poet in love – the courtship of Charles Wesley, 1747–1749', *Methodist History*, 29 (1991), 235–47.

27 Rack, *Reasonable Enthusiast*, 253.

28 Rack, *Reasonable Enthusiast*, 262; Baker, *Charles Wesley as Revealed by his Letters*, 68–9.

29 Rack asserts that this has been common assessment: 'It has been generally supposed that his marriage and family had much to do' with his withdrawal from itinerancy; Rack, *Reasonable Enthusiast*, 254.

30 Rack, *Reasonable Enthusiast*, 255.

31 Tyerman, 2.271. Tyerman argues that Charles gave up the itinerancy to avoid conflicts with preachers in 1756.

32 Rack, *Reasonable Enthusiast*, 255.

33 See particularly the letters to Charles Wesley collected in the Early Methodist Volume, MARC, ref. EMV.

34 For further discussion of John Wesley and early Methodists' ideas towards sexuality and marriage, see Anna M. Lawrence, '"I thought I felt a sinful desire": the question of celibacy for eighteenth-century Methodists', in *Bulletin of the John Rylands University Library of Manchester*, 87 (1) (Spring 2005), 177–93.

35 Conversations with Gareth Lloyd have been particularly helpful in empha-

sizing this divide between the Wesleys. Lloyd's work on Charles Wesley under-lines the divisions of labour, and he fleshes out the important leadership of the underrated brother. He maintains that followers of Methodism turned to Charles more often for real, human leadership in a way, and a primary example of his leadership was his healthy family life. See also Gareth Lloyd, 'Charles Wesley: A New Evaluation of his Life and Ministry'.

36  *CWJ*, 2.55.

37  John Johnson, 'Account of Himself' in Early Methodist Volume, 3 November 1767, MARC, 93.

38  See letters to Charles Wesley in the Early Methodist Volume, MARC; George Downing to Charles Wesley, 15 November 1758, DDPr 1/22, MARC; Joseph Cownley, 9 May 1774, DDPr 1/104, MARC. One can also see Wesley's compassion towards other Methodists in the deaths of their children in various passages of his journal as well as letters, such as Charles Wesley to Sarah Wesley, 1 March 1850, DDWES, 4/57, MARC.

39  John Valton to Charles Wesley, 3 April 1787, DDPr 2/59, MARC.

40  Anna M. Lawrence, 'The Transatlantic Methodist Family: Gender, Revolution and Evangelicalism in America and England, *c.* 1730–1815 (PhD dissertation, University of Michigan, 2004), 144–201; Lawrence, 'I thought I felt a sinful desire' 181–2; Diary of John Valton, MARC diaries collection.

41  Charles Wesley to Sarah Gwynne junior, 26 January 1749, MARC, DDWES, 1/40.

42  Ibid. Cf. Romans 8.38–9.

43  See Charles Wesley to Sarah Gwynne junior, [25 or 27 December 1748], MARC, DDCW, 5/10.

44  Charles Wesley to Sarah Gwynne junior, 17 September 1747, MARC, DDCW, 5/2.

45  *CWJ*, [19 April 1748] 2.12.

46  *CWJ*, [19 April 1748] 2.12.

47  *CWJ*, [19 April 1748] 2.12.

48  Lloyd, 'Charles Wesley', 102. Lloyd has a significant discussion of issues arising from the previous scholarly uncertainty over this date. Shorthand entries, such as the one containing the record of Charles' proposal, have been omitted from reproductions of the journal, particularly Thomas Jackson's edition. Lloyd argues that this has skewed our understanding of the relationship between John and Charles Wesley. See Kimbrough and Newport, *The Journal of Charles Wesley, in loc.*

49  Quoted from Lloyd, 'Charles Wesley' 102.

50  *CWJ*, [19 April 1748] 2.12.

51  Lloyd, 'Charles Wesley', 102–3. Lloyd argues extensively that this period of courtship, which overlaps with the failed courtship between John Wesley and Grace Murray, marked a separation between John and Charles Wesley. Lloyd's argument concludes that Charles saw his brother's relationship with Murray as a threat to his bond with John, and that his effective prevention of John's marriage to Murray soured their relationship for good. While jealousy may have played a larger role than we have previously imagined, there is also strong evidence that Charles felt that this particular match was unsuitable, because of their differences in class and status. Charles had also felt that this would single out one Methodist woman, and make others feel cheated by this preferment. Another strong factor against John marrying anyone was his clear ambivalence over romantic attach-

ments and his general emotional unsuitability, and Charles would have been very aware of these shortcomings. See Lloyd, 'Charles Wesley', 100–28.

52 'MS Deliberate': Hymn 2; *Charles Wesley: A Reader*, 313.

53 'MS Deliberate': Hymn 2; *Charles Wesley: A Reader*, 314.

54 'MS Deliberate': Hymn 4; *Charles Wesley: A Reader*, 314–15.

55 Charles Wesley to Sarah Gwynne, 12 August 1748, MARC, DDCW, 5/5.

56 Charles Wesley to Sarah Gwynne, 10 November 1748, MARC, DDCW, 5/8.

57 Charles Wesley to Sarah Gwynne, 14 December [1748], MARC, DDWES, 4/55.

58 Charles Wesley to Sarah Gwynne junior, [25 or 27 December 1748], MARC, DDCW, 5/10.

59 Charles Wesley to Sarah Gwynne junior, 15 January 1749, MARC, DDCW, 5/20.

60 Charles names the author of this false revelation as 'our weak S.[ister] Aspurnall'. See Charles Wesley to Sarah Gwynne junior, 15 January 1749, MARC, DDCW, 5/20.

61 Gill, *Charles Wesley: The First Methodist*, 135–6.

62 Charles Wesley to Sarah Gwynne junior, 15 January 1749, MARC ref. DDCW 5/20.

63 Charles Wesley to Sarah Gwynne junior, 15 January 1749, MARC ref. DDCW 5/20.

64 Martha Hall to Charles Wesley, 17 April 1749, MARC, DDWES 1/34.

65 Baker, 60, 65, 67; Gill, 134, 141.

66 Lloyd, 'Charles Wesley', 104–12.

67 *CWJ*, [11 November 1748] 2.44.

68 Charles Wesley to Sarah Gwynne junior, [25 or 27 December 1748], MARC, DDCW, 5/10.

69 For instances of John's participation in the marriage agreement, see Charles Wesley to Sarah Gwynne junior, 26 January 1749, MARC, DDWES, 1/40 and *CWJ*, [17 December 1748], 2.46–7.

70 Charles Wesley to Sarah Gwynne junior, 15 January 1749, MARC, DDCW, 5/20.

71 Sarah Gwynne junior to Charles Wesley, 19 January 1749, MARC, DDWES, 1/48.

72 Charles Wesley to Sarah Gwynne junior, 15 January 1749, MARC, DDCW, 5/20.

73 Charles Wesley to Sarah Gwynne junior, 15 January 1749, MARC, DDCW, 5/20.

74 Charles Wesley to Sarah Gwynne junior, 15 January 1749, MARC, DDCW, 5/20.

75 Lloyd makes the argument that this was not simply an economic difficulty, but that John Wesley was afraid of how this marriage would separate the brothers, and that he may have felt betrayed by Charles telling others before him of his formal intentions. To be fair, John Wesley had been the first person Charles Wesley had told about his feelings towards Sarah during Charles' time in Ireland. However, it does appear that he waited some time until he confirmed the seriousness of this affair to John, seven months after he had made his first proposal. See Lloyd, 'Charles Wesley', 105.

76 Quoted from Lloyd, 'Charles Wesley', 104.

77 Lloyd, 'Charles Wesley', MARC, 108.

78 Charles Wesley to Sarah G. Wesley, undated [1756], MARC, DDWES, 4/ 76.

79 Sarah Gwynne to Charles Wesley, 19 January 1749, MARC, DDWES, 1/48.

80 Sarah Gwynne to Charles Wesley, 19 January 1749, MARC, DDWES, 1/48.

81 *CWJ*, [17 December 1748], 2.46–7.

82 *CWJ*, [18 February 1749], 2.52.

83 *CWJ*, [18–27 February 1749], 2.52–3.

84 *CWJ*, [1 April 1749], 2.54.

85 *CWJ*, [2 April 1749], 2.54.

86 *CWJ*, [3 April 1749], 2.54. In his journal, Charles wrote that John also was opposed to signing 'his own agreement', presumably referring to the marriage settlement and his publications.

87 *CWJ*, [7 April 1749], 2.55.

88 *CWJ*, [8 April 1749], 2.55.

89 *CWJ*, [8 April 1749], 2.56.

90 *CWJ*, [8 April 1749], 2.56.

91 *CWJ*, [22 April 1749], 2.57.

92 It is important to state here that his withdrawal from itinerancy seemed to have little to do with his family obligations. He was increasingly alienated from the brotherhood of preachers, and for a variety of reasons was not as skilled as his brother at leading the preachers. See Lloyd, especially 181–94.

93 *CWJ*, [19 February, 1749] 2.52.

94 For more on how itinerant preachers viewed the pressures of family during this period, see Lawrence, 'The Transatlantic Methodist Family', 218–53.

95 Charles Wesley to Sarah Wesley, 24 February 1759, MARC, DDWES, 4/4.

96 *CWJ*, [29 November 1753] 2.95–6.

97 *CWJ*, [2 December 1753] 2.97.

98 *CWJ*, [2 December 1753] 2.96.

99 Brailsford, *A Tale of Two Brothers*, 246. At the time of Sarah's infection, Sarah's sister Becky had recently been inoculated for smallpox, a new practice at the time, and it was not clearly understood that the newly inoculated was also a carrier for the disease. Unwittingly, Sarah and her family were living with someone who was highly contagious.

100 *CWJ*, [3 December 1753] 2.100.

101 *CWJ*, [6 December 1753] 2.100.

102 Gill, *Charles Wesley: The First Methodist*, 156.

103 Quoted from Tyson, *Charles Wesley: A reader*, 334–5.

104 This theme of rivalry between earthly and divine loves is central to my work on early Methodists in 'The Transatlantic Methodist Family', especially 144–201. Also see Brailsford, 248–9, for her commentary on the themes of this specific poem.

105 Sarah Wesley to Charles Wesley, 6 July 1768, MARC, DDWES, 1/50.

106 Sarah Wesley to Charles Wesley, 11 July 1768, MARC, DDWES, 7/20.

107 See George Downing to Charles Wesley, 15 November 1758, MARC, DDPr, 1/22; Joseph Cownley, 9 May 1774, MARC, DDPr, 1/104; Charles Wesley to Sarah Wesley, 1 March 1850, MARC, DDWES, 4/57.

108 John Collinson to Charles Wesley, 11 September 1772, MARC, DDWES, 1/114.

109 Charles Wesley to Sarah Wesley, 7 April 1757, MARC, DDWES, 4/57.

110 Charles Wesley to Sarah Wesley, 10 July [1764], MARC, DDWES, 4/5; Charles Wesley to Sarah Wesley, n.d., MARC, DDWES, 4/17; Charles Wesley to

Sarah Wesley, n.d., MARC, DDWES, 4/37; Charles Wesley to Sarah Wesley, 14 June [1763], MARC, DDWES, 4/77.

111  For more on this idea, see Lawrence, 'The Transatlantic Methodist Family', 202–53.

112  John Wesley, *The Letters*, John Telford, ed., 8.35.

113  Charles Wesley to Sarah G. Wesley, undated [1756], MARC, DDWES, 4/75.

# 27. Purge the Preachers: The Wesleys and Quality Control

## RICHARD P. HEITZENRATER

About a decade into the Methodist Revival, the Wesleys discovered serious problems within the ranks of the preachers. At a conference of preachers in Leeds on 15 May 1751, John Wesley 'particularly inquired concerning their grace, and gifts, and fruit'.[1] As a result, he found reason to doubt the condition of one preacher, James Wheatley, a cobbler, who had been a Wesleyan itinerant preacher for nearly a decade.[2]

During the following weeks, the situation deteriorated rapidly and the Wesleys' attempts to maintain discipline within the increasingly variegated movement were severely tested. The initial blow came from several women who accused Wheatley, a lay preacher at Bradford-upon-Avon, of sexual indiscretions, which simply poured fuel upon the fire of opposition that had tormented the movement since its inception. The story of the manner in which the Wesleys confronted the ensuing crisis presents a fascinating picture of the internal workings of Methodist leadership at mid-century during one of the movement's greatest challenges.

## Discipline in the societies

From the beginning of the Revival, Charles Wesley had qualms about lay preachers, who were generally uneducated men and often lacked other talents that Charles considered requisite to ministry. However, the spread of the Methodist Revival depended upon preachers other than Anglican clergy, who were slow to associate with the Wesleys. Providing lay preachers for the spreading movement presented two challenges: to recruit and retain *enough* leaders to serve the growing number of societies; and also to make sure that the preachers were *adequate* to the task.

Concern for both discipline and doctrine became a hallmark of the Wesleyan movement at a very early stage. The Wesleyan Revival attracted a pot-pourri of adherents and would-be spiritual leaders, from Quakers to Baptists and evangelicals of every ilk.[3] Discipline and unity, if not uniformity, became problems that reached every level of the Methodist societies. Quarterly examination and purges of members became a regular feature of Methodism by 1743. Only those who passed muster were given quarterly membership tickets. Charles

was apparently even tougher than John in these examinations, at times fer-
reting out 'counterfeits and slackers' among those who had survived John's
questioning.[4]

The inclusion of preachers who had a variety of doctrinal positions, and in
some cases questionable personal histories, necessitated similar controls, mon-
itoring and education. To these ends, John developed an annual Conference of
full-time preachers, attendance by invitation, tried first in 1743 and formalized
the following year. These Conferences included the few Anglican clergy who
aligned with the Methodists, but consisted primarily of lay preachers. In 1746
they developed a list of questions that became a standard tool for examining
the preachers.[5] First, the Wesleys tried to observe whether the person might
have the gifts and grace for ministry – the talents requisite to the task and the
manifestations of God's presence in their life and work. They also tested the
preachers' effectiveness – whether or not their preaching bore fruit.

The process of issuing class tickets to members upon quarterly examination, begun in the early 1740s, was matched for preachers in November 1749,
when the method for receiving the new preachers included their receiving a
copy of the doctrinal and disciplinary *Minutes* of the Conferences from 1744 to
1748 (published in 1749), with a note inscribed inside the front cover indicating
that 'So long as you freely consent to and earnestly endeavour to walk according to the following rules, we shall rejoice to go on with you hand in hand.'[6]
This note in its successive versions, signed by John Wesley, was in effect their
certification as a Methodist preacher 'set apart' by Wesley.

High standards of discipline were expected throughout the societies,
especially among the leadership. While visiting Cornwall in July 1747,[7]
John expelled nearly a third of the Methodist exhorters[8] in the area. In 1748,
Wesley extended this examination process to the class leaders, looking carefully at 'their grace, their gifts, and the manner of meeting their several
classes'.[9] Careful discipline and examination was becoming the norm for the
Methodists at every level.

## Tensions between the brothers

For several years, however, the two brothers had sparred over the level of
requirements necessary to provide an adequate preaching ministry in the
local Methodist societies. Charles would have preferred to rely solely on
evangelical Anglican clergy. Once the principle of lay preaching had been
established, however, the brothers continued to disagree over the relative
weight given to the three requirements: gifts, grace and fruits.

The interaction between the Wesley brothers on leadership standards also
highlighted several differences of opinion. These issues included the question of priority between gifts and grace, Charles always stressing the former.
He could also be a harsh critic of John's preaching. After hearing him on one
occasion in January 1751, he candidly noted in his own manuscript journal
(in shorthand), 'I thought he misspent his strength in trifles.'[10] The brothers
also differed on other issues, such as what would cause or constitute separation from the Church of England, and whether or not Methodist preachers

should continue to ply their trade on the side while preaching among the societies.

Other personal strains between the brothers at this time further complicated the situation, including the longtime older–younger brother sibling tensions (not to be overlooked as a factor in many situations throughout their lives) and the friction caused by their marriages. During the period April 1749 to February 1751, Charles married Sarah Gwynne, accompanied by some financial arrangements made grudgingly by John; John's impending marriage to Grace Murray was aborted by Charles' interference in arranging her quick marriage to one of the preachers, John Bennet;[11] and John's quiet marriage to a wealthy widow, Molly Vazeille, took place in spite of Charles' opposition and disappointment.[12] The personal tensions between the brothers had never been worse.

In March of 1751, Charles and John attempted a reconciliation, recognizing that their deteriorating relationship was exacerbated by a growing lack of 'mutual confidence'. John, in fact, expressed a willingness to incorporate his brother more fully into the leadership of the movement. But Charles, who had not fully travelled in the connexion for some time, was not ready to accept his brother's entreaty to 'engage' for the coming year.[13]

## The Wheatley affair

The Wheatley affair in 1751 simply confirmed Charles' negative opinions about the lay preachers. For a decade, he had complained to his brother John about their inadequacies.[14] As early as 1741 he advised his older sibling, 'The lion is easier kept out than turned out; therefore discard Acourt.'[15] Although John was unquestionably the leader of the Wesleyan Revival, his younger brother never hesitated to speak his mind concerning the need for adequate leadership in the movement.

In June 1751 Charles was asked by the Methodists in Bradford to bring Wheatley there to answer for his 'horrible practices'. Charles investigated the situation on the spot, taking testimony from at least seven women whom Wheatley had 'abused'. He then travelled to Bristol and chastised Wheatley, who 'seemed willing to confess'. When taken to Bearfield[16] on 25 June and confronted by two of his victims, who 'proved their charge to his face', Wheatley pleaded guilty[17] but justified his actions and claimed (as Charles recorded) that he would 'expose *all* our preachers, who, he said, were like himself'.[18]

Charles prevailed upon John to draw up a resolution that Wheatley 'should not preach' and asked John to read it to Wheatley's face in front of the women.[19] But at that point, Wheatley became totally recalcitrant and refused to submit to the Wesleys' wishes, insisting that he would preach occasionally in the Methodist societies.[20] For two days, the Wesleys pressed Wheatley, trying to get him to withdraw voluntarily, and although he shifted so far as to feign penitence, John saw only proof of the opposite, and listed the marks of his obvious lack of true repentance: Wheatley 'never *owned* one tittle but what he knew we could prove; he always *extenuated* what he could not deny, he as constantly *accused* others as excused himself, saying many had been guilty of *little imprudences* as well as he; and in doing this, he told several palpable *untruths*, which he well knew so to be'.[21]

Since Wheatley had accused all the preachers of being gross sinners, the Wesleys tested his charges by calling in ten preachers, each of whom asked the accuser, 'What sin can you charge me with?' Wheatley remained silent through the whole charade, which convinced the Wesleys that he was a 'willful liar'.[22] Charles ended his account of the event by noting, 'However, it put my brother and me upon a resolution of strictly examining into the life and moral behaviour of every preacher in connexion with us; and the office fell upon me.'[23]

The situation that arose in 1751 presented a confluence of factors that have never been fully related before. For John, however, the potential scandal was primarily an opportunity to get his brother to participate more actively in the movement, especially in exercising leadership, which they nominally shared.[24] If Charles were put in charge of examining the preachers, then, rather than just complaining about them, he would be responsible for doing something about the matter of establishing and maintaining qualified lay preachers. In order to keep an adequate number of leaders, John made it very clear that Charles should not only weed out the inadequate preachers but also recruit good preachers to fill their places.

## The state of the Societies

Charles accepted his assignment eagerly. He set out on his inquisitorial journey the very next day after his joint session with Wheatley and John. His travels over the next three months would take him on an itinerary that resembles the rough shape of an ampersand, between Bristol, Manchester, Epworth, Newcastle, Birmingham, Oxford and London. He would visit societies in all of the Methodist circuits in England, save Cornwall, towards which John headed.[25] A careful examination of Charles' actions and methods during this trip displays not only the state of Methodism at the time but also Charles' principles, his manner of leadership and his relationship both to the preachers and to his brother.

During this visitation itinerary, Charles did not travel alone or make his judgements and decisions singly. Rather, he was accompanied on the trip by several people, in various configurations at different times. He set out with Francis Walker,[26] Sarah Perrin,[27] his wife Sally and her sister Becky. These compatriots often participated in the inquiry process, even if informally, and made very helpful comments along the way, in some cases transmitting those opinions to John Wesley, generally in support of Charles' conclusions.

Charles' journal record for his travels in July sounds more like a triumphant preaching mission than an inquisitorial visitation. The extensive journal letters that Charles sent to John were presumably intended to report in detail on his activities – it seems somewhat odd that the narrative tells primarily of a constant sequence his effective preaching engagements, along with a few comments about the condition of some Methodist societies, most of which were holding fast to the faith.[28] For several weeks in these letters he says hardly a word about examining any preachers.

Charles does, however, occasionally note some problems confronting a few societies. West of Birmingham, notorious for its anti-Methodist mobs, Charles faced the typical riotous behaviour of rowdies who disrupted his preaching and threw dirt in his face.[29] In other places the societies suffered from physical and theological attacks: in Wednesbury, a strong society of 300 had been reduced to 70 'weak, lifeless members', the result of persecution and the 'vain janglings' of the predestinarians.[30] Charles seems to have shaped these accounts to show his older brother that he himself was both a powerful preacher and an effective leader – able to face persecution as well as arbitrate problems within the societies.

After three weeks, however, Charles wrote a letter to John from Leeds saying that his 'chief design for coming seems likely to succeed'.[31] He spelled out this design in mid-August: '. . . my *most important* concern [is] to purge the Church, beginning with the labourers'.[32] For instance, Charles intentionally kept Michael Fenwick close by in order 'fully [to] prove him', but promised John that he would 'do nothing rashly and believe nothing without full proof'. He also told John that he found three more women 'whom the shepherd had well nigh devoured', a reference to the continuing saga of James Wheatley. Charles' opinion of the scoundrel was never stronger: 'Never, never must he hope to be received again amongst us!'

Besides the journal and letters, Charles created other documents that indicate he had already begun not only to plan his task seriously but also to evaluate some of the preachers. He made notes relative to this assignment in a small notebook headed, 'The Preachers, 1751'.[33] During the first week of his journey, Charles noted that in Worcester he had stopped Thomas Walker from giving up his trade to become a preacher, and pointed out that 'upon the strictest inquiry, I cannot discover that he has much, if any, gift for preaching'. A week later he records comments that he wrote to the Nottingham society, informing them that Joseph Leigh was 'a weak man of little understanding and less grace'. He added that he felt Leigh was 'unstable as water, therefore altogether unfit to direct and instruct others'. He warned them: 'Beware then how ye suffer him to speak, pray, or meddle at all with our Society. He is not one of us.'[34]

In this little notebook Charles also began to collect 'hints for conversation' selected from his brother's letters.[35] These concerns included faithfulness to the Church of England,[36] loyalty to the Methodist connexion, steadfastness in the faith, uprightness of life and willingness to study and to save souls. John exhibited dismay at Charles' strictness in testing the gifts of ministry in potential recruits and therefore reiterated his basic principle to Charles: 'My counsel is not to check the young ones, without strong necessity. If we lay some aside, we *must* have a supply, and of the two, I prefer grace before gifts.' The implication of John's preference is that more preachers would pass muster on the basis of spirituality than of talent. Charles' reaction was to ask, 'Are not both indispensibly necessary?' Before their different views could create a chasm, John tried to bridge the gap with the comment, 'Let these things drive us two close together, and 'tis worth all the cost.' To which Charles responded, 'Amen with all my heart, in the name of God! But *can* we unite unless it be given us from above?'

As for the problem of new recruits, Charles had his own view: 'Should we not first regulate, reform, and bring into discipline, the preachers we *have*, *before* we look for more?' The listing of preachers in November 1749 indicated that there were two dozen 'helpers' ('set apart' as preachers) and just over a dozen probationers ('on trial') to cover the nine circuits in England, Wales and Ireland, which included nearly fifty localities that had Methodist societies. Some of these were already known to be problems, such as Wheatley and Fenwick. John, worried that Charles' approach would diminish the supply of preachers, strongly reiterated his point: 'We must have forty itinerant preachers, or drop some of our societies. You cannot so well judge of this, without seeing the letters I receive from all parts.'[37]

Charles' unrecorded response to this high-handed remark must have convincingly stated the depth of the problem, as evidenced by the turnabout in John's next response: 'So much the more freely and firmly do I acquiesce in the determination of my brother, that it is far better for us to have ten, or six, preachers who are alive to God, sound in the faith, and of one heart with us and with one another, than fifty of whom we have no such assurance.'[38]

Within a week, John expelled a preacher and wrote to Charles: 'O that you and I may arise and stand upright! I quite agree with you. Let us have but six, so we are all one. I have sent one more, J. Loveybond,[39] home to his work. We may trust God to send forth more labourers.' John then added an admonition: 'Only be not unwilling to receive them when there is reasonable proof that He has sent them.'[40]

## Thoughts on the state of Methodism

While in Leeds on 24 July, Charles fell victim to a fever and was confined to bed for several days in Miss Norton's house.[41] During that period, while in the midst of a 'shivering fit', he dictated a document to Sarah Perrin that recorded what he called 'my confused thoughts concerning the state of the Church'.[42] That Charles and John would both refer to the Methodists during this period as 'the Church' is a fascinating bit of confused ecclesiological diction.[43] Nevertheless, Charles' two-page account is a telling indictment of the leadership within Methodism.[44]

Charles' 'thoughts' begin with his general conviction concerning the problem: 'Unless a sudden remedy be found,' he states, *'the preachers will destroy the work of God.'* He then proceeds to analyse the cause of the problem, evident first in the vocational ambiguity and confusion among many preachers.

What has well nigh ruined as many of them is idleness, the consequence of their having been taken from their trade. Most of them were as mere novices, as Michael Fenwick, without experience or stability, as fit to command an army as guide a Christian flock. Hence they quickly run themselves out of breath, losing first their grace, then their gifts and success. The unusual respect they met with turned their heads. The tinner, barber, thatcher, forgot himself, with his business, and immediately set up for a gentleman, and then – looked out for a fortune, having lost his only way of maintaining himself or family.

Charles also saw a second problem with some, most notably Wheatley: 'Some have been betrayed by pride into still grosser sins; and are likely, unless stopped in time, to do the Devil more service than ever they have done God.'

A third major problem was more doctrinal:

> Some have fallen into grievous errors and must therefore be put away. What then will become of them? Will they not shut the door against us, in whatsoever new places they come? Will they not cause the same confusion that is now in Wales? Will not each, in time, set up for himself, like Kendrick, and make a new party, sect, or religion? Or supposing my brother and I have authority enough to quash them while we live, who shall stop them after our death? It does not satisfy my conscience to say, 'God will look to that'. *We* also must look to it ourselves, if we would not tempt God and act the part of rash enthusiasts. *We* must use all probable means of preventing so great an evil, as a *real schism entailed on the Church. We* are justly answerable for the consequences of our own indiscretion and negligence. *We* are in conscience bound to hinder as much as in us is, our sons in the gospel from ruining their own souls and theirs that hear them.

Charles states his solution to these problems in the strongest terms: 'The most effectual, the *only* way (in my judgement) is *To set them to work again.*' This proposal is directly counter to his brother's principle, stated in a letter in mid-July: 'The least I can say to any of those preachers is, "Give yourself wholly to the work and you shall have food to eat and raiment to put on".'[45] But John also recognized the potential problem of the preachers leaving their trade and having too much time on their hands, as he admitted to Charles: 'What is it has eaten out the heart of half of our preachers, particularly those in Ireland? Absolutely idleness: their not being constantly employed.'

John had a different solution for this situation and told Charles to ask of each preacher, 'How do you spend your time from morning to evening?' John would give them a choice: 'Either follow your trade or resolve before God to spend the same hours in *reading* which you used to spend in working.'[46]

But Charles was very strongly opposed to taking the preachers from their trade and closed his 'thoughts' with a proposed series of steps to help solve the problem of idleness:

1.  That every preacher (excepting a very few) who has a trade return to it and labour with his own hands . . .
2.  That no future preacher be ever taken from his business or even permitted to preach till the point be settled, 'How is he to be maintained?'
3.  That no one be allowed to preach with us, till my brother and I have heard him *frequently* ourselves and talked largely with him, and each of us kept him with us, till *all the three are equally satisfied.*

Charles' conviction about the matter of preachers having a trade is reinforced by several other comments in this document,[47] which lead toward some very practical considerations: 'His trade leaves him no vacant time for sauntering, gossiping, fortune-making, and if he is inclined to marry, the Church is secure against being burdened with his wife and children.'

## Examining individual preachers

Charles had put his thoughts on paper in case he did not survive the fever,[48] but within a week he felt good enough to ride out 'to confer with the preachers and others'.[49] There is no indication of who was there or what happened, but we can be assured that the agenda of his inquisition was never far from his mind.

Two days later he heard Michael Fenwick preach. From his account, we gain some insight into the intensity of Charles' pursuit. His reaction was devastating: 'Such a preacher have I never heard and hope I never shall again! It was beyond all description! I can't say he preached false doctrine, or true, or any doctrine at all, but pure unmixed nonsense. Not one sentence did he utter that could do the least good to any one soul.' The performance was such a fiasco that Charles was tempted to step in to put a halt to it: 'He set my blood a galloping, and threw me into such a sweat that I expected the fever to follow.' When it was finally over, Charles (at the request of some of the leaders) went to the desk and spoke to 'the poor dissatisfied hearers,' taking no notice of Fenwick,[50] of whom he was 'infallibly sure, that if ever he had a gift for preaching, he has now *totally* lost it'.

Charles then 'spoke closely' with Fenwick, who was 'utterly averse to working'. But Charles was firm, telling him plainly that 'he should either labour with his hands or preach no more'. The young man confessed that leaving his trade had been his ruin but also complained about pressure from John Wesley. When Charles said that he could 'repair the injury by setting him up again in his barber's shop', Fenwick yielded.[51]

Before he left Leeds, Charles also met with Eleazer Webster, a 'self-hardened slave of sin', to whom he spoke 'fully' and finally silenced him.[52] In the month leading up to this point, Charles had dealt with at least five problem preachers. Having silenced James Wheatley and Eleazer Webster, he now sent Michael Fenwick back to his trade and prevented Thomas Walker from leaving his trade to become a preacher. He also warned the Methodists in Nottingham against hearing Joseph Leigh.[53]

## Preliminary Conferences with the preachers

His critical psyche invigorated and his health strengthened, Charles set out on 7 August for the two-day trip to Newcastle, his entourage now enhanced by Miss Naylor, William Shent and brother Lambertson. Charles spent the day after their arrival 'in conference with the preachers'. His journal letter makes no further comment about the occasion: no listing of participants, no listing of agenda and no indication of results. But the purpose of the conference would have been obvious to all, and the intended result was a tightening up of the reins on the preachers. His two local conferences, the earlier one at Leeds and this one at Newcastle, were preparatory to a larger regional Conference to be held a month later in Leeds.

Charles wanted people to know that he was there to be tough on the preachers. The day after the Newcastle conference, he wrote to John Bennet, thanking him for giving information about an inadequate preacher:

Your last helped on the work of God for which he has sent me into his vineyard at this time, and it supplied me with more abundant proof of R[obert] G[illespie]'s utter unworthiness to preach the gospel. I have accordingly stopped him, and shall tomorrow send him back to his proper business.[54]

In this private note to a close acquaintance, Charles could not resist adding a comment comparing his brother's inept creation of this debacle with his own resolution of the problem: 'A friend of ours (without God's counsel) made a preacher of a tailor. I, with God's help, shall make a tailor of him again.'[55]

Having made the point that he was exercising rigour, Charles announced that he would be at Leeds on 11 September 'to meet in conference as many of the preachers as can be got together'. He then gives Bennet a dual task: 'Bring you all you can, and give notice everywhere, I have silenced another scandalous preacher, and sent a third back to his trade.' Charles wants the people to know that he is serious about purging the preachers.

During August, Charles examined several other preachers in the Newcastle area and exercised his authority to weed out the chaff. His comments are telling: the drummer was perhaps okay with soldiers but not as an itinerant;[56] two preachers needed more reproof than encouragement;[57] one exhorter was encouraged not to leave his business.[58] A typical example of Charles' method of inquiry is evident in his encounter with one preacher near Newcastle:

I had some conversation with one, who thinks himself called to preach.[59] He told me himself that he had preached a long time in Scotland, and had not been instrumental in converting a single soul. 'But you might as well preach to the stones,' he added, 'as to the Scots'.

I could not find that he had had better success in other places, yet I would not judge of his gifts till I had heard him myself. This morning I did so, but not to my satisfaction. He made nothing out; spoke nothing that could either inform the understanding or affect the heart. But, to the best of my present judgment, *vox est praeteritque nihil*.[60]

For Charles, listening to the preacher was a crucial part of the process. He felt that he should not rely on rumours or reputation, but rather personally analyse the ability of the preacher to convey a message that could inform as well as inspire.

Back in Leeds at the beginning of September, Charles heard Fenwick again (he adds, hopefully, 'for the last time'). Fenwick tried to make up for his own deficiencies by using memorized paragraphs from John's printed sermons. Charles reacted sarcastically: '*Ohe, iam satis est.*[61] . . . Some things which he spake *were* very good, when my Brother spake them.'[62]

Charles also consulted with old reliable friends such as Christopher Hopper, and talked with many of the newer ones directly. Some passed muster, such as Richard Wendells and Thomas Mitchell. Several of his examinations, however, drew negative results: Eleazer Webster fell short, John Bennet had far more zeal than direction, David Trathen and Thomas Webb were rooted in predestination. Of the latter he was convinced: 'These I cannot keep.' Notice the use of the first-person pronoun.

## The Leeds Conference

The well-advertised Conference began at Leeds on Thursday 11 September. More than a dozen preachers had a note from Charles as a ticket of admission.[63] Four others came who were not admitted to the morning session.[64] Charles' own account of the occasion in a journal letter to his brother[65] begins with a very innocuous statement: 'Had anyone asked me the end of our Conference, I could not have told him, only that I came to make observations, to get acquainted with the preachers, and [to] see if God had anything to do with us, or by us.' However, the preachers certainly gained a rather explicit idea of what was in store for them in the opening verses of a 12-verse hymn of Charles' composition, with which they began the Conference:

Arise, thou jealous God, arise,
    Thy sifting power exert,
Look through us with thy flaming eyes,
    And search out every heart.

Our inmost souls Thy Spirit knows,
    And let Him now display
Whom Thou hast for Thy glory chose,
    And purge the rest away.[66]

At the conclusion of the hymn, Charles began to talk, 'without design' (he reported to brother John) 'of the qualifications, work and trials of a preacher, and what I thought requisite of men that acted in concert'. The group spent the bulk of three hours examining the 'preliminaries and disciplines', to which all present agreed.

After the lunch break with three compatriots at Miss Norton's,[67] Charles personally interviewed two of the preachers who had not been admitted to the morning session. He decided to admit one, Mortimer, but rejected the other, William Darney. The latter's reaction to the questioning illustrates the strong feelings some of his confrontational interviews elicited:

His stiff-neckedness I knew of old and was now resolved to bend or break him. The preachers had informed me of his obstinate behaviour toward my patient (too patient) brother at the last conference; besides his scandalous begging wherever he comes, and railing at his brethren or whomsoever he is displeased with. At Epworth he got more clothes than his horse can carry. They were ashamed to see the bags and bundles which he carried. I told him these things in few words, for he soon took fire and flew out, as I expected, into such violence of behaviour that I thought he would have beat me. I left him raging like a wild bull in a net and went to the preachers.[68]

Charles opened his heart 'fully and freely' during the afternoon session, talking of both 'the work and the workmen'. Remarkably, he makes no comment about Michael Fenwick's deficiencies in this context. His concluding comment echoes his brother's frequent note: 'We parted in the spirit of love.'

At William Grimshaw's request,[69] Charles agreed to give William Darney another hearing the following morning, at what might be considered a rump session of the Conference.[70] Darney once again denied all charges against him, though William Shent seemed to prove them all. Charles offered to forget the past on condition that, for at least half a year, Darney would abide by three restrictions: refrain '(1) from railing, (2) from begging, (3) from printing – any more of his nonsense'. This proposal brought a torrent of abuse upon the examiner:

'Nonsense!' quoth he. 'Nonsense? What? Do you call my hymns nonsense! They are not mine but Christ's. He *gave* 'em me, and Mr. John [Wesley] had nothing to say against them, and Mr. Grimshaw and Milner have recommended them. Here they are! What fault can you find with them.'[71]

When Darney threw his newly printed hymn book on the table, Charles picked it up and began reading in the middle of some of Darney's doggerel:

There's Brother-Tost and Wrangle,
When Satan souls do strangle.[72]

As Charles read on, the other preachers soon drowned him out by the 'violence of their applause'. Grimshaw and Milner immediately apologized for having recommended the work, but Darney persisted in claiming that 'it was all divine'.

Charles ended the episode, 'having turned [Darney] inside out', by compromising. In the light of the stated restrictions, especially to print no more books without the Wesleys' 'imprimatur', Charles agreed to allow him to preach among the Methodists, but only 'as a probationer'. Charles told John in the journal letter that he would not admit Darney to the Conference, 'that he might be humbled by perceiving I made a difference betwixt him and our preachers'.

Before the small session broke up at midday, Charles tried to resolve other tensions and 'stave off' a rupture among the 'confederates' present. Bennet convinced Charles that he had no design to set up a separate party.[73] Charles bound Bennet and Swindells together, hoping to set them both right and keep them from 'Satan's messengers'. In the end, the group agreed to postpone any final opinions until the next 'general conference'. Charles then noted that after they 'settled the affairs of the Church [!] the best we could', they all parted as friends.

## Final leg of the tour

Charles remained in the Leeds area for a few days, visiting the societies in Birstall, Bradford, Skircoat Green, Keighley and Haworth. Charles had some faint words of praise for Bennet, who preached at Birstall 'to the satisfaction of all'. However, the evaluation of other preachers pales in comparison with Charles' description of his own work along the route. The listeners come to life under his preaching and are greatly moved. At Haworth, the 'multitude' who could not get in the church cried and begged for him to preach in the churchyard, where he stood on a tombstone and spoke to a crowd he estimated at between three and four thousand. That afternoon at two, he reports, he returned and preached to twice that number.[74]

At Skircoat Green,[75] Charles attributed the 'backwardness' and lack of life among the society members to the 'many teachers' that had sprung up from within their own Society. On questioning, one of these 'burst out into tears and offered to leave off preaching entirely'. Charles decided he did not have the time to break another one of them, a 'stubborn, stiff-necked, mischievous man' (as 'hardened' as Darney), who not only quarrelled with others continually but also felt he was 'above all advice'.

On 16 September, Charles had one last skirmish with Darney himself, at Grimshaw's instigation. Charles told Darney again ('as warily and gently as I could') that he was not to use any of his own verses in any Methodist society, except perhaps Grimshaw's or Bennet's. This comment touched a raw nerve.[76] Darney's roaring and railing astonished everyone present, and his outrageous behaviour led his old friend[77] Grimshaw to give him up as 'the most obstinate unpersuadeable man he ever saw'. Grimshaw concluded that Darney needed not only to be conquered, but 'humbled and broken to pieces'. Grimshaw and William Shent were to enforce the restrictions on Darney, explicitly under the authority of both Wesley brothers (since Darney felt that John was more accepting of his work). The written stipulation stated that if he ever used his own verses in a Methodist society, 'in that society *he shall preach no more*'. Charles felt (or at least hoped?) that this arrangement would put an end to the problem.

The following day, Charles and his entourage set out for London. In Manchester he examined the society and made a 'mystic' mad by questioning his grace. Here also he heard John Bennet preach on a Saturday morning, which several listeners noted was 'with the demonstration of the Spirit'. Charles also took time to visit his old friend, Dr Byrom (inventor of the shorthand the Wesleys used), who made a valuable contribution to the inquisition by 'fairly and calmly' telling him 'what he felt was amiss in us'. Charles appreciated the candour: 'Of such reprovers, how shy are we by nature? Yet such are our best friends.'

While in Birmingham, Charles wrote to Bennet, trying to patch up any tensions from the Leeds Conference, saying that he felt 'more united to you than ever'. He also encouraged Bennet to help enforce the effort against disputes and 'vain janglings' among the preachers in his area (especially Trathen and Webb). But Charles was probably not prepared for Bennet's response, which criticized him for promoting 'unChristian behaviour' toward Webb. Bennet was very open in suspecting Charles' sincerity, and charged both him and John with using guile, imposing 'unscriptural things, and assuming arbitrary power'. He also pointed out that to preach 'sinless perfection at all and pressing even holiness in general' had done a great deal of harm. Bennet thus concluded that he could not 'in conscience put my neck again under your yoke'. Given Bennet's recent history, Charles could not be held fully accountable for Bennet's attitude toward the Wesley brothers.[78] This reaction also indicates that, once Charles was no longer breathing down their neck, the preachers were prone to return to their former attitudes. They also seem better able to express themselves more honestly and fully on paper than face to face.

Charles' trip, which had now turned back to a preaching tour, proceeded to Oxford, where some conversation with two 'serious scholars' put him 'in mind of the first Methodists'. In those closing days of September, Charles heard more bad news about two problem preachers, Trathen and Webb, and wrote to the stewards of their societies with instructions to stop them from preaching. Of some preachers, such as Swindells, he speaks kindly; of others, however, he is torn between thinking them 'very honest or very false', believing (again hoping?) the former. In spite of his attempts at playing the 'enforcer', Charles did have a soft heart and was in some ways as hopeful as was his brother John that God would transform the hearts and minds of their compatriots.

## Results of the circuit of inquiry

Charles arrived in London on 4 October, more than two weeks before his brother John returned from his two-month tour of Cornwall and the West Country.[79] As John headed back to London, he noted in his journal the evident change in the Bristol Society on 1 October: the members were now as 'calm and well united together as if James Wheatley had never been'.[80] This turned out, however, to be the calm before another storm.

Charles appears to have enjoyed exercising his supervisory power during his circuit of inquiry, even if his effectiveness depended occasionally upon invoking his brother's name. He had preached to many lively societies and examined many preachers: he sent some back to their trade, encouraged others not to leave their business, reprimanded a few, tried to discipline a couple, and probably more than fulfilled his assigned mission. In the flush of his success, his courage was bolstered and he was ready not only to report these activities to his brother but also to press for some actions that he knew, from past experience, John might resist. If John wanted him to exercise an important role of leadership in the Methodist movement, he was now ready to do so – with certain stipulations that would guarantee an equal role for Charles.

John's journal and correspondence give very little information regarding what occurred between him and Charles in the succeeding weeks.[81] From Charles' side, however, we discover an interesting set of events that illustrate both the level of concern that Charles had developed on the matter of the preachers, the extent of the tension that still existed between the brothers, and Charles' strategy for confronting his brother with the realities of the situation.

Charles was in London at the beginning of November when he received a letter from Sarah Perrin, who was at home in Bradford. She and Charles' wife, Sarah, had conversed with John, an event which Charles' wife had not reported fully to him. Sarah Perrin summarized it as follows:

> I spoke my thoughts freely and told him the danger the work was in of being destroyed unless an immediate stop was put to some preachers who do not live the gospel. I likewise told him you could not labour in the work

on faith unless he would agree by written Articles between you to let none labour with you but such as both consented to. He told me if you would agree to take one third of the travelling work upon you, he would agree to that; otherwise, he could not because it would be impossible for you to have any knowledge of the preachers.

In these few words, Sarah touches on several key issues: the danger of inadequate preachers, the need for equality in shared governance, the necessity of articles of agreement. She also provides John's primary response to her list of complaints, especially his unwillingness to turn over an equal share in the work, largely because of his superior knowledge of the work in the connexion. She then tells Charles of several places that are suffering either from the lack of a preacher or the 'lame work' of specific preachers, whom she names.[82] At the end of the summary, she laments, 'My heart is pained for these things and I am ready to cry out, Who is on the Lord's side?'[83]

The fact that Sarah Perrin, Wesley's former housekeeper at Kingswood, would confront him in person with these weaknesses within the movement discloses a picture of Wesley and Methodism that is not often portrayed – a leader who could be approached and criticized by a woman who was, granted, a friend but certainly not one of the public leaders of the movement.

Another friend of the brothers soon entered the scene – as an arbiter, the result of an earlier agreement between John and Charles. Vincent Perronet, of Shoreham, offered his home as the location for a consultation to work out the disagreements resulting from Charles' purge of the preachers. Charles was sceptical, evidenced by his preliminary letter to Perronet two days before the meeting: 'Things are come to a crisis. Without a miracle I fear he will not hold to reasonable terms, and if he utterly refuses, I doubt my own patience and rationality.'[84] He also gives Perronet the latest word on Fenwick:[85] John has promised to take him back again. But Charles is adamant: 'I shall stand in the gap as long as I can.' As for articles of agreement, the crux of any solution, Charles lays out his position:

If our friend [John] arrives to see no articles of my drawing up, he shall draw them up himself, only he must oblige himself to consult me on taking on the putting out. This is the whole of my demand, the one condition of my entire union with him. But this implies that he should not readmit them without my concurrence, whom at his desire I have put away.[86]

Charles' record of the meeting two days later indicates a sincere and common desire for union in order to promote 'the glory of God and the salvation of souls'. They then agreed on two main points. The first fulfilled Charles' main demand: 'To concur or *act in concert* with respect to the preachers, so as neither to admit or refuse any but such as *both* of us admitted or refused.' And the second spelled out the specific details: that neither of them would receive any of the nine preachers listed, all of whom had been culled out during Charles' northern itinerary – James Wheatley, Eleazer Webster, Robert Gillespie, James Watson, Michael Fenwick, John Maddern, David Trathen, Thomas Webb, William Darney.[87]

Charles came away from this meeting, however, without a signed agreement, or 'signed articles', largely because Perronet suggested that to urge John on this matter would appear to mistrust him. John had suggested another method of putting such matters in writing: 'To have a book of the preachers and try to enter the names of received or regulated preachers, and when anyone hereafter has to be put away, to put out his name with me in the place of all the others.'[88]

Charles' suspicion of John's spinelessness, however, was supported two days later. Fenwick had successfully lobbied John, asking pardon for going to the Calvinist Tabernacle, and prevailed upon John to let him live at the Foundery. John even agreed to buy his horse, promising the inept preacher that 'if his gifts should return by and by', he would get his horse back. Charles viewed this whole episode as a direct breach of their agreement ('our articles'). He immediately rode to Newington and searched out his brother to complain, 'with all the address and gentleness I was master of'. At the same time, Charles was careful to profess an 'ardent desire of union'.

John's response totally surprised Charles – he did not attempt to excuse himself but, as Charles said, 'took advantage of my past dispassion and graciously told me he might have confidence in me – if I would do exactly as he did in London, and if I would be civil and good to his wife'. These were, in fact, two of the hardest conditions John could have placed upon Charles in these circumstances: to act just as his older brother did, and to be kind to a woman he despised.

During these events, Sarah Perrin wrote to Charles, encouraging his efforts to help the people called Methodists, who are 'longing for faithful ministers' and have a 'hunger for the sincere milk of the word'.[89] They are, in fact, able to 'distinguish those who instead of bread give them a stone'. But she also bemoans the consequences of 'suffering some preachers to go forth . . . who haven't grace to adorn the gospel they preach'. Among the preachers she criticizes specifically is Burton Wells, whom she and others have already begged Charles to prevent from preaching in their circuit.

Sarah holds back nothing as she attempts to 'deliver my own soul'. Sarah lays the blame for this situation right at the feet of John Wesley, 'the very source of the affliction', since he has not failed to prevent, but has knowingly sent out preachers of whose incompetence and/or iniquity he had been warned. Having herself heard many 'servile accounts' of people like Gillespie, Wheatley and Fenwick, Sarah reiterates that other preachers are not only embarrassed by the actions of these incompetents but also by the inaction of the leadership in allowing them to continue. She cannot believe that John continues to waffle on the status of Fenwick, for instance, whose preaching (she claims) anyone 'who could distinguish right from wrong' would think to be 'more like a burlesque upon reason than being to God'.[90] She names others, such as Thomas Williams in Ireland, who are not (in her view) up to the task. She thinks John 'greatly deserves' regulation, and points out that the lay preachers not only loathe the Wesleys and do not love God, but also 'do much more hurt to the cause of God than any of the clergy can do'.

There was little in this letter that was new to Charles, and in spite of Sarah's bad news and very critical views, he continues to exhibit more resilience during this period than one might suspect. Nevertheless, the pressure on him was not over. On 5 December (probably before he received Sarah's letter), Charles talked again with the number one offender, James Wheatley, who claimed that events 'obliged' him to 'leave the Church'.[91] He also threatened to take a thousand people with him and encourage all the lay preachers to follow. Charles feared that Wheatley's own actions might, in fact, precipitate the event they feared, namely 'a real schism'.[92] In the depths of this conundrum, Charles asked himself the question he could not avoid: 'If it came to this, should I leave the Church or the Methodists?' The weight of evidence suggests that Charles would never leave the Church, a view his next observation reinforces: 'Does not Mr. Lunell rightly call the Methodists a seminary for Dissenters?'[93]

Charles then began another list of questions for his next conference with John, which illustrate his growing testiness. Two of the questions focus on John's unwillingness to deal mutually with incompetent preachers:

> If you knew of any scandalous behaviour of a preacher, would you not hold it from me? Would you not screen him for a full inquiry? Why have you never mentioned Fellow to me? Is not the case for sparing him fair? The case for not communicating less, proved? Could you stop a preacher if you would? [Charles then lists two examples: Madren, Fenwick].[94]

Charles is still not convinced that John has the backbone necessary to deal squarely with either the preachers or with him. He also points out that John has not lived up to the articles of agreement to which they agreed (presumably orally) at Shoreham: 'Was it not a breach of articles or no, encouraging Fenwick, by taking him into our house? Have you seen the articles now?'[95]

And as for John acting by himself in this matter (which includes *both* receiving and expelling), Charles sees no precedent for it in the Church: 'Do you look upon our saying as but one thing, not to receive or reject singly? What single bishop ever took upon him to ordain?'

But the most searching question, which comes from Charles' pained heart at this point, is nearly hidden in the middle of the list: 'Will you release me of any farther concern for the preachers?' It seems that Charles might have a double edge to this question: either, 'Would you please put me out of my misery and take this responsibility from me?'; or, 'Have your continued actions, in fact, released me from the responsibility that you earlier appeared to have given me?'.

To add to Charles' misery, during the first week in December he also received one of the most devastating letters written by his older brother. John had apparently just discovered the letter that Charles had written to Lady Huntingdon in August, in which Charles explained that his primary reason for keeping the preachers in their trades was to break John's power and 'reduce his authority' over the preachers.[96] John always chafed at any suggestion that he desired power. In an uncommon moment of retaliation, John suggested that Charles (apparently unsatisfied with his generous annual stipend of £150 per year) was skimming money from the quarterly contributions in the societies, designed for operating expenses and benevolent work. John accused

Charles of 'robbing the spittle' or poor fund, a common phrase for the 'mean-est form of profiteering'.[97] Having fallen into a litigious mode of late, John offered to enter into mediation again on this matter, if Charles so desired.

The matter apparently blew over, though the details of the period are cloudy, since both brothers had stopped keeping a journal. John was continu-ing to consider the standards for preaching, however, evident in a letter he wrote in mid-December, outlining what he meant by 'preaching the gospel' and 'preaching the law'. In 32 paragraphs, John laid out his balanced view of the need for both law and gospel. He especially criticized the so-called 'gos-pel preachers' and their *'new* method of "preaching Christ"' whereby they bleat out some facile words from the pulpit about simply having faith in the blood of Christ and totally ignore the necessity of obeying the will of God through holy living.[98] He and Charles continually witnessed the ill effects of shallow solifidianism within the Methodist societies, encouraged by inad-equate preaching. And the recent crisis gave him specific examples to cite by name in this letter, preachers whose preaching resembled 'an unconnected rhapsody of unmeaning words' – namely, David Trathen, Thomas Webb, Robert Swindells, John Maddern, and the best example of the dangers of anti-nomianism, James Wheatley.[99] If anyone thought the Methodist Revival had no doctrinal standards, or that their doctrines had no moral consequences, this treatise 'On Preaching Christ' put that misjudgement to rest.

Another problem that arose during December resulted from John's deci-sion to settle the preaching houses on trust deeds that prevented anyone from preaching therein save persons appointed by the Wesley brothers or William Grimshaw. This new arrangement, first implemented in Birstall in August 1750, was the model for the deed signed by the trustees at Bolton on 24 December 1751, without the knowledge of their preacher, John Bennet. When Bennet discovered this action, which he considered high-handed, he railed against Wesley in the presence of his congregation, saying 'many bitter things about Wesley' and then spreading his arms and crying, 'Popery! Popery! Popery! I have not been in connexion with him these three years; neither will I be any more.'[100] Bennet waited for Wesley to visit three months later, however, before having a final confrontation on the matter.

## Covenants among the preachers

In the face of continuing challenges, disaffection, departures, expulsions and ambiguity, the Wesley brothers attempted to clarify the situation in mid-January 1752. At a private meeting, again in the presence of Vincent Perronet as the arbitrator, the two brothers signed an accord with six articles that spelled out their working relationship:

With regard to the preachers, we agree:

1. That no one shall be permitted to preach in any of our societies till he has been examined both as to his gifts and grace, at least by the assistant, who, sending word to us, may by our answer admit him as a local preacher.

2. That such a preacher be not immediately taken from his trade but expected to follow it with all diligence.
3. That no person shall be received as a travelling preacher or taken from his trade by either of us alone, but by both conjointly giving him a note under both our hands.
4. That neither of us will readmit a travelling preacher laid aside without the consent of the other.
5. That if we should ever disagree in our judgment, we would refer the matter to Mr. Perronet.
6. That we will endeavor to be patterns of all we expect of our preachers, particularly of zeal, diligence, and punctuality in the work. By constantly preaching and meeting the societies, by visiting yearly Ireland, Cornwall, and the north, and England; by superintending the whole work and every branch of it, with all the strength which God shall give.

We agree to the above written, till this day the next year.

John Wesley
Charles Wesley[101]

The first five issues are obviously from Charles' agenda: concern for gifts as well as grace; leaving preachers in their trades; requiring written conjoint action by both brothers; arbitration by Mr Perronet in cases of disagreement. Article 6 is apparently John's attempt to get diligent participation from Charles in sharing the superintendence of the whole work, in return for his own agreement to the first five points. No doubt Charles could also hope that the last point would keep John's nose to the grindstone as well.

This clearing of the air between Charles and John paved the way for a larger meeting of the preachers in the London area, at which a new sense of discipline could be implemented. One of the evident problems over the previous months had been the prevalence of false accusations based on inaccurate information. To confront this problem, John called a conference for 29 January 1752. The preachers in attendance were asked to sign the following document, written in John Wesley's hand:

It is agreed by us whose names are underwritten:

1. That we will not listen or willingly inquire after any ill concerning each other;
2. That if we do hear any ill of each other, we will not be forward to believe it;
3. That as soon as possible, we will communicate what we hear, by speaking or writing to the person concerned;
4. That till we have done this, we will not write or speak a syllable of it to any other person whatsoever;
5. That neither will we mention it, after we have done this, to any other person;
6. That we will not make any exception to any of these rules, unless we think ourselves absolutely obliged in conscience so to do.[102]

This document was signed by 13 preachers, including both of the Wesleys.[103] But nothing in these agreements in January touched on one of the larger continuing issues in Charles' mind. Charles brought the matter to the fore in a subsequent document (in his hand), dated 16 March 1752, and signed by the Wesleys and four other preachers:

> We whose names are underwritten, being clearly and fully convinced, (1) that the success of the present work of God done in great measure depend on the entire union of all the labourers employed therein; [and] (2) that our present call is chiefly to the members of that Church wherein we have been brought up; are absolutely determined, by the grace of God,
>
> 1. To abide in the closest union with each other, and never knowingly or willingly to hear, speak, do or suffer anything which tends to weaken that union;
> 2. Never to leave the communion of the Church of England without the consent of all whose names are subjoined.[104]

This document summarized the intent of the 29 January document in one article and added another article that was just as important to Charles. It became the model for similar covenants that were signed in subsequent Conferences.[105]

## The model deed

Having received ambiguous signals from Charles, Bennet had announced his departure from the connexion (and his intention to take his society in Bolton with him) in December 1751, at the time of the trust deed controversy. He would not have been the first to leave, of course, but the revised status of the property put the issue in a new light.

John arrived in the area with his wife and step-daughter at the end of March 1752.[106] Bennet confronted him in Bolton on 1 April, privately telling him that there was a great deal of uneasiness in the society over the preaching house 'being made over or given by the trustees to him and his brother . . . for the use of all preachers that preached their doctrine and not otherwise'. Bennet recommended to Wesley that 'in order to make peace' he simply buy back the preaching house. Wesley did not respond. When Bennet then revealed that a local lawyer suggested prosecuting Wesley for receiving property that was not the trustees' to give away, Wesley 'broke out into a passion'. He told Bennet to go ahead with the suit – that he was ready to spend 500 guineas to defend himself and his actions.

Before the conversation was over, Mrs Wesley entered the room 'in a great rage', protesting any 'underhand dealings'. She claimed that Bennet was 'in the gall of bitterness and the bond of iniquity' and was 'a very bad man'. One might not expect Mrs Wesley to have any higher opinion of Mr Bennet, given his previous history with her husband. On the other hand, it is somewhat surprising to see Mrs Wesley bursting into a crucial conversation on matters of connexional polity and politics.

Wesley proceeded from this conversation to the service and preached a sermon on the righteousness of Christ. The congregation, spurred by Bennet, felt that Wesley preached an 'imputed righteousness', contrary to his supposed principles. In his diary, Bennet filled several pages supporting his claim that Wesley contradicted his own writings, only demonstrating, however, that Bennet himself did not have a clear grasp of the developing Wesleyan doctrines of justification and sanctification.[107] Bennet's intent, of course, was to show the irony of Wesley, who had drawn up the deed requiring proper Methodist preaching, not following his own strictures.

After the service, Wesley tried to calm the trustees on the property issue by agreeing to buy the house. When the discussion began to touch on doctrine, however, Wesley rose again in a passion and proceeded to call Bennet a 'knave and a villian'. Mrs Wesley, not to be outdone, then told Bennet to 'get out of the room and be gone'. Bennet's further exposition of the doctrinal problem did nothing to solve the dispute, and the confrontation ended. For Wesley, it was just another day and another problem, not the worst one he had faced in the previous six months. He did not bother to mention anything about the confrontation in his journal.

## Conclusion

The events during the months between March 1751 and 1752 display the confluence of several key problems within the leadership of the Wesleyan movement. The obvious primary difficulty is the lack of good doctrine and discipline among the lay preachers, which came to the fore with the incidents surrounding James Wheatley and became even more apparent in the work of William Darney, Michael Fenwick, John Bennet and others. John Wesley saw this issue as an occasion to draw his brother further into the leadership of the movement, allowing him some responsibility in an area of special concern to Charles. A second major problem, however, that interweaves with the first is found in the heightened tensions between John and Charles Wesley, both of whom had gone through several trying experiences in recent months that tested their sibling relationship in new ways.

Add to those problems, current at the turn of the 1750s, the issues of longer duration – the question of separation from the Church, some preachers' desire for ordination, the use of the sacraments in the societies, and the attempt to sort out doctrinal emphases – and the picture becomes even more complicated. Charles' recent lack of participation in the leadership of the movement, and the brothers' longtime differences on some issues of polity and doctrine, exacerbated a complicated set of circumstances that developed during 1751. The story we have outlined above, however, demonstrates several important aspects of the situation that are central to the story but not often noticed or highlighted. These may be enumerated as follows.

1. Effective discipline among the preachers was a difficult problem. It was especially difficult to dissociate individual preachers completely from the Wesleyan connexion. The names of 'problem' preachers enumerated in this story, such as Wheatley, Darney and Fenwick, keep appearing back on the scene, not only during these few months but sometimes for years to come.

There are several reasons for this situation. (a) The preachers could be expelled, but it took a concerted connexional effort to keep them from preaching among the societies. Wesleyan preachers could be officially certified, even with written proof, but it was difficult to force all the societies to accept only the preachers approved by the Wesleys. Even the development of a Model Deed was not always a final solution, as seen in the case of Bennet. (b) No one could prevent people from claiming to be 'Methodist', a term that was applied to many different groups with different theological positions – a term that eventually became a generic designation for dissenting evangelical fanatics. (c) John had a degree of trust in God's power over human nature (or was just plain naïve or gullible, depending on one's view), and seemed unwilling to concede that anyone was really intractably inadequate. Charles tried to appear firm toward the inept preachers, but at times appeared nearly as hopeful as his brother that God will reform rather than condemn them.

2. In Charles' own accounts of this period, he portrays himself as more than just his brother's 'enforcer,' weeding out inept and problematic preachers, but rather as a positive leader who provides a model of preaching and spiritual effectiveness among the societies. Charles' apparent intention is to show his older brother that he can exercise leadership within the movement on several levels, thus contradicting his older brother's image of him as a person who has distanced himself from the life of the societies.

3. Ironically, Charles seems to have made many, if not most, decisions on his own during this trip, in spite of his later desire for two-way consultation with John at every step. There are instances when it appears that Charles shores up his authority by mentioning explicitly his brother's name, although it is not clear whether Charles was fully comfortable having to rely on this tactic.[108] While Charles seems to have assumed that John had in fact given him singular authority to act, John subsequently seems reticent to allow Charles to exercise equal power with him in the leadership of the movement.

4. Charles seems to place himself in a real conundrum *vis à vis* his brother's position against taking preachers from their trades. John asked the preachers to give themselves full time to the work (supported by a small allowance), but wanted them to spend as much time reading as they used to spend working.[109] Charles' desire to keep preachers working at their trades would make it more difficult for such 'part-time' preachers to become educated and thereby cultivate their 'gifts', which Charles nevertheless was wont to emphasize. Charles might not have actually trusted the preachers to educate themselves, in spite of the prolific publishing programme that the Wesleys carried out for their edification. Or Charles may have been blinded in this matter by his desire to preserve the preachers from economic dependence upon John, which he viewed as the root of John's unwarranted power over them.

5. Women had an active role in helping to evaluate the preachers, both in this particular set of events and in a similar manner throughout the whole movement. Sarah Perrin not only travelled with the examining party but also contributed to the final evaluation by writing letters and conversing directly with John Wesley as well as Charles about the matter, seeming to be fully candid in the disclosure of very specific information. Charles' wife and sister also felt free to join in the process in the same fashion. Even Mrs John Wesley

(Molly) seems to have had no qualms about participating in conversations with recalcitrant preachers such as John Bennet, and telling them just what she thought of their character and capabilities. These involvements fit nicely into the larger picture of John's extensive correspondence with women during his ministry, which includes questions concerning the adequacies or inadequacies of many of the Methodist preachers.

6. The brothers worked hard at trying to co-operate, but pushed each other to the edge of their patience, speaking their minds, chancing alienation, at times even requiring mediation. But throughout this whole period they never gave up on the possibility of working in union with each other. They each tried to hold to some principles that, while not diametrically opposite, were constantly in tension. Charles' emphasis on gifts resulted in a winnowing of the preacher list to levels nearly inadequate to service the societies. And Charles' adamant attachment to the Church made it difficult for him to see the intent and value of John's innovations that challenged tradition. John's ebullient reliance upon God's grace in all things sometimes made him look naïve and subject to connivance on the part of some preachers.

7. The interaction of tensions from many sources made the actions and decisions of this period even more difficult for the brothers. Both of the brothers' marriages heightened the tension between them, neither being particularly favourable to the other's desires. Then Charles nearly caused an irreparable breach by arranging the marriage of Grace Murray (John's fiancée) to John Bennet, one of Wesley's preachers. The preachers already had a tendency to play the brothers off against each other, like children manipulating their parents separately. Many of the preachers suffered from divided loyalties, trying to be responsible to the Wesleyan connexion but also serving the needs of local societies.

8. The problem preachers usually exhibited a combination of inadequacies. Even Wheatley's moral turpitude was combined with supposed illiteracy. And the fatal combination in many cases included some form of final intransigence or insubordination.

The developments within the tangled web of circumstances during this period led to several important features that became fixtures in Methodism. The Conference of preachers shortly became an annual event, to which John Wesley especially invited preachers who had any kind of disciplinary or doctrinal problem. The examination of the preachers became a regular part of the annual Conference, for all the preachers in attendance (new and old) every year. The written covenant of union became a document that preachers were frequently expected to sign, especially in times of internal conflict. The Model Deed soon became a legal requirement for all the preaching houses, so as to establish a means of enforcing doctrinal standards in the preaching and the appointment system. And the treatise 'On Preaching Christ' provided a lasting summary of the Wesleyan balance between law and gospel.

At the same time, other features of these events remained in the category of informal approaches. The Wesleys continued to solicit the opinions of women on important matters of polity and discipline, but never worked them into the top levels of the hierarchy of the movement. Relationships with Anglican priests continued to develop on a very limited and personal level, rather than any greater institutional support from the established Church. The preachers continued to press for more independence, more rights, more power, more democracy, but that was a battle not to be won, at least during Wesley's lifetime.

And Charles himself, after this one major fling at exercising leadership within the movement, retired back into the folds of his family, leaving the operation of the connexion to his older brother. In future skirmishes with his brother, Charles seems to have preferred sniping from the outskirts rather than trying to effect change from the centre. While John seemed to be energized by controversy, such conflicts seemed to wear Charles down. A decade after these events, Charles was drawn into another controversy with John, focused on the interlocking questions of ordination, the sacraments and separation from the Church of England. By that time, however, Charles was largely on the sidelines, and although he continued to exert his influence to prevent his brother from taking unwise steps, he had removed himself from the centres of authority and rarely even attended Conference.[110]

But this one flurry of activity on Charles' part, and the concessions that he won from his brother on several matters of importance, gave the signal that he was a force to be reckoned with, not only because of the strength of his convictions and the power of his arguments, but also his ability to muster support from the preachers in the connexion and from the clergy of the Church, with whom he was closely aligned. It is a tribute to Charles Wesley that pastoral leadership in the Methodist heritage has become a ministry that is a disciplined balance of gifts and grace, conceived as a part of the larger work of God in the Church universal.

## Notes

1 At a similar conference in Bristol two months earlier, John had pointed out what was 'amiss or wanting' in any of the brethren. John Wesley, *Journal and Diaries III* (15 March 1751), W. Reginald Ward and Richard P. Heitzenrater, eds, in *BE*, 20.380.

2 Ibid., 20.389n. Wheatley had been a Methodist preacher since 1742. His notoriety was evident as early as April 1744 when he was attacked by a mob in Bristol, causing the mayor to come and read the Riot Act (1715) to the mob, ordering them to disperse. *BE*, 20.23–4. See also, Elizabeth J. Bellamy, *James Wheatley and Norwich Methodism* (Peterborough: Methodist Publishing House, 1994), 21.

3 See Henry Rack's discussion of this phenomenon, in which he calls Wesley the 'great cannibalizer' of local revivals. *Reasonable Enthusiast: John Wesley and the Rise of Methodism,* 2nd edn (Nashville: Abingdon, 1992), 214. In any case, the spreading of Methodist societies certainly represented an amalgam of people with different backgrounds, interests, doctrine and levels of discipline.

4 Charles Wesley, *Journal and Letters* (London: Conference Office, 1849), 1, 305; hereafter cited as *CWJ*.

5 *Minutes of the Methodist Conferences* (London: John Mason, 1862), 1.30–31 (14 May 1746, Question 8); see also 564–5. Another more extensive list was added two decades later; ibid, 566–9.

6 Qu. 18 (4). This minute outlined four steps for receiving 'helpers'. The Minutes of the 1749 Conference, in John Jones' hand, are in the Methodist Archives, Rylands University of Manchester. See the first known use of this note in John Bennet's copy of the published *Minutes* (1749) given to him in March 1751, also in the Methodist Archives (hereafter MA). A note similar to this, within a copy of the 'Large' *Minutes*, became a standard means of indicating that a preacher was accepted into and in good standing within the connexion.

7 During a visit to the area shortly before this, Charles noted, 'I did not know till now, that an holiday in Hell is always an holiday in St. Ives'. *MS Journal Letter* (30 July 1746), in MARC, hereafter cited as *MS Journal Letter* (and date of entry). These letters, now in preparation for publication, cover only selected blocks of time but are often more detailed than the MS Journal itself.

8 Exhorters were local leaders (not full-time 'travelling preachers') who occasionally spoke to their fellow Methodists, exhorting them to lead a Christian life.

9 *Minutes*, 1, 40 (2 June 1748), Question 9, 'What can be done in order to purge and quicken the Society?'

10 Charles Wesley, *MS Journal* (13 January 1751), in MARC; hereafter cited as *MS Journal* (and date of entry). This thick volume is more chronologically comprehensive than the journal letters.

11 See *BE*, 20.300n, for a summary of this development.

12 A day or so before the marriage, Charles met John at the Foundery, and noted in his journal, 'heard my brother's lamentable apology which made us all hide our faces'. *MS Journal* (17 February 1751).

13 *MS Journal* (22 March 1751). On 1 June of that year, in the same spirit of peace, Charles visited Lady Huntingdon, 'forgot all that is past, and sealed the reconciliation' with her.

14 Charles no doubt saw Wheatley's alleged immorality as only part of the problem, since he was also accused of illiteracy and poor speech, which may have resulted from Wheatley's heavy Welsh accent. Bellamy, 21.

15 A would-be preacher with a questionable reputation. *MS Journal* (20 June 1740).

16 Bearfield was on the north edge of Bradford-upon-Avon.

17 John's account says that Wheatley 'cavilled at one or two trifling circumstances but allowed the substance of what they said to be true'. *BE*, 20:.395.

18 *MS Journal* (25 June 1751); cf. John's account, which claims that Wheatley accused other preachers of also exercising 'little imprudences'. *BE*, 20.396.

19 *MS Journal* (23 June 1751). See letter to Wheatley, 'that wonderful self-deceiver and hypocrite' – 'Because you have wrought folly in Israel, grieved the Holy Spirit of God, betrayed your own soul into temptation and sin, and the souls of many others whom you ought, even at the peril of your own life, to have guarded against all sin; because you have given occasion to the enemies of God, whenever they shall know these things, to blaspheme the ways and truth of God: We can in no wise receive you as a fellow labourer till we see clear proofs of your real and deep repentance. Of this you have given us no proof yet. You have not so much as named one single person in all England or Ireland with whom you have behaved ill, except those we knew before. The least and lowest proof of such repentance which we can receive is this: that, till our next conference (which we hope will be in October), you abstain both from preaching and from practising physic. If you do not, we are clear, we cannot answer for the consequences.' Signed by both John Wesley and Charles Wesley, *Journal and Diaries III* (25 June 1751), in *BE*, 20.395.

20 Wheatley moved his operation to Norwich in late August 1751, where he was known as a 'Methodist' but openly disowned by the Wesleys.

21 *Journal and Diaries III* (8 July 1751), in *BE*, 20.396.

22 John's account illustrates either his abiding hope that God would work in such people's lives or his indefatigable gullibility regarding the intransigence of human nature, noting in several places, for instance, signals that he had not given up hope that 'Almighty Love might at length bring him to true repentance'. *Journal and Diaries III* (8 July 1751), in *BE*, 20.396

23 *MS Journal* (28 June 1751).

24 Since his marriage to Sally Gwynne in the spring of 1749, Charles had virtually left the itinerancy as he settled into a home in Bristol and began with his wife to raise a family, quite different from the model of the itinerant preacher promoted by his brother John.

25 As of 1749, there were nine circuits or regional groups of Methodist societies, including two in Ireland.

26 A Methodist preacher and good friend of Charles.

27 A close friend of the Wesleys, Sarah had been assigned as housekeeper of Kingswood School, just outside Bristol, and was in a respected position with a full range of responsibilities that entailed close communication with the Wesleys, especially Charles, who lived in Bristol. At this time, she lived in Bradford-upon-Avon. See Gareth Lloyd's important article on her correspondence, now housed in MARC: 'Sarah Perrin (1721–87); Early Methodist Exhorter' in *Proceedings of the Wesley Historical Society*, 41 (No. 3, April 2003).

28 For example, he noted on 21 July that his hearers 'filled the valley and side of the hill, as grasshoppers for multitude. Yet my voice reached the most distant, as I perceived by their bowing at the holy name'. *MS Journal Letter*. He appears to be telling his brother that he also can draw crowds by field preaching.

29 *MS Journal* (6 July 1751); see also a letter to Mr Baily in John Wesley's journal at about this time, which describes in some detail similar attacks upon the Methodists in Lincolnshire, asking that the offenders try to understand their doctrine of 'inward religion' and realize that, in a Protestant country, 'every man *may* think for himself, as he *must* give an account for himself to God'. *BE*, 20.396–7.

30 *MS Journal* (6 July 1751).

31 Charles Wesley, MS letter to John Wesley (in shorthand; 22 July 1751).

32 Charles Wesley, MS letter to John Bennet (11 August 1751).

33 Presently in the MARC; hereafter cited as *MS Preachers*.

34 *MS Preachers*, 1.

35 Each excerpt is carefully dated and represents the only record we have of these particular letters.

36 In the middle of July, John expressed some concern about the rumour that Charles Skelton and James Cownley 'frequently and bitterly rail against the Church'. In response, Charles raised the question, 'What assurance *can* we have that they will not forsake it, at least when we are dead? Ought we to admit any man for a preacher *till* we can trust his invariable attachment to the Church?' Skelton soon left Methodism and settled in Southwark as an Independent minister.

37 *MS Preachers* (letter from John, 8 August 1751).

38 *MS Preachers* (letter from John, 21 August 1751).

39 *MS Preachers* (letter from John, 24 August 1751). Charles' reaction to hearing Loveybond preach ('most miserably') earlier that year had included a typical reaction: 'By how many degrees are such preachers worse than none!' *MS Journal*

(15 April 1751). John's reticence to be critical was overcome slowly, as illustrated by his note of concurrence to Charles on 3 August that he would deal not only with disorderly walkers, but also with triflers, effeminate men, and busybodies: 'I spoke to one this evening, so that I was even amazed at myself'. *MS Preachers*; cf. *Works*, 26.473.

40 Charles transcribes this one sentence admonition into *MS Preachers* in shorthand.

41 Charles points out in his journal that Miss Norton 'quitted' her house for the Wesley entourage, including Sarah Perrin.

42 This document, in Charles Wesley's hand without the later additions (see below, fn. 44), is in *MS Preachers* (pp. 2–5) and provides the quotations in this section.

43 John is quoted as having written on 20 July, 'The Church, that is, the Societies, both *must* and *shall* maintain the preachers we send among them, or I will preach among them no more.'

44 Frank Baker appraises this document cautiously as a 'candid (though maybe incorrect) diagnosis of the growing pains from which Methodism was suffering' but quotes it at some length in *Charles Wesley as Revealed by his Letters* (London: Epworth Press, 1948), 83–5.

45 *MS Preachers*; quoted in Wesley, *BE*, 26.471 (20 July 1751).

46 *MS Preachers*, July 27, quoted in Wesley, *BE*, 26.473 (27 July 1751). This principle (to read all morning or at least five hours a day) is at the heart of Wesley's comments at the 1766 conference, later inserted in the 'Large' *Minutes* (beginning in 1770), concerning the idleness of the preachers, which should be overcome by reading more books, to which some preachers apparently objected that they had no taste for reading, and to which Wesley responded: 'Contract a taste for it by use, or return to your trade'. *Minutes*, 1.68, 518.

47 For instance, a strong restatement of his proposed principle: 'That man, who disdains to work with his own hands (after the great Apostle's example), is no fellow-labourer for us.' His reasoning has both an administrative and pragmatic rationale: 'The man who consents to labour at his calling approves his obedience and humility, both to us and the Church; by being constantly employed he escapes a thousand shams, stops the mouths of gainsayers, relieves the poor people of a grievous burden; and if God withdraws his gift, he is but where he was'.

48 The extant copy of these 'confused thoughts' in Charles' hand (see fn. 38 above) does not include a second section, which apparently was included in the copy written in Sarah Perrin's hand (a week after Charles dictated the first portion to her) and posted to Lady Huntingdon. The letter was intercepted, however, by Mr Doleman and carried to John Wesley, who seems not to have received it until the beginning of December (he was travelling in Cornwall from mid-August to mid-October), but then reacted very strongly to the sentiments expressed in the second section, which stated: 'The second reason I have for insisting on the labourers keeping themselves (which I cannot mention to my brother lest it should be a reason with him against it) is, namely, it will break his power; their not depending on him for bread, and reduce his authority within due bounds, as well as guard against that rashness and credulity of his which has kept me in continual awe and bondage for many years. Therefore, I shall insist on their working as the one point, the single condition of my acting in consort with him, because without this, I can neither trust them nor him.' Charles Wesley, letter to Lady Huntingdon (misdated 4 August 1752, i.e., 1751), in Sarah Perrin's hand. MARC. See John's letter to Charles in reaction to this, in *Letters II* (4 December 1751), in *BE*, 26.479–80.

49 *MS Journal Letter* (3 August 1751).

50 He noted in the *MS Journal* (5 August 1751). that Fenwick had been 'late superintendent of all Ireland'. The other quotations in the paragraph are from Charles' *MS Journal Letter* of the same day.

51 *MS Journal* (5 August 1751).

52 *MS Journal* (5 August 1751), and *MS Preachers*, 1.

53 Thomas Jackson claims that the 'direct object of his mission' was simply to detect sin among the preachers (such as was found in Wheatley) and that he found none. Such whitewashing of history is typical of nineteenth century Methodist literature. Jackson, *Life of Charles Wesley* (New York: Lane & Sandford, 1842), 442.

54 Charles Wesley, MS letter to John Bennet (11 August 1751).

55 Charles Wesley, MS letter to John Bennet (11 August 1751).

56 *MS Journal* (16 August 1751).

57 *MS Journal* (19 August 1751).

58 *MS Journal* (26 August 1751).

59 This phrase is an ironic twisted echo of the language found in the 1746 questions for those who think they are called by the Holy Spirit to be preachers. This interview took place on 12 and 13 August. *MS Journal*.

60 'His preaching is archaic and useless'. Charles Wesley, *MS Journal Letter* (13 August 1751; cf. 12 August).

61 Horace, *Satires*, I.5.11–12. 'Hey, now that is enough!'

62 *MS Journal Letter* (4 and 6 September).

63 Charles reported the attendees to be William Grimshaw, John Milner, John Nelson, William Shent, Christopher Hopper, Thomas Colbeck, Jonathan Reeves, John Bennet, Paul Greenwood, Michael Fenwick, Titus Knight, Robert Swindells and Matthew Watson.

64 These were Mr Mortimer, William Darney, Thomas Webb, and David Trathen.

65 John Wesley was travelling in Cornwall at this time and did not return to London until mid-October. Letters were probably directed to him at various places during his preset itinerary (see fn. 71 below).

66 See George Osborn, *Poetical Works of John and Charles Wesley* (London: 1868), 8.404–5 for all 12 verses.

67 Miss Norton herself would become a divisive force in the Leeds society. Frank Baker, *William Grimshaw; 1708–63* (London: Epworth, 1963), 154.

68 *MS Journal Letter* (11 September 1751).

69 Grimshaw, the incumbent of Haworth, was a longtime friend of the Wesleys and had recently been named by them in the Model Deed as the effective leader of the movement, in case the Wesley brothers died. See, Baker, *Grimshaw*, 154–5, 160.

70 Only about half the attendees from the previous day were present: Charles, William Grimshaw, John Nelson, William Shent, Christopher Hopper, John Bennet and Milner.

71 *MS Journal Letter* (12 September 1751).

72 *MS Journal Letter* (12 September 1751). Charles' report records the first line fairly well, but not the second. The actual text, verse 88 (of 104) in the first hymn in the book, entitled 'The Progress of the Gospel in divers Places of Great Bratain [*sic*],' reads as follows:

There is Brother *Tost* and *Wrangle*
  of late they have begun

To seek, let them never strangle,
    but thy Work carry on.

William Darney, *A Collection of Hymns* (Leeds: James Lister, [1751]), 20. Verse 32 spoke of Leeds:

In *Leedes*, and many Towns around,
    the work goes sweetly on;
There's many hear the Gospel Sound,
    and to the Saviour turn.

Other towns mentioned in the hymn include Birstall, Wakefield, Bradford, Baildon, Keighley, Haworth (Grimshaw's home), Halifax, Skircoat-Green, and several other smaller places. Lister, the publisher of this volume, had also printed a hymn collection for Benjamin Ingham, a former Oxford Methodist, in 1747.

73 Grimshaw testified that Bennet was 'as honest-hearted a man as any among us'. This and subsequent quotations in this section are from Charles' *MS Journal Letter* for this period.

74 It could be noted that the total population of the largest city in the region, Leeds, was not much more than this in 1750, and the borough of Haworth in 2001 had a population of 3390.

75 A very small community two miles south of Halifax.

76 Charles says 'I wounded him in the most sensible part.'

77 Charles adds 'and admirer' in shorthand.

78 See Simon Ross Valentine, *John Bennet and the Origins of Methodism and the Evangelical Revival in England* (Lanham: Scarecrow Press, 1997), 245, 249–52.

79 John had apparently been able to keep in touch occasionally with Charles, who recorded extracts from their correspondence during their travels. They no doubt had shared their itineraries before parting in June and would have been able to exchange letters with about a week's turnaround.

80 John Wesley, *Journal and Diaries III* (Nashville: Abingdon, 1980–96), in *BE*, 20.403.

81 He records virtually nothing between his return to London at the end of October 1751 and the middle of March 1752. There are three or four journal entries for November, which take up about a page, then an account of an earlier incident, which is followed by a gap until March. His correspondence for the period is likewise very sparse and not very helpful in this particular matter.

82 Especially the preachers at Bearfield, Bristol, Bradford and Salisbury.

83 MS letter, Sarah Perrin to Charles Wesley (4 November 1751), in MARC.

84 *MS Preachers* (23 November 1751). Charles' transcript of this letter and most of the material in his notebook from this point on (including a second letter from Sarah Perrin) are written in shorthand.

85 Charles noted parenthetically, 'of his fame you have heard' (in shorthand).

86 *MS Preachers* (23 November; in shorthand).

87 *MS Preachers* (25 November 1751; in shorthand).

88 *MS Preachers* (25 November 1751; in shorthand).

89 *MS Preachers* (2 December 1751). This letter is transcribed by Charles in shorthand, from which the following quotations are taken.

90 She names three preachers who explicitly have agreed with her on this matter and supports her continuing fears in this regard by pointing out that Fenwick was currently in London trying to gain consent from John to continue preaching.

91  *MS Preachers* (5 December 1751; in shorthand).

92  Ibid. Charles saw the potential of separation heightened if they began licensing the preaching houses.

93  Ibid. Probably William Lunnel of Dublin, a banker and supporter of the Wesleys until he left the connexion shortly before his death in 1774. *BE*, 20.187n.

94  *MS Preachers* (2 December 1751). This letter is transcribed by Charles in shorthand, from which the following quotations are taken.

95  Ibid. It appears that Charles has by now written out the Articles.

96  See above, footnote 42. In *MS Preachers*, Charles had recorded his own thoughts in response to a letter from John in August: 'I am told from Bristol you rule the preachers with a rod of iron. They complain of it all over England.'

97  Letter to Charles Wesley, *Letters II* (4 December 1751), *BE*, 26.480–1 and n.

98  Or 'speaking much of the promises, little of the commands'. John had, of course, just published three sermons the previous year that dealt with the same issues: sermons 34–36, 'The Original, Nature, Use, and Properties of the Law' and 'The Law Established Through Faith' (I and II). See *BE*, 2.1–43.

99  These preachers listed by John account for nearly half of the list that Charles and he agreed to expel on 27 November 1751.

100  *BE*, 26.491–2n.

101  *MS Preachers* (16 January 1752; in shorthand)

102  John Wesley, *Letter II* (29 January 1752), in *BE*, 26.490.

103  Signers were: John Wesley, Charles Wesley, John Trembath (one whom John had listed as a 'gospel preacher'), Vincent Perronet, Jonathan Reeves (whom Charles had earlier said 'needed reproof more than encouragement'), Joseph Cownley (of whom John had complained that he 'frequently and bitterly rail[ed] against the Church'), Charles Perronet, Thomas Maxfield (who later became a problem over perfectionism), John Downes, John Jones (who later left the movement), John Nelson, William Shent and John Haine. Ironically, Reeves left Methodism and became ordained in the Church of England.

104  In John Wesley, *Letters II* (16 March 1752), in *BE*, 26.491. Signers were Charles Wesley, William Shent, John Wesley, John Jones, John Downes and John Nelson.

105  Such as the Conferences of May 1754 and later, especially in times of crisis, and fairly regularly after 1769.

106  The following material concerning John and Molly Wesley's confrontation with Bennet is largely summarized from Bennet's diary and found in Simon Ross Valentine, *Mirror of the Soul: The Diary of an Early Methodist Preacher* (Peterborough: Methodist Publishing House, 2002), 211–16.

107  Also the more subtle areas of active and passive righteousness, as well as the issue of causation.

108  It is difficult, in fact, to know how much Charles actually relied on his brother during this trip – the details of their communication is sketchy at best; see fn. 59 and 71 above.

109  John never completely gives up this approach, but recognizes the complexity of the issue; see *Minutes*, 1.78–9 (1768, Question 22)

110  In 1785, when Charles again followed his growing pattern of not attending Conference, John wrote to him: 'If you will go hand in hand with me, do. But do not hinder me if you will not help. Perhaps, if you had kept close to me, I might have done better. However, with or without help, I creep on.' John Telford, ed., *Letters of the Rev. John Wesley* (London, 1931), 7.285.

# 28.  Charles Wesley and Contemporary Theology

## SUSAN J. WHITE

By his own admission, Charles Wesley lived much of his life in the shadow of his elder brother John, who, as he says, 'always had the ascendant over me'.[1] Of course a broader look at the parallel lives of the Wesley brothers shows this was not uniformly the case. Not only did they confront one another on major issues of the polity and praxis of the religious revival they unleashed, but a considerable body of Charles' work published for the use of 'the people called Methodists', including the largest collection of his sacred poetry on biblical themes, his *Short Hymns on Select Passages of the Holy Scripture* (1762), was published without John's editorial influence. However, the impression of inequality in the relationship between the two brothers remains strong, and is affirmed by those who were acquainted with them both. For example, an Oxford contemporary opined that he had 'never observed any person have a more real deference for another, than [Charles] had for his brother . . . He followed his brother entirely.' The same person goes on to add: 'Could I describe one of them, I should describe both.'[2] Many of John and Charles Wesley's Methodist followers could say much the same, and it has been common to speak of 'The Wesleys' as if they were a single, undifferentiated individual.

Certainly the 'ascendancy' of John over his younger brother has carried over into theological writing in the Methodist tradition. In his contribution to a volume on a Wesleyan theological response to poverty, S T Kimbrough Jr, who has produced some of the most exacting work on Charles Wesley's poetry, acknowledges that 'the church's memory of Charles' message to the poor is miniscule at best'.[3] Until very recently, this can probably also be said of Charles' message on most other topics of theological concern to Methodists. Because the historical–theological debates surrounding the role of Charles Wesley's thought in the formation of the Methodist tradition[4] have not been settled in Charles' favour, not even his strongest advocates (J. E. Rattenbury, for example) have been able to make a sufficiently convincing case for his inclusion on historical grounds. As a result, the term 'Methodist theology' has all too often meant 'theology rooted in the writings of John Wesley with the writings of Charles thrown in on occasion where needed'.[5]

## Four difficulties

This persistent failure to take Charles Wesley seriously as a Methodist theologian in his own right is the first difficulty we face if we wish to speak of the ways in which Charles Wesley might serve as a resource for the task of expounding a contemporary Methodist theology. Until quite recently, materials for the study of Charles' work have not been readily available, and denominational hymnals have been the primary way of accessing any writing with the name 'Charles Wesley' attached.[6] Happily, this problem has begun to be recognized and rectified, as the pages of this current book testify. Much of Charles' unpublished work – not only his religious poetry, but a significant number of his sermons, important letters and journal entries as well – is now available in critical editions, material long out of print has been reprinted, and several scholars have taken up Charles' life and work as their primary research interest.[7] In addition, a number of significant monographs focused on specific themes in Charles Wesley's theology have also been published in recent years.[8] But even with this renewal of interest and access, the more general familiarity with Charles Wesley's writing is diminishing as the number of Charles Wesley hymns in denominational hymnals dwindles.[9]

An additional, and perhaps more serious, difficulty in finding a place for Charles in the Methodist theological enterprise is rooted in the methodological challenges presented by the predominant genre through which his thought is embodied. It is a fairly straightforward task to apply the dogmatic content of the kind of letters and journal entries, expository sermons, biblical commentaries and treatises through which John expounded the theology of 'evangelical Arminianism' to the expansion of a particular theological motif. Although Charles' writing certainly includes these kinds of materials, it is of course the enormous output of religious poetry which expresses his theological vision most fully. In his analysis of Charles Wesley as a poet, Kenneth D. Shields points out that the problem is compounded by the fact that Charles Wesley conformed his style not to the prevailing conventions of the day, but to the musical settings which allowed them to be sung by the Methodist people.[10] For those who wish to take seriously modern schools of literary criticism, the task of interpreting his poetry is made even more complex, as the place of historical context becomes less relevant and even the category 'meaning' has begun to be quite slippery. In short, as difficult as it may be to translate theology into poetry, it is at least as difficult to translate poetry into theology, especially to a contemporary culture which has largely stopped reading any form of poetry at all.

The third difficulty is related to the one to which reference has already been made above, namely the personal and theological 'ascendancy' of John over Charles. It is clear that, with certain notable exceptions, the two brothers were in genuine agreement on significant doctrinal matters: prevenient grace, the work of the Holy Spirit, redemption in Christ, the quest for holiness, the nature of the Church and sacraments, and the content of social ethics. Indeed, it has been something of a 'Methodist parlour game' to find passages in John's treatises which correlate with stanzas in Charles' hymns. But we have tended to presume that this was a 'one-way street', with Charles simply putting John's theological insights into poetic forms.[11] More recently, however, Charles Wesley scholars have begun to suggest that the lines of influence might well have gone both ways, and that Charles' poetry very likely gave rise to new and significant theological insights on his brother's part. We stand at the very beginning of the journey toward establishing what elements of Charles' religious poetry and prose can be isolated as an independent theological resource.

The fourth and final difficulty arises from the use to which Charles' work has most often been put: as spiritual nurture for generations of Methodist worshippers who sang his words in church and meditated on them as a constituent element of their private prayer. Charles' poetry was meant to be sung and not read, and has been the principal means by which a specifically Methodist theology was and is internalized by most ordinary Methodist Christians.[12] But this devotional context has tended to insulate it from rigorous analysis and critique. Charles' writing has been so closely associated with religious subjectivity, with spiritual insight and experience, that to remove it to a more objective and analytical arena for application to the establishment of the baselines of Methodist theology seems to degrade it somehow. As an integral part of Methodist ritual, Charles' work inhabits a 'consecrated realm', and to many it seems somehow inappropriate to subject it to the rough-and-tumble of theological argument.[13]

All of this raises a number of important questions for those who wish to see a well-grounded and well-balanced contemporary exposition of Methodist doctrine, one which takes the unique contributions of *both* Wesley brothers seriously in the formation of a theology which is truly 'Wesleyan'. How have these kinds of challenges to the task of appropriating Charles' thought affected the most recent generation of Methodist theologians? Have they been able to overcome these difficulties, or have they been so daunted by them that Charles' work remains marginal in their work? And if so, what, precisely, is lost in the silencing of Charles' distinctive theological voice?

## Charles Wesley's place in contemporary Methodist systematic theology

The renaissance of Wesleyan theology in the past two decades, particularly in the United States, has provided new energy in the exploration not only of classical doctrinal themes but also of matters of immediate contemporary concern from an explicitly Methodist perspective. While in the past we might have spoken of systematic theology undertaken by people who just happen to be Methodists,[14] now we can speak with some confidence of Methodist systematics, and with this shift, scholars seeking to ground themselves in a distinctively Methodist way of doing theology have a range of resources at their disposal.[15] Much of this recent activity has centred upon the Oxford Institute of Methodist Theological Studies, which brings together scholars within the Wesleyan traditions ('those who stand in the tradition of John and Charles Wesley') every five years under the auspices of the World Methodist Council and which tackles a particular theme at each meeting.[16] Kingswood Books, an imprint of Abingdon Press based in Nashville, Tennessee, not only puts the papers from these meetings into print, but also has taken as a mandate the publication of the best of the new wave of Methodist systematic theology, covering a breadth of topics from Trinity to ecumenism and from process theology to political ethics. Scholars at all stages of their academic careers have taken up the task of the renewal of Methodist theology for the third millennium, producing monographs and contributing essays to edited volumes and academic journals.[17] There has also been an attempt at a thorough-going Methodist systematic theology by Walter Klaiber and Manfred Marquardt.[18] While the contributors to this renaissance of Methodist theology take a wide variety of approaches to the task, they all have one thing in common: they are fundamentally concerned with how the varied peculiarities of the Methodist intellectual inheritance might inform current issues of theology and praxis.

One might think that this state of affairs would augur well for Charles Wesley. The most recent generation of Methodist systematicians is not primarily concerned with re-hashing the place of the Wesleys within their eighteenth-century context and in the initial formation and progress of the Methodist worldview (although they certainly do not ignore these matters). They feel free, within limits, to take up the various components of the tradition and to use them creatively in new frames of reference; they do not tend to set their course invariably by the use to which those components have been put in the past. So Charles' rather marginal status in the history of Methodist theologizing should not constrain them from finding an important place for him in the future of Methodist theologizing as they envision it.

But a survey of the recent literature gives a rather mixed picture. Some authors claim quite overtly that Charles has very little place in the configuration of a twenty-first-century Methodist doctrine. Some wish to make this claim based on the internal limitations of the Methodist 'tradition'. For example, Thomas Langford, who was at the forefront of the movement to rejuvenate a specifically Wesleyan form of theology, is quite clear:

> The Wesleyan tradition has been built upon the foundation of John Wesley's sermons and biblical commentaries, 'our doctrines'; has given shape to the moral life, 'our disciplines'; has sung the hymns of Charles Wesley, 'our hymns' and has studied Wesley's other writings and edited works, 'our literature'.[19]

In other words, doctrine is rooted in John's work; singing Charles' hymns is an aspect of Methodist praxis, distinctive but not determinative. In another essay specifically focused on Charles Wesley as a theologian, Langford describes the historic place of Charles' poetry in the formation of eighteenth-century Wesleyan theology, but misses the opportunity to situate him as a resource for Methodist theologians today. Similarly, the opening overview essay in *Charles Wesley: Poet and Theologian* concludes with a clarion call for further research on the theological interpretation of Charles' writing, for ecumenical approaches to his work, and for 'a complete and critical edition of Charles Wesley's works for the sake of future research', but not for a thoroughgoing integration of Charles' thought into the contemporary exposition of Methodist theology.[20]

Many Methodist systematic theologians simply continue the long tradition of displacing Charles' contributions to the margins of Wesleyan theology. The *Epworth Review* volume 'The Millennium Challenges to Methodist Theology' is a case in point. A chapter by Henry Rack, 'John Wesley as Theologian', is not paralleled by one entitled 'Charles Wesley as Theologian', and indeed Charles hardly gets a mention anywhere in this forward look at the future of Wesleyan theology. Some theologians continue the habit of collapsing the two brothers into one. In his otherwise splendid treatment of the theology of the natural world, *God of Nature God of Grace: Reading the World in a Wesleyan Way*, Michael Lodahl quotes extensively (even as a part of the title) from Charles' religious poetry. But only John's name appears in the index, and some of Charles' verse is attributed to 'John and Charles Wesley'. Several books expounding what is described as a 'Wesleyan' theology fail to mention Charles at all.[21] And in some cases mention of his work seems to be something of an afterthought. In the main body of Klaiber and Marquardt's Wesleyan systematic theology, for example, Charles Wesley is given scant attention and only one example of his verse is quoted (although arguments in the text are sometimes buttressed by quoting one of the hymns in the footnotes).

Occasionally we find the theology embedded in the hymns dismissed, implicitly or explicitly, as not as 'elevated' as discursive theology. The 'Editorial' in the issue of the *Epworth Review* on Methodist theology for the new millennium suggests this when it says that 'folk theology lends itself to singing and hymnody, as countless hymnbooks demonstrate when they reproduce even the tiniest output from Charles . . .'[22] But even the article in this issue entitled 'Developing Theology at the Grassroots' does not mention the singing of Charles Wesley's hymns as a part of the nurture of lay theologians.[23]

But the story is not uniformly bleak. Some writers do take for granted Charles' place in the formation of contemporary Methodist doctrine, without seeing the need to argue for it. In one passage in *In Search of the Catholic Spirit: Methodists and Roman Catholics in Dialogue* which contrasts Roman Catholic and Methodist theologies of the church, David Chapman says that,

> Methodists will more readily appreciate the language of John Paul II when he speaks of 'a ministry which presides in truth and love' so that the ship of the Church 'will not be buffeted by the storms and will one say reach its haven' These same scriptural categories of truth and love are also present in the hymns of Charles Wesley from where they have found their way into Methodist ecclesiology.[24]

Mark Stamm approaches Charles' work in much the same way in his attempt to explicate a contemporary eucharistic theology for the Methodist Churches. He moves seamlessly from the quotation of the Wesley hymn, 'O the depth of love divine' to statements about what 'we', the Methodist people, believe: '. . . we do not know exactly how God accomplishes it [the grace of the Supper]. We do, however, know the means appointed: bread and wine received in thanksgiving for all that God has done in Christ.'[25]

A number of recent authors are willing to include Charles' work where it buttresses doctrine already expounded in other forms by John. They do this with varying levels of confidence, however, and some are happiest when John Wesley gives his tacit permission, for example when he himself uses Charles' work in this way.

> . . . One of his [John's] last sermons was devoted to the theme that human life in this world is a protracted *illusion* when compared with the wonderful *realities* of life after death. John closed this sermon with one of Charles Wesley's hymns: 'Vanish then this world of shadows, Pass the former things away!' . . .[26]

In Theodore Runyon's important book on the ways in which John Wesley's theology can shape Methodist thinking on issues of current concern (*The New Creation: John Wesley's Theology Today*),[27] he takes pains to point to those places where Charles Wesley's verse further explicates and expands John's thought on diverse issues, from the Moravian 'stillness' doctrine to perfection, from eucharistic presence to sanctification.

A small number of those involved in the renaissance of Methodist systematic theology have given Charles Wesley serious attention as a significant source for contemporary theological reflection. Perhaps because his work has always been so closely associated with Christian worship, those interested in the renewal of sacramental theology and praxis have found Charles' thought, particularly as it is expressed in the hymns, especially fruitful. Laurence Stookey, for example, ends a long exposition of Charles' ecclesiology and eucharistic theology with the observation:

> Time fails to tell of [Charles] Wesley's potential contribution to other key interests in liturgical renewal: baptism and other aspects of Christian initiation, the liturgical calendar; reform of the wedding and funeral; and the like. But even a limited examination reveals the way in which in our age Charles Wesley can serve as one of our mentors for, and contributors to, the reform and renewal of the church's worship.[28]

Geoffrey Wainwright, in his plea for resistance to the 'neo-Saballenianism' and creeping Unitarianism infecting services of Christian worship and sacramental life looks to the emphatic trinitarianism of Charles Wesley's theology for support.[29] The voices of both Charles and John are weighted equally in the argument; Wainwright quotes in full one of Charles' baptismal hymns ('Come Father, Son, and Holy Ghost') and one of his Eucharistic hymns ('Father, thy grace we claim'), giving them equal standing alongside John's sermons 'The New Creation' and 'On the Trinity'.[30] In his efforts toward a reconstruction of Methodist eucharistic theology, Mark Stamm also gives Charles a good hearing, with a careful exegesis of a number of the eucharistic hymns, and particularly 'Victim Divine'. Stamm is entirely willing to move directly from the theological content of Charles' verse to contemporary doctrinal standards, as in, for example, his statement about the notion of eucharistic sacrifice: 'That Charles Wesley used such an obviously catholic term to describe the sacrament reminds us once again that persons of Methodist heritage should not speak of the sacraments as empty signs.'[31] But this positive attitude is not exclusive to liturgists and sacramental theologians. S T Kimbrough Jr, having argued that Charles Wesley intended the kind of 'gospel poverty' described in his hymns to be both an 'ultimate social principle and an 'ultimate theological imperative', suggests to his readers that:

> ... Charles Wesley's telescopic way of focusing the character and nature of the poor, the vicarious role of the poor in the world, the nature of the community of believers and its mutual sharing of resources, and particularly the powerful concepts of gospel poverty and perfect poverty, can help individual Christians and the corporate body of the Church in the new millennium to discover viable life with the poor and hence with Jesus Christ, the Savior. In fact, Charles can help all Christians learn to seek perfection without both self-divestment and life with and among the poor may indeed be futile.[32]

Other Methodist systematic theologians highlight the special attributes of verse as a carrier of theological content. In his essay in *The Poor and the People Called Methodists*[33] Ted A. Campbell uses a significant number of examples from Charles' work to explore 'the image of Christ in the poor' in Wesleyan thought, contrasting the two brothers' approach to the theme of poverty. Campbell argues that Charles' poetry makes a clear and compelling case that in both caring for the poor and in embracing voluntary poverty ourselves we are coming close to the heart of God. For John, the rich simply owe the poor courtesy and respect as a Christian moral imperative; for Charles, the poor are especially beloved of Christ ('Jesus' bosom friends', those who 'share his condition' and are marked by 'distinguished grace'). Campbell notes that:

> ... [I]t would be fair to conclude that, at many points, Charles Wesley's verse comes closer to the distinctiveness of mendicant understandings of the poor than John Wesley's prose. Perhaps that has something to so with the particular personality of Charles in contrast to John, but it may have something to do with the nature of poetry as contrasted with prose, *for poetry sometimes carries echoes of notions that have long since perished in prose.*[34]

Of course there are other significant ways in which poetry is better able to carry theological meaning than prose, and we shall come to this again below.

A few writers do contrast the thinking of John and Charles on particular theological issues where they disagree. For example, Richard P. Heitzenrater in his essay 'The Poor and the People Called Methodist' distinguishes Charles' attitude toward the poor with that of his brother:

> On the one hand, although 'perfect poverty' was an ideal that Charles Wesley had enunciated for the Methodists in his hymns, John's quarterly allowance was twice the poverty level and five times that of many Methodist preachers. [John] Wesley's views of providence also led him occasionally to see poverty as God's punishment to bring people to an awareness of their sin.[35]

Later in that same volume, Ted A. Campbell contrasts the two brothers' thought, observing that 'Charles Wesley's verse embodies much more of the medieval sense of the saving significance of Christ's poverty, of the distinct love that Christ has for the poor, and even of a distinct call to a life of renunciation and voluntary poverty.' (Theodore Runyon makes the same kind of point in *The New Creation* when he discusses the Wesley brothers' dispute over the doctrine of entire sanctification.)[36]

There are some themes which authors admit Charles having expressed with more cogency and clarity than his brother. In discussing the centrality of love in Methodist theology, John B. Cobb states that 'rhetorically, the centrality of divine love comes to expression most powerfully in the hymns of early Methodism'. He goes on to cite Charles' hymn 'Love divine, all loves excelling' as a case-in-point, with an extended commentary.

> Since the main issue in Wesley's day was to relate this understanding of God as Love Divine to the idea of God's omnipotent sovereignty, it is interesting to note here the appearance of 'almighty' in the second verse. Many prayers and hymns address God as 'The Almighty' rather than Love Divine. The Wesleys did not avoid the language of divine power, but they were careful about the unqualified use of power rhetoric, or allowing that rhetoric to shape the discourse as a whole.[37]

Cobb sets the tone here for those who would wish to take Charles' poetry seriously as a source of Wesleyan theology. But sadly it is the only example in *Grace and Responsibility* of the use of Charles Wesley's thought to make a theological point.

In sum, while contemporary systematic theologians have not ignored Charles Wesley altogether in the formation of a modern Wesleyan theology, and the materials for Charles Wesley research are becoming increasingly available, there is little evidence that many have been convinced by J. E. Rattenbury's assertion that 'Charles' and not John's was the most effective and comprehensive statement of Methodist doctrine'.[38] Finding the voice of Charles Wesley in the work of the most recent generation of Methodist systematicians is something of a treasure hunt. And this is both because of the paucity of references, and because some of Charles' writing is misattributed to John.

But all of this raises important questions: What would mean to Wesleyan systematic theology if Charles Wesley began to be seen as a primary and indispensable resource? What is lost by a failure to integrate Charles fully within the contemporary Methodist theological renewal? To conclude this essay, I would like to suggest five ways in which the inclusion of Charles' theological voice would enhance the twenty-first-century Methodist theological project.

## Integration

The kind of integrated approach represented in Charles Wesley's thought brings together various clusters of elements. S T Kimbrough Jr claims that the great contribution of Charles' approach to theology is that it provides a paradigm that integrates 'head, heart and hands'.[39] Geoffrey Wainwright highlights a different combination: 'The incandescent orthodoxy of Charles Wesley's hymns

– resulting from the fusion of Scripture, the dogmatic tradition, and personal experience – may have been equalled but was never bettered in Christian history.[40] On those occasions where Charles found himself at odds with John's theological vision, it was usually the result of this demand that the inner and outer dimensions of the faith be held together. (This was surely the cause of Charles' intractability on the question of the Moravian 'stillness'.)

The postmodern situation has encouraged this kind of multi-faceted and integrated approach to all of its intellectual projects, including the doing of theology. The most potent approaches to the theological task in our time have centred upon this expectation: liberation theology, which holds the classical elements of theology together with politics; feminist and black theology, which hold them together with gendered and racially-sensitive forms of social analysis respectively; modern forms of evangelical theology, which hold them together with religious experience. If Methodist theology is to join their company, and speak with some potency and authority to those for whom the old analytical modes of discourse have lost their force, then the 'head, heart, and hands' approach of Charles Wesley is indispensable.

## Empathy and affect

One of the words that is often used, both by his contemporaries and by later biographers, to describe Charles, is 'warmth'. He is compassionate towards human frailty, concerned with maintaining the bonds of friendship as a spiritual and theological discipline, and able to talk about love not only as a theological virtue, but also as a human experience of inestimable worth.[41] Charles' affective piety shines throughout his religious poetry and his prose; and the full range of human emotion, from grief to joy, from shame to anger, from fear to love, is represented. Affect is not simply incidental to the theologizing that he does, but is a necessary and indispensable part of it.

But of course it is love that is the beginning and end of Charles Wesley's theological vision, with all other characteristics of mind, heart and action radiating from that centre in concentric circles.:

> Hence may all our actions flow,
> Love the proof that Christ we know;
> Mutual love the token be,
> Lord, that we belong to Thee:
> Love, thy image love, impart
> Stamp it on our face and heart;
> Only love to us be given,
> Lord, we ask no other heaven.[42]

Charles' presumption is that since love is essence of God and of the God–human relationship, the understanding of which is the object of our theological quest, it is only by approaching the task with love that we can hope to know when we have come close to the truth.

Many intellectual heirs of Kant would still want to argue that the activity

of theologizing at its highest is meant to be cool and detached, that it must
be able to claim 'objectivity' and 'balance' in order to have anything valid to
say at all. But since Schleiermacher and those who followed in the philosophical trajectory he set, the presumption that the doing of theology necessarily
requires a 'disembodied person'[43] has begun to be challenged, with more and
more attention being paid to the place of affect not only as a fit subject of
theological enquiry, but as a necessary component of the theological enterprise itself. But Charles Wesley, even caught up as he was in the middle of the
intellectual project we have come to call the Enlightenment, seemed to know
intuitively what came to Schleiermacher a century later as a revolutionary
thought: 'Affect precedes reason.' So in allowing the voice of Charles Wesley
to penetrate our theological method we are on the way to becoming truly
'contemporary theologians' in this important respect.

## Doxology

If we are to take our fellow Methodist Geoffrey Wainwright seriously, doxology is not only the proper mode for Christian living, but for doing theology
as well. The whole substance of Christian faith and action can be presented, as
he does in his magisterial *Doxology: The Praise of God in Doctrine, Faith and Life*,[44]
according to the pattern whereby the Church offers worship to God through
Jesus Christ in the power of the Holy Spirit. *Doxology* is the only example of a
full-scale systematic theology worked out by a Methodist theologian (it is not,
nor does it claim to be, an explicitly *Methodist* systematic theology) which cites
Charles Wesley more often than his brother: Charles merits nearly five times
the number of mentions given to John, and his work is given equal weight
with that of more usually-cited discursive theologians.

To integrate Charles' work, and particularly his religious poetry where his
doxological intent is most transparent, more fully into the Wesleyan theological enterprise, is to push toward this kind of doxological form of theology.
Wainwright sums up his whole with the final stanza of Charles Wesley's
hymn 'Love divine, all loves excelling':

Finish then Thy new creation,
Pure and spotless let us be,
Let us see Thy great salvation,
Perfectly restored in Thee;
Changed from glory into glory,
Till in heaven we take our place,
Till we cast our crowns before Thee,
Lost in wonder, love, and praise![45]

Wainwright says this: 'At its own provisional conclusion a systematic theology
may open into direct prayer for the unfettered circulation of glory which will
be both God's kingdom and our salvation.' Theology is done within the recip-
rocal relationship between God and humankind, which, Wainwright says, 'is
both the condition and content of Christian worship'.

But there is a second aspect to this doxological way of doing theology. Underlying so much of Charles Wesley's work – his religious poetry, as well as his sermons and letters – is a single aim: the transformation of the human mind and heart. He knows intuitively that it is primarily through imagery, and not rational argumentation, that hearts are 'strangely warmed' and made vulnerable to God's love. 'It is towards poetry that the "ecstatic reason", as some have called it, of the religious believer presses when it comes to speech.'[46] Again, in this Charles Wesley takes his place as a contributor to the modern discussions on the nature of theological discourse. He would surely have understood the recent arguments for an understanding of theology as a kind of 'performative rhetoric', in which one can speak meaningfully of 'truthful performance' or 'untruthful performance'.[47] To allow Charles to teach us ways of doing doxological theology and ways of shaping a theological rhetoric that issues in truthful performance is to be both fully Wesleyan and fully contemporary in our approach to God-talk.

### An understanding of metaphorical nature of biblical and theological language

S T Kimbrough Jr remarks (rather cautiously, perhaps) that Charles Wesley 'moved back and forth between a literalistic and non-literalistic view of biblical interpretation, although the latter seems to be more dominant than the former'.[48] But elsewhere he makes a stronger case for the place of the 'hermeneutic of imagination in Charles' work, acknowledging his fidelity to 'traditional authorities and worlds of meaning', while at the same time 'open to new categories of meaning'.[49] Kimbrough laments that modern biblical interpretation has left little room for any form of imagination, 'especially poetical imagination', in the interpretive enterprise, but that the result of this in Charles' writing is that the 'dramatic mythology of the bible comes alive'.

This is a kind of imaginative freedom which is not found in John's exacting exegetical work. In our *An Introduction to World Methodism*, Kenneth Cracknell and I cite the hymn 'Wrestling Jacob' as an example of this kind of freedom. Based on the Genesis text on Jacob wrestling with the stranger (Genesis 32.24–32), Charles casts the singer of the hymn in the role of Jacob, who speaks of the one wrestled with as a 'Traveller Unknown'. As in the biblical text, the singer, like Jacob, demands a blessing, and to know the name of the contender.

> It is here that the hymn diverges from the Genesis text; the singer asks the contender to speak, and to 'tell me if thy Name is LOVE' . . . It is only then that we learn the identity of the one with whom the singer wrestles. "Tis Love! 'Tis Love! Thou diedst for me/I hear thy whisper in my heart!/The morning breaks, the shadows flee,/Pure Universal love thou art:/To me, to all, thy bowels move –/Thy Nature, and Thy Name, is Love'.[50]

As in all of these poems based on scripture texts, the imaginative use of scripture is not for its own sake but for the sake of the spiritual nurture of the singer, and indeed for the people called Methodists as a whole. The ancient story is collapsed into the singer's contemporary situation; here the singer stands in the place of Jacob and knows the helplessness of the struggle and the joy in the Name revealed. In Kimbrough's words, 'It seems self-evident for Wesley that the drama of Scripture and of life anticipates and requires the wedding of faith and imagination through which a sense of the unknown comes.'[51]

The same is true when Charles translates doctrine into poetry. The sense of the heightening of metaphorical power is achieved by the piling up and juxtaposing of doctrinal and biblical imagery, and the turning of the focus toward the first person subject, as one can see in one of the eucharistic hymns:

> The Arm that smote the parting Sea
> Is still stretched out for us, for me,
> The Angel-God is still our guide,
> And, lest we in the Desert faint,
> We find our Spirits' every want
> By constant Miracle supplied.
>
> Thy Flesh for our Support is given,
> Thou art the Bread sent down from Heaven,
> That all Mankind by Thee might live;
> O that we evermore may prove
> The Manna of thy quickening Love,
> And all they Life of Grace receive.[52]

The central place of the imagination, of image and metaphor in theological method is increasingly recognized as a necessity in theological methodology.[53] Dietrich Ritschl has put it most cogently: 'Ideas have as complex a connection with images, feelings, and imagination as with words: they are generated through images and also lead to new images . . . Theology has been haunted down the centuries by the danger of a positivistic understanding of word and language.'[54] To give Charles Wesley a central place in the Wesleyan theology of the future will allow us to tap into this rich vein of metaphorical theology and biblical interpretation.

## Conclusion

The recent renaissance of Wesleyan systematic theology shows some genuine hope that the work of Charles Wesley is beginning to be more fully integrated within contemporary Methodist doctrine. With new editions of his unpublished poetry, his letters and sermons and his journals, we are beginning to have good resources for ascertaining Charles' distinctive theological vision, for disentangling his views from those of his elder brother, and for understanding his place in the gradual formation of the Methodist tradition. We are also beginning to recognize that the ways in which Charles did his theologizing parallel important trends and presuppositions in contemporary theological method. It remains to be seen, however, if Charles' voice can be viewed as something more than just incidental and accessory to the theological enterprise.

Those who choose to follow the example of Charles Wesley's integrated, affective, doxological and metaphorical theology will surely reap for themselves a rich harvest of insight. In addition, the Church and the wider world have a stake in such a process as well. As the Church seeks to rekindle the religious imaginations of those who are mired in the prosaic and the mundane, those who would look to Charles Wesley as a guide for their work will have much to contribute. And as the world asks religious people to provide potent and engaging alternatives to the increasingly influential forms of literalistic interpretations of texts, interpretations which are fuelling so much of the tension and terror around the globe, those who would reach back to claim the work of Charles Wesley as a model may have things of inestimable value to contribute to that task as well. Surely even his most ardent proponents would be unlikely to claim that Charles Wesley is the answer to all the problems of global unrest and malaise in the Church. But on this, the three-hundredth anniversary of his birth, it is surely right and proper to call upon him to lend us a hand in this work.

## Notes

1 Letter to Dr Chandler, in Tyson, *Charles Wesley: A reader*, 59.

2 Quoted in Brailsford, *A Tale of Two Brothers*, 130. Not all interpreters concur with this assessment, however. Eric Routley says of the brothers Wesley: 'They were in some ways complementary; yet, in fact, they saw less of one another than brothers engaged in such work as theirs might be expected to do, and their approach to religion and life differed in matters so fundamental that open disagreement between them was not only possible, but was probably as infrequent as it was only because they spent so little time in company.' Erik Routley, *The Musical Wesleys* (London: Herbert Jenkins, 1968), 28.

3 S T Kimbrough Jr, 'Charles Wesley and the Poor', in D. Meeks, ed., *The Portion of the Poor: Good news to the poor in the Wesleyan tradition* (Nashville: Kingswood, 1995), 167.

4 See Richard P. Heitzenrater, 'Charles Wesley and the Methodist Tradition', in S T Kimbrough Jr, ed., *Charles Wesley: Poet and theologian* (Nashville: Kingswood, 1992), 176–85.

5 Henry Rack claims that even attention to John Wesley as a theologian is a quite recent development. 'Until well into the present century [that is, the twentieth century] few scholars regarded Wesley as a theologian at all, still less as a theologian with an independent and distinctive approach to theology.' H. Rack, 'John Wesley as Theologian', in *The Epworth Review: The millennium challenges Methodist Theology* 27:1 (January 2000), 43. For a survey of the changing approach to John Wesley, see Randy Maddox, 'Rethinking an Inheritance: Wesley as Theologian in the History of Methodist Theology', in R. Maddox, ed., *Rethinking Wesley's Theology for Contemporary Methodism* (Nashville: Abingdon, 1998).

6 Richard Heitzenrater observed in 1992 that the key to a better understanding of Charles Wesley's role in the development of the Methodist tradition would be the publication of critical editions of his work. While acknowledging that 'several important contributions have been made' to this task, 'I would hope', he writes, 'that in the next decade we would see even greater strides in the preparation and

production of this material.' Heitzenrater, 'Charles Wesley and the Methodist Tradition', in Kimbrough, ed., *Charles Wesley: Poet and theologian*, 185.

7 This output began with three good introductions to Charles Wesley's work by Frank Baker: *Charles Wesley as Revealed by his Letters* (1948), *The Representative Verse of Charles Wesley* (1962) and *Charles Wesley's Verse: An introduction* (1964). More material became available in a reprinting of CWJ by Baker Book House in 1980. Kimbrough and Beckerlegge's three-volume *The Unpublished Poetry of Charles Wesley*, and Newport, *Sermons*, gave scholars a good sense of the breadth of Charles Wesley's thought. Miscellaneous prose works were offered in Tyson, *Charles Wesley: A reader*. Tyson, Kimbrough and Newport are the scholars who have most emphatically taken up Charles Wesley as their principal research area. Charles Wesley studies will be enormously aided with the appearance of Kimbrough and Newport's full edition of the Charles Wesley journal (Abingdon, 2007) and by Newport and Lloyd's two-volume critical edition of Charles Wesley's letters, forthcoming from Oxford University Press.

8 See, for example, Gilbert L. Morris, 'Imagery in the Hymns of Charles Wesley' (PhD Dissertation, University of Arkansas, 1981); Barbara Ann Welch, 'Charles Wesley and the Celebrations of Evangelical Experience' (PhD Dissertation, University of Michigan, 1971); James C. Ekrut, *Universal Redemption, Assurance of Salvation, and Christian Perfection in the Hymns of Charles Wesley* (M.Mus. thesis, Southwestern Baptist Theological Seminary, Fort Worth, Texas, 1978); James A. Townsend, *Feelings Related to Assurance in Charles Wesley's Hymns* (PhD Dissertation, Fuller Theological Seminary, 1979); John R. Tyson, *Charles Wesley's Theology of the Cross: An Examination of the Theology and Method of Charles Wesley as seen in his Doctrine of the Atonement* (PhD Dissertation, Drew University, Madison New Jersey, 1983) and idem *Charles Wesley on Sanctification: A biographical and theological study*; Wilma Jean Quantrille, *The Triune God in the Hymns of Charles Wesley* (PhD Dissertation, Drew University, Madison, New Jersey, 1989); Richard Fleming, *The Concept of Sacrifice in the Eucharistic Hymns of John and Charles Wesley* (DMin thesis, Southern Methodist University, Dallas, Texas, 1979).

9 Having made the claim that 'One of the main vehicles for teaching "our doctrines" was "our hymns"', Geoffrey Wainwright recalls: 'My mentor Raymond George used to say that Methodist hymnals got successively worse as the proportion of Wesleyan hymns in them declined.' Wainwright then offers up a *cri de coeur*: 'Can some other English-speaking churches – who were showing signs of taking into their liturgical practice what we had best to offer – help Methodists to regain the Wesleyan hymns? Or will the cultural pressures of the early twenty-first century be too much for us all?' 'Ecumenical Challenges to Methodism', in *The Epworth Review: The millennial challenges Methodist theology*, 27.1 (January 2000), 70.

10 Kenneth D. Shields, 'Charles Wesley as Poet', in Kimbrough Jr, ed., *Charles Wesley: Poet and theologian*, 66.

11 It has been common to describe the hymns as 'Mr. Wesley's [i.e., John's] hymns', as we find in the first American Methodist Discipline (1784).

12 As noted above, Geoffrey Wainwright claims that 'One of the main vehicles for the teaching of "our doctrines" has been "our hymns".'

13 As Teresa Berger points out, even the Charles Wesley literature has had a devotional cast. T. Berger, 'Charles Wesley: A Literary Overview', in S T Kimbrough Jr, ed., *Charles Wesley: Poet and theologian*, 22–3.

14  In Britain these would include Gordon Rupp and Philip Watson; and in the United States, Robert Cushman, Carl Michaelson and, more recently, Geoffrey Wainwright, who is cited below in another context.

15  This is headed by a recent attempt at a Methodist systematic theology by Walter Kaiber and Manfred Marquardt, *Gelebte Gnade: Grundruss einer Theologie der Evangelisch-methodistischen Kirche* (Stuttgart: Christliches Verlagshaus GmbH, 1993) translated into English as *Living Grace: An Outline of Methodist Theology* (Nashville: Abingdon, 2001); Albert Outler, *Evangelism and Theology in the Wesleyan Spirit* (Nashville: Discipleship Resources, 1996); John B. Cobb, *Grace and Responsibility: A Wesleyan theology for today* (Nashville: Abingdon, 1995); Joerg Rieger and John J. Vincent, *Methodist and Radical: Rejuvenating the tradition* (Nashville: Kingswood, 2003); M. Douglas Meeks' three edited volumes, reflecting the collaborative work done at the Oxford Institute of Theology, *The Future of the Wesleyan Theological Tradition* (Nashville: Abingdon, 1985); *The Portion of the Poor: Good news to the poor in the Wesleyan tradition, Trinity, Community and Power: Mapping trajectories in Wesleyan theology;* and *Wesleyan Perspectives on the New Creation* (Nashville: Abingdon, 2004); Randy Maddox, ed., *Rethinking Wesley's Theology for Contemporary Methodism* (Nashville: Kingswood); Theodore Weber, *Politics and the Order of Salvation: Transforming Wesleyan political ethics* (Nashville: Abingdon, 2001); Bryan P. Stone and Thomas Jay Oord, eds, *Thy Nature and Thy Name is Love: Wesleyan and process theology in dialogue* (Nashville: Kingswood, 2001); and S T Kimbrough Jr's edited volume, *Charles Wesley: Poet and theologian.* Kingswood Books, a sub-set of Abingdon Press based in Nashville, Tennessee, has taken as a mandate the publication of the new wave of Methodist theology. Paul Chilcote, ed., *The Wesleyan Tradition: A paradigm for renewal* (Nashville: Abingdon, 2002); Tyson, *Charles Wesley on Sanctification.* These volumes are augmented by a number of shorter articles in scholarly journals. See also Clarence Bence, 'Processive Eschatology: Wesleyan Alternatives', in *Wesleyan Theological Journal* 14:1 (1979).

16  M. Douglas Meeks has edited a number of volumes of the papers presented at these meetings: *The Future of the Wesleyan Theological Tradition* (Nashville, TN: Abingdon, 1982); *What Should Methodists Teach: Wesleyan traditions and modern diversity* (Nashville: Kingswood, 1987); *The Portion of the Poor: Good news to the poor in the Wesleyan tradition, Trinity, Community and Power: Mapping trajectories in Wesleyan theology* (Nashville: Kingswood); and *Wesleyan Perspectives on the New Creation.*

17  Senior scholars include the late Albert Outler, *Evangelism and Theology in the Wesleyan Spirit,* John B. Cobb, *Grace and Responsibility: A Wesleyan theology for today* and Thomas A. Langford, *Practical Divinity: Theology in the Wesleyan tradition* (Nashville: Abingdon, 1983) and scholars at mid and early career include Randy Maddox, *Rethinking Wesley's Theology for Contemporary Methodism and Aldersgate Reconsidered* (Nashville: Kingswood, 1990) and Bryan P. Stone and Thomas Jay Oord, eds, *Thy Nature and Thy Name is Love: Wesleyan and process theology in dialogue;* Joerg Rieger, *Methodist and Radical: Rejuvenating the tradition,* 2003 and Paul Chilcote, ed., *The Wesleyan Tradition: A paradigm for renewal* (Nashville: Abingdon, 2002) and Theodore Weber, *Politics and the Order of Salvation: Transforming Wesleyan political ethics.*

18  *Living Grace: An outline of Methodist theology* (Nashville: Abingdon, 2001).

19  *Practical Divinity,* 13.

20  T. Berger, 'Charles Wesley: A Literary Overview', in S T Kimbrough Jr, ed., *Charles Wesley: Poet and theologian,* 28–9.

21 See, for example, the published papers from the ninth Oxford Institute of Theology, M. Douglas Meeks, ed., *The Portion of the Poor: Good news for the poor in the Wesleyan tradition*.

22 'Editorial', *Epworth Review: The millennial Challenges to Methodist Theology* 27:1 (January 2000); 6.

23 Kathleen Bowe, 'Developing Theology at the Grassroots', 64–8.

24 David Chapman, *In Search of the Catholic Spirit: Methodists and Roman Catholics in dialogue* (London: Epworth, 2004), 217–18.

25 Mark Stamm, *Sacraments and Discipleship: Understanding baptism and the Lord's Supper in a United Methodist context* (Nashville: Discipleship Resources, 2001), 102.

26 R. Maddox, 'Nurturing the New Creation', *in Wesleyan Perspectives on the New Creation*, 22. David Chapman does something similar in his conclusion to the story of the progress of ecumenical dialogue between Methodists and Roman Catholics, when he concludes his exposition of Charles Wesley's hymn 'Weary of all this worldly strife', taking care to note that John had appended it to the published version of his treatise 'on the Catholic Spirit'. Chapman, *In Search of the Catholic Spirit*, 262–3. 'Charles Wesley: Mentor and Contributor to Liturgical Renewal', in Kimbrough, ed., *Charles Wesley: Poet and theologian*, 154.

27 Theodore Runyon, *The New Creation: John Wesley's theology today* (Nashville: Abingdon, 1998).

28 Laurence Hull Stookey, 'Charles Wesley: Mentor and Contributor to Liturgical Renewal', in S T Kimbrough Jr, ed., *Charles Wesley: Poet and theologian*, 154.

29 I try to enlist him for support in a similar cause in *Whatever Happened to God the Father?: The Jesus heresy in modern worship* ([Penryn, Cornwall?]: Methodist Sacramental Fellowship, 2002).

30 Wainwright, 'Sacraments in Wesleyan Perspective', in *Worship With One Accord: Where liturgy and ecumenism meet* (Oxford: Oxford University Press, 1997), 120–2.

31 Mark W. Stamm, *Let Every Soul be Jesus' Guest: A theology of the open table*, (Nashville: Abingdon, 2005). Tom Albin suggests that those with interest in the renewal Methodist sacramental theology would be much helped by giving attention to some of Charles' hitherto unpublished work, including an eight-page manuscript from 1779 which contains a treatise 'On the Weekly Sacrament'. Albin, 'Charles Wesley's Other Prose Writings, in S T Kimbrough Jr, ed., *Charles Wesley: Poet and theologian*, 95. See further, Newport, *Sermons*, 280–6.

32 S T Kimbrough Jr, 'Perfection Revisited: Charles Wesley's Theology of 'Gospel Poverty' and 'Perfect Poverty', in Richard Heitzenrater, ed., *The Poor and the People Called Methodists* (Nashville: Kingswood, 2002), 118–19.

33 Richard Heitzenrater, ed., *The Poor and the People Called Methodists*.

34 Ted A. Campbell, 'The Image of Christ in the Poor', in Heitzenrater, *The Poor and the People Called Methodists*, 56. Emphasis added.

35 'The Poor and the People Called Methodists', in Heitzenrater, ed., *The Poor and the People Called Methodists*.

36 See T. Runyon, *New Creation*, 230.

37 John B. Cobb, *Grace and Responsibility*, 58–9.

38 E. J. Rattenbury, *The Evangelical Doctrines of Charles Wesley's Hymns*, 61.

39 S T Kimbrough Jr, 'The Portion of the Poor', 167.

40 'Ecumenical Challenges for Methodism in the twenty-first century' in Epworth Review 27:1, p. 70.

41 *The Poor and People Called Methodists*, 126.

42 *PW*, 1.354.

43 See Fergus Kerr, *Theology after Wittgenstein* (Cambridge: Cambridge University Press, 2003).

44 G. Wainwright, *Doxology: The Praise of God in Doctrine, Faith and Life* (Oxford: Oxford University Press, 1980).

45 *PW*, 4.219–20.

46 Wainwright, *Doxology*, 203.

47 See Stanley Hauerwas and James Fodor, 'Performing Faith: The Peaceable Rhetoric of God's Church', in S. Hauerwas, *Performing the Faith* (Grand Rapids: Brazos Press, 2004).

48 Kimbrough, 'Charles Wesley and Biblical Interpretation', in Kimbrough, ed., *Charles Wesley: Poet and theologian*, 109.

49 Kimbrough, 'Charles Wesley and Biblical Interpretation', 113ff.

50 Kenneth Cracknell and Susan J. White, *An Introduction to World Methodism* (Cambridge: Cambridge University Press, 2005), 152.

51 S T Kimbrough, 'Charles Wesley and Biblical Interpretation', 118.

52 Charles Wesley, *Hymns on The Lord's Supper* (Bristol: Felix Farley, 1745), no. XCII, 78–9.

53 See, for example, Sallie McFague, *Metaphorical Theology*, for a good statement of the place of metaphor in theological method.

54 D. Ritschl, *The Logic of Theology* (Minneapolis: Fortress, 1982), 15–16.

# Bibliography

Compiled by Donald A. Bullen

## A complete list of works relating to Charles Wesley

Adams, Charles, *The Poet Preacher: A brief memorial of Charles Wesley, the eminent preacher and poet, Five illustrations*, New York: Carlton & Porter, 1859.

Albin, Thomas R. and Oliver A. Beckerlegge, *Charles Wesley's Earliest Evangelical Sermons: Six shorthand manuscript sermons now for the first time transcribed from the original*, Ilford: Wesley Historical Society in association with Robert Odcombe Associates, 1987.

Allchin, A. M., *Participation in God: A forgotten strand in Anglican tradition*, Wilton, CT: Morehouse-Barlow, 1988.

Allen, Cecil J., 'John and Charles Wesley', *Hymns and the Christian Faith*, pp. 55–66, London: Pickering and Inglis, 1966.

Arnold, Richard, *English Hymns of the Eighteenth Century: An anthology*, New York: P. Lang, 1991.

Armstrong, Thomas, 'The Wesleys – Evangelists and Musicians', *Organ and Choral Aspects and Prospects*, ed. Max Hinrichson, 95–106, New York and London: Hinrichson, 1958.

Atmore, Charles, 'Charles Wesley', in *The Methodist Memorial: Being an impartial sketch of the lives and characters, of the preachers, who have departed this life*, Bristol: R. Edwards, 1801.

Baker, Frank, *A Union Catalogue of the Publications of John and Charles Wesley*, Durham, NC: The Divinity School, Duke University, 1966.

Baker, Frank, *A Wesley Bibliography: An introduction to the publications of John and Charles Wesley*, 2 vols, 1985.

Baker, Frank, *Charles Wesley as Revealed by his Letters*, Wesley Historical Society Lectures no. 14, London: Epworth Press, 1948.

Baker, Frank, ed., *Charles Wesley's Verse: An introduction*, London: Epworth Press, 1964, second ed., 1988.

Baker, Frank, *John Wesley and the Church of England*, Nashville: Abingdon Press, 1970.

Baker, Frank, ed., *Representative verse of Charles Wesley*, London: Epworth Press, 1962.

Baker, Frank, *Selective Representative Verse of Charles Wesley* [With plates, including a portrait and facsimiles], London: Epworth Press, 1962.

Baker, Frank, *William Grimshaw; 1708–63*, London: Epworth Press, 1963.

Barker, Esther T., *Lady Huntingdon, Whitefield, and the Wesleys*, Maryville, TN, 1984.

Barry, Jonathan and Kenneth Morgan eds, *Reformation and Revival in Eighteenth-Century Bristol*, Wesley Theological Seminary Library, Produced for the Society by Alan Sutton Pub. Limited, 1994.

Beckerlegge, Oliver A., *Charles Wesley, Poet*, Ilkeston, Derbyshire: Moorley's Print & Publishing, 1990, This paper was read at the October 1990 meeting of the Wesley Fellowship in Nantwich, Cheshire.

Beckerlegge, Oliver A., *John Wesley's Writings on Roman Catholicism*. Selected, arranged and edited by Oliver A. Beckerlegge, London: Protestant Truth Society, 1993.

Beckerlegge, Oliver A., *The Shorthand of Charles Wesley*, Madison, NJ: Charles Wesley Society, 2002.

Bellamy, Elizabeth J., *James Wheatley and Norwich Methodism*, Peterborough: Methodist Publishing House, 1994.

Belshaw, Robert R., *John Lee and Charles Wesley's Hymns: An appreciation*, Dublin: the University Press by Ponsonby & Gibbs, 1902.

Benson, Joseph, *Hymns for Children selected chiefly from the publications of John & Charles Wesley, and Dr. Watts*, G. Story, 1806, also under title *Hymns for Children: selected chiefly from the publications of the Rev. John & Charles Wesley, and Dr. Watts, and arranged in proper order*, London: T. Blanshard, 1814.

Benson, Joseph, *The Life of the Rev John de la Flechere*, London: Thomas Cordeux, 1806.

Berger, Teresa, *Theology in Hymns? A study of the relationship of doxology and theology according to A collection of hymns for the use of the people called Methodists (1780)*. translated by Timothy E. Kimbrough, Nashville: Kingswood Books, 1995.

Best, Gary, *Charles Wesley: A biography*, Peterborough: Epworth, 2006.

Bett, Henry, *The Hymns of Methodism*, London: Epworth Press, 1st edn 1913, 3rd edn revised and enlarged, 1945.

Bible, Ken, *Wesley Hymns*, Kansas City: Lillenas Publishing Co., 1982.

Bird, Frederick, *Charles Wesley and Methodist Hymns*, Andover: Warren F. Draper, 1864. An article with the same title appears in *Bibliotheca 21*, 127–62, 284–318, 1864.

Bird, Frederic M., *Charles Wesley seen in his finer and less familiar poems*, R. Worthington, 1878 [1866].

Birtwhistle, Allen, *Seek Ye First: A Series of Six Meditations Based on Charles Wesley's Hymn, 'Come O Thou Traveller Unknown'*, London: Epworth Press, 1969.

Body, Alfred H., *John Wesley and Education*, London: Epworth Press, 1936.

Bowmer, John C., *Charles Wesley: the poet of Methodism*, Sunderland, Wesley Historical Society, North-East Branch, 1988.

Brailsford, Mabel R., *A tale of two brothers: John and Charles Wesley*, London: Hart-Davis and New York: Oxford University Press, 1954.

Brawley, Benjamin G., 'Charles Wesley and His Age' in *History of the English Hymn*, 89–119, New York: Abingdon Press, 1932.

Brecht, M. *et al.* eds, *Pietismus und Neuzeit: ein Jahrbuch zur Geschichte des neueren Protestantismus* vol. 17, 1991, Göttingen: Vandenhoeck & Ruprecht, 1991.

Brose, Martin E., *Charles Wesley (1707–1788) Tagebuch 1738*, übersetzt und kommentiert von Martin E. Brose, Stuttgart: Christliches Verlagshaus, 1992.

Brose, Martin E., *Charles Wesley: der methodistische Liederdichter*, Stuttgart: Christliches Verlagshaus, 1999.

Brose, Martin E., *Zum Lob befreit: Charles Wesley und das Kirchenlied*, Stuttgart: Christliches Verlagshaus, 1997.

Browlie, John, 'Charles Wesley' in *Hymns and Hymn Writers of the Church Hymnary*, 131–7, London: H. Frowde, 1899.

Brown, Robert W., *Charles Wesley: Hymnwriter: Notes on research carried out to establish the location of his residence in Bristol during the period 1749–1771*, Bristol: The Author, 1993.

Brown, Earl Kent, *Women of Mr Wesley's Methodism*, New York: Edwin Mellen Press, 1983.

Burgess, William Penington, *Wesleyan Hymnology : or, A companion to the Wesleyan hymn book: comprising remarks, critical, explanatory and cautionary, designed to promote the more profitable use of the volume*, 2nd edn, London: John Snow, 1846.

Burton, Jack R., *The Richest Legacy: The eucharistic hymns of John and Charles Wesley*, Norwich: F. Crowe and Sons, 1981.

Bush, George W., *A Charge to Keep*, New York: William Morrow & Company, 1999.

Butler, David, *Methodists and Papists: John Wesley and the Catholic Church in the eighteenth century*, London: Darton Longman and Todd, 1995.


Caldecott, William Shaw, *Good Works; or, 'Things that accompany salvation': being a series of chapters on the Methodist rules [of John and Charles Wesley]*, London 1876.

Campbell, Ted A., *John Wesley and Christian Antiquity: Religious vision and cultural change*, Nashville: Kingswood Books, 1991.

Capon, John, *John and Charles Wesley: The preacher and the poet*, London: Hodder and Stoughton, 1988.

Carter, David, *Love Bade Me Welcome: A British Methodist perspective on the church*, Peterborough: Epworth Press, 2002.

Catalogue of the Charles Wesley papers, Manchester: John Rylands University Library, vols 1 and 2, 1994.

Cate, Margaret Davis, *The Wesleys on Saint Simons Island*, The Commission on Archives and History, South Georgia Conference, United Methodist Church, 1971.

Challoner, Richard, *A Caveat Against the Methodists*, London, printed for M. Cooper, 3rd edn, 1787.

Chapman David, *In Search of the Catholic Spirit: Methodists and Roman Catholics in Dialogue*, Peterborough: Epworth Press, 2004.

Chilcote, Paul Wesley, 'A faith that sings: the renewing power of lyrical theology' [with special reference to Charles Wesley], in *The Wesleyan Tradition: A paradigm for renewal*, Paul Wesley Chilcote, ed., Nashville: Abingdon Press, 2002.

Chilcote, Paul Wesley, *John Wesley and the Women Preachers of Early Methodism*, London: Scarecrow Press 1991.

Chilcote, Paul Wesley, *Recapturing the Wesleys' Vision: An introduction to the faith of John and Charles Wesley*, Leicester: InterVarsity Press, 2004.

Chilcote, Paul Wesley, ed., *The Wesleyan Tradition: A paradigm for renewal*, Nashville: Abingdon Presss, 2002.

Christensen, Michael J., and Jeffery Wittung, eds, *Partakers of the Divine Nature*, Rutherford, NJ: Fairleigh Dickinson University Press, 2006.

Christophilus, *A Serious Inquiry whether a late epistle from the Rev. Mr. Charles Wesley to the Rev. Mr. John Wesley be not an evident mark of their being unhappily fallen into one of the . . . wiles of the Devil, . . . by inducing their hearers to have too high an opinion of them, as the peculiar servants of God*, London: Printed for the author, 1755.

'A Churchman', *Methodist Episcopacy: A tract, containing authentic documents from the writings of the Rev. Messrs. John and Charles Wesley, Rev. Dr. Coke, Bishop White, and others, submitted to the candid consideration of the reader, by a churchman ...*, Delaware, OH: Printed by Ezra Griswold, 1823.

Clapper, Gregory Scott, *As if the Heart Mattered: a Wesleyan spirituality*, Nashville: Upper Room Books, 1997.

Clark, Elmer T., *Charles Wesley*, published jointly by the World Methodist Council and Association of Methodist Historical Societies, 1964/1976.

Clark, Elmer T., *Charles Wesley, the Singer of the Evangelical Revival*, Nashville: The Upper Room, 1957.

Clarke, Adam, *Memoirs of the Wesley Family*, London: J. & T. Clarke, and sold by J. Kershaw, 1823, also T. Tegg & Son, 1826.

Cobb, John B., *Grace and Responsibility: A Wesleyan Theology for Today*, Nashville: Abingdon Press, 1995.

Cole, Richard Lee, *The Wesleys (John and Charles) in Cork*, Cork, 1917, reprinted from *The Daily Christian advocate*.

Colquhoun, Frank, *Charles Wesley, 1707–1788: The poet of the evangelical revival*, London: Church Book Room Press, 1947.

Colquhoun, Frank, *Hymns that Live: Their meaning and message*, London: Hodder and Stoughton, 1986.

Cooke, Frances E., *Footprints, [Biographies of John and Charles Wesley, George Fox, Mohammed, John Huss and John Falk]*, London: Sunday School Association, 1875.

Cooper, Arnold H., *The Intercession of our Lord: Charles Wesley's eucharistic hymns today*, Oxford: Westminster College, 1996.

Creamer, David, *Methodist Hymnology: Comprehending notices of the poetical works of John and Charles Wesley, showing the origin of their hymns in the Methodist Episcopal, Methodist Episcopal south, and Wesleyan collections; also, of such other hymns as are not Wesleyan, in the Methodist Episcopal hymn-book, and some account of the authors, with critical and historical observations*, New York: published for the author, 1848.

Crichton, Mitchell, T., *Charles Wesley: Man with the dancing heart*, Kansas City: Beacon Hill Press, 1994.

Christophers, Samuel Woolcock, *The Epworth Singers and Other Poets of Methodism*, London: Haughton & Co., 1875.

Cumbers, Frank H., *My Wondering Soul: Scenes from the life of Charles Wesley*, London: Epworth Press, 1957. (An Epworth Play).

Curnock, Nehemiah, *The Journal of the Rev. John Wesley, A.M.*, 8 vols, 1909, reprinted and enlarged, London: Epworth Press, 1938.

Daines, Barrington, *Miscellanies*, London: J. Nichols, 1781.

Dallimore, Arnold.A., *A Heart Set Free: the life of Charles Wesley*, Westchester, IL: Crossway Books, 1988.

Dallimore, Arnold A., *Susanna: the mother of John and Charles Wesley*, Darlington: Evangelical Press, 1992.

Davie, Donald, 'The Classicism of Charles Wesley', in *Purity of Diction in English Verse*, 70–81, London: Chatto and Windus, 1952.

Davies, G. C. B., *Early Cornish Evangelicals*, London: SPCK, 1951.

Davies, Rupert E., 'John and Charles Wesley', 'The Revival', and 'The Theology and the Hymns of the Revival' in *Methodism*, pp. 38–104, London: Epworth Press, 1963.

Davies, Rupert E., A. Raymond George and Gordon Rupp, eds, *A History of the Methodist Church in Great Britain*, 4 vols, London: Epworth Press, 1965–88.

Demaray, Donald, 'John Wesley: preaching principles and practice', in *Kerygma and Praxis*, ed. W Vanderhoof and D. Basinger, Rochester, NY: Roberts Wesleyan College, 1984.

Douglass, Paul F., *Wesleys at Oxford: The religion of university men*, Bryn Mawr, PA: Bryn Mawr Press, 1953.

Drew University Library, *Resources for Wesley and Methodist Studies in Drew University Library*, Madison, NJ: [Drew University Library], 1974.

Dudley-Smith, Timothy, *A Flame of Love: A personal choice of Charles Wesley's verse*, London: Triangle, 1987.

Duffy, E., 'Wesley and the Counter Reformation', *Revival and Religion since 1700: Essays for John Walsh*, eds J. Garnett & C. Matthew, London: Hambledon Press, 1993.

Dutton, W. E., ed., *Hymns on the Lord's Supper: The eucharistic manuals of John and Charles Wesley*, Bull Simons, 1871, 2nd edn, John Hodges, 1880.

Edwards, Maldwyn L., *Family Circle: A Study of the Epworth household in relation to John and Charles Wesley*, London: Epworth Press, 1949.

Edwards, Maldwyn L., *John Wesley and the Eighteenth Century: A study of his social and political influence*, London: Epworth Press, 1st edn 1933, rev. edn, 1955.

Edwards, Maldwyn L., *Sons to Samuel*, London: Epworth Press 1961.

Emurian, Ernest K, *Charles Wesley: A play in three scenes*, Portsmouth, VA: Elm Avenue Methodist Church [n.d.]

Findlay, George H., *Christ's Standard Bearer: A study in the hymns of Charles Wesley as they are contained in the last edition, 1876, of 'A Collection of Hymns for the Use of the People Called Methodists'*, London: Epworth Press, 1956.

Fish, Henry, ed., *A Poetical Version of Nearly the Whole of the Psalms of David by Charles Wesley*, 2nd edn, London: James Nichols for the editor, sold by John Mason, 1854.

Flew, R. Newton, *The Hymns of Charles Wesley, a study of their structure*, WHS Lecture, London: Epworth Press, 1953.

Flint, Charles Wesley, *Charles Wesley and his Colleagues*, Washington: Public Affairs Press, 1957.

Forsaith, Peter S., *A Kindled Fire: John and Charles Wesley, and the Methodist revival in the Leeds area*, Leeds: the author, 1988.

Forsaith, Peter S., *Unexampled Labours: The letters of the Revd. John Fletcher of Madeley to leaders in the Evangelical Revival*, Peterborough: Epworth, 2007.

Freeman, C. B., *Charles Wesley: The poet and the editors*, London: SPCK, 1958.

Frost, Brian, 'The Idea of Fullness in the Hymns of Charles Wesley', in *We Belong to One Another: Methodist, Anglican and Orthodox essays*, pp. 48–61, ed. A. M. Allchin, London: Epworth Press, 1965.

Funston, John Wesley, *The Wesleys in Picture and Story: An illustrated history of the life and times of John and Charles Wesley*, Mount Morris, IL: Kable Brothers, 1939.

Gamble, T., *The Love Stories of John and Charles Wesley*, Savannah: Review Publishing and Printing, 1927.

Gentry, Peter W., *Heritage in the Warmed Heart: our holiness roots*, Kansas City: Beacon Hill Press, 1986.

Gilbert, John P., *Praising the God of Grace: The theology of Charles Wesley's hymns*, Nashville: Abingdon Press, 2005.

Gill, Frederick C., *Charles Wesley: The first Methodist*, London: Lutterworth Press, 1964.

Gordon, Alexander, 'Charles Wesley', in vol. 20 of *Dictionary of National Biography*, edited by Leslie Stephen, 1213–4, London: Smith, Elder, 1885–1900.

Green, F. Pratt, *Twenty-six Hymns*, London: Epworth Press/Methodist Publishing House, 1971.

Green, Richard, *The Works of John and Charles Wesley: A bibliography containing an exact account of all the publications issued by the brothers Wesley, arranged in chronological order, with a list of the early editions, and descriptive and illustrative notes*, London: C. H. Kelly, 1896.

Green, V. H. H., *Young Mr Wesley*, London: St Martin's Press, 1961.

Gregory, Benjamin, 'Charles Wesley', in *Champions of the Truth: Short lives of Christian leaders in thought and action*, ed. A. R. Buckland, London: Religious Tract Society, 1963.

Gregory, Jeremy, '"In the Church I will live and die": John Wesley, the Church of England, and Methodism', in William Gibson and Robert G. Ingram ed. *Religious Identities in Britain, 1660–1832*, Aldershot: Ashgate, 2005, 147–78.

Gumbs, Wycherley, *Singing Redemption Songs: (a commentary on the hymns published in the Methodist Hymns book 1933, with special emphasis on the hymns written by Charles Wesley)*, St Thomas, Virgin Islands, 1990.

Haas, A. B., *Charles Wesley*, Boston: Papers of the Hymn Society of America, 1957.

Halévy, E., *The Birth of Methodism in England*, Chicago: University of Chicago Press, 1971.

Hampson, John, *Memoirs of John Wesley*, 3 vols, Sunderland: for John Hampson, 1791.

Handel, George F., *The Fitzwilliam Music never before Published: Three hymns, the words by the late Rev. Charles Wesley . . . Set to Music by George Frideric Handel . . . 1826. George Frideric Handel, The Complete Hymns & Chorales*, facsimile ed., with an Introduction by Donald Burrows, London: Novello, 1988.

Hanson, Derrick G., *Favourite Hymns: Their stories and their meaning, vol. IV, the hymns of Charles Wesley*, Liverpool: Grasshopper Publishing, 2004.

Harrison, G. Elsie, *Son to Susanna: The Private Life of John Wesley*, London: Ivor Nicholson and Watson, 1937.

Hart, Elizabeth, *All Loves Excelling: Daily meditation with Charles Wesley*, Peterborough: Methodist Publishing House, 1997.

Heitzenrater, Richard P., *Mirror and Memory: Reflections on early Methodism*, Nashville: Abingdon Press, 1989.

Heitzenrater, Richard P., *The Elusive Mr Wesley*, 2nd edn, Nashville: Abingdon Press, 2003.

Heitzenrater, Richard P., ed. *The Poor and the People Called Methodists*, Nashville: Kingswood Books, 2002.

Heitzenrater, Richard P., *Wesley and the People Called Methodists*, Nashville: Abingdon Press, 1995.

Hempton, David, 'John Wesley and England's Ancient Regime', *The Religion of the People: Methodism and Popular Religion*, London: Routledge, 1996, 77–90.

Hempton, D., 'John Wesley and the Rise of Methodism', *John Wesley Tercentenary Essays: Proceedings of a conference held at the University of Manchester, June 2003*.

Edited by Jeremy Gregory, *Bulletin of the John Rylands University Library of Manchester*, 85, nos. 2 and 3, Summer and Autumn, 2003.

Hempton, David, *Methodism and Politics in British Society 1750–1850*, London: Hutchinson, 1984.

Hempton, David, *Methodism: Empire of the Spirit*, New Haven: Yale University Press, 2005.

Hempton, David and John Walsh, 'E. P. Thompson and Methodism', *God and Mammon: Protestants, money and the market, 1790–1860*, ed. Mark A. Noll, Oxford and New York: Oxford University Press, 2001.

Herbert, Chesley Carlisle, 'Charles Wesley, the Poet–Theologian of Methodism', in *The Theologians of Methodism*, 48–59, Nashville: Publishing House of the Methodist Episcopal Church, South, 1895.

Hildebrandt, Franz, *Christianity according to the Wesleys*: the Harris Franklin Rall lectures, 1954, delivered at Garrett Biblical Institute, Evanston, Illinois, London: Epworth Press, 1956.

Hildebrandt, Franz, *Wesley Hymn Book*, London: A. Weekes, 1959.

Hodges, H. A. and A. M. Allchin, *A Rapture of Praise: Hymns of John and Charles Wesley*, selected, arranged and introduced by H. A. Hodges and A. M. Allchin, London: Hodder & Stoughton, 1966.

Hogue, W. T., *Living Hymns of Charles Wesley, the Singing Saint: Hymns that are immortal*, Minneapolis: Light and Life Press, 1957.

Holifield, E. Brooks, *Health and Medicine in the Methodist Tradition*, New York: Crossroad, 1986.

Hoole, Elijah, *Byrom and the Wesleys*, London: William Nichols, 1864.

Horton, Peter, *Samuel Sebastian Wesley: A life*, Oxford: Oxford University Press, 1964.

Houghton, Edward, *The Handmaid of Piety: And other papers on Charles Wesley's hymns*, Quacks Books in association with the Wesley Fellowship, 1992.

*Hymns & Psalms*, London: Methodist Publishing House, 1983.

*Hymns & Songs*, London: Methodist Publishing House, 1969.

Jackson, Francis M., *Index to the Library Edition of Thomas Jackson's Life of Charles Wesley*, published for the Wesley Historical Society by C. H. Kelly, 1899.

Jackson, Thomas, *Aids to Truth and Charity: A letter addressed to William Fitzgerald, D.D., bishop of Cork, Cloyne, and Ross, being a vindication of John and Charles Wesley, George Whitefield, and their people against his censures contained in a volume entitled Aids to Faith, edited by William Thomson, D.D., Lord Bishop of Gloucester and Bristol*, London: J. Mason, 1862.

Jackson, Thomas, ed., *The Lives of Early Methodist preachers: Chiefly written by themselves/edited, with an introductory essay, by Thomas Jackson*, London: Wesleyan Conference Office, 1837 and subsequent editions.

Jackson, Thomas, *Memoirs of the Rev. Charles Wesley . . . Being an abridgement of his Life in two volumes*, London: John Mason, 1848.

Jackson, Thomas, ed., *The Journal of the Rev. Charles Wesley, M.A., sometime student of Christ Church, Oxford : to which are appended selections from his correspondence and poetry with an introduction and occasional notes by Thomas Jackson*, London: Wesleyan Methodist Book-Room, 1849, Grand Rapids: Baker Book House, 1980, 2 vols.

Jackson, Thomas, *The life of . . . Charles Wesley . . . comprising a review of his poetry: sketches of the rise and progress of Methodism: with notices of contemporary events and characters*, London: John Mason, 1841.

Jackson, Thomas, ed., *The Works of John Wesley*, London: John Mason, 1831.

Jarboe, Betty M., *John and Charles Wesley: a bibliography*, ATLA bibliography series 22, Metuchen, NJ: American Theological Library Association and London: Scarecrow Press, 1987.

Jasper, David, 'Religious Thought: Wesley, Swedenborg' in Raimond, Jean, Watson, J. R. eds, *A Handbook to English Romanticism*, New York, St Martin's, 1992.

Jones, Arthur E. Jr, and Lawrence O. Kline, eds, *A union checklist of the publications of John and Charles Wesley* (based upon *The works of John and Charles Wesley: a bibliography by Richard Green*), edited for the Methodist Librarians Fellowship, Madison, NJ: Drew University, 1961.

Jones, Dora M., *Charles Wesley: A Study*, London: Epworth Press, 1919.

Kaiber, Walter, and Manfred Marquardt, *Gelebte Gnade: Grundriss einer Theologie der Evangelisch-methodistischen Kirche*, Stuttgart: Christliches Verlagshaus GmbH, 1993. English translation: *Living Grace: An outline of Methodist theology*, Nashville: Abingdon Press, 2001.

Kalas, J. E., *Our First Song: Evangelism in the hymns of Charles Wesley*, Nashville, TN: Abingdon, 1984.

Kassler, Michael, and Philip Olleson, *Samuel Wesley (1766–1837): A source book*, Aldershot: Ashgate, 2001.

Kay, J. Alan, ed., *Wesley's Prayers and Praises: A selection of little-known hymns by Charles Wesley, to which have been added a few by his brother, the whole being arranged for use mainly in private devotion*, London: Epworth Press, 1958.

Kimbrough, S T Jr, *A Heart to Praise My God: Charles Wesley's hymns for today*, Nashville: Abingdon Press, 1996.

Kimbrough, S T Jr, ed., *Songs for the Poor: Hymns by Charles Wesley*, New York: Mission Education and Cultivation Program Dept., General Board of Global Ministries, United Methodist Church, 1993.

Kimbrough, S T Jr, ed., *Charles Wesley: Poet and theologian*, Nashville, TN: Kingswood Books, 1992. (Chapters by Thomas R. Albin, Frank Baker, Oliver A. Beckerlegge, Teresa Berger, Horton Davies, Richard P. Heitzenrater, S T Kimbrough Jr, Thomas Langford, R. Leaver, Kenneth D. Shields, L. Stookey. All but three of the chapters in this volume originated as papers presented at the 1st Charles Wesley Publication Colloquium, Center of Theological Inquiry, Princeton, S., 1989.)

Kimbrough, S T Jr, 'Kenosis in the nativity hymns of Ephrem the Syrian and Charles Wesley', *Orthodox and Wesleyan Spirituality*, edited by S T Kimbrough Jr, Crestwood: St Vladimir's Seminary Press, 2002.

Kimbrough, S T Jr, *Lost in wonder: Charles Wesley, the meaning of his hymns today*, Nashville: The Upper Room, 1987.

Kimbrough, S T Jr, ed., *Orthodox and Wesleyan Scriptural Understanding and Practice*, St Vladimir's Seminary Press, 2005.

Kimbrough, S T Jr, ed., *Orthodox and Wesleyan Spirituality*, Crestwood, NY: St Vladimir's Seminary Press, 2002.

Kimbrough, S T Jr, 'Perfection Revisited: Charles Wesley's Theology of "Gospel Poverty" and "Perfect Poverty"', *The Poor and the People Called Methodists*, Richard P. Heitzenrater, Nashville: Abingdon Press, 2002, 101–19.

Kimbrough, S T Jr, *Songs for the world : hymns*, Nashville: General Board of Global Ministries, 2001.

Kimbrough, S T Jr and Oliver A. Beckerlegge, eds, *Hymns for Ascension-Day by Charles Wesley. And, Hymns of petition and thanksgiving for the promise of the Father (Hymns for Whitsunday) by John and Charles Wesley*, Reprint edition, Madison, NJ: Charles Wesley Society, n.d.

Kimbrough, S T Jr and Oliver A. Beckerlegge, eds, *The Unpublished Poetry of Charles Wesley*, 3 vols, Nashville, TN: Abingdon/Kingswood, 1988, 1990, 1992.

Kirk, John, *Charles Wesley, the Poet of Methodism: A Lecture*, Hamilton: Adams, 1860.

Lampe, John Frederick, *Hymns on the Great Festivals, and Other Occasions*, Madison, NJ: Charles Wesley Society, 1996.

Langford, Thomas A., *Practical Divinity: Theology in the Wesleyan tradition*, Nashville: Abingdon Press, 1983.

*The Last Days of Charles Wesley*, New York: Tract Society (18p tract, nineteenth century).

Lavington, G., *The Enthusiasm of Methodists and Papists Compared*, London: J. and P. Knapton, 3rd edn, 1752.

Lawson, John, *A Thousand Tongues: The Wesley hymns as a guide to scriptural teaching*, Carlisle: Paternoster Press, 1987.

Lawson, John, ed., *The Christian Year with Charles Wesley: Being a devotional companion to the Book of Common Prayer*, London: Epworth Press, 1966.

Lawson, John, *The Wesley Hymns as a Guide to Scriptural Teaching*, Grand Rapids: Francis Asbury Press, 1988.

Leger, J. A., ed., *John Wesley, John Wesley's Last Love*, London: J. M. Dent & Sons, Ltd, 1910.

Lenhart, Thomas E., *A Checklist of Wesleyan and Methodist Studies, 1970–1975*, Evanston, IL: Institute for Methodist Studies and Related Movements, Garrett–Evangelical Seminary, 1976.

Lenton, John, *My Sons in the Gospel*, Loughborough: Wesley Historical Society, 2000.

Lightwood, James T., *Hymn Tunes and Their Stories*, rev. edn, London: Epworth Press, 1905, 1923.

Lightwood, James T., *Methodist Music in the Eighteenth Century*, London: Epworth Press, 1927.

Lightwood, James T., *Samuel Wesley, Musician: The story of his life*, London: Epworth Press, 1937.

Lightwood, James T., *Stories of Methodist Music: Nineteenth century*, London: Epworth Press, 1928.

Linnell, C. L. S., ed., *The Diaries of Thomas Wilson*, London: SPCK, 1964.

Lloyd, Gareth, *Catalogue of the Charles Wesley Papers*, John Rylands University Library of Manchester, Methodist Archives and Research Centre, 1994.

Lockwood, J. P., *The Western Pioneers: Boardman and Pilmoor*, London: Wesleyan Conference Office, 1881, 69–70.

Lofthouse, William F., 'Charles Wesley', in *A History of the Methodist Church in Great Britain*, ed. Gordon Rupp and Rupert Davies, London: Epworth Press, 1965, 113–44.

Ludwig, Charles, *Susanna Wesley: Mother of John and Charles*, Milford, MI: Mott Media, 1984.

Lynch, Elizabeth Kurtz, 'John Wesley's editorial hand in Susanna Annesley Wesley's 1732 'Education' letter', in *John Wesley; Tercentenary Essays*, ed.

Jeremy Gregory, Special Edition of the *Bulletin of the John Rylands University Library of Manchester* 85 (2005 for 2003), 195–208.

McClintock, John, 'Wesley, Charles', in Vol. 10 *Cyclopedia of Biblical, Theological and Ecclesiastical Literature*, New York: Harper and Bros., 1886.

McMullen, Michael D., ed., *Hearts Aflame: Prayers of Susanna, John and Charles Wesley*, London: Triangle, 1995.

Macquiban, Timothy S. A., 'Dialogue with the Wesley's: remembering their origins' [the place of John and Charles Wesley in shaping British Methodist theology since 1932, as reflected in Methodist Conference reports and publications of the book room], *Unmasking Methodist Theology*, eds Clive Marsh, Brian E. Beck, Angela Shier-Jones and Helen Wareing, London: Continuum, 2004, 17–28.

Macquiban, Timothy S. A., *Grievous Wolves, Unlettered Disciples or Ministers to the Glory of God?*, unpublished paper, 1994.

Macquiban, Timothy S. A., ed., *Pure, Universal Love: Reflections on the Wesleys and inter-faith dialogue*, Oxford: Applied Theology Press, 1995.

Maddox, Graham, ed., *Political Writings of John Wesley*, Bristol: Thoemmes Press, 1998.

Maddox, Randy L., ed., *Aldersgate Reconsidered*, Nashville: Kingswood Books, 1990.

Maddox, Randy L., *Responsible Grace: John Wesley's practical theology*, Nashville,: Kingswood Books, 1994.

Maddox, Randy L., ed., *Rethinking Wesley's Theology for Contemporary Methodism*, Nashville: Abingdon Press, 1998.

Manning, Bernard Lord, *The Hymns of Wesley and Watts: Five informal papers*, London: Epworth Press, 1942, reissued: Peterborough: Epworth Press, 1988.

Marks, Harvey Blair, 'Charles Wesley', *The Rise and Growth of English Hymnody*, New York: Fleming H. Revell Co., 1937.

Martin, A. W. Jr, *A Diary of Devotion: A month with John and Charles Wesley*, Batesville: Britton & Britton, 2002.

Matthews, H. J., *Old Marylebone and Some of its Famous People: The Brownings, Charles Dickens, Charles Wesley, Lord Nelson, Lord Byron, Francis Bacon*, London: Simpkin Marshall Limited, 1946.

Meeks, M. Douglas, *The Future of the Wesleyan Theological Tradition*, Nashville: Abingdon Press, 1982.

Meeks, M. Douglas, ed., *The Portion of the Poor: Good news to the poor in the Wesleyan tradition*, Nashville: Kingswood Books, 1995.

Meeks, M. Douglas, *What Should Methodists Teach: Wesleyan traditions and modern diversity*, Nashville: Kingswood Books, 1987.

Meistad, Tore, 'The Missiology of Charles Wesley and its links to the Eastern Church', *Orthodox and Wesleyan Spirituality*, ed. S T Kimbrough Jr, Crestwood: St Vladimir's Seminary Press, 2002.

*Methodism and Popery Dissected and Compared; and the doctrines of both proved to be derived from a Pagan origin: including an impartial and candid enquiry into the writings of St Paul*, London, 1779.

*Methodist Worship Book*, Peterborough: Methodist Publishing House, 1999.

Milburn, Geoffrey E., *The Travelling Preacher: John Wesley in the North-East of England, with details also of the work of Charles Wesley and other early Methodist preachers*, revised edn, Peterborough: Methodist Publishing House on behalf of the Wesley Historical Society, North-East Branch, 2003.

*Minutes of the Methodist Conferences from the first held in London by the late Rev. John Wesley, A.M. in the Year 1744*, 4 vols, London: Methodist Conference Office, 1812–18.

Mitchell, T. C., *Charles Wesley: Man with the dancing heart*, Kansas City: Beacon Press, 1994.

Moore, Henry, *The Life of Mrs Mary Fletcher*, Birmingham: J. Peart,1817.

Moore, Henry, *The Life of the Rev. John Wesley A.M. Fellow of Lincoln College, Oxford in which are included the life of his brother the Rev Charles Wesley . . .*, 2 vols, London, J. Kershaw, 1824–25, also New York: N. Bangs and J. Emory for the Methodist Episcopal Church, 1826.

Morgan, K., ed., 'Methodist Testimonies from Bristol' in J. Barry and K. Morgan eds, *Reformation and Revival in Eighteenth Century Bristol*, Bristol Record Society. Publications XLV, Bristol: Bristol Record Society, 1994.

Myers, Elizabeth P., *Singer of Six Thousand Songs: A life of Charles Wesley*, London: T. Nelson, 1965.

Myles, William, *A Short Chronological History of the Methodists*, Rochdale, NY: J. Hartley, 1798.


Nelson, John, *et al*, *Wesley's Veterans*, 7 vols, London: Charles A. Kelly, 1912.

Newport, Kenneth G. C., *The Sermons of Charles Wesley: A critical edition*, with introduction and notes, Oxford and New York: Oxford University Press, 2001.

Newport, Kenneth G. C. and Gareth Lloyd, 'George Bell and Early Methodist Enthusiasm: A New Source from the Manchester Archives', *Bulletin of the John Rylands University Library of Manchester* 80 (1998), 89–101.

Newton, John A., *Heart Speaks to Heart: Studies in ecumenical spirituality*, London: Darton, Longman and Todd, 1994.

Newton, John A., 'John and Charles Wesley: Brothers in Arms', *Proceedings of the Charles Wesley Society* 5 (1998): 11–21.

Newton, John A., *John and Charles Wesley: Brothers in arms*, Cornish Methodist Historical Association Occasional Publication' No. 27, Carharrack, the Association, 2004.

Newton, John A., *Susanna Wesley and the Puritan Tradition in Methodism*, revised edn, Peterborough: Epworth Press, 2002.

Nuelsen, J. *Jean Guillaume de la Flechere: der erste schweizerische Methodist*, Zurich: 1929.

Nystrom, Carolyn, *The Wesleys – Amazing Love: 6 studies for individuals or groups with study notes*, Leicester: InterVarsity Press, 2002.


O'Leary, Arthur, *Miscellaneous Tracts by the Rev Arthur O'Leary*, 2nd edn, Dublin: John Chambers, 1781.

Olleson, Philip, *Samuel Wesley: the man and his music*, Woodbridge: Boydell & Brewer, 2003.

Osborn, G., *Outlines of Wesleyan Bibliography; or, A record of Methodist literature from the beginning. In two parts: the first containing the publications of John and Charles Wesley . . . the second, those of Methodist preachers . . .*, London: Wesleyan Methodist Conference Office, 1869.

Osborn, G., *The Poetical Works of John and Charles Wesley . . . together with the poems of Charles Wesley not before published*, 13 vols, London: Wesleyan–Methodist Conference Office, 1869–1872.

Outler, Albert, *Evangelism and Theology in the Wesleyan Spirit*, Nashville: Discipleship Resources, 1996.

Outler, Albert C., ed., *John Wesley*, New York: Oxford University Press, 1964.

Pawson, John, *The Letters of John Pawson (Methodist Itinerant, 1762–1806)*, ed. John C. Bowmer and John A. Vickers, Peterborough: Methodist Publishing House on behalf of the World Methodist Historical Society, 1994.

Pearce, John, *The Wesleys in Cornwall: Extracts from the journals of John and Charles Wesley and John Nelson*, Truro: D. B. Barton, 1964.

Perkins, E. Benson, *Charles Wesley: A short life.* (Reprinted from "Fifty Hymns by Charles Wesley"), London: Epworth Press, 1957.

Pfatteicher, Helen Emma, 'Charles Wesley', in *In Every Corner Sing*, Allentown: Muhlenberg Press, 1954, 98–101.

Piette, M., *John Wesley in the Evolution of Protestantism*, London: Sheed & Ward, 1979.

Powell, Samuel M., 'A Trinitarian Alternative to Process Theism', in *Thy Nature and Thy Name is Love: Wesleyan and process theologies in dialogue*, edited by Bryan P. Stone and Thomas Jay Oord, Nashville: Kingswood Books, 2001.

Pratt, Andrew, *O for a Thousand Tongues: The 1933 Methodist Hymn Book in context*, Peterborough: Epworth, 2004.

Priestly, Joseph, ed. *Original Letters by the Rev. John Wesley . . . with Other Curious Papers . . .* Birmingham: Thomas Pearson, 1791.

Rack, Henry D., 'Doctors, Demons, and Early Methodist Healing', in *The Church and Healing*, (ed.), W. J. Shields, Studies in Church History xix, Oxford: Basil Blackwell, 1982, 150–1.

Rack, Henry D., *Early Methodist Experience: Some prototypical accounts*, Religious Experience Unit, Westminster College, Oxford, Occasional Papers, Second Series No. 4, 1997.

Rack, Henry D. *Reasonable Enthusiast: John Wesley and the rise of Methodism*, 3rd edn, London: Epworth Press, 2002.

Rack, Henry D. 'Wesley, Charles (1707–1788)', *Oxford Dictionary of National Biography*, Oxford: Oxford University Press, 2004.

Rack, Henry D., 'Wesley Portrayed: Character and Criticism in some early Biographies', *Methodist History*, XLIII (2), 2005.

Rattenbury, J. Ernest, *The Conversion of the Wesleys: A critical study*, London: Epworth Press, 1938.

Rattenbury, J. Ernest, *The Eucharistic Hymns of John and Charles Wesley: To which is appended Wesley's Preface extracted from Brevint's Christian sacrament and sacrifice, together with Hymns on the Lord's supper*, London: Epworth Press, 1948.

Rattenbury, J. Ernest, *The Evangelical Doctrines of Charles Wesley's hymns*, 3rd edn, London: Epworth Press, 1954, 1st edn, 1941.

Reed, Alfred Hamish, *Notes on Autograph Letters of John and Charles Wesley in the Alfred and Isabel Reed Collection at the Dunedin Public Library*, Dunedin, 1972.

Rieger, Joerg and John J. Vincent, *Methodist and Radical: Rejuvenating the Tradition*, Nashville: Kingswood Books, 2003

Rogal, Samuel J., *A Biographical Dictionary of 18th Century Methodism*, Lampeter: Mellen Press, 1997–99.

Rogal, Samuel J., *John and Charles Wesley*, Twayne's English Authors Series, Boston: Twayne Publishers, 1983.

Rogal, Samuel J., *Old Testament Prophecy in Charles Wesley's Paraphrase of Scripture*, Bristol: New Room Bristol Pamphlet, 1984.

Rogal, Samuel J., *Susanna Annesley Wesley (1669–1742): a biography of strength and love: (the mother of John and Charles Wesley)*, Bristol, IN: Wyndham Hall Press, 2001.

Rogal, Samuel J., *The Occasional Hymns of Charles Wesley: Their historic viewpoint*, Bristol: New Room Bristol Pamphlet, 1979.

Rogal, Samuel J., *The Role of Paradise Lost in the Works of John and Charles Wesley*, Bristol: New Room Bristol Pamphlet, 1979.

Rogers, Donald G., *A Selection of John and Charles Wesley's Hymns on the Lord's Supper*, Exeter: Methodist Sacramental Fellowship, 1995.

Routley, Erik, 'Charles Wesley and His Family', in *A Panorama of Christian Hymnody*, Collegeville: Liturgical Press, 1979, 25–32.

Routley, Erik, *The Musical Wesleys*, London: Jenkins, 1968.

Rowe, K., 'The Search for the Historical Wesley', *The Place of Wesley in the Christian Tradition*, ed. K. Rowe, Metuchen, NY: Scarecrow Press, 1976.

Runyon, Theodore, *The New Creation: John Wesley's theology today*, Nashville: Abingdon Press, 1998.

Runyon, Theodore, ed., *Wesleyan Theology Today*, Nashville: Kingswood Books, 1985.

Rupp, E. Gordon, *Religion in England 1688–1791*, Oxford History of the Christian Church, ed. Henry and Owen Chadwick, Oxford: Clarendon Press, 1986.

Ryle, J. C., *Christian Leaders of the 18th Century*, London: Charles J. Thynne, 1885.

Sackett, A. B., *John Jones: First after the Wesleys*, WHMS, 1972.

Samuels, Joel L., *The Writings and Theology of John and Charles Wesley: An introductory bibliography*, 1993 and 1995. In the Wesley Library, Wesley Theological Seminary, Washington DC.

Schmidt, M., *John Wesley: A theological biography*, Engl. Trans., 3 vols, London: Epworth Press, 1973, II (2) 118–74.

Selen, M., *The Oxford Movement and Wesleyan Methodism in England 1833–1882: A study in religious conflict*, Lund: Lund University Press, 1992.

Sell, Alan P. F., *The Great Debate: Calvinism, Arminianism and salvation*, Worthing: H. E. Walter, 1982.

Short, Roy Hunter, *My Great Redeemer's Praise: The Methodist witness in the Wesley hymns*, Nashville: Methodist Evangelistic Materials, 1960.

Simon, John S., *John Wesley: The last phase*, 2nd edn, London: Epworth Press, 1962.

Smith, Mrs Richard, *The Life of the Rev Mr Henry Moore*, London: Simpkin and Marshall, 1844.

Smith, Timothy L., ed., *The Pentecost Hymns of John and Charles Wesley with a Devotional Commentary*, Kansas City: Beacon Hill Press, 1982.

Smith, Timothy L., Roy S. Nicholson, Sr, and T. Crichton Mitchell, 'Hymnology: The Theology of the Wesleys' Hymns', Chapter 22 in *A Contemporary Wesleyan Theology: Biblical, systematic and practical* ed. Charles W. Carter, Grand Rapids: Francis Asbury Press, 1983.

Southey, Robert, *The Life of Wesley: And rise and progress of Methodism*, London: Longman, Hurst, Rees, Orme and Brown, 1820 (Harper & Brothers, 1847, 1858 and other editions).

Spurgeon, Charles Haddon, *The Two Wesleys*: a lecture delivered in the Metropolitan Tabernacle Lecture Hall on December 6th 1861.

Stamm, Mark W., *Let Every Soul be Jesus' Guest: A theology of the open table*, Nashville: Abingdon Press, 2005.

Stamm, Mark W., *Sacraments and Discipleship: Understanding baptism and the Lord's Supper in a united Methodist context*, Nashville: Discipleship Resources, 2001.

Stanley, A. P., 'John and Charles Wesley', in *Addison to Blake: Selections with critical introductions*, Vol. 3, London: Macmillan, 1903.

Stevenson, George J., 'Charles Wesley, A.M., the Poet of Methodism', in Vol. 1, *Methodist Worthies: Characteristic sketches of Methodist preachers of the several denominations, with historical sketch of each connexion*, London: T. C. Jack, 1884–6.

Stevenson, George J., *City Road Chapel, London*, London: G. J. Stevenson, 1872.

Stevenson, George J., *Memorials of the Wesley Family*, London: S. W. Partridge Co., 1876.

Stevenson. George J., *The Methodist Hymn Book [by J. and C. Wesley] and its associations. With notes by W. M. Bunting, and an introductory poem by B. Gough*, London, Edinburgh 1870.

Stevick, Daniel B., *The Altar's Fire: The Lord's Supper, 1745, introduction and comment*, Peterborough: Epworth, 2004.

Stoeffler, F. Ernest, 'Pietism, the Wesleys, and Methodist beginnings in America' in F. E. Stoeffler, ed., *Continental Pietism and Early American Christianity*, Grand Rapids: Eerdmans, 1976.

Stone Bryan P. and Thomas Jay Oord, eds, *Thy Nature and Thy Name is Love: Wesleyan and process theologies in dialogue,* Nashville: Kingswood Books, 2001.

Stookey, Laurence Hull, *The Wesleys and the Saints.* [n.p., n.d.]

Stream, Carol, 'The Wesleys : Charles and John', *Christian History* 69 (2001).

Streiff, P., *Reluctant Saint: A theological biography of Fletcher of Madeley*, Peterborough: Epworth Press, 2001.

Sykes, Norman, *Church and State in England in the XVIII Century*, Cambridge: Cambridge University Press, 1934.

Tabraham, Barrie W., *Brother Charles*, Peterborough: Epworth Press, 2003.

Tailford, Patrick, *et al.*, *A True and Historical Narrative of the Colony of Georgia in America from the first settlement thereof until this present period*, Charles-Town, SC: 1741.

Taves, Ann, *Fits, Trances and Visions: Experiencing religion and explaining experience from Wesley to James*, Princeton: Princeton University Press, 1999.

Telford, John, ed., *Early Journals of Charles Wesley*, London: Charles H. Kelly, 1909.

Telford, John, ed., *Portraits: Sayings and portraits of Charles Wesley with family portraits, historic scenes, and additional portraits of John Wesley*, London: Epworth Press, 1927.

Telford, John, ed., *The Letters of John Wesley, A.M.* 8 vols, London: Epworth Press, 1931.

Telford, John, *The Life of Charles Wesley*, Religious Tract Society, 1886, Revised and enlarged, London: Wesleyan Methodist Book Room, 1900.

Telford, John, *The Methodist Hymn-Book Illustrated*, London: Epworth Press, 1906, ed. 1929, completely revised 1934.

Telford, John, *The Treasure House of Charles Wesley: A short anthology of the evangelical revival*, London: Epworth Press, 1933.

Thomas, Gilbert Oliver, 'Brother Charles', Chapter 11 in *Builders and Makers: Occasional studies*, London: Epworth Press, 1944.

Todd, J., *John Wesley and the Catholic Church*, London: Hodder & Stoughton, 1958.

Tooms, L. E., 'Cross,' in George Buttrick, ed., *Interpreters Dictionary of the Bible*, 5 vols, Nashville: Abingdon Press, 1962, Vol. I, 745–6.

*Two-Hundred-and-fiftieth Anniversary of the Birth of Charles Wesley, 1707–1957: Souvenir programme*, Nelson and Knox, 1757, reprint edition, Belfast: Wesley Historical Society, Irish Branch, n.d..

Tyerman, Luke, *The Life and Times of John Wesley, M.A.*, London: Hodder & Stoughton, 1871.

Tyerman, Luke, *The Oxford Methodists*, London: Hodder & Stoughton, 1873.

Tyerman, Luke, *Wesley's Designated Successor*, London: Hodder & Stoughton, 1882.

Tyson, John R., ed., *Charles Wesley: A reader*, Oxford: Oxford University Press, 1989, 2001.

Tyson, John R., *Charles Wesley on Sanctification: A biographical and theological study*, Grand Rapids: F. Asbury Press, 1986, also Schmul Publishing Co. Inc, 1992.

Tyson, John R., 'The Lord's Supper in the Wesleyan tradition', J. Heidinger II, ed., *Basic United Methodist beliefs*, Wilmore: Good News Books, 1986.

Tyson, John R., *Samuel Wesley: The man and his music*, Ipswich: Boydell Press, 2003.


Valentine, Simon Ross, *John Bennet and the Origins of Methodism and the Evangelical Revival in England*, London: Scarecrow Press, 1997.

Valentine, Simon Ross, *Mirror of the Soul: The diary of an early Methodist preacher*, Peterborough: Methodist Publishing House, 2002.

Vallins, George H., *The Wesleys and the English Language: Four essays*, London: Epworth Press, 1957.

Vickers, John, *Charles Wesley*, Peterborough: Foundery Press, 1990.


Wainwright, Arthur W., editor, in collaboration with Don E. Saliers, *Wesley–Langshaw correspondence: Charles Wesley, his sons, and the Lancaster organists*, Atlanta: Scholars Press, 1993.

Wainwright, Geoffrey, *Doxology: The praise of God in worship, doctrine and life*, New York: Oxford University Press, 1984.

Wainwright, Geoffrey, ed., *Hymns on the Lord's Supper, by John Wesley and Charles Wesley*, Madison, NJ: Charles Wesley Society, 1995.

Wainwright, Geoffrey, *Methodists in Dialogue*, Nashville: Kingswood Books, 1995.

Wainwright, Geoffrey, 'Trinitarian Theology and Wesleyan holiness' [in the writings of John and Charles Wesley] in S T Kimbrough Jr, ed., *Orthodox and Wesleyan Spirituality*, Crestwood: St Vladimir's Seminary Press, 2002.

Wainwright, Geoffrey, *Wesley and Calvin: Sources for theology, liturgy and spirituality*, Melbourne, Uniting Church Press, 1987.

Wainwright, Geoffrey, *Worship With One Accord: Where liturgy and ecumenism embrace*, New York: Oxford University Press, 1997.

Wakefield, Gordon, 'John and Charles Wesley: a tale of two brothers', in G. Rowell ed., *The English Religious Tradition and the Genius of Anglicanism*, Wantage: Ikon, 1992.

Wakefield, Gordon, *Methodist Spirituality*, Peterborough: Epworth Press, 1999.

Wakely, Joseph Beaumont, *Anecdotes of the Wesleys: Illustrative of their character and their personal history . . . With an introduction by J. M'Clintock*, London: Frome, 1869.

Wallace, Charles, ed., *Susanna Wesley: The complete writings*, New York: Oxford University Press, 1997.

Waller, Ralph, 'Hymns of Charles Wesley', *Joy of Heaven: Springs of Christian spirituality*, ed. Benedicta Ward and Ralph Waller, London: SPCK, 2003, 109–20.

Walsh, J., 'Methodism and the Mob', *Popular Belief and Practice*, Studies in Church History, vol. 8, ed. G. J. Cuming and Derek Baker, Cambridge: Cambridge University Press, 1972, 213–27.

Waterhouse, John W., *The Bible in Charles Wesley's Hymns*, Manuals of Fellowship; No. 5, Peterborough: Epworth Press, 1954.

Watson, J. R., *Pitying Tenderness and Tenderest Pity: The hymns of Charles Wesley and the writings of St Luke*, The A. S. Peake Memorial Lecture, The Methodist Conference, Torquay, 2005 published in *Epworth Review* 32:3 (2005), 33–8.

Watson, Philip S., *Anatomy of a Conversion: The message and mission of John & Charles Wesley*, Grand Rapids: Francis Asbury Press, 1990.

Watson, Philip S., *The Message of the Wesleys: A reader of instruction and devotion*, Macmillan, 1964, London: Epworth Press, 1965.

Watson, Richard, *Vie du révérend Jean Wesley . . . avec quelques details sur son frère le révérend Charles Wesley . . .: On y a joint quelques morceaux sur les ancêtres de Wesley, etc., du révérend H. Moore et du docteur Southey Traduit de l'anglais sur la quatrieme edition . . .* [vol. 1], Delay, Libraire, 1840.

Watson, R. and K. Trickett, *Companion to Hymns & Psalms*, Peterborough: Methodist Publishing House, 1988.

Watters, Philip S., *A Hymn Festival Service Commemorating the 250th Anniversary of the Birth of John Wesley*, Boston: Hymn Society of America, 1957.

Wearmouth, R. H., *Methodism and the Working Class Movements of England, 1800–1850*, London, Epworth Press, 1937.

Wearmouth, R. H., *Methodism and the Common People of the Eighteenth Century*, London: Epworth Press, 1945.

Wearmouth, R. H., *Some Working Class Movements of the Nineteenth Century*, London, Epworth Press, 1948.

Weber, Theodore, *Politics and the Order of Salvation: Transforming Wesleyan Political Ethics*, Nashville: Abingdon, 2001.

Wesley, Charles, *The Fitzwilliam Music never before Published, Three Hymns, the Words by the late Rev. Charles Wesley . . . Set to Music by George Frederic Handel . . . 1826.*

Wesley, Charles, *Hymns for Our Lord's Resurrection*, Introduction and Notes by Oliver A. Beckerlege, Madison, NJ: Charles Wesley Society, 1992.

Wesley, Charles, *Hymns for the Nativity of our Lord*, Madison, NJ: Charles Wesley Society, 1991.

Wesley, Charles, *Hymns for the Use of Families, and on Various Occasions*, William Pine, 1767.

Wesley, Charles, *Hymns. Selections: Charles Wesley seen in his finer and less familiar poems*, Hurd and Houghton, 1867 (a collection of his hymns).

Wesley, Charles, *Sacred poetry : selected from the works of the Rev. Charles Wesley*, Protestant Episcopal Society for the Promotion of Evangelical Knowledge, 1864. (Edited by a lay member of the Protestant Episcopal Church.)

Wesley, Charles, *Sermons by the late . . . Charles Wesley . . . with a memoir of the author by the editor*, ed. Mrs Sarah Wesley, London: Baldwin, Cradock and Joy, 1816.

Wesley, Charles, *Short Hymns on Select Passages of the Holy Scriptures*, 2 vols, Bristol: Felix Farley, 1762.

Wesley, John, *A Collection of Hymns for the Use of the People called Methodists*, eds

Franz Hildebrandt and Oliver A. Beckerlegge. New York: Oxford University. Press, 1983.

Wesley, John, *A Collection of Tunes: Set to music, as they are commonly sung at the Foundery*, London: A. Pearson, 1742.

Wesley, John, *A Short Account of the Life and Death of the Rev John Fletcher*, London, 1786.

Wesley, John, *A Word To a Protestant*, 8th edn, London, 1745.

Wesley, John, *Explanatory Notes upon the New Testament*, reprint edition, Epworth Press, 1976.

Wesley, John, *Sacred Harmony, or A choice collection of psalm and hymn tunes in two or three parts for the voice, harpsichord & organ*, London, 1780.

Wesley, John, *Select Hymns with Tunes Annext: Designed chiefly for the use of the people called Methodists*, London, 1761.

Wesley, John, *The Works of John Wesley: The bicentennial edition*, ed. Richard Heitzenrater, Nashville: Abingdon Press, various dates.

Wesley, John and Charles Wesley, *Hymns on the Last Supper*, Bristol: Felix Farley, 1745.

*Wesleyan Methodist Hymn Book*, London: Wesleyan Conference Office, 1904.

*Wesley's Hymns and New Supplement with Tunes*, London: Wesleyan Conference Office, 1877.

Weyer, Michel, 'Neuerscheinungen zu John und Charles Wesley' in *Jahrbuch für Pietismus und Neuzeit*, vol. 17; ed. M. Brecht. (Bibliographical essay.)

Whaling, Frank, *John and Charles Wesley: Selected prayers, hymns, journal notes, sermons, letters and treatises*, New York: Paulist Press, 1981.

White, Susan, *Whatever Happened to God the Father?: The Jesus heresy in modern worship*, Methodist Sacramental Fellowship, 2002.

Whitehead, John, *Life of John Wesley and Charles Wesley*, 2 vols, London: S. Couchman, 1793–6.

Whitehead, John, *Some Account of the Life of the Rev. Charles Wesley, A.M. late Student of Christ-Church, Oxford. Collected from his private journal*, London, printed by Stephen Couchman; and sold by Dan. Taylor, 1793; 2nd edn, Dublin: John Jones, 1805.

Whitehead, John, *The Life of the Rev. Charles Wesley: Late student of the Christ-Church, Oxford, collected from his private journal*, Dublin: John Jones, 1805.

Whitehead, John, *The Life of the Rev. John Wesley: Collected from his private papers and printed works; and written at the request of his executors. To which is prefixed some account of his ancestors and relations; with the life of the Rev. Charles Wesley, collected from his private journal, and never before published. The whole forming a history of Methodism, in which the principles and economy of the Methodists are unfolded*, London: Stephen Couchman, 1793.

Whitely, Jesse T., *Mottoes of Methodism: From the prose writings of Rev. John Wesley and the poetical writings of Rev. Charles Wesley: with scripture texts for every day of the year*, New York: Phillips & Hunt, and Cincinnati: Walden & Stowe, 1883.

Wilder, Franklin, *The Methodist Riots: The testing of Charles Wesley*, Great Neck: Todd and Honeywell, 1981.

Williamson, Glen, *Sons of Susanna*, Wheaton, IL: Tyndale House Publishers, 1991.

Winchester, Elhanan, *An Elegy upon Messrs. John and Charles Wesley, George Whitefield, and John de la Fletcher ...* Weathersfield: printed by Isaac Eddy, 1815.

Winters, William, *An Account of the Remarkable Musical Talents of Several Members of the Wesley Family, collected from Original Manuscripts, &c., with Memorial*

*Introduction and Notes*, F. Davies, 1874.

Wiseman, F. Luke, *Charles Wesley and his Hymns* (Reprinted from *A New History of Methodism*, 1909), London: Epworth Press, 1938. (Wesley Bi-centenary Manuals No. 6).

Wiseman, F. Luke, 'Charles Wesley and the Hymn Writers of Methodism', *A New History of Methodism*, Vol. 1, eds W. J. Townsend, H. R. Workman and George Eayres, London: Hodder & Stoughton, 1909, 237–54.

Wiseman, F. Luke, *Charles Wesley: Evangelist and poet*, Nashville: Abingdon Press, 1932, London: Epworth Press, 1933.

Wood, Paul, *Charles Wesley: Études*, Rouen: A.-C. Cornier, 1907.

Wright, David, *Thirty Hymns of the Wesleys*, Carlisle: Paternoster Press, 1985.


Young, Carlton R., *An Introduction to the New Methodist Hymnal*, Nashville: United Methodist Publishing House/Graded Press, 1966.

Young, Carlton R., *Music of the Heart: An anthology: John & Charles Wesley on music and musicians*, Carol Stream: Hope Publishing, 1995.

Young, Norman, *Charles Wesley: A tribute*, pamphlet in library of The Nazarene Bible College, Colorado Springs, n.d.

Yrigoyen, Charles, *Praising the God of Grace: The theology of Charles Wesley's hymns*, Nashville: Abingdon Press, 2005.

## Charles Wesley Society (Founding Meeting October 1990)

Charles Wesley, Bristol: William Pine, *Hymns on the Trinity*, 1767, (A Facsimile Reprint), Madison, NJ: The Charles Wesley Society, 1998.

Kimbrough, S T, Jr, ed., *Hymns on the Great Festivals, and Other Occasions*, Madison, NJ: The Charles Wesley Society, 1996. (Facsimile of the first edition of 1746.)

Papers presented at the fifth annual meeting of the Charles Wesley Society, October, 1994, The Society, Archives and History Center, Drew University, 1996.

Papers presented at the sixth annual meeting of the Charles Wesley Society, October 1995, The Society, Archives and History Center, Drew University, 1997.

Papers presented at the seventh annual meeting of the Charles Wesley Society, November 1996, The Society, Archives and History Center, Drew University, 1998.

Papers presented at the eighth annual meeting of the Charles Wesley Society, August 1997, The Society, Archives and History Center, Drew University, 1999.

Papers presented at the ninth annual meeting of the Charles Wesley Society, November 1998, The Society, Archives and History Center, Drew University, 2001.

Papers presented at the eleventh annual meeting of the Charles Wesley Society, July 2000, The Society, Archives and History Center, Drew University, 2002.

Papers presented at the fourteenth annual meeting of the Charles Wesley Society: October 2001, The Society, Archives and History Center, Drew University,

2004. Note that it was in fact the twelfth annual meeting although the title says that it was the fourteenth. Attendance and papers were limited because of the terrorist attacks in September 2001 and this volume includes papers delivered at earlier meetings of the Society in years for which papers had not been published. Subjects include: Frank Baker, 'The metamorphoses of Charles Wesley's Christmas hymns, 1739–88. (pp. 43–59), Elizabeth A. Buckroyd, 'A consideration of the undated *Hymns for children*', (pp. 61–80), S T Kimbrough 'A bibliography of translations of Wesley hymns', (pp. 13–42), J.R. Tyson, 'The Lord of life is risen: theological reflections on *Hymns for our Lord's resurrection* (1746)', pp. 81–101.

# Articles

Adams, Charles, 'The Poet Preacher: A Brief Memorial of Charles Wesley', *Methodist Quarterly Review* 13, p. 459, 1859 (also New York: Carlton & Porte, 1859).

Adams, Charles, *The Poet Preacher: A Brief Memorial of Charles Wesley* [review] in *Methodist Review* 41, p. 499, 1859.

Albin, Thomas R., 'Charles Wesley's Earliest Evangelical Sermons', *Methodist History* 21, pp. 60–2, 1982.

Anderson, Fred R., review of *Lost in Wonder: Charles Wesley, the Meaning of His Hymns Today*, by S T Kimbrough Jr in *Theology Today* 45, p. 264, 1988.

'Anecdotes of the late Charles Wesley, Esq.', *Wesleyan Methodist Magazine* 57, pp. 514–9, 1834.

'Anecdotes of the late Charles Wesley, Esq', *Methodist Review* 16, pp. 437–43, 1834.

Baker, Donald, 'Charles Wesley and the American Loyalists', *Proceedings of the Wesley Historical Society* 35, pp. 5–9, 1965.

Baker, Donald, 'Charles Wesley and the American War of Independence', *Methodist History* 5, pp. 5-37 1966. The same title appears in *Proceedings of the Wesley Historical Society* 34, pp. 159–64, 1964 and in *Proceedings of the Wesley Historical Society* 40, pp. 125–134, 165–82, 1976.

Baker, Frank, 'A poet in love – the courtship of Charles Wesley, 1747–1749', *Methodist History* 29, pp. 235–47, 1991.

Baker, Frank, 'Charles Wesley's Hymns for Children', *Proceedings of the Wesley Historical Society* 31, pp. 81–5, 1957.

Baker, Frank, 'Charles Wesley's Productivity as a Religious Poet', *Proceedings of the Wesley Historical Society*, 47, pp. 1–12, 1989.

Baker, Frank, 'Charles Wesley's Scripture Playing Cards', *Proceedings of the Wesley Historical Society* 29, pp. 136–8, 1954.

Baker, Frank, 'Charles Wesley to Varanese (possibly Sally Kirkham)', *Proceedings of the Wesley Historical Society* 31, pp. 97–104, 1946.

Baker, Frank, 'Investigating Wesley family traditions [genealogical table]', *Methodist History* 26, pp. 154–62, 1988.

Baker, Frank, 'Prose writings of Charles Wesley', *London Quarterly and Holborn Review* 182, pp. 268–74, 1957.

Baker, Frank, review of *A Heart Set Free: The Life of Charles Wesley* by Arnold A. Dallimore, in *Catholic Historical Review* 75, p. 521, 1989.

Baker, Frank, review of *Charles Wesley: The First Methodist* by Frederick C. Gill, in *Duke Divinity School Review* 30, pp. 212–13, 1965.

Baker, Frank, review of *A Song for the Poor: Hymns by Charles Wesley* ed. Timothy E. Kimbrough and S T Kimbrough Jr, in *Methodist History* 32, pp. 201–2, 1994.

Baker, Frank, 'The Birth of Charles Wesley', *Proceedings of the Wesley Historical Society* 31, pp. 25–6, 1957.

Baker, Frank, 'Thomas Maxfield's first sermon' in *Proceedings of the Wesley Historical Society* 27, pp. 7–15.

Bangs, Carl O., 'Historical theology in the Wesleyan mode' [reply, Leon O. Hynson], *Wesleyan Theological Journal* 17, pp. 85–92, 1982.

Bartels, Laura A., 'Hymns of the Status Quo: Charles Wesley on the Trinity', *Wesleyan Theological Journal* 38: 2, 2003.

Beach, Waldo, review of *The Unpublished Poetry of Charles Wesley*, v. 1; ed. by S T Kimbrough Jr and Oliver A. Beckerlegge in *Hymn* 44, p. 48, 1993.

Beach, Waldo, review of *The Unpublished poetry of Charles Wesley*, v. 2; ed. by S T Kimbrough Jr and Oliver A. Beckerlegge in *Hymn* 44, p. 48, 1993.

Beckerlegge, Oliver A., 'An Attempt at a Classification of Charles Wesley's Metres: a Contribution to the Study of English Prosody', *London Quarterly and Holborn Review* 169, pp. 219–27, 1944.

Beckerlegge, Oliver A., 'Charles Wesley's Politics', *London Quarterly and Holborn Review* 182, pp. 280–91, 1957.

Beckerlegge, Oliver A., 'Charles Wesley's Vocabulary', *London Quarterly and Holborn Review* 193, pp. 152–61, 1968.

Bence, Clarence, 'Processive Eschatology: Wesleyan Alternatives' in *Wesleyan Theological Journal* 14:1, 1979.

Benson, George, 'Wesley Souvenirs', *Connoisseur* 24, pp. 238–40, 1909. (Contains some of Charles Wesley's musical manuscripts).

Bett, Henry, 'A Detail of Pronunciation in Wesley's Hymns', *Proceedings of the Wesley Historical Society* 14, pp. 78–80, 1923.

Bett, Henry, 'A French Marquis and the Class Meeting', *Proceedings of the Wesley Historical Society*, pp. 43–5, 1931–2.

Bett, Henry, 'An Unpublished Latin Letter to Zinzendorf by Charles Wesley', *Proceedings of the Wesley Historical Society* 15, pp. 166–8, 1926.

Bett, Henry, 'Archaisms in Wesley's Hymns', *Proceedings of the Wesley Historical Society* 8, pp. 85–90, 1911.

Bett, Henry, 'Some Classical Allusions in Hymns of the Wesleys', *Proceedings of the Wesley Historical Society* 9, pp. 116–20, 1914.

Bett, Henry, 'Some Latinisms in the Wesleys' Hymns', *London Quarterly and Holborn Review* 163, pp. 308–19, 1938.

Bible, Ken, 'The Wesleys' Hymns on Full Redemption and Pentecost: A brief comparison', *Wesleyan Theological Journal* 17, pp. 79–87, Fall 1982.

Bird, Isabella L., 'The Wesleys and their Hymns', *Littel's Living Age* 100, pp. 112–17, 1989; 101, pp. 368–75, 1989.

Bowmer, John C., 'The Churchmanship of Charles Wesley', *Proceedings of the Wesley Historical Society* 31, pp. 78–80, 1957.

Brantley, Richard E., 'Charles Wesley's Experiential Art', *Eighteenth-Century Life* 11, pp. 1–11, 1987.

Bridgen, T., 'Pascal and the Wesleys', *Proceedings of the Wesley Historical Society*, 7, p. 61, 1910.

Brose, Martin E., 'Die Feuer-Metapher in frühen Methodismus: drei Briefe von Samuel und Susanna Wesley aus dem Jahre 1709' [and other examples of fire imagery in Charles Wesley's writings], *Mitteilungen der Studiengemeinschaft f r*

*Geschichte der Evangelisch-Methodistischen Kirche*, 21:2, pp. 12–17, 2000.

Brose, Martin E., '"My Dear Charles": zwei Briefe von Susanna Wesley (1669–1742) aus dem Jahr 1738 an ihren Sohn Charles (1707–1788)', *EmK Geschichte*, 24: 2, pp. 5–13, 2003.

Bryant, Barry E., 'Trinity and Hymnody: The doctrine of the Trinity in the hymns of Charles Wesley', *Wesleyan Theological Journal* 25, pp. 64–73, 1990.

Burham, Elizabeth, 'Susanna Wesley's Influence upon the Hymnody of Her Sons', *Methodist Review* 112, pp. 540–50, 1929.

Burtt, Percy E., 'Comparison of Charles Wesley and Isaac Watts', *Pittsburgh Christian Advocate* 77, 17, p. 21, 1910.


Campbell, Ted A., 'John Wesley and the Legacy of Methodist Theology', *Bulletin of the John Rylands University Library of Manchester*; 85:2–3, pp. 405–420, 2004.

Capey, A. C., 'Charles Wesley and his literary relations', Retford: Brynmill Press, 1983, Offprinted from '*The Gadfly*', 6:1, pp. 17–26.

Capon, John, 'John and Charles Wesley: The preacher and the poet', *Churchman* 102, p. 359, 1988.

'Charles and Sarah Wesley', *Quiver* 13, pp. 171–3, 310–12, 374–8, 1878.

*Charles Wesley Seen in His Finer and Less Familiar Poems* [review] in *Methodist Review* 49, pp. 304–6, 1867.

Church, Leslie F., 'Charles Wesley: The man', *London Quarterly and Holborn Review* 182, pp. 247-253, 1957.

Cole, Charles E., ed., Special issue: The United Methodist bicentenary, *Quarterly Review* 4, pp. 3–100, 1984.

Colquhoun, Frank, 'Charles Wesley's Eucharistic Hymns', *Churchman* 63, pp. 103–7, 1949.

Coulton, B. in 'Tutor to the Hills: The early career of John Fletcher' in *Proceedings of the Wesley Historical Society* 47:3, p. 97, 1989.

Crooks, George R., 'Charles Wesley and his Poetry', *Methodist Quarterly Review* 31, pp. 378–87, 1849.


Dale, James, 'Charles Wesley, the Odyssey, and Clement of Alexandria' *Methodist History 30*, pp. 100–102, 1992 (also published in *Proceedings of the Wesley Historical Society* 48, pp. 150–152, 1992) (nautical imagery in Wesley hymns).

Dale, James, 'Some Echoes of Charles Wesley's Hymns in his Journal', *London Quarterly and Holborn Review* 184, pp. 336–44, 1959.

Davies, W. R. 'John Fletcher's Georgian Ordinations and Madeley Curacy', *Proceedings of the Wesley Historical Society* 35:3, pp. 139–142, 1968.

'Description of the monuments, erected in the City–Road Chapel', *Methodist Review* 6, pp. 431–5, 1823.

Dinwiddie, Richard D., 'Two Brothers who Changed the Course of Church Singing', *Christianity Today* 13, pp. 30–4, 1984.

Doughty, William L., 'Charles Wesley, Preacher', *London Quarterly and Holborn Review* 182, pp. 263–7, 1957.

Dowdy, Roger, 'A Service of Wesley Hymns [bibliography]', *Journal of Church Music* 30, pp. 5–7, 1988.

DuBose, Horace Mellard, 'John Fletcher and matrimony', *Methodist Quarterly Review* 65, pp. 780–2, 1916.

Dudley-Smith, Timothy, 'Charles Wesley: A hymnwriter for today', *Hymn* 39, pp. 7–15, 1988.

Eayrs, George, 'Charles Wesley's Engagement: Light from unpublished letters', *Proceedings of the Wesley Historical Society* 36, pp. 33–5, 1967.

Ellingworth, Paul, "I' and 'We' in Charles Wesley's Hymns', *London Quarterly and Holborn Review* 188, pp. 153–64, 1963.

Flowers, Margaret G., Wayne Gordon McCown and Douglas Russell, '18th-century Earthquakes and Apocalyptic Expectations: The hymns of Charles Wesley', *Methodist History* 152, pp. 222–35, 2003–4.

Floy, James, Review of *A Collection of Hymns for the Use of the Methodist Episcopal Church*, *Methodist Review* 26, pp. 165–206, 1844.

Floy, James, 'The Methodist Hymn-Book' [review article], *Methodist Review* 26, pp. 165–206, 1844.

Fox, Adam, 'Hymns and Charles Wesley', *Spectator* 169, pp. 306–7, 1942.

Fox, Michael V., Review of Dallimore, Arnold A., *A Heart Set Free: The Life of Charles Wesley*, *Journal of Biblical Literature* 108, pp. 510–12, 1989.

Freeman, C. B., 'Charles Wesley: The poet and the editors', *Theology* 61, pp. 503–7, 1958.

Frost, Francis, 'Biblical Imagery and Religious Experience in the Hymns of the Wesleys', *Proceedings of the Wesley Historical Society* 42, pp. 158–66, 1980.

Frost, Francis, 'Christ in the hymns of Charles Wesley: A spirituality for the unity of Christians', *The Unity of Christians: the Vision of Paul Couturier*, ed. Mark Woodruff, a special edition of *The Messenger of the Catholic League*, No 280, October 2003–February 2004, pp. 76–90.

Galloway, Charles B., 'Charles Wesley, the Hymnist of the Ages', in *The Wesley Bi-Centenary Celebration in Savannah, GA*, pp. 55–74, Savannah Morning News Print, 1903.

Gill, Thomas H., 'Charles Wesley', *Congregationalist* 6, pp. 513–29, 1877.

Gill, Thomas H., 'Watts and Charles Wesley Compared', *Congregationalist* 7, pp. 129–44, 1878.

Gillespie, Norman, 'New Light on a Source of Charles Wesley and Thomas Morell'. *Notes and Queries* 31, pp. 10–11, 1984.

Glen, R., 'Man or Beast? English Methodists as animals in 18th century satiric prints', *Connecticut Review* 15:2, Fall, 1993.

Green, Roger, review of Dallimore, Arnold A., *A Heart Set Free: The Life of Charles Wesley*, *Fides et Historia* 23:9, pp. 120–3, 1991.

Green, Roger, review of Tyson, John R., *Charles Wesley: A Reader*, *Fides et Historia* 23, pp. 120-123, 1991.

Gregory, T. S., 'Charles Wesley's Hymns and Poems', *London Quarterly and Holborn Review* 162, pp. 253–62, 1957.

Guorion, Vigen, 'Divine Therapy,' *Theology Today* 61:3, pp. 309–321, October 2004.

Hale, John G., 'Charles Wesley and Methodist Hymns', *Boston Review* 5, pp. 296–305, 1865.

Harrison, Archibald W., 'Restoration of Charles Wesley's Tomb', *Proceedings of the Wesley Historical Society* 17, pp. 145–50, 1930.

Hawn, C. Michael, 'Hymnody for Children, pt 1', *Hymn* 36, pp. 19–26, 1985.

Heitzenrater, Richard P., 'Charles Wesley Letter on Lay Preaching and Separation [1756]' *Methodist History* 22, 1984.

Heitzenrater, Richard, P., 'John Wesley's Earliest Sermons,' *Proceedings of the Wesley*

*Historical Society* 36, pp. 112–13, 1970.

Herklots, H. G. G., review of J. Alan Kay, ed., *Wesley's Prayers and Praises: A Selection of Little Known Hymns by Charles Wesley*, *Church Quarterly Review* 160, pp. 408–9, 1959.

Higgs, James, 'Samuel Wesley: His life, times, and influence on music,' *Proceedings of The Musical Association*, 20th Sess, 1893–94.

Hildebrandt, Franz, 'The Wesley Hymns', *Asbury Seminarian* 14:1, pp. 16–47, 1960.

Hobbs, R. Gerald, 'With a Thousand Tongues: The Wesleys and Christian song' *Touchstone* 3, pp. 18–29, 1984.

Hodgson, E. M., 'John or Charles Wesley', *Proceedings of the Wesley Historical Society* 41, pp. 73–6, 1977.

Hodgson, E. M., 'Poetry in the Hymns of John and Charles Wesley', *Proceedings of the Wesley Historical Society* 38, pp. 131–5, 161–5, 1972.

Holland, Bernard C., 'The Conversions of John and Charles Wesley and their Place in Methodist Tradition', *Proceedings of the Wesley Historical Society* 38, pp. 46–53, 65–71, 1972.

Hospital, Clifford G., 'My Chains Fell Off, My Heart Was Free: Another perspective on the hymns of Charles Wesley', *Touchstone* 9, pp. 7–19, 1991.

Houghton, Edward, 'John Wesley or Charles Wesley?', *Hymn Society of Great Britain and Ireland Bulletin* 9, pp. 93–9, 1979.

Houghton, Edward, 'Poetry and Piety in Charles Wesley's Hymns', *Hymn* 6, pp. 77–86, 1955.

Houghton, Edward, 'Wrestling Jacob', *Evangelical Quarterly* 50, pp. 104–8, 1978.

Hower, Robert G., review of *A Heart Set Free: The Life of Charles Wesley* by Arnold A. Dallimore, *Evangelical Journal* 7, pp. 40–1, 1989.

Hower, Robert G., review of *Charles Wesley: A Reader* by John Tyson, *Evangelical Journal* 10, p. 83, 1992.

Jackson, Thomas, 'Life of Charles Wesley', *Methodist Quarterly Review* 24, pp. 112–41, 1842.

Jackson, Thomas, The Life of the Rev Charles Wesley [review] in *Methodist Review* 24, pp. 469–70, 1842.

Jackson, Thomas, *The Life of the Rev Charles Wesley*; 2 v. [review] in *Methodist Review* 23, pp. 632–3, 1841.

Jackson, Thomas, *The Life of the Rev Charles Wesley*, 2 v. [review] in *Methodist Review* 24, pp. 112–41, 1842.

'Jackson's life of Rev Charles Wesley' [review article], *Methodist Review* 24, pp. 112–41, 1842.

Johnson, Dale, 'Is This the Lord's Song? Pedagogy and polemic in modern english hymns', *Historical Magazine of the Protestant Episcopal Church*, 48, pp. 195–218, 1979.

Johnson, Ronald, 'Charles Wesley and J. S. Bach', *Choir and Musical Journal* 39, pp. 34–6, 50–1, 1948.

Jones, Richard G, 'Where Earth and Heaven Combine' [Charles Wesley's hymn 'Let earth and heaven combine', *Expository Times* 114, pp. 85–7, 2002–3.

Kay, J. Alan, 'Charles Wesley', *London Quarterly and Holborn Review* 182, pp. 241–6, 1957.

Kellett, E. E., 'The Poetic Character of Wesley's Hymns', *Methodist Recorder*, pp. 10–11, 18 August 1910.

Kellock, John M., 'Charles Wesley and his Hymns', *Methodist Review* 112, pp. 527–39, 1929.

Kerr, Ernest, 'On Mending Charles Wesley', *London Quarterly and Holborn Review* 172, pp. 353–9, 1947.

Kimbrough, S T Jr, 'Charles Wesley as a Biblical Interpreter', *Methodist History* 26, pp. 139–53, 1988.

Kimbrough, S T Jr, 'L'Hymnographie de Charles Wesley: art théo-poétique ou chant?', *John Wesley: actes du colloque à l'occasion du tricentaire de la naissance du fondateur du méthodisme, Faculté de Théologie de l'Université de Lausanne, 12–13 juin 2003*, Lausanne: Éditions du Centre Méthodiste de Formation Théoloique, pp. 61–77, 2003.

Kimbrough, S T Jr, 'Die Psalmlyrik Charles Wesleys: zwei Richtungen seiner Interpretation', *Theologie für die Praxis*, 8, pp. 22–34, 2002.

Kimbrough, S T Jr, 'Lyrical Theology', *Journal of Theology* 98, pp. 18–43, 1994.

Kimbrough, S T Jr, Review of *Charles Wesley, A Reader* by John R. Tyson, *Methodist History* 29, pp. 54–8, 1990.

Kimbrough, S T Jr, 'The Founding Meeting of the Charles Wesley Society', *Methodist History* 29, pp. 251–61, 1991.

Knickerbocker, Waldo E., 'Arminian Anglicanism and John and Charles Wesley', *Memphis Theological Seminary Journal* 29, pp. 79–97, 1991.

Kolodziej, Benjamin A., 'Isaac Watts, the Wesleys and the Evolution of the 18th-century English Congregational Song', *Methodist History*, XLII, pp. 236–48, 2003–4.

Lawrence, Anna M., '"I thought I felt a sinful desire": the question of celibacy for eighteenth-century Methodists', *Bulletin of the John Rylands University Library of Manchester*, 87:1, pp. 177–93, 2005.

Lawson, John, 'The Poetry of Charles Wesley', *Emory University Quarterly* 15, pp. 31–47, 1959.

Lawson, John, 'The Conversion of the Wesleys: 1738 reconsidered', *Asbury Theological Journal* 43, pp. 7–44, 1988.

Lee, Umphrey, Review of *A Tale of Two Brothers* by Mabel R. Brailsford, *Religion in Life* 24, pp. 471–3, 1955.

Lewis, Edwin, Review of *The Eucharistic Hymns of John and Charles Wesley* by John E. Rattenbury, *Religion in Life* 18, pp. 613–14, 1949.

'Life of Rev J Wesley' [review article] in *Methodist Review* 8, pp. 305–14, 1825.

'Life of the Rev John Wesley [review article] in *Methodist Review* 8, pp. 141–9, 1825.

Lightwood, James T., 'Handel's Original Tunes to Charles Wesley's Hymns', *Choir and Musical Journal* 31, pp. 53–5. 101–3, 1930.

Lloyd, A. Kingsley, 'Charles Wesley's Debt to Matthew Henry', *London Quarterly and Holborn Review* 171, pp. 330–7, 1946.

Lloyd, Gareth, '"A Cloud of Perfect Witnesses": John Wesley and the London disturbances 1760–1763', *Asbury Theological Journal* 56:2, 57:1, pp. 116–36, 2001/2002.

Lloyd, Gareth, 'Sarah Perrin (1721–1787) – Early Methodist Exhorter', *Methodist History* 41, pp. 79–88, April 2002.

Lofthouse, William F., 'John Wesley's Letters to his Brother', *London Quarterly and Holborn Review* 185, pp. 60–5, 1960.

McAdoo, Henry R, 'A Theology of the Eucharist: Brevint and the Wesleys', *Theology* 97, pp. 245–56, 1994.

McLamore, Alyson, '"By the Will and Order of Providence": The Wesley family concerts, 1779–1787', *Royal Musical Association Research Chronicle* 37, pp. 71–220, 2004.

Madden, Deborah, 'Experience and the Common Interest of Mankind: The enlightened empiricism of John Wesley's Primitive Physick', *British Journal for Eighteenth-Century Studies* 26, pp. 41–54, 2003.

Maddox, Randy L., Review of *John and Charles Wesley: A Bibliography*, ed. Betty M. Jarboe, *Journal of Religion* 69, p. 604, 1989.

Maddox, Randy L., 'The Collection of Books owned by the Charles Wesley Family' (now in the John Rylands Library), *Wesleyan Theological Journal* 38:2, pp. 175–216, 2003.

Manning, Bernard L., 'The Evangelical Doctrines of Charles Wesley's Hymns', *London Quarterly and Holborn Review* 166, pp. 459–63, 1941.

Manning, Bernard L., 'The Recall to Religion in the Hymns of Charles Wesley', *London Quarterly and Holborn Review* 163, pp. 475–91, 1938.

Manning, Bernard L., 'Wesley's Hymns Reconsidered', *London Quarterly and Holborn Review* 165, pp. 19–30, 134–65, 1940.

Marlatt, Earl, Review of *Representative Verse of Charles Wesley* ed. Frank Baker, *Religion in Life* 32, p. 650, 1963.

Maser, Frederick E., 'An hitherto "unpublished letter" of Charles Wesley', *Methodist History* 29, pp. 248–52, 1991.

Maser, Frederick E., 'Charles Wesley and his biographers', *Methodist History* 29, pp. 47–51, 1990. (Bibliography.)

Mitchell, T. Crichton, 'Response to Dr. Timothy Smith on the Wesleys' Hymns', *Wesleyan Theological Journal* 16:2, pp. 48–57, 1981.

Moore, Henry, *The Life of the Rev John Wesley and the Rev Charles Wesley*; v.1. [review] in *Methodist Review* 8, pp. 141–9, 1825.

Moore, Henry, *The Life of the Rev John Wesley and the Rev Charles Wesley*; v 2 [review] in *Methodist Review* 8, pp. 305–14, 1825.

Moore, Jacob, 'Anecdotes of Mr Charles Wesley', *Methodist Review* 8, pp. 314–16, 1825.

Nelson, J. Robert, 'What Methodists Think of Eucharistic Theology', *Worship* 52, pp. 409–24, 1978.

Newport, Kenneth, G. C., 'Charles Wesley and the Articulation of Faith', *Methodist History* 152, pp. 33–48, 2003–4.

Newport, Kenneth G. C., 'Charles Wesley's Interpretation of Some Biblical Prophecies according to a Previously Unpublished Letter Dated 25 April, 1754', *Bulletin of the John Rylands University Library of Manchester* 77, pp. 31–52, 1995.

Newport, Kenneth G. C., 'Methodists and the Millennium: Eschatological Belief and the Interpretation of Biblical Prophecy in Early British Methodism', *Bulletin of the John Rylands University Library of Manchester* 78, pp. 103–22, 1996.

Newport, Kenneth G. C., 'The French Prophets and Early Methodism: Some New Evidence', *Proceedings of the Wesley Historical Society* 50, pp. 127–40, 1996.

Newport, Kenneth G. C., 'Premillennialism in the Early Writings of Charles Wesley', *Wesleyan Theological Journal* 32, pp. 85–103, 1997.

Nicholson, Norman, 'Wesley and Watts', *Times Literary Supplement*, pp. 44–5, 6 August 1954.

Noble, Mark, 'Romanticism and the Hymns of Charles Wesley', *Evangelical Quarterly* 46, pp. 195–222, 1974.

Noll, Mark A., 'Romanticism and the hymns of Charles Wesley', *Evangelical Quarterly* 46, pp. 195–223, 1974.

Nuttall, Geoffrey F., 'Charles Wesley in 1739', *Proceedings of the Wesley Historical Society* 42, pp. 181–5, 1980.

Nutter Charles S., 'Charles Wesley as a Hymnist', *Methodist Review* 108, pp. 341–57, 1925.

Olleson, Philip, 'The Wesleys at Home: Charles Wesley and his children', *Methodist History* 36:3, 1998.

Outler, Albert C., 'John Wesley: Folk-Theologian', *Theology Today* 34, pp. 150–60, 1977.

Paananen, Victor N., 'Martin Madan and the Limits of Evangelical Philanthropy', *Proceedings of the Wesley Historical Society* 40, pp. 57–68, 1958.

Platt, Frederic, 'Charles Wesley's Bristol House', *Proceedings of the Wesley Historical Society* 18, pp. 137–43, 1932.

Plumb, J. H., 'The New World of Children in Eighteenth-Century England', *Past and Present* 67, pp. 64–95, 1975.

Preston, Novella D., 'Charles Wesley, Preacher as Well as Poet', *Church Musician* 13, pp. 14–15, 1962.

Quantrille, Wilma J., 'A Woman Responds to Charles Wesley', *Methodist History*, pp. 199–212, 1991.

Quiller-Couch, Arthur, 'Sir A. Quiller-Couch on the Wesley Hymns', *Choir and Musical Journal* 12, pp. 86–8, 1921.

Rack, Henry D., 'Charles Wesley and the Irish Inheritance Tradition', *Proceedings of the Wesley Historical Society* 53:4, pp. 117–26, 2002.

Rack, Henry D., 'John Wesley as Theologian', *Epworth Review* 27:1 pp. 43–7, 2000.

Rack, Henry D., 'Wesley, Charles' (including 'Wesley Sarah' [Charles Wesley's wife]), *Oxford Dictionary of National Biography* vol. 58, p. 180, Oxford: Oxford University Press, 2004.

Rack, Henry D., 'Wesley Observed,' *Proceedings of the Wesley Historical Society* 49:1, p. 17, February 1993.

'Rev Charles Wesley, MA' [portrait only] *Methodist Review* 8, p. 289, 1825.

Richardson, Paul A., review of *Lost in Wonder: Charles Wesley, the Meaning of His Hymns Today* by S T Kimbrough Jr, *Review and Expositor* 86, p. 291, 1989.

Richardson, Paul A., review of *Charles Wesley: Poet and Theologian* ed. by S T Kimbrough Jr, *Journal of Church and State* 35, pp. 634–5, 1993.

Roberts, Griffith T., 'Charles Wesley's Right to Preach Throughout England and Ireland', *Proceedings of the Wesley Historical Society* 21, pp. 31–2, 1937.

Rogal, Samuel J., 'Old Testament Prophecy in Charles Wesley's Paraphrase of Scripture', *Christian Scholar's Review* 13, pp. 205–16, 1984.

Rogal, Samuel J., 'The Contributions of John and Charles Wesley to the Spread of Popular Religion', *Grace Theological Journal* 2, pp. 233–44, 1983.

Rogal, Samuel J., 'The Occasional Hymns of Charles Wesley: Their historic viewpoint', *Cresset*, pp. 8–12, 1979.

Rogal, Samuel J., 'The Role of Paradise Lost in Works by John and Charles Wesley',

*Milton Quarterly* 13, pp. 114–19, 1979.

Rogal, Samuel J., 'Scripture References, Allusions and Echoes in Works by Charles and John Wesley', *Trinity Journal* 25, pp. 75–91, 2004.

Rousseau, G. S., 'John Wesley's Primitive Physic (1747)', *Harvard Library Bulletin* 169, p. 23, 1979.

Routley, Erik, 'Charles Wesley and Matthew Henry', *Congregational Quarterly* 33, pp. 345–51, 1955.

Routley, Erik, 'The Case Against Charles Wesley', *Hymn Society of Great Britain and Ireland Bulletin* 4, pp. 252–9, 1960.

S., G. M. 'Charles Wesley', *Monthly Religious Magazine* 22, pp. 217–33, 1859.

Sellers, William E., 'The Wesleys and Garth', *Wesleyan Methodist Magazine* 135, pp. 372–6, 1917.

Sellers, William E., 'The Wesleys and Trevecca', *Wesleyan Methodist Magazine* 135, pp. 538–42, 1912.

Severs, George, 'Anticipation and the Proleptic Adjective in Charles Wesley's Hymns', *Proceedings of the Wesley Historical Society* 8, pp. 184–8, 1912.

Sharpe, Eric J., 'Gentle Jesus, Meek and Mild: Variations on a nursery theme, for congregation and critic', *Evangelical Quarterly* 53, pp. 149–64, 1981.

Shelton, R. Larry, review of *A Heart Set Free: The Life of Charles Wesley* by Arnold A. Dallimore, *Christian Scholar's Review* 19, pp. 298–300, 1990.

Shepherd, Thomas Boswell, 'And Can It Be? An analysis of a hymn by Charles Wesley', *London Quarterly and Holborn Review* 170, pp. 445–8, 1945.

Shepherd, Thomas Boswell, 'The Children's Verse of Dr. Watts and Charles Wesley', *London Quarterly and Holborn Review* 164, pp. 173–84, 1939.

Shields, Kenneth D., review of *The Unpublished Poetry of Charles Wesley* Vol. 1, ed. S T Kimbrough and Oliver Beckerlegge, *Methodist History* 29, pp. 126–7, 1991.

Smith, C. Ryder, 'The Richmond Letters of Charles Wesley', *Proceedings of the Wesley Historical Society* 22, pp. 150–4, 183–8 and 23, pp. 7–14, 1940.

Smith, Timothy L., 'The Holy Spirit in the Hymns of the Wesleys' [reply, T. C. Mitchell pp 48-57], *Wesleyan Theological Journal* 16:2, pp. 20–47, 1981.

Smith, Warren Thomas, 'The Wesleys in Georgia: An evaluation', *Journal of the Interdenominational Theological Center* 6, pp. 157–67, 1979.

Snape, Michael Francis, 'Anti-Methodism in Eighteenth-Century England: The Pendle Forest Riots of 1748', *Journal of Ecclesiastical History* 49, pp. 257–81, 1998.

'Some Account of Mrs Sarah Wesley (Relict of the Rev. Charles Wesley, M.A.)', *Methodist Magazine* 6, pp. 447–52, 1823.

Sowton, Stanley, 'The Schooldays of Two Famous Boys: John and Charles Wesley at Charterhouse and Westminster', *Methodist Recorder*, p. 10, 7 December 1933.

Speck, W. A., 'Will the Real Eighteenth Century Stand Up?', *Historical Journal* 34, 1991, pp. 203–6.

Stamp, John S., 'Memoir of the Rev. Charles Atmore', *Wesleyan Methodist Magazine*, 1845; pp. 14–15.

Stevenson, Robert M., 'The Musical Wesleys', *Religion in Life* 16, pp. 589–93, 1947.

Strickling, George F., 'Charles Wesley – The Indomitable!', *Choral and Organ Guide* 6: 3, pp. 30–1, 1953.

Studwell, William E., 'Glory to the New-Born King!', *Journal of Church Music* 21: 10, pp. 2–6, 1979.

Supplee, G. William, 'Charles Wesley: Persecuted hymn writer', *Eternity* 21:10, p. 36, 1970.

Swift, Wesley F., 'Brothers Charles and John', *London Quarterly and Holborn Review* 182, pp. 275–80, 1957.

Swift, Wesley F., 'Portraits and Biographies of Charles Wesley', *Proceedings of the Wesley Historical Society* 31, pp. 86–92, 1957.

Swift, Wesley F., review of *Charles Wesley and His Colleagues* by Charles Wesley Flint with introductory notes by Gerald Kennedy, G. Bromley Oxnam, and Norman Vincent Peale in *London Quarterly and Holborn Review* 183, pp. 68–9, 1958.


Taylor, Vincent, review of *The Hymns of Charles Wesley: A Study of their Structure* by Robert Newton Flew in *Expository Times* 65, p. 160, 1954.

'Together in God's Grace', *Reformed World* 39, 1986–7.

Tucker, Karen Beth Westerfield, '"On the Occasion": Charles Wesley's hymns on London earthquakes of 1750', *Methodist History* 42, 2003–4, pp. 197–221.

Tyson, John R., 'An Instrument for Sally: Charles Wesley's shorthand biography of an early methodist layman, John Davis,' *Methodist History* 30:2, pp. 103–8, 1992.

Tyson, John R., 'Charles Wesley,' *Dictionary of Evangelicalism*, Leicester: InterVarsity Press, pp. 710–12, 2003.

Tyson, John R., 'Charles Wesley – A Man of Singing Faith,' *Challenge to Evangelicalism Today*, 17:2, pp. 10–11, 1982.

Tyson, John R., 'Charles Wesley and Edward Young: Eighteenth century poetical apologists,' *Methodist History*, 27:2, pp. 110–19, 1989.

Tyson, John R., 'Charles Wesley and the German Hymns,' *Hymn*, 35:3, pp. 153–8, 1983.

Tyson, John R., 'Charles Wesley Evangelist: The Unpublished Newcastle Journal,' *Methodist History* 25:1, pp. 41–61, 1986.

Tyson, John R., 'Charles Wesley, Pastor: A glimpse inside the shorthand journal,' *Methodist Quarterly Review* 4:1, 1984, pp. 9–22, 1984.

Tyson, John R., 'Charles Wesley: Preacher, teacher and singer of revival,' *Preacher's Magazine*, pp. 54–60, 1987.

Tyson, John R., 'Charles Wesley's Sentimental Language,' *Evangelical Quarterly* 57: 3, pp. 269–75, 1985.

Tyson, John R., 'Charles Wesley's Theology of Redemption,' *Wesleyan Theological Journal* 20:2, pp. 7–29, 1985.

Tyson, John R., 'Christian Liberty as Full Redemption: Charles Wesley's approach,' *Wesleyan Theological Journal* 38:2, pp. 143–75, 1982.

Tyson, John R., 'God's Everlasting Love: Charles Wesley and the predestinarian controversy,' *Evangelical Journal* 3:2, pp. 47–63, 1963.

Tyson, John R., 'The Lord of Life is Risen: Theological reflections on *Hymns for our Lord's Resurrection* (1746)' *Charles Wesley Society Newsletter*, 4:1, pp. 4–25, 1994.

Tyson, John R., 'The Transfiguration of Scripture: Charles Wesley's Poetical Hermeneutic,' *Asbury Journal*, 47:2, pp. 17–42, 1992.

Tyson, John R., 'The Wesleyan Hymns – Then and Now,' *Challenge for Evangelism Today* 26:2, p. 5, 1993.

Tyson, John R., 'The Wesleys at Home: Charles Wesley and his children', *Methodist History* 36, pp. 139–52, 1998.

Tyson, John R., and Douglas Lister, 'Charles Wesley, Pastor: A glimpse inside his shorthand journal', *Quarterly Review* 4:2, pp. 9–21, 1984.

Van Doornik, Merwin, 'Your Master Proclaim: A tribute to John and Charles Wesley', *Reformed Worship* 8, pp. 14–16, 1988.

Van Pelt, John Robert, 'The Eucharistic Hymns of the Wesleys', *Religion in Life* 22, pp. 449–54, 1953.

Vickers, Jason, E., 'Charles Wesley's Doctrine of the Holy Spirit: A vital resource for the renewal of Methodism today' *Asbury Journal* 61:1, 2006.

Vilain, Robert, 'Charles Wesley (1707–1788)' [significance in Methodism; text of Christ Church Gaudy Oration, 1988], *Proceedings of the Wesley Historical Society* 47, pp. 38–43, 1989.

Wainwright, Geoffrey, 'Ecumenical Challenges to Methodism', *Epworth Review* 27:1, 69–76, 2000.

Wainwright, Geoffrey, 'Wesley and the communion of saints', *One in Christ* 27:4, pp. 332–45, 1991.

Wakefield, Gordon, 'John Wesley and Ephraem Syrus,' *Hygoye: Journal of Syriac Studies* 1: 2, p. 8, 1998.

Wakefield, Gordon S., 'Littérature du désert chez John Wesley', *Irénikon* 51, pp. 155–70, 1978.

Wakeley, Joseph B., *Anecdotes of the Wesleys* [review] in *Methodist Review* 51, pp. 459–60, 1869.

Wallace, Charles, '"Some Stated Employment of Your Mind": Reading, writing, and religion in the life of Susanna Wesley', *Church History* 58:3, pp. 354–66, 1989.

Wallwork, Norman, 'Hymns on the Lord's Supper', *Proceedings of the Wesley Historical Society* 43, pp. 92–4, 1982.

Walsh, J. D., 'Elie Halévy and the Birth of Methodism', *Transactions of the Royal Historical Society*, 5th series 25, pp. 1–20, 1975.

Walsh John, 'Religious Societies: Methodist and Evangelical, 1738–1800', *Voluntary Religion* eds W. J. Sheils and Diana Wood, 23, pp. 279–302, 1986.

Ward, W. R., review of *John and Charles Wesley: A Bibliography* ed. Betty M. Jarboe, in *Journal of Ecclesiastical History* 40, p. 468, 1989.

Watson, J. R., 'An Ovidian Source for Charles Wesley?', *Bulletin of the Hymn Society of Great Britain and Ireland* 209, pp. 271–5, 1996.

Watts, A. McKibbin, 'John and Charles Wesley: radical reactionaries?', *Touchstone* 6, pp. 13–26, 1988.

Watts, A. McKibbin, ed., 'John and Charles Wesley: 250th anniversary of their conversion', *Touchstone* 6, pp. 4–37, 1988.

Wesley, Charles, 'Poetical Epistle of Charles Wesley to his brother John', *Methodist Quarterly Review* 4, pp. 755–60, 1881.

Wesley, Sarah (Miss), 'Some Account of Mrs. Sarah Wesley, Relict of Charles Wesley', *Wesleyan Methodist Magazine* 46, pp. 506–11, 1823.

Westermeyer, Paul, ed., 'Charles Wesley's Hymns', *Hymn* 39, pp 7–53, 1988.

Westra, Helen, review of *A Heart Set Free: The Life of Charles Wesley* by Arnold A. Dallimore, in *Calvin Theological Journal* 24, pp. 331-332, 1989.

Whyte, Alexander, 'Gentle Jesus, Meek and Mild; Some notes of a lecture on Charles Wesley's children's hymn in Free St. George's, Edinburgh', *Sunday Magazine* n.s. 28, pp. 324–6, 1899.

Wilson, John W., 'Handel and the Hymn Tune, 1: Handel's tunes for Charles Wesley's hymns' [musical examples], *Hymn* 36:4, pp. 18–23, 1985.

Winter, Lovick Pierce, 'Charles Wesley in America', *Methodist Quarterly Review* 65, pp. 71–84, 1916.

Yrigoyen, Charles, Jr, review of *John and Charles Wesley: A Bibliography* ed. Betty M. Jarboe, in *Methodist History* 26, p. 258, 1988.

Zeitz, Lisa M., 'What Sweeter Musick': The politics of praise in Herrick's 'Christmas Caroll' and Wesley's 'Hymn for Christmas-Day', *English Studies in Canada* 14, pp. 270-285, 1988.

## Dissertations/Theses

Adams, Nelson F., *The Musical Sources for John Wesley's Tunebooks: The genealogy of 148 tunes*, unpublished DMA thesis, Ann Arbor: University Microfilms International, 1973.

Baker, D. S., *Hymns on Patriotism: Unpublished poems of Charles Wesley*, University of Birmingham, 1960.
Berry, Herbert Eugene, *A Program for the Nurturing of Catholic Eucharistic Piety among United Methodists through the Study of Pertinent Writings of J. and C. Wesley*, Indianapolis: Christian Theological Seminary, 1987.
Brose, Martin E., *The Literary and Liturgical Background of the Funeral Hymns of John and Charles Wesley*, Typescript thesis in Duke University Library, 1999.
Byrum, Roy Delbert, *Theological Implications in the hymns of Charles Wesley*, Duke University, 1945.

Caldwell, John Michael, *The Methodist Organization of the United States, 1784–1844: An historical geography of the Methodist Episcopal Church from its formation to its division*, University of Oklahoma, 1983.

Dale, James, *The Theological and Literary Qualities of the Poetry of Charles Wesley in Relation to the Standards of his Age*, University of Cambridge, 1960.
Denyer, A. S., *The Catholic Element in the Hymns of Charles Wesley*, University of Leeds, 1943.
Downes, James Cyril Thomas, *Eschatological Doctrines in the Writings of John and Charles Wesley*, University of Edinburgh, 1960.

Ekrut, James, *Universal Redemption: Assurance of salvation, and Christian perfection in the hymns of Charles Wesley with a poetic analysis and tune examples*, South-Western Baptist Theological Seminary, 1978.

Flemming, Richard L., *The Concept of Sacrifice in the Eucharistic hymns of John and Charles Wesley*, Southern Methodist University, 1980.
Forsaith, Peter S., *The Correspondence of the Revd John W. Fletcher: Letters to the Revd Charles Wesley, considered in the context of the Evangelical Revival*, Oxford Brookes University, 2003.
Fraser, M. Robert, *Strains in the Understandings of Christian Perfection in Early British Methodism (England)*, Vanderbilt University, 1988.

Gallaway, Craig B., *The Presence of Christ with the Worshipping Community: A study in the hymns of John and Charles Wesley*, Emory University, 1988.

Hannon, E., *The Influence of Paradise Lost on the Hymns of Charles Wesley*, MA, University of Columbia, 1985.

Hodgson, E. M., *The Poetry of John and Charles Wesley with Special Reference to their Hymns'* University of London, 1970.

Ingles, Faith Petra, *The Role of Wesleyan Hymnody in the Development of Congregational Song*, Combs College of Music, 1986.

Lawrence, Anna M., *The Transatlantic Methodist Family: Gender, revolution and Evangelicalism in America and England, c. 1730 –1815*, University of Michigan, 2004.

Lewis, Mary Frances, *Charles Wesley's Contribution to Hymnology*, Union Theological Seminary, 1957.

Lloyd, Gareth, *Charles Wesley: a new evaluation of his life and ministry*, University of Liverpool, 2002.

Madden, Deborah, *Pristine Purity: Primitivism and practical piety in John Wesley's Art of Physic*, University of Oxford, 2003.

Martin, John T., *The Wesleyan Doctrine of the Eucharist: its salvific and ethical implications*, Wesley Theological Seminary, 1976.

McCommon, Paul C., *The Influence of Charles Wesley's Hymns on Baptist Theology*, Southern Baptist Theological Seminary, 1948.

Morris, Gilbert Leslie, *Imagery in the Hymns of Charles Wesley*, University of Arkansas, 1969.

Osterman, Eurydice V., *Hail the Day*, University of Alabama, 1988.

Quantrille, Wilma Jean, *The Triune God in the Hymns of Charles Wesley*, Drew University, 1989.

Rench, Larry B., *The Function of the Hymns of Charles Wesley in his Ministry During the Years of 1738–1788*, Point Loma College, 1978.

Renshaw, John Rutherford, *The Atonement in the Theology of John and Charles Wesley*, Boston University School of Theology, 1965.

Roth, Herbert John, *A Literary Study of the Calvinistic and Deistic Implications in the Hymns of Isaac Watts, Charles Wesley and William Cowper*, Texas Christian University, 1978.

Sheffler, Samuel Lee, *Communicating the Gospel to a Rural Church through the 'Sermons' of the Wesleys*, Drew University, 1982.

Shepherd, Neville T., *Charles Wesley and the Doctrine of the Atonement*, University of Bristol, 1999.

Smith, Chester Burl, *Influences of Moravian Mysticism Appearing in the Hymnody of the Wesleys*, Butler University, 1958.

Thompson, Leon E., *Teaching Some Basic Wesleyan Doctrines through the Use of Charles Wesley's Hymns*, Candler School of Theology at Emory University, 1988.

Townsend, James A., *Feelings Related to Assurance in Charles Wesley's Hymns*, Fuller Theological Seminary, 1979.

Tseng, Y. D., *Charles Wesley and His Poetry*, University of Oxford, 1936.

Tyson, John R., *Charles Wesley's Theology of the Cross: An examination of the theology and method of Charles Wesley as seen in his doctrine of the atonement*, Drew University 1983.

Uphaus, Dwight Leslie, *A Set of Wesley Hymns Suited to Worship in the Church of the Nazarene Arranged for Choir and Congregation*, University of Missouri, 1981.

Vetter, Joseph, *A Critical Analysis of the Soteriological Beliefs of Charles Wesley*, Dallas Theological Seminary, 1980.

Webster, Robert, *Methodism and the Miraculous: John Wesley's Contribution to the Historia Miraculorum*, University of Oxford, 2006.

Webster, Robert, *'Methodist Bitches': The Anti-Methodist Representations of Bishop George Lavington, William Hogarth, and Richard Graves*, unpublished MA thesis, University of the South, 2001.

Welch, Barbara Ann, *Charles Wesley and the Celebrations of Evangelical Experience*, University of Michigan, 1971.

## Poetry and Hymnology

Anon., 'By a Friend', *Verses occasioned by the death of the Rev. Charles Wesley, who died March 29, 1788, aged eighty*, London: T. Scollick, 1788.

Barrow, James, *An Elegy Occasioned by the Death of the Rev. Charles Wesley, M.A., Who Departed this Life March the 29th 1788 in the 80th Year of His Life*, London: Scollick, 1788.

Burrows, Donald, ed., *George Frideric Handel, The Complete Hymns & Chorales*, Facsimile ed., with an Introduction by Donald Burrows, London: Novello, 1988.

Creighton, James, *Elegiac Stanzas Occasioned by the Death of the Rev. Charles Wesley, A.M. late of Christ-Church College, Oxford: Who Departed this Life, March 29, 1788, in the Eightieth Year of His Age*, London: printed for the author, and sold by T. Scollick; and J. Buckland, 1788.

Gough, Benjamin, 'In Memoriam. Charles Wesley, Hymnologist', in *The Methodist Hymn Book and its Associations*, ed. George J. Stevenson, London: Hamilton, Adams & Co., 1870.

Kenton, James, *Thoughts (in verse,) Sacred to the Memory of the Rev. Charles Wesley, who Died March 29th, 1788; in the Eightieth Year of his Age*, London: printed for the author, by J. Moore; and sold by T. Scollick, 1788.

Kresensky, Raymond, 'Poem for Charles Wesley', *Christian Century* 59, p. 629, 1942.

# Index of Names and Subjects

on preaching Christ 502
*Primitive Physic* 230
and Roman Catholicism 134, 141–3,
146, 155–6, 159
Wesley, John (CW's son 'Jacky') 127,
477–9
Wesley, Mary ('Molly', née Vazeille;
John Wesley's wife) 10, 44, 504,
506–7
Wesley, Samuel (CW's brother)
critical of CW 81
marriage 86 n31
relationship with his mother 70–71
Wesley, Samuel (CW's father) 65, 70
epitaph 266
library 78
Wesley, Samuel (CW's son) 124–5
children 136
conversion to Roman Catholicism
133–5, 144, 157–9
education 130–31
marriage 135–6
musical talent 127–31, 420, 421,
427–9, 431
Wesley, Sarah (CW's daughter) 119, 124
after CW's death 104, 119
character 4
on CW's ceasing itinerancy 45
encouraged to read 74, 131
writing 4, 131
Wesley, Sarah (née Gwynne; CW's
wife)
accepts CW's proposal 352
after CW's death 104
and CW's itinerancy 43–4, 489
musicianship 419–20
Wesley, Susanna (CW's mother) 70–84
burial 65, 84
child-rearing methods 60, 70, 72–5,
125

critical of CW's views 80–81
epitaph 83–4
holds services at home 64, 82, 415
old age 70, 80
reading 78–9, 143, 266
views on conversion 80
Wesley, Ursula (née Berry) 86 n31
West Street chapel 111, 442 n57
Westell, Thomas 91–2, 93
Westminster School 415
Whaling, Frank 451
Wheatley, James 44, 93, 230, 487, 488–9,
490, 499, 501, 502
White, Alex 342
Whitefield, George
in Bristol 49
criticized by Susanna Wesley 82
disagrees with Wesleys over
Calvinisim 154, 191
evangelism 49, 120
and open-air preaching 42
in Sheffield 49
Whitehead, John 2–3, 4, 48, 71, 323
Wilberforce, William 29
Wilford, Priscilla 29
Wilkins, John 328
Williams, Joseph 60–61, 307, 321–2
Williams, Thomas 500
women
and evaluation of preachers 506–7
as preachers 103–4
Woolf, Francis 90
Worcester 490
Wordsworth, William 23
Wren, Brian 406, 408
Wroot 86 n30
Wynn, W. W. 420

York 22
Young, Edward 24